ollins
s of
orld
r II

Collins

Atlas of World War II

JOHN KEEGAN

First published in 2006 by
COLLINS
HarperCollinsPublishers
77-85 Fulham Palace Road
Hammersmith, London W6 8JB

The Collins website address is **www.collins.co.uk**

Collins is a registered trademark of HarperCollins Publishers

British Library Cataloguing in Publication Data:
A catalogue record is available from the British Library

Printed and bound in Hong Kong by Printing Express

ISBN-10: 0-00-721465-0
ISBN-13: 978-0-00-721465-5

The Collins Atlas of the Second World War
edited by
John Keegan

Atlas prepared for Collins by Martin Brown

Editorial Direction: Fiona Hobbins
Editing: Christopher Summerville
Proof-reading: Jodi Simpson
Indexing: David Moody

Picture Credits
Front cover © CORBIS
10-11 Hulton-Deutsch Collection/CORBIS; **22-23** Hulton-Deutsch Collection/CORBIS; **64-65** Bettmann/CORBIS; **108-109** Bettmann/CORBIS; **142-143** Hulton-Deutsch Collection/CORBIS

The introduction to the original Times version of this atlas, written in 1989, emphasised the degree to which the then frontiers of the world's states, particularly those of Eastern and Central Europe, had been determined by the events of the war and the treaties that concluded it. This new edition of the *Atlas* still reveals the effects of the Second World War, but events that have taken place since 1989 have modified them, particularly in Europe.

The most important of these events has been the collapse of communism in 1989 and the years following. The most apparent effect has been the termination of the division of Germany following the dissolution of the Warsaw Pact and the withdrawal of the Group of Soviet Occupation Forces in Germany. Germany now occupies much the same territory as it did in 1937, the main difference being that its frontier with Poland now lies 100 miles to the west and that the remnant of East Prussia – from 1945–1990 known as the Soviet territory of Kaliningrad – has become a sort of no man's land. Berlin (a divided and occupied city for nearly fifty years after 1945) is now restored as the capital of the Federal Republic.

The wars in the Balkans in the 1990s, which owed their origins largely to the civil conflicts originating in the Second World War, have changed the region's political geography radically. Yugoslavia, a product of the Versailles Treaty, has ceased to exist and its territory has been divided between its ethnic regions, bringing back into being Serbia, and establishing Croatia and Macedonia as independent states.

The fall of communism has had direct effects on the Soviet Union, the heartland of communism itself. Component republics of the old Soviet Union (accorded a cynical independence by the Soviet Moscow government and acting in theory as the seat of pan-Soviet power, practically as the successor of the Tsarist imperial regime) have realised their theoretical independence to become fully independent and sovereign. Those that have benefited most are the larger, more industrialised westerly republics, such as Ukraine and Belarus; the most successful are the Baltic States which, having miraculously survived Soviet efforts to Russify them during 1940–1990, very rapidly regained true independence and sovereignty as soon as they were permitted to assert their historic nationalisms. At the Soviet margins, weaker nationalities (as in Moldova and Bessarabia) have also regained independence, though without succeeding in creating strong governments or economies. In former Soviet Central Asia, the Muslim republics emerged with an independence not enjoyed since the mid-nineteenth century, but their governments depend for support either on Moscow or on arrangements made with the United States.

The Second World War remains the most potent agent of boundary change since the Treaty of Versailles; knowledge of its events is key to understanding the political geography of the world.

John Keegan
January 2006

CONTENTS

MILITARY FORMATIONS AND UNITS

National colours
(arrow/unit/symbol colours)

- British and Commonwealth
- American
- French
- Soviet
- Chinese
- German and German satellites
- Italian
- Japanese
- other, specified on maps

Military craft
(coloured according to nationality)

- bomber
- fighter bomber
- fighter
- troop carrier
- heavy aircraft carrier
- light aircraft carrier
- battle ship
- heavy cruiser
- light cruiser
- destroyer
- patrol/escort vessel
- oil tanker
- submarine

General military symbols
(mostly coloured according to nationality)

- ---XXXXX--- boundary between units (with appropriate size qualification)
- army base
- garrisoned city/town
- airforce base
- naval base
- army/navy movement
- retreat (unless otherwise specified)
- air track
- frontline
- fortified frontline
- air raid
- airborne landing
- sinking (coloured according to nationality of vessel)
- minefield
- gun emplacement
- battle

Many of the colours and symbols used in this atlas are common to each map. This general key should be used as a guide to understanding them. Exceptions and additional symbols are keyed on the individual maps.

Military units: types
(coloured according to nationality)

- infantry
- cavalry
- mechanised unit
- armour
- airborne
- naval troops
- air force unit

Military units: types
(coloured according to nationality)

XXXXX NAME/NUMBER COMMANDER	army group
XXXX NAME/NUMBER COMMANDER	army/fleet/air force
XXX TYPE/NUMBER	corps
XX TYPE	division
X TYPE	brigade
III TYPE	regiment
II TYPE	battalion
I TYPE	company

e.g. the German Army Group South, commanded by Rundstedt appears as:

the 9th Australian Armoured Division appears as:

General cartographic symbols

- village/town/city
- built-up area
- road (at larger scales)
- railway (at larger scales)
- river
- canal
- wadi
- swamp/marsh
- coral reef
- national border
- oilfield
- mountain peak

A military unit is a force composed of troops of the same arm of service, e.g. an infantry company or an artillery battery. A formation is a force composed of units of different arms of service. The smallest true formation is a division, though brigades usually contain units of different arms and are conventionally regarded as formations.

A battalion is a unit 600–1,000 strong; a regiment, composed of three battalions, is about 3,000 strong; a brigade, which contains two regiments or several battalions, varies in strength between 3,000 and 6,000; a division has three brigades with supporting troops and is about 15,000 strong; a corps contains at least two divisions, an army at least two corps and an army group at least two armies.

Battalions are commanded by lieutenant colonels, regiments by colonels, brigades by brigadiers, divisions by major generals and corps by lieutenant generals; armies and army groups are commanded by lieutenant generals, generals or (field) marshals as appropriate. Conventionally, the ranks from brigadier to marshal are represented by one, two, three, four or five stars.

There are many national exceptions to these broad rules. The British Army, for example, calls armoured and artillery battalions 'regiments'; a British infantry regiment, on the other hand, is not a tactical unit but a historical parent unit of independent battalions. In the German Army, battalions were often commanded by majors and divisions by lieutenant generals. In many armies the brigade does not exist or else is an independent organisation outside a division. The Soviet Union, in the Second World War, called army groups 'Fronts'; there were higher headquarters called 'theatres' or 'directions'. The United States Army called infantry brigades 'regimental combat teams' and armoured brigades 'combat commands'.

Size also varied greatly from country to country. Japanese formations were generally smaller than their Western equivalents; Chinese formations were often so weak as not to deserve their designations. German formations grew smaller during the war, as losses had their effect; Soviet formations, by contrast, were often skeletal in 1941–42 but regained strength as the war progressed. The formations and units of all armies, even those with ample manpower, lost strength significantly during periods of intense fighting.

TERMS AND ABBREVIATIONS

Selected terms and abbreviations

Abwehr The intelligence department of the German Armed Forces. Abwehr had three divisions: i) espionage with specialist groups (military, technical, political and economic), ii) sabotage and iii) counter-espionage. From 1938, Abwehr was run by Admiral Wilhelm Canaris. After his implication in the plot against Hitler (in 1944), the organisation was absorbed into the SS (RSHA VI).

AEAF Allied Expeditionary Air Force.

AEF Allied Expeditionary Force.

AIF Australian Imperial Forces.

Anti-Comintern Pact Joint declaration by Germany and Japan, issued on 25 November 1936, that they would consult and collaborate in opposing the Comintern or Communist International. It was acceded to by Italy in October 1937, and later became the instrument by which Germany secured the loyalty of its Romanian, Hungarian and Bulgarian satellites, and attempted to bind Yugoslavia. See also Comintern, Tripartite Pact.

ANZAC Australia and New Zealand Army Corps.

AVG American Volunteer Group (Flying Tigers) of pilots fighting for Chiang Kai-shek.

BEF British Expeditionary Force. Name given in both World Wars to British troops serving in France at the outbreak of hostilities and thereafter. In the Second World War, the BEF was evacuated by sea from Dunkirk (26 May–4 June 1940) and other parts of France in the face of overwhelming German strength.

Blitzkrieg Lightning war. An expression widely used by the late 1930s to describe new forms of fast, mobile warfare based around a core of tanks, armoured vehicles and battlefield aircraft. German military leaders never used the term themselves, but it was popularly applied to the startling and swift victories won by the German armed forces between 1939 and 1941 against Poland, France and the Soviet Union. German operations were performed to a regular pattern. The weak point in the enemy front was identified, and while conventional forces contained the sectors of either side, heavy tank and air strikes through the chosen corridor of attack occured until breakthrough was achieved. Armoured forces then continued to penetrate enemy territory while infantry and motorised columns destroyed remaining enemy strongpoints. Speed was essential to success. All armed forces were compelled to adopt a variety of German operational strategies before the end of the war.

Brandenburgers German Special Force set up by the Abwehr in 1939 and originally composed of small groups in civilian clothes, who were sent in ahead of the main fighting force to seize or demolish key targets.

CAS Chief of Air Staff (Britain).

CCS Combined Chiefs of Staff (Allied).

Chetniks Members of a Serbian nationalist group that operated underground during WWII during the German occupation of Yugoslavia. Initially received support from Allies, but this support was transfered to Communist Partisans led by Tito.

Chindits Long-range penetration troops used behind Japanese lines.

CIGS Chief of the Imperial General Staff (British).

CINCAF Commander-in-Chief, Allied Forces.

CINCMED Commander-in-Chief, Mediterranean Fleet (US).

CINPAC Commander-in-Chief, Pacific Area Fleet (US).

CINCPOA Commander-In-Chief, Pacific Ocean Area (US).

CINCSWPA Commander-in-Chief, Southwest Pacific Area (US).

Comintern Lenin inaugurated the Comintern at the Communist Third Socialist International in 1919, with the object of establishing Communist domination of all socialist movements throughout the world. The Comintern's endeavours to foster revolution, most especially in Germany and Spain, were generally unsuccessful. In 1943, during the Second World War, the USSR dissolved the Comintern to calm the misgivings of its Western allies.

Commandos British Special Force, composed of elite, all volunteer troops, was employed largely for raids along the coast of German-occupied Europe. They were formed into brigades, each usually comprising four units of about 500 men. The first brigades comprised British personnel only, but subsequently an international brigade of Free French, Dutch, Polish, Belgian and other volunteers, was formed. The Commandos fought in many theatres, including Norway, the Mediterranean, France and South East Asia; they were also heavily involved in the 1944 campaigns in Italy, during the Normandy landings and in subsequent battles in the West. Hitler regarded them as saboteurs in uniform, who should be shot on sight or on capture.

Einsatzgruppe German and Axis operational group of German security police for extermination missions in occupied territory. In the German-occupied territories of eastern Europe they formed punishment and extermination squads operating immediately behind conventional forces.

Far East Command (Soviet) New theatre level of command, controlling three Fronts (Army Groups) – Transbaikal, First and Second Far Eastern – set up for the Manchurian operation in August 1945, under Marshal Vasilevski. Previously the Fronts had been controlled directly from the Stavka in Moscow, but the distance of the theatre from Moscow and the problems of co-ordinating the operations of three fronts (1.5 million men) over an area the size of the whole of western Europe necessitated an 'intermediate, operational-strategic level of command'.

Final Solution Endlösung. Term usually applied to a decision or decisions taken by Hitler and other National Socialist leaders in late 1941 for the annihilation of the European Jews. No clear decision has ever been found but most historians agree that the process was launched in the last two months of 1941. For the next three years Jews were murdered in mass in purpose-built killing centres.

FFI French Forces of the Interior.

FHO Fremde Heere Ost (Foreign Armies East). German intelligence organisation specialising in the Soviet Union, run first by Colonel Kinzel and then, from late spring 1942, by General Gehlen.

GAU Glavnoye Artilleriyskoye Upravleniye (Soviet Main Artillery Directorate). Commanded during the war by Colonel General of Artillery N.D. Yakovlev, the directorate was responsible not only for the design and supply of artillery pieces and shells, but also for small arms and ammunition, rockets and aircraft armament. *GAU* representatives supervised production in factories dispersed throughout the USSR.

GC&CS British Government Code and Cypher School, at Bletchley Park.

Gestapo Geheime Staatspolizei. Originally part of the Prussian State Police, this force was moulded by Göring, then Himmler into the primary security organisation of the Third Reich. As part of the RSHA, from 1939, it acted against political opponents of the Nazis both inside and outside Germany and hunted down Jews.

GHQ General Headquarters.

GKO/GOKO Soviet State Defence Committee.

GOC General Officer Commanding (Soviet).

HIWI Hilfsfreiwillige. Auxiliary (Russian) Volunteers in the German armed forces, 1941–45.

IA/IND Indian Army.

JCS Joint Chiefs of Staff (US).

KMG Konno-Mekhanizirovannaya Gruppa (Soviet Cavalry-Mechanised Group). The mixed mobile formation of cavalry, motor transport and armour used on the Eastern Front and in Manchuria. KMGs were formed in order to capitalise on the Red Army's large cavalry forces, which were of particular value in difficult terrain, but stiffened with armour and firepower.

Kristallnacht On 19 November 1938 'The night of broken glass'; some 100 Jews were killed and many synagogues burned down in coordinated attacks against Jews and Jewish property throughout Germany and Austria.

LCA Landing Craft Assault (US).

LRDG Long-Range Desert Group (Allied).

LRPG Long-Range Penetration Group (US).

LSD Landing Ship Dock (US).

MAAF Mediterranean Allied Air Force.

MAC Mediterranean Air Command.

MI5 The British Security Service, responsible for counter-intelligence. Originally a branch of Military Intelligence, it came under the supervision of the Home Office. It acted against enemy agents attempting to operate in Britain and the Empire and monitored the activities of potentially subversive organisations and individuals. It proved itself to be particularly effective against German spies operating in Great Britain and consequently ran a highly successful series of double agents.

MI6 The British Secret Service, also known as the Secret Intelligence Service (SIS). Its function was to gather information from foreign sources and, with most of its European networks overrun by the German occupation, made extensive use of intelligence gathered by the Resistance. Once a branch of Military Intelligence, MI6 was under the administrative control of the Foreign Secretary. It was responsible for the important codebreaking establishment, the Government Code and Cypher School (GC&CS) and its most important product, Ultra.

***Motti* tactics** Motti is Finnish for a small log of firewood, specifically a reference to cutting up roadbound armoured columns into vulnerable sections, like a string of sausages. A tactic employed by the Finnish Army during the war with the USSR (1939-40). In these motti battles, Finish troops, clad in white to camouflage them against the snow, and moving swiftly on skis, penetrated deep behind Soviet lines to destroy supply bases, disrupt communications and attack the enemy. Targets were usually first bypassed, then taken in rear.

MTB Motor Torpedo Boat (US).

NATO North Atlantic Treaty Organisation formed in 1949.

Nazi Party Acronymic form for Hitler's Nationale Sozialistische Deutsche Arbeiterpartei (National Socialist German Workers' Party), the only legal political movement in Germany between 1933 and May 1945.

NKVD Narodny Komissariat Vnutrennykh Del (People's Commissariat of Internal Affairs). The Soviet commissariat (later ministry) responsible for running the Soviet police and security services during the 1930s. In 1934 the NKVD took over the running of the camp system (Gulag) in addition to its other police powers. The NKVD fielded a police militia of around 750,000 which was used during the war to maintain discipline in the Soviet armed forces and to investigate and punish alleged cases of cowardice or dereliction of duty. NKVD motorised troops were used in the defence of Kiev in 1941, and the NKVD 21st division in the defence of Leningrad. The NKVD was responsible for a number of notorious atrocities including the massacre of Polish officers in the Katyn forest in 1940 and the mass deportation of the peoples of the Caucasus in 1943–44. In 1943 the NKVD was reformed; its security functions were taken over by a new commissariat, the NKGB.

Ob *Oberbefehlshaber* (Commander-in-Chief).

OKH see OKW

OKW Oberkommando der Wehrmacht. The High Command of all German armed forces created in 1938, with Hitler at its head. The OKH (Oberkommando des Heeres), the High Command of the German Army, together with the OKL (Oberkommando der Luftwaffe), the High Command of the Air Force, and the OKM (Oberkommando der Kriegsmarine), the High Command of the Navy, came under the authority of the OKW. After the Germans were held by the Soviets before Moscow (December 1941), Hitler assumed personal command of the German Army, taking direct responsibility for operations. A few months later he appointed Speer as Armaments Minister and held regular conferences thereafter on economic and technical questions, extending his role in the war effort ever more widely. The OKW organisation was run by a *chef de cabinet*, Field Marshal Wilhelm Keitel, and an operations chief, Colonel-General Alfred Jodl.

OSS Office of Strategic Services. The US secret military agency, responsible to the Joint Chiefs of Staff. Created by President Roosevelt in 1942, its first director was General William Donovan (1883–1959), previously Co-ordinator of Information, who had studied resistance groups, and the British SOE. Under his leadership OSS worked closely with SOE, and developed a network of special units throughout the world, which gathered intelligence and sent agents to help resistance organisations.

PCNL Polish Committee of National Liberation.

Pact of Steel Formal alliance signed on 22 May 1939, between Germany and Italy (Axis Pact).

Pluto Pipe Line Under The Ocean. Code name for the oil pipeline laid under the English Channel to supply the Allied armies in North West Europe, 1944.

RAAF Royal Australian Air Force.

RAF Royal Air Force (British).

RAN Royal Australian Navy.

Rangers American Special Force formed and organised into battalions. Unlike the British Commandos, the Rangers usually operated in concert with conventional forces, being detailed specific tasks within combined operations. In this capacity, they played a crucial role in the development of amphibious landing techniques in numerous operations in the Pacific.

Their most outstanding exploits – by the 2nd and 5th battalions – were the assaults on the Pointe du Hoc and the Pointe de la Percée during the Normandy landings (June 1944) when, equipped with grapnels, ropes and ladders, they scaled the cliffs, intending to silence heavy German defensive guns.

RCAF Royal Canadian Air Force.

RCN Royal Canadian Navy.

RN Royal Navy (British).

RNZAF Royal New Zealand Air Force.

RNZN Royal New Zealand Navy.

SAS Special Air Service (British).

SCAEF Supreme Commander Allied Expeditionary Force.

Scorched earth The policy of destroying, mainly by fire, everything in the path of an advancing army, to prevent their living off occupied land; it was adopted by Stalin during the German invasion of the USSR in 1941.

SHAEF Supreme Headquarters Allied Expeditionary Force.

SIS Secret Intelligence Service. The US Army cryptographic unit formed in the inter-war years under the leadership of William Friedman. Renamed the Signal Security Service and, later, the Signal Security Agency, it was responsible for unravelling the Japanese Purple diplomatic cipher and handling the intelligence they obtained codenamed Magic.

SIS Secret Intelligence Service (British) *see* M16.

SOE Special Operations Executive (British). Formed in July 1940 out of two small SIS and War Office departments, SOE's remit was, in Churchill's words to 'Set Europe Ablaze' and to foment resistance in German- and, later, Japanese-occupied territories. It supplied organisers, instructors, communications, weapons and equipment to tens of thousands of resisters throughout the war. Its relations with other government bodies and the military establishment were not always harmonious and this contributed to its disbandment in 1946.

SS Schutzstaffel. The elite arm of the NSDAP established by Hitler in 1925 as his personal bodyguard. In 1929 it was taken over by Heinrich Himmler who led the SS until 1945. It recruited only those regarded as the racial elite. In 1939 Hitler agreed to allow an 'armed SS' (Waffen-SS) to be formed but by 1943 there were four divisions, principally armoured. Following SS Adolf Hitler division's success in halting a Soviet advance at Kharkov, the Waffen SS was rapidly expanded by conscripting throughout the Reich and occupied territories, reaching a strength of 40 divisions by 1945. They were noted for their ruthless efficiency and cruelty, especially in anti-partisan warfare in the USSR and Italy, and in quelling both the ghetto and 1944 uprisings in Warsaw. They saw action as front line troops in every theatre of the German war.

Stavka Supreme High Command of the Soviet Union. Stavka is an old Russian word for a warrior chief's encampment, and implies the highest military-political authority. In the First World War, the Stavka had been the headquarters of the Russian Supreme Commander, first Grand Duke Nikolay Nikolayevich, then Tsar Nicholas II himself. In the Second World War, the Stavka of the Main Command (Glavnogo Komandovaniya) was set up on 23 June 1941, by an order of the USSR Council of People's Commissars and the Party Central Committee. It included People's Commissar of Defence Timoshenko (President), Voroshilov, Molotov, Stalin, Zhukov (Chief of the General Staff), Budenny and Admiral Kuznetsov. On 10 July it was renamed Stavka of the Supreme Command (Verkhovnogo Komandovaniya) and on 8 August Stavka of the Supreme High Command (Verkhovnogo Glavnokomandovaniya) when Stalin adopted that title. Stavka controlled military activity of all the Soviet Union's Armed Forces, but under the direction of the State Defence Committee (GKO), thus fulfilling the Leninist principle of 'unity of political and military direction of armed struggle'. Communication between Stavka and commanders of fronts was accomplished by inviting the latter to Stavka briefings, and also by sending Stavka representatives to supervise and advise Front headquarters and co-ordinate operations on more than one front. Eminent Stavka representatives were Zhukov, Vasilevskiy, Voroshilov, Timoshenko, Shaposhnikov, Antonov, Novikov, Kuznetsov and Voronov.

TF Task Force (Allied, navy).

TG Task Group (Allied, navy).

Tripartite Pact Agreement signed on 27 September 1940 between Germany, Italy and Japan, setting up a political alliance (the Rome-Berlin-Tokyo Axis) and promising military aid if any member was attacked by a state not already at war.

Ultra The code name (and attached security classification) given to the British system for intercepting, decrypting, interpreting and distributing German signals encyphered on the Enigma machine. The product of the system was known as 'Ultra intelligence'. The system control on the Government Code and Cypher School (GCCS) of Bletchley Park.

USSAF US Army Air Force (formerly US Army Air Corps).

USAAC US Army Air Corps. *see* USAAF.

USN US Navy.

USS US Ship.

USSTAF US Strategic Air Force.

Volksdeutsche People of German extraction who lived outside Germany, especially in the former Habsburg Empire. Hitler was concerned to gather those Volksdeutsche who had settled in other countries back into the Reich. The Voksdeutsche who lived in occupied countries were given special privileges and positions of authority.

Waffen SS see SS.

Wehrmacht The armed forces of Germany. *see* OKW.

PART 1 THE PRE-WAR WORLD

europe after the **first world war**

1919 to 1936

- **1919 (28 June)** Treaty of Versailles
- **1922** Rapallo Pact between Germany and USSR
- **1922 (30 October)** March on Rome; Mussolini becomes Italian Prime Minister
- **1923** French and Belgians occupy the Ruhr
- **1932 (July)** German election; Nazi party becomes largest but without majority
- **1933 (January)** Hitler becomes Chancellor of National Coalition Government
- **1934** 'Night of the Long Knives'; Nazis purge Sturm Abteilung
- **1935 (March)** Saar restored to Germany

The First World War ceased with the armistice of 11 November 1918. Germany gave in – her empire in collapse, her towns in uproar, her army in retreat. The terms of the peace, decided at Paris in 1919, were such that Germany would not be able to fight again. Her overseas empire was confiscated. The navy was impounded, and at Scapa Flow it was to be sunk by the crews themselves. Allied troops occupied strategic points on the western German border. Imports of food were strictly controlled; cities starved, and an epidemic in Central Europe killed some 10 million more people than the war itself.

The aftermath of the war was apparent for some time. In Russia the civil war effectively came to an end only in February 1921, when the last anti-Bolshevik forces evacuated the Crimea, bound for exile. The Habsburg monarchy in Central Europe had disintegrated in October 1918, and warring went on between its 'successor states'. The two dominant nationalities had been the Germans, in the western part, and the Hungarians in the east. The rule of both was now overthrown: the Czechs and Slovaks asserted independence, ruling over a new state, which mainly in its western part (the Sudetenland), contained three million Germans. Poland re-emerged with many Germans living within its borders. Yugoslavia combined Serbs, Croats, Slovenes and others; Romania took Transylvania, Bessarabia and southern Dobruja in eastern Hungary. Hungary, reduced by almost two-thirds of its historic area, briefly passed under Communist rule, until counter-revolutionary forces regained control in 1919.

Under the Treaty of Versailles, signed on 28 June 1919, Germany lost Alsace-Lorraine to France, and territories in the east, to the newly-reconstituted Polish Republic, as well as areas to Denmark, Lithuania and Belgium. She had to accept limitation of her armed forces to 100,000 men – a police force, in effect – and occupation of strategic places on the east bank of the Rhine by Allied forces for 15 years. The Saar, with important mineral reserves, was handed to France for the same period. In principle (confirmed in 1921), Germany had to agree to pay 'reparations': an annual sum ostensibly designed to compensate the victims of German aggression, but really intended, by removing gold reserves, to prevent the German economy from ever recovering. To justify this, the Allies made the German delegates agree that Germany (as distinct from the imperial regime) had caused the war in 1914.

Other treaties between 1919–22 were similarly felt by the losing parties to represent injustice. The Treaty of Saint Germain, in September 1919, settled the fate of most Germans – now known as *Volksdeutsche* – living in the old Habsburg monarchy. Austria was created, more or less by decree of the Allies, to prevent Germans there from joining the German Republic (as they had almost overwhelmingly voted to do); other parts of the monarchy were consigned to Italy, Yugoslavia, Romania, Czechoslovakia and Poland. Although independent, Austria was also required to pay reparations. Hungary's new borders were dictated by the Treaty of Trianon in June 1920. Turkey and Bulgaria, former allies of Germany, also lost territory – in the Turkish case a vast amount, to newly-devised states in the Middle East, including Palestine, which, as a 'Jewish national home', was passed to Britain as a League of Nations mandate. The various wars came to an end with recognition by the new Soviet state of national borders with Poland, the Baltic States and Finland (the Treaty of Riga, 1921).

Europe had been dramatically redrawn, but national hatreds had not been overcome – very far from it. The Western Powers claimed superior morality, and devised the League of Nations at Geneva, at American instigation, as a means of sustaining the political and moral status quo. But the question remained: would the combined weight of the victorious Allies be strong enough to enforce the post-war settlement?

This proved not to be the case. The US had entered into war with Germany in 1917 and soon relapsed into isolation, keen only to recoup her outstanding loans in Europe. The French insisted on full reparations, and allying with the new successor states; the British now wished to restore her gradually to the European community of nations. German reparations could only be paid by an export surplus, which would dent Britain's own exports. Britain, therefore, opposed French demands for reparations, and was upset when the French occupied the Ruhr in 1922–23.

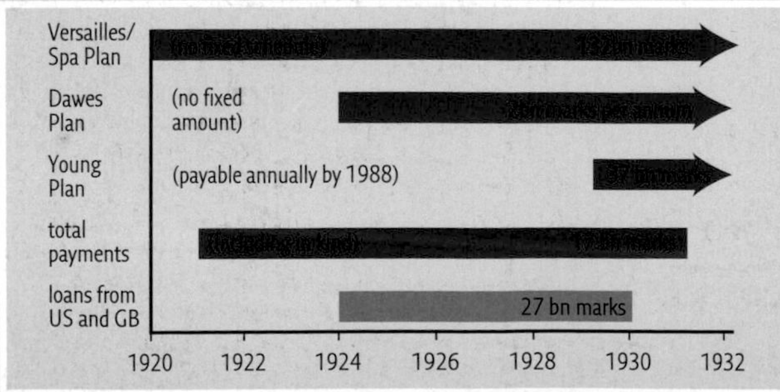

Inflation of mark 1919–23

Dec. 1919 £ 1 = 20 marks
Dec. 1920 £ 1 = 250 marks
Dec. 1921 £ 1 = 1,000 marks
Dec. 1922 £ 1 = 35,000 marks
Nov. 1923 £ 1 = 50 bn marks

mark payments at gold prices

2 **The dismemberment of Germany, the heavy economic restrictions imposed on it, and the question of reparation payments, led to economic collapse and political turmoil under the Weimar Republic.**

2 german reparations, 1920–32

http://history.acusd.edu/gen/text/versaillestreaty/vercontents.html The complete treaty with all 440 articles, with maps charts and photographs
http://mars.wnec.edu/~grempel/courses/germany/lectures/25naziorigins.html Origins of the Nazi Party

Germany was in a state of internal chaos. The empire had gone – the Kaiser in exile in Holland – and an uneasy republic took its place, named after the town of Weimar, where the republican government went to escape rebellion in Berlin. An ultra-democratic constitution was devised, in February 1919. But it was assailed from the Left (Spartakists in 1918–19. Comintern in 1921 and 1923) and the Right (Friekorps rebellion and Kapp Putsch, 1919–20 and Hitler's Munich Putsch, November 1923). Lack of central control and the occupation of much of Germany's industrial heartland by the Allies meant that finances became a nightmare. By November 1923, when a new, stable currency was introduced, there were over 50 thousand million marks to the pound sterling.

In 1924 the mark stabilised and the Weimar Republic entered a period of relative calm. Germany was admitted to the League of Nations. Economic recovery went ahead just the same, and in 1925 there was an accord of the Western Powers, which led to the Treaty of Locarno. By this, German statesmen – Gustav Stresemann in particular – 'accepted' reparations and the new western borders, though not the eastern ones. The Soviet Union had even concluded a pact with Germany in 1922 (the Treaty of Rapallo). But nationalist hatreds were ever-present and the economic recovery of the 1920s was only able to keep them in check for a few years. In the 1930s European rivalries would once again breakout.

1 The post-war settlement was arrived at in a series of treaties devised by the major powers in sessions in and around Paris between 1919 and 1920. Heavy territorial penalties were imposed on Germany, Austria, Hungary, Bulgaria and Turkey. Though not party to the settlement, the new Soviet state also lost extensive pre-war Russian territory in Poland, the Baltic states and Romania. The gainers were the eight new national States created in central and eastern Europe. Despite the Allies' desire to satisfy demands for self-determination by the peoples of the old empires, they left large minority groups living under the rule of other nationalities, creating an unstable foundation for the new post-war order.

1929 to 1939

- **1932** Antonio de Salazar becomes dictator of Portugal
- **1933** Germany becomes single-party dictatorship
- **1934** Konstantin Päts imposes one-party rule in Estonia
- **1934 (25 July)** Austrian Nazi assassination of Chancellor Dollfuss
- **1934 (9 October)** King Alexander of Yugoslavia assassinated
- **1935** Greece becomes a military dictatorship
- **1937 (12 June)** Red Army leaders purged
- **1937 (28 May)** Chamberlain becomes British Prime Minister

By the summer of 1929, the West had returned to guarded optimism: the disasters following the First World War appeared to be at an end. The world's economy was recovering, and internally, the various new states created after 1919 appeared to be more stable. This situation came to an end in October 1929, when the US Stock Exchange on Wall Street dramatically collapsed. Now an unreal speculative boom turned into an equally unreal collapse. Exports everywhere declined – by the autumn of 1932 to one-third of their level in 1929.

This meant worldwide unemployment. In the first instance, it affected the ship-building and heavy-industrial areas. But since these, in turn, now purchased fewer of the necessities of life, it affected food production – farmers soon found that they had no takers for their products, and in the first half of the 1930s, people went hungry while farmers destroyed their produce. This, then, was 'the Great Depression'.

Unemployment, bitter farmers, and the instability of foreign exchange resulted in the widespread disruption of political patterns. In the more prosperous countries of the West, which had reserves upon which to fall, Right and Centre, or moderate Left and Centre, held the ring. Liberal economics, whether in the form of Roosevelt's 'New Deal' or the National Government in Great Britain, struggled to maintain concensus through a slow and patchy revival. Elsewhere the solutions were more extreme. Outstanding among them were those of Adolf Hitler in Germany and Josef Stalin in the USSR. Hitler, long a nationalist agitator, had steered his national socialist (Nazi) party into a position of parliamentary dominance in Germany by 1932. He became Chancellor of Germany in 1933. Stalin emerged after Lenin's death in 1924 as the dominant figure in the USSR; in 1929 he proclaimed as the original idea of communism the collectivisation of agriculture and the forced industrialisation of the Soviet Union, to be effected by a programme of Five Year Plans. Both leaders turned towards radical solutions. In March 1933 Hitler received almost 45 per cent of the votes, and together with the few per cent awarded to the conservative Right, ran Germany. Stalin was equally determined to show that the original Communist alternative to capitalism was not dead.

Hitler wanted to restore Germany to her former glory as the lynch pin of a modern European superstate, and as the effective ruler of Eastern and Central Europe. Stalin seemed to be set on a Communist empire, its frontiers unclear, but undoubtedly oriented to the West. Both leaders voiced strong dissatisfaction with the apparent weakness of the belt of new states, which, since 1919, had forced a buffer zone between them. Britain and France, now cast in the role of forces of moderation, were faced with a dilemma. The British Prime Minister, Neville Chamberlain, thought he was dealing with 'two mad dogs'. Which dictator would be the most amenable to reason? At first, this seemed to be Hitler; after all, enlightened British opinion had said for some years that Germany ought to be given her rightful place in Europe. Thus, Hitler's strong arm tactics were tolerated. He was allowed to re-arm, by conscription, in 1935; he was allowed to re-occupy the Rhineland, militarily, in 1936. He was variously told that Germany might, in due course, have back her colonies in Africa and when in March 1938 Germany re-occupied Austria (the *Anschluss*), this too passed without more than paper protest. In September 1938 Hitler was also granted the (mainly) German-populated

2 The Great Bull Market of 1928 gave way to a precipitous fall in stock prices in October 1929. The Slump saw a drastic drop in the level of prices coupled with a moderate decrease in volume, which produced a decline in the value of world trade. The consequent slump in commodity prices caused severe hardship and dislocation in many countries. Multilateral trade and payment was replaced by a system of increasingly closed currency and trading blocs.

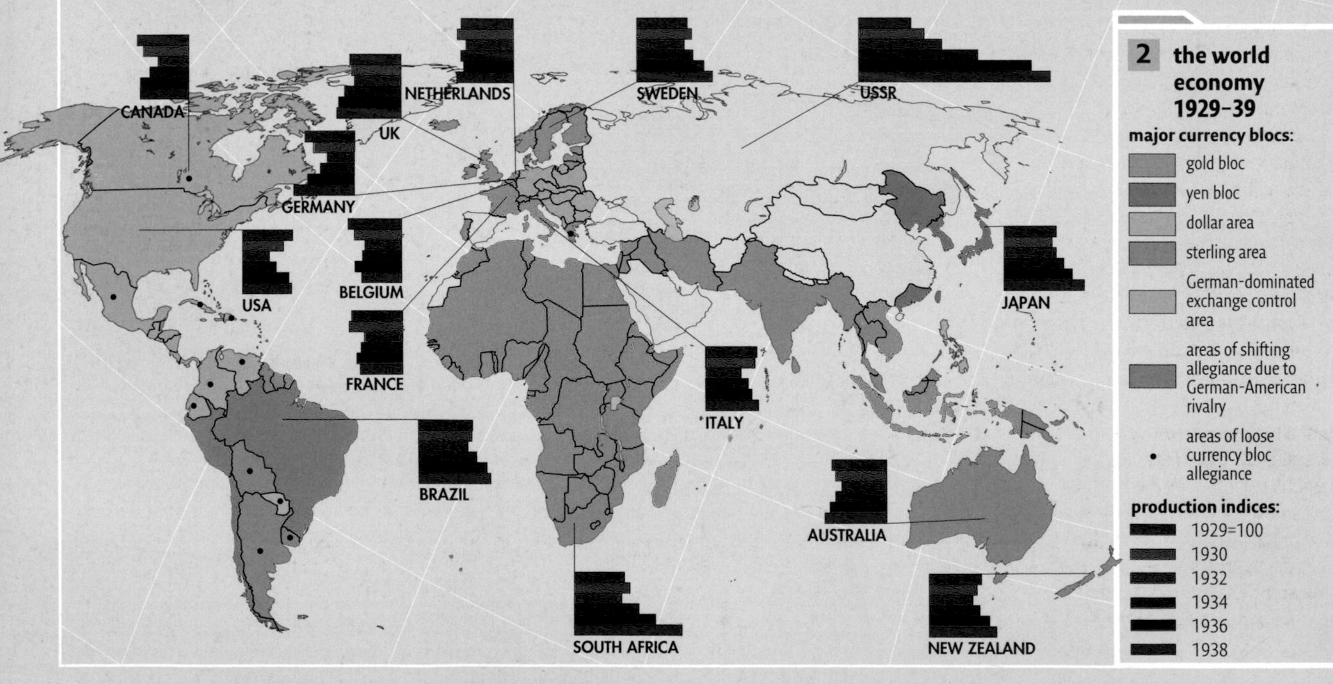

www.freedomhouse.org/reports/century.html
Survey of democracy in the 20th century
www.giles.34sp.com/
National Archive site for 1901 Census of England and Wales

1 At the beginning of the 1920s most European states were democracies. By 1939 most were dictatorships, some Fascist, some Nationalist, some Royalist. The new states created at Versailles faced numerous difficulties in establishing a modern parliamentary system. The slump exacerbated domestic political tensions. Europe's population began to move towards radical extremes – Communist, Nationalist or Fascist. Democracy survived in Britain and France, the Low Countries and Scandinavia, but in these countries too there developed native Fascist and Communist movements which threatened democratic stability.

parts of Czechoslovakia, at the agreement of Munich, where Chamberlain and the French Prime Minister, Daladier, met Hitler, with Mussolini's mediation.

Later on, the Munich agreement counted as shameful – the hand-over of an ally. At the time, it made sense to most people. There seemed to be a Fascist conspiracy, of Mussolini, Franco and Hitler. Everyone dreaded another world war. The French had built a huge defensive wall, the Maginot line, but had no plans to attack. The British needed time to build up their air force and their air defence, while also facing colonial rivalry with Italy in Africa and in the Mediterranean, and Japan in the Far East. But Hitler now showed that he regarded Munich not as a settlement but as a payment on account. German rearmament proceeded and in March 1939 Hitler seized Bohemia and Moravia, Slovakia becoming a client state. The British now saw Hitler as marching towards world conquest – an impression reinforced by Nazi atrocities against Jews and non-Germans. British guarantees were given to Poland and Romania; the French reluctantly followed; the US refused to be involved.

If the Western Powers were seriously to resist Hitler, they could only practically do so if they had an alliance with the Soviet Union. They did approach Stalin, but it remains unclear whether their approach was seriously made, or seriously entertained. The Red Army at this time was very weak, Stalin having purged much of its higher officer-corps, and in any case the Western Powers were reluctant to upset Nazism only to put communism in its place. In the event, Hitler approached Stalin, offering to partition Poland and Eastern Europe, and a pact was concluded in late August 1939. With the assurance of Stalin's help, Hitler invaded Poland on 1 September. The British and French saw no option but to declare war, which they did on 3 September, after their ultimatum had been rejected.

1920 to 1934

- **1919** 'May 4th' movement launched by Chinese student protesters
- **1921** Chinese Communist Party formed
- **1921-2** Washington Conference attempts to regulate situation in East Asia
- **1924** Kuomintang government established in Canton
- **1926** Chiang Kai-shek begins reunification of China (Northern Expedition)
- **1927** Chiang Kai-shek suppresses Communists at Shanghai
- **1930** Chaing Kai-shek launches operations against Chinese Communists
- **1934** Long March of Chinese Communists begins

In the opening decades of the twentieth century, China was to play a part in East Asian politics not dissimilar to that played by the Balkan states in European politics: it was a forum for Great Power rivalry, dissent and - eventually - open hostilities. In the last six decades of the nineteenth century various European powers and the United States compromised China's sovereignty and integrity by a series of unequal treaties that exacted from China territorial, commercial, financial and extra-territorial concessions.

Although the Western Powers wanted the ruling Manchu dynasty to survive as guarantor of their privileges, they wanted it sufficiently weak to be unable to challenge them; the effect of their actions, however, was to undermine the authority of the dynasty and to generate political pressures within China that erupted in the revolution of October 1911, the overthrow of the 250-year-old Manchu dynasty, and the inauguration of a republic in February 1912.

The erosion of Manchu authority after 1900 coincided with an intensification of Great Power rivalries within China, the most important of which was the conflict of interest between Russia and Japan. The latter, which had escaped subjugation to the Western Powers largely because China attracted so much of their predatory attention, emerged upon the China scene in 1895, when it defeated Manchu forces in Korea and Manchuria. However, the gains Japan made, ratified at the Treaty of Shimonoseki, were stripped by the Triple Intervention of France, Germany and Russia. Thereafter, Russo-Japanese estrangement deepened as Russia sought to secure for herself an exclusive sphere of influence in Korea and Manchuria, both of which Japan considered vital to her own security and economic interests. The Russo-Japanese war of 1904–05 saw Japanese forces victorious in both Korea and southern Manchuria and paved the way for a post-war rapprochement that allowed Japan to take control of Korea (1910), while Manchuria was divided between Japan and Russia. Here they worked together against other powers in the preservation of their respective spheres of interest, and after 1912 arranged for a division of Mongolia between themselves in the event of a disintegration of China.

The First World War witnessed both the eclipse of European power and influence and the progressive weakening of central authority in China: developments that Japan sought to put to her advantage in the form of the 'Twenty-one Demands' of 1915. Though forced by international pressure to moderate her position, the 'Twenty-one Demands' revealed the extent of Japanese ambitions: in effect, Japan aimed at reducing China to a position of dependency upon her. Japan secured from China recognition of certain of her claims, but their acceptance by the government of Yüan Shih-k'ai fatally compromised the latter's hopes of founding his own dynasty and set in train a series of revolts and mass demonstrations that were to lead to the collapse of central authority in China after Yuan's death in 1916.

1 The privileged positions that the Great Powers had established in China survived the revolution of 1911–12, but president Yüan Shih-k'ai's attempt in 1915 to install himself as emperor destroyed the authority of central government. Secession by Kwangsi and revolt throughout the country left provincial military governors with effective local power as Yüan's party, the Peiyang, split between Anhwei and Chihli factions. Chang Tsolin, later head of the Fengtien, established himself in Manchuria, and the most important of the old-guard revolutionaries, Sun Yat-sen, began to create a power base in the south. After 1918, virtually every province was beset by local power struggles as the main factions fought for control of north China and the Yangtze valley; but a clear split emerged between these warlord factions and the south.

2 From 1928 to 1937 much of China was brought under the control of Chiang Kai-shek after a period of warlordism had brought China into political chaos. Chiang set up his capital at Nanking, where he launched the 'New Life Movement', a quasi-Fascist renewal of Chinese culture and values against Westernism and Marxism.

www.newton.mec.edu/Angier/DimSum/Chiang%20Kai%20Shek.Bio.html
Photographs and biography of Chiang Kai-shek
www.spartacus.schoolnet.co.uk/2WWchaing.htm
Chiang Kai-Shek and the Kuomintang

Between 1918 and 1928 China was savaged by a series of violent clashes between a variety of individuals and factions that made and broke a bewildering sequence of alliances with one another in a naked struggle for power. Motivated more by self-interest than by political idealism, rival warlords sought to ensure their own power bases through the prevention of the emergence of a single centralising authority. Yet in terms of the events that were to lead to the outbreak of the Second World War, the period between 1918 and 1928 was critical, for this 'warlord era' presented all the Powers with the problem of deciding which individual or faction to support at any particular time, and to what purpose.

For Japan this problem was particularly acute, because her extensive interests in China were mainly concentrated in Manchuria, which was the fief of Chang Tso-lin, who hoped to establish his authority throughout northern China, but whose capacity to rule Manchuria effectively weakened in the period. As a result, the Japanese Army in Manchuria and northern China became gradually involved in China's interminable wars, in defence of what were felt to be Japan's national interests. These were both undefined and constantly widened as the Japanese Army sought to take further advantage of Chinese weakness. Further, after 1921, there emerged at Canton a Nationalist authority – the Kuomintang – under Sun Yat-sen, which embraced a genuine, if conveniently vague, political programme, dominated by an ambition to end the state of civil war in China by a twin policy of conquest and political mobilisation. With Soviet support, the Canton government spent the period before 1926 consolidating its authority in the south before beginning the Northern Expedition against the warlords on and beyond the Yangtze.

Within six months Nationalist armies secured the upper Yangtze, Nanking and Shanghai, but in mid-1927, faced by military reverses around Hsüchow and the realisation that its Communist allies were intent on a seizure of power on their own behalf, the Kuomintang turned upon the Communists and thereafter sought a series of arrangements with northern warlords that would preserve the existing political and social order, while ensuring at least nominal Kuomintang authority throughout China.

Various wars continued into 1929, but in October 1928 the Kuomintang authorities established themselves in Nanking as the National Government of China and in so doing presented the prospect of bringing some form of order to China as a whole. Its attempts to bring Manchuria into its fold led to an ill-judged war with the Soviet Union in 1929 that was to be very significant for the future: it revealed Chinese ambitions and the threat these presented to all the powers that depended upon Chinese divisions for the preservation of their interests; it also revealed Chinese weaknesses. By 1930, the Japanese decided that it was time to act decisively to defend their interests in mainland Asia, firstly in Manchuria, then in China itself.

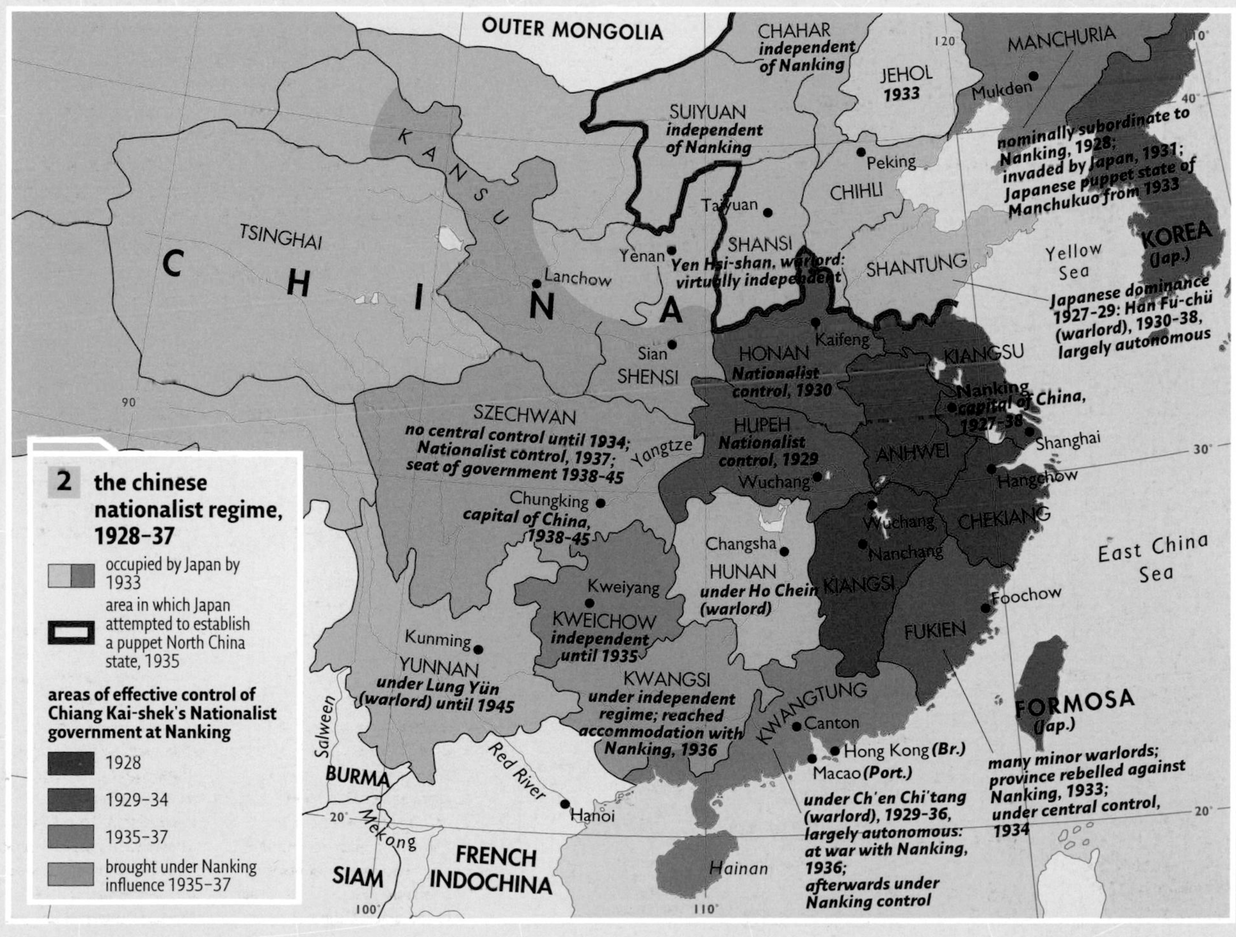

2 the chinese nationalist regime, 1928–37

japanese expansion

1931 to 1941

- **1931** Japanese occupy Manchuria
- **1932** 'Manchukuo' Republic set up in China by Japan
- **1933** Japan leaves League of Nations
- **1934** Japan declares 'Amau Doctrine' (Japanese sphere of influence in East Asia)
- **1936** Japanese military take over government
- **1936** Japanese sign anti-Comintern pact with Germany
- **1937** beginning of full-scale war between Japan and China
- **1938** Japanese install puppet government of Chinese Republic of Nanjing

The decade following the end of the First World War saw Japan observe considerable restraint towards China and the Western Powers. This moderation, however, survived neither the emergence of a Nationalist government in Nanking nor the onset of the Great Depression in 1929. The former was an explicit threat to Japan's existing privileges and future ambitions in China; the latter intensified Japan's search for raw materials and markets in a drive towards self-sufficiency. These developments, combined with the Japanese Army's acquired habit of intervention in Chinese affairs without reference to Tokyo and a hardening Nationalist view that Manchuria and Mongolia were natural areas of Japanese interest, led to the Japanese occupation of Manchuria.

A five-month campaign brought the Japanese effective control of the Chinese province, and on 18 February 1932, a Japanese puppet assembly proclaimed the independence of Manchuria; in March a new state, Manchukuo, was promulgated with the last emperor of China, Pu-yi, the successor to the Manchu throne, installed at its head. This declaration of independence, however, defined the neighbouring Chinese province, Jehol, as part of this new state, and in January and February 1933 the Japanese occupied the recalcitrant territory. Over the next two years a policy of alternating inducements and threats was used to force extensive concessions from the Chinese in the areas beyond the Great Wall.

After July 1937, the Japanese Army embarked upon the full-scale invasion and conquest of northern and central China. As in 1931, however, the driving force behind Japanese aggression was the suspicion that China was attempting to settle her domestic quarrels in order to resist her neighbour; following the Long March (1934–35), when the Communists withdrew from their southern bases to the north-west, the Sian agreement (Dec. 1936) brought an uneasy end to nearly a decade of civil war between the Nationalists and Communists. In northern China the Japanese made extensive gains, but on the lower Yangtze they were bitterly opposed around Shanghai, which was not taken until November. Nanking fell the following month amid scenes of mass butchery and rape on the part of Japanese. It was not until May 1938, however, that the capture of Tungshan allowed the Japanese to link their conquests in northern and central China: thereafter the Japanese advanced up the Yangtze to secure Hankow and Wuchang in October. Having lost Canton in the same month, the Chinese made no attempt to defend the great cities of the middle Yangtze.

Chiang refused various overtures for peace, and Japan sought to counter Chiang's obstinacy by sponsoring Chinese regimes at both Peking and Nanking, but these were too weak to make them genuine alternatives to Chiang's regime at Chungking. The Japanese were without the means of fully occupying the areas they already held, and further conquests only threatened further complications. In 1941 the Japanese nevertheless occupied the major coastal cities south of the Yangtze, as their attention turned to the possibility of isolating Chungking from all outside sources of support. The defeat of France in 1940 placed Indo-China in pledge to the Japanese, and in September 1940 Japanese forces moved into northern Indo-China; in July 1941 Japan forced the Vichy authorities to accept a joint protectorate over Indo-China. These moves prompted the United States to impose sanctions on Japan, thereby setting in train the events that were to lead to the outbreak of the Pacific war in December. But the war in China was to continue under its own complex terms of conduct until the final Japanese capitulation in August 1945.

1 manchuria, 1931–32

- railways under Japanese control
- Japanese advances, 1931
- Japanese garrisons, 1931
- Japanese control by Sept. 1931
- railways under Soviet control, 1931
- Japanese control by Aug. 1932
- areas of Manchurian resistance
- target area of Japanese subversion and inducement, 1932–37
- area from which Chinese regular forces effectively expelled, 1935
- area of Japanese attempt to establish puppet North China State, 1935

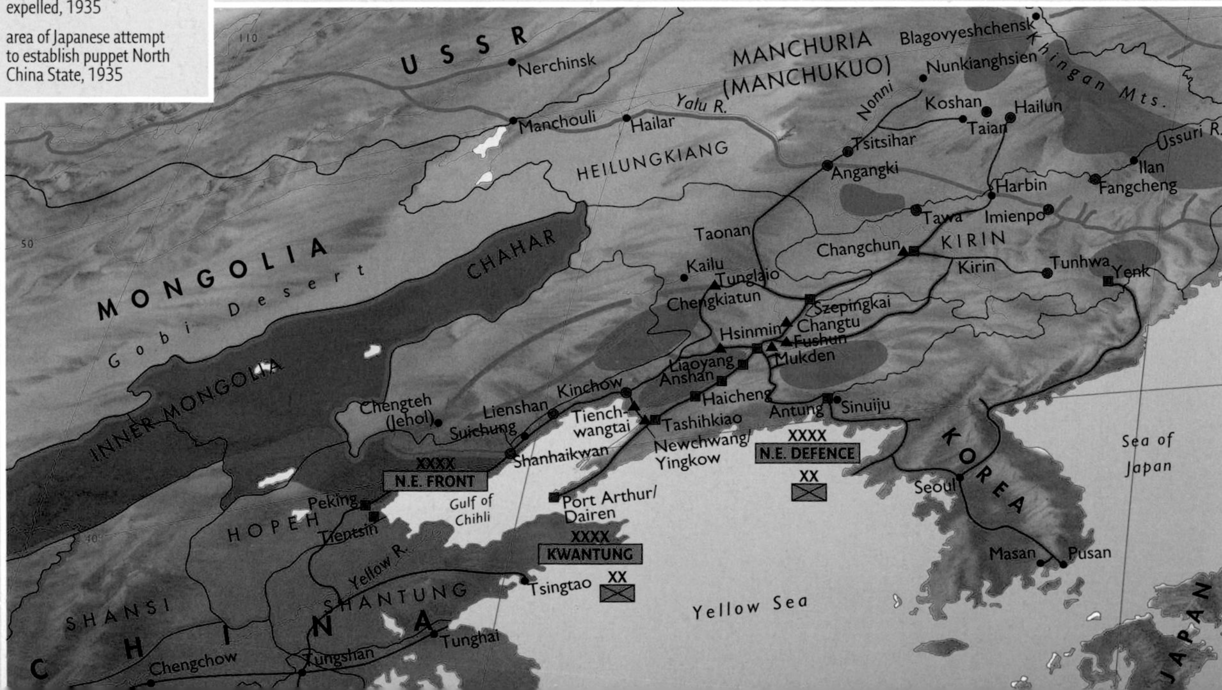

www.johndclare.net/EL5.htm
Japan's invasion of Manchuria
www.fas.harvard.edu/~asiactr/sino-japanese/
A study of the Sino-Japanese war

1 Since the Russo-Japanese war of 1904–05, both powers had coveted the Chinese province of Manchuria. Their influence was extended by the construction of railways; the Japanese also maintained military bases around the Gulf of Chihli. A swift Japanese campaign, conducted along the railway lines (September 1931–February 1932) drove the forces of the local warlord, Chang Hsueh-liang, from the province. The Soviets garrisoned the northern borders, and their attempts to stem Japanese expansion led to battles at Changkufen (1938) and Nomonhan Bridge (1939). Japanese attention now turned to the consolidation by coercion, then military force, of Jehol (January–February 1933) and Chahar and Hopeh (by mid-1935).

2 The full-scale invasion of China began with a drive from positions north of Peking (July 1937) and amphibious landings at Shanghai (November 1937). Gains in the north were extensive and rapid despite the Nationalist/Communist alliance (from December 1936). Within a month Nanking had fallen, the Nationalist government withdrawing to Chungking in Szechwan.

3 The consolidation of Japanese gains from 1938–41 was gradual and incomplete: the Yangtze cities fell easily, but Communist partisans disputed the northern territories, and the southern ports were gained in a series of amphibious operations designed to cut off Chungking from external aid.

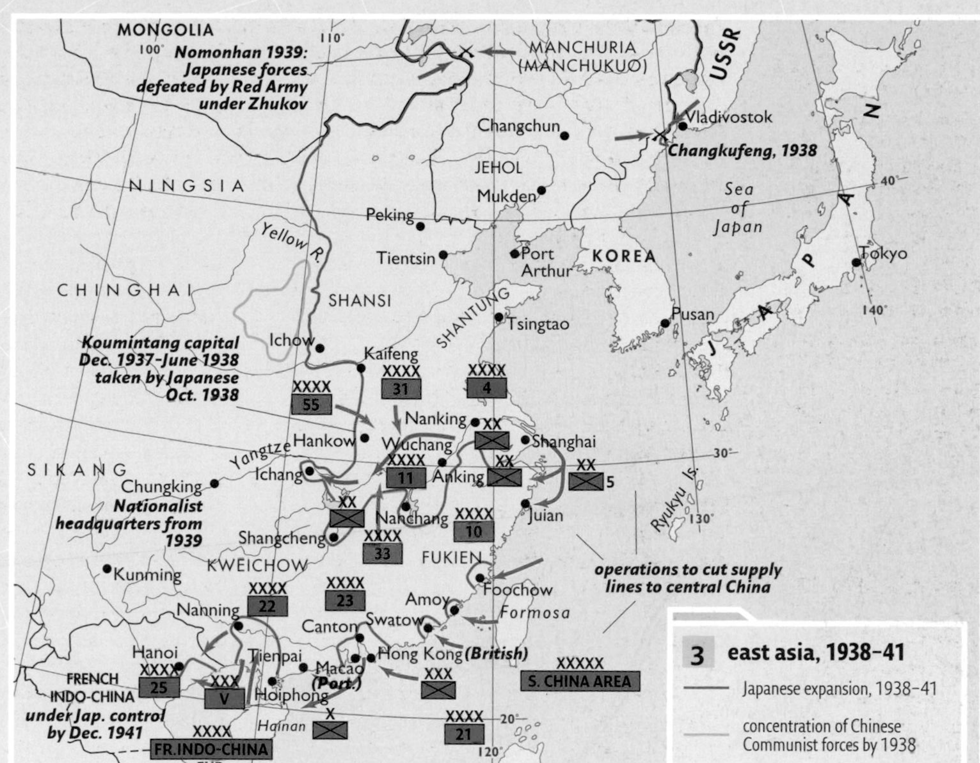

3 east asia, 1938–41
Japanese expansion, 1938–41
concentration of Chinese Communist forces by 1938

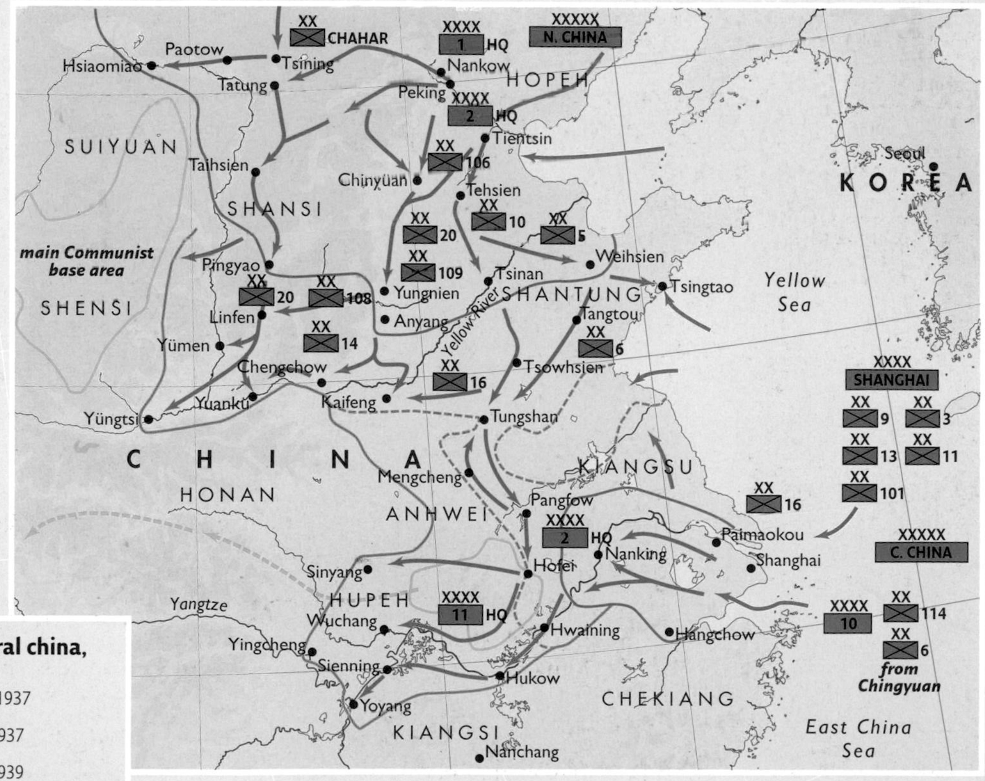

2 northern and central china, 1937–39
Japanese front line, Dec. 1937
Chinese front line, Dec. 1937
Chinese front line, Dec. 1939
movements of Communist units

fascism in europe

1922 to 1939

- **1935** Mussolini launches war against Ethiopia
- **1936 (7 March)** Germany reoccupies the Rhineland
- **1936 (18 July)** Spanish civil war starts
- **1937 (27 April)** Axis bombing destroys Guernica
- **1938** The *Anschluss;* German troops enter Austria
- **1938 (30 September)** Britain, France, Germany and Italy agree the transfer of Sudetenland to Germany
- **1938 (9 November)** *Kristallnacht* anti-Jewish pogrom
- **1939 (January)** Spanish civil war ends
- **1939 (23 August)** German-Soviet Non-aggression Pact signed

Fascism was founded by Benito Mussolini, a left-wing agitator in Italy who, in 1915, broke with the main strain of Italian socialism and became a Nationalist. Fascism was characterised by extreme nationalism and dictatorship with the concomitants of militarism, secret police and violent anti-Marxism (although several of the leading Fascists began as figures of the Left, and continued to preach egalitarianism and anti-capitalism). The externals of Fascism everywhere were much the same, usually derived from Italian models: the 'Roman Salute', with arm outstretched, as answer to the Marxists' clenched-fist-in-anger; black shirts, as counterpart to Garibaldi's red ones.

There was a Fascist style in architecture (a bombastic classicism), broad-ranging propaganda, youth organisations and a commitment to remodelling all social institutions. All Fascist movements had their 'Leader' – Duce, Führer, Jefe. Beyond these common features, however, the movements usually defined as fascist varied greatly in terms of their ambitions and the degree of political success.

In only two major states did fascist movements achieve political power. In Italy Mussolini, head of the Italian Fascist Party, founded in November 1921, was invited to become prime minister in October 1922 by the Italian king; in Germany Adolf Hitler, leader of the National Socialist Party, founded in 1920, was invited to become chancellor in January 1933 by the ageing president, Field Marshal von Hindenburg. In both cases the two political movements profited from a period of economic turmoil; a parliamentary system that failed to deliver stable government; deep popular hostility towards communism; and the collaboration of traditional conservative elites who thought they could exploit fascist movements to break the influence of the left. In both cases street violence accompanied the electoral path to power. The fascist 'squads' in Italy and the paramilitary SA organisation in Germany sought out political enemies and murdered or violated them.

When they came to power Mussolini and Hitler were part of political coalitions. The dictatorship usually associated with fascist political systems was constructed only after they had come to power. In Italy Mussolini altered the electoral law to produce a fascist majority in 1924, and finally established single-party power and an authoritarian dictatorship in 1925–26. Hitler was granted an 'Enabling Law' in March 1933 which formed the basis of his dictatorship. During that year the other parties were outlawed and in 1934, with the death of Hindenburg, Hitler became supreme leader or Führer, answerable to no-one. During the year the first concentration camps were set up and thousands of political opponents murdered or imprisoned at the hands of the SA and a new secret police force, the Gestapo. In Mussolini's Italy political opponents were exiled or imprisoned and a secret police, the OVRA, was set up. Civil liberties were suspended and the parties came to exert an increasingly 'totalitarian' control over the population. In both states laws were passed discriminating against the Jews as enemies of the race.

Both leaders had territorial ambitions and a strong desire to forge a new imperial state – Mussolini in the Mediterranean and Africa, Hitler in Central and

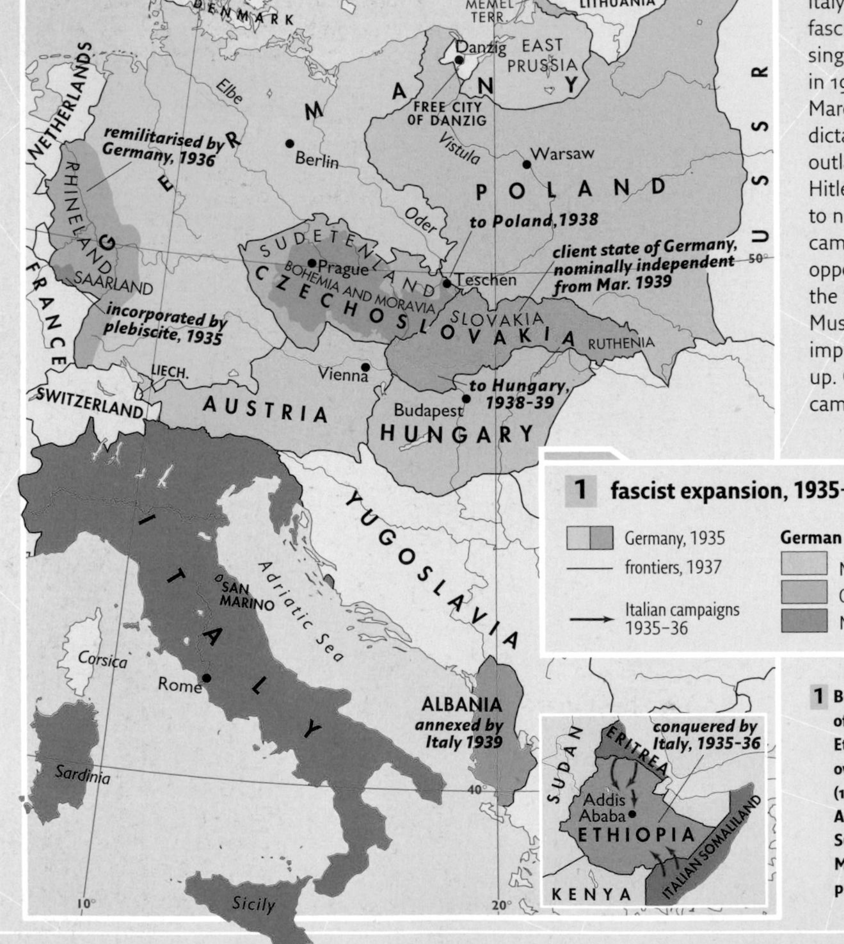

1 Between 1935 and 1939 Italy and Germany began programmes of imperial expansion. In 1936 Italy completed the conquest of Ethiopia and occupied Albania in 1939. Germany under Hitler overturned the Versailles settlement by taking back the Saar (1935), remilitarising the Rhineland (1936), incorporating Austria (March 1938), compelling Czechoslovakia to cede the Sudetenland (October 1938) and occupying Bohemia and Moravia (March 1939). Hitler's invasion of Poland finally provoked Britain and France into war.

www.spartacus.schoolnet.co.uk/Spanish-Civil-War.htm
Comprehensive guide to the Spanish civil war
www.calvin.edu/academic/cas/gpa/index.htm
Information about and original documentation of Nazi propaganda

3 electoral performance of the nazi party in sept. 1930 and march 1933

NSDAP % share of vote

50–59 | 40–49 | 30–39 | 20–29 | 10–19 | 0–9

Kiel, Rostock, Königsberg, Hamburg, Bremen, Stettin, Hanover, Berlin, Kassel, Cologne, Leipzig, Dresden, Breslau, Nuremberg, Stuttgart, Munich, GERMANY — 1933 — 1930

3 The most disruptive change came in Germany. The electoral triumph of Nazism which secured 44% of the vote in March 1933, encouraged radical right-wing movements in the rest of Europe. Hitler and his closest associates used the means of democracy in order to subvert it.

Eastern Europe. Mussolini began a period of active expansion in 1935 when he launched war against the independent African kingdom of Ethiopia. A year later, with Ethiopia conquered, he declared a new Italian empire. In spring 1939 Italy occupied Albania. A large rearmament programme was initiated for the next stage of Italian expansion in the 1940s. To help achieve this Mussolini inaugurated a policy of economic 'autarchy' or self-sufficiency, cutting back on exports and boosting domestic production. In Hitler's Germany the same pattern can be traced: economic stabilisation around policies of autarchy, the initiation of a major programme of rearmament and the onset of territorial expansion to overturn the Versailles settlement and begin a phase of German imperialism. In March 1936 the Rhineland was remilitarised, in February 1938 Austria was occupied and forcibly united with Germany (to the delight of the many Austrian fascists), and in October 1938 the German-speaking areas of Czechoslovakia were incorporated into Germany. German rearmament, organised through a Four-Year Plan set up in October 1936, was planned to reach a peak in the early 1940s when Hitler expected a war in the east to establish German empire.

The success of Mussolini and Hitler encouraged many imitators, from the Iron Guard fascists in Romania to the British Union of Fascists under Oswald Moseley. A small fascist movement in Spain, the Falange, took an active part alongside Franco in the Spanish civil war, where nationalist and fascist forces destroyed the Second Republic after three years of vicious fighting. But only during the war did fascist regimes, puppets of Germany and Italy, appear in other European states.

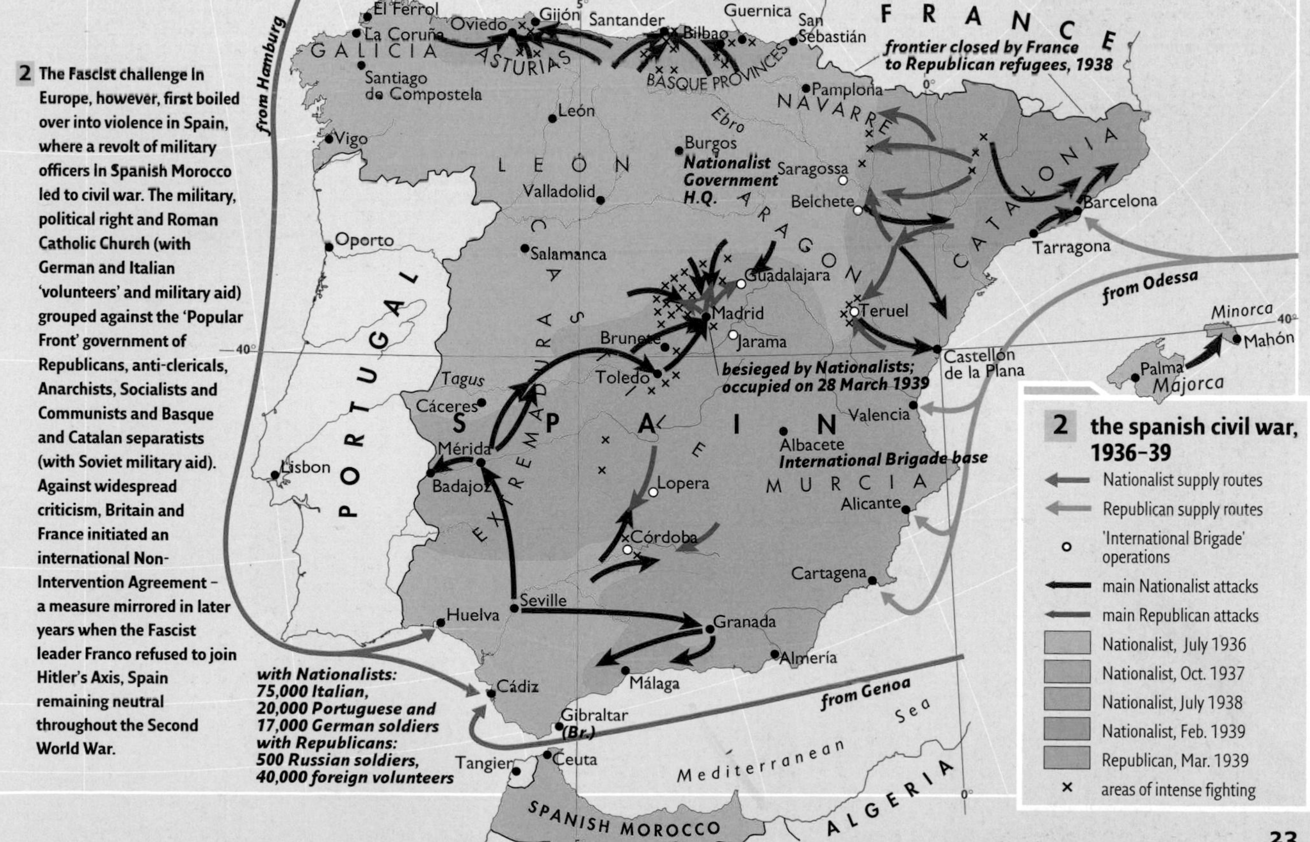

2 The Fascist challenge in Europe, however, first boiled over into violence in Spain, where a revolt of military officers in Spanish Morocco led to civil war. The military, political right and Roman Catholic Church (with German and Italian 'volunteers' and military aid) grouped against the 'Popular Front' government of Republicans, anti-clericals, Anarchists, Socialists and Communists and Basque and Catalan separatists (with Soviet military aid). Against widespread criticism, Britain and France initiated an international Non-Intervention Agreement – a measure mirrored in later years when the Fascist leader Franco refused to join Hitler's Axis, Spain remaining neutral throughout the Second World War.

2 the spanish civil war, 1936–39

- Nationalist supply routes
- Republican supply routes
- 'International Brigade' operations
- main Nationalist attacks
- main Republican attacks
- Nationalist, July 1936
- Nationalist, Oct. 1937
- Nationalist, July 1938
- Nationalist, Feb. 1939
- Republican, Mar. 1939
- × areas of intense fighting

PART 2 THE AXIS ADVANCES

september 1939

1 September Germans invade Poland, annex Danzig; Great Britain and France demand withdrawal

3 September Great Britain, France, Australia and New Zealand declare war on Germany

5 September Germans cross River Vistula

10 September BEF moves to France

12 September Chamberlain rejects Hitler's peace plans

17 September USSR invades eastern Poland

23 September Soviet-German demarcation line reached

27 September Warsaw surrenders

29 September partition of Poland

30 September General Sikorski sets up Polish government in exile in Paris

The Polish campaign was the shortest and most decisive of all German aggressions of the Second World War, of which it marked the opening stage. Between 1 and 19 September 1939 German armies broke through Poland's northern, western and southern frontiers and completed whirlwind advances that overwhelmed the much weaker Polish forces; their destruction was consummated by the intervention of the Soviet Army, which began to advance into eastern Poland on 17 September.

The concessions of territory under the Versailles Treaty to the reborn state of Poland were the most resented grievances felt by Germany in the inter-war years. Resentment focused particularly on the loss of direct access to East Prussia, through the creation of the Polish Corridor to the Baltic, of the German-speaking city of Danzig and of the partly German-speaking regions of Silesia. Hitler placed the repossession of these areas high on his list of 'territorial ambitions', even though the integrity of Poland was guaranteed by France (1921) and, from 31 March 1939, by Britain .

On 25 March 1939, Hitler told the German Army Staff that the time had come to consider solving the 'Polish problem' by military means. On 3 April he set 1 September as the date for an attack. On 28 April he abrogated the German–Polish non-aggression treaty of 1934 and on 23 May he warned his generals to expect war. Hitler was confident that Britain and France would not honour their pledge to Poland and ignored all the evidence to the contrary. To ensure the isolation of Poland he finally overcame his ideological scruples and agreed a Non-Aggression Pact with the USSR, signed in Moscow on 23 August, which included a secret protocol dividing Eastern Europe into spheres of influence.

Germany deployed five armies totalling 1,500,000 men for the offensive. The Poles, who began military preparations in July, had succeeded in mobilising one million when, following German-staged frontier incidents, the Germans attacked at dawn on 1 September. The Luftwaffe attacked Polish air bases throughout the country: many obsolete aircraft were destroyed, although the Polish air force destroyed or damaged 564 German planes. Aerial attacks against Polish defences and cities continued throughout the campaign. A German naval bombardment destroyed the defences of Gdynia, near Danzig, and much of the Polish Fleet on the first day.

On the ground, the German advance was quick. The Polish High Command, in the hope of preserving its western industrial region, had rejected the option of making a stand on the river line of the Narew–Vistula–San. Instead the Polish armies were deployed at the frontiers, which the Germans quickly broke through, thereafter encircling the isolated Polish forces. Without armour or mechanical transport, the Poles were unable to manoeuvre on the battlefield against invaders armed with nearly 2,000 modern tanks.

The German penetration of the frontiers was complete by 5 September. By 7 September Tenthth Army, advancing from the south, was within 40 miles of Warsaw, which the Polish government had left the day before. The Eighth and Fourteenth Armies had kept

1 **The Polish government in 1939 was the first to stand up to Hitler. Foreign Minister Josef Beck argued that Germany was bluffing and its military strength exaggerated. Boosted by a guarantee of support from Britain and France, the Polish Army drew up defence plans. Poland's 37 divisions and 200 aircraft would fight a brief holding action and then withdraw to central Poland to fight in front of Warsaw. They had few tanks, relying on cavalry for mobility. During August 1939 troops and arms were smuggled into Danzig by German forces in East Prussia. On the night of 31 Aug. SS units captured the city, and the following day German soldiers began the invasion of Poland.**

www.worldwar2database.com/html/poland.htm
The German invasion of Poland
www.kasprzyk.demon.co.uk/www/WW2.html
Poland during the Second World War

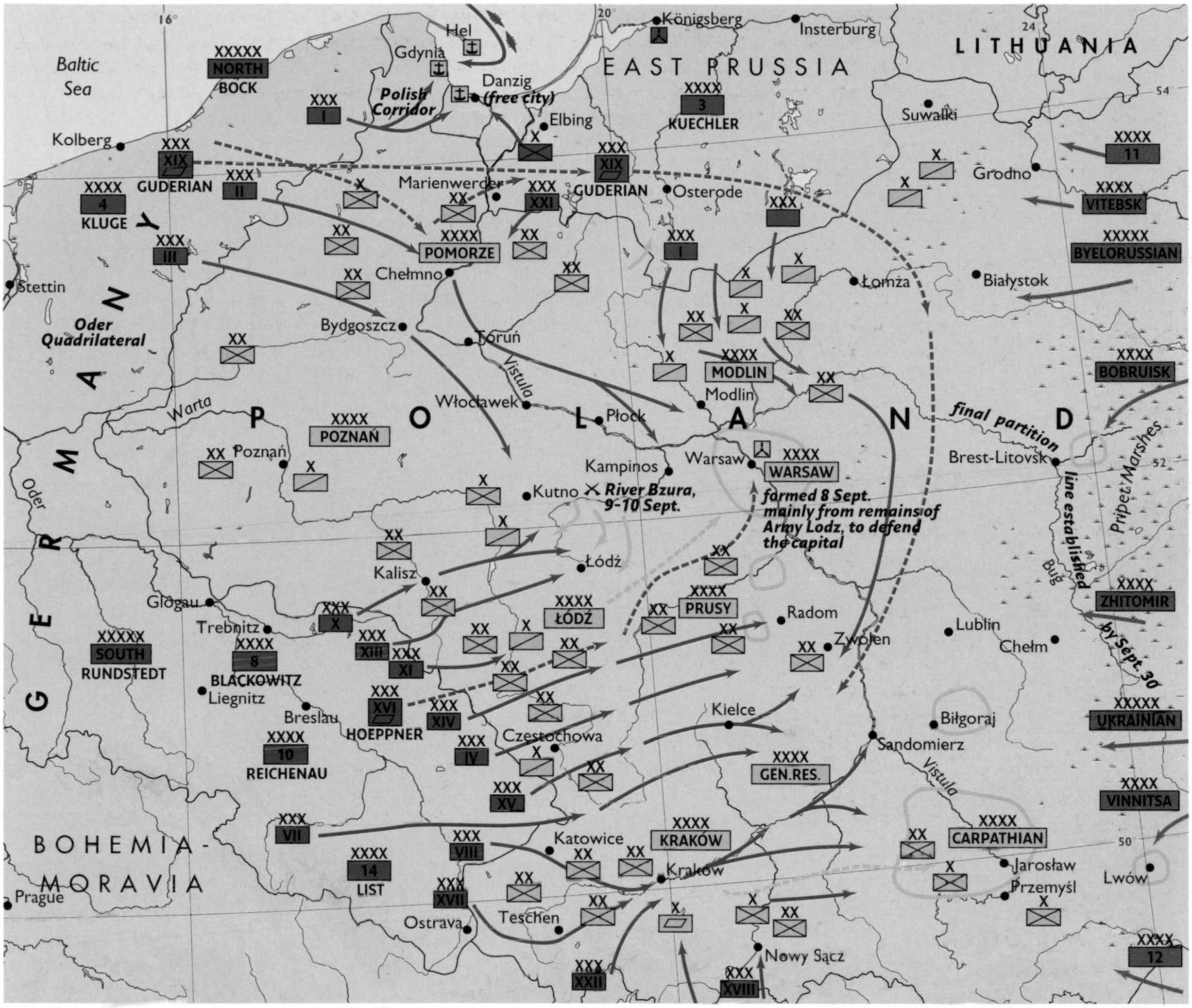

pace to the west, capturing the Silesian industrial region. From the north, Fourth and Third Armies had advanced rapidly, the latter being 25 miles from Warsaw by 7 September. Most of the Polish forces were then confined within their encircling pincers, concentrated in two large pockets around Kutno and Warsaw. The German plan had expected this outcome. Reports that Polish forces were escaping eastwards prompted a revision on 11 September to extend the envelopment beyond the River Vistula. A spirited Polish counter-offensive west of Warsaw on the River Bzura was crushed by 17 September.

On that day, two Soviet Fronts, the Belarussian and Ukrainian, marched into Poland from the east. The Soviets apparently overcame their initial unreadiness in order to prevent German occupation of eastern Poland. They met little resistance.

This first example of German Blitzkrieg tactics – fast moving armoured thrusts supported by air strikes, penetrating deep behind enemy defences to create encirclements that could be mopped up later – had proved a total success.

The Germans took 694,000 prisoners; 100,000 Poles escaped into Lithuania, Hungary and Romania, many eventually joining the Allies in the West. German losses were 13,000 killed and 30,000 wounded. Polish losses were 70,000 killed and 133,000 wounded against the Germans. Losses at Soviet hands have never been accurately calculated.

2 poland, 1–28 sept. 1939

2 **The German plan involved a textbook breakthrough, the cutting of the Polish Corridor, encirclement of the Poles and annihilation within pincer jaws centred on Warsaw, while the Luftwaffe destroyed much of the air force on the ground. The Poznan Army, isolated by the initial German advance, turned east on 10 Sept. and attempted to break across the River Bzura. This initiative was contained by the Germans around Kutno and the pocket surrendered on 17 Sept. Meanwhile, Guderian's panzers took Brest-Litovsk (17 Sept.), while Lwów fell on 19 Sept. Warsaw, heavily bombed, capitulated on 27 Sept. The Russians invaded on 17 Sept., German advance units withdrawing behind a pre-agreed partition line. At this stage many Polish combatants surrendered to the Germans in preference to confronting the Soviet Army.**

scandinavia

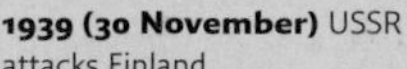

1939 to 1940

- **1939 (30 November)** USSR attacks Finland
- **22 November** strong Finnish counter-attack
- **29 November** Finnish victory at Suommusalmi
- **1940 (1 January)** Soviet offensive against Finns
- **1 February** Soviets attack in Karelia
- **12 February** Finish defences crack
- **13 March** Treaty of Moscow ends the 'Winter War'
- **7 April** Allied forces sail for Norway
- **9 April** Germans occupy Denmark and invade Norway
- **10 May** Norway capitulates; Norwegian government in exile set up in London (from 5 May)

Between the invasion of Poland in September 1939 and the campaign in the West in May 1940, Germany and the USSR transformed, by force or diplomacy, the political geography of the Baltic. The Baltic States, together with Finland, had been allocated to the Soviet sphere of influence by a secret protocol to the Ribbentrop-Molotov Pact of 23 August 1939.

From late September, the Baltic States were forced to sign treaties allowing the basing of Soviet troops on their territory and in June 1940 were definitively occupied, and subsequently annexed as Soviet republics. Finland was confronted on 12 October by Soviet demands to cede a 30-year lease on bases in Karelia, Hangö on the Baltic, and the Rybachi Peninsula and Petsamo in the Arctic. On 26 November the USSR staged an incident that provided the pretext for attack along the whole Finno-Soviet border. The Finns had time to mobilise 200,000 men against one million Soviets. Mannerheim, the Finnish commander, put six of his nine divisions in Karelia, two north of Lake Ladoga with one in reserve. The northern front was held by scattered units. Encirclement tactics (*motti*), and pinpoint assaults on targets such as field kitchens, allowed Finnish units to inflict humiliating defeats on the Red Army north of Lake Ladoga in December, particularly at Tolvayarvi and Suomussalmi. Meanwhile, Mannerheim held Karelia and counter-attacked on 23 December. The Soviets regrouped and on 1 February opened a final offensive. Its sheer weight forced the Finns to sue for peace on 6 March; a treaty of 12 March ceded to the USSR all the territory demanded before the outbreak. Finnish fatal casualties exceeded 24,000, Soviet 200,000, many killed by cold or deprivation.

Soviet aggression against Finland focused Allied and Axis attention on Scandinavia. The German Navy was

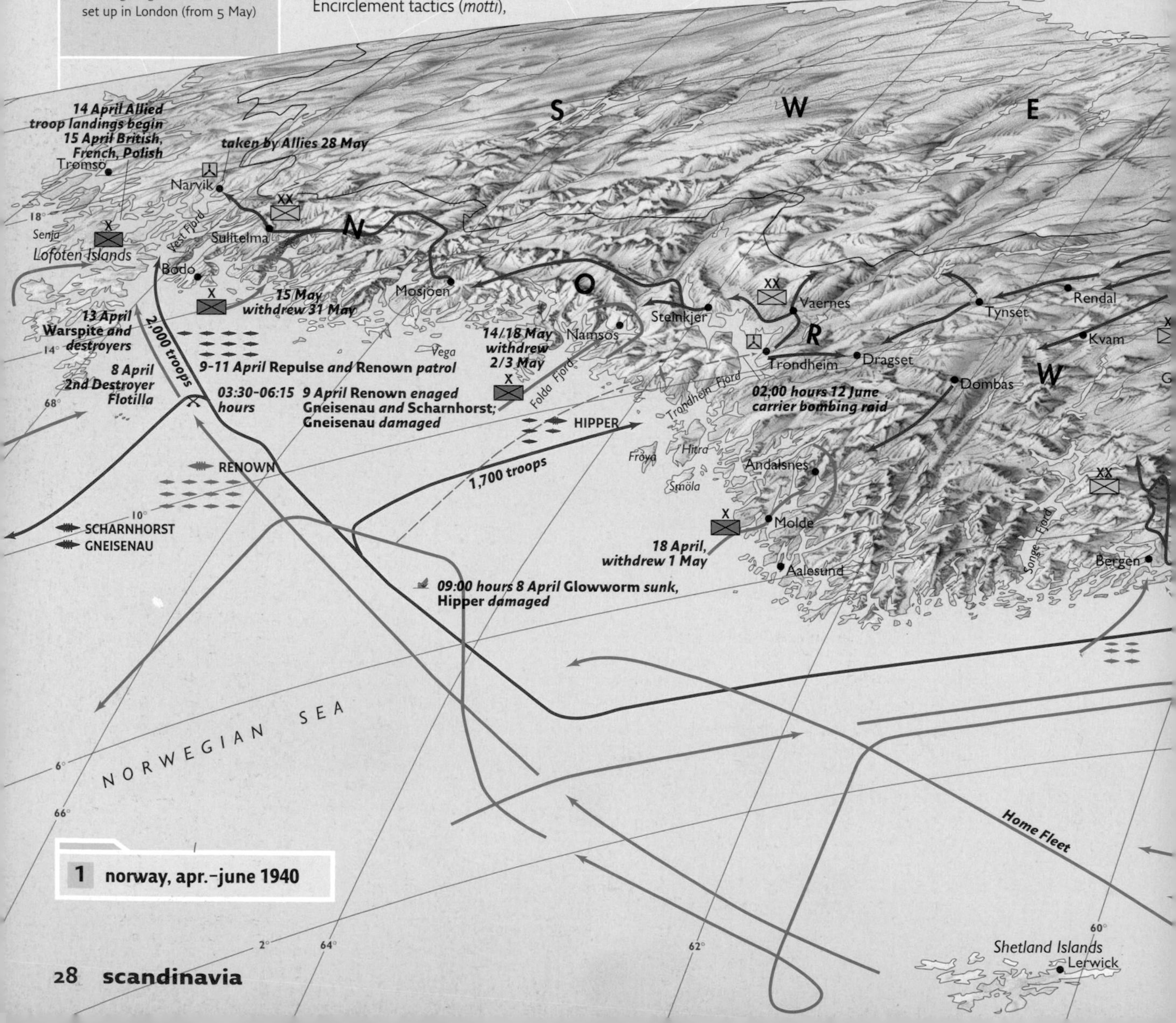

1 norway, apr.–june 1940

www.magweb.com/sample/sconflic/c003wese.htm
The German invasion of Norway
www.kaiku.com/winterwar.html
The Soviet-Finnish 'Winter War'

anxious to acquire bases there, both to protect the iron ore trade with Sweden and to outflank the Royal Navy's dominance of the North Sea. Angered by British violation of neutral Norwegian waters to recover British prisoners from a German merchantman (the *Altmark* incident 16 February 1940) and encouraged by the Norwegian Nazi Vidkun Quisling's claim of local enthusiasm for the German cause, Hitler ordered General Falkenhorst to plan for an invasion of Norway on 21 February.

The British and French considered their own plans for landings in Norway. They were forestalled, however, by the Germans on 9 April, who launched a brilliantly conceived combined operation. Denmark capitulated immediately. Norway, where German sea and airborne forces landed at Oslo, Kristiansand, Stavanger, Bergen, Trondheim and Narvik, held out longer. Norwegian troops resisted resolutely in the north and were joined by Franco-British forces at Trondheim (18 April) and Narvik (14 April). In two battles in the Narvik fjords (10 and 13 April), the Royal Navy inflicted heavy losses on the German covering force. In fierce fighting around Trondheim, British, French and Polish troops were forced to evacuate or surrender by 3 May. The battle at Narvik persisted until 4 June (Allied attention by then concentrated on the Battle of France), but German reinforcements forced an Allied evacuation on 8 June. The withdrawal turned into near disaster as the Allied convoys were harried by German battleships in the North Sea, resulting in the loss of six British vessels; the cruiser, evacuating the King and government of Norway, narrowly escaped. The Norwegian Army concluded an armistice on 9 June and Quisling was installed as puppet ruler.

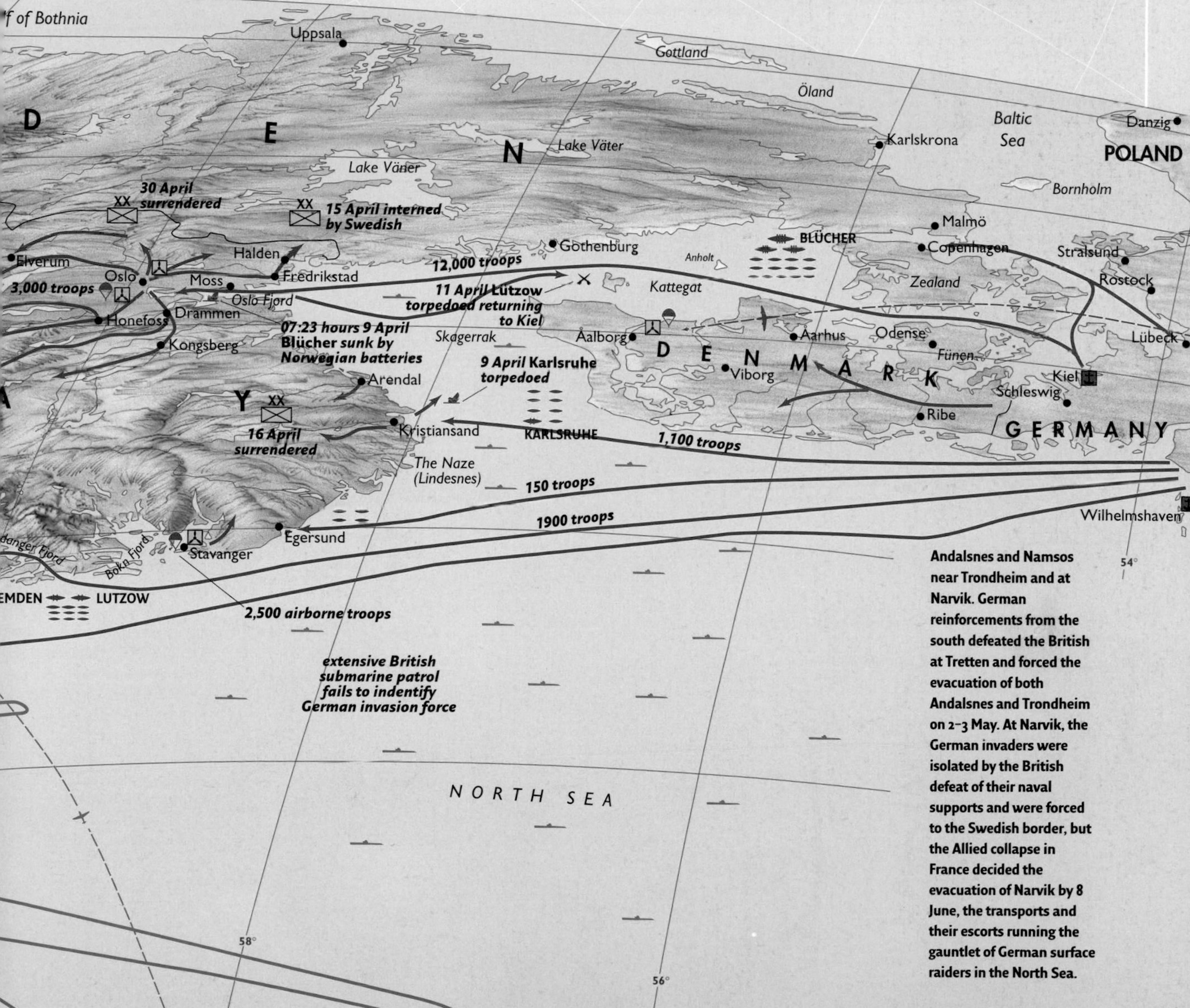

1 **Germany invaded Norway on 9 Apr. At Oslo, Norwegian shore batteries sank the cruiser *Blücher* before it could land troops, allowing the government to escape north, and then to England. The city was captured by an airborne landing. At Stavanger, Kristiansand, Bergen, Trondheim and Narvik, the Germans got ashore on schedule. Once the Germans were established, the small Norwegian army (15,000) resisted, reinforced by British and French troops, who landed at Andalsnes and Namsos near Trondheim and at Narvik. German reinforcements from the south defeated the British at Tretten and forced the evacuation of both Andalsnes and Trondheim on 2–3 May. At Narvik, the German invaders were isolated by the British defeat of their naval supports and were forced to the Swedish border, but the Allied collapse in France decided the evacuation of Narvik by 8 June, the transports and their escorts running the gauntlet of German surface raiders in the North Sea.**

the low countries

1940

- **15 January** Belgium refuses Allied request to pass through her territory
- **10 May** Chamberlain resigns; Churchill becomes new Prime Minister; Germany attacks Holland, Belgium and Luxembourg
- **11 May** Rapid German advances; Fort Eden Emael taken by airborne assault
- **14 May** German air raid on Rotterdam
- **15 May** Holland capitulates; government in exile set up in London; German forces cross River Meuse
- **18 May** Antwerp captured
- **20 May** German forces reach the Channel
- **26 May–3 June** 350,000 Allied troops evacuated from Dunkirk beaches
- **27 May** Belgian Army capitulates

Hitler announced his intention to attack in the west to his generals on 27 September 1939, the day Poland capitulated. He wanted the campaign completed before winter and demanded a plan. That plan was submitted by OKH on 19 October: Operation Yellow called for a drive to the Dutch and Belgian coasts, to secure a base for further operations by land, sea and air against the French and British. It dissatisfied Hitler, who wanted a more decisive outcome. OKH demurred, while bad weather forced successive postponements.

Operation Yellow was finally cancelled when German officers carrying secret documents compromised it by force-landing at Mechelen in Belgium on 9 January 1940. The plan replacing it (Operation Sichelschnitt) was the brainchild of a critic of OKH, General von Manstein. It coincided with Hitler's own ideas, and with his backing, was transformed by OKH into a grand design (24 February) to encircle and destroy the Anglo-French armies in northern France.

The French, with their British allies, depended on the Maginot Line to defend the Franco-German frontier. That, with neutral Belgium, was to be covered, in the event of a German invasion, by rushing the Allies' mobile forces to the line of the River Dyle and hinging their right flank on the Ardennes, which was believed 'untankable'. This latter assumption proved dangerously ignorant. The Germans had performed extensive exercises to test the viability of an armoured thrust through the Ardennes forest, allowing them to bypass the Maginot Line. In fact their tactical thinking was based on the combined use of armoured thrusts and advance units of mobile sappers. Operation Sichelschnitt planned to drive the armoured columns of Army Group A across the Ardennes and across the Meuse, the most formidable of the river obstacles, at Sedan, Monthermé and Dinant. The columns were then to swing north-west and drive for the Channel coast near Abbeville, trapping the French First Army Group and the British Expeditionary Force with their backs to the sea. Airborne and ground forces would, meanwhile, overwhelm the defences of neutral Holland, while the main weight of Army Group A fell on the Belgians. The role of Army Group C, which had been allotted no armour, was to engage the garrison of the Maginot Line, which it was to penetrate if possible.

Numbers on each side were approximately equal. The Germans deployed 136 divisions against 94 French, 12 British (comprising almost the whole of Britain's army strength), 22 Belgian and 9 Dutch. Allied tanks

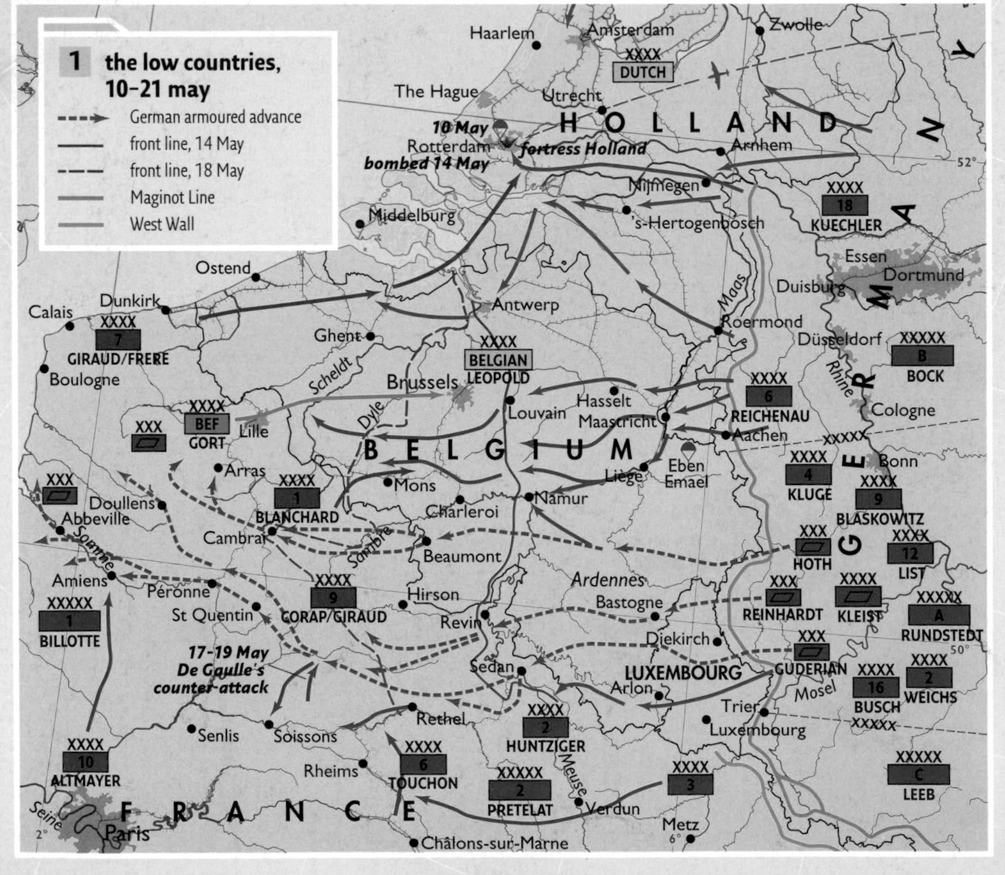

1 **The campaign in the Low Countries was, on the German part, a masterly piece of detailed planning and accurate execution, pin-pointing the weakness of Allied response. The German attack, Operation Sichelschnitt (Sicklestroke), bypassed the Maginot Line to the west, encircled the Dutch and Belgian armies and pinned the BEF and the First French Army Group against the Channel. The overall success of the campaign relied upon a series of detailed airborne and river crossing manoeuvres. The first crossing of the Meuse was achieved by 7th Panzer Division (Rommel) early on 13 May at Dinant, with Guderian's Panzer Group crossing later that day at Sedan. The British mounted an armoured counter-attack on the spearhead of the German panzer corridor at Arras halting the advance and causing heavy losses of men and equipment. The panzer thrust managed, however, to reach the coast by 21 May.**

www.historylearningsite.co.uk/blitzkrieg.htm
The German military tactic of speed and surprise
http://news.bbc.co.uk/1/hi/uk/765004.stm
History of the Dunkirk evacuation

numbered 4,200 to 2,500, though the Germans were superior in aircraft for the campaign: 3,200 to 1,800. The Allied divisions, however, were of very uneven quality, and few were pure tank formations. The Germans, by contrast, had organised their tanks into ten panzer divisions, strongly supported by tactical air forces, massing the majority under Army Group A for the Meuse crossings. The German Army also had a clearcut offensive doctrine, later to be called blitzkrieg, while the Allies thought in defensive terms. They also had a muddled chain of command and there was only patchy enthusiasm for the war among the rank and file.

Germany began its attack on 10 May. In Holland the Dutch Army was organised around Rotterdam, Amsterdam and Utrecht (Fortress Holland). The Dutch had not fought a war since 1830. German parachutists penetrated Fortress Holland and secured bridgeheads for airborne troops and tank columns. French relieving columns were turned back and on 14 May – after the Luftwaffe had carried out a threat to bomb Rotterdam, causing 30,000 civilian casualties, and German ground troops had made contact with the parachutists – Holland surrendered.

The Belgian Army was also committed to the defence of the national fortresses, particularly on the Meuse; it was to fight with great bravery after the defences of Belgium were compromised on 10 May, when German glider troops neutralised the fortress defending the Meuse crossing at Eben Emael. On the next day, the Belgian Army began to fall back to the Dyle, where the French First Army Group (with most of the French mobile and armour divisions and the BEF under its command) had arrived. But by 15 May the German Eighteenth Army was outflanking them from Holland in the north, while the Sixth was pressing against the Dyle Line itself. Meanwhile, Army Group A had crossed the Meuse at Dinant and Sedan on 13 May, and Monthermé on 15 May. As French resistance collapsed on that sector, Army Group A's eight panzer divisions drove into northern France.

Gamelin, French supreme commander, acquiesced in the withdrawal of the First Army Group and the BEF from the Dyle to the Scheldt on 16 May and tried to organise realignments and counter-attacks to save his crumbling front. Armoured thrusts by the French, under de Gaulle, at Laon (17–19 May) and by the British at Arras (21 May) dented but did not cut the German panzer corridor. The latter illustrated the lack of German awareness of their enemy's weakness, as the German divisional commander, Rommel, believed he had been attacked by five tank divisions. Nevertheless, the German panzers had reached St Quentin on 18 May and Abbeville on 20 May. French counter-attacks, ordered by Weygand (who succeeded Gamelin on 19 May) also failed at Cambrai and Amiens on 22–23 May.

German attacks separated the Belgian Army from the BEF on 25 May, forcing Belgium's capitulation on 28 May. Meanwhile, the BEF and the French forces were being forced back into what would become the Dunkirk perimeter. Successive water lines surrounding the port were judged by Hitler so serious an obstacle to his tanks that he ordered their halt on 23 May. This apparent error of judgement gave the trapped armies a glimmer of hope. On 26 May, the British government authorised Gort to withdraw the BEF to Britain, and evacuation (Operation Dynamo) began the next day. A portion of the French Army continued to defend Lille until 1 June. The rest, with the BEF, was shipped from the Dunkirk beaches. By 4 June, when evacuation ceased, 338,226 men had been taken off, two-thirds British. Relentless German pressure on the pocket resumed on 26 May, but was restrained by brave resistance and fierce intervention by the RAF, which flew 2,739 sorties. Almost all the heavy equipment of the BEF and First Army Group was lost or left behind, but Britain at least had the core of an army with which to prepare the defence of the United Kingdom. The Germans, meanwhile, turned south.

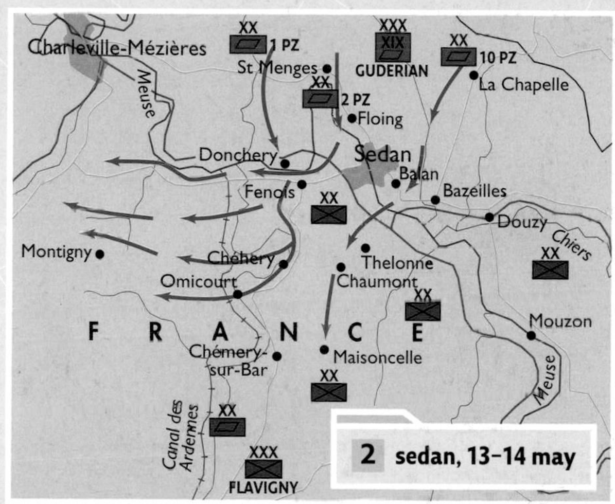

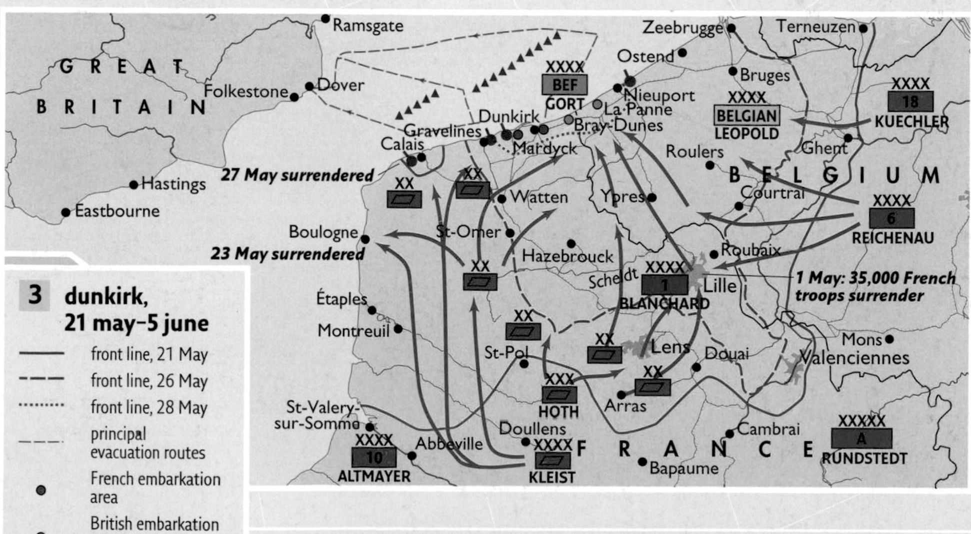

3 Operation Dynamo, begun on 27 May, was designed to withdraw the survivors of the BEF, and as many of the French as possible, to Britain. Fierce defence of the water lines surrounding Dunkirk allowed 336,000 soldiers (including 110,000 French) to be taken off by 4 June. The Germans were then within 1 1/4 miles of the sea. An armada of small boats participated in Operation Dynamo, but most troops were evacuated by the Royal Navy, which, despite RAF cover, bore both fighter-bomber attack and coastal battery fire.

june 1940

- **3 June** Germans take 40,000 prisoners at Dunkirk
- **10 June** Italy declares war on Britain and France
- **14 June** Germans enter Paris
- **16 June** Reynaud resigns; Marshal Pétain forms new French government
- **22 June** Franco-German armistice signed (effective from 25th) at Compiègne
- **23 June** First British commando raid at Boulogne
- **28 June** Britain recognises General de Gaulle as Free French leader
- **30 June** Germans occupy the Channel Islands

While Weygand's plan to halt the German advance to the sea by counter-attacks towards Arras and Amiens had been tried and failed, he had been organising a new defensive line (the Weygand Line) along the Somme and Aisne. Reinforcements and surviving elements of the battle in the north had been deployed in a new Fourth Army Group (Huntziger), which together with Second and a reorganised Third, was ordered to hold 225 miles of front with only 50 divisions. German strength, at over 120 divisions, was unimpaired. The French air force had received reinforcements from the RAF and still operated 1,000 aircraft, but more than half the French tanks had been lost in the defence of Belgium.

The Germans aligned most of their panzer divisions in two groups (Kleist and Guderian) opposite Amiens and Rheims, as the spearheads of Army Groups B and A. They attacked on 5 and 9 June respectively. The French, in the path of Army Group B, resisted valiantly – as did those in the coastal pocket around St Valéry-en-Caux (surrendered 12 June; the defenders included the British 51st Highland Division). But by the night of 8 June, Bock had broken through towards Paris and the next day Rundstedt attacked towards Rheims. He met three days of fierce resistance but on 11 June the collapse of the French in front of Bock forced Rundstedt's opponents to retreat behind the Marne. On 12 June, Guderian's panzer group (now joined by Kleist) broke through to the east of Paris.

Reynaud's government had left Paris for Tours on 10 June, at the head of a vast efflux of fugitives (*l'exode*), which was to leave the city apparently almost deserted when the Germans entered on 14 June. Churchill, making his fourth visit to France since he had become Prime Minister on 10 May, visited Reynaud at Tours on 11 June to urge continued resistance. When he returned to England he took with him General Charles de Gaulle, whom Reynaud had appointed Under Secretary for War, after his valiant effort to blunt the German advance at Laon (17–19 May), as an ally against the peace party in his cabinet. At de Gaulle's prompting, Churchill proposed on 16 June an 'indissoluble union' of Britain and France as a testimony of their determination to fight Germany to the end. But the proposal was unacceptable to the peace party, which on the night of 16 June appointed Marshal Philippe Pétain head of government. Early the following morning he decided to renegotiate for an armistice. On 18 June de Gaulle made his historic broadcast from London establishing a 'Free France' to carry on the fight.

Within France, however, the advance of the German Army proceeded almost unchecked. Bordeaux had become the seat of French government on 14 June, and by that date Army Groups B and A had crossed the Seine and were pressing forward towards the Loire, while C had broken the Maginot Line near Saarbrücken. On 15 June it was broken again near Colmar and the remnants of the French Second Army Group, encircled by Army Group C near Epinal, surrendered on 22 June.

In places the French continued to resist the advance of Army Groups B and A, notably at Saumur on the Loire, where the students of the famous cavalry school held the bridges against the tanks of Army Group B, 19–20 June. On 19 June, however, Pétain had formally petitioned the Germans for an armistice. On 21 June a French armistice delegation was taken by the Germans to the forest near Compiègne, site of the German armistice of November 1918, where, on the next day, in a conspicuously humiliating gesture, Hitler signed the terms in the same railway carriage in which the Germans had agreed to the end of the First World War.

The armistice did not take effect until 25 June, when Italy, which had come into the war on 10 June, also signed. Mussolini, hoping for victories as spectacular as the German, attacked the French defenders of the Alps on 20 June but achieved no success at all. Italy was nevertheless allotted a zone of occupation in Provence. The German zone of occupation delineated by the armistice was smaller than that captured by the German armies, which, by 22 June, had advanced almost to Bordeaux and south of Lyons. The unoccupied zone, with its seat of government at Vichy, eventually comprised France south of the Loire, less its Atlantic and Alpine frontiers. The French Empire and the French Fleet, which based itself in the Mediterranean and North African ports, remained under the control of Pétain's Vichy government. Vichy remained, in name, a sovereign government and was permitted an 'armistice army' of 100,000 men, but Paris and the territory outside the unoccupied zone came under the German military administration. Nevertheless, substantial numbers of French troops and naval vessels had been evacuated to Britain. De Gaulle and his adherents were declared traitors by the Vichy government.

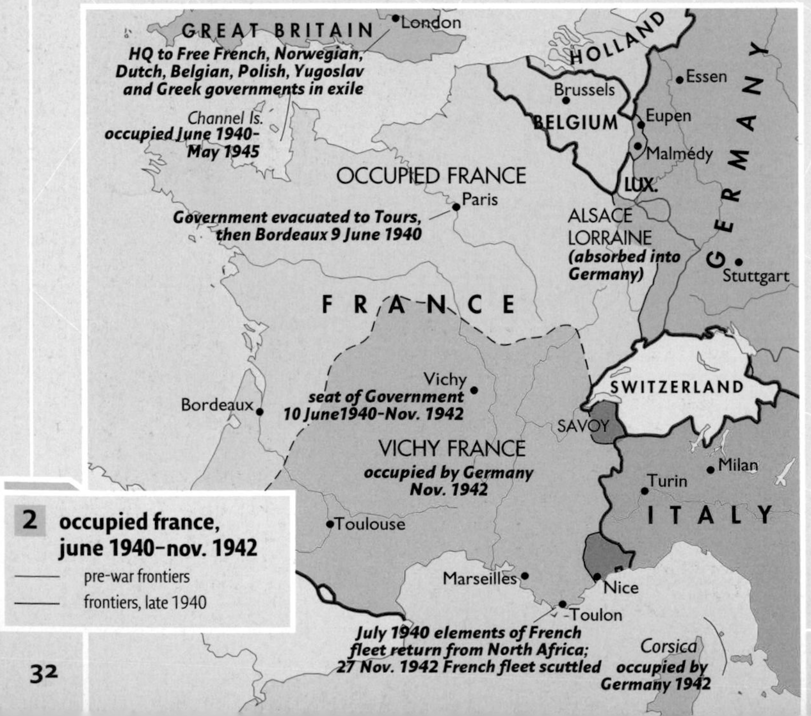

2 occupied france, june 1940–nov. 1942

pre-war frontiers
frontiers, late 1940

www.bbc.co.uk/history/war/wwtwo/launch_ani_fall_france_campaign.shtml
The fall of France
www.diggerhistory.info/pages-enemy/vichy.htm
The Vichy government in France

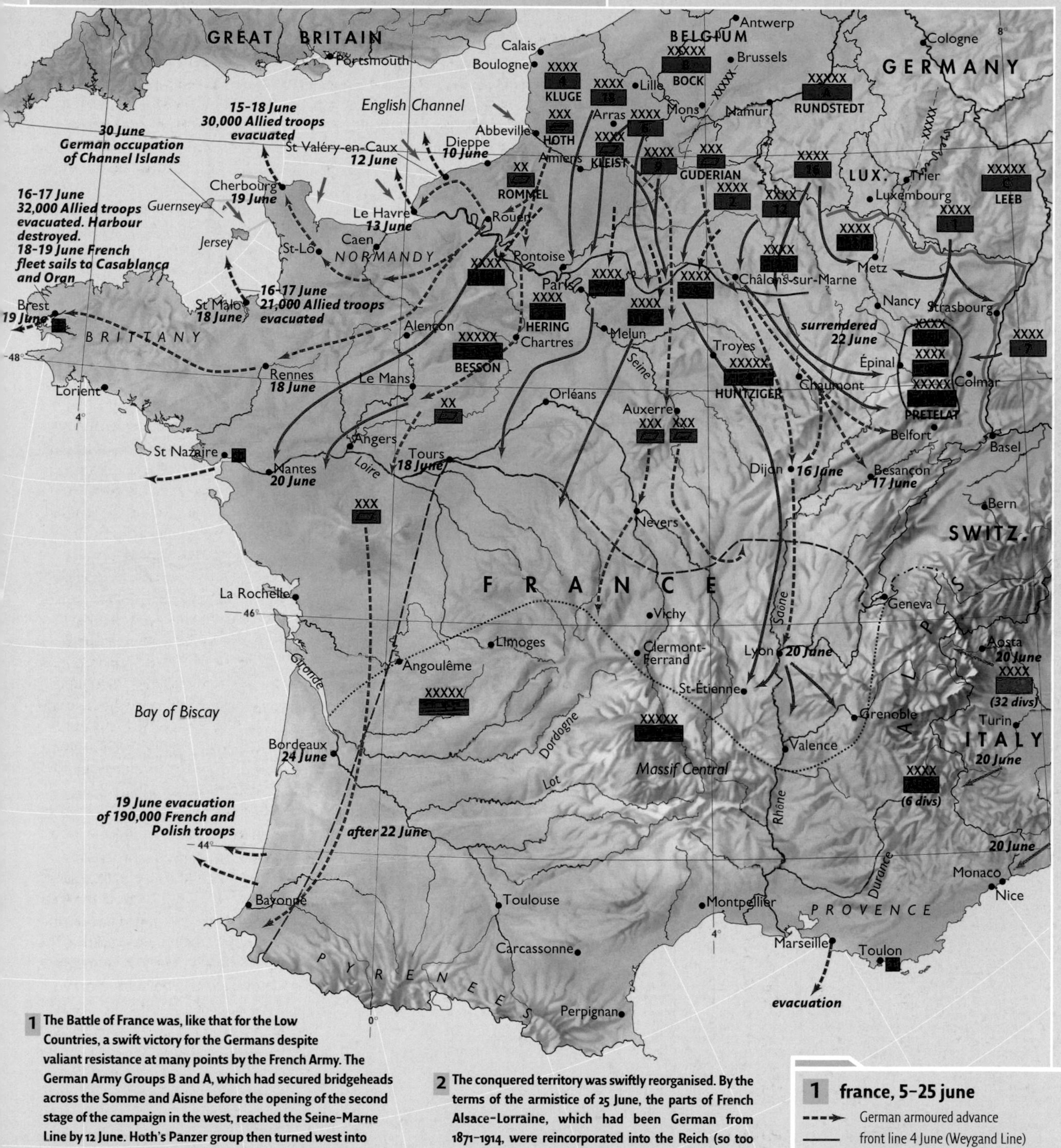

1 The Battle of France was, like that for the Low Countries, a swift victory for the Germans despite valiant resistance at many points by the French Army. The German Army Groups B and A, which had secured bridgeheads across the Somme and Aisne before the opening of the second stage of the campaign in the west, reached the Seine-Marne Line by 12 June. Hoth's Panzer group then turned west into Brittany, capturing Brest on 19 June. Guderian's Panzer group turned east, helping Army Group C to encircle the remnants of the French Second Army Group. Kleist's Panzer group spearheaded the advance into central France. The line of the Loire was reached on 17 June and the Gironde and lower Rhône by 25 June. Some of Kleist's tanks penetrated as far as the Pyrenees before withdrawing. The Italian Army, which attacked on 20 June, was held at the border by six French divisions.

2 The conquered territory was swiftly reorganised. By the terms of the armistice of 25 June, the parts of French Alsace-Lorraine, which had been German from 1871–1914, were reincorporated into the Reich (so too were Belgian border districts). Nice and Savoy were occupied by Italy. France as far north as the Loire, together with the Atlantic coast, was placed under German military adminstration. The capital of Pétain's État Français was established at Vichy. The French Empire remained under the control of Vichy. It included Syria-Lebanon, Algeria, Tunisia and Morocco, French West Africa, Madagascar, French Guiana and Indo-China.

1 france, 5–25 june
- German armoured advance
- front line 4 June (Weygand Line)
- limit of German advance by armistice, 22 June
- demarcation between German-occupied France and Vichy administration following armistice
- naval actions against land forces
- main French evacuation routes
- Maginot Line

battle of the **atlantic I**

september 1939 to march 1941

- **1939 (10 September)** Battle of Atlantic begins; Allied loses 53 ships for 2 U-boats
- **30 September** *Graf Spee* sinks first ship
- **14 October** HMS *Oak Royal* sunk in Scapa Flow by U47
- **November** Allied shipping losses: 21 ships of 51,600 tons
- **18 November** German magnetic mines inflict heavy damage on British shipping
- **23 November** Magnetic mines analysed by British and counter-measures taken
- **13 December** Battle of River Plate; *Graf Spee* scuttled (16th)
- **1940 (28 February)** British Ultra team breaks the Enigma Code
- **20-22 September** U-boat Wolf Packs attack Convoy HX-72, sinking 12 ships totalling 78,000 tons
- **18-19 September** Sunderland flying boat detects U-boat using ASV1 radar for first time

The defeat of the German Navy in the First World War stemmed from its attempt to conduct a campaign against Allied merchant shipping from a position of strategic and numerical weakness. Despite its awareness of the reasons for its previous defeat, the German Navy entered the Second World War committed to the same attritional doctrine that had failed it after 1917 and was forced to operate under the same handicaps as in the First World War.

German naval strategy in 1939 – tonnage warfare – was based on a simple calculation: if 750,000 tonnes of British shipping could be sunk every month, over a 12-month period, then Britain would be forced to surrender. At this time Britain, totally dependent upon the sea for over 60 million tonnes per annum of imports, had some 22 million tonnes of shipping, over half of which was available after September 1939 for oceanic trade. Germany began the war with 57 submarines (not the 350 deemed necessary to complete Britain's defeat) but it was her intention to develop her campaign against shipping by using mines, aircraft and warships, and auxiliary raiders. It was after June 1940 when the acquisition of bases in Norway and France allowed German aircraft and submarines to reach into the Atlantic, far beyond the range of effective escort cover, that the campaign against Allied shipping was joined on a significant scale by aircraft and raiders for the first time. The peak of their efforts, however, passed very quickly. Though five warships broke into the Atlantic in the first half of 1941 the loss of the *Bismarck* revealed the danger of operating surface units without air support in waters patrolled by Allied aircraft; RAF raids on Brest led to the withdrawal of major warships to Germany in February 1942. Auxiliary raiders disguised as unarmed merchantmen continued to set sail until October 1942 and to operate until October 1943, but their activities after 1941 were largely neutralised by the extension of convoys throughout the Atlantic; thereafter they were exiled to the more distant and less rewarding waters of the Indian and Pacific Oceans. The Luftwaffe ceased to be a major factor in the Battle of the Atlantic after June 1941 because of its commitments on the Eastern Front.

After the German use of magnetic mines (in autumn 1939 and of acoustic mines in autumn 1940) in British home waters was countered, U-boats were the primary instrument in the German campaign against Allied commerce throughout the war. In this initial period the Allies were at their weakest. There was no comprehensive convoy system throughout the Atlantic; and with convoys poorly protected there was no good reason for the German Navy and Luftwaffe to run risks by directing their main efforts against escorted merchantmen when so much shipping remained outside convoy. Of the 1,787 Allied and neutral merchantmen sunk between September 1939 and June 1941, only 362 were sunk in convoy.

Only in this initial period of the war, therefore, were the Germans able to conduct a balanced campaign against Allied shipping; but even though at this time German submarines commanded considerable success, most notably in autumn 1940, various developments indicated that Germany's tonnage warfare strategy was failing at this early stage. The invasions of Norway and the Netherlands had forced their shipping into British ports; further, rationing and the strict control of shipping

1 the north atlantic, sept. 1939–may 1940

- Allied merchant ships sunk by U-boats
- U-boats sunk
- major convoy routes
- air escort cover

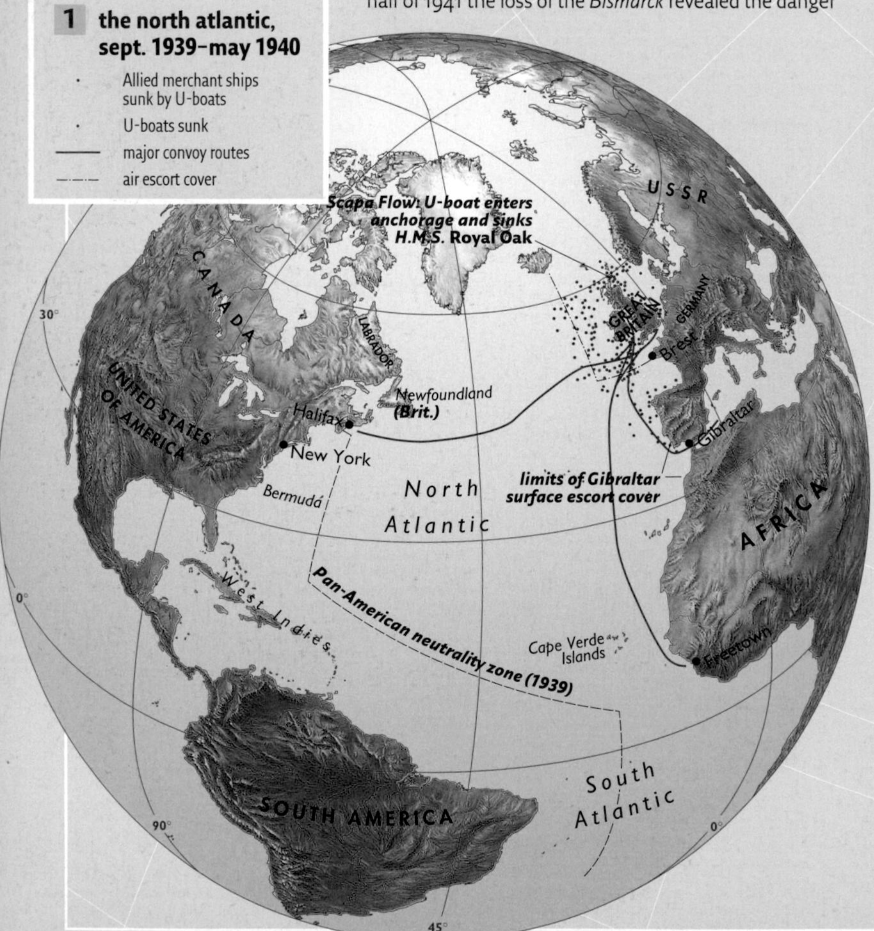

1 **The European war began in September 1939 with the German Navy (apart from two raiders in the Atlantic) unable to carry the campaign against Allied shipping outside the North Sea, the English Channel and the Western Approaches; as a consequence, the bulk of Allied shipping losses was incurred in these areas, with German milling activity causing a severe disruption of coastal shipping in the North Sea. By having virtually the whole of the U-boat arm available for operations in September 1939, however, the German Navy trapped itself in a pattern of operations that hindered the long-term expansion of the U-boat service in the first phase of the war. As a result, sinkings by submarines in the first ten months of the war fluctuated considerably. The German conquest of France, however, changed the strategic pattern of the war at sea; possession of naval bases on the French Atlantic coast gave German submarines and aircraft direct access into the Atlantic and forced the British to divert shipping from the south-west approaches to the north-west. With isolated exceptions, the south-west approaches remained closed to Allied shipping until 1944.**

www.iwm.org.uk/upload/package/8/atlantic/campaign.htm
The Imperial War Museum guide to the Battle of the Atlantic
www.mariner.org/atlantic/
The Mariners' Museum guide to the Battle of the Atlantic

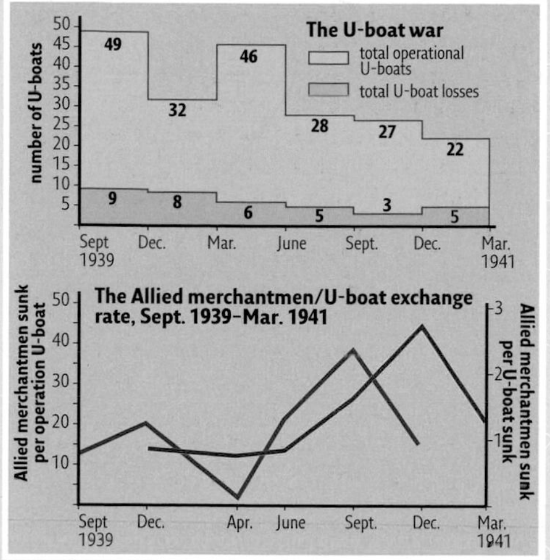

Allied merchant ship losses, Sept. 1939–Mar. 1941

date	U-boat	aircraft	mine	warship raider	merchant raider	E-boat	unknown and other causes	quarterly totals
Sept.–Dec. 1939	421,156 (114)	2,949 (10)	262,697 (79)	61,337 (15)	none	none	7,253 (4)	755,392 (222)
Jan.–Mar. 1940	343,610 (108)	33,240 (20)	167,357 (50)	1,761 (1)	none	none	2,467 (2)	548,435 (181)
Apr.–June 1940	372,160 (78)	276,950 (77)	153,591 (53)	25,506 (2)	40,631 (6)	7,701 (5)	155,636 (78)	1,032,175 (299)
July.–Sept. 1940	758,778 (153)	179,804 (63)	55,300 (26)	none	194,647 (30)	29,836 (15)	14, 398 (10)	1,232,763 (297)
Oct.–Dec. 1940	711,610 (132)	90,080 (32)	133,641 (72)	69,719 (14)	131,366 (18)	10,448 (3)	31,404 (11)	1,178,268 (282)
Jan.–Mar. 1941	566,585 (101)	281,216 (88)	57,199 (39)	187,662 (37)	114,222 (25)	23,340 (12)	23,115 (15)	1,253,339 (317)

totals by theatre, Sept. 1939–Mar. 1941

Atlantic Ocean	Mediterranean	Indian Ocean	Pacific Ocean
5,605,449 (1,533)	84,394 (17)	210,005 (31)	99,531 (15)

figures show tonnages, with numbers of ships in backets

space reduced Britain's import needs by more than half in the course of the war. Moreover, despite German success – which in this period peaked in April 1941 with the fourth highest Allied losses of the entire war – sinkings registered per operational U-boat began to decline in 1941, as did the direct exchange rate between sinkings of merchantmen and U-boats. In effect, therefore, as convoys became more widespread and better protected, the U-boats found it increasingly difficult to sink merchantmen and throughout this period they were never able to sustain a rate of sinkings that approximated to the original tonnage warfare requirements. Meanwhile, problems of extending the U-boat arm meant that after eighteen months of war, its operational strength was less than half that of September 1939. Lastly, as British counter measures in the eastern Atlantic became increasingly effective – the convoy system in the North Atlantic being extended in spring 1941 – the U-boats were forced both to turn their attention to convoys and to move westwards in an attempt to find victims beyond the range of British aircraft. As they did so, however, there emerged the danger of a German clash with the United States, a clash which, despite the increasingly obvious American determination to ensure Britain's survival, Hitler desperately wished to avoid until the defeat of the USSR.

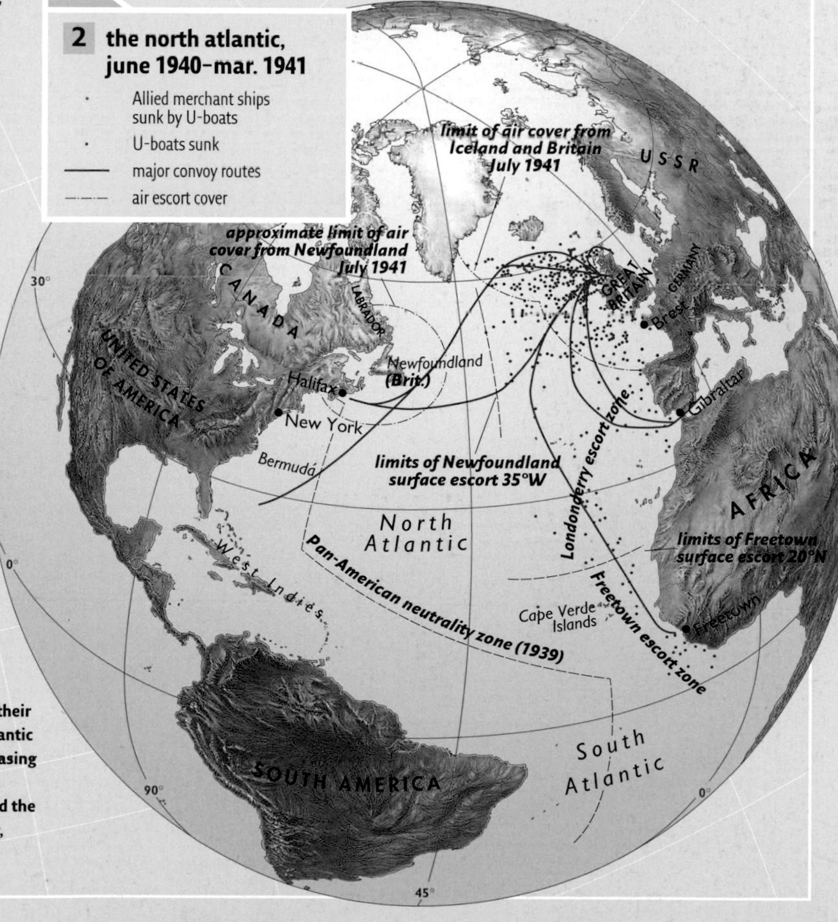

2 **After June 1940 the campaign against Allied shipping was joined on a significant scale by aircraft and raiders. The peak of the warship effort was made in the first half of 1941 when five ships broke into the Atlantic, but the loss of the *Bismarck* and RAF raids on Brest led to the withdrawal of heavy warships to Germany in February 1942; thereafter, German warships were used as a threat to Arctic convoys. The last of the disguised raiders was sunk in October 1943, though their activities were dissipated after 1941 by the extension of the Atlantic convoy. German submarines, however, now commanded increasing success, reaching a high point in October 1940 when they sank 352,407 tonnes of shipping. The gradual extension of convoy and the development of British air bases in Iceland after 1940, however, forced the U-boats westwards.**

1940 to 1941

- **1936 (3 August)** Italy annexes Ethiopia
- **1939 (2 August)** Wavell made Commander-in-Chief in Near East; extended to E. Africa, Iraq and Persian Gulf by 3 September
- **1940 (12 February)** Australian and New Zealand troops land at Suez
- **30 July** French North African and Syrian armies demobilised
- **3–19 August** Italy occupies British Somaliland
- **13 September** Italians invade Egypt; take Sollum
- **9 December** British Western Desert offensive Operation Compass
- **1941 (22 January)** Tobruk falls to British and Australians
- **6 February** British and Australians capture Benghazi

The strategic situation in the Mediterranean and North Africa was transformed by the German invasion of France in June 1940. Hitherto the overwhelming naval and military power of the French and British in the region, assured by their respective fleet bases spanning the Mediterranean, had deterred Italy from intervening on the side of its ally, Germany. Mussolini's decision to join in the defeat of France (10 June) was partly prompted by his desire to profit from an altered balance of power in the Mediterranean.

The neutralisation of French naval power left the Italian Navy the largest in the Mediterranean. Further, Italian ground forces, stationed in Libya, Ethiopia, Eritrea and Italian Somaliland, formed the largest combatant group in North Africa. Britain was confronted with a possible cross-Channel invasion and seemed unlikely to be able effectively to support her forces beyond Europe. Seizing what he perceived as an initiative, Mussolini ordered offensives against the frontiers of the Sudan (Kassala and Gallabat, captured 4 July), Kenya (Moyale, captured in July) and British Somaliland (occupied 5–19 August). On 13 September a large Italian army entered Egypt from Libya but halted on 18 September, after advancing 60 miles, to construct a forward base at Sidi Barrani. These early successes were soon to be reversed.

The British and de Gaulle's Free French began taking action against the Vichy government's forces in Africa soon after the French capitulation, the better to consolidate their control of the continent. Under the terms of the armistice with Germany, Vichy retained control of the French overseas empire and the forces within it, including the French Fleet, which had taken refuge at Oran and Mers-el-Kebir in Algeria. On 3 July the British Mediterranean Fleet, following Vichy's refusal to immobilise its navy, bombarded those ports, sinking a battleship, damaging three other large warships, and killing 1,300 French sailors: an act that outraged France. However, the French squadron in Alexandria was surrendered to the British without loss, and various French warships still in British ports were seized. When, on 23–25 September, a British naval force, with de Gaulle on board, approached Dakar in French West Africa (Senegal) and landed a force, it was driven off. Free France's only success at this stage of the war was to rally the remote colonies of Equatorial Africa and Congo.

On land the British went over to the offensive in Egypt on 9 December. The operation had been planned to last only five days but its success led Wavell, the desert commander, to enter Libya in early January 1941 and thereafter to capture Bardia (5 January) and Tobruk (22 January). He then divided his force, sending the 7th Armoured Division across the desert to meet the 6th Australian Division advancing along the coast. On 5 February they joined hands at Beda Fomm, having advanced 500 miles, capturing 130,000 prisoners and much equipment.

The British offensive in East Africa opened on 19–20 January 1941, when forces in the Sudan invaded Eritrea and northern Ethiopia. Three weeks later, a second front was opened when Cunningham's offensive from Kenya into Italian Somaliland and southern Ethiopia was launched on 11 February. British Somaliland was reoccupied by a force which landed from Aden at Berbera on 16 March. By 25 February most of Italian Somaliland had been occupied. Addis Ababa, the Ethiopian capital, fell on 6 April. Italian resistance was strongest in the north, where a bitter battle for the mountain position of Keren did not end until 26 March. The Duke of Aosta, Italian Commander-in-Chief, then withdrew to Amba Alagi where, after more fighting, he surrendered on 16 May. Isolated forces continued resistance until 3 July. Some 420,000 Italian troops, including Africans, had been killed or captured in East Africa, against 3,100 British Commonwealth casualties. The victory restored the Emperor Haile Selassie of Ethiopia to his throne.

The initiative had now returned to British hands. The problem of supply and coordination between London and eastern Africa still remained, as did substantial areas of Vichy territory. But if the latter could be contained, and the substantial Commonwealth troops east of Aden be fully exploited, Allied control of the eastern Mediterranean and the Middle East might be assured. But the advent of German forces in the Balkans and Mediterranean would alter this balance.

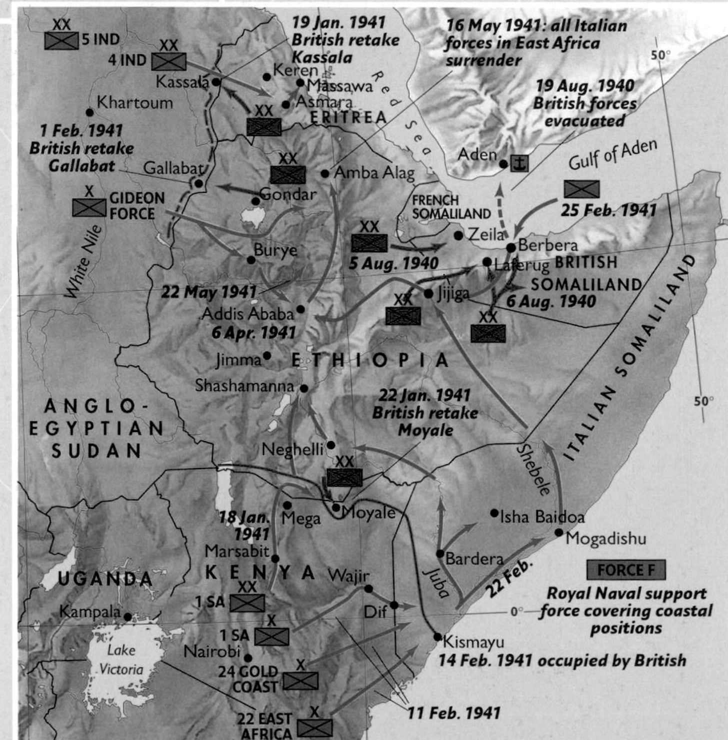

www.answers.com/topic/destruction-of-the-french-fleet-at-mers-el-kebir
The destruction of the French Fleet at Mers-el-Kebir
www.nationmaster.com/encyclopedia/Operation-Compass
The British counter-attack against the Italian invasion of Egypt

1 Hitler had no plans for involvement in Africa, but the terms of the French armistice in June 1940 allowed France to retain control of her colonies and protectorates in North and West Africa, and her mandated territories in Syria and Lebanon, together with local military forces. These posed a potential threat to British control of the Mediterranean, exercised through her bases at Gibraltar and Malta and the garrison in Egypt; Britain also had colonial forces in the Sudan, Kenya and British Somaliland. With the entry of Germany's ally, Italy, into the war (10 June) the struggle for control of Africa broke out. The Free French leader de Gaulle, through his emissary Leclerc, succeeded in rallying French colonies in Equatorial Africa (August–October 1940), but an attempt to seize Senegal (23–25 Sept.) failed. The French Fleet in Mers-el-Kebir and Oran was bombarded by the British (3 July) on its refusal to scuttle, join forces or sail to a British or French Caribbean port. Of its battleships, *Bretagne* was sunk, *Dunkerque* and *Provence* damaged and *Strasbourg* escaped to Toulon.

2 Mussolini, keen to take advantage of British weakness in the area in order to expand his African colonies, launched offensives in East Africa from July. With the exception of the occupation of British Somaliland (5–19 Aug.) these failed. A British counter-offensive provoked heavy fighting around Keren in mountainous northern Eritrea. The first battle (3–13 Feb. 1941) was an Italian defensive victory; in the second (15–26 Mar.1941) the British took the position and began a victorious advance.

3 The Italian offensive into Egypt began on 13 Sept. but was not followed up, allowing a British counter-offensive (9 Dec.) to gain the initiative, forcing the surrender by February 1941 of large Italian forces.

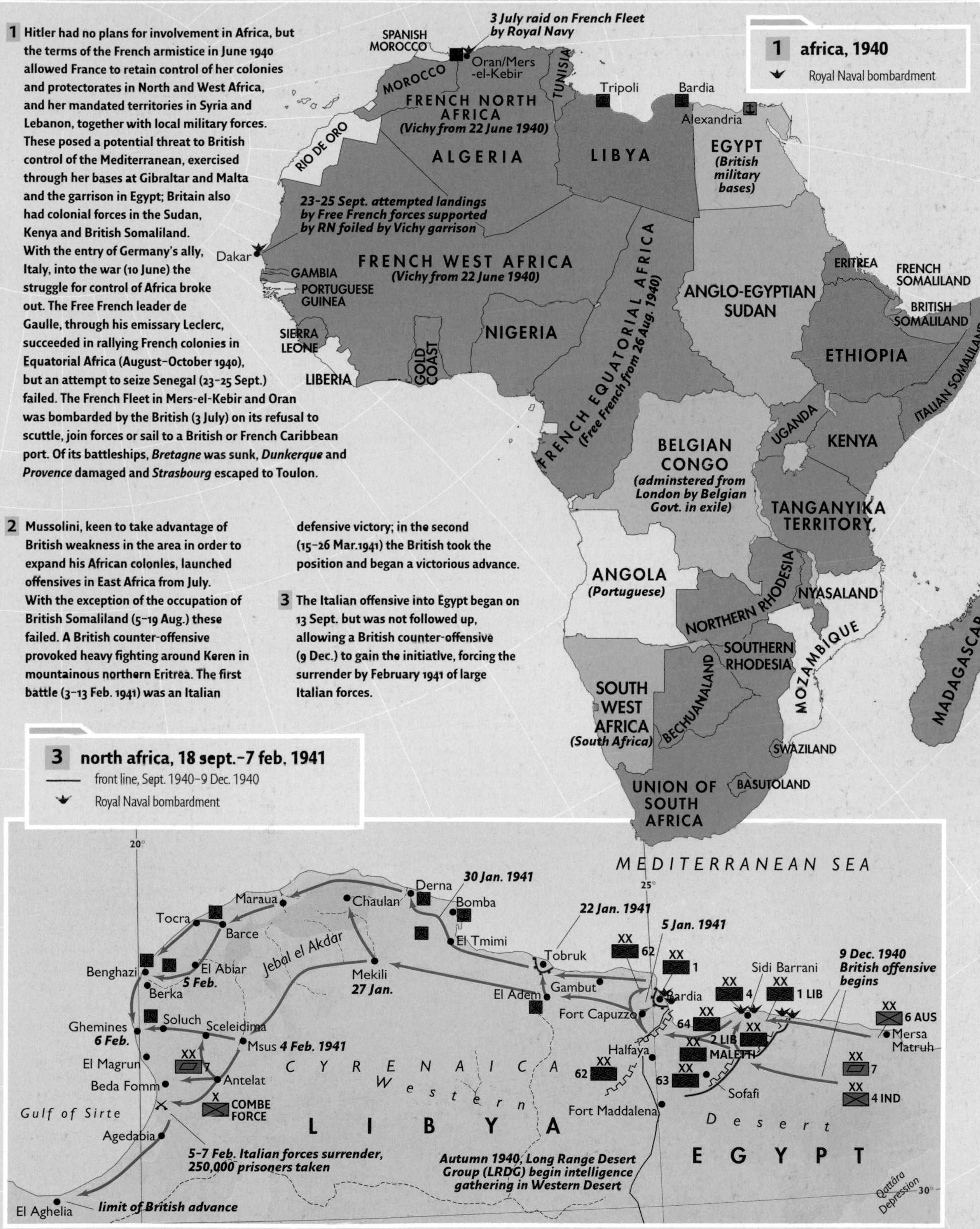

air war in europe I

1940 to 1941

- **1940 (10 July)** Battle of Britain begins; Luftwaffe attack Channel convoys
- **12 August** Portsmouth heavily bombed
- **13 August** 'Eagle Day' of Battle of Britain
- **25 August** First RAF raid on Berlin
- **7 September** 'The Blitz' begins
- **15 September** Battle of Britain Sunday
- **15 October** 400-bomber raid on London

With the defeat of France in June 1940 Hitler hoped that Britain would sue for peace. When Britain refused any offer to end the war, Hitler ordered an invasion of Britain. On 16 July the directive for Operation Sealion was issued. The directive ordered the German air force (Luftwaffe) to overpower the RAF as the prelude to a cross-Channel invasion. For the first time a battle was to be fought between aircraft that would alter the course of the war.

The Luftwaffe was poorly prepared for the conflict. Heavy losses were sustained in the invasion of France. German aircraft lacked sufficient range or bomb-carrying capacity to mount a major campaign over hostile territory against a well-armed adversary. German airmen lacked experience of this kind of campaign, and, most important of all, German fighter range was too short to cover more than a small part of southern England for even limited periods, allowing the RAF to stay out of range and to regroup in relative safety to the north and west.

The British had been preparing since 1937, though the RAF was still short of pilots and of combat experience. Britain now possessed radar and a comprehensive air defence organisation. British fighter units were at last stocked with the fast monoplane fighters, Hurricanes and Spitfires, in large numbers – almost 700 by June 1940. Moreover, British factories, bullied by Lord Beaverbrook, Minister for Aircraft Production, were turning out over 400 fighters a month by late 1940; Germany produced on average fewer than 200 a month.

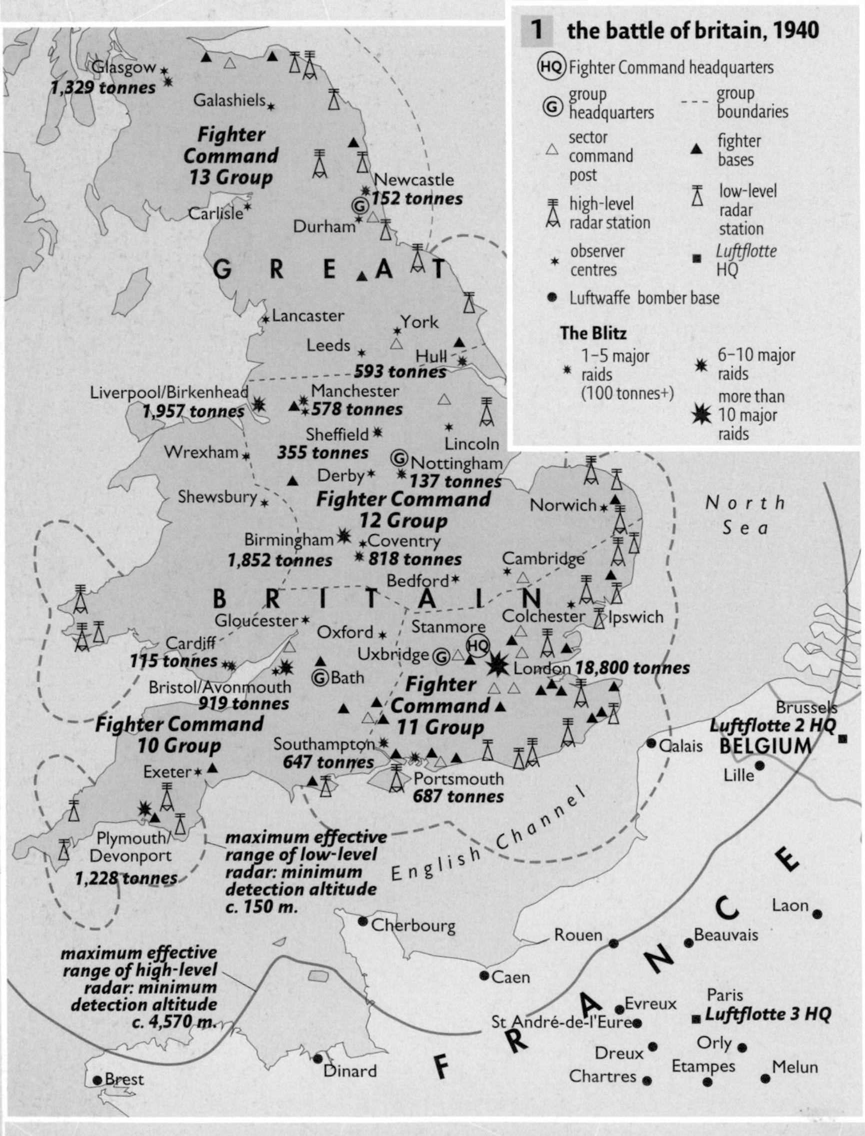

1 the battle of britain, 1940

HQ Fighter Command headquarters
G group headquarters
group boundaries
sector command post
fighter bases
high-level radar station
low-level radar station
observer centres
Luftflotte HQ
Luftwaffe bomber base

The Blitz
1–5 major raids (100 tonnes+)
6–10 major raids
more than 10 major raids

Glasgow 1,329 tonnes
Galashiels
Fighter Command 13 Group
Newcastle 152 tonnes
Carlisle
Durham
GREAT BRITAIN
Lancaster
York
Leeds
Hull 593 tonnes
Liverpool/Birkenhead 1,957 tonnes
Manchester 578 tonnes
Sheffield 355 tonnes
Lincoln
Wrexham
Nottingham 137 tonnes
Derby
Shewsbury
Fighter Command 12 Group
Norwich
North Sea
Birmingham 1,852 tonnes
Coventry 818 tonnes
Cambridge
Bedford
Gloucester
Oxford
Stanmore
Colchester
Ipswich
Cardiff 115 tonnes
Uxbridge
London 18,800 tonnes
Bath
Bristol/Avonmouth 919 tonnes
Fighter Command 11 Group
Fighter Command 10 Group
Southampton 647 tonnes
Calais
Brussels
Luftflotte 2 HQ
BELGIUM
Lille
Exeter
Portsmouth 687 tonnes
Plymouth/Devonport 1,228 tonnes
maximum effective range of low-level radar: minimum detection altitude c. 150 m.
English Channel
Cherbourg
Laon
Rouen
Beauvais
maximum effective range of high-level radar: minimum detection altitude c. 4,570 m.
Caen
FRANCE
Evreux
Paris
St André-de-l'Eure
Luftflotte 3 HQ
Dreux
Orly
Chartres
Etampes
Melun
Brest
Dinard

1 Until the summer of 1940, air warfare in Europe had largely consisted of close support for ground armies, and the bombing of 'defended' cities (Warsaw, Rotterdam) by the Luftwaffe. The 'knock-out blow' from the air, initially feared by all participants, did not materialise. After the invasion of France the situation altered, and aircraft came into their own. Between late July and mid-September 1940 the Luftwaffe sought to defeat the RAF to pave the way for Operation Sealion, a German invasion of southern England. The resulting engagement – the Battle of Britain – proved to be the first serious setback the Germans encountered. The Germans underestimated the tenacity and complexity of the British defence. When radar and Observer Corps intelligence showed approaching German aircraft, details were sent directly to Fighter Command HQ and the Fighter Group operations rooms. The Group then gave instructions to Sector commanders who put their squadrons on alert. On a final order from Group HQ, the Sector commander ordered combat. The Sector retained control over the aircraft in the air when in radio contact. After that, squadron leaders took operational control. This proved a quick and effective chain of command and contributed much to the eventual success of the RAF in the battle. Frustrated at the lack of success against the RAF, the Luftwaffe switched to night bombing of cities in September. Over 35,000 tonnes of bombs were dropped for the loss of 650 German aircraft. London was attacked 19 times between September 1940 and May 1941 with about 19,000 tonnes of bombs. The bombers were sent to attack rail centres, docks, munitions works and government buildings. Much of the destruction occurred instead in civilian residential areas close to strategic targets. The campaign was finally cancelled in order to conserve forces for the coming Russian offensive. The Blitz failed to force Britain out of the war, and resulted in further improvements in British defences.

www.battleofbritain.net/
The Battle of Britain
www.raf.mod.uk/bob1940/bobhome.html
The RAF's account of the Battle of Britain

From July 1940, mixed groups of German bombers and dive-bombers, escorted by fighters, attacked British airfields, air depots and radar stations within range of their bases in France and the Low Countries. Luftwaffe intelligence reported, incorrectly, by mid-August that the task was almost complete. Though there were times when the sheer weight of German forces threatened to overwhelm the defences of the Kent and Sussex sectors, airfields were rapidly repaired and a stream of replacement aircraft and pilots ensured that the overall strength of Fighter Command actually rose during August and September. By contrast, German fighter units declined in operational strength from over 700 in July to 275 by 1 October. The Ju-87 dive-bomber, so effective in the land battles, proved vulnerable and was withdrawn. No target system was attacked with sufficient intensity to create a critical situation for the defenders. By mid-September, after high losses of pilots and planes, the Luftwaffe halted its offensive and Operation Sealion was postponed indefinitely. From July to October the RAF lost 915 aircraft; the German air force 1,733.

Hitler, preparing to turn east against the Soviet Union, agreed to try a heavy bombing offensive. In mid-September the Luftwaffe switched from day to night attacks against military and economic targets in Britain's major cities. Helped by good electronic navigation aids, German airmen made devastating attacks on 16 major cities and ports over a six-month period. But the Luftwaffe suffered continued attrition of aircraft and crews, lacked pilots and navigators with training for long-range flying and bombardment, and lacked aircraft with sufficient range and lifting-power to deliver a crucial blow. Though heavy damage and high civilian casualties were sustained, neither was as great as those for which the British government had planned. British war production was not greatly affected and morale remained intact. In the early spring, Hitler ordered an end to the bombing. The first strategic air campaign was a failure.

The defeat of the Luftwaffe in 1940 saved Britain from an invasion her badly depleted army could hardly have repelled. But British air leaders did not learn from the German failure. Instead they began a limited offensive against German targets using a similar medium, twin-engined bombers. During 1941 the campaign built up steadily, directed first at strategic economic and military targets. These attacks proved so inaccurate that Bomber Command was compelled to switch to 'area bombing'. Churchill saw this as the only way Britain could fight back in 1940 and 1941, and wanted the German civilians to 'feel the weight of the war'. Thus, the foundations were laid for the great bombing offensives conducted later in the war.

2 The RAF began bombing strategic economic sites (oil, transport, docks etc.) in Germany in May 1940. The campaign was soon extended to cover German-occupied territory. The difficulty in locating sites at night resulted in general attacks on industrial areas rather than specific targets – the origin of 'area bombing'. By the end of 1941 the RAF had dropped 50,000 tonnes on Europe, almost as much as Germany had dropped on Britain.

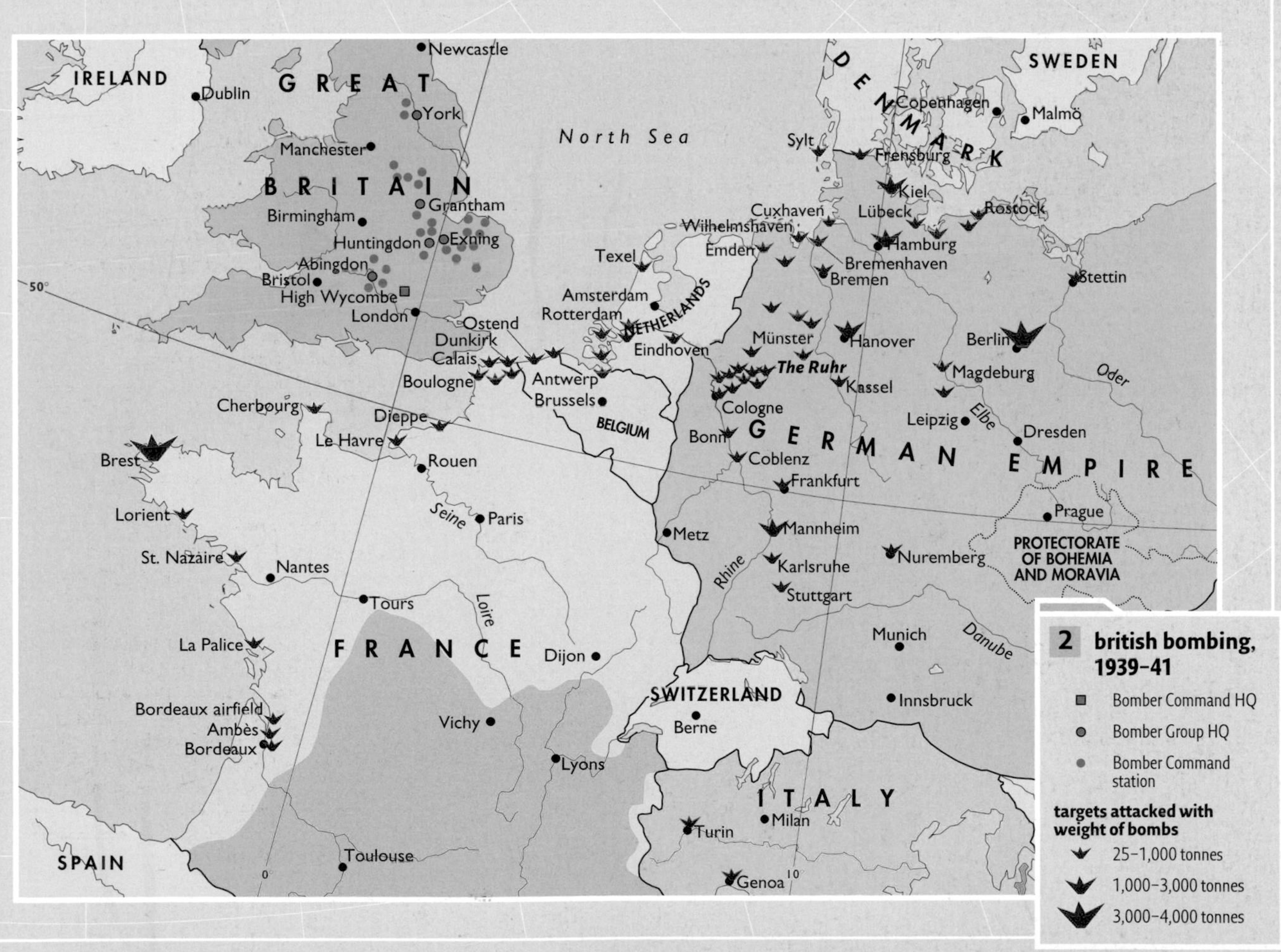

1941

- **1939 (7 April)** Albania annexed by Italy
- **13 April** Britain and France guarantee security of Greece and Romania
- **1940 (20 November)** Hungary and Romania enter into Tripartite Pact with the Axis powers; Bulgaria joins 1 March 1941 and allows German troops to enter Sofia
- **28 October** German troops enter Romania via Hungary. Italy invades Northern Greece
- **1941 (4 March)** British troops arrive in Greece
- **25 March** Yugoslavia joins Tripartite Pact leading to anti-Royalist coup (26–27 March) and repudiation of treaty
- **April 1941** German forces invade Yugoslavia and Greece
- **27 April** Athens falls to Germans
- **31 May** British retreat from Crete

The Balkans, source of the disagreements that had precipitated the First World War, remained isolated from the course of the Second throughout the first year. In June 1940, however, the Soviet Union made on Romania the territorial claims agreed with Germany in the Ribbentrop-Molotov Pact of 22 August 1939. It annexed the provinces of Bessarabia and northern Bukovina (the former had been Russian before 1917; the latter had not). Germany and Italy accepted these annexations in the Vienna Award of 30 August 1940, which also returned northern Transylvania to Hungary and southern Dobruja (September 7) to Bulgaria. Romania's shrunken frontiers were, however, guaranteed by Italy and Germany.

Hitler was anxious to secure access to Romania's oil fields at Ploesti, which were to remain Germany's main source of supply throughout the war. He was also suspicious of Soviet ambitions in the Balkans, particularly as his intention to attack the USSR grew during the autumn of 1940; in September he sent a 'military mission' of an army division to Romania and Hungary, binding them into the Tripartite Pact (signed between Germany, Italy and Japan on 27 September). Bulgaria, which Hitler was simultaneously wooing away from dependence on the USSR, joined the pact on 1 March 1941.

Hitler's aim of transforming the Balkans into a satellite region by peaceful diplomacy was disturbed on 28 October 1940 by Mussolini's unprovoked invasion of Greece from Albania. Mussolini, whose part in the defeat of France had been inglorious, hoped to confront his fellow dictator with a military triumph of his own. He believed Greece would collapse when attacked. On the contrary, the Greeks resisted stiffly and then, with the assistance of British air units landed in the Peloponnese (from 3 November), counter-attacked. By mid-December, the Italians had been driven back 50 miles within Albania and by 1 March most of the south was in Greek hands. Mussolini's initiative infuriated Hitler: it both provided Britain with a pretext to intervene and heightened Soviet suspicions of his policy towards Bulgaria, which the Soviet government had earmarked as a satellite of its own. At Hitler's meeting with Molotov in Berlin on 11–12 November the Soviet Foreign Minister declared Russia's intention of extending a unilateral guarantee of Bulgaria's frontiers, with the aim of securing bases from which it could exercise closer control over the exit from the Black Sea. It was Molotov's attitude here that stiffened Hitler's resolve to attack the USSR.

In the meantime, however, Hitler had ordered the Army General Staff (4 November) to prepare plans for an attack on Greece (Operation Marita). This was to be mounted from Bulgaria, where German engineers began to bridge the Danube on 28 February 1941 to permit the assault force in Romania to reach its attack positions. Yugoslavia, across which he also required transit rights, had resisted his diplomacy thus far, but on 25 March agreed to join the Tripartite Pact. Two days later, the Yugoslav government was deposed by a military coup. Hitler at once included the invasion of Yugoslavia in his general plan. The military government of Yugoslavia sought, but was denied, Soviet assistance; its mission to Moscow secured a meaningless treaty of friendship on 5 April. On the next day, German forces opened an attack from southern Germany, Romania and Bulgaria. An air attack on Belgrade (6 April) killed 17,000 citizens and on 10 April Yugoslav resistance began to collapse when the predominantly Croatian Fourth and Seventh Armies mutinied. An autonomous Croat government welcomed the Germans into Zagreb the same day.

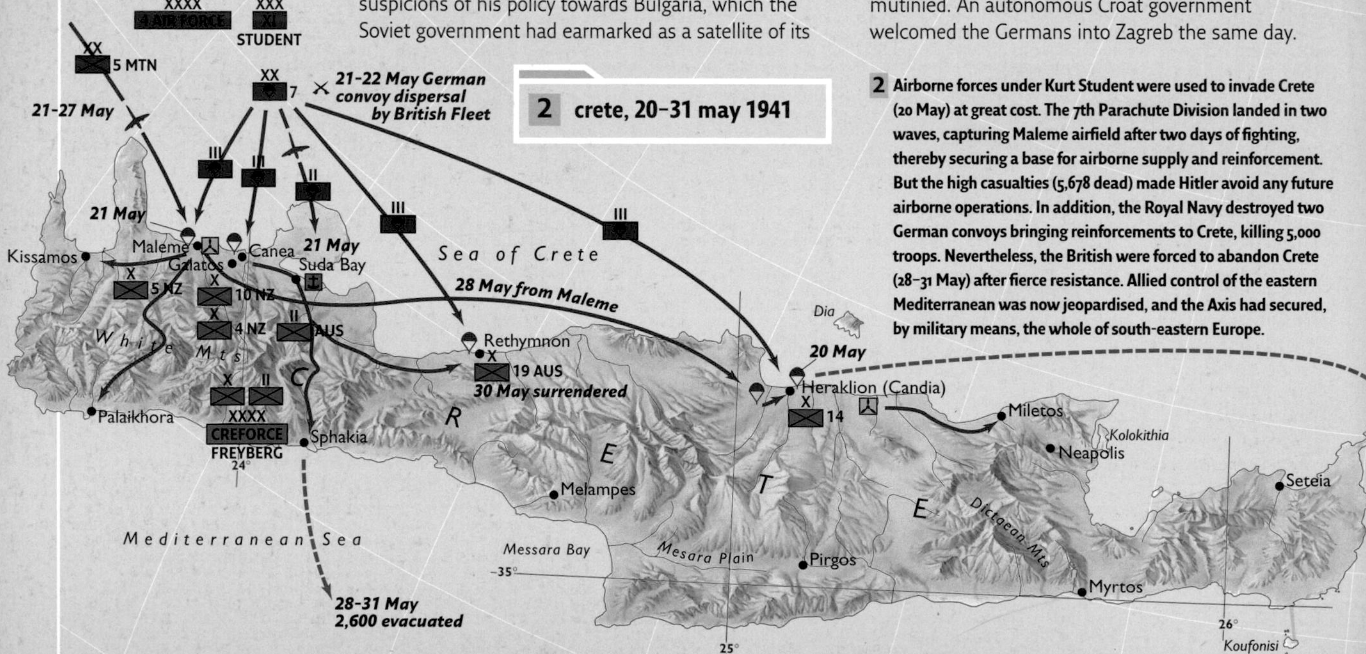

2 crete, 20–31 may 1941

2 Airborne forces under Kurt Student were used to invade Crete (20 May) at great cost. The 7th Parachute Division landed in two waves, capturing Maleme airfield after two days of fighting, thereby securing a base for airborne supply and reinforcement. But the high casualties (5,678 dead) made Hitler avoid any future airborne operations. In addition, the Royal Navy destroyed two German convoys bringing reinforcements to Crete, killing 5,000 troops. Nevertheless, the British were forced to abandon Crete (28–31 May) after fierce resistance. Allied control of the eastern Mediterranean was now jeopardised, and the Axis had secured, by military means, the whole of south-eastern Europe.

www.crete-1941.org.uk/
Historical account of the German invasion of Crete in May 1941
www.feldgrau.com/greecewar.html
The German invasion of the Balkans

Belgrade fell two days later and the government asked for an armistice on 14 April. Serbian resistance began almost at once, with the formation of royalist *Chetnik* groups in the mountains.

In Greece the government was committed, for political reasons, to defending the Metaxas Line along the Bulgarian frontier with Thrace (promised to Bulgaria as a bribe for joining the Tripartite Pact). Its main force was therefore in the wrong place to resist the Germans when they crossed the Yugoslav frontier on to April. A British expeditionary force, which had been sent to Greece from Egypt in March, also found itself in the wrong place and was quickly forced to retreat. German troops captured Athens on 27 April and the British evacuated the Peloponnese, with heavy losses, on 30 April. The British fugitives joined a garrison sent to Crete the previous October. Hitler decided to take the island from them, and in the airborne Operation Mercury (20–31 May), captured the Maleme airstrip and forced the British to evacuate to Egypt from the southern harbour of Sphakia. German seaborne reinforcements suffered heavily from British naval attack, although losses were not as severe as those of the British.

Hitler's Balkan Blitzkrieg not only inflicted humiliation and heavy casualties on the British, it also compromised their strategic position in the eastern Mediterranean. It opened up the immediate danger that Hitler would establish a centre of power in the Levant, threatening the British forces in Egypt and the Middle East; it put paid to hopes that Turkey might soon be brought into the war on the Allied side. The extension of Axis control over the Balkans also robbed Britain of its last potential foothold in Europe and committed it to acting against the Wehrmacht on land through guerrilla and resistance forces only. For the Germans, however, the guerrilla war in Yugoslavia would prove the costliest in occupied western Europe.

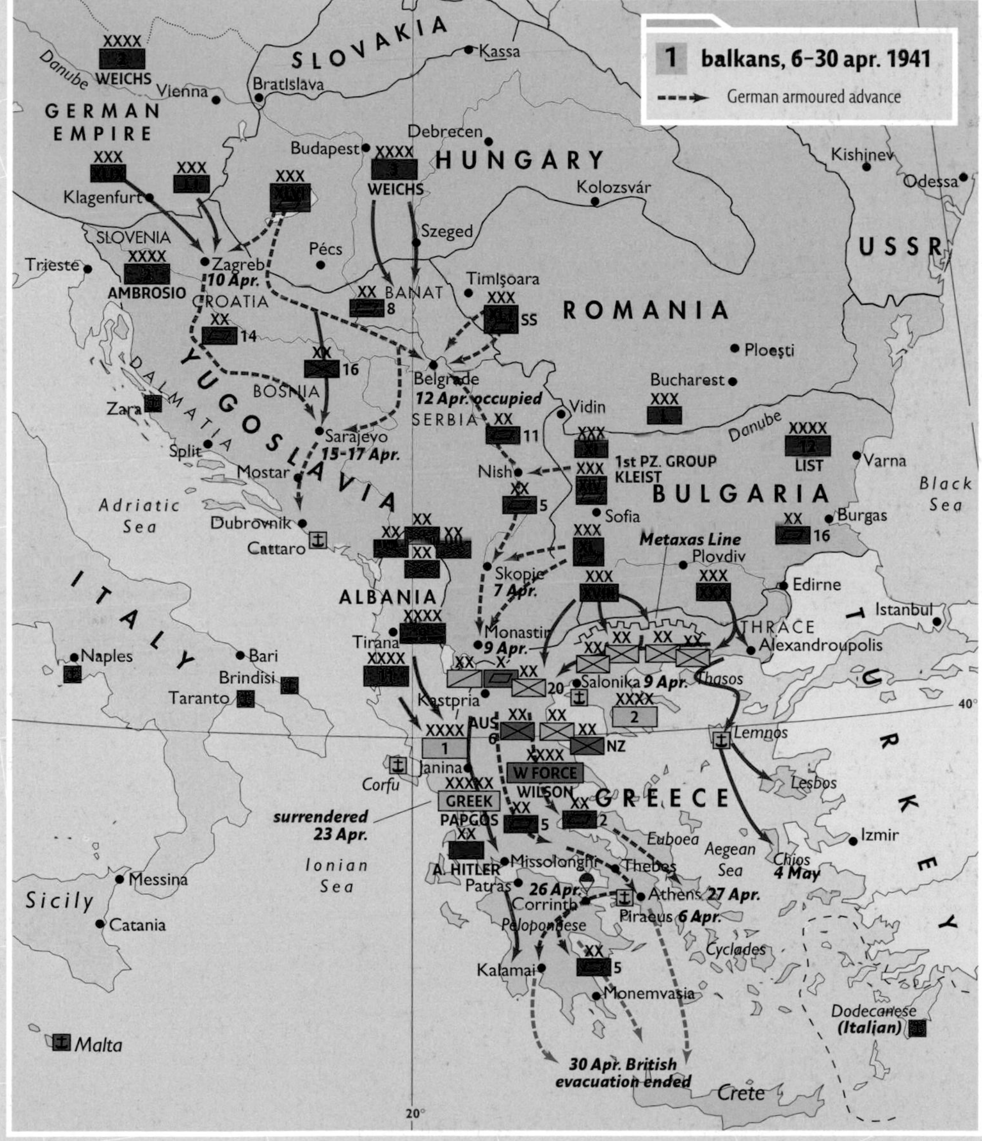

1 Until 1940, various diplomatic moves and territorial changes in the Balkans failed to maintain the status quo of the major European powers. Hitler's plans for peacefully securing the area for the Axis, in the Tripartite Pact, were undermined by Mussolini's invasion of Greece (28 Oct. 1940). Unexpectedly, the Greeks fought back, driving the Italians deep into Albania by 23 Dec. British forces occupied Crete and Lemnos (31 Oct.) and RAF units arrived in the Peloponnese (3 Nov.) to provide support. British carrier aircraft attacked the Italian Fleet in harbour at Taranto (11 Nov.), damaging three battleships and forcing its withdrawal to Italy's west coast. Hitler determined (4 Nov.) to divert resources to contain the problem. A German offensive opened (6 Apr.) with advance bombing and armoured units entering Yugoslavia, forcing a surrender by 14 Apr. A two-pronged assault on Greece, into Thrace and through Macedonia, forced through the Greek defensive lines. British troops, landed on Greece on 4 Mar., were evacuated to Crete on 30 Apr. as German armoured divisions poured south, supporting advance airborne landings at Corinth. The British lost over 25,000 troops dead or captured, along with six cruisers, seven destroyers lost and five battleships and an aircraft carrier damaged.

june to july 1941

- **22 June** Germany invades USSR; Italy and Romania declare war on USSR
- **23 June** Hungary and Slovakia declare war on USSR
- **23 June** Germans cross river Bug; destruction of Soviet Air Force
- **28 June** Germans capture Minsk
- **30 June** Germans encircle Soviet forces in 'Białystok pocket'
- **1 July** Germans capture Riga
- **3 July** Stalin calls for 'scorched earth' policy in broadcast
- **10 July** Germans cross River Dnieper
- **21 July** Moscow bombed
- **22 July** German advance halted through exhaustion

The scale of Operation Barbarossa overwhelms the imagination. On 22 June 1941 armies of three million men on either side, with air and naval support, were aligned along the German/Soviet frontier; the potential area of operations covered half of Europe. The German High Command knew that, like earlier invaders, they had to destroy the defending army before it could retreat into the vastness of the Russian interior and prolong the campaign into the winter.

Germany's armoured forces offered the only chance of success. Concentrated on narrow sectors, the four Panzer Groups had to trap the first strategic echelon of Soviet armies west of the River Dnieper. The early days of the campaign saw dramatic advances by the armoured forces, averaging 30 or more kilometres a day. Behind them marched the infantry divisions, which could not maintain half the Panzers' speed. As the gaps opened, armoured forces had to be committed to holding objectives rather than pressing eastwards. The German armoured force was too small for the task and it was further hampered by the inadequate Soviet road and rail network. The armoured forces began to run short of fuel and every other sort of supply. The maintenance problems caused by Russian roads exceeded all expectations and the tank strength of German divisions dropped by half in the first month of war.

In the first weeks of the war German forces achieved vast encirclements and hundreds of thousands of prisoners were captured. Despite the shock of the German surprise attack, there was no dramatic collapse of Soviet will power. Whenever German planners had faced the strategic and logistic impossibilities of the invasion of the USSR, they had conjured them away by assuming that the Soviet soldier was either racially inferior or would not fight to defend the Bolshevik state. They had also over-estimated the effect of the purges of the 1930s on the Soviet officer corps. A third mistake was to underestimate the ability of the Soviet government to generate reserves. Divisions and whole armies disappeared in the frontier battles but by mid-July the number of Soviet divisions had risen from 170 to 212, although only 90 were at anything like their proper establishment. This reveals the hollowness of much of the western debate about Operation Barbarossa. Even had it been possible to start earlier, to agree on Moscow as the main objective, and to concentrate armoured forces to reach it, the capital would have been defended as fiercely as Leningrad or Stalingrad were in their turn. What is more, Panzer divisions were hardly ideally suited to street fighting and they would inevitably have become exhausted.

1 **The Barbarossa Plan can be divided into two sectors and three phases. The bulk of the German force was concentrated north of the Pripet Marshes in Army Groups North and Centre. Army Group Centre was to shatter the Soviet force in Belarus and then assist Army Group North in clearing the Baltic area and capturing Leningrad. In the southern sector Army Group South was to launch a pinning attack from Romania, while its Panzer Group drove to the River Dnieper and then south to envelop the Soviet force in the Ukraine. In the second phase, Moscow would be the objective in the north, while Army Group South occupied the Donets Basin and threatened the Caucasus.**

1 the german plan

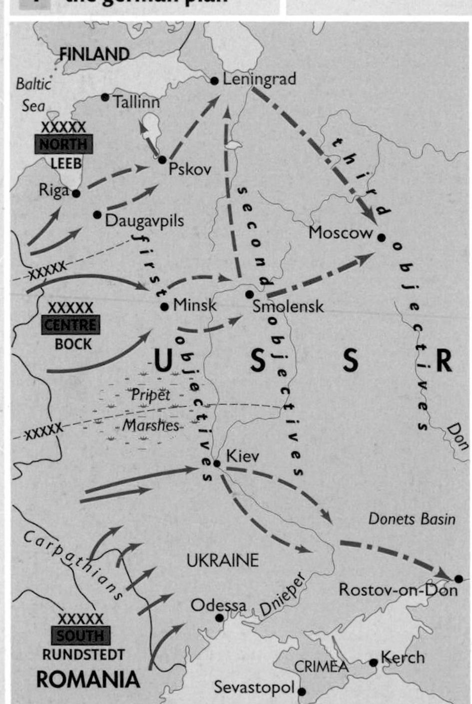

2 **On 22 June 1941 the bulk of the Soviet forces in the USSR were deployed in the territories occupied since 1939. The border armies were grouped under military districts, which would form front headquarters in wartime. Soviet armoured forces were organised into mechanised corps, distributed among the districts. The corps had only recently been formed and were not properly equipped or trained. The Red Army lacked armoured groupings to compare with the German Panzer Groups. Behind the first echelon of armies, four new armies were beginning to form up from the interior military districts, two each in rear of the Kiev and Western Special Military Districts. The Germans had a general idea of the Soviet deployment, though they overestimated the strength of the infantry armies and seriously underestimated the Soviet armoured strength. The German assault began with a shattering series of air attacks, disrupting headquarters and supply dumps and destroying the bulk of the Soviet Air Force on the ground. German air superiority was assured, limiting Soviet ability to manoeuvre, particularly in the Pripet and Baltic areas, where tanks soon became bogged down in the swamps if they could not use the roads. Army Group North made excellent progress, capturing the bridges at Daugavpils on 26 June and crossing the River Velikaya on 4 July. However, Panzer Group 4 reached the River Luga on 14 July but was delayed for nearly three weeks to allow the Eighteenth Army to catch up. Army Group Centre also ran to plan initially. Panzer Groups 2 and 3 completed a double envelopment at Minsk on 28 June, leading to the capture of 280,000 men. However, success on this scale brought its own problems: liquidating the pocket took days, delaying the advance on Smolensk, while Soviet reinforcements were concentrated in the area. Most of the city was in German hands by 17 July but Soviet resistance continued. At this point Hitler intervened, overruling the Army High Command's desire to press on for Moscow, and insisting that Panzer Group 3 support Army Group North against Leningrad, while Panzer Group 2 swung south into the Ukraine where the Germans were falling behind their timetable. The South West Front under General Kirponos was the strongest Soviet grouping, particularly in armour, and a series of counter-attacks checked the German onslaught. At the end of the first week in July, Panzer Group 1 had not passed the Zhitomir–Berdichev Line, although Soviet resistance further south was beginning to crumble.**

www.geocities.com/Area51/Cavern/2941/
Historical account of the Eastern Front
www.achtungpanzer.com/gen2.htm
Generaloberst H. W. Guderian, German Panzer Army commander during Operation Barbarossa

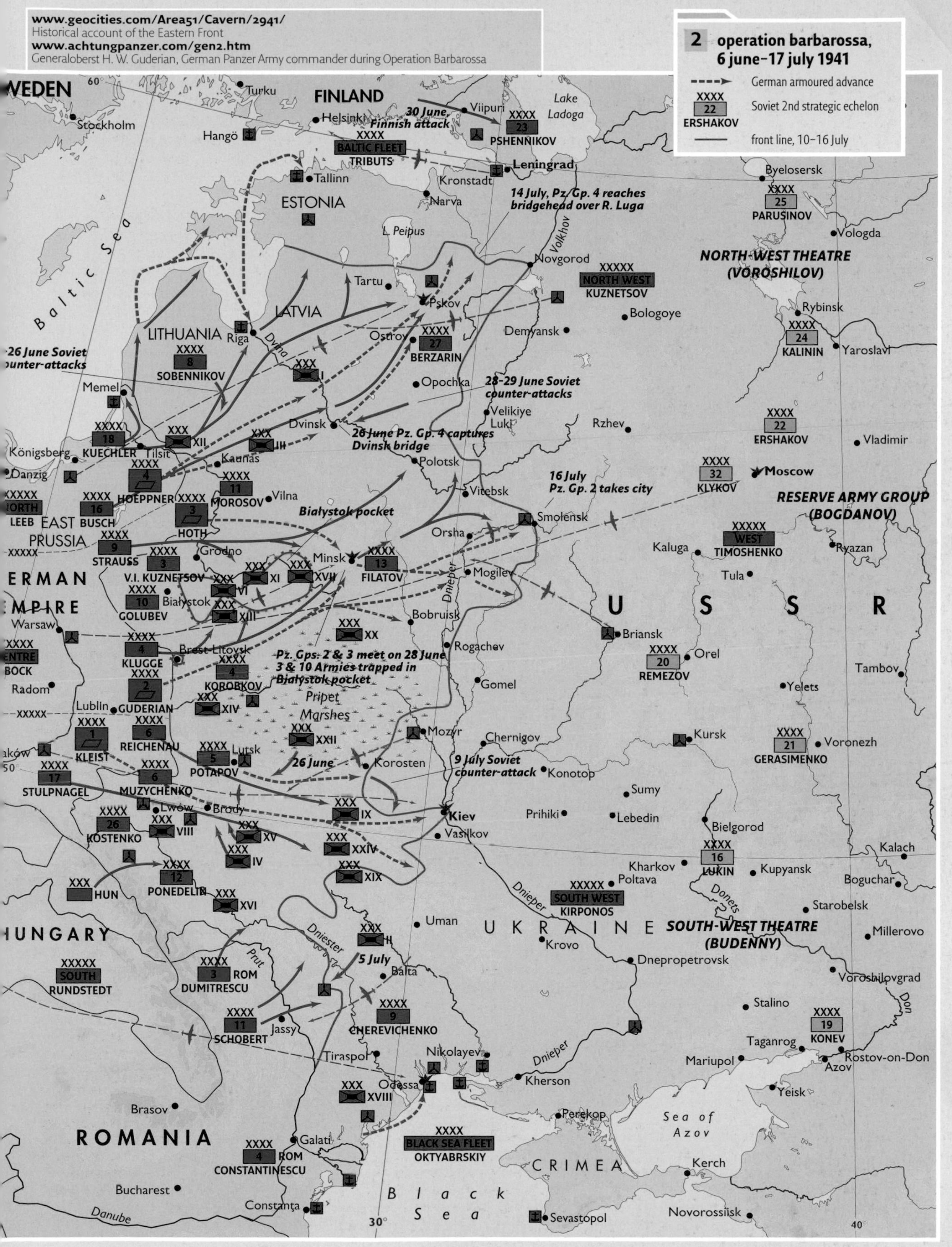

july to september 1941

- **5 August** Siege of Odessa begins
- **7 August** Stalin becomes Supreme Commander
- **19 August** Germans surround Leningrad
- **24 August** Finns surround Soviets at Viipuri
- **1 September** Soviets counter-attack at Gomel
- **5 September** Germans occupy Estonia
- **12 September** first snows slow German offensive
- **15 September** Siege of Leningrad begins
- **19 September** Germans take Kiev and Poltava

By 17 July the German Army was beginning to confront the problems of its own success. The leading Panzer divisions were 300-400 miles inside Russia, stretching the German supply chain to its absolute limit. Behind those spearheads laboured the infantry and there were many pockets of Soviet troops still capable of resistance.

In particular the High Command was concerned by the remnants of several Soviet armies, known to the Germans as the Fifth Army, in the Pripet Marshes. Roads were jammed with columns of vehicles and horse wagons. The Soviet railways used broad-gauge track, so it was necessary not only to repair combat damage, but to convert the lines to the standard gauge used by Germany. Delay was inevitable while the Army Groups brought up their stocks of ammunition and fuel to the required level. Most of their soldiers' food was expected to be foraged from the country, but the Soviets had used 'scorched earth' tactics as they retreated. As supplies came up, and quartermasters worked miracles of improvisation, new advances became possible until again the armour outran its supplies.

This logistic background is vital to an understanding of operations in this period. At its start, for example, XLI Panzer Corps of Panzer Group 4 was within 80 miles of Leningrad, but it had less than half its ammunition establishment. Although General Hoepner, commander of the Panzer Group, suggested trying to seize Leningrad with just this one force, the Army Group could not guarantee to supply it. On the Smolensk-Moscow axis there was hardly any progress at all for over two months. This was partly because Hitler insisted on diverting Army Group Centre's Panzer Groups elsewhere, but also because of the supply problem. As Army Group Centre waited for supplies to come forward, Soviet counter-attacks, such as at Elnya (30 Aug.-8 Sept.) made heavy demands on ammunition stocks, which actually decreased during August and early September. Not until the Soviet offensive was exhausted was it possible to build up the supply base for an attack on Moscow.

The German High Command was also worried by its continually increasing casualty figures. By 13 July the German Army had lost 92,120 killed, wounded and missing (3.6 per cent of the field army). A month later the total had risen to 389,924 in all (10 per cent of the field army). By the end of September casualties stood at 551,039 - 16.2% of the field army. Replacements totalled only about half this figure, so that the German army was now more than 200,000 men below strength.

On the Soviet side, although casualties were several times worse, reinforcements continued to arrive. New armies were created and moved to the most threatened sectors of the line, especially in front of Moscow. Equipment was in short supply but by reducing the size of divisions a reserve was created. Divisional artillery strengths were halved, which made it possible to form new artillery regiments and divisions, as the Reserve of the High Command. These formations played a key role all through the war; they were moved around the front to create vital superiorities at crucial points, both in attack and defence. Similar reserves were created for other arms of the service and the air force.

The Soviet Army was gradually learning how to fight. From the catastrophes of 1941 a new generation of soldiers was arising. Among those whose names first came to notice in this period were Koniev, Rokossovsky, Malinovsky, Vlasov and others, who would rise to command armies and, later, fronts. Junior commanders and soldiers were now veterans. There remained a serious shortage of trained staff officers, which would limit the Red Army's capabilities for another year or two. However, the Soviets were learning fast and the army was clearly not going to collapse.

1 **From the middle of July Army Group South, which had made least progress in the first month of the war, began to break Soviet resistance in the Ukraine. The Eleventh and Seventeenth Armies began to converge on Uman and a Soviet attempt to withdraw was frustrated when Panzer Group 1 swung south from the Kiev axis. Between 3-10 Aug. 100,000 Soviet troops were captured in the Uman pocket. Further south the Fourth Romanian Army had advanced to Odessa but the garrison, the Independent Coastal Army, held out from 5 Aug. until evacuated to the Crimea in early October. The defence could not prevent the Eleventh Army's advance across the Ukraine with support from Panzer Group 2. The Eleventh Army advanced into the Crimea while the remains of the Southern Front struggled to hold the River Donets. As the battle for Smolensk drew to a close, the German High Command debated Army Group Centre's next objective: Hitler would not give priority to Moscow and insisted that Panzer Group 3 should assist Army Group North with a thrust to cut communications between Moscow and Leningrad, although the area was not suited to armoured operations. Panzer Group 2 was ordered south to meet the main body of Panzer Group 1 near Konotop. The advance on Moscow was to be continued by infantry, which needed some weeks to build up the supplies required. Panzer Groups 1 and 2 met south of Romny on 15 Sept., trapping 650,000 troops in the Kiev pocket. The South West Front commander, General Kirponos, was killed at this time, completing the collapse of command and control in the area. Only about 150,000 Soviet troops escaped from the Kiev pocket. Army Group North's advance got under way again on 8 Aug. By 21 Aug. Panzer Group 4 had reached Novgorod but a counter-attack in the Staraya Russa area temporarily checked its southern corps. The delay was not long and on 8 Sept. Army Group North reached Lake Ladoga at Shlisselburg, isolating Leningrad. Hitler decided not to storm the city but to leave it to starve under Luftwaffe bombardment. In Karelia the Finns pressed forwards but could not make a final push to link up, thus leaving open a lifeline across Lake Ladoga. Meanwhile, the Eighteenth Army had been clearing the Baltic States, forcing the abandonment of the Baltic Fleet's bases. Success on the flanks, with his objectives apparently almost in German hands, encouraged Hitler to look again at Moscow. Deciding that Soviet resistance must be near its last gasp, on 6 Sept. he authorised the envelopment of Vyazma, to be followed by an advance to Moscow. However, Army Group Centre's supplies had been depleted in beating off Soviet counter-attacks at Elnya and Groups 2, 3 and 4 faced complicated re-organisation to create the necessary strike groups. The rest of Sept.ember was devoted to these preparations and the front remained static, though not inactive.**

http://history.acusd.edu/gen/WW2Timeline/BARBAROS.HTML
Chronology of events during the Eastern front campaign
www.carpenoctem.tv/military/zhukov.html
Georgi Konstantinovich Zhukov, Soviet military leader

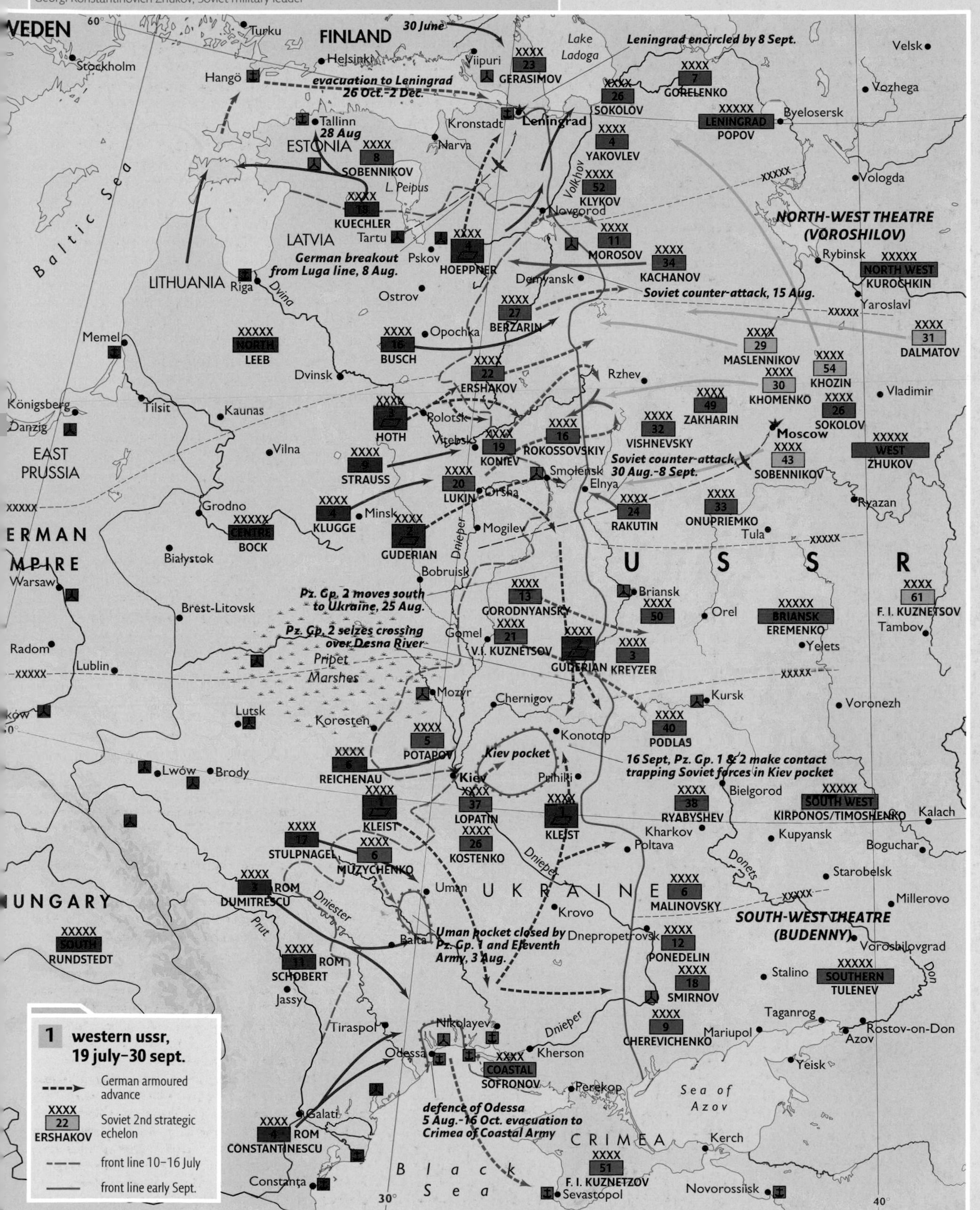

- **1941 (21 September)** Zhukov takes charge of Moscow defence
- **30 September onwards** Operation Tyhoon – German advance on Moscow
- **19 October** state of siege declared in Moscow; Stalin decides to stay in the capital
- **30 November** German units 12 miles from centre of Moscow
- **5 December** Germans abandon attack on Moscow

Hitler's Directive No. 35 of 6 September finally made Moscow the objective of the 1941 campaign. Although Army Groups North and South were to continue to advance towards Leningrad and Rostov, the bulk of German armour, the 2nd, 3rd and 4th Panzer Groups, were to concentrate under Army Group Centre. Completion of their existing missions and regrouping would take the rest of September.

The German plan for Operation Typhoon, the assault on Moscow, followed the standard pattern. Panzer forces would penetrate deeply, creating vast encirclements to be annihilated by the infantry armies. However, once again the German High Command was neglecting Russian geography and counting on the collapse of Soviet resistance. October brought the autumn rains and the *rasputitsa* (the roadless season). Most Russian roads were unmetalled and unusable in spring and autumn – the bulk of the German Army would simply stick where it was. November might bring a brief respite before the notorious Russian winter but pre-war plans had assumed that only a garrison of 60 divisions would be left in the USSR by then.

On the Soviet side the situation was critical. Only 90,000 tired troops stood between the Germans and Moscow. However, Stalin had been convinced that Japan was about to strike south in the Pacific, so he could afford to move properly trained and combat-tested divisions from the Far East. Zhukov was to take command of the Western Front for the Battle of Moscow and around him were now grouped the best of the younger generals. The balance of quality still favoured the Germans but it was far more even than three months earlier.

At first Operation Typhoon seemed to be running to schedule and thousands of prisoners fell into German hands at Vyazma and Briansk. By mid-October there were signs of panic in Moscow, which was put under a state of siege on the 19th. At the front, Soviet resistance continued, as strong counter-attacks at Kalinin and Mtsensk indicated. Early in November the German High Command finally admitted that the Soviet Union could not be beaten in 1941.

1 moscow 30 sept.– 5 dec. 1941

- German armoured advance
- XXXX 26 SOKOLOV — Soviet reserve
- front line, 30 Sept.
- front line, 30 Oct.
- front line, early Dec.

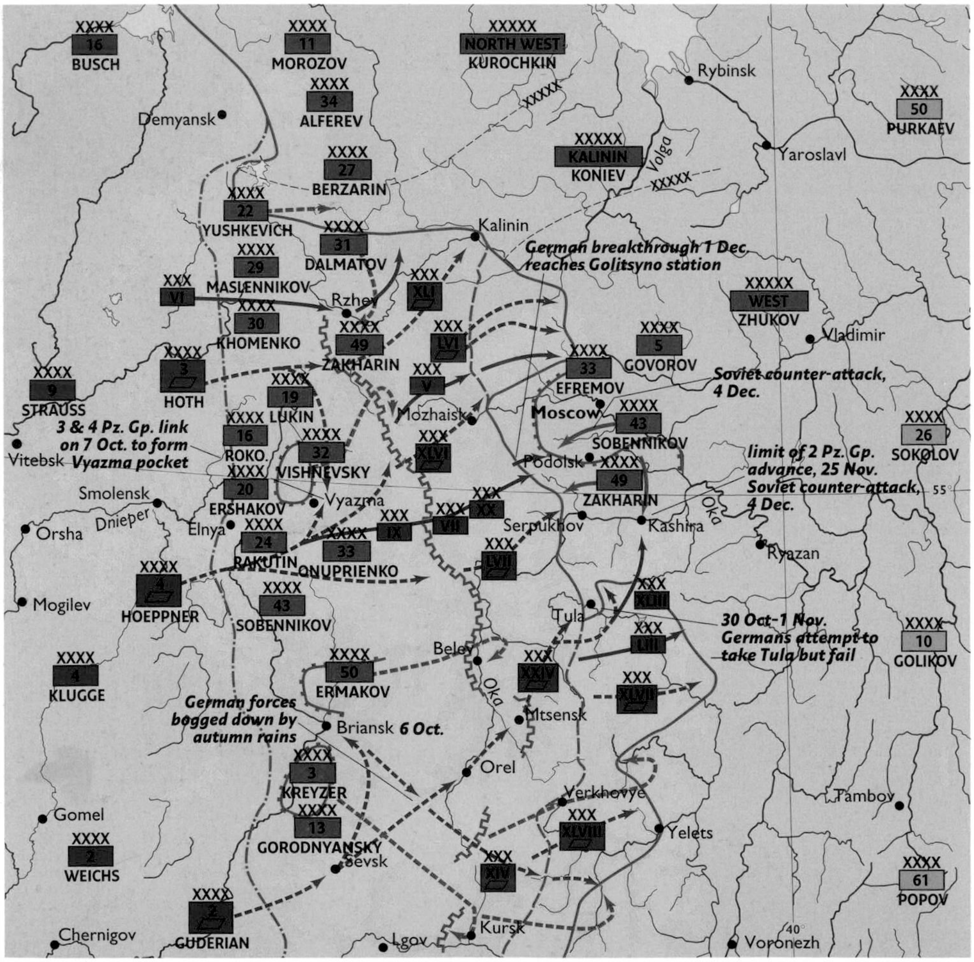

1 In spite of severe reductions in German combat efficiency as a result of the initial success of Operation Barbarossa, Hitler was convinced that a decisive victory in 1941 would finish Soviet resistance for good: Moscow was only 40 miles from the German front line in early November. The assault on Moscow began on 30 Sept. when the 2nd Panzer Group broke through the Thirteenth Army and threatened Orel and Briansk, forcing the Third and Fiftieth Armies to attack eastwards to escape encirclement. On 2 Oct. the 3rd and 4th Panzer Groups joined the offensive, splintering the Soviet defences. In the Vyazma pocket large parts of six Soviet armies were trapped, bringing the German bag of prisoners to 700,000 in three weeks. However, the onset of the autumn rains and the need to clear up the pockets slowed the German advance, and Soviet resistance at Tula, Kalinin and in the Mozhaisk Line was stubborn. The second phase of the German offensive began on 15 Nov. It was an attempt to encircle Moscow from the Tula and Kalinin areas but only slow progress was made.

www.answers.com/topic/battle-of-moscow
The Battle of Moscow
www.bbc.co.uk/history/war/wwtwo/soviet_german_war_01.shtml
History of the Soviet–German War

In this final stage of the campaign the Germans continued to attack because to yield the initiative and go over the defence entailed a greater risk. New thrusts in mid-November and the first days of December brought their leading elements almost to the Moscow city limits, but each advance was halted more rapidly than the last. However, the German High Command continued to believe that the Red Army must be equally exhausted and that victory would go to the side that hung on to the last battalion. In fact the Russians had concentrated nine reserve armies along the front and were debating when and where to use them. Stalin would not allow this reserve to be sucked into the Moscow battle and during November it was decided that the German Army had almost reached exhaustion. The counter-offensive was timed to begin immediately after the arrival of the winter frosts because German tanks and other equipment would cease to operate in the extreme cold, while Soviet equipment had been designed to cope with the conditions.

The first weeks of the Soviet counter-offensive seemed to justify their calculations. The extreme cold sapped the German soldiers, will to fight and immobilised their equipment. As units were forced to retreat, much of their equipment was left behind. A major command crisis followed on the German side. Hitler was most unwilling to permit withdrawals. The army commanders continued to demand freedom of action as they saw their troops sacrificed to no effect. The Army Group commanders were the middle-men between Hitler and their subordinates. The result was a dramatic change of personnel as Hitler sacked all three Army Group commanders and several Army commanders, including Guderian, in the first month of the Soviet offensive. He then assumed direct command of the German Army himself.

In the short term, events justified Hitler. The Red Army began the second phase of its winter campaign in mid-January, maintaining pressure in the Western Front sector while expanding the offensive on either flank. The aim was to encircle Army Group Centre. The concept was excellent but the Soviets lacked the resources to maintain major thrusts into an enemy position. Thanks to the losses of 1941 they were short of tanks, and brigades were the largest armoured formations available to them. The I Guards Cavalry Corps managed to penetrate the German lines and an airborne corps was dropped in driblets near Vyazma. On Hitler's order the German Army held 'hedgehogs' around the main centres of communication, however weak the garrison, and the Soviet attackers did not possess the artillery, tanks and supplies to break through. The spring *rasputitsa* only confirmed the stalemate. When Hitler repeated his calls for 'fanatical resistance' in future years, the German Army would be facing an enemy who had grasped the slender opportunity to create strength in depth.

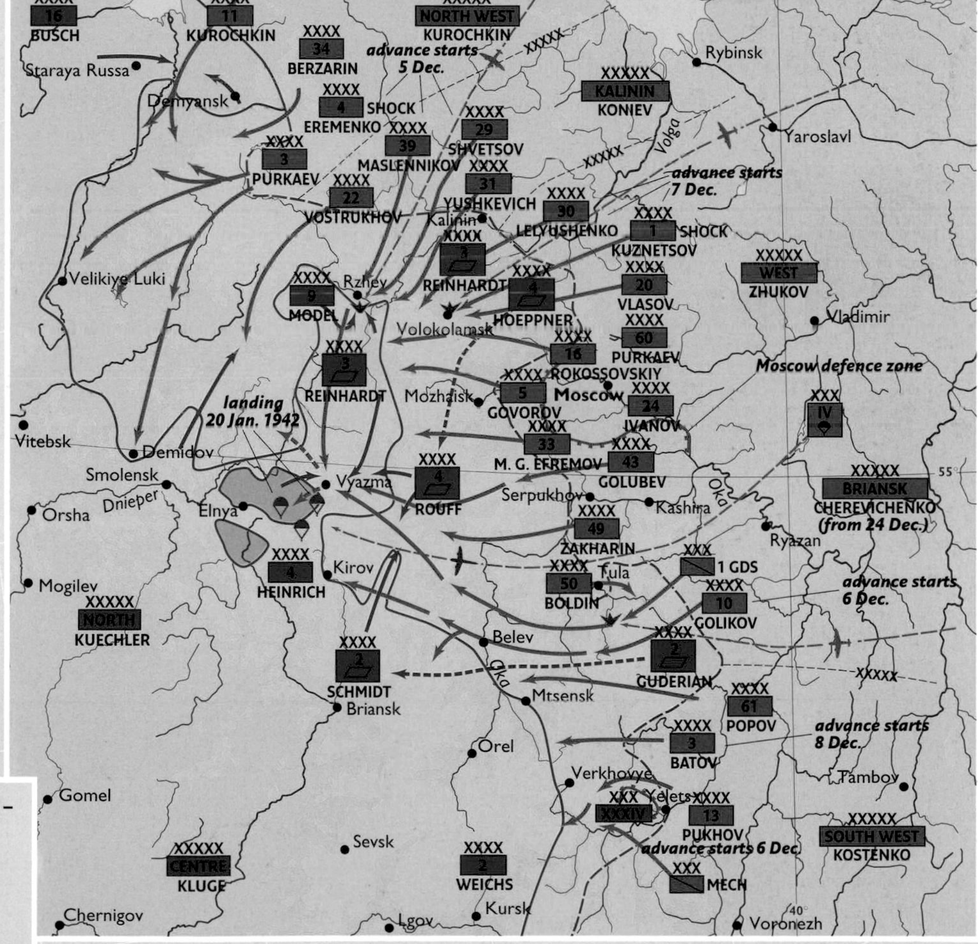

2 At the beginning of December winter struck; facing 30 or more degrees of frost the exhausted German troops could advance no further. Meanwhile, by transferring units from the Far East and raising new formations, the Soviet High Command had conjured up reserves for a decisive counter-offensive. The Soviets had also created new formations – Shock Armies – designed for counter-offensive thrusts. The first phase began on 6 Dec., when Zhukov unleashed the First Shock Army, and Twentieth and Tenth Armies. The German salients north and south of the city collapsed and with the threat to Moscow removed the Soviet Army began to attack all along the front. Although airborne and cavalry corps penetrated the German rear areas there was no general retreat. By the spring the two sides had fought to a standstill.

2 moscow 6 dec. 1941–30 apr. 1942

- – – – front line, 5–6 Dec. 1941
- —— front line, end Apr. 1942
- ▇ encircled Soviet partisan resistance

ukraine and crimea

november 1941 to july 1942

- **1941 (9 November)** Germans take Yalta
- **22 November** Germans take Rostov-on-Don
- **28 November** Germans lose Rostov-on-Don
- **29 December** Soviets retake Kerch
- **1942 (5 January)** Soviets control Kerch peninsula; Stalin orders general offensive
- **28 January** Timoshenko's forces advance in the Ukraine
- **30 March** Soviet counter-offensive ends; Germans much weakened
- **8 May** German summer offensive begins (28 June on southern front)
- **16–17 May** Germans capture Kerch and halt Soviets east of Kharkov
- **5 June** Germans besiege Sevastopol
- **3 July** Germans capture Sevastopol
- **4 July** Germans reach River Don on a wide front, crossing on a 150-mile-wide front from 30 July

At the end of 1941, German forces along the whole Eastern Front from the Baltic to the Black Sea were deployed in a row of defensive areas, nicknamed 'hedgehogs'. Hitler ordered the savagely mauled German forces to stand fast, attempting to construct defensive positions in ground frozen as hard as steel, which could only be excavated with explosives. However, the Germans had made spectacular headway. In the south, they had reached Taganrog, near where the Don flows into the Sea of Azov, and held all the Crimean peninsula except for the fortress of Sevastopol itself, in the west, and (temporarily) the Kerch peninsula in the east. The main hedgehogs in this area were Kharkov, Artemovsk and Taganrog.

On 5 January 1942, Stavka met and Stalin outlined his plans. The Germans were in disarray as a result of their defeat at Moscow and were obviously badly kitted out for the winter. Now was the time to counter-attack and the plans were cast on a grandiose scale. The Red Army's first significant success had gone to Stalin's head. During November and December, the Russians had launched a counter-offensive north of Rostov-on-Don, symmetrical to that at Tikhvin, near Leningrad. Stalin planned to attack outwards in every direction, attempting to relieve Leningrad, destroy Army Group Centre and liberate the Donbass and Crimea. Events overtook the planning. On 1 January South-West Front had launched an attack in the Kursk area against German Army Group South, which lasted 70 days and developed into the *srazheniye* (operational level battle) of Kharkov. From 18–22 January, Sixth and Fifty-Seventh Armies carved out a 20-mile-deep breakthrough south of Balakleya, German divisions on either side at Balakleya and Slaviansk holding the shoulders of the breakthrough in what would become the text book German response to the rupture of their front. On 27 January the Soviets captured Lozovaya, an important rail junction at the head of the salient they had carved out, the only major shift in the shape of the front lines in the south during the first third of 1942.

1 Between the battle of Moscow at the end of 1941 and May 1942, the front overall remained surprisingly stable, apart from Soviet gains round Moscow and the creation of the Izyum salient between Jan. and May 1942.

1 eastern europe, may–july 1942

- front line, May 1942
- front line, July 1942

Further south, the Germans were in control of most of the Crimea. They had attacked across the Perekop isthmus, devoid of cover, at the end of September 1941, and by 16 November had captured all the peninsula apart from Sevastopol, the great fortress and naval base. Eleventh Army, assisted by elements of Third Romanian Army, now began the Siege of Sevastopol.

Sevastopol was ringed by forts, with armoured emplacements buried deep in concrete and rock. The garrison, augmented by withdrawing troops, numbered up to 106,000 soldiers and sailors. First attempts to overrun the fortress on 30 October were easily beaten off: the main assault was delayed as the bombardment could not start until 17 December. On 25 December the Soviets began Operation Kerch-Feodosiya (an amphibious assault) on the east side of the Crimea peninsula. The objective was seizure of the Kerch peninsula and the creation of favourable conditions for recapturing the rest of the Crimea. The amphibious assault was carried out by the Transcaucasus Front, part of the Black Sea Fleet, and the Azov Flotilla. Over 250 naval and merchant vessels and 660 aircraft helped lift Soviet troops back across the Straits of Kerch, seizing bridgeheads on the north-east littoral of the Kerch peninsula and on 29 December, under cover of superior naval forces, the port of Feodosiya itself. The Germans and Romanians recaptured Feodosiya by 18 January, but by this time the Straits of Kerch had frozen so the Soviets were less dependent on the port for supplying their forces in the bridgehead. Heavy fighting continued through February, and the Soviets made several attempts to break out of Sevastopol, but after the beginning of March exhaustion ensued on both sides.

During this time, Soviet forces remained locked in Sevastopol, although only one German corps and one Romanian division were there to contain them. Meanwhile, Operation Bustard, the German recapture of Kerch, took place between 8–18 May. This accomplished, Eleventh Army faced the hardest task of all; the capture of Sevastopol. The Germans deployed the largest artillery piece ever built, known as 'Gerät' to Krupps, who made it, but nicknamed 'Big Dora' by the troops. The bombardment and infantry attack went on from 7 June for 27 days. The Soviet troops, sailors and marines fought on, even when the installations were torn open, the Germans using toxic smoke (one of the few occasions in the Second World War when chemical weapons were used) to kill them in their subterranean strongholds. At the last moment some top officers and officials were taken off, on Stalin's orders, by submarine: the rest fought to the death.

www.worldwar2.ro/operatii/?article=10
The Crimean campaign
http://en.wikipedia.org/wiki/Battle_of_Sevastopol
The Siege of Sevastopol

To the north, the bulge around Izyum had held, providing the opportunity for a concentric attack on Kharkov from there to the north-west and from Volchansk to the east. The new head of Fremde Heere Ost, Gehlen, predicted such an attack: it materialised between 12 and 29 May. This anticipated a German plan, Operation Fridericus, to pinch out the Izyum salient. In some desperation, the southern pincer of Operation Fridericus was launched by Army Group Kleist on 17 May, and succeeded in cutting off the salient.

Meanwhile, on 5 April Hitler committed himself to a drive on the flanks, in particular in the south, towards supplies of oil and grain, hoping also to influence Turkey to join the German side and cut Western supply lines through Iran. Soviet resistance would first be crushed between the Donets and the Don, then German forces would drive down to the Caucasus, between the Black Sea and the Caspian. The operation, first named Siegfried, was renamed Operation Blau (Blue). Stalin received hard intelligence of the German plans, but was convinced that Operation Blau was a massive strategic feint to draw off forces from Moscow. In their attempt to break Soviet resistance in the pivotal region of the Don, in order then to drive south, the Germans were drawn inexorably east, towards Stalingrad.

2 **The war in the Ukraine and Crimea began to resemble the First World War: it was characterised by Soviet offensives flowing between German hedgehogs, which held firm. The highly mobile characteristics of the early German offensives disappeared. The largest Soviet operation was the attempt to capture Kharkov (12–29 May 1942). In the first three days the Soviets in the south penetrated up to 30 miles. XXI Tank Corps, however, was committed too late (17 May) to exploit the breakthrough. When the Germans launched Operation Fridericus, on the same day, Stalin refused to break off the offensive to defend against the German pincers closing in on the rear. Army Group Kleist and Sixth Army met south of Balakleya (23 May). Only 22,000 Soviets managed to break out of the salient and back to the north bank of the Northern Donets: 200,000 were taken prisoner. To the south, von Manstein's Eleventh Army and Third Romanian Army conquered all the Crimea apart from Sevastopol itself in late 1941. The Siege of Sevastopol was interrupted by the Soviet Kerch–Feodosiya amphibious landing, which recovered the Kerch peninsula. The Germans drove the Soviets off it again in May and resumed the assault on Sevastopol.**

2 ukraine and crimea, nov. 1941–june 1942

German armoured advance

Nov.–Dec. 1941, Rotov-on-Don operations
front line, 17 Nov.
front line, 21 Nov.
front line, 2 Dec.
Soviet counter-attacks

Dec. 1941–Jan. 1942, Kerch- Feodosiya operations
Soviet position in Dec.
German front line, 2 Jan.–8 May

May–June 1942, German offensive
front line, 27 June
front line, 6 July
front line, 11 July
front line, 23 July

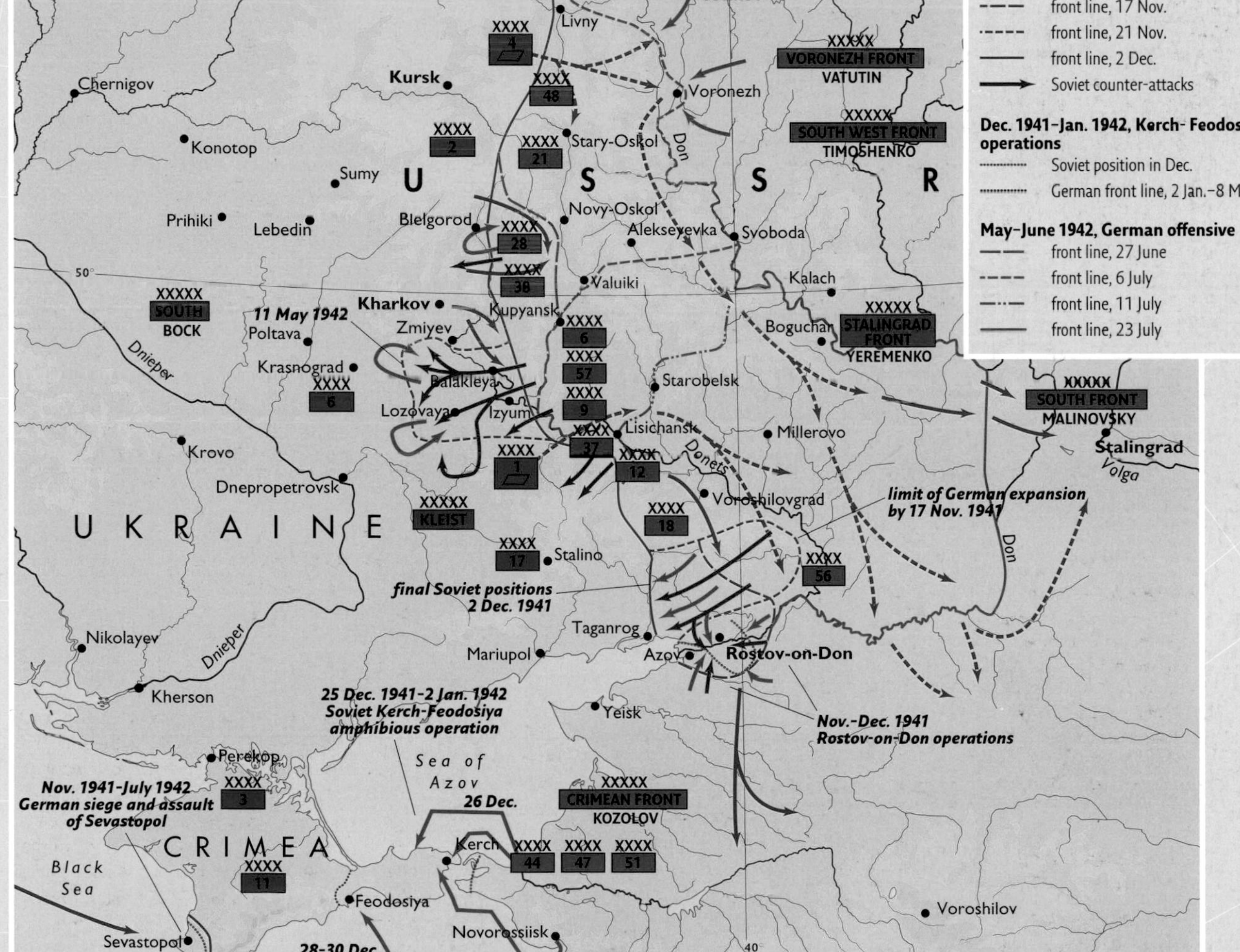

leningrad

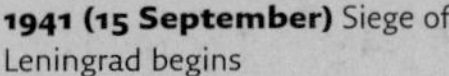

1941 to 1943

- **1941 (15 September)** Siege of Leningrad begins
- **9 November** Tikhvin falls to the Germans; recaptured 9 December
- **22 November** 'Ice Road' opened
- **1942 (22 October)** unsuccessful large-scale German assaults
- **1943 (18 January)** blockade ended
- **1944 (February)** siege raised

The Tsarist capital of St Petersburg, renamed Petrograd in 1914 in an anti-German gesture, and Leningrad from 1924, has always had a unique character, to which the memory of the '900 days' of siege, between September 1941 and 1944, has contributed.

The German Army Group North had Leningrad as its objective when it invaded the USSR on 22 June 1941. Spearheads of German Army Group North (Leeb) reached the Luga river, 60 miles south of Leningrad in mid-July 1941, by which time the Finnish Army had reached the northern shore of Lake Ladoga. The Finns refused to act in direct co-operation with Army Group North, however, and Leeb completed the encirclement of Leningrad on 15 September. A rapid thrust by Army Group North in late July, when its defences were disorganised, could probably have seized the city, but Hitler insisted on diverting forces to help Army Group Centre assault Moscow.

Leningrad had been under martial law since June; defence was commanded by Lt-Gen. Popov. The first long-range artillery shell fell on the city on 1 September, and by 8 September the city was cut off from land communication with the rest of the Soviet Union. At this time its population was about 2.5 million, plus about 100,000 refugees and the entire Baltic Fleet. On 12 September there remained in the city enough flour for 25 days, cereals for 30, meat for 22, fats for 45 and sugar for 60. Trains that might have been used to bring more into the city in preparation for a siege were being used to evacuate industry. A small amount of food was brought by barge across Lake Ladoga until the fall of Tikhvin to the Germans (9 November). Any meat and meat substitutes went to the defending troops: the search turned to bread. At first, brewing malt and animal feed were added to bread, but soon artificial substitutes were sought. A method of making cellulose flour from shell packing was developed at the Leningrad Scientific Institute. Wallpaper was stripped and the paste and size used in artificial bread; dead horses, dogs and cats were processed into food – all of which combined to give a working man about one tenth of the normal calorific intake. The sewage system broke down at the beginning of the siege as a result of bombing and shelling, but soon the excrement froze, reducing the danger of infection. Conditions in the overcrowded hospitals, without sanitation, heating or medicines, were indescribable.

After the fall of Tikhvin a lifeline road was built through the forest, without engineering equipment and under German artillery fire. Thousands died in its construction. The longed-for freeze, which would permit supplies to be dragged over the ice of Lake Ladoga was delayed, but only three days after the road was completed Soviet troops under Gen. Meretskov recaptured Tikhvin (9 Dec.), promising a more reliable route. Bridges had to be repaired and the last leg into the city had to go over the ice. On 25 December the bread ration was raised slightly. On that day alone 3,700 people died of starvation, out of 52,000 recorded deaths in that month. The official death toll for the siege of Leningrad is 632,000 although the victims probably numbered nearer one million.

1 leningrad, 10 july–9 nov. 1941

front lines

- 9 July
- 7 August
- 8 September
- 26 September
- 9 November

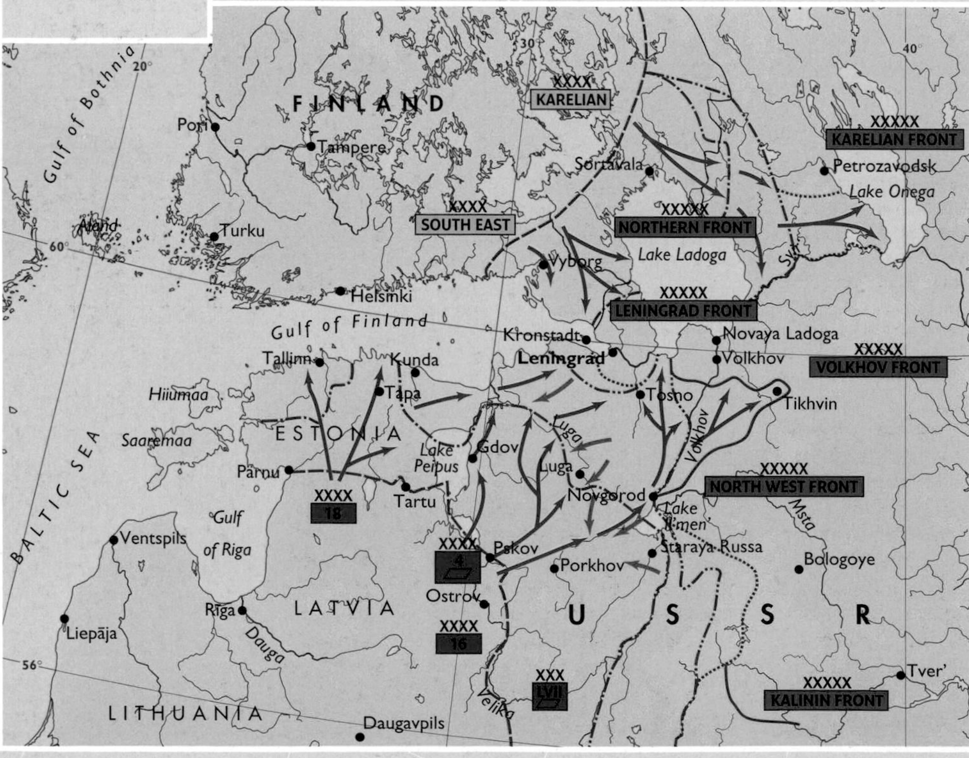

1 By 8 Sept. German forces were within ten miles of Leningrad. With the fall of Tikhvin (9 Nov.) a new 200-mile supply road surfaced with branches of trees, often on top of men who had died building it, had to be constructed. It was finished on 6 Dec.

www.bbc.co.uk/history/war/wwtwo/leningrad_betrayal_01.shtml
The Siege of Leningrad
www.saint-petersburg.com/history/siege.asp
The Siege of Leningrad

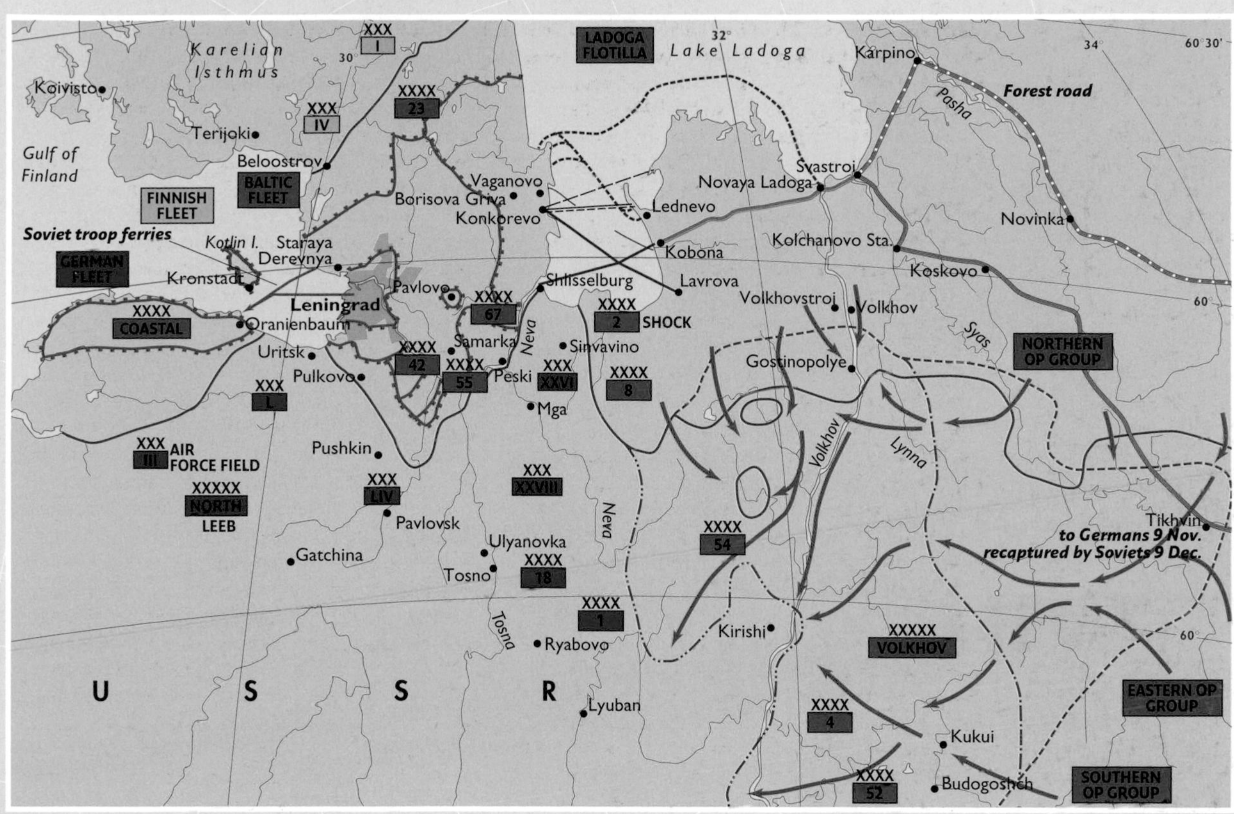

2 **On 9 Dec. Tikhvin was recaptured, with 7,000 German casualties, and Meretskov pushed the Germans back, west of the River Volkhov. The 'Road of Life' across the Lake presented more problems. The ice needed to be a uniform 200mm (8 inches) thick to bear the weight of trucks; this was not reached until the end of Nov. On 26 Nov. a convoy brought in 33 tonnes of food: 100 tonnes a day were needed to keep the city alive, but this was only occasionally achieved. The Germans lacked the strength to storm the Soviet city defences or to overcome the seaward protection of the Baltic Fleet and the great fortress of Kronstadt. The first attempt to break the blockade occurred in the first Operation Sinyavino (Sept. and 20–29 Oct. 1941), and then in Operation Lyuban, (Jan.–Apr. 1942). Other Soviet operations on this front were designed to pin down German forces away from Leningrad. The second Operation Sinyavino (19 Aug.–10 Oct. 1942), failed to break the land blockade but it interrupted German preparations for storming the city and forced the Germans to move Eleventh Army from the Crimea to help repel Soviet forces. The blockade was finally broken on 18 Jan.1943, as Sixty-Seventh Army of the Leningrad Front and new Second Shock Army of the Volkhov Front met at Workers' Estate no. 5.**

2 the siege of leningrad, 18 sept. 1941–18 jan. 1943

front line, 11 Nov. 1941
front line, 7 Dec. 1941

supply routes

prior to fall of Tikhvin
after fall of Tikhvin
water routes
ice roads
ice railways
underwater signals cable, laid 29 Oct. 1941
underwater electric cable, laid summer and autumn 1942
underwater pipeline

The German air and artillery offensive was regular rather than intense. During the course of the Battle of Leningrad about 150,000 artillery shells, over 100,000 incendiary and over 4,600 high explosive bombs fell on the city. The Leningrad Front, pushing outwards, and the Volkhov Front, pushing from the east, attempted to break the blockade from August to October 1941 (Operation Sinyavino) and January to April 1942 (Operation Lyuban), but without success. The Baltic Fleet covered Soviet moves and attacked the Germans with its aircraft, coastal artillery and naval gunfire from warships. On 12 January 1943, formations of the Sixty-Seventh Army of the Leningrad Front (Govorov) and Second Shock Army of the Volkhov Front (Meretskov) began Operation Iskra (Spark), to break the blockade. On 18 January 1943 forward units met at Workers' Housing Estate no. 5. The blockade was broken. A corridor 5–7 miles wide was forced open between the northernmost German troops and Lake Ladoga, through which a railway line and a road were built in 17 days. The blockade was broken, but the '900 days' would not be over until the Leningrad-Novgorod operation finally dislodged Army Group North in February 1944.

pearl harbor and the pacific

december 1941

- **Nov. 26** Japanese Fleet under Vice-Admiral Chuichi Nagumo leaves the Kurile Islands for Hawaii, maintaining radio silence and taking a northerly route to avoid detection
- **Nov. 28** Intercepted dispatch from Tokyo to the Japanese embassy in Washington confirms that Japan was now preparing to go to war
- **Dec. 7** Japanese Navy attacks Pearl Harbor
- **Dec. 8** Japanese invade Philippines, Siam and Malaya
- **Dec. 10** Guam falls to the Japanese
- **Dec. 11** Germany and Italy declare war on the United States
- **Dec. 23** Wake Island falls to the Japanese
- **Dec. 25** Hong Kong falls to the Japanese

The plan of campaign with which Japan went to war in December 1941 was one of great complexity, involving a series of elaborate operations spread across the International Date Line and seven time zones. Its main provisions called for initial attacks designed to eliminate both American naval power in the central Pacific and British power in the Far East; the occupation of the Dutch East Indies; and the creation of a defensive perimeter around conquered South East Asia.

Japan's first moves involved two operations separated by more than 100 degrees of longitude – landings in the early hours of 8 December in southern Siam and northern Malaya by formations from Yamashita's Twenty-Fifth Army, and, some thirty minutes later (but on the morning of the 7th), strikes by carrier aircraft against the US Pacific Fleet at its base at Pearl Harbor in Hawaii.

Thus far in the war no single operation had involved the use of more than a single carrier and a handful of aircraft. For the strike against Pearl Harbor the Japanese committed their entire first-line strength of six fleet carriers (with over 460 aircraft) in a two-wave attack under the command of Admiral Nagumo. The element of surprise was almost total, resulting in the destruction or disablement of 18 US warships, although some of these were subsequently refitted.

On 11 December, the Japanese attempt to secure Wake was repulsed without a single man being landed on the atoll, the Japanese losing one transport and two destroyers in the process. This was the only occasion during the Pacific war when an assault landing was prevented, but success proved short-lived. Stung by failure, the Japanese detached two of Nagumo's returning carriers to support a renewed and successful attack on 23 December.

In the western Pacific, Japanese forces very quickly secured an overwhelming advantage over American and Allied forces. On the first day of hostilities Japanese aircraft from Formosa effectively destroyed American air power on Luzon, while amphibious forces secured Batan Island on the approaches to the Philippines. On 10 December Japanese units from Fourteenth Army came ashore on Camiguin Island and on northern Luzon, while on 12 December a formation from the Palaus landed in southern Luzon. By the time of the main landings in Lingayen Gulf on 22 December the defeat of the Philippine garrison was assured. By that time, the Japanese were also in the process of occupying the few places of any importance in Sarawak and British North Borneo. In addition, the 38th Infantry Division had cleared the British from the New

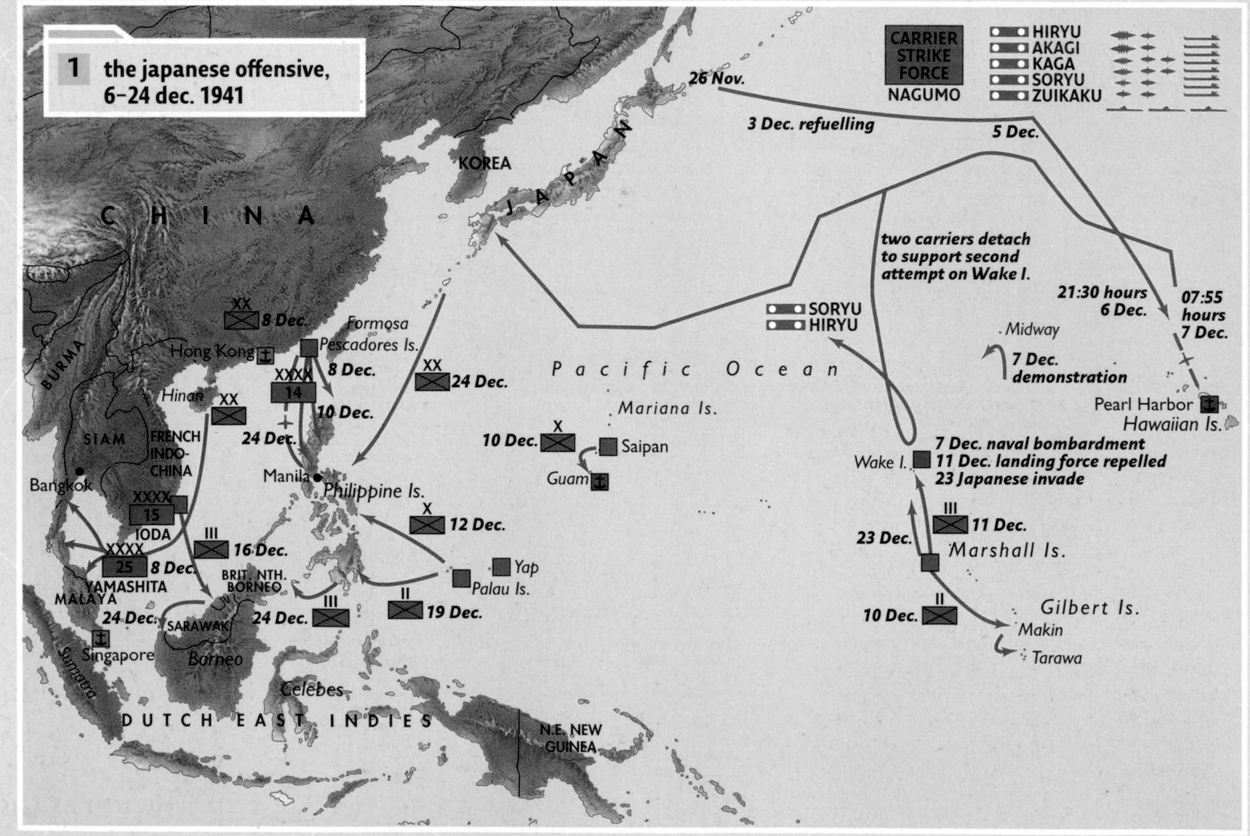

http://plasma.nationalgeographic.com/pearlharbor/
Pearl Harbor virtual war maps, survivors' personal stories and rare photographs
www.history.navy.mil/photos/events/wwii-pac/pearlhbr/pearlhbr.htm
Overview and special image selection of Pearl Harbor

Territories on the Chinese mainland and had established itself on Hong Kong Island, which fell on Christmas Day.

To the south the Japanese completed their occupation of Siam, and forced that country into an alliance, at the same time inflicting a series of costly and demoralising defeats on British forces in northern Malaya. After having sunk two British capital ships in the Gulf of Siam on 10 December, the Japanese enjoyed an overwhelming superiority both in the air and at sea, not merely in Malaya but throughout South East Asia: their enemies had been reduced to increasingly ineffective responses to events that were clearly beyond their control.

By the end of December 1941 the Japanese held the initiative throughout the theatre of operations; but the most stunning of their initial victories at Pearl Harbor contained within itself the seeds of ultimate defeat. For all its apparent success, the attack did not damage a single aircraft carrier or submarine, while the power stations, docks, machine shops and oil-storage facilities of the base were unscathed. Thus the foundations of a reconstituted fleet and the base from which it was to operate remained intact. But perhaps more significantly, by attacking Pearl Harbor at the start of the war, the Japanese sought to demoralise and divide American opinion: instead their attack united American society and provided it with a single aim – total victory. For the moment, however, victory seemed to be a monopoly of the Japanese.

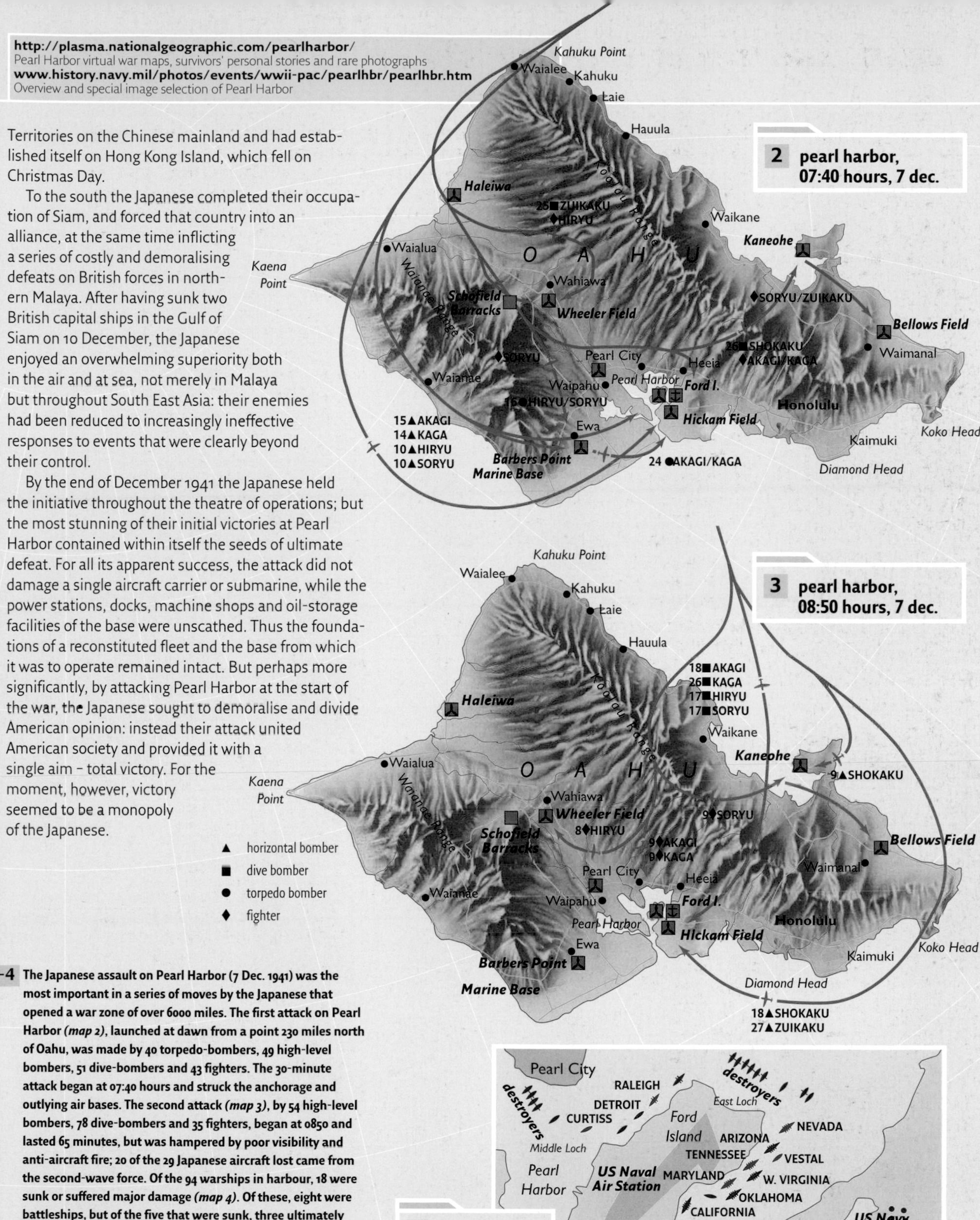

1-4 **The Japanese assault on Pearl Harbor (7 Dec. 1941) was the most important in a series of moves by the Japanese that opened a war zone of over 6000 miles. The first attack on Pearl Harbor *(map 2)*, launched at dawn from a point 230 miles north of Oahu, was made by 40 torpedo-bombers, 49 high-level bombers, 51 dive-bombers and 43 fighters. The 30-minute attack began at 07:40 hours and struck the anchorage and outlying air bases. The second attack *(map 3)*, by 54 high-level bombers, 78 dive-bombers and 35 fighters, began at 0850 and lasted 65 minutes, but was hampered by poor visibility and anti-aircraft fire; 20 of the 29 Japanese aircraft lost came from the second-wave force. Of the 94 warships in harbour, 18 were sunk or suffered major damage *(map 4)*. Of these, eight were battleships, but of the five that were sunk, three ultimately saw service again. There were no US carriers in the anchorage. Of the 394 US aircraft on the island, 188 were destroyed and another 159 damaged. On the same day, Guam was occupied, after a token resistance on the part of its 365-man garrison, by a 5,000-strong force from Saipan. The defence of Hong Kong was recognised as hopeless.**

malaya and **singapore**

december 1941 to february 1942

- **1941 (7 December)** Japanese land in Siam and Malaya, bomb Singapore
- **10 December** HMS *Repulse* and HMS *Prince of Wales* sunk during Japanese air attack
- **19 December** Georgetown abandoned by British
- **1942 (6 January)** Battle of Slim River, Malaya
- **11 January** Japanese enter Kuala Lumpur
- **30 January** British withdraw into Singapore, destroying the causeway
- **7 February** Japanese land on Singapore Island
- **15 February** British surrender at Singapore; 130,000 prisoners

The Japanese plan for breaking British colonial power based in Malaya and Singapore was the most complex of their first-phase operations. It involved formations from two armies in a series of separated landings throughout southern Siam and northern Malaya, plus the movement of forces into Siam from French Indo-China, followed by various moves against British positions in southern Burma, Tenasserim and the movement of formations by rail to northern Malaya. The arrival in Singapore of two British capital ships on 4 December was an additional hazard, threatening Japanese operations in the Gulf of Siam.

The British situation was no less complicated. As early as 1937 the British had realised that the guns of Singapore would prevent a direct seaborne attack on the base, and that as a result any Japanese move against Singapore had to be made from the north through Malaya. The denial of landing beaches in northern Malaya and airfields at Singora and Pattani was thus essential to the defence of Malaya. In December 1941, however, when Britain still hoped to avoid providing Japan with a pretext for war, their occupation could not be and was not attempted. But in the absence of a preventive move into southern Siam the British forces in northern Malaya were saddled with defensive commitments that were beyond their practical resources; at the same time the British command was not prepared to abandon northern and central Malaya in order to concentrate their forces for a defence of Johore. The British military position in Malaya on the eve of war thus was one of dispersal and weakness.

The landings of the 5th Infantry Division at Singora and Pattani on 8 December were thus unopposed by the British and while the Imperial Guards Division occupied Bangkok and the 18th Infantry Division all but met disaster amidst the surf and defences of Kota Bharu, the 5th, with armoured support, developed a two-pronged attack into northern Malaya, slashing through the British positions at Betong on 10 December, thereby threatening Kuala Kangsar and outflanking British forces in Kedah and west of the Perak river. By the 21 December British formations had been given permission to withdraw behind the river, the intention being to fight a series of delaying actions while defensive positions were prepared in central and southern Malaya, but in the event this intention fell apart for two reasons. First, the Eleventh Indian Division could not fight delaying actions while simultaneously preparing defensive positions; its attempt to do both ended in disastrous defeat on the Slim river on 7 January. Second, while the British had no answer to the Japanese tactic of encirclement through the jungle, the Japanese arrival on the Strait of Malacca, with assault boats moved from Singora, provided the Japanese with the means to turn British positions on either flank. These two developments rendered northern Johore indefensible, but the evacuation of the mainland – completed on 31 January – and the destruction of the causeway and main water supply between Johore Bahru and Singapore Island ensured the fall of Singapore. After fierce initial exchanges the Japanese secured the western part of Singapore Island by the 11 February. After the surrender four days later, about 130,000 British Commonwealth soldiers were taken prisoner in the greatest single defeat in British history: about the same number of Chinese were killed after the fall of the city by a Japanese army that incurred a mere 3,000 casualties in the course of the whole campaign.

2 **The Japanese Twenty-Fifth Army concentrated its full strength of three Divisions for the invasion of Singapore on the west of the island (8–9 Feb.), while the British concentrated on the defence of the naval and air installations on the east. The Japanese pushed swiftly to the outskirts of the city itself, where, despite vigorous defensive fighting, the British surrendered on 15 Feb.**

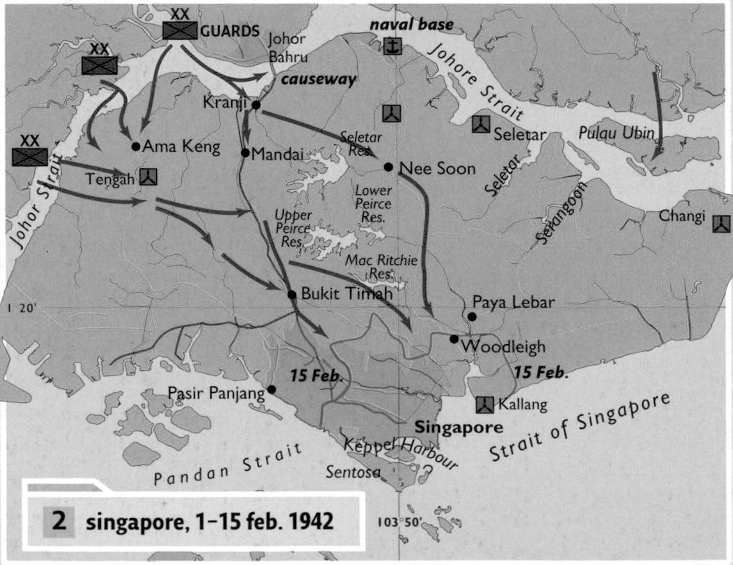

2 singapore, 1–15 feb. 1942

1 **Control of the Gulf of Siam was crucial to Japanese success, and with the sinking of the *Repulse* and the *Prince of Wales*, and having secured Singora and Patani airfields, and effected amphibious landings on the north Malayan coast , the Japanese were able to advance on two main fronts. The strategic advantage of holding a position on the Ledge (on the Siamese border), was recognised but not realised in practice. Forcing successive British retreats into the interior as they moved down the less populated east coast, the Japanese dealt with a series of defended positions along the west coast by using hook actions. Bearing round the defenders by penetrating the dense jungle, and after the fall of Penang, by amphibious hook manoeuvres launched down the coast, the Japanese Army confounded the defenders. Planned delaying actions failed after the capture of Ipoh and Kampar, and the strain of successive withdrawals and rearguard actions culminated in a major British defeat at Slim River. Although Johore now seemed indefensible, the 8th Australian Division inflicted a sharp defeat on the Japanese at Gemas (14 Jan.), but again Japanese flanking attacks, simultaneously breaking through British positions on the lower Maw and effecting a landing behind the Batu Pahat (16 Jan.), almost trapped the Australians. The whirlwind advance was temporarily halted at great cost at Parit and Pelandok (20–23 Jan.), but with the capture of Endau (21 Jan.) Johore was lost. Bombing raids over Singapore Island dislocated local services and hampered the civilian evacuation, but failed to stop reinforcements arriving.**

www.britain-at-war.org.uk/Malaya_and_Singapore/body_index.htm
The fall of Malaya and Singapore
www.historylearningsite.co.uk/fall_of_singapore.htm
The fall of Singapore

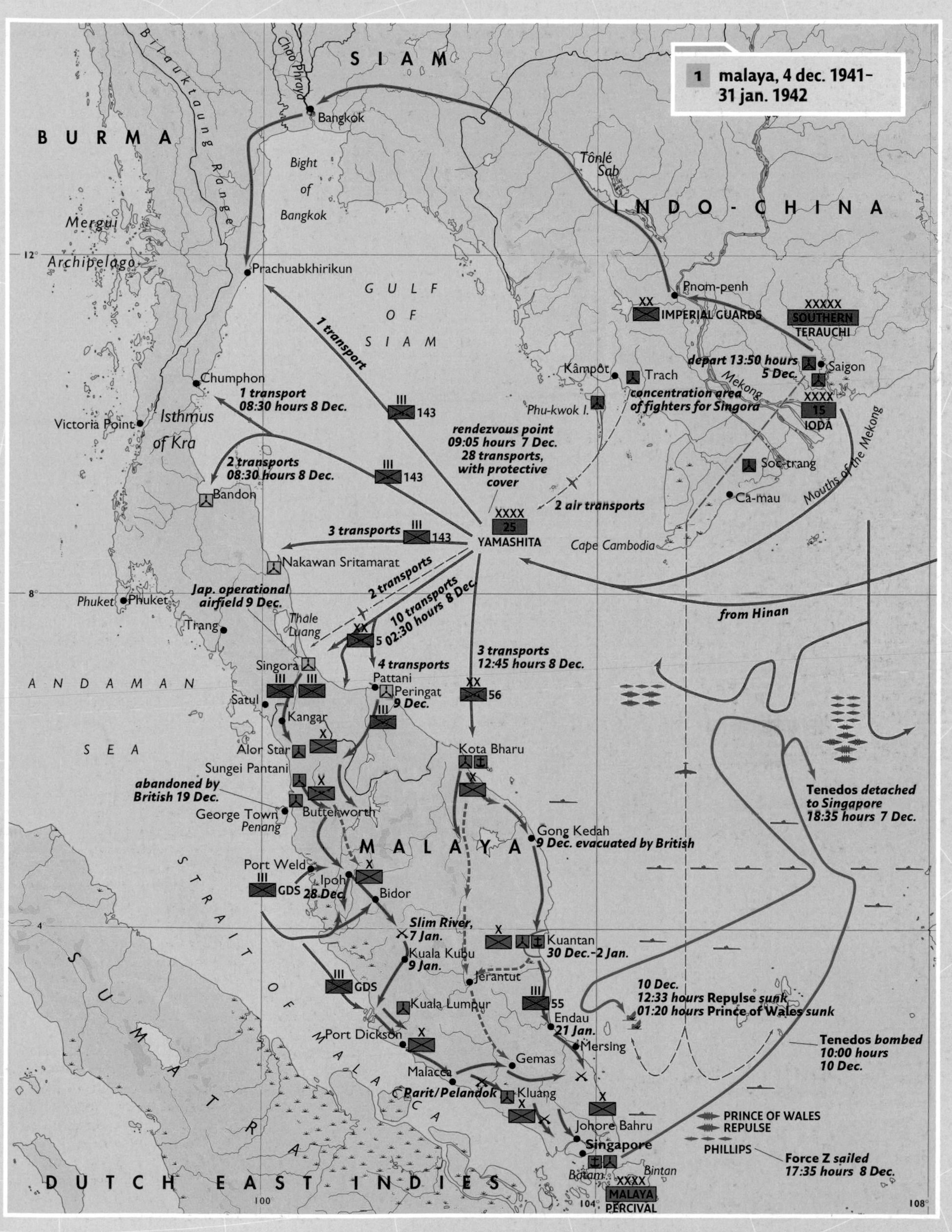

december 1941 to june 1942

- **1941 (December 10)** Japanese land on Luzon
- **22 December** Japanese land at Lingayen Gulf
- **1942 (2 January)** Japanese capture Manila and Cavite naval bases
- **22 January** Americans retreat into Bataan peninsula
- **2 March** Japanese invade Mindanao
- **9 March** General Yamashita appointed Commander-in-Chief in Philippines
- **3 April** new Japanese offensive on Bataan
- **9 April** General King surrenders on Bataan
- **11 April–5 May** 'Bataan Death March'

From the start of the Philippines campaign Japanese forces enjoyed advantages bestowed by possession of the initiative and superior geographical position that ensured victory over a garrison that was ill-led, dispersed amongst the eleven main islands of the group, and in effect abandoned to its fate by the United States from the first day of the war.

Pre-war American planning for the defence of the Philippines had been based on the premise that American forces in the islands would be able to withstand a siege until the Pacific Fleet was able to fight its way across the western Pacific to effect their relief. To this very dubious assumption was grafted in 1941 the concentration of heavy bomber forces on Luzon, primarily for deterrence purposes, and the assertion by the US commander in the islands, Lt-Gen. Douglas MacArthur, that his forces would be able to prevent Japanese landings anywhere in the Philippines. The unreality of all three aspects of American policy was revealed during the first day of the Pacific war, the crippling of the Pacific Fleet being accompanied by Japanese landings on Batan Island and an attack by Formosa-based naval bombers on Clark and Nichols airfields that caught most of the US planes on the ground and undispersed. With this one strike (some ten hours after the Pearl Harbor attack) the Japanese destroyed 103 American aircraft and ensured themselves air superiority for the remainder of the campaign. The Asiatic Fleet and surviving American bombers were withdrawn from Luzon after December 14.

The Japanese followed up their occupation of Batan with landings in northern and southern Luzon isolating the main US force around Manila. Meanwhile, Davao was secured in Mindanao. These successes provided the Japanese with a stranglehold on the Philippines even before the main forces landed.

The Luzon landings were executed in the expectation that the Americans would attempt to defend Manila, the dispersal of the Japanese effort being intended to ensure the capital's rapid encirclement. On December 23, however, MacArthur took the decision to withdraw his forces into the Bataan peninsula. In its anxiety to secure Manila, the Fourteenth Army missed the significance of the American redeployment and by 2 January some 80,000 American and Filipino troops had successfully moved into Bataan, though little effort had been made to stock the rugged peninsula in advance of their arrival.

Before the start of hostilities it had been the Japanese intention to complete the occupation of the Philippines before developing an offensive into the East Indies, but the ease with which its forces secured their objectives on Luzon and Mindanao prompted the Japanese High Command to recast its plans, the Fourteenth Army being ordered to release its air support and one division for operations in the Indies on 2 January. The start of these operations had been foreshadowed since Christmas Day, when Japanese forces occupied Job (on the approaches to Borneo) but this change of plan left the Fourteenth Army outnumbered 3:1 on Bataan and unable to bring the campaign on Luzon to a speedy conclusion. The Fourteenth Army had some initial successes, but lacked the strength to break through the last American line of defence. Forced on to the offensive while fresh formations were moved to Luzon, the Fourteenth Army thereafter relied upon a two-month siege to weaken the American garrison. On 22 Feb., when the Dutch East Indies was rapidly falling into Japanese hands, MacArthur was ordered to transfer his headquarters to Australia. On 11 Mar., four torpedo boats evacuated to Mindanao and thence Australia, MacArthur, his family and personal staff, and President Quezon with the Philippine gold reserve. The rapid collapse of American resistance on Bataan led to a general surrender on the peninsula on 8 April.

With the fall of Bataan the Americans retained only four island forts in Manila Bay in the north, plus the Visayans and most of Mindanao. While, after clearing Bataan, the Japanese prepared to assault the American headquarters on Corregidor, two regiments brought from Malaya to Davao set about securing the central and southern Philippines. When Corregidor surrendered on 7 May after a month-long bombardment, and an assault supported by tanks on the previous day, the Japanese refused to accept the surrender of the fortress without a general American surrender throughout the Philippines; an inability to resist this demand and a concern to avoid any massacre of prisoners, wounded and civilians ensured that the Japanese had their way. The result was the only surrender in history to a foreign enemy by an American army in the field. Though many Filipino troops chose to go into the hills rather than into captivity, the surrender of 7 May brought organised resistance in the Philippines to an end, and ensured the largely unopposed occupation by the Japanese of various islands thus far beyond their reach.

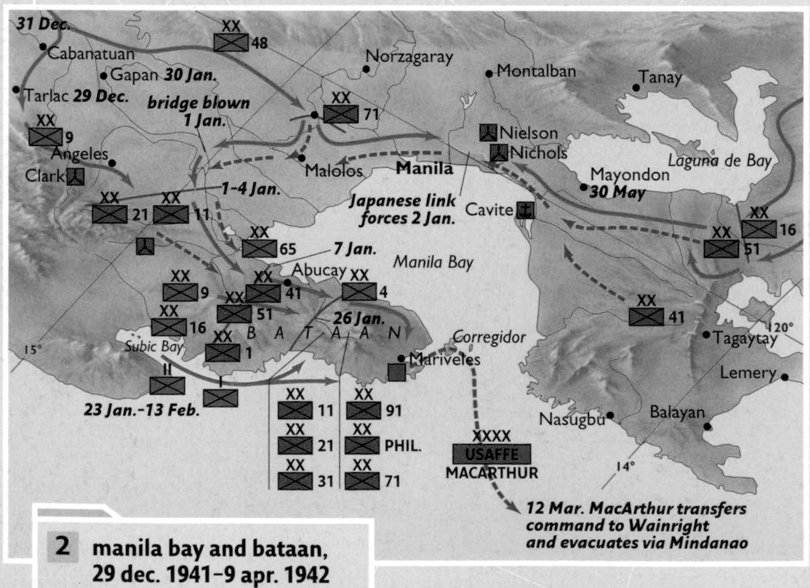

2 manila bay and bataan, 29 dec. 1941–9 apr. 1942

www.geocities.com/Pentagon/6315/bataan.html
The American defeat at Bataan
http://en.wikipedia.org/wiki/Battle_of_the_Philippines_(1941-42)
Battle of the Philippines

1-2 **The Japanese assault on Luzon began on two fronts: in the north the occupation of Batan Island was followed by landings on Camiguin and at Aparri and Vigan (10 Dec.), while Legaspi in southern Luzon was secured on 12 Dec., isolating US forces in central Luzon. While these landings were followed by unopposed advances towards central Luzon, a regiment from the Palaus secured Davao on southern Mindanao (19 Dec.). Following the main force landings at Lingayen Gulf (22 Dec.) and Lamon Bay (24 Dec.), MacArthur began a withdrawal into the Bataan peninsula. US formations conducted a phased withdrawal from Lingayen Gulf, while divisions from southern Luzon moved via Manila and San Fernando into the peninsula. Here the main line of US resistance astride Mt Natib was breached between 10 and 22 Jan., forcing a US withdrawal to the Bagac-Orion line by 26 Jan. Despite major assaults either side of Mt. Samat, and three attempts to land forces behind the US lines between 23 Jan. and 6 Feb., the depleted Japanese Army spent two months laying siege to the trapped defenders, only resuming the offensive with fresh formations on 3 Apr. Following the final US withdrawal to Corregidor (3 Apr.) the Japanese turned to the southern Philippines, occupying Cebu city and various towns on Panay (16–20 Apr.) which brought them control of the Visayans, the same two regiments then moving on to ensure Japanese control of western Mindanao by 7 May.**

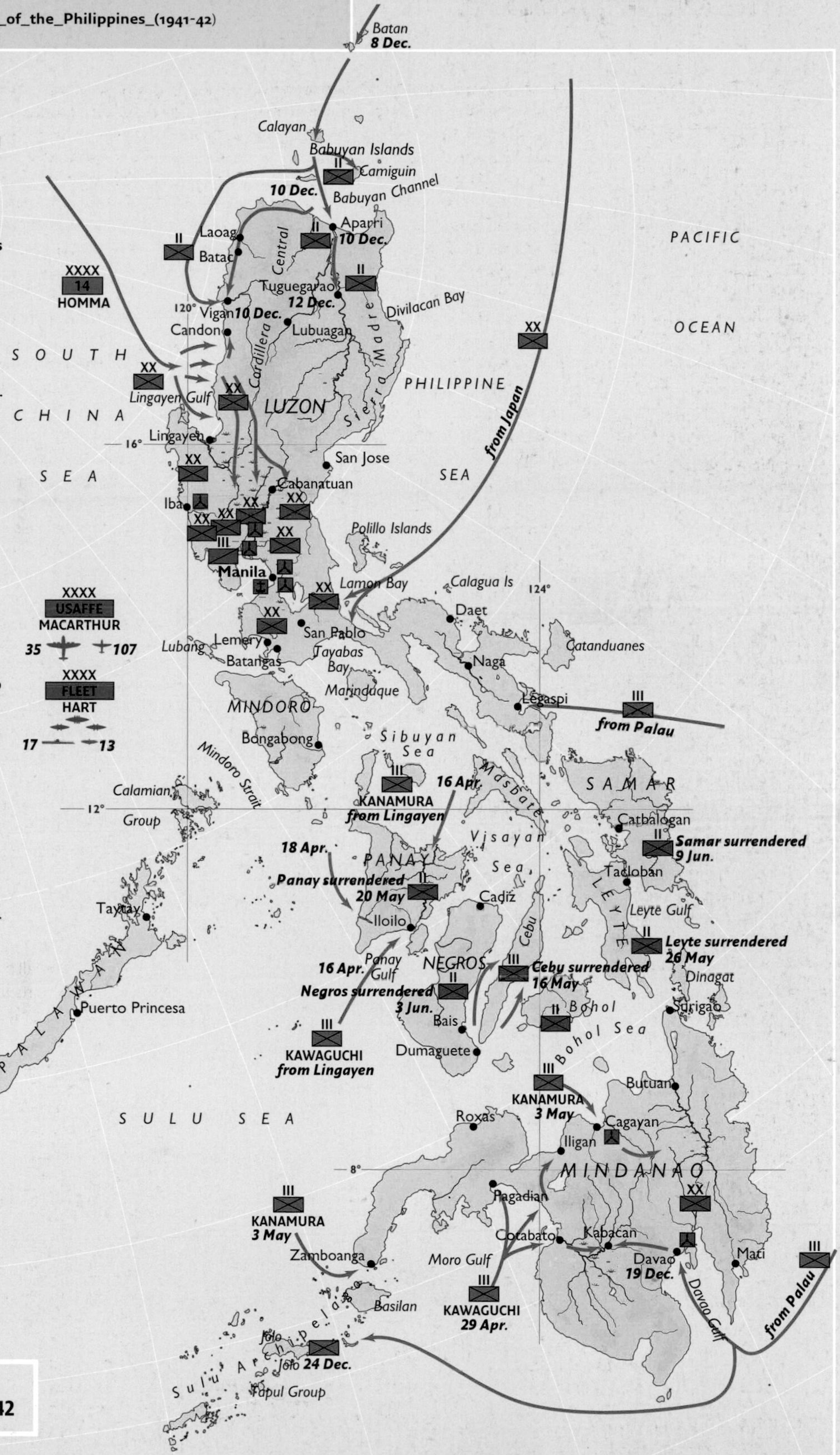

1 the philippines, 8 dec. 1941–9 june 1942

the **east indies**

january to may 1942

- **11 January** Japanese capture Tarakan in Dutch East Indies
- **22 January** Japanese planes attack New Guinea
- **23 January** Japanese land on Rabaul
- **24 January** Battle of Macassar Strait
- **1 February** US carrier attack on Gilbert and Marshall Islands
- **19 February** Japanese invade Bali; Carrier aircraft bomb Darwin
- **9 March** Dutch East Indies capitulates
- **18 March** Surprise 'Doolittle Raid' on Japan by Mitchell B25 bombers
- **4–8 May** First carrier versus carrier battle of Coral Sea

The new year in 1942 found Japan in a position of contrasts. Militarily, the first three weeks of the Pacific war had brought her a series of overwhelming victories in Malaya, the Philippines and the western Pacific, and her general victory throughout South East Asia was assured. Politically, on New Year's Day, 26 nations indicated, in the declaration of the United Nations, that they would wage total war until victory was won over the Axis powers. Thus, while operations then in hand in South East Asia would go forward to an end that Allies and Japanese alike could foresee, Japan was presented with the problem of how the war was to be prosecuted to a successful conclusion once the initial phase of conquest was complete.

The conquest and consolidation of the East Indies – for the most part in Dutch colonial hands – would be the economic jewel in the crown of the new Japanese empire, but as the defensive perimeter was extended east, became something of an Achilles' heel. Only the British possessions on Borneo played unwilling host to Japanese operations in 1941. Miri was secured by an independent formation from southern Indo-China on 15 December, Kuching being occupied on Christmas Day and the Dutch airfield at Singkawang in late January. From Miri, too, Japanese forces moved to occupy British North Borneo, Sandakan being taken on 17 January. By then, however, the main Japanese offensive into the Indies had opened with landings at Tarakan (10 January) and Menado the next day. From these two ports the Japanese could develop their offensive either side of Macassar, thereby dividing Allied attention and resources, but their next moves, on Balikpapan and Kendari, were accompanied by a carrier strike on Rabaul and the occupation of this base and of Kavieng. Possession of the great natural harbour at Rabaul provided the Japanese with the base from which to secure the upper Solomons and eastern New Guinea, but for the moment Japanese attention centred on Borneo and Macassar, where, despite losses incurred off Balikpapan on 24 January, the Japanese moved in strength to secure Macassar city on 8 February after having occupied Amboina, and its airfield, on 31 January. With the occupation of Bandlermasin on 10 February by a force that advanced overland after first being landed on Laut Island, the Japanese by mid-February dominated the approaches to Java.

2 the pacific, mid-1942

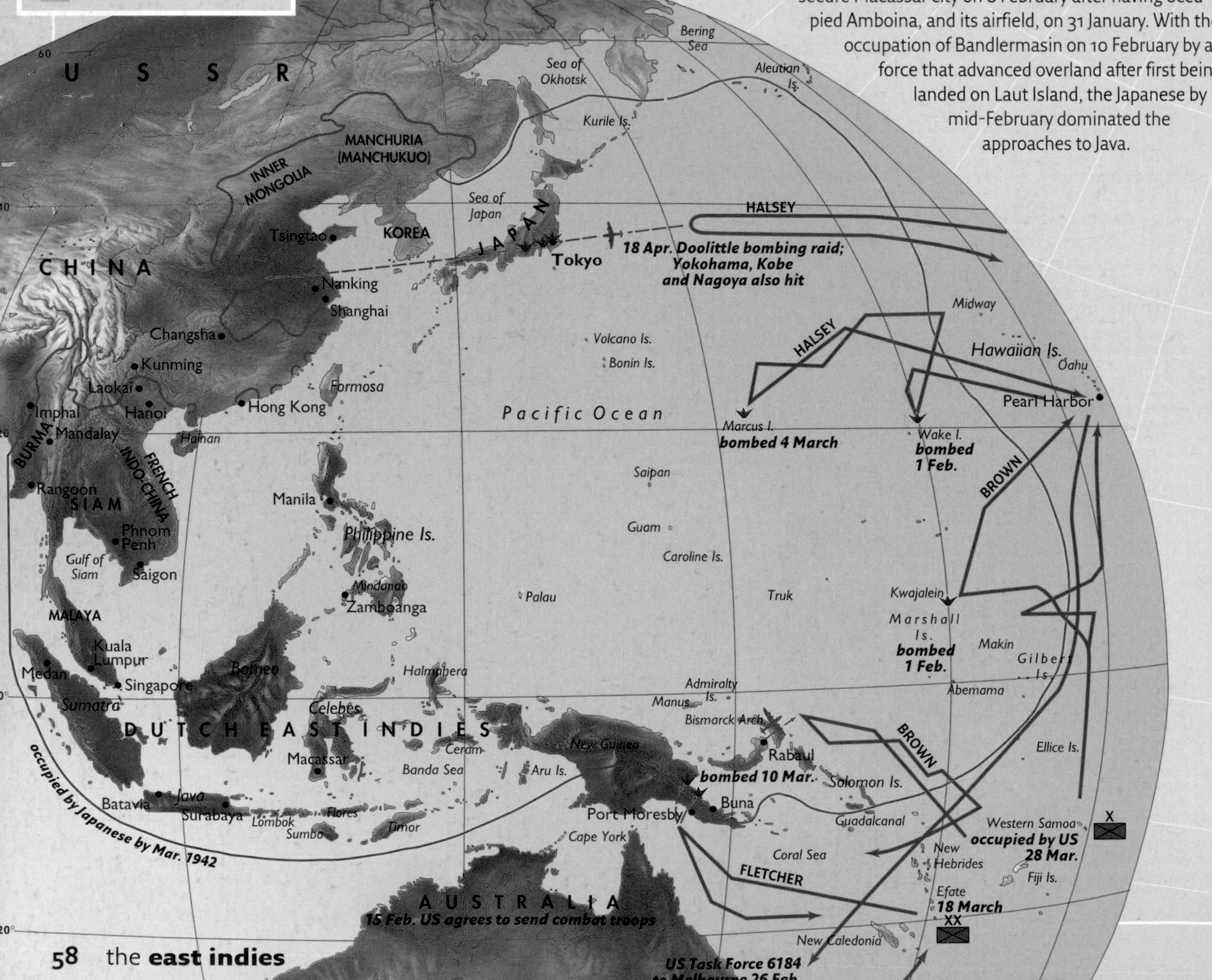

www.doolittleraid.com/
The Doolittle Raid on Japan
www.history.navy.mil/photos/events/wwii-pac/coralsea/coralsea.htm
Overview of the Battle of Coral Sea

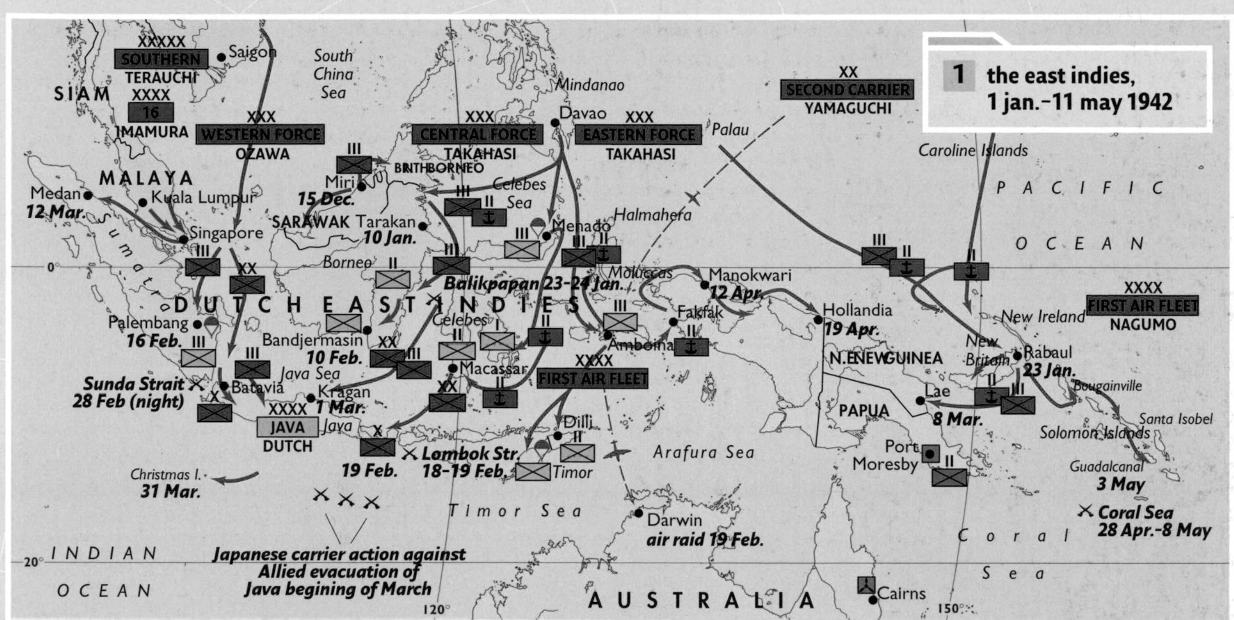

The reduction of Singapore was the *sine qua non* for an assault on the East Indies, and with the assault on the island on 8 February the Japanese moved to secure Palembang by combined airborne and amphibious assault on the 14 February. Palembang and its refineries were occupied on 17 February, when the Allied evacuation of southern Sumatra was complete. Thereafter the main Japanese blows fell in the east, the carrier force, supported by bombers from Kendari and Amboina, reducing much of Darwin to debris on 19 February, while assault forces landed on Bali (also on the 19th) and in both Dutch and Portuguese Timor (20 February). With Japanese forces simultaneously working their way around western Borneo, the Allied defeat on Java was assured even before the Japanese landings on the island on the night of 28 February/1 March.

Various Japanese landings had been disputed, inconclusively, by Allied naval forces, but the assault on Java committed the Allies to a decisive naval action in the eastern Java Sea, two cruisers and three destroyers being lost in a vain attempt to get amongst the transports carrying the 48th Infantry Division to Kragan. After this action, surviving Allied warships in the Java Sea were hunted to destruction by Japanese naval units, while to the south of Java the carrier force dealt with Allied shipping trying to escape from the island. Only at Bantam Bay did Allied cruisers manage to engage Japanese transports, and paid the inevitable price for their fleeting success, the Japanese being able to come ashore in western Java across the wide front and to secure Batavia on 5 March. With the Dutch surrendering throughout the Indies on 9 March and their allies following suit on the 12th, the Japanese were able to proceed with the immediate unopposed occupation of northern Sumatra and of northern New Guinea from Boela to Hollandia between 31 March and 19 April.

By mid-April, however, Japanese policy for the next phase of operations had been settled. The UN declaration and American carrier operations in early 1942 convinced the Japanese High Command that offensive operations would have to be undertaken in order to complete the destruction of the American carrier formations and to force the United States to the compromised peace she so disdained.

The plan of campaign that was devised during March, and accepted on 5 April, provided for an attack on the Aleutians and Midway, in the course of which American carrier forces were to be brought to battle and destroyed. Thereafter Japanese forces were to secure New Caledonia, Fiji and Samoa in July before taking Johnson Island in August, the Hawaiian Islands being the obvious target for subsequent operations. Various American carrier operations against the Marshall Islands, Rabaul, Wake and Marcus between 1 February and 4 March had achieved negligible results, though they served to underline the Japanese need to bring about the defeat of enemy carrier forces at the earliest possible opportunity, but in Huon Gulf, American carriers achieved successes against Japanese shipping supporting the landings at Lae and Salamaua; this left Japanese forces in the South West Pacific without the means to proceed with their next operations, the occupation of Tulagi in the Solomons and Port Moresby in New Guinea. With Japanese intelligence suggesting the continued presence of two American carriers in the South West Pacific after March, the decision to seek a decisive battle in the central Pacific was followed by the strange decision to detach two fleet carriers to support the operations against Tulagi and Port Moresby, before the central Pacific undertaking began. The result – the Battle of the Coral Sea – was not merely the first carrier engagement in history but the first strategic defeat incurred by Japanese forces in the Second World War. Despite sinking the carrier USS *Lexington*, the Japanese called off their attempt to invade Port Moresby and withdrew. It proved to be the point at which the flow of Japanese successes in the area was finally stemmed, allowing the Allies gradually to consolidate their strength.

1-2 **The invasion of the East Indies (*map 1*) illustrated the Japanese mastery of combined operations, a skill which the Allies would have to master before registering any successful responses. A series of audacious US carrier raids in the first four months of 1942 (*map 2*) boosted US morale, none more so than the 'Doolittle' air raid on Japan's premier cities, but it was not until the battle in the Coral Sea that a significant US victory could be recorded.**

december 1941 to may 1942

16 January Japanese invade Burma from Siam

29 February Britain promises full dominion status to India after the war

8 March Japanese enter Rangoon

10 March General Stilwell appointed Chief of Staff in China

19 March General Slim takes charge in Burma

4 April fires sweep Mandalay after Japanese bombing

29 April Japanese seize Lashio and cut Burma Road

1 May British evacuate Mandalay

2 May British retreat over Irrawaddy

24 May General Stilwell arrives in Delhi after 20-day trek through jungle

Until 1941, the defence of Burma ranked below that of the West Indies in the list of British strategic priorities. The Japanese occupation of southern Indo-China in July 1941, however, presented Burma with a real external threat, but the higher claim of Malaya and Singapore on military resources meant that in December 1941 the military establishment in Burma consisted of a few combat aircraft and the equivalent of one division.

For Japan, Burma's occupation would sever the Chinese Nationalists' main line of communication with the outside world (via Lashio and Rangoon) and would provide defence in depth to the southern resources area. The Japanese High Command thus earmarked the Fifteenth Army for operations in Burma after the occupation of Siam was complete.

The Fifteenth Army, with just one regiment under command, occupied the Kra Isthmus between Prachaub and Nakhorn on 8 December, to secure the rear and the lines of communication of the Twenty-Fifth Army as it advanced into Malaya. Victoria Point airfield was secured on 16 December, but it was not until then that the Fifteenth Army began operations in earnest. Airfields at Tavoy and Mergui were secured and from them Japanese fighters were able to escort bomber raids on southern Burma for the first time. By the end of January the port of Rangoon had been brought to a standstill.

The main Japanese effort was made, however, on the Raheng–Moulmein track. The Fifteenth Army had two half-strength divisions under command when it crossed the border on 20 January, but these possessed superiority of numbers over a defence divided between Tenasserim and the Shan States, and which was committed to defending Burma east of the Salween. Despite the arrival at Rangoon of four brigades in the six weeks before the city's fall, the destruction of the 17th Indian Division doomed the capital, and with it any British hope of holding Burma.

It had been the original Japanese intention to secure Rangoon and then to advance into central Burma, and with the end of the other campaigns in South East Asia the Japanese were able to move the equivalent of three divisions by sea to Burma within seven weeks of the capture of Rangoon. The Fifteenth Army quickly developed its offensives in the Irrawaddy–Sittang valleys, despite the presence there of Chinese forces (which were dispersed, equivalent to no more than a division, and, on the Sittang, were not mutually supporting). The first crucial clash around Toungoo was won by the Japanese. Critically, the Japanese secured intact the bridge over the Sittang and were able to develop an offensive through the mountains that resulted in the capture of Lashio on 28 April. Four days later the Japanese secured Mandalay and with it control of central and northern Burma.

The formal decision to abandon Burma was not taken until 25 April, by which time the withdrawal was threatened as much by the approach of the monsoon as by the advancing Japanese. In the first week of May the last British formations in Burma, plus one Chinese division, abandoned the lower Chindwin and began to trek to Imphal, while the remainder of the Fifth Chinese Army withdrew into northern Burma and thence either to Assam or northern Yunnan. Parts of the Sixth Chinese Army contrived to remain in the eastern Shan States, but on the Sixty-Sixth Army's front the Japanese advanced into Yunnan and established themselves on the Salween, where they were to remain until late 1944.

The Japanese presence in most of Burma preoccupied British strategy in the East until 1944. Supplies to Nationalist forces in China were disrupted, but the incipient threat to India was never realised, although an assault on Ceylon and other ports signposted disruption of shipping in the Indian Ocean and caused fears of Japanese designs on Madagascar.

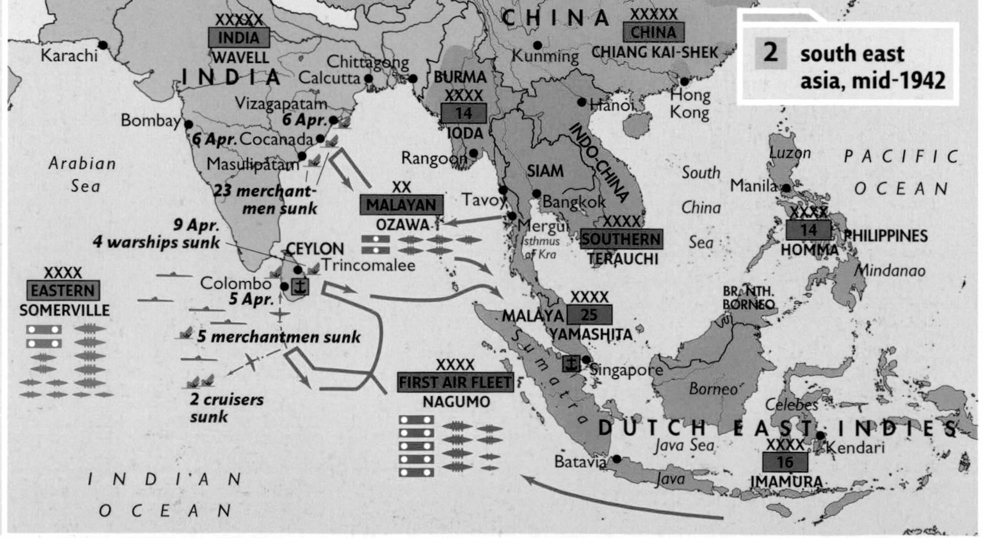

2 **Japan's employment of the carrier strike force in the Indies in early 1942 left it ideally placed to raid Ceylon. It sailed from Kendari on 2 Mar. and raided Colombo, surprisingly ineffectively, on 5 Apr., but its aircraft found and destroyed two British heavy cruisers. The British force sought to join battle under cover of night, but on 7 Apr. it was given discretion to withdraw, which it did. Meeting no effective opposition, the Japanese raided Trincomalee on 9 Apr., sinking four warships and auxiliaries, including the *Hermes*, the first carrier to be sunk by carrier aircraft attack. Supporting operations were conducted by submarines that sank five merchantmen off the west coast of India, and by a carrier-cruiser force that sank 23 merchantmen and raided various cities in eastern India. The blow to British prestige and trade in the Bay of Bengal was considerable, but strategically the Japanese raid achieved little of consequence.**

http://homepages.force9.net/rothwell/burmaweb/japinvade.htm
The Japanese invasion of Burma
www.burmastar.org.uk/
The Burma Star Association

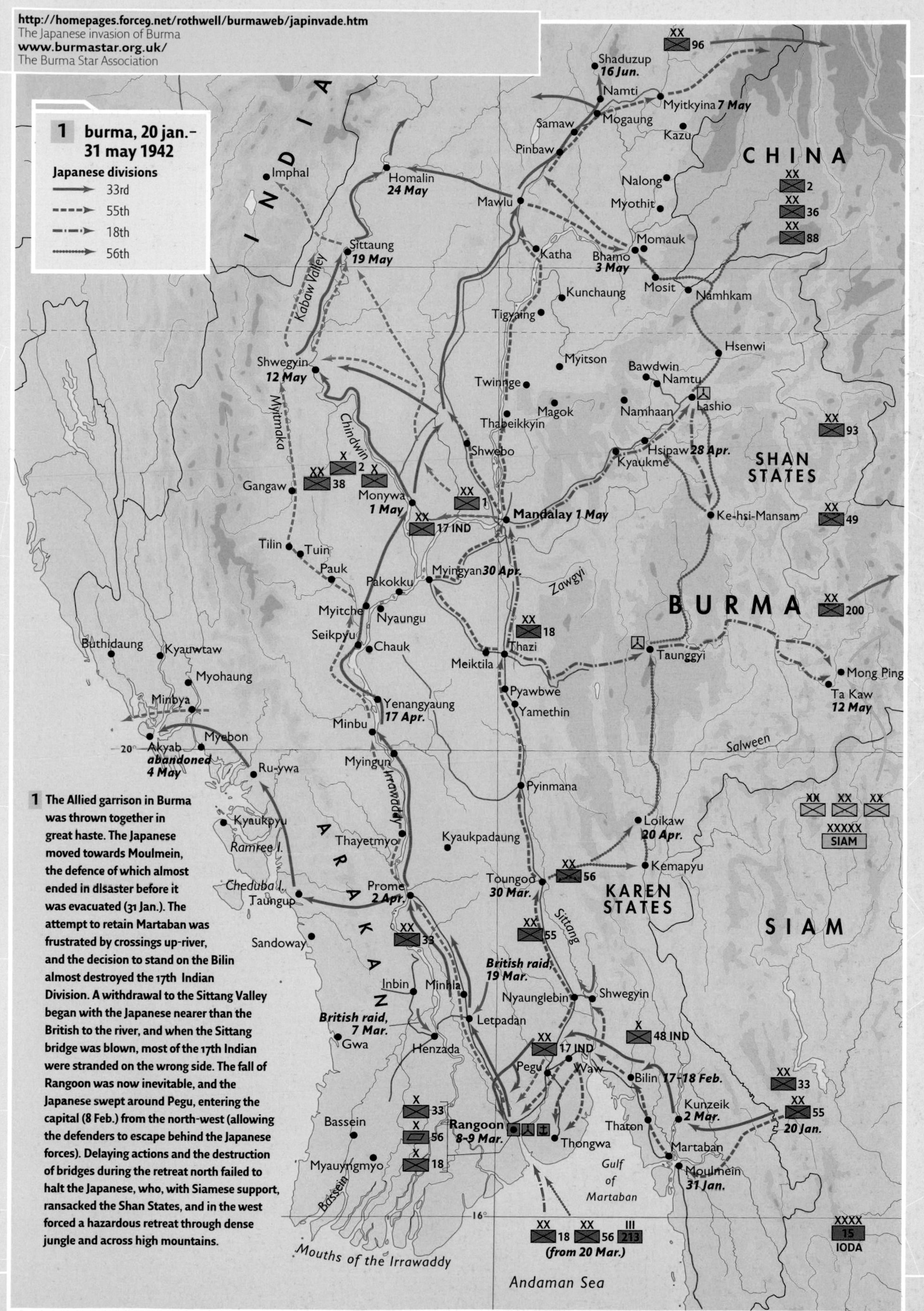

1 The Allied garrison in Burma was thrown together in great haste. The Japanese moved towards Moulmein, the defence of which almost ended in disaster before it was evacuated (31 Jan.). The attempt to retain Martaban was frustrated by crossings up-river, and the decision to stand on the Bilin almost destroyed the 17th Indian Division. A withdrawal to the Sittang Valley began with the Japanese nearer than the British to the river, and when the Sittang bridge was blown, most of the 17th Indian were stranded on the wrong side. The fall of Rangoon was now inevitable, and the Japanese swept around Pegu, entering the capital (8 Feb.) from the north-west (allowing the defenders to escape behind the Japanese forces). Delaying actions and the destruction of bridges during the retreat north failed to halt the Japanese, who, with Siamese support, ransacked the Shan States, and in the west forced a hazardous retreat through dense jungle and across high mountains.

1940 to 1942

- **1941 (2 February)** Rommel arrives in Tripoli
- **30 March** Afrika Korps offensive in Cyrenaica
- **1 April** Raschid Ali seizes power in Iraq
- **4 April** Afrika Korps captures Benghazi
- **13 April** Rommel's forces surround Tobruk
- **28 April** Germans take Sollum
- **30 April** Iraqi troops surround RAF airbase at Habbaniya
- **8 June** British, Australian, Indian and Free French forces invade Syria

As early as October 1940 Hitler had considered the strategic merit of extending his war against Britain into the Middle East. Mussolini at first resented German involvement in what he regarded as Italy's particular sphere of operations, but after his humiliation in Egypt at the hands of the British and in Albania at the hands of the Greeks, he could no longer sustain the pretence that he did not need German help. Hitler arranged for the despatch of German troops to Libya at a meeting with the Italians on 19-20 January 1941. The Deutsches Afrika Korps (DAK), of 5th Motorised and 15th Panzer Divisions, began to arrive at Tripoli on 12 February. It was commanded by Erwin Rommel, a tank strategist who had tasted victory in Belgium and France.

The British were keenly aware of the problem posed by the increasing Axis presence in the Mediterranean. New supply lines to the British garrisons in Egypt and East Africa had to be created as alternatives to hazardous Mediterranean routes. The problem was eased by Commonwealth troops from India, Australia, New Zealand and South Africa, who were relied upon to shore up the British presence in Africa.

Rommel opened his offensive at El Agheila, lightly held by the British 2nd Armoured Division. Wavell's Western Desert Force had been heavily depleted by transfers to Greece; its air support amounted to only 30 aircraft but fortunately the Axis air forces were not strong. El Agheila fell at once and Mersa Brega, in its immediate rear, on 31 March. Despite orders to the contrary, Rommel continued his advance into Cyrenaica. He organised his mobile forces into three columns, one to follow the coast road, the two others to use desert tracks to cut off the British from the rear. The British withdrew to the Mekili-Wadi Cuff Line. Although the Germans found difficulty navigating the desert tracks, and had to be led by Rommel in person on the night of 5 April, the British decided to withdraw again on 6 April, making for Gazala, losing in the process their two leading generals, Neame and O'Connor, who were captured by an Axis patrol. Mekili was abandoned after a three-day stand (6-8 April). The Australian 9th Division withdrew into Tobruk, which was surrounded by 11 April.

Rommel, who could not advance leaving Tobruk to his rear, now decided to make a deliberate assault on the defences. It opened on the night of 30 April/1 May and achieved some success. The Australians, heavily supported by artillery, virtually destroyed half the attacking German tanks, and Paulus, who had arrived from Berlin to oversee Rommel's decisions, refused to permit the attack to be renewed. He ordered instead that priority should be given to establishing a defensive line west of Tobruk at Gazala, while reinforcements and supplies were accumulated. His signal to Berlin revealing this change of intention was intercepted by *Ultra* and prompted Churchill to order Wavell, to whom the Tiger convoy had brought 240 tanks on 12 May, to undertake a counter-offensive. Code named Brevity, it was launched by 7th Armoured and 22 Guards Brigade at Sollum on 15 May, but in too little strength. The British took the outer defences of Sollum, Halfaya and Fort Capuzzo but were counter-attacked and forced to withdraw. On 26 May the Germans recovered the remnants of the ground lost

1 **The war in the Western Desert developed badly for the Allies after the arrival of German forces in Libya. The success of Rommel's opening offensives was overwhelming, and his response to the British Operations Brevity (15–26 May) and Battleaxe (15–17 June) led to the isolation of Tobruk and counter-offensives at Sollum, Halfaya and Fort Capuzzo, which eventually drove the British east of the Egyptian border.**

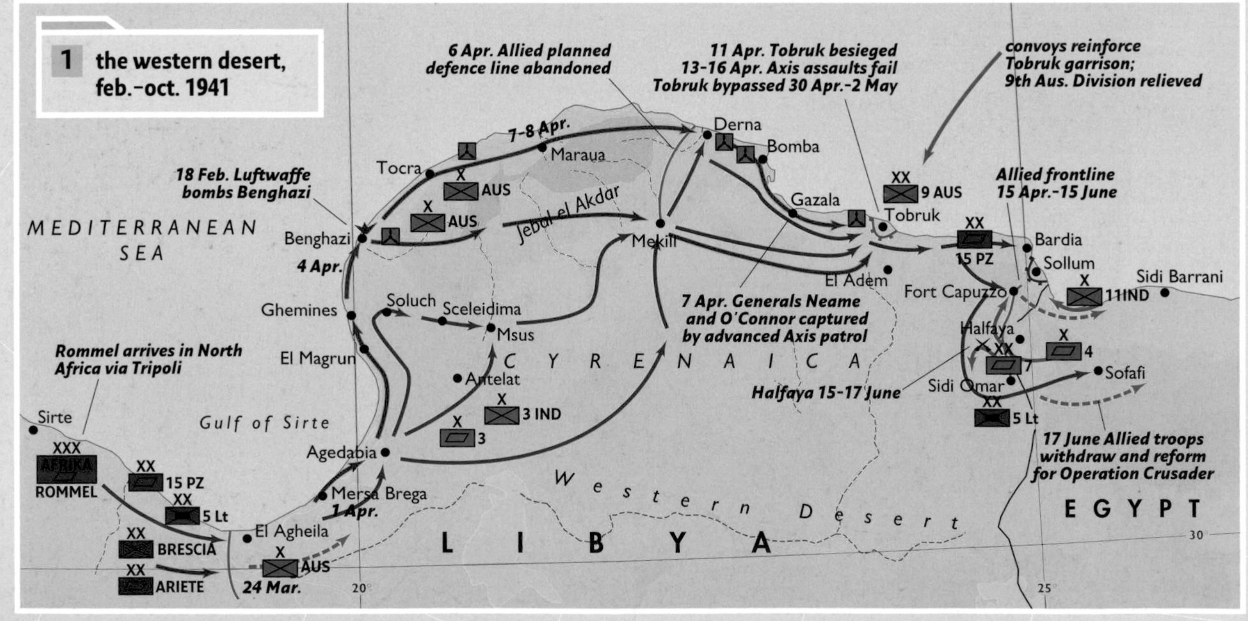

www.achtungpanzer.com/gen1.htm
Biography of General Rommel
www.bbc.co.uk/dna/ww2/A1057565
The Allied campaign in Syria

in Operation Brevity and there was then a pause until the opening of Wavell's equally unsuccessful Operation Battleaxe on 15 June, which failed to penetrate the forward Axis line near Bardia, and indeed resulted in a British retreat well inside the Egyptian border.

The British had had greater success, meanwhile, in offsetting indirect German penetration of the Middle East, and by June 1941 the Soviet Union had joined the Allied cause. It became essential to ensure supply lines to her, via the Gulf and Persia, and to secure the Middle East in general, not least because of the Gulf oil reserves. On 3 April the pro-British Regent of Iraq, Emir Abdullah, had been overthrown in a coup led by the pro-Axis General Rashid Ah. On 29 April he invested the British air base at Habbaniya, near Baghdad, to forestall the build-up of British troops in the country, where they had the right to use the port of Basra. Fighting broke out at Habbaniya on 2 May and a relief force, Habforce, left Transjordan on 13 May. It was attacked by Luftwaffe aircraft operating from Syria and Iraq but forced its way into Baghdad between 27–30 May. Rashid Ah fled to Persia and Abdullah was restored on 30 May. Evidence of German involvement in Syria, where French forces were loyal to Vichy, prompted Churchill to organise a four-pronged assault, beginning on 23 June. From Palestine the Allies advanced on Beirut and Damascus, while the Iraq Habforce and 10th Indian Division advanced to Homs and Aleppo. Most made slow progress, but supported by naval gunfire, the 7th Australians broke through to Beirut on 6 July and in a five-day battle forced Dentz, the Vichy commander, to sue for terms. The armistice, signed on 14 July, allowed French troops to return to France if they chose. Only 5,700 out of 38,000 surviving troops opted to join de Gaulle's Free French.

Both British reliance on Commonwealth troops east of Suez and the security of the Indian Ocean shipping lanes were threatened by the Japanese entry to the war in December 1941. Fear of Japanese plans to establish submarine bases in Vichy Madagascar prompted, in May 1942, a British/South African invasion and protracted campaign; this completed Allied control between 30° and 90° East, driving a wedge between the Axis powers in Europe and Asia. Now British strategy in the west would centre upon the Western Desert.

2 A campaign to secure Vichy territories in the Middle East proved a bitter fight, as did the British invasion of Madagascar a year later. Nevertheless, with Vichy and pro-Axis elements west of Egypt eliminated, essential supply routes to the USSR via Persia could be established, and the vital oil resources of the Gulf guaranteed to the Allies.

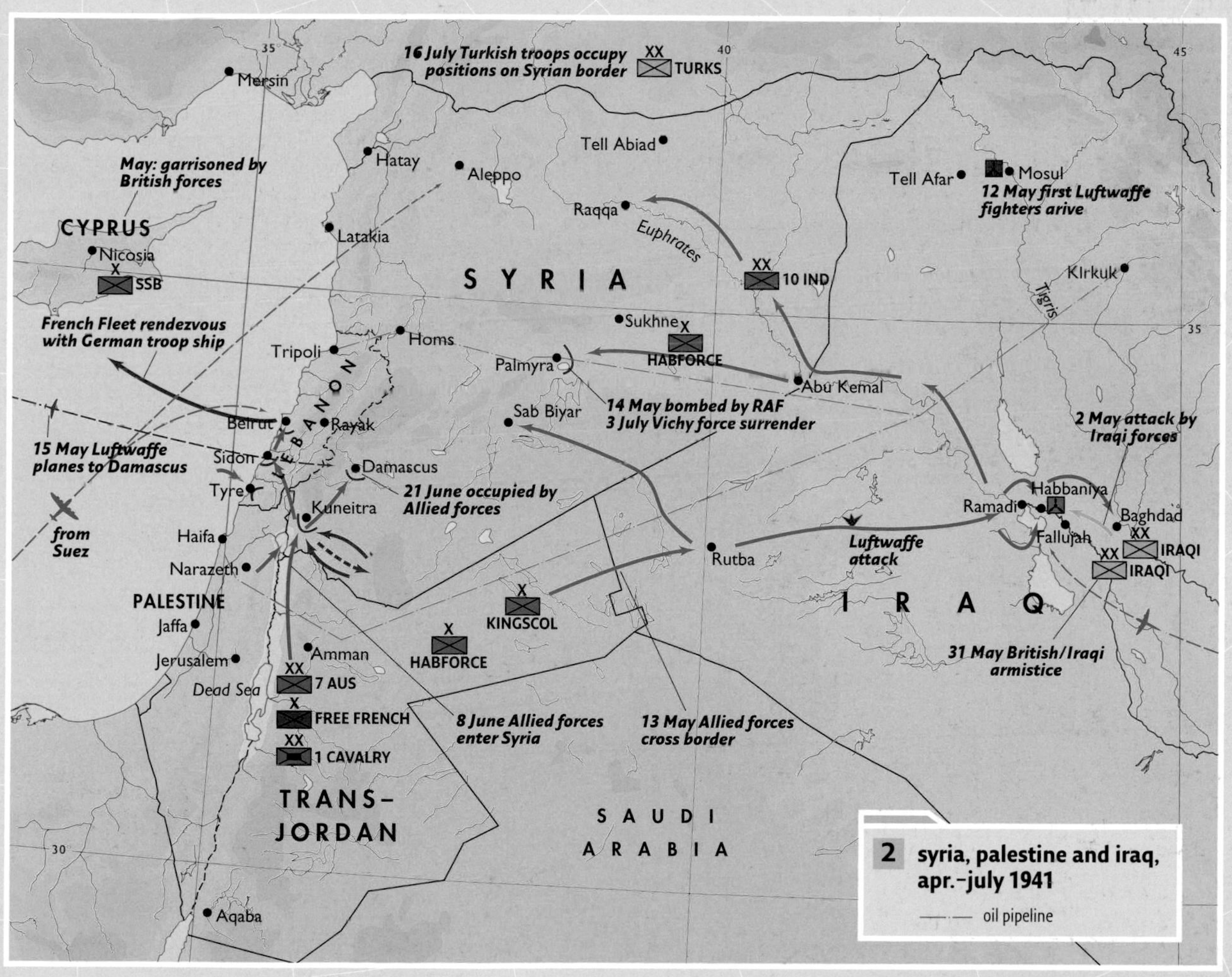

nov. 1941 to july 1942

- **1942 (2 January)** British and South Africans recapture Bardia
- **26–30 May** Rommel attacks and outflanks Gazala line
- **28 May** Bir Hakeim tank battle; Free French hold out
- **17 June** British garrison Tobruk and retreat to Egypt
- **30 June** Germans reach El Alamein

Leaving Tobruk under siege, and advancing to the Egyptian border in March-April 1941, Rommel then consolidated his positions near Sollum. General Claude Auchinleck, who had succeeded Wavell as Middle East Commander on 5 July, began planning a counterstroke – Operation Crusader – with Western Desert Force (redesignated Eighth Army on 18 December) in August. The relief of Tobruk and the reoccupation of Cyrenaica were the principal aims of the operation. It was to be commanded by Lt.-Gen. Alan Cunningham, the victor of the East African campaign.

The outbreak of war with Japan had syphoned off many Far Eastern Commonwealth reinforcements. The importance of maintaining a Mediterranean supply route from Great Britain and her transatlantic allies, and of retaining Malta, midway between Gibraltar and Alexandria, was critical. German bombing of the island had begun in late 1940, but RAF units resolutely resisted the almost continuous Luftwaffe assault and a series of major supply convoys began to force a passage through the hazardous narrows south of Sicily and Sardinia.

In the Western Desert, by November 1941, the Eighth Army outnumbered the combined Axis force (c. 118,000 men to c. 113,000), had 680 tanks (with 500 in reserve or in supply) to Rommel's 390 and 1,000 British planes confronted 320 Axis aircraft. Thus, Operation Crusader, opening on 28 November, and taking Rommel by surprise, should have succeeded. It did not. An initial break-out from Tobruk was contained, as was the major offensive by XXX Corps. Cunningham was replaced by Lt.-Gen. Neil Ritchie, who restored the Allied offensive, causing Rommel to retreat west of Tobruk, abandoning Italian forces at Bardia and Sollum (surrendered 17 December) and reaching Gazala (7 December) then El Agheila by the end of the year.

1 tobruk, 18 nov.–8 dec. 1941

Allied position, 24:00 hours 19 Nov.
Afrika Korps, 9–26 Nov.
Afrika Korps, 27 Nov.–7 Dec.

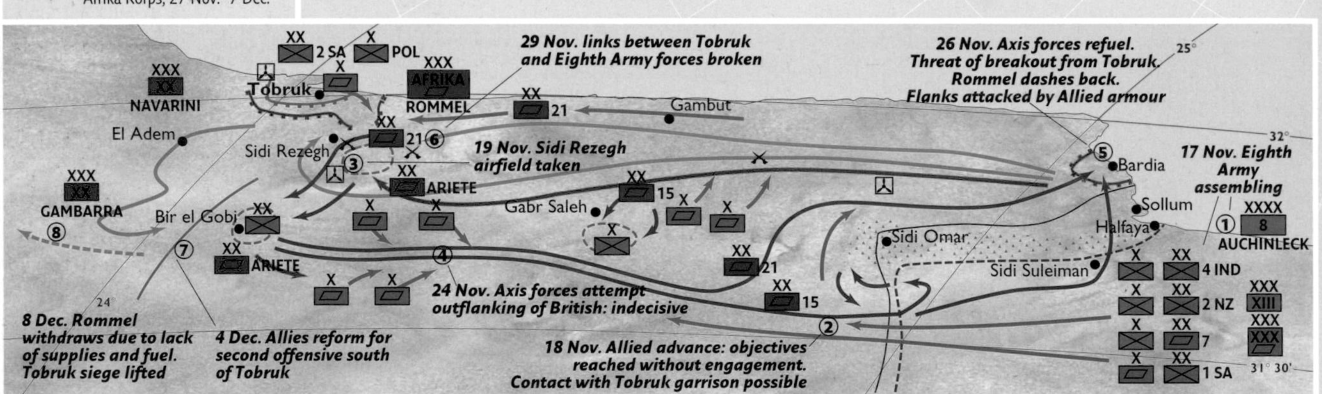

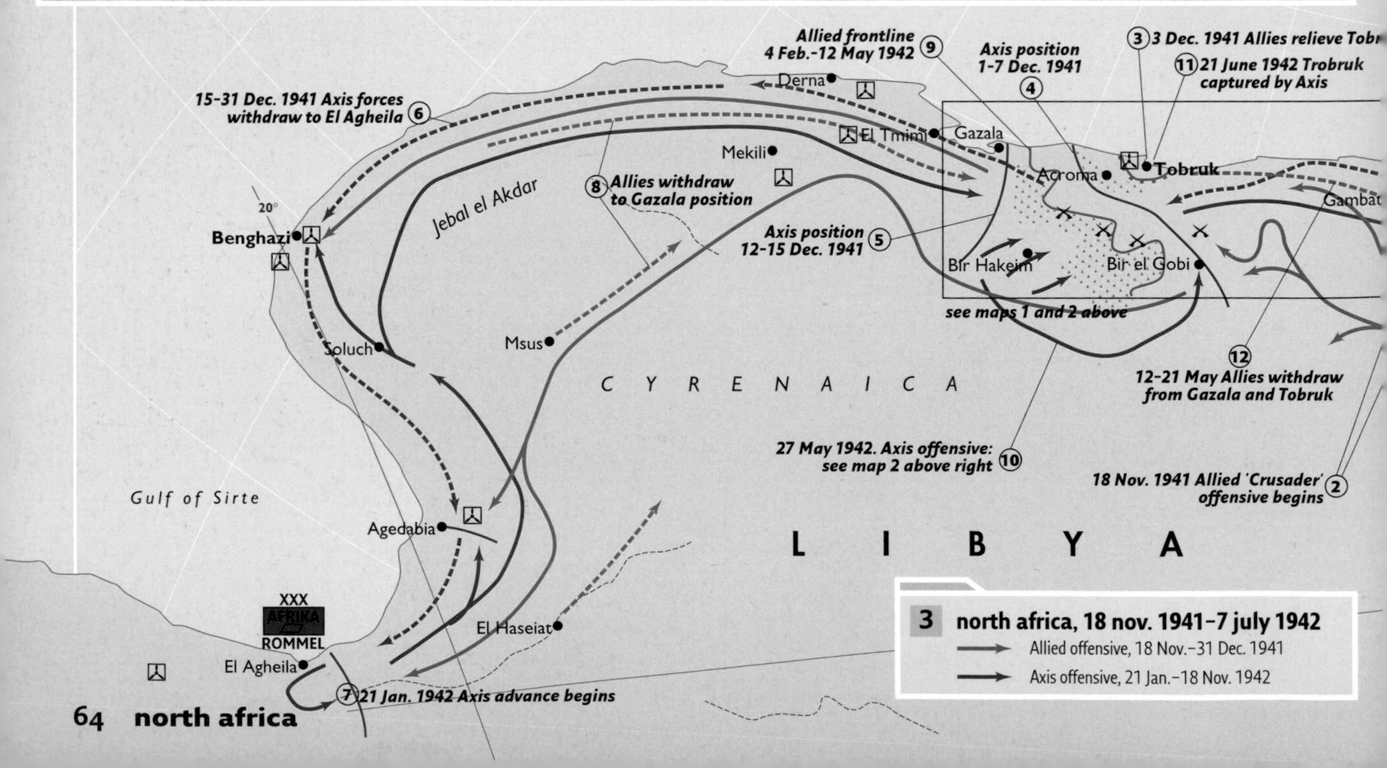

Allied frontline 4 Feb.–12 May 1942 (9)
Axis position 1–7 Dec. 1941 (4)
(3) 3 Dec. 1941 Allies relieve Tobr
(11) 21 June 1942 Trobruk captured by Axis
15–31 Dec. 1941 Axis forces withdraw to El Agheila (6)
Derna
El Tmimi
Gazala
Mekili
Acroma
Tobruk
Gambut
Jebal el Akdar
(8) Allies withdraw to Gazala position
Benghazi
Axis position 12–15 Dec. 1941 (5)
Bir Hakeim
Bir el Gobi
see maps 1 and 2 above
Soluch
Msus
C Y R E N A I C A
(12) 12–21 May Allies withdraw from Gazala and Tobruk
27 May 1942. Axis offensive: see map 2 above right (10)
18 Nov. 1941 Allied 'Crusader' offensive begins (2)
Gulf of Sirte
Agedabia
L I B Y A
AFRIKA
ROMMEL
El Haseiat
El Agheila
(7) 21 Jan. 1942 Axis advance begins

3 north africa, 18 nov. 1941–7 july 1942

Allied offensive, 18 Nov.–31 Dec. 1941
Axis offensive, 21 Jan.–18 Nov. 1942

www.bbc.co.uk/dna/ww2/A1124777
The Siege of Tobruk
www.geocities.com/firefly1002000/crusader.html
The Allied offensive Operation Crusader

The familiar desert warfare phenomenon of over-extension now worked to Rommel's benefit. He had retreated with his main base at Tripoli, where a major supply convoy arrived on 5 January 1942. Eighth Army, by contrast having advanced over 300 miles in three weeks, was at the extremity of its lines of communication, undersupplied and off-balance. Sensing its weakness, Rommel went over to the counter-offensive on 21 January and quickly drove it back to Gazala, 30 miles west of Tobruk, by 4 February. Both sides stood on this line throughout the spring, gathering reinforcements.

Rommel attacked again on 26 May. He had 560 tanks, of which 240 were Italian and outclassed; the British had 700, including 200 new American Grants, with powerful 75mm guns. Rommel swung his armour around the southern end of the heavily mined Gazala front, but within three days withdrew into a *kessel* (cauldron) inside British lines. There he resisted heavy attacks, then broke eastwards, driving the British before him. The Tobruk garrison was forced to surrender (21 June) and Eighth Army retreated 300 miles to the Alam Halfa-Alamein Line (7 July). Operation Crusader had proved a costly failure.

1-3 **The period between Nov. 1941 and July 1942 (*map 3*) saw the most extended advances and retreats by British and Axis forces of the whole Desert War. The relief of Tobruk and the clearing of Cyrenaica formed the core of the British Crusader plan. When Auchinleck attacked the Axis forces besieging Tobruk (*map 1*), 70th Division broke out to join XIII Corps which was working westward along the coast. This breakout was held and Rommel counter-attacked towards Sidi Rezegh. Only when faced with the pincers of XIII and XXX Corps did Rommel retire (27 Nov.). On 29 Nov. XIII Corps made contact with the Tobruk garrison but it was broken the next day. After heavy fighting the siege was finally raised, after 240 days (8 Dec.); Rommel had begun his retreat to El Agheila the day before. Now both sides gathered their strength. Rommel's true strength was in his mobile forces south of the Trigh Capuzzo road. With these he attacked (*map 2*) south of the heavily mined line engaging the British in heavy tank fighting around 'Knightsbridge'. When his tank losses became too high (30 May) he withdrew to the *kessel* area where he could be supplied through the British minefields. Ritchie was overwhelmed by Rommel's breakout (11 June) and forced to retreat eastward, leaving Bir Hakeim in German hands. Tobruk sustained siege only for one week (14–21 June) before surrendering.**

2 gazala and tobruk, 27 may–21 june 1942

Afrika Korps, 27 May–5 June
Afrika Korps, 11 June–21 June

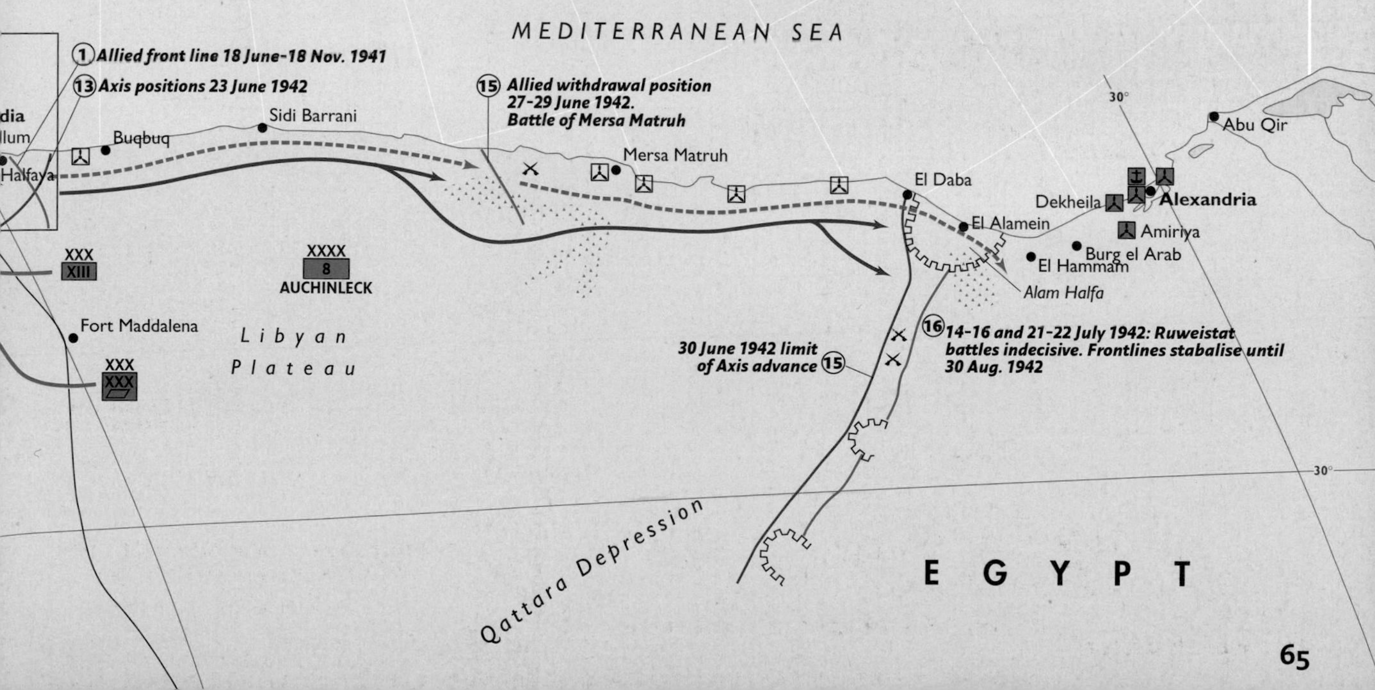

PART 3 TURNING THE AXIS TIDE

the **greater german reich**

1939 to 1943

- **1940 (4 January)** Göring takes control of German war production
- **29 May** German-Romanian arms and oil pact
- **1941 (1 August)** US oil embargo against 'aggressor' states
- **1942 (8 February)** Albert Speer made German Arms Minister
- **1943 (2 December)** Hitler calls up German youth
- **1944 (22 July)** Göbbels appointed Plenipotentiary for Total War
- **1944 (18 October)** *Volksturm*, the last ditch people's army created in Germany

The early successes in Europe gave Nazi leaders the opportunity to begin the building of what they called the 'New Order' - a redrawing of the boundaries of Europe to establish a European states system with Germany as the dominant imperial power. Germany was to become the new Rome, ruling Europe from the ethnic heartland, either through direct annexation (Austria, Bohemia-Moravia and Western Poland), or through satellite states (Ukraine, Slovakia, Croatia, Norway, Holland) with their own governments and Nazi commissioners in residence. The other major states, either through alliance or defeat, would retain a restricted autonomy in a German-dominated Europe.

The wartime administration of Europe already reflected these distinctions, though the requirements of war left much of the continent under formal military control. The New Order was to be constructed with the peace.

This order was effectively an economic as well as a political one. The economic resources of the whole continent were to be regulated or influenced from Berlin; Germany would become the major industrial state, selling its goods to the more agrarian, primary-resource-producing states on its borders. A large, new central-eastern industrial region stretching from Silesia to the Black Sea would provide Germany with high living standards, and change the balance of the European industrial economy. The German domination and exploitation of the European economy became accomplished fact by the middle of the war. Conquered Europe gave 90 billion marks to the German war effort; a stream of vital materials, food and labour flowed into the Reich. German businesses, state and private, organised the takeover of much of European industry.

It was Hitler's view that the war was a final war for the future - not only of Germany, but of European culture - and that it should be fought to the bitter end. For this reason he ordered the full use of economic resources in Germany from the start of the conflict. By mid-1941, almost two-thirds of the industrial workforce was engaged in filling war orders - more than in Britain. Living standards were reduced sharply from the very start, with rationing being introduced for almost all major consumer goods and food. The rationing system worked well and black-marketeering was controlled through draconian punishments for both the seller, and receiver, of illicit goods. Consumption levels in Germany dropped much lower than in Britain or the US. By the end of the war, over half the German workforce was made up of women, and economic life was dominated by war production and the impact of strategic bombing. The German arms industries performed poorly in the early years of the war, but the rationalisation of industry enforced by Albert Speer (from 1942 onwards) trebled arms output in two years. In 1943, Göbbels called for all-out war.

The German empire in Eastern and Central Europe was the product of a broad imperial vision. Plans were drawn up to transform the political and ethnic geography of the region, moving Slavic populations eastwards, expecting up to 30 million to die of starvation and disease while the rest inhabited a rump Siberian state or worked as labourers for the German imperial rulers. The Jews of the region were to be systematically slaughtered in the so-called 'Final Solution' to the Jewish question (*Endlösung der Judenfrage*). This part of the programme was savagely completed between 1941 and 1944.

As the war progressed, Hitler drew more of its conduct under his direct control. In 1941, he took over command of his armies; in the same year, he began to direct war production and weapons development more closely. No decision could be taken without direct reference to Hitler, or more often, to one of his immediate subordinates, Bormann, Keitel and Lammers - the 'Committee of Three'. Popular enthusiasm for the Party began to wane as the war went sour, but ordinary Germans kept their belief in the Führer, and his ability to save them from disaster, for much longer. The myth of the Führer only began to pall after Stalingrad and Hamburg. By then it was fear of the Soviets that kept many Germans fighting, as well as fear of the SS, which used the war crisis to increase its power in Germany with savage policing methods. The more brutal the Nazi movement became, the less attractive many Germans found it. As the German New Order collapsed around them, the German people became resigned and apathetic. They called the moment of defeat 'Hour Zero'.

2 All the heavy industry of the occupied areas was taken over, the bulk of it by the state-run Reichswerke Hermann Göring, a giant holding-company employing one million people, with assets all over Europe, from the iron-ore fields of Lorraine to the steel mills of the Ukraine. Europe was exploited as a source of raw materials and labour. Some workers came willingly, lured by higher wages and regular employment, but most were compelled to work in Germany. By 1944, six million foreign workers helped to treble German war production.

2 the german war economy, 1939–45

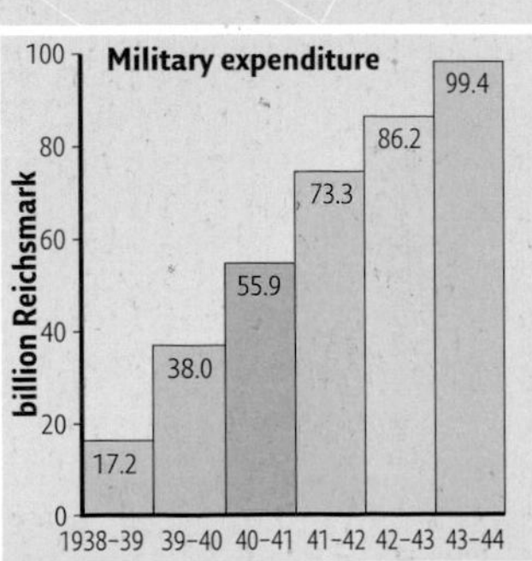

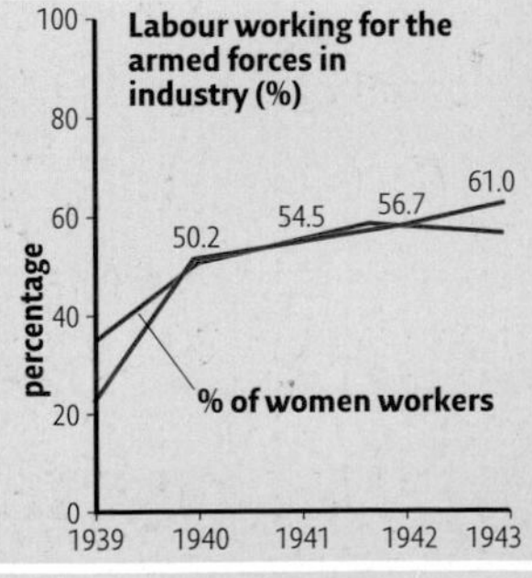

Armaments output

	1940	1941	1942	1943	1944	1945
aircraft	10,257	11,776	15,409	24,897	39,807	7540
tanks artillery	2200	5200	9300	19,800	27,300	n/a
pieces	6000	30,000	69,000	157,000	361,000	n/a
munitions (tonnes)	865,000	540,000	1,270,000	2,558,000	3,350,000	n/a

www.thirdreichpages.com/
Education and information about the Third Reich
www.bbc.co.uk/bbcfour/audiointerviews/profilepages/speera1.shtml
Radio interview with Albert Speer

1 the third reich, 1939–43

1 By 1941, German rule extended into 15 European countries; only neutral governments in Sweden, Spain, Switzerland and Portugal retained any real independence. German officials and leaders began to plan the New Order in Europe from early on in the war. Conquered Russia was to be organised as a series of provinces of the German empire, with a rump Siberian state for the Soviet population, kept out of Europe by a series of large German garrisons. Conquered populations would be resettled, Germanised or exterminated. Europe was to be linked by a network of new motorways spreading from Paris to the Crimea.

german persecutions

1933 to 1945

- **1935 (15 September)** announcement of Nuremberg Laws
- **1938 (9–10 Nov.)** *Kristallnacht* – pogrom against German Jews
- **1939** Himmler begins official extermination of disabled
- **1941–42** Einsatzgruppen murder Jews in USSR
- **1942** German genocide of Jews begins in full (to 1945); Wannsee Conference; 'The Final Solution'
- **1943 (April)** armed revolt in Warsaw ghetto
- **1942–45** as many as 3.7 million Jews die in Nazi death camps, 5.7 million in total

From his very first days as German Chancellor in 1933, Adolf Hitler introduced laws that victimised and persecuted political opponents, the socially 'undesirable' and various racial groups. Outstanding among his victims were the Jews. Within two years, Germany's half million Jews had been isolated from German life, and driven out of their professions. As many as 250,000 found refuge abroad, including 50,000 who were given a haven in Britain. But for those who remained, the future was one of continuing persecution.

In November 1938, some 100 Jews were killed, and many synagogues burned down, in coordinated attacks on Jews and Jewish property throughout Germany and Austria (*Kristallnacht*). The German occupation of Bohemia and Moravia in March 1939 brought a further half million Jews under German rule. But as they, too, were severely discriminated against, and sought to flee, fewer and fewer governments were willing to take in Jewish refugees.

The German conquest of Poland added a further two million Jews under German control. No decision had yet been taken on their treatment. From the autumn of 1939 they were driven into purpose-built ghettos where they were compelled to survive from their own meagre resources. The ghettos became crude prisons, where thousands died from malnutrition and disease. In 1940 Hitler explored the idea of deporting all Jews to the island of Madagascar but failure to defeat Britain cut off any

1 The German persecution of the Jews moved from the discrimination against German Jews in the 1930s, through the policy of isolation in ghettos in 1940 and 1941, to the final stage of physical extermination, aimed at the entire Jewish population of occupied and satellite Europe.

www.holocaust-history.org/
The Holocaust History Project archive of documents, photographs, recordings and essays
www.ushmm.org/outreach/nlaw.htm
The Nuremberg Race Laws

prospect of mass overseas deportation. Only early in 1941 were orders given to exterminate some categories of Jews in the forthcoming invasion of the USSR, home, in Hitler's warped view, to the Jewish-Bolshevik world conspiracy.

From the start of the Barbarossa campaign Jews were singled out for murder, either as alleged partisans or communist functionaries, or in a wave of German-inspired pogroms in Poland and the Baltic States. The murder squads of security police (the Einsatzgruppen) killed Jews in reprisal for the murder of German soldiers: the largest single act, – the killing of 30,000 at Babi Yar outside Kiev – was in retaliation for the death of German officers from Red Army booby traps in the city. From August 1941 they were ordered to kill women and children as well, and by the end of the year one million Jews had been killed in cold blood. From November 1941 German Jews were also shipped to the East and the killing was extended to the Jewish population of the whole of German-occupied Europe. When and why the decision was taken to begin the so-called 'Final Solution' has never been established with certainty, but most historians agree that it came in the last two months of 1941, almost certainly in reaction to what Hitler saw as Jewish efforts to involve the US in the war and so create a global coalition against Germany. Hitler believed that the war he was fighting was essentially a war against the Jews.

To complete the annihilation of the Jews, Himmler's SS camp organisation began building special extermination sites from late 1941 where Jews would be killed on arrival in gas chambers using carbon monoxide poisoning or, at Auschwitz, the pesticide agent Zyklon-B. The first death camp was opened at Chelmno (December 1941), followed within a few months by further death camps at Belzec, Sobibor, Treblinka and Maly Trostinets. By 1945, more than 2.5 million Jews had been murdered in these five camps.

For non-Jewish victims of Nazi persecution – Communists and homosexuals among them – terrible tortures had been devised since 1933 in a series of concentration camps, of which Sachsenhausen, Buchenwald and Dachau, in Germany itself, were among the first. Jews were also sent to these camps, and many were murdered there. Mauthausen in Austria, Natzweiler in Alsace, and Stutthof in Poland, were particularly notorious. In the summer of 1940 the Germans set up a punishment camp specifically for Poles, at Auschwitz. In the summer of 1942 this camp was extended, and gas chambers built, so that Jews could be brought there from all over Europe. Hundreds of thousands of Jews were sent to the barracks at Auschwitz, and became slave labourers. But as many as one million, mostly women and children, old people and the sick, were gassed within a few hours of their arrival at the camp. Several hundred thousand gypsies were also murdered at Auschwitz, and at some of the other death camps.

By the end of 1943, most of the death camps had completed their horrific work and been closed down. The gas chambers at Auschwitz, and at another camp in Poland, Majdanek, continued almost until the arrival of the Soviet Army. Those still alive in the slave labour barracks at Auschwitz and elsewhere as the Soviets approached were sent by the Germans on marches westwards. Tens of thousands, emaciated and starving, died or were shot on these death marches. Those who survived were brought to concentration camps in Germany, among them Dachau and Belsen. By the time the British and US forces reached these camps, tens of thousands more had died of starvation.

The total number of Jews who were murdered between 1939 and 1945 is in the region of 5.7 million. Hundreds of thousands of gypsies were also murdered, as were more than 100,000 Germans and Poles who had been judged by the German euthanasia programme to be too mentally ill or physically retarded to be allowed to live. Three million non-Jewish Polish civilians and one million Serbs, as well as hundreds of thousands of slave labourers from Western Europe and the Balkans, were also killed by the Germans, or died of hunger and ill-treatment during the war years. As many as four million Soviet prisoners of war were murdered by the Germans; some were killed at Auschwitz, but most were left to die, confined in camps without food or medical help.

More than any other single factor, the Nazi policies of persecution and extermination of Jews and other groups provoked global condemnation, which found expression during the war in the establishment of the War Crimes Commission.

2 birkenau death camp

2 **Birkenau was one of three concentration camps built around the town of Auschwitz in Poland. Founded in October 1941, it was used as an extermination centre using Zyklon-B gas. An estimated 1.1 million died at Auschwitz.**

1 the holocaust, 1933–45 (left)

- greatest extent of Axis power, 1942
- 1,000 planned deaths according to 'Final Solution', 20 Jan. 1942
- *1,000* estimated actual (Jewish) deaths, Sept. 1939–Mar. 1945
- ○ main concentration camp, with date of foundation
- ● camp built for implementation of 'Final Solution' (from 1942)
- ● euthanasia centre
- ■ mass murder site
- ▲ major ghetto
- ■ location of Einsatzgruppe

clandestine war

1940 to 1945

1940 (July) Special Operations Executive (SOE), often known as 'The Baker Street Irregulars', initiated by Winston Churchill and Hugh Dalton

1941 (6 May) SOE's 'F Section' despatches first agent into France

1942 (27 May) Attempted assassination of Reinhard Heydrich in Prague (dies of wounds 4 June)

10 June Reprisal massacre at Lidice for Heydrich's death

1943 (28 February) Operation Gunnerside; Norwegian commandoes destroy the Norsk-Hydro heavy water plant at Vemork

1946 SOE dissolved with much of its influence reverting to MI6

The use of covert techniques to achieve both conventional military objectives and to promote political indoctrination was a particular feature of the Second World War. The development of Special Forces was one aspect of this; German Brandenburgers often operated in plain clothes (Danzig 1939, Rotterdam 1940) in advance of conventional forces. The Soviet NKVD operated widely throughout Europe, activating partisans and resistance groups from existing Communist cells. But the British SOE and American OSS were to become unique.

Fears at Germany's rapid territorial expansion in Europe in the 1930s and the impact of irregular operations witnessed during the Irish and Spanish civil wars encouraged the British War Office and the Secret Intelligence Service (SIS) to establish special departments to study this form of warfare. Military Intelligence Research (MIR) and SIS, Section D had begun their work before the outbreak of the Second World War and some, albeit inadequate, plans had been laid for sabotage, subversion and guerrilla operations in Europe in the event of hostilities breaking out. However, the triumph of Germany's armed forces in the summer of 1940 and the occupation of most of continental Europe left Britain desperately seeking to employ virtually any means of striking back. Accordingly, in July, the Special Operations Executive (SOE) was formed to foment resistance, and, in Churchill's words, 'to set Europe ablaze'. Section D and MIR were amalgamated and the new organisation was placed under the auspices of the Ministry of Economic Warfare.

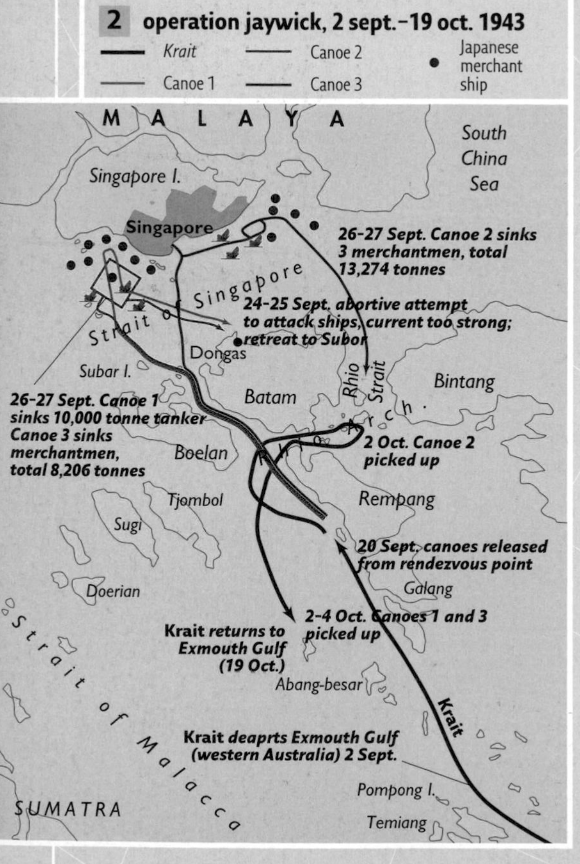

2 **Clandestine operations in Japanese-occupied territory were limited by obvious problems of racial appearance, and by Japanese anti-imperialist propaganda. Nevertheless, in South East Asia British, US and Asian agents were inserted into Japanese-held territory to gather intelligence, co-ordinate guerrilla operations and carry out sabotage attacks against communications and enemy shipping. The most successful action was Operation Jaywick, mounted by SOE's India Mission but launched from Australia. After a long and hazardous voyage in a captured fishing boat (the *Krait*), the raiding party transferred to canoes for the attack on Japanese merchant ships at anchor in Singapore harbour. Using limpet mines, the saboteurs sank over 30,000 tonnes of enemy shipping and made a successful escape. An attempt to repeat the operation in Oct.1944 proved disastrous – the entire sabotage party was killed or captured and executed in July 1945.**

In spite of Churchill's support, SOE's relations with the services and other government departments, notably SIS, were not always harmonious. The diversion of ships and aircraft to assist in their operations, together with the secondment of high calibre service personnel to man the new organisation brought considerable criticism. Furthermore, SOE's activities were, on occasion, at variance with Foreign Office policy and relations with SIS were frequently acrimonious – intelligence gathering and subversive operations were largely antipathetic, and the two bodies constantly vied for control of spheres of influence, resources and personnel.

Nevertheless, agents were recruited, trained and inserted into all the occupied countries of Western Europe, where they helped to organise, supply and instruct resistance groups. Special attention was paid to the development of armed groups that could be controlled from London and activated in the event of an Allied invasion. Their task was to attack enemy communications and divert resources away from the main battle front. This achievement, similar to that of the Central Staff of the Partisan Movement on the Eastern Front, was of great importance. In addition, SOE was called upon to help train members of the armies-in-exile and liaise with their governments in employing them in particular acts of sabotage, assassination and even kidnapping.

The outbreak of the war with Japan resulted in the need for SOE to expand its activities into Asia, and, at the same time, provoked the formation of a complementary American organisation, the Office of Strategic Services (OSS). Fortunately, American deference for British experience and expertise helped to promote a high degree of Allied cooperation and SOE and OSS worked together in Europe and the Far East.

The often spectacular and controversial nature of clandestine operations and post-war revelations about its most celebrated agents and operations have given SOE and OSS a prominence out of all proportion to their overall contribution to the war effort. The expansive claims made for some of the most famous coups – such as the raid on the Norsk-Hydro heavy water plant and the assassination of Heydrich – have been a result of self-justification in the face of criticism of irregular operations. However, it may be argued that clandestine warfare was at its most efficacious not necessarily in dramatic, single actions but in its small-scale, attritional effects. Morale in the countries occupied by the Axis forces was undoubtedly lifted by the knowledge of Allied operations within enemy territory, and the supply of weapons and explosives transformed the civilian population into an immensely potent force for resistance.

www.bbc.co.uk/history/war/wwtwo/soe_gallery.shtml
The SOE and some of the equipment and gadgets that it used
www.dva.gov.au/media/publicat/2003/jaywick/
Operation Jaywick, the Allied raid on Japanese merchant ships at Singapore

1 Britain's SOE was the main Allied organisation engaged in clandestine operations in occupied Western Europe. Divided into 'country' sections, it worked closely with the governments-in-exile, although the harmoniousness of its relations and the nature of its operations varied immensely. In the Balkans and Italy, its operatives were attached to partisan groups to help furnish them with weapons and supplies and to liaise with SOE and Allied headquarters. In North West Europe its agents generally operated undercover, building up networks to carry out sabotage and preparing the resistance for a concerted effort in support of the Second Front. Although some agents and supplies were landed by sea, most of this type of work was carried out by RAF Special Duties Squadrons. These specialist units operated from bases in Britain, North Africa and Italy and dropped or collected agents as far afield as Poland and Estonia. France was at the forefront of SOE's plans due to its proximity to Britain, its political and economic importance and its selection as the location of the Second Front. No less than six separate SOE sections operated into it, in addition to other British organisations, the American OSS, Free French services and the Soviet NKVD.

1 special operations executive in europe, 1940–45

- ■ SOE main base
- ● SOE secondary base
- ★ SOE operation

resistance in western europe

1940 to 1945

- **1940 (June 14)** Germans enter Paris
- **25 September** Quisling government in Norway
- **1941 (19 July)** BBC broadcasts 'V' for Victory declaring resistance in occupied Europe
- **20 October** German commander of Nantes shot by Resistance; 50 hostages shot in reprisal
- **1944 (1 February)** French Forces of the Interior formed to coordinate Resistance
- **4–6 June** Resistance disrupts German communications in advance of Normandy landings
- **10 June** Massacre at Oradour-sur-Glane near Lomoges by SS
- **11 July** French Resistance rising at Vercors (until 29 July)
- **22 August** rising in Paris, prior to liberation by Allied forces

The speed and completeness of the German victory in Western Europe in 1940 resulted in the absence of any significant plans for resistance to occupation. Shocked by military defeat and cowed by the full weight of the Nazis' well-honed forces of repression, opposition to German rule was initially uncoordinated and small scale. Instead, large sections of the population sought to conform to the new status quo and endeavoured to recreate a form of pre-war normality.

In contrast, the Fascist Parties of the newly conquered countries anticipated that the new conditions would enable them to seize power. But even trusted leaders such as Quisling in Norway and Mussert in Holland were allowed by the German occupiers to exercise only limited political control. Nevertheless, the rewards of outright collaboration proved too strong for many to resist, with hundreds of thousands volunteering to work for the occupying forces. Consciences were salved to a great extent by Germany's attack upon the Soviet Union in 1941, and for those who enlisted in the Waffen-SS collaboration became less of a betrayal of nationalist ideals and was elevated to the level of a 'crusade' against communism.

Arguably the first acts of resistance were offered by those who fled from occupation in order to maintain the struggle from exile. The heads of state of Holland, Norway, Yugoslavia, Greece and Luxembourg and the Belgian, Czechoslovakian and Polish governments-in-exile became the figureheads behind which their nations' resistance could develop. The need to secure a widely accepted leadership was highlighted by the problems encountered by General de Gaulle, the Free French leader, whose most senior governmental position had been a brief term as Under-Secretary of State for War.

However, the impact of the exiled forces on the war constituted far more than just a moral stimulant to resisters who had stayed at home. Polish armies in exile fought in Norway, the Soviet Union, North Africa, Italy and the Low Countries. Polish, Czech, French and Belgian pilots played an important role during the Battle of Britain, while the adherence of the Norwegian, Danish and Dutch merchant marine to the Allied cause helped offset British losses sustained as a result of U-boat attacks. Similarly, substantial French and Polish forces made significant contributions to Allied campaigns in the Mediterranean and North West Europe.

Meanwhile, the initial acts of resistance in occupied Europe were of necessity primarily passive. Members of the occupying forces were 'cold-shouldered' by the civilian population, who further expressed their sentiments with a proliferation of anti-German graffiti. More overt acts soon followed, and in spite of the apparent omnipotence and omniscience of the German security forces, public demonstrations were made. In Holland in 1941 a general strike was called to protest against anti-Semitic and anti-labour legislation. A year later, Norwegian teachers refused en masse to sign a declaration of allegiance to the new regime. Ideological and cultural resistance was also maintained by a clandestine press that flourished in all of the occupied countries. France, Poland and Holland each produced over a thousand illegal newspaper titles, and tens of millions of books, pamphlets and newssheets combatted Nazi propaganda throughout occupied Europe. Much of the news was acquired from BBC radio broadcasts, which were banned by the German authorities; listening to these was, in itself, a punishable act of resistance.

Increased self-confidence amongst resisters within the occupied countries and the establishment of Allied organisations such as the SOE to assist them resulted in increased subversive activity. The SOE and, later, the NKVD and OSS, provided trained agents to coordinate groups and instruct them in the use of explosives and firearms. More importantly, complex wireless and courier links were forged with the 'free' world, enabling resistance to be integrated into Allied strategy.

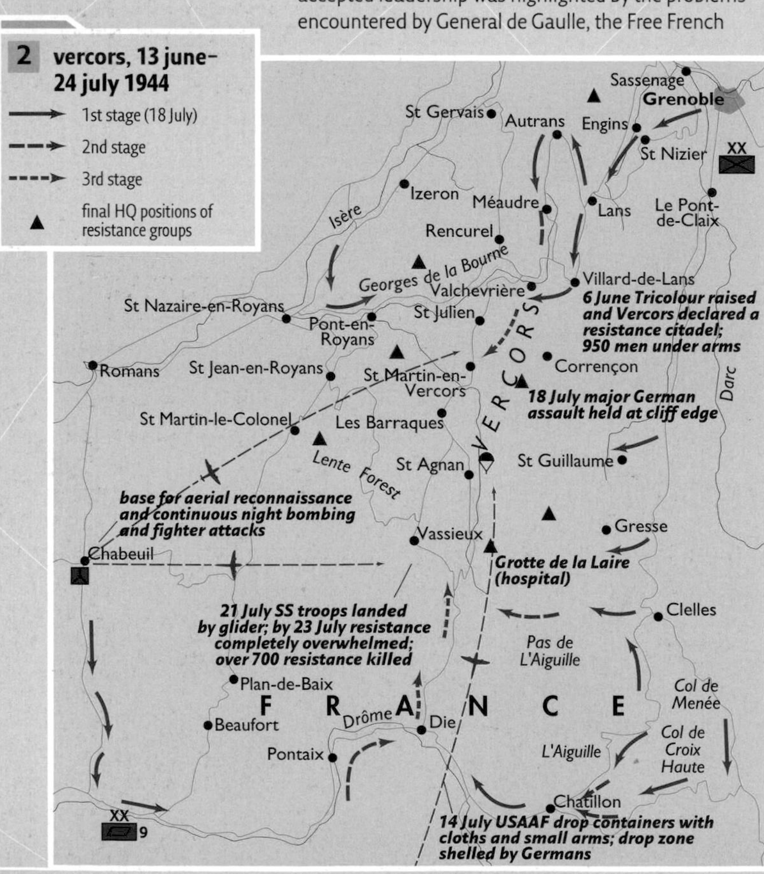

2 **The mountainous redoubt of the Vercors plateau, long a safe rallying point for French resisters, declared itself free from German rule. Anticipating substantial Allied air-drops of supplies, and only a brief period of armed resistance prior to Allied landings in Provence and Normandy, the French conducted a vigorous defence of the crevassed terrain. However, in the ensuing clashes the inadequately armed *Maquis* proved to be no match for well-equipped and -trained troops, supported by artillery, tanks and aircraft.**

www.spartacus.schoolnet.co.uk/FRresistance.htm
The French Resistance during World War Two
www.oradour.info/
German reprisal massacre and destruction of the French village of Oradour-sur-Glane

Invaluable work was carried out on escape lines that helped fugitive Allied servicemen and refugees to the safety of neutral Spain, Switzerland and Sweden. While this made a useful contribution to the Allied war effort by allowing highly trained aircrew to return to active service, the resistance played an even more important role on the Second Front. Widespread attacks were made on French road, rail and telephone communications in support of the Normandy invasion and sabotage was carried out as far afield as Scandinavia to prevent German reinforcements reaching the front. Furthermore, their efforts forced significant German resources to be diverted to internal security tasks at a time when they were needed badly elsewhere.

Less successful were over ambitious attempts made by resistance groups to engage German forces in open conflict rather than hit-and-run guerrilla warfare. The crushing of the Vercors uprising contrasted with the achievements attained in France, Belgium and Italy when the resistance acted in close concert with advancing Allied ground units.

But the resistance's greatest triumphs were not in moonlight raids on enemy communications nor the highly emotional scenes of liberation in Paris, Brussels or Genoa, but in the consistent flow of vital intelligence to the Allies throughout the war. One network alone, the Belgian Service Clarence, had 1,500 agents and supplied SIS with a range of information from bomb damage in Berlin to concentration camps in Poland, and from daily troop movements to railway traffic. Similarly, Danish and Polish cells secured important details of German V-weapons; the Poles also relayed intelligence from agents operating behind the German front as far east as the Caucasus, while French agents passed crucial intelligence to Allied planners on German defences and troop movements in Normandy.

1 **The task facing the German occupying forces in Western Europe was eased by the absence of any substantial political or military focus for resistance. The onus of maintaining control of the conquered territories lay less with the Wehrmacht than with the German security services and paramilitary collaborationist units such as the *Milice* in France and the *Schalburg Korps* in Denmark. Wholesale arrests of likely dissidents neutralised potential sources of resistance while the captives provided useful hostages should the need arise for reprisals to be exacted against the civilian population. In spite of such measures, myriad resistance organisations gradually formed from a wide range of political, religious, professional and ethnic groupings.**

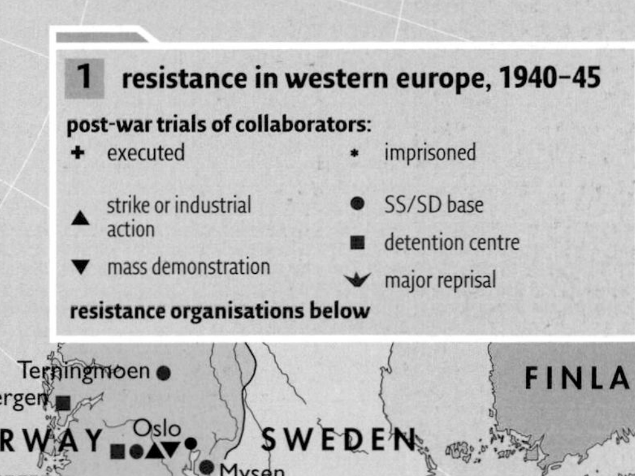

BELGIUM
Front de l'Independence (Communist); L'Armée Secréte; Legion Belge; Groupe Mobile des Partisans + 230, *c.50,000

FRANCE
Marquis (originally forced-labour evaders, later general term for partisan secret armies, in occupied France); OCM (former Army officers); Libération-Nord (trade unions); Front National (Communists); in March 1943 all merged to form MUR. In unoccupied France, Combat, Libération (trade unions); Franes-Tireurs. After Feb. 1944 French Forces of the Interior (FFI) formed amalgamating MUR, ORA (disaffected Army resisters) and FTP (Communist partisans). By 1944 c. 400,000 resisters, (only c. 166,000 armed) + 2093, * 39,000 (excluding c. 10,000 court martial executions)

ITALY (after Sept. 1943)
National Liberation Committee (CLN); National Liberation Council for Northern Italy; 'Garibaldi' (Communist partisans). By 1944 c. 200,000 behind German lines

NORWAY
MILORG (1944: 35,000 resisters); HL; Arbejdstjeneste-Komite; Kretsen + 25, * 18,000

DENMARK
Prinserne; Danmarks Frihedsraad; BOPA (Communist); Holgar Danske. By 1944, 25,000 resisters + 46, * 14,495

HOLLAND
Resistance Council (RvZ); Geuzen; Knokploegen; Ordedienst; BS; LO. By 1944 c. 2000 resisters + 36, * c. 50,000

battle of the atlantic II

april 1941 to march 1943

- **1941 (4 April)** German raider *Thor* sinks armed mechant cruiser *Voltaire*
- **11 April** USN covers to 26°W, British to 35°W
- **15 April** RAF Coastal Command under RN control increases cover
- **7 May** captured German ship provides secret Enigma code papers
- **27 May** *Bismarck* sunk
- **1 July** USN aircraft start anti-sub patrols from Newfoundland
- **31 October** U-boat sinks US destroyer *Ruben James*; first American loss
- **1942 (13 January)** German U-boats start Operation Paukenschlag on east coast of America, sinking 150,000 tonnes
- **1943 (5–20 March)** Biggest convoy battle of the war; Convoys SC122 and HX229 lose 22 ships of 140,800 tonnes - crisis point of the Battle of Atlantic

At various times between April 1941 and March 1943, the initiative in the campaign against Allied shipping changed hands. In general terms, at least superficially, events seemed to favour the Axis cause. As the British Admiralty subsequently noted, the German U-boats never came as close to severing Allied communications across the North Atlantic as in the first twenty days of March 1943.

In that month U-boats sank 108 of a total Allied merchantman loss of 120 vessels, not the heaviest monthly loss of the war, but potentially much more serious than previous losses because of the heavy concentration of sinkings among escorted merchantmen - 72 in all.

In retrospect, however, the German success of March 1943 can be seen as exceptional, at very best a partial and flawed success achieved against the general trend of the Battle of the Atlantic. In this one month the German U-boats achieved their highest monthly return at the expense of convoyed shipping in the course of a campaign that saw a toll of 30 escorted merchantmen sunk by U-boats exceeded in only five months: after March 1943, German monthly returns fell dramatically as the battle turned against the U-boats.

The long-term trends of the Battle of the Atlantic in this phase of the war were such that, by spring 1942, the German Navy could predict ultimate defeat, even in the midst of a period of unprecedented success. It could do this as a result of its recognition of the coming together of various unfavourable conditions. Outstanding among these was the fact that, after May 1941, the U-boats had been left to carry the burden from surface forces, raiders and the Luftwaffe. Moreover, after mid-year, an increasing number of U-boats were diverted to the Mediterranean. This reassignment was partly an attempt to prop up a faltering Italy and partly a result of Hitler's determination to avoid a clash with the United States. The latter, despite its neutral status, was intent upon an increasingly belligerent forward strategy in the North Atlantic.

Thus the second half of 1941 saw the main U-boat effort made in the eastern Atlantic, where British escorts were most heavily concentrated; by the end of the year the U-boats, for the first time, incurred significant losses in attacks on convoys. The American entry into the war in December 1941, however, necessarily provided the Germans with the opportunity to sink merchantmen with little risk off the US eastern seaboard, rather than face the uncertainties of battle in the eastern Atlantic. As a result of first an American unwillingness and then American difficulties in organising convoys along the eastern seaboard and in the Caribbean, the U-boats enjoyed massive success in these waters in the first six months of 1942. Thereafter the main combat zone switched back to mid-ocean as the American introduction of convoys forced the U-boats away from the western Atlantic. The field of operations available to the U-boats was already becoming limited.

For nine months after this change the battle between escort and submarine was evenly balanced, at least in terms of losses. Growing submarine numbers, both in commission and operational, ensured that Allied losses remained uncomfortably high. Moreover, the second half of 1942 saw the introduction, on a large scale, of extended U-boat scouting lines; further, German naval intelligence held distinct advantages as a result of its ability to read British naval and maritime signals. But in terms of sinkings per operational boat per month, the German effort was in decline, and returns after August 1942 would have been very low but

1 the north atlantic, apr.–dec. 1941

- Allied merchant ships sunk by U-boats
- U-boats sunk
- major convoy routes

Jan Mayen I. occupied by US, 11 July 1942. Escorts refuel here
Apr. 1941: limit of anti-submarine escort 35°W
limit of Allied air cover
June 1941: transatlantic convoys escorted all the way
July 1941: Freetown-Gibraltar-London convoys escorted all the way
limits of US merchant responsiblity zone (declared Apr. 1941)

1 With the United States still neutral the burden of convoying ships remained until Dec. 1941 with British and Canadian forces. As more ships sailed, the organisation of convoy operations became ever more complex. Four separate escort groups had to be coordinated for each convoy. U-boat production was rising, as were operational losses helped by the bombing of U-boat bases on the west coast of France. While Allied air cover was better than in 1940, there was still a severe shortage of aircraft, and none that could close the air gap: delivery of long-range US Liberators was still 18 months away. Coastal Command began to take deliveries of Hudsons and Catalina flying boats in December, but detection of U-boats leaving their major operating bases in the Bay of Biscay remained poor. However, the use of bases in neutral Iceland, first by the British, then by the Americans (after 11 July 1942) increased the area of the North Atlantic that could be covered by air patrols.

www.bbc.co.uk/history/war/wwtwo/battle_atlantic_01.shtml
A guide to the Battle of the Atlantic
www.theworldatwar.com/feature.htm
The Battle of the Atlantic with audio and multi-media clips

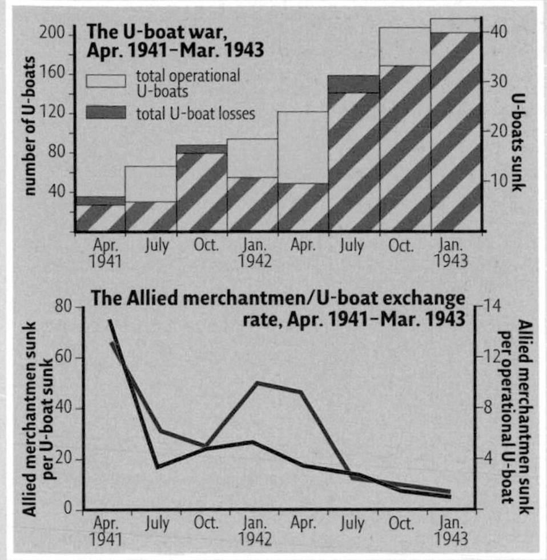

Allied merchant ship losses, Apr. 1941–Mar. 1943 tonnages (nos. of ships)

date	U-boat	aircraft	mine	warship raider	merchant raider	E-boat	unknown and other causes	quarterly totals
Apr.–June 1941	885,010 (162)	531,170 (222)	63,408 (25)	none	76,401 (13)	4,299 (3)	70,680 (34)	1,630,968 (443)
July–Sept. 1941	377,341 (98)	73,949 (45)	24,931 (19)	7,500 (1)	35,904 (6)	10,195 (5)	7,798 (7)	537,616 (168)
Oct.–Dec. 1941	342,820 (71)	131,087 (45)	85,304 (28)	6,661 (2)	none	21,020 (9)	319,743 (216)	906,635 (371)
Jan.–Mar. 1942	1,341,778 (242)	246,183 (18)	34,183 (18)	19,347 (9)	8,591 (2)	951 (1)	202,305 (203)	1,933,703 (533)
Apr.–June 1942	1,739,146 (343)	196,707 (42)	53,730 (23)	100,001 (20)	99,024 (15)	none	13,092 (13)	2,213,703 (132)
July.–Sept. 1942	1,505,880 (302)	192,371 (36)	8,905 (2)	3,188 (1)	76,312 (11)	49,762 (9)	10,147 (4)	1,846,573 (365)
Oct.–Dec. 1942	1,679,393 (272)	63,707 (9)	7,767 (8)	7,925 (1)	10,698 (2)	20,433 (13)	4,556 (2)	1,794,489 (308)
Jan.–Mar. 1943	1,189,833 (208)	90,706 (16)	53,782 (14)	none	7,040 (1)	4,858 (1)	11,591 (3)	1,357,810 (243)

totals by theatre, Apr. 1941–Mar. 1943

Atlantic Ocean	Mediterranean	Indian Ocean	Pacific Ocean
8,631,152 (1,727)	1,032,733 (271)	838,511 (231)	1,043,328 (467)

for German successes in the Arctic. There the combination of U-boats, air attack and the presence of major German warships in the Norwegian fjords led to the temporary suspension of Allied convoys to the USSR in late summer 1942.

This decline of German returns stemmed from the fact that just as U-boat numbers had increased since the start of the war so had British escort strengths. By late 1942, the number of escorts per convoy hovered around the five mark, but the presence of ever more convoys denied German submarines the easy pickings on which they depended for success. In 1942, 962 merchantmen sailing independently were sunk, 840 by German submarines, but as the convoy system was extended, so the U-boats were forced to turn their attention to convoys and battle with escorts that were both individually and collectively far more formidable than in 1940 and 1941. Compounding German difficulties after 1942, was the fact that British naval intelligence both penetrated German signals security and took steps to ensure the security of its own signals. After January 1943, and with the exception of a brief period when a German procedural change denied the British access to German signals, Ultra intercepts meant the balance of advantage in intelligence matters increasingly favoured the British. The period of temporary British blindness was March 1943, which was in effect the swansong of the U-boats in the Second World War.

2 **The entry of the US into the war led to an extension of U-boat warfare to the eastern seaboard of the US. Still unconvinced by the effectiveness of the convoy system, the Americans were later to be persuaded by the huge numbers of losses they suffered. By February, however, a reduction in losses from submarine attacks led to growing British confidence that the threat could be mastered. March was to reverse the trend: U-boats sank more than twice as many escorted merchantmen than in any other single month of the war. U-boats relied upon an absence of air cover, and upon dense radio traffic with their command in Germany. Radio interception and Ultra decrypts, and continuous air cover, introduced by the Allies in spring 1943, dramatically increased the security of Allied convoys in the North Atlantic.**

may to june 1942

1942 (30 May) US task force sets out for Midway

4 June US Navy sinks four Japanese carriers and destroys 300 aircraft

7 June Japanese invade Aleutian Islands

The Japanese had no opportunity either to evaluate the lessons of the Battle of the Coral Sea or to recast their plans: they were committed to establishing a Central Pacific perimeter, upon which any American offensive actions would be met. The failure off the Louisiades was dismissed as a local setback; the absence of two fleet carriers from the forthcoming operation was recognised to be serious, but with virtually the entire Combined Fleet committed to the offensive the Japanese remained supremely confident.

With eight carriers deployed for the offensive the Japanese had good reason for confidence, but the pattern of deployment that had almost led to disaster in the Coral Sea – a dispersal of strength amongst widely separated formations that were not mutually supporting – was to be repeated. Their plan called for a diversionary attack on certain islands in the Aleutians, the neutralisation and occupation of Kure and Midway, and the annihilation of any enemy carrier force that gave battle. Against an ill-prepared or surprised foe such a plan might have succeeded, but by May 1942 the Americans were neither. Their recent ability to read Japanese operational signals enabled the Americans to identify the critical weaknesses of the Japanese plan – the broad dispersal of force, the relative smallness of Nagumo's carrier force and its vulnerability in the opening phase. With the Japanese able to use only four carriers for this task, the Americans appreciated that if they could deploy three carriers on the enemy's disengaged beam, there was a reasonable chance of turning the tables of Nagumo.

From the outset Japanese plans miscarried. First, submarines tasked to scout the Hawaiian Islands arrived late and failed to detect the US carrier Task Forces, which were moving to attacking positions north of Midway. Second, a planned reconnaissance of Pearl Harbor by flying boats from the Marshalls had to be cancelled; Nagumo was not informed of either development. Thus, as he bore down on Midway at a time when Kakuta's carriers began a desultory attack on Dutch Harbor (3 June), Nagumo had no reason to assume that US carrier forces were at sea.

The battle that unfolded on 4 June was settled for the Japanese by an unfortunate sequence of events. Nagumo's air groups struck Midway at dawn, and were ineffectually counter-attacked thereon by planes from the base. But during these exchanges Nagumo's seaplanes discovered the US carrier Task Force 17, which, with Task Force 16, attacked the Japanese carrier force after it had recovered the Midway attack groups but before it was able to launch its own attack. Three of Nagumo's carriers were crippled. When finally Nagumo's dive-bombers struck the USS carrier *Yorktown*, the Americans were already preparing a coup de grace. Nagumo's flagship, the *Hiryu*, was in flames before dusk. The operation was doomed before the main body forces under Yamamoto, Kurita or Kondo had even reached the battle zone. The Americans declined to be drawn into a surface action, and conducted a limited pursuit only when it was

2-5 midway, 04:00 hours, 4 june–24:00 hours, 6 june

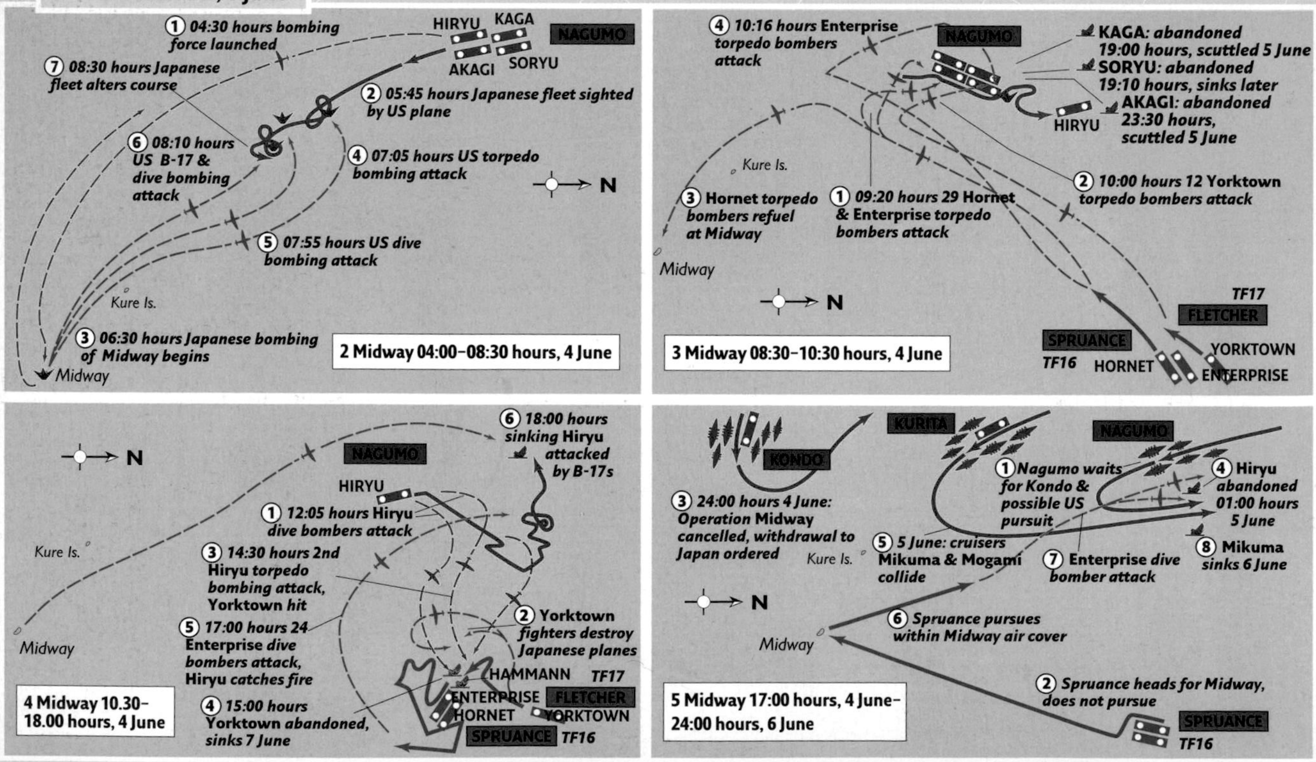

2 Midway 04:00–08:30 hours, 4 June

3 Midway 08:30–10:30 hours, 4 June

4 Midway 10.30–18.00 hours, 4 June

5 Midway 17:00 hours, 4 June–24:00 hours, 6 June

www.history.navy.mil/photos/events/wwii-pac/midway/midway.htm
Overview and a selection of images of the battle
www.bbc.co.uk/history/war/wwtwo/battle_midway_01.shtml
Description and images of the battle

clear that the Japanese were withdrawing; by reversing the element of surprise and securing overwhelming superiority in the air, American control of the Central Pacific remained intact.

At Midway the Americans won a crushing victory – the first irreversible Allied victory of the war; it was marred only by the loss of the *Yorktown* and the destroyer *Hammann*, and by the Japanese occupation of Attu and Kiska in the Aleutians. The two warships were lost as a result of an attack by the submarine I-168 at 13:36 hours on 6 June, the *Hammann* sinking immediately, while the *Yorktown* succumbed finally on the 7th. The capture of Attu and Kiska had no strategic significance: the Japanese took the islands for political and propaganda reasons. Nothing could disguise, within the Imperial Navy's High Command, the enormity of its defeat. It marked the end of the period of seemingly overwhelming Japanese advantage; the next phase of naval war was to be fought by more evenly matched antagonists.

1-5 **Following an opening air strike on Dutch Harbor, Nagumo's first carrier strike force closed for battle. At 04:30 hours on the 4 June, Nagumo committed just under half his strike aircraft against Midway from a position some 250 miles north-west (*map 2*). At 05:45 hours a Midway-based Catalina found him. US carriers then turned towards an enemy that had to hold his course for Midway in order to recover his strike force. The *Yorktown*, obliged to recover her aircraft, became separated from TF16, but from 06:00 hours Midway, and from 07:02 hours TF16, began to launch their aircraft against Nagumo's carriers. The Japanese strike against Midway, therefore, was the first to be delivered. As the Japanese emerged from these attacks, however, they became aware of the presence of a US Task Force off their port beam (*map 3*). The Americans' first attacks, by Devastator torpedo-bombers, incurred heavy losses without recording a single hit, but they served to disorganise Nagumo's formation. Further attacks, by Dauntless dive-bombers from the *Enterprise* and *Yorktown*, accounted for the *Akagi*, *Kaga* and *Soryu*. The *Hiryu* was not attacked and in the course of the afternoon (*map 4*), her aircraft twice found and attacked the *Yorktown*, after which *Yorktown* was abandoned. Dauntlesses flown from *Enterprise* and *Hornet* caught the *Hiryu* just before sunset. The Americans then set course to the east and away from the area of the day's battle (*map 5*). The Japanese response was to try to reach Midway and detect and destroy the US carrier formations during the hours of darkness using their surface forces, which now included Yamamoto's 1st Fleet. But by turning away after dusk, TF16 denied the Japanese any chance of forcing a night action. Soon after midnight the Japanese abandoned the attempt. In the early hours of 7 June TF16 turned for home.**

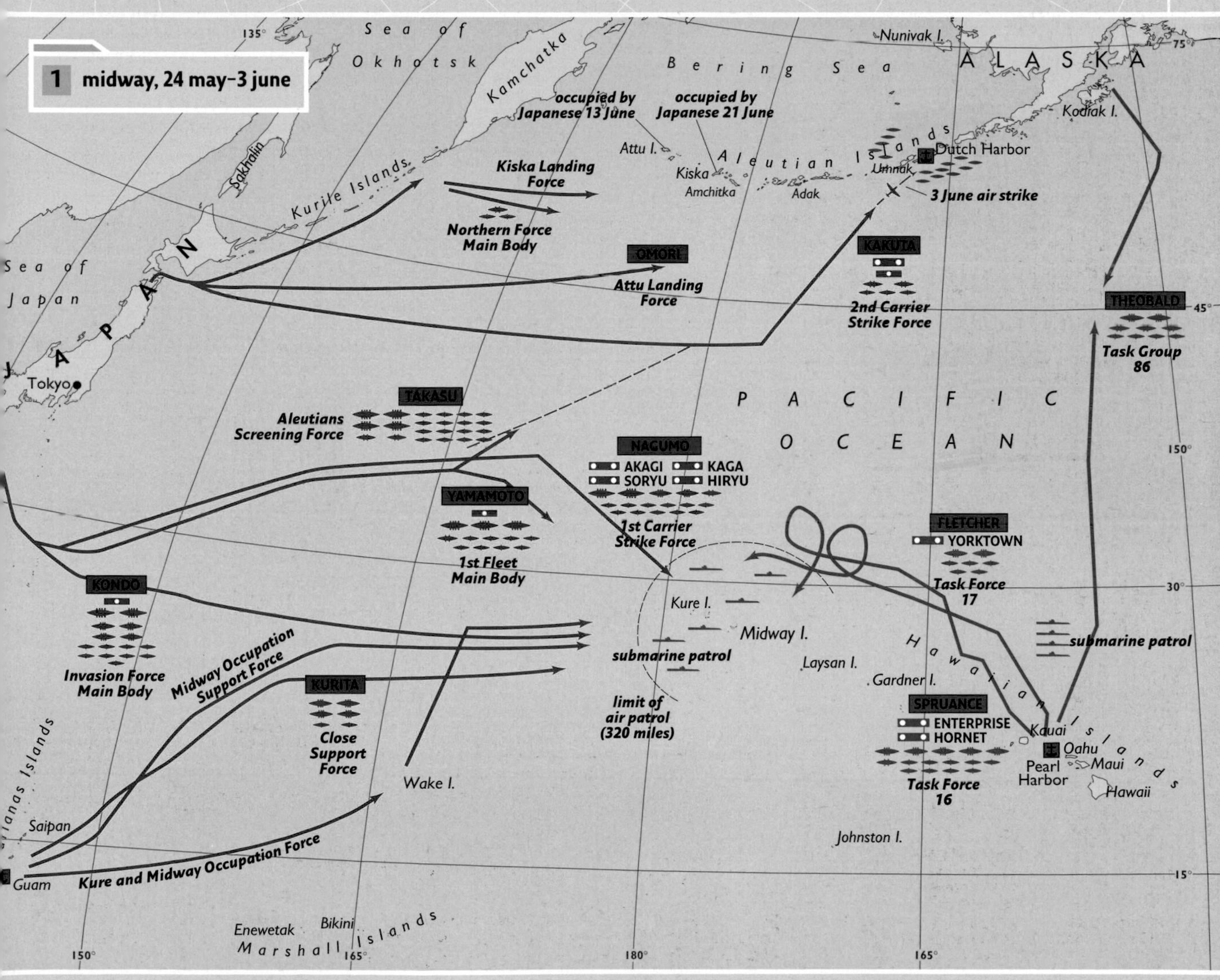

stalingrad I

july to november 1942

- **17 July** Germans take Voronezh
- **19 August** General Paulus orders Sixth Army to take Stalingrad
- **1 September** fierce fighting around the city
- **13 September** German's 'final' offensive
- **14 October** Hitler orders East Front troops to stand fast; second 'final' offensive at Stalingrad
- **19 November** Soviet counter-attack west of Stalingrad
- **23 November** German Sixth Army surrounded

Stalingrad, formerly Tsaritsyn, now modern Volgograd, was the site of the most titanic and terrible battle of the Second World War, the first really significant defeat inflicted on Nazi Germany's land forces. Stalin's association with the city went back to the Civil War, when he had been instrumental in its defence. It was also symbolic, and strategically important, for Hitler. By 1942 Stalingrad was a sprawling conurbation stretching for 30 miles along the west bank of the Volga, nowhere more than three miles wide. It was a crucial industrial and communications centre, dominating the north-western approaches to the Caucasus.

By July 1942 it was obvious that the main German thrust had turned south-east; Army Group A to the south and the Caucasus, Army Group B to the Don. On 23 July, German units broke through to the western bank of the Don near Kamensk and in the first week of August the Soviets suffered disaster in the Don bend. Defence of Stalingrad was now in the hands of two fronts: Stalingrad (Gordov) to the north, and the new South East (Yeremenko) to the south. By the night of 23 August, Rostov-on-Don had fallen to the Germans and the Soviets were fast running out of space into which to retreat. The Volga was the final defensive line. Evacuation of industry and planting demolition charges in the Stalingrad factories were forbidden. Stalin had committed the Soviets to a terrible battle of attrition. From 23 August, when the Germans reached the Volga to the north, Stalingrad was under constant air attack, and as German and other Axis troops closed in on the city, Soviet Russia had reached perhaps the critical point of the war.

On 10 September General Alexander Lopatin was dismissed from command of Sixty-Second Army, now on the defence of Stalingrad, and replaced by Lt.-Gen. Vasily Chuikov. His arrival coincided with the ferocious German assault against the centre sector of Stalingrad itself, on 13 September. By this time Sixty-Second Army had been bombed and shelled to pieces, divisions numbering a couple of hundred rather than the regulation 10,000. Seven thousand

1-2 In 1942 central Stalingrad straggled along 12 miles of the River Volga. In the centre lay Mamayev Kurgan on Hill 102, a key point for which the struggle never slackened. Soviet positions on the eastern bank were relatively safe and here most of the artillery was concentrated. In mid-August, Germans forces crossed the narrow strip of land that separates the Don and Volga to close in on Stalingrad. By 12 Sept. the city proper was completely surrounded on the west bank, so that the Soviets could only get in and out by river. Mamayev Kurgan, Chuikov's Sixty-Second Army HQ, the Barricades, Red October and Tractor factories were all key objectives, taken and retaken many times. German air superiority made the daytime particularly dangerous for the Soviets, but they frequently recovered lost ground during the night. The Central Station and the engineers' houses nearby were also important objectives, the latter giving a field of fire over the main Volga jetty. Soviet artillery was concentrated on the east bank, firing across the river. Some of Sixty-Second Army's artillery, however, remained on the west bank, including the very short-range Katyushu rocket launchers, which by 14 Oct. had to back right into the water of the Volga to get the necessary angle of fire. The battle was a perfect illustration of the huge numbers of troops a large city like Stalingrad could absorb. The German assault, designed to overrun the factory districts (14 Oct.) failed despite the use of three infantry divisions and over 300 tanks. Such forces were simply lost, sucked into the blazing maelstrom of Stalingrad.

2 stalingrad, 13 sept.–19 nov. 1942

- front line, 13 Sept.
- front line, 15 Sept.
- front line, 28 Sept
- front line, 1 Nov.
- Soviet fighter sweeps
- Soviet supply lines

XXXXX B WEICHS
XXX XLVIII
XXXX 4 VON RICHTHOFEN
XXXX 4 VON SCHWEDLER
XXX SHTAKHEL GROUP
Minina
Yelshanka
Stalingrad n… stat…
3
5

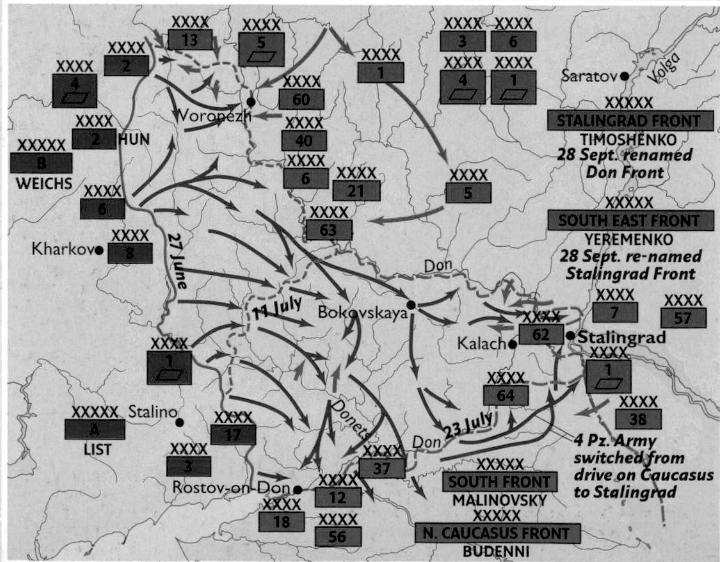

http://users.pandora.be/stalingrad/
History, images and maps of the Battle of Stalingrad
www.spartacus.schoolnet.co.uk/GERpaulus.htm
General Friedrich Paulus and the Battle of Stalingrad

workers had been formed into people's militia units to defend their factories, and women and children evacuated to the east bank.

Chuikov's HQ on Mamayev Kurgan, a Scythian tumulus on Hill 102 commanding the central and northern suburbs, became the centre of an inferno as German troops, fighting with unequalled savagery and determination, hacked their way through the city. On 14 September, they occupied engineers' houses near Stalingrad Central Station and brought the main landing stage on the river under accurate machine-gun fire, proceeding to fight their way into the area of the grain elevator. Sixty-Second Army, reinforced by 13th Division, moved into the city centre during the night and managed to claw a foothold on the west bank despite murderous German gunfire. Stalingrad Central Station changed hands four times during that day: the whole city became a blazing furnace of burned out buildings and small, savage actions. On the 17 September Chuikov moved his HQ near the Red October factory. The fighting continued without let up amidst the lurid glow of blazing buildings and illumination shells, while small boats ferried ammunition and brought the wounded back across the river alight with burning oil. There were renewed German surges on 27 September, when 80 tanks moved on the Red October factory. During the night the Soviet 193rd Rifle Division was ferried across the Volga to retake it. By 5 October the Germans occupied the northern landing stages, and Stalin ordered them to be prised away from the river. A huge bombardment, lasting 40 minutes, by 300 guns and five regiments of Katyusha multiple rocket launchers smashed German units preparing to break into the Tractor factory and the Barricades gun factory. The Germans then launched an attack of even greater ferocity and by the 16 September had taken the Tractor plant and appeared about to take Barricades, but the Soviets held on in parts of the factory until the 23 September.

Meanwhile, the German command was receiving reports of Soviet redeployment north of the Don. The only way out was to take Stalingrad, and soon, and in a desperate attempt to do this, they piled in more resources. On 11 November the last great German attempt to break through to the Volga split Chuikov's bridgehead for the third time. The Red October factory was in German hands; Soviet units and formations were, at best, down to about a tenth of regulation strength, and running out of ammunition and food. By 17 November the Soviet situation was desperate and to make things worse the Volga was beginning to freeze. So far the battle of Stalingrad had cost the Germans 700,000 men killed, wounded, prisoners and missing, and 1,000 tanks, over 2,000 guns and 1,400 aircraft destroyed.

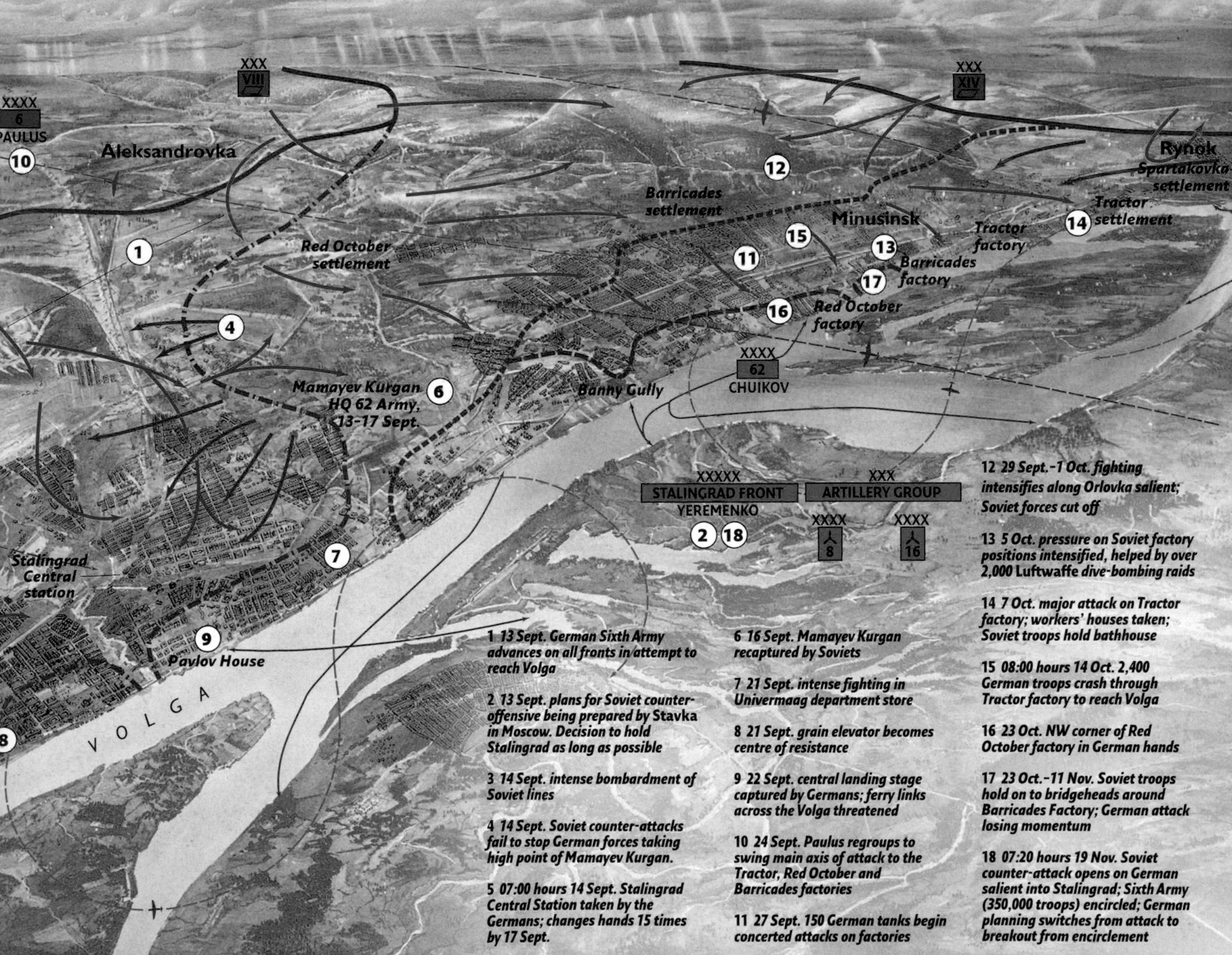

1942 to 1943

- **1942 (9 August)** Germans capture Krasnoda, Maikop and Stavropol
- **12 August** Germans advance in Kuban region
- **28 December** Hitler withdraws Army Group A from Caucasus
- **1943 (6 February)** Soviets reach Sea of Azov to cut off Army Group A

The first phase of the German summer offensive of 1942 had brought them to the River Don. In the second phase, Army Group A was tasked with Operation Edelweiss, the capture of the Caucasus oilfields at Maikop, Grozny and Baku. These would be a considerable prize for the German economy in themselves, but in terms of grand strategy the arrival of German troops in the Caucasus offered even more dazzling rewards. Turkey might be coerced to join the Axis powers, and the Deutsches Afrika Korps' success in North Africa might mean a joint encirclement of British possessions in the Middle East and the Mediterranean could become an Axis lake.

But dreaming over a map and fighting over the ground were entirely different. From Rostov to Baku was the same distance as from the Polish-Soviet frontier to Rostov – and the terrain grew increasingly difficult. The eastern half of the land between the Caspian Sea and the Black Sea is a roadless desert. In the western half the German armies were restricted to two narrow axes, either along the Black Sea coast, and then inland from Sukhumi to Tiflis, or north of the Caucasus via Armavir, Grozny and Makhach Kala to Baku. Soviet reinforcements faced a long haul round to the front, but they could at least use the Caspian route from Astrakhan to Makhach Kala, while also bringing some forces up from the Turkish border.

Operation Edelweiss began on 25 July and for the first two or three weeks Army Group A swept forwards, advancing up to 30 miles a day. The Soviet forces defending the Caucasus had not yet recovered from their earlier defeats. But by the middle of August German daily progress was averaging only one or or two miles a day. As the terrain became more difficult Army Group A also found its forces being drained away to the Stalingrad front. In particular the Luftwaffe's 4th Air Fleet, planned to provide essential tactical air support, was ordered to concentrate its resources against Stalingrad. At the same time new commanders and fresh troops arrived on the Soviet side. Among them was Lavrenti Beria with internal security troops of the NKVD; these would ensure that German hopes of an anti-Soviet rising by the non-Soviet people of the Caucasus would be dashed by the harsh repression of any possible discontent.

German and Romanian mountain troops were committed to the battle but the Red Army held on. Within the mountain passes the fighting turned into a series of platoon-level battles for individual positions. Hitler refused to consider the evidence of difficult terrain, adverse weather and diminishing resources and continued to press General List, commanding Army Group A,

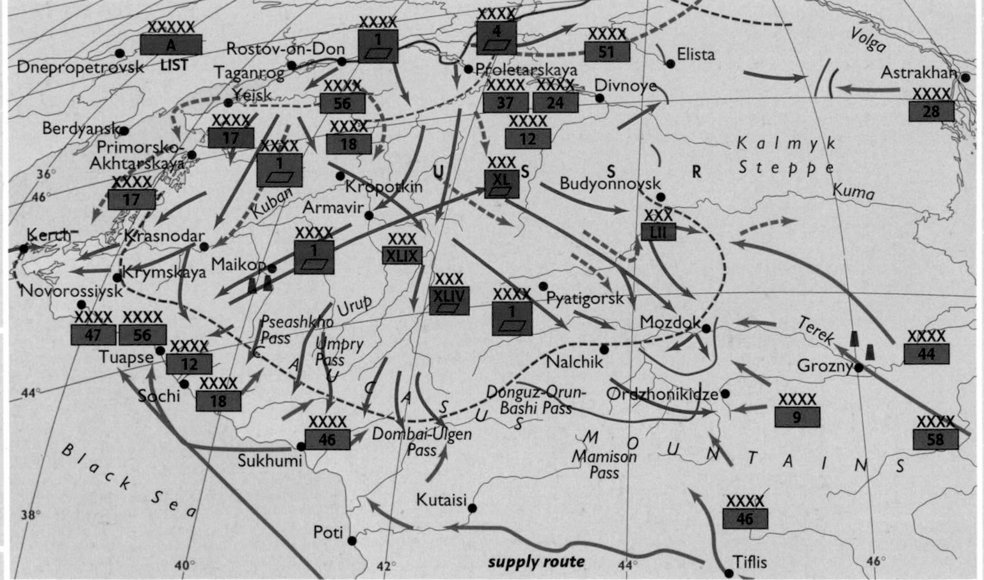

1 the caucasus, july–nov. 1942

- Soviet front line, 25 July
- Soviet front line, 25 Aug.
- German position, 1 Aug.
- German position, 25–28 Aug.

1 **The German advance into the Caucasus began on 25 July 1942 when Army Group A advanced rapidly from the River Don. By 9 Aug. it had reached the Krasnodar–Stavropol–Maikop Line. However, the foothills of the Caucasus began to slow down the advance and each side split its forces. German Seventeenth Army, supported by Romanian Third Army, fought the four Soviet armies of what became known as the Transcaucasus Front's Black Sea Group for control of the coastal road from Novorossiysk to Sukhumi. With the aid of Operation Blücher II (2 Sept., an amphibious assault across the Kerch Strait to clear the Taman Peninsula), Seventeenth Army reached Novorossiysk on 6 Sept., but by 11 Sept. the front line was stuck at a cement factory on the outskirts: it remained there for 360 days. Attempts to thrust through the mountains to the coast made only slightly faster progress before the arrival of winter made any advance impossible. In the east First Panzer Army had the apparently easier task of skirting the Caucasus to the north against the opposition forces of the Northern Group. LII Corps crossed the Terek at Mozdok on 2 Sept. but was then held in its bridgehead by Soviet counter-attacks. Hopes were raised by two more bursts of progress, along the line of the Terek in late September and to Nalchik in late October but winter rain and snow brought operations to an end on 9 Nov. The Soviet counter-offensive in the Caucasus was to exploit the over-extension of the German forces and the winter conditions. It formed only part of a general counter-offensive all along the front.**

www.worldwar2.ro/operatii/?article=13
The Taman offensive (1943) in the Caucasus south-west region
www.spartacus.schoolnet.co.uk/GERkliest.htm
Paul von Kleist, German forces commander during the latter stages of the Caucasus campaign

to continue his advance. List was forced to resign on 10 September and for some time Army Group A was left without a commander, while Seventeenth Army and First Panzer Army dealt directly with Hitler's headquarters.

On the Soviet side the Supreme Commander was equally intrusive. In considering plans for the 1942 winter offensive Stalin rejected the Transcaucasus Front's proposal to put the main axis north of the Caucasus, against First Panzer Army, aiming at Maikop. In Moscow a more ambitious plan had been developed, which hoped to encircle Army Group A and destroy it totally. This was to be achieved by Southern Front thrusting down through Salsk to Tikhoretsk, while the Black Sea Group struck north from Tuapse to Krasnodar to link up with Southern Front at Tikhoretsk. It was another plan which offered a dramatic victory on the map but which ignored the reality of the ground. There was no reason why Soviet troops should find it any easier to conquer the ground and the weather than the Germans had.

The final plan involved two attacks. The first, Operation Mountains, was to be launched at Goryachi Klyuch and on to Tikhoretsk; the second, Operation Sea, was an amphibious assault to clear Novorossiysk and threaten the Taman Peninsula. However, foul weather delayed preparations and grew worse as Operation Mountains got under way. The landing at Novorossiysk failed to capture the city but did leave a small bridgehead (Malaya Zemlya) to the south, which remained in Soviet hands through the summer. The numerous small landings along the coast in this campaign were typical of the Soviet approach to amphibious assault during the Second World War, which was very different to the experience of the Western Allies. There were no major overseas assaults; instead amphibious forces were used for outflanking moves over short distances. Such assaults were often rapidly improvised; it was thus easy to see why the Soviets became impatient with Western delays in mounting Operation Overlord.

The clearing of the Caucasus was only part of the Soviet winter offensive of 1942–43, which turned the tide of German success in the east. It denied Germany the oilfields at Baku, upon which Hitler had pinned substantial hopes.

2 **In the overall plan for the Soviet 1942 winter offensive, the Transcaucasus Front was to cooperate with the Southern Front in trapping Army Group A before it could withdraw through Rostov. But the Black Sea Group made only slow progress in appalling weather along the Tuapse–Krasnodar–Tikhoretsk axis. In the north, First Panzer Army was allowed to withdraw steadily from river to river, despite Stavka's attempts to speed up the movement of the Northern Group. A great threat to First Panzer Army was the Southern Front's progress to the River Manych, but the line held long enough for First Panzer to escape and join Manstein's counter-offensive at Kharkov. Seventeenth Army was left holding a large bridgehead on the Taman Peninsula, the *Gotenkopf* position. But during the summer attention was focused in the north, and the front remained static in the Caucasus. On 9 Sept. the Taman offensive opened with an amphibious assault directly into the harbour of Novorossiysk. In the next month frontal pressure, combined with small-scale amphibious outflanking moves along the coast , cleared the Taman Peninsula, although the bulk of Seventeenth Army was able to cross the Kerch Strait back into the Crimea.**

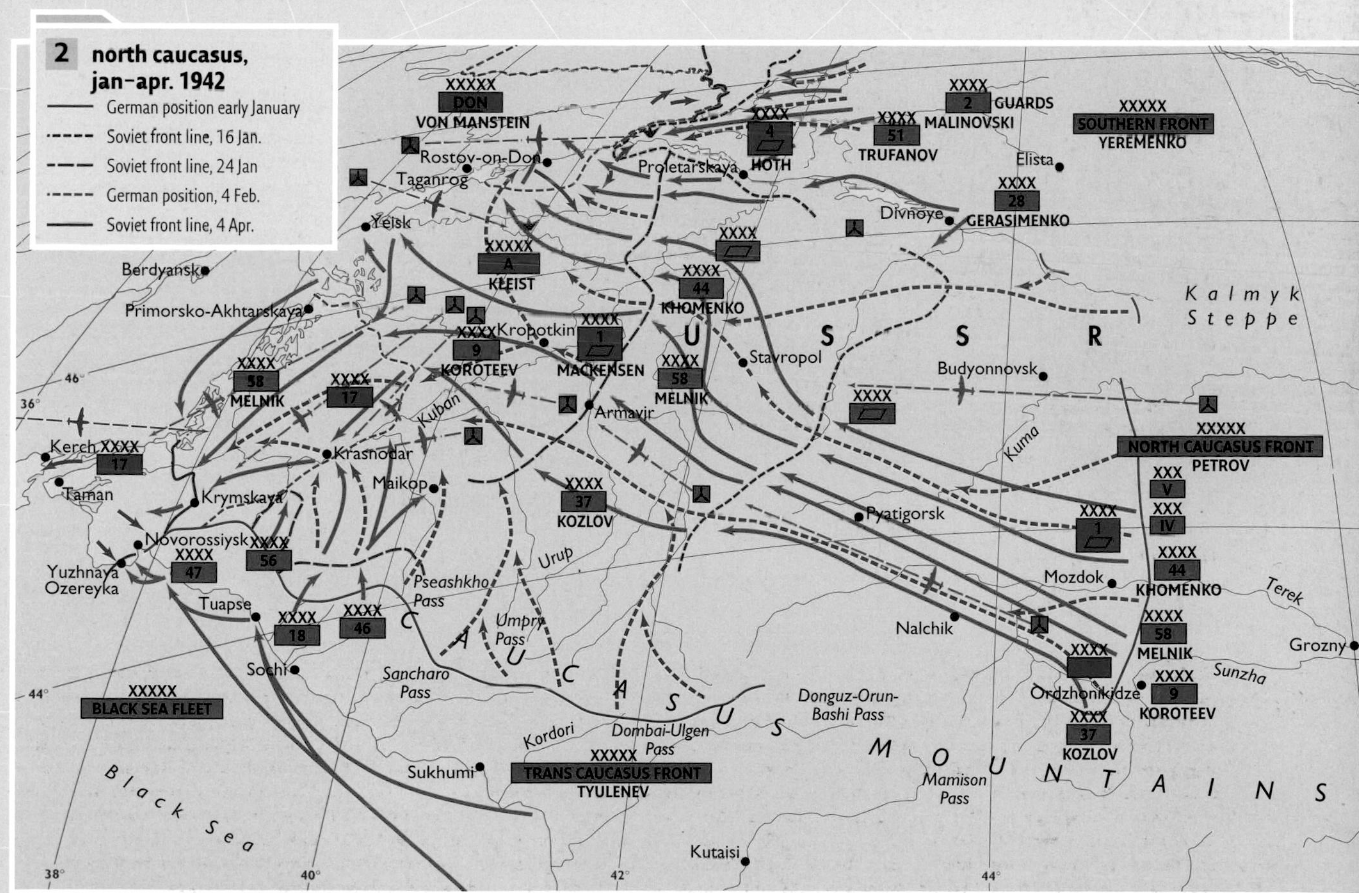

stalingrad II

- **1942 (19 November)** Soviets launch Operation Uranus to entrap the German Sixth Army at Stalingrad
- **23 November** forward units of the South-West and Stalingrad Fronts link to cut off Germans
- **1942 (8 January)** German Sixth Army refuses surrender demand
- **21 January** Soviets capture airfield supplying Stalingrad
- **31 January** General Paulus surrenders
- **2 February** remaining German pockets surrender at Stalingrad

At midnight on Wednesday 18 November Chuikov, commanding Sixty-Second Army in Stalingrad, was told to stand by for new orders. The next morning an 80-minute artillery preparation would herald Operation Uranus, a counter-offensive using over one million Soviet soldiers with over 13,000 guns, 894 tanks and 1,150 aircraft, slicing from north and east far behind and forward German troops still assailing Chuikov's ragged perimeter. The first wisps of snow had fallen on 16 November. During the night of the 18/19 November, snow clouds brought freezing fog and thicker snow, swathing the tortured terrain in a white mantle and reducing visibility to zero. At 07:20 hours the guns were loaded; at 07:30 hours they fired on what was to be named, from 1944, 'Artillery Day', and at 08:50 hours the infantry attack went in.

Plans for the counter-offensive, the second phase of the Stalingrad battle, were first presented to Stalin on 13 September. There were two main tasks: first, the encirclement of the force operating within the Stalingrad area, and second, its annihilation. To capitalise on the relative ineffectiveness of Romanian forces, the blows had to be struck far back on the flanks; until then, Stalingrad itself had to hold. In Operation Command No. 1 of 14 October, Hitler brought the German summer offensive to a close, believing that defence of the present positions would suffice until a final annihilating blow could be struck in 1943. On 23 October, Zeitzler, Chief of the General Staff, reiterated this, stressing that the Soviets were in 'no position to mount a major offensive with any far-reaching objective'. In fact, Soviet preparations were well advanced. Only Gehlen, head of the intelligence organisation Fremde Heere Ost, appears to have had the knowledge or imagination to predict either limited operations against Third Hungarian Army or operations over the Don on a larger scale against the Italian and Hungarian armies, on 12 November.

In retrospect, the German position looks terribly vulnerable. Von Manstein, appointed to command new Don Army Group on 20 November, said that the attempt to gain the Volga by taking Stalingrad as a set-piece battle was only admissible on a very short term basis. To have such a major force bogged down at Stalingrad for weeks with inadequately protected flanks was 'a cardinal error'. The German command structure was 'utterly grotesque'. Army Group A, to the south, was commanded by Hitler on a part-time basis; Army Group B had no less than seven armies, including four allied, an impossible span of control and divided loyalties as to the chain of command which would hamper German response to the well organised and meticulously planned Soviet blow.

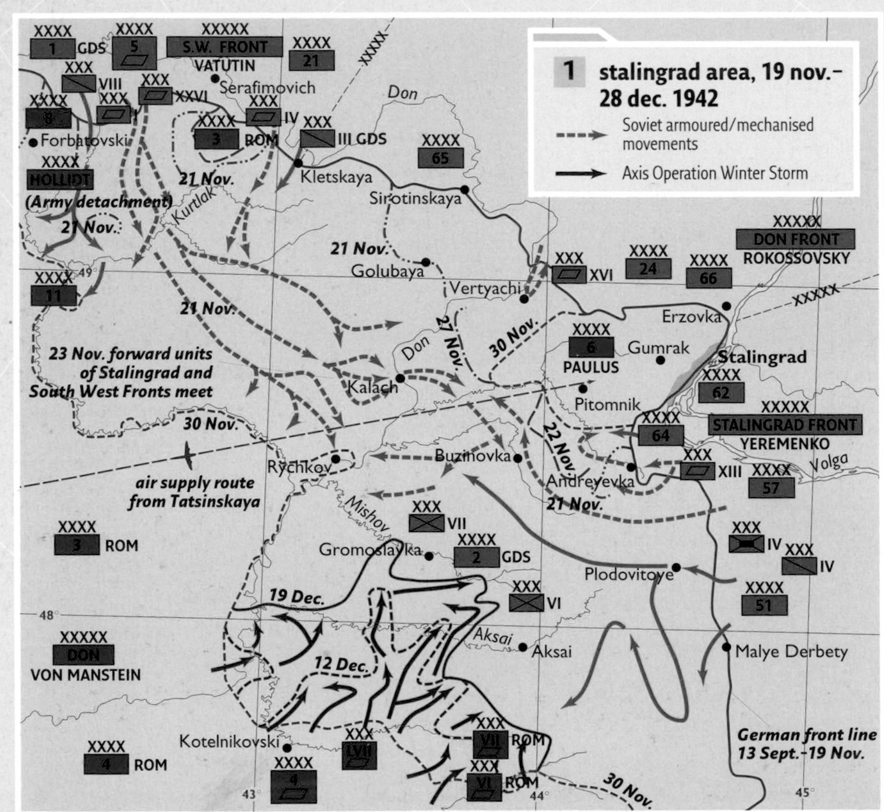

1 The main thrust of Operation Uranus, to encircle Axis forces in the Stalingrad area and then annihilate them, was launched on 19 Nov. As Soviet units of the South West Front ripped an 8-mile gap in the defences, Romanian divisions began to disintegrate and fell back, pursued by tank columns across the Don Steppe. The assault of the Stalingrad Front (20 Nov.) was delayed two hours (08:00 to 10:00 hours) because the weather conditions made it impossible to observe fire. During the following night a 20-mile-wide gash was torn in Fourth Panzer Army's eastern flank and the HQ had to withdraw. On the morning of 23 Nov. forward brigades (South West Front) and Stalingrad Front met in the vicinity of Kalach trapping what they believed to be 90,000 enemy troops in an encirclement 200 miles in circumference. It was at least two and a half times that number. First German transport aircraft flew into the ring on 25 Nov., where the beleaguered Sixty-Second Soviet Army still held its precarious positions on the west bank. The German attempt to relieve the pocket, Operation Winter Storm, was launched on 12 Dec. from the area of Kotelnikovski. Fifty-Seventh Panzer Corps was across the Aksai and reached the River Mishov, within 30 miles of the siege front (19 Dec.). The attempt to relieve Sixth Army had failed.

www.stalingrad-info.com/
Images, maps and descriptions of the Battle of Stalingrad
http://216.198.255.120/germanpart/winterstorm.htm
The German attempted relief of the Sixth Army, Operation *Winter Storm*

The Soviet counter-offensive opened on 19 November as South West Front and Sixty-Fifth Army of the Don Front struck from the north, pushing the breakthrough to 20 miles by the end of day one. The next day the southern pincer (Stalingrad Front) attacked. On 23 November mobile units of the two fronts met on target in the Kalach area blocking Sixth Army's resupply and exit routes. In a giant Cannae that would have appealed to the Soviet General Staff, the Soviets had trapped a major enemy force in a pocket extending about 30 miles from west to east and 25 from north to south. There seem to be no definitive figures as to the number of troops in the pocket: von Manstein reckoned that estimates over 300,000 (the official Soviet estimate is 330,000) were exaggerated: 200,000 to 220,000 was probably a reliable estimate

Von Manstein considered it imperative to get Sixth Army out. The Soviets would obviously do everything in their power to destroy Sixth Army and might also push mechanised forces across the large Don bend towards Rostov, threatening to cut off Army Group A as well. The force in the pocket needed 550 tonnes of supplies a day, but might make do with 400 until the ration dumps already in the pocket could be supplied by air: Göring boasting that it could. Hitler remained determined to leave Sixth Army in 'Fortress Stalingrad', perhaps supplying it through a land corridor.

The Soviets, having completed their encirclement and bolstered up the inner and outer fronts, launched their first attack on Sixth Army on 2 December. By this time, the Germans had made plans for the relief attempt, Operation Winter Storm, launched on 12 December. The grotesque command relationships hampered attempts to get Sixth Army out of the pocket: Paulus seemed determined to obey Hitler's order to hold, while on 19 December von Manstein, as his immediate superior, ordered Sixth Army to begin breaking out to the south-west. The German dilemma was insoluble. Leaving Sixth Army and a large part of Fourth Panzer tied down around Stalingrad placed the Army Group as a whole in a very vulnerable position. But Sixth Army was too weak to attempt to make contact with relief forces by breaking out and at the same time to hold its perimeter. Should Paulus obey Hitler or von Manstein?

Meanwhile the Soviet Operation Kol' tso (Ring), to destroy the encircled garrison, proceeded. By 26 December Paulus was radioing that he could not hold out for long and that he had received only 70 tonnes of supplies that day. In a last, almost comic, gesture to induce Sixth Army to hold on, Hitler promoted Paulus with indecent rapidity, first to Colonel General, then to Field Marshal. By 24 January 30,000 wounded had been flown out and the garrison was ordered to break up into small groups. On 31 January the southern group of German forces, including Paulus, surrendered; on 2 February, the northern surrendered: 91,000 officers and men were taken prisoner; about 140,000 had died in the pocket in January. The Battle of Stalingrad had destroyed Sixth Field and Fourth Panzer Armies, Third and Fourth Romanian and Eighth Italian. In all the Battle of Stalingrad may have cost the Germans as many as one and a half million men killed, wounded, missing and prisoner, nearly a quarter of their strength on the eastern front.

Von Manstein believed that Sixth Army was a necessary sacrifice: other sectors of Army Group B's front were weakly held and had Sixth Army not put up fierce and prolonged resistance, in spite of cold, hunger and shortage of ammunition, the Soviet victory on the southern front might have been even more crushing.

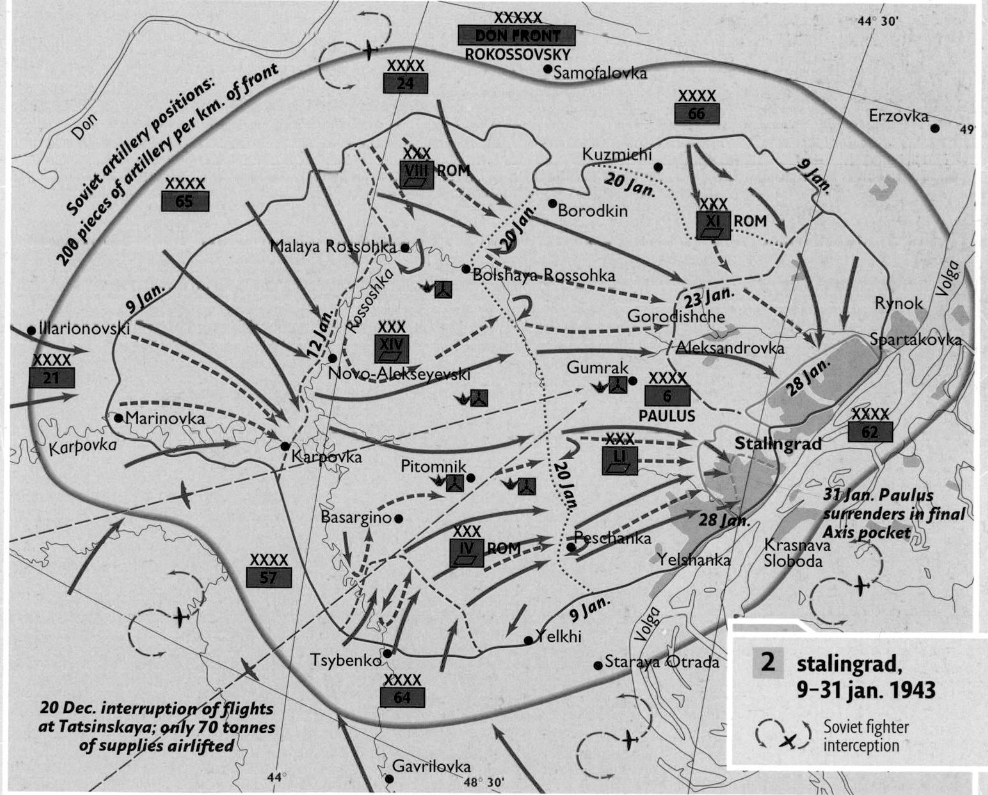

2 Five Soviet armies now surrounded Paulus's Sixth Army and units of Fourth Panzer. The Don Front was charged with liquidating the encircled force, after the Germans rejected an ultimatum (10 Jan.). By 9 Jan. the western edge of the pocket was 25–30 miles from the Volga. By 16 Jan. the Soviets were seven miles from Stalingrad, by the 25 Jan. German positions were reduced to two pockets in the city itself, opposite Krasnaya Sloboda and Zaytsev Island. On the 26 Jan. the Soviets reached the slopes of Mamayev Kurgan, on which the snow had never settled: the heat of the constant shell and bomb bursts had melted it off. The southern group, including Paulus, now a Field Marshal, surrendered on 31 Jan., the northern on 2 Feb.

southern soviet union

february to june 1943

- **1943 (8 February)** Soviet Army captures Kursk
- **16 February** Soviet Army captures Kharkov
- **2–4 March** Germans defeat Third Tank Army at Kharkov
- **14 March** Germans retake Kharkov
- **26 March** spring thaw halts fighting

The final destruction of Sixth Army at Stalingrad on 2 February made a renewed Soviet surge possible beyond the outer front of the Stalingrad encirclement. By 2 February the Soviets had advanced beyond the outer front established by Little Saturn - the Middle Don Operation - at the end of December, to the Don in the south, the Northern Donets and then a line running north some 50 miles east of Bielgorod and Kursk.

The Soviets now planned a renewed surge. Exactly as had happened a year before, winter victory made Stalin and Stavka over-ambitious. Three fronts, Voronezh, South West and Southern, would liberate the second largest political entity in the USSR: Ukraine. As well as over-ambitious, it seemed that Stalin could not choose between occupation of territory and control of its resources on the one hand, and destruction of enemy forces, as objectives on the other. The Stavka directive of 6 February ordered South West Front to cut off the Donets group of German forces and drive it into isolation in the Crimea. To the north, Soviet forces would strike into the rear of Army Group centre through Briansk and Smolensk, and, further north still would wipe out the Demyansk Pocket and open the way to the relief of Leningrad.

Soviet South West Front attacked on 29 January and Voronezh Front on 2 February. German Army Group Don still occupied the 'balcony' between the Don and Donets rivers, placing it in danger of immediate encirclement. On 6 February Von Manstein met Hitler to elicit approval to withdraw from the eastern part of the area. Characteristically Hitler at first refused, then agreed. By 9 February the Soviets had taken Bielgorod

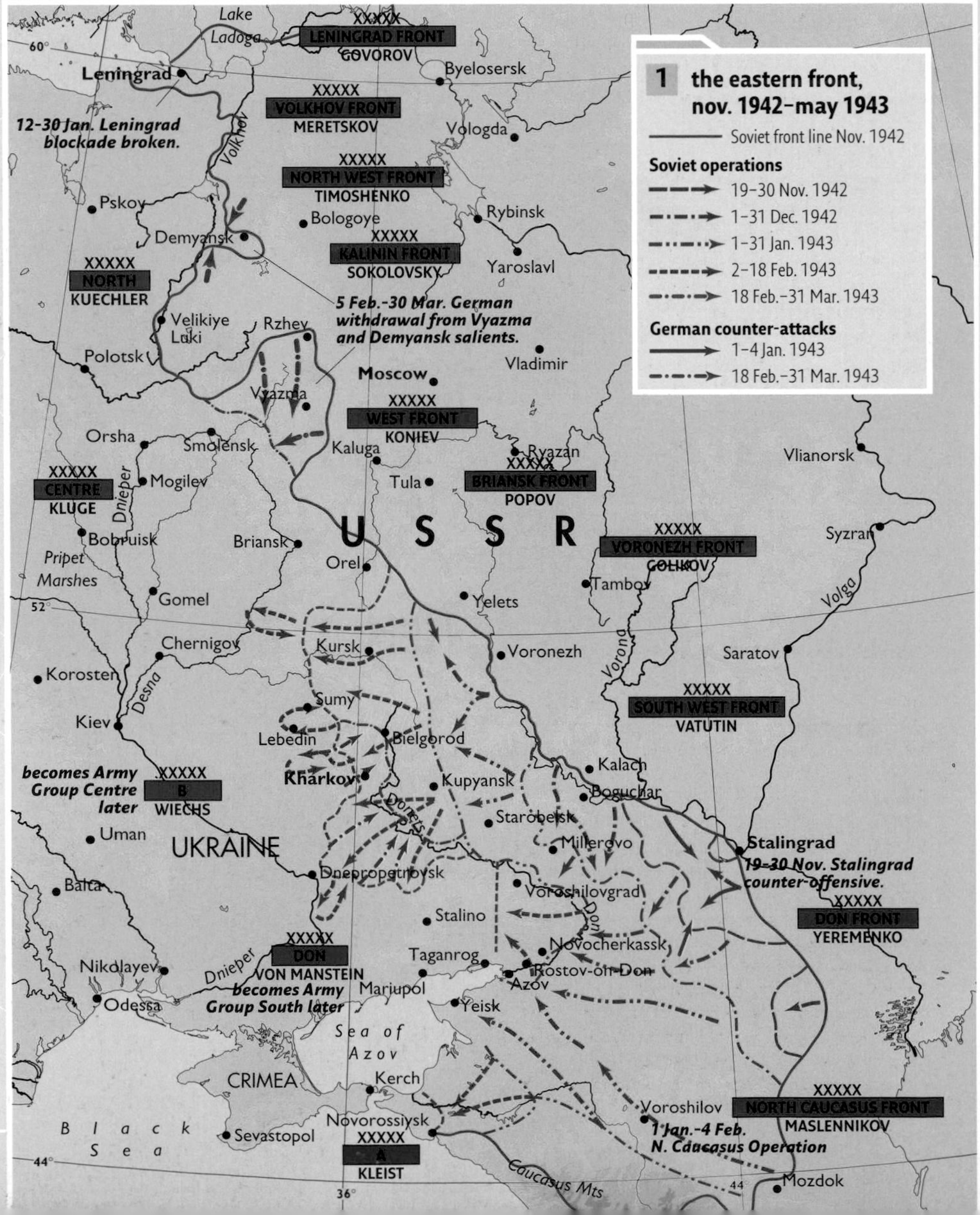

1 the eastern front, nov. 1942–may 1943

Soviet front line Nov. 1942

Soviet operations
- 19–30 Nov. 1942
- 1–31 Dec. 1942
- 1–31 Jan. 1943
- 2–18 Feb. 1943
- 18 Feb.–31 Mar. 1943

German counter-attacks
- 1–4 Jan. 1943
- 18 Feb.–31 Mar. 1943

12–30 Jan. Leningrad blockade broken.

5 Feb.–30 Mar. German withdrawal from Vyazma and Demyansk salients.

19–30 Nov. Stalingrad counter-offensive.

1 Jan.–4 Feb. N. Caucasus Operation

becomes Army Group Centre later

becomes Army Group South later

1 **The Stalingrad counter-offensive (19–30 Nov.), and Operation Little Saturn (16–30 Dec.) had brought Soviet forces to the middle reaches of the Don. During January 1943, Voronezh, South West, Don, Stalingrad and Southern Fronts pushed German forces back to the Lower Don, and a line east of Bielgorod and Kursk. The Soviet advance continued (2–28 Feb.), into the western Donets area, which von Manstein had eventually persuaded Hitler to relinquish. A further penetration took the Soviets almost to Dnepropetrovsk.**

www.achtungpanzer.com/gen8.htm
Erich Von Manstein, commander Army Group South
www.bbc.co.uk/history/historic_figures/stalin_joseph.shtml
Biography of Joseph Stalin (1879–1953)

and Kursk, north of Kharkov. Army Group B now faced a superiority of (in German estimation) up to 8:1. By mid-February, the danger of encirclement of the entire German southern wing from the north had become acute, but these very dispositions created the potential for a counter-stroke.

Kharkov, the fourth largest city in the Soviet Union, was a prestigious prize and on 13 February Hitler ordered it to be held at all costs. The SS Panzer Corps there had no intention of being encircled, however, and pulled out on the 15 Febraury. Kharkov fell to the Soviets the next day, opening a 100-mile breach between German Army Group B and Don, the latter renamed South. The Germans now shelved plans for expansion in the Caucasus: Army Group A became a reservoir of forces for Army Group South. On 19 February Fourth Panzer Army executed a counter-stroke, hitting the Soviet forces trying to drive a wedge down to the Dnieper, in the flank. The battle between the Donets and the Dnieper raged until 2 March, by which time Army Detachment Hollidt had held the River Mius and First and Fourth Panzer Armies had severely mauled Soviet forces in the area, counting 23,000 dead, 615 tanks captured, but only 9,000 Soviet prisoners, most Soviets able to escape across the frozen Donets.

The next German counter-attack came on 7 March. Fourth Panzer Army hoped to break into the rear of the Voronezh and Central Fronts, cutting them off in the Kharkov area and thus creating what Stalin subsequently called a 'German Stalingrad'. Voronezh Front withdrew 60 to 100 miles, forming the southern face of the huge Kursk salient, about half the size of England. The muddy season gave an advantage to the Germans now going onto the defence, but it provided a menacing springboard for Soviet attacks to south and north into the flanks of Army Groups South and Centre. The sooner the Germans attacked, the less prepared the defence of the salient would be. This was the rationale behind Operation Zitadelle, originally timed to start in early May. Had it been launched then, it might have worked, but it was delayed to June, and then the beginning of July.

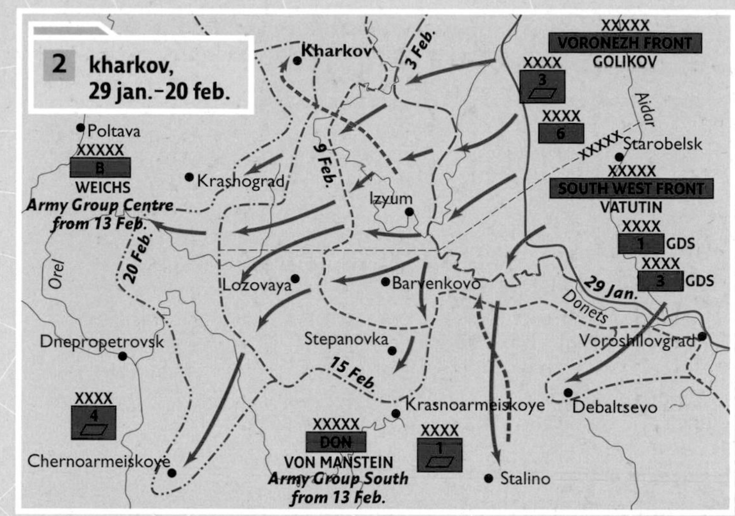

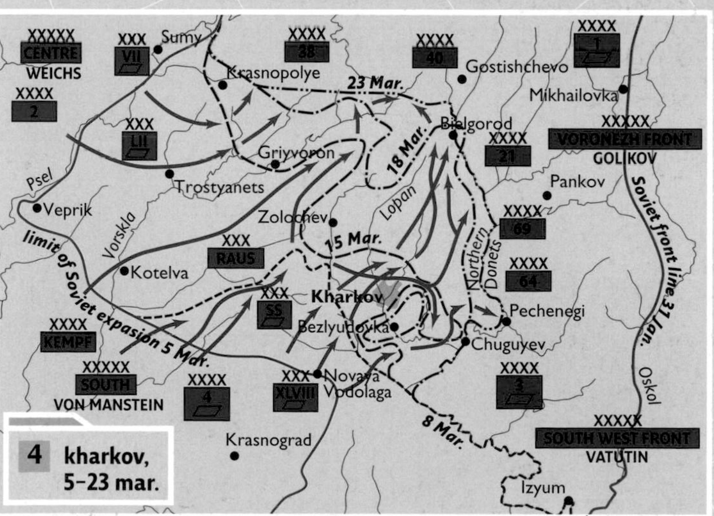

2-4 The battles for Kharkov fell into two phases. During the Soviet offensive phase (2 Feb.–3 Mar. 1943), forces of Voronezh Front and Sixth Army of South West Front attacked with the aim of destroying the main forces of Army Group B south of Kharkov, although the city itself, which fell on 16 Feb., was a prestigious bonus (*map 2*). This very success invited (19 Feb.) a German counter-stroke (*map 3*), masterminded by von Manstein commanding Army Group Don (renamed South from 13 Feb.). To the north (15–28 Feb.) Soviet North West Front (Timoshenko) was ordered to liquidate the pocket of German troops around Demyansk (*map 1*), facilitating thrusts into the rear of German forces besieging Leningrad. On 7 Mar. Fourth Panzer Army attacked towards Kharkov (*map 4*), aiming not so much to retake the city as to destroy Soviet forces located there. While protected by the thawing Donets from an attack in Voronezh Front's rear, the Soviets lost Kharkov on 14 Mar. The result of operations in the southern theatre was the formation of the southern face of the great Kursk salient, which would be the objective of Germany's last major offensive in the east: Operation Zitadelle.

battle of the atlantic III

april to september 1943

- **1943 (1 April)** convoy protection improved; British and Canadians in the north, USN in the south
- **28 April** Battle of Convoy ONS-5, the turning point in the Atlantic; seven U-boats sunk
- **30 April** RN 'Support Groups' provide improved protection
- **22 May** Admiral Dönitz suspends U-boat operations in North Atlantic
- **June** Allied shipping losses: down to 28; zero to U-boats
- **1 July** new Allied shipping tonnage overtakes losses
- **3 August** U-boats abandon Wolf Packs for independent patrols
- **18 September** Wolf Pack raids resumed in North Atlantic

Given the dependence of their future operations - especially the build-up and supply for Operation Overlord - upon the defeat of the U-boats, the Americans and British agreed at the Casablanca conference (January 1943) that priority had to be placed upon winning the Battle of the Atlantic. By March 1943 the increased U-boat losses indicated that a major new aspect of the struggle was developing: additional very long-range aircraft were allocated to the battle, and their intervention is generally considered to have been crucial to the defeat of the U-boats in May 1943.

In reality, the losses sustained by the U-boats in May 1943 were the result not of any single cause, however important, but of a combination of factors. The defeat of the U-boat campaign against Allied shipping lay not simply in the reverses sustained in May 1943 – when 41 U-boats were destroyed – but in the fact that in July and August 1943 the U-boat arm sustained defeats of similar severity. Though losses in these months – 37 and 25 respectively – were less than in May they were sustained by a force that had regrouped and reorganised after the May debacle, and had intended to mount a sustained, massed offensive to regain the initiative. Thus the losses in July and August were more profound than those of May, and August 1943 marked the real Allied victory in the Battle of the Atlantic; thereafter, the U-boat arm was never again able to mount a sustained threat to Allied communications in the North Atlantic. After August 1943 the primary role of the U-boats was to tie down and distract disproportionately large Allied naval forces, while a new generation of submarines was developed.

The Allied victory in the North Atlantic between May and August 1943 was the product of four related developments: the organisational, tactical and technical superiority of convoy escorts over the U-boats became apparent for the first time; Allied air power became increasingly effective; better intelligence concerning U-boat movements became available via Ultra intercepts; and finally German errors in the conduct of operations. Possibly the Allied victory might have been won before spring 1943 had it not be for Operation Torch, which tied down substantial escort forces until this time, but in this period various technical developments – ship-borne radar and direction-finding equipment, improved asdic detection equipment, more powerful depth-charges and new and more accurate firing patterns – allowed convoys to be accorded an adequate scale of escort protection. In its conventional form, the submarine was incapable of the tactical or technological development required to counter the increases in escort numbers and advances of anti-submarine technology: further, in its conventional form the submarine could not withstand the introduction of Allied air power to the Battle of the Atlantic in spring 1943.

The latter took three forms – the escort carrier, very long range (VLR) patrol aircraft operating in direct support of convoys, and standard patrols over transit areas. All three forms were small-scale at this time. In March 1943 the Allies deployed just 18 VLR aircraft, nine of which were assigned patrol duties, but by May 1943 total strength had risen to 49 aircraft, and this total allowed between 12 and 15 of their number to spend an average of three hours with convoys beyond 650 miles from land on every day of May 1943; thus, with a small number of escort convoys, the Allies acquired the ability

1 the north atlantic, mar.–may 1943

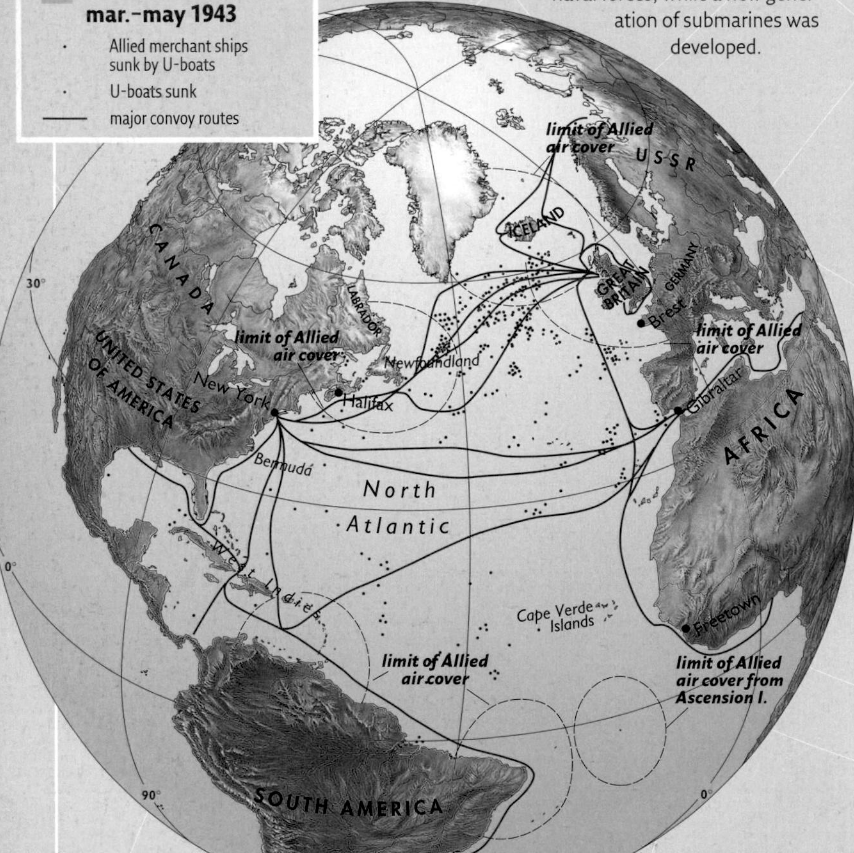

1 **March 1943 was a decisive month in the Battle of the Atlantic. German operational U-boat strengths had reached a peak. This was reflected in the fierceness of the convoy battles in previous months. Changes in the Allied convoy organisation, however, began to reap results. Most ships sailing off the US and Caribbean coast were now convoyed with a dramatic fall in sinkings. Further reductions in sinkings in April and May were achieved by more effective air cover: escort carriers appeared on some Atlantic convoys, and many more aircraft were made available for convoy duties. As German losses mounted and exchange rates fell, much of the attention of the battle turned upon operations in the Bay of Biscay. More aircraft became available for patrols, and in April were provided with 10cm radar sets, undetectable by U-boats. In July, of 86 U-boats that crossed the Bay, 55 were sighted, 16 sunk by aircraft, and six forced to turn back. The cost was 14 aircraft. By August, however, better German air-cover, the use of Spanish coastal waters to gain access to the Atlantic and a return to single, submerged sailings, reduced U-boats losses in the Bay.**

www.liverpoolmuseums.org.uk/maritime/exhibitions/boa/home.aspl
A guide to the Battle of the Atlantic from the Merseyside Maritime Museum
http://uboat.net/
Information on German U-boats used during World War Two

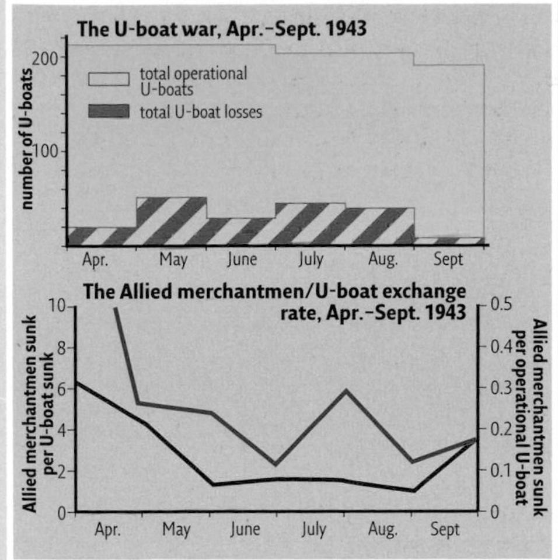

Allied merchant ship losses, Apr.–Sept. 1943 tonnages (nos. of ships)

date	U-boat	aircraft	mine	warship raider	merchant raider	E-boat	unknown and other causes	monthly totals
April	327,943 (56)	3,034 (2)	11,961 (5)	none	none	1,742 (1)	none	344,680 (64)
May	264,852 (50)	20,942 (5)	1,568 (1)	none	none	none	12,066 (2)	299,428 (58)
June	95,753 (20)	6,083 (3)	4,334 (3)	none	17,655 (2)	none	none	123,825 (28)
July	252,145 (46)	106,005 (13)	72 (1)	none	7176 (1)	none	none	365,398 (61)
August	86,579 (16)	14,133 (5)	19 (1)	none	none	none	19,070 (3)	119,801 (25)
September	118,841 (20)	22,905 (4)	4,396 (3)	none	9,977 (1)	none	300 (1)	156,419 (29)

totals by theatre, Apr.–Sept. 1943

Atlantic Ocean	Mediterranean	Indian Ocean	Pacific Ocean
744,507 (130)	246,889 (55)	322,080 (54)	84,341 (16)

figures show tonnages, with numbers of ships in backets

both to harry U-boats gathering around convoys and to attack in mid-ocean where U-boats had to run on the surface in order to recharge their batteries. The spring months witnessed a German attempt to counter the Allied ability to find surfaced submarines as they crossed the Bay of Biscay at night, by sailing in daylight and fighting the aircraft in the process: this error provided the patrols with their only period of substantial success in the entire war.

The combination of air power and increased escort effectiveness was, in technical terms, decisive in bringing about the defeat of the U-boat arm. Nevertheless, the U-boat arm was at that time in qualitative decline anyway, because of enforced dilution arising from its rapid expansion in previous years. In any event, even had the successes of 1942 been sustained throughout 1943, this could not have secured a German victory, for the extension of convoy struck at the very effectiveness of a U-boat service that achieved its greatest returns at the expense of merchantmen sailing independently. More importantly, by March 1943, US shipyard production had outstripped Allied shipping losses. It was with this complex interplay of factors that the critical point of the Battle of the Atlantic was passed in 1943, ensuring the Allies against defeat.

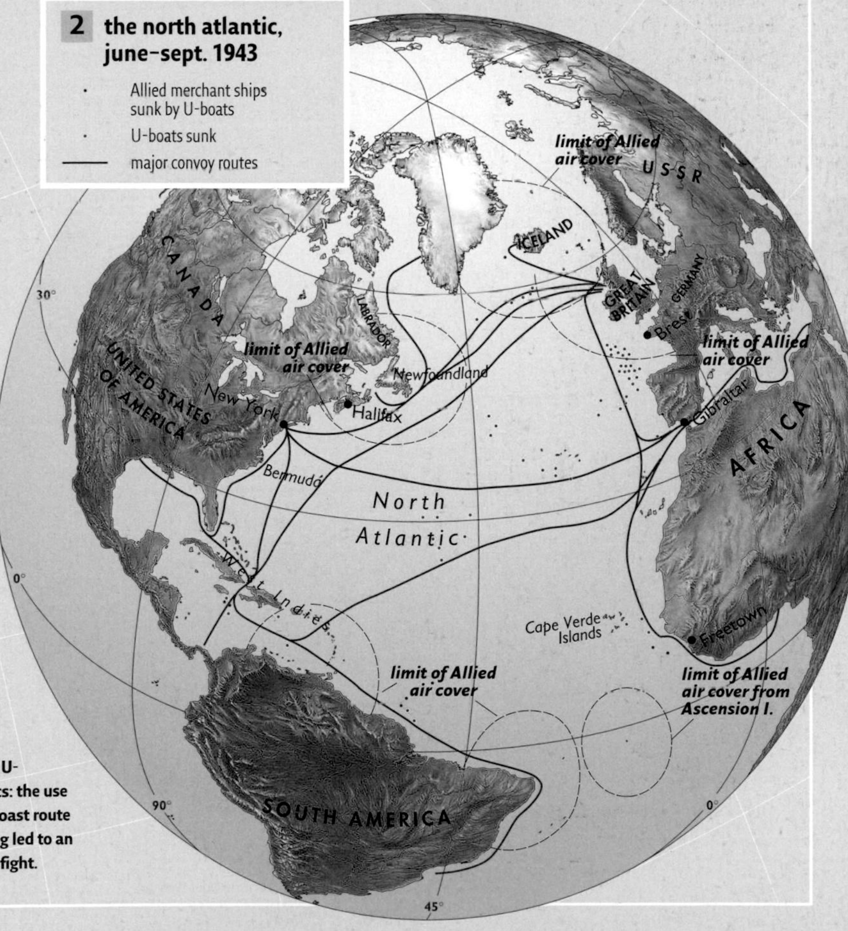

2 June 1943 was the quietest month in the North Atlantic: U-boats concentrated on soft targets off the west coast of Africa and Brazil. The combination of increased patrols in the Bay of Biscay, rising numbers of escorts and difficulties in deciphering the new Allied codes introduced in May led Dönitz to recall U-boats for the fitting of new anti-aircraft and snorkel devices, and to attempt to persuade Hitler to encourage more Navy/Luftwaffe cooperation. In July 1943 Allied ship production exceeded, for the first time, losses from enemy action. Thereafter, the Allies produced an average of 5,000 gross tonnes more per month than they lost. By September, however, U-boats returned to the North Atlantic in numbers with new tactics: the use of snorkel to recharge batteries while submerged, the Spanish coast route to the North Atlantic and increased use of mid-Atlantic refuelling led to an increase in sinkings. The U-boats had by no means given up the fight.

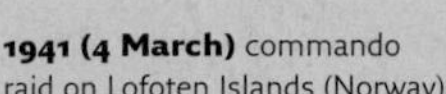

1939 to 1945

- **1941 (4 March)** commando raid on Lofoten Islands (Norway)
- **17 November** Keyes Raid - abortive commando raid on Rommel's HQ in North Africa
- **1942 (27 February)** Bruneval commando raid captures German secret radar
- **28 March** commando raid on St Nazaire
- **19 August** Dieppe Raid; 6,000 men suffer 50 per cent casualties
- **4 October** commando raid on Sark
- **18 October** Hitler orders execution of all captured commandos
- **11-12 December (night)** Operation Frankton, commando raid against Axis shipping on the Gironde river

The creation of Special Forces - military formations comprising teams of specially trained soldiers for unconventional combat missions - was a particular feature of the Second World War. All the major combatant nations developed Special Forces, most usually as a supporting arm of conventional forces, but it was the British who made the most use of them.

The Germans set up the first Special Forces of the war, Construction Battalion 800, organised by the Abwehr in 1939 and made up of small parties in civilian clothes who operated ahead of conventional forces to seize or demolish key points. They first went into action on 1 September 1939 against Poland, later expanding to regimental strength under the name Brandenburg and serving in every theatre of Germany's war.

On 3 June 1940 Winston Churchill addressed a minute to the Chiefs of Staff calling for raiding forces to keep the German forces on the coasts of occupied Europe tied down. Within two months eleven Commando units had been formed, each of 500 volunteers. One of these, No. 2 Commando, eventually became the Parachute Regiment. The first Commando raid (night, 24/25 June) was carried out by No. 11 Independent Company, part of a unit raised for special operations in the Norwegian campaign, since the Commandos were still forming, but that against Guernsey a month later did include No. 3 Commando.

Three Commandos were raised in late summer 1940 from volunteers in the Middle East. At the same time, the Long Range Desert Group (LRDG) came into being. It was to provide invaluable intelligence through infiltration of the Axis lines via the open desert flank. In early 1941 three UK-raised Commandos combined with a Middle East Commando to form Layforce. This carried out Commando operations on the North African and Syrian coasts, but much of it was lost on Crete in May. This put the future of the Commandos in the Middle East in jeopardy, but Auchinleck backed a new unit, the Special Air Service (SAS), designed to infiltrate enemy lines to destroy aircraft on the ground. By the end of the war the SAS had grown into a brigade-sized unit and was active in behind-the-lines operations in both north-west Europe and Italy. The Middle East, however, soon became swollen by 'private armies' - among them the Special Boat Squadron, which specialised in landing on enemy-held coasts, Popski's Private Army (Libyan Arab Force Commando) and the 1st Special Service Regiment. However, coordinating their activities became increasingly difficult.

During 1941 the Commandos in Britain began to make a name for themselves, especially as a result of the Lofoten Islands and Vaagsö raids. With RAF Bomber Command, they were seen as the only means of striking directly at the Germans. Increasingly, however, it was realised (especially after the disastrous Dieppe raid, August 1942) that the war in Western Europe and the Mediterranean could only be won through successful major landings on hostile coasts. Consequently, Special Forces organisations came to be raised for this purpose. The Combined Operations Pilotage Parties (COPPs) specialised in examining potential landing beaches and No. 30 Commando mirrored the German Abwehrkommando, whose purpose was to accompany assaulting troops and seize enemy papers and equipment. The Commandos themselves came to play a major role in spearheading amphibious assaults from the Madagascar landings in May 1942 onwards.

In Burma there was further scope for Special Forces, such as the long-range penetration groups, the Chindits,

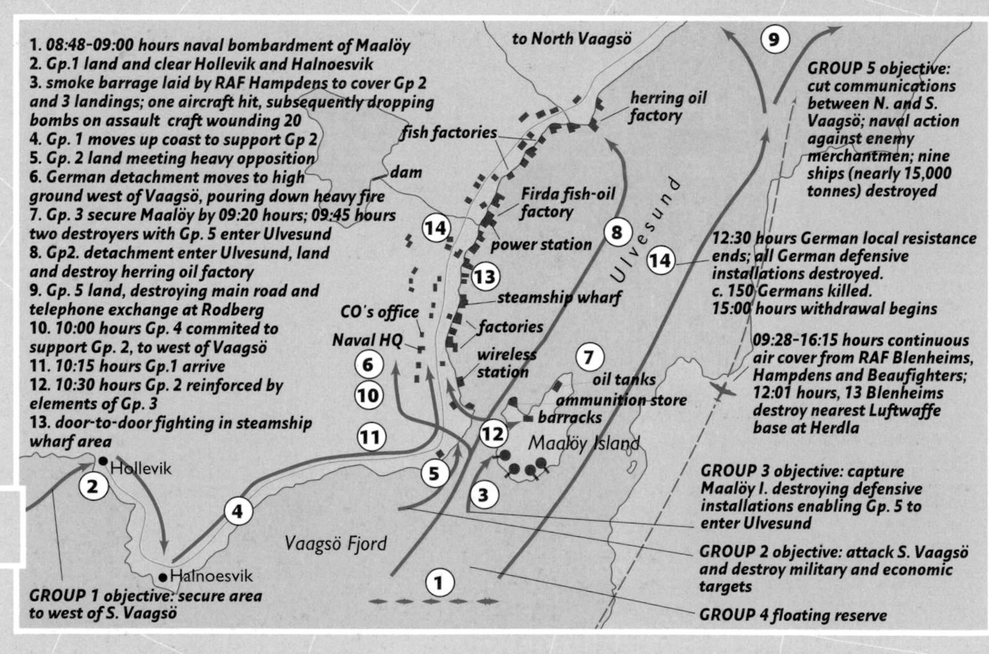

2 the vaagsö raid, 27 dec. 1941

2 The Vaagsö raid in December 1941 was an early Commando operation to destroy German military installations. The Commandos were split into five groups - one to prevent German reinforcements being sent to the town of South Vaagsö from the north, one to attack the town itself, one to deal with Maalöy, one to attack a strongpoint at Hollevik, and one as a floating reserve. The force arrived off Vaagsö at dawn on 27 Dec. RAF Blenheims and Hampdens laid a smokescreen and the Royal Navy bombarded German batteries on Maalöy prior to the Commando attack using landing craft. Resistance was fierce in South Vaagsö, but all objectives were achieved at a cost of 19 killed. The Commandos destroyed port and military installations, brought back nearly 100 German prisoners and some volunteers for the Norwegian Free Forces.

www.combinedops.com/vaagso.htm#The%20Raid
Operation Archery: the Vaagsö raid
www.royalmarinesregimental.co.uk/histcockmain.html
Operation Frankton: the 'Cockleshell Heroes' raid

their US equivalent, Merrill's Marauders, and V-Force, an information-gathering and sabotage group of indigenous tribesmen led by British officers. The Pacific theatre also spawned the US equivalents to the Commandos, the Rangers (Army), who also fought in Europe, Raider (Marine) battalions, the Seabees – the US Navy's Construction Battalions, which cleared beach, harbour and airfield obstacles – and the Australian Coastwatchers, who reported on Japanese movements. In the final months of the war, the Japanese instituted suicide kamikaze wings to combat the US Navy, while in Germany young volunteers joined the *Wehrwolf*, units designed to attack Allied forces as they advanced into the Reich.

While sometimes unpopular and regarded with suspicion by conventional forces, there is no doubt that Special Forces, when properly handled, made an important contribution to raiding, intelligence-gathering and Combined Operations.

1 Special operations in Norway were a vital means of keeping up the pretence that the Allies intended to invade it. Cross-Channel raids ceased at the end of 1943 for fear that they would encourage the Germans to strengthen their coastal defences, although there was another flurry in May 1944 to make final checks on beach obstacles. Many more operations were planned than those shown on the map. North Africa and the Mediterranean provided much scope for special operations and many demolition raids were carried out. Numerous SAS and SBS reconnaissances were also undertaken. From the invasion of Sicily onwards Special Forces remained active in the Aegean, Balkans, Adriatic and Italy.

air war in europe II

1941 to 1943

- **1941 (13 March)** devastating night raids on Glasgow and Clydeside leave two-thirds of population homeless
- **1–9 May** Liverpool Blitz
- **10 May** climax of London Blitz
- **1942 (14 February)** Area bombing directive shifts RAF from specific to general urban targets
- **1 March** RAF '1,000 Bomber' raid on Cologne
- **23 April** 'Baedeker' raids against Britain's catherdal cities begins
- **15 August** Pathfinder force created in Britain
- **1943 (25–28 July)** first firestorm raid on Hamburg

Before the outbreak of war only two air forces, the RAF and the US Army Air Corps, were committed to strategic bombing as a central part of air strategy. Air leaders in both countries believed that it was possible to destroy the war-willingness of enemy countries by attacking their industries and civilian workforces from the air, cutting off supplies to the armed forces, and increasing popular demands for peace.

It was evident, however, from early in the war that the RAF lacked the technical means to carry this strategy out. Not until large numbers of heavy four-engined bombers were available with sufficient trained air crews could a bombing offensive be launched with any chance of success. Only from 1942, with the larger Lancaster and Stirling bombers coming into service, and with the arrival in Britain of the US 8th Air Force – built around the high-performance four-engined B-17 'Flying Fortress' and the B-24 Liberator – was an offensive possible that could bring real strategic results.

RAF Bomber Command never deviated from the view that the bombing campaign was worth the effort. Even in the difficult early years of the war, plans were drawn up for a systematic attack on German industrial target-systems. Priority was given to oil and power, with transport and the aircraft industry high on the list. But the RAF lacked good navigational aids and escort fighters, and was compelled to fly only at night under clear skies, and to aim at whole cities rather than particular factories. As a result, Bomber Command, led from February 1942 by Air Marshal Arthur Harris, moved by default to a strategy of 'area

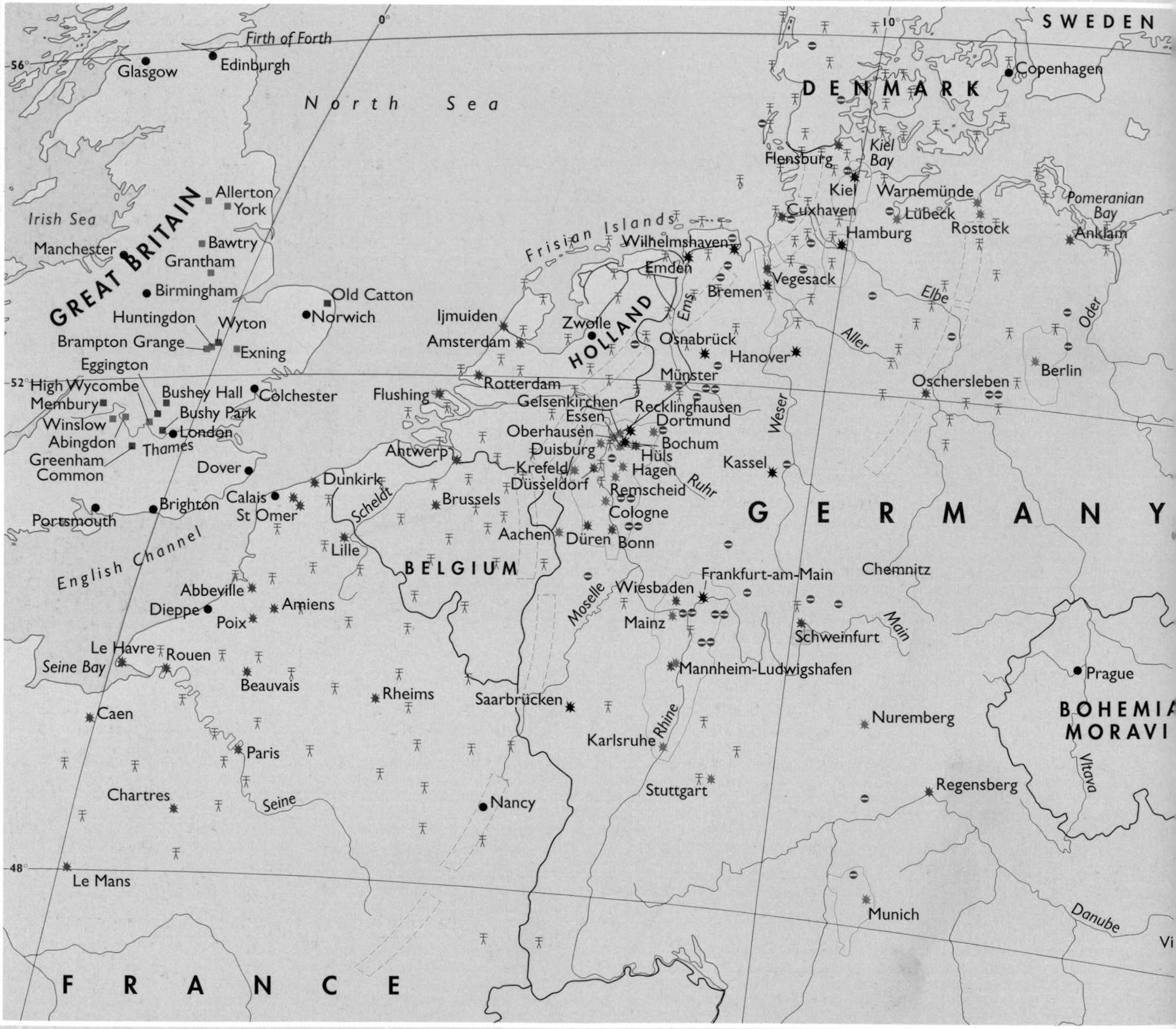

www.bbc.co.uk/history/historic_figures/harris_sir_arthur_bomber.shtml
Air Marshall, Sir Arthur 'Bomber' Harris
www.historylearningsite.co.uk/thousand_bomber_raid.htm
'1,000 Bomber Raid' on Cologne

bombing'. It was argued that even attacks of an indiscriminate type would disrupt the local economy and undermine war-willingness.

The USAAF took a different view. American planners believed in precision bombing by day, using large, well-armed bombers that could fight their way to the target and back. The Air Corps, under General 'Hap' Arnold, drew up detailed bombardment plans even before American entry in to the war. American airmen favoured oil, electric power, the aviation industry, transportation, chemicals and machinery as major targets, but unlike the RAF insisted that it was also necessary to attack the Luftwaffe as an 'intermediate target'. Without destroying German air defence, it was argued, the strategic offensive would be blunted, as the Luftwaffe had been in 1940. When US bombers arrived in Britain in 1942, in small numbers and poorly prepared, they were sent in precision daylight attacks to bomb industrial and air force targets.

The Allied campaign in 1942 was very limited. This was a period of apprenticeship as bomber commanders learned tactics, trained crews and built up a satisfactory ground organisation. In May a '1,000 Bomber Raid' was launched against Cologne, but this was not typical of the offensive. It was a spectacular demonstration to the Germans of the growing power and confidence of the RAF, and a reply to critics at home. The bombing offensive only became a major campaign following the Casablanca meeting between Roosevelt and Churchill in January 1943, from which came the directive for a 'Combined Bombing Offensive'. By then very large numbers of bombers were in the pipeline, and both Western Allies were under pressure from Stalin to relieve the pressure on Soviet forces in the east. The bombing offensive was a kind of second front, forcing the Germans to divert aircraft and resources to combating the threat from the air. Both Bomber Command and the 8th Air Force began systematically to bomb German targets deeper and deeper within German territory, the Americans hitting specific industrial targets, the RAF attacking cities with devastating effects. In Hamburg in late July bomber forces created the first 'firestorm' destroying 70 per cent of the city and killing over 40,000 people.

During 1943 the German defences began to organise more effectively to counter the bombing. General Kammhuber built a defensive line of anti-aircraft and searchlight batteries in northern Germany, Holland and Denmark, supplemented by an expanded home fighter force for day and night combat. By the late autumn the balance was swinging in favour of the defence: during the intensive raids on Berlin (1943) RAF Bomber Command sustained losses that forced major attacks to cease. In the 8th Air Force attack on the ball-bearing plants at Schweinfurt in October the bomber streams were harried on the outward and homeward journey, losing 65 bombers out of a force of 291. These rates of attrition were unacceptable. Not until long-range fighters were available to escort the bombers to their targets, and not until heavy damage was inflicted on the Luftwaffe, could the offensive hope for greater success. The failure to break down the German defences echoed the German defeat over Britain in 1940, and raised the powerful argument that bombers might be better employed helping the ground forces. By the end of 1943 the bombing campaign was yet to prove its worth.

1 **From May 1940 RAF Bomber Command undertook a strategic bombing campaign against individual cities and military targets in Germany and occupied Europe from the Baltic to western France, but their effect was limited by poor accuracy, limited range and growing German defences. In 1942 the US 8th Air Force joined the campaign and began a series of precision daylight raids on specific industrial targets. In 1943 the Luftwaffe dropped only 2,298 tonnes on Britain (graphs left), a fraction of the amount carried by the RAF in a single raid. The air war now turned upon the economics of production and supply, and the Allies gained the upper hand.**

1 the bombing of germany, 1941–43

- Bomber Command main HQs
- US 8th Air Force group HQs
- target bombed by RAF
- target bombed by USAAF
- target bombed by RAF and USAAF
- German radar station
- German night fighter station
- anti-aircraft batteries
- searchlight batteries

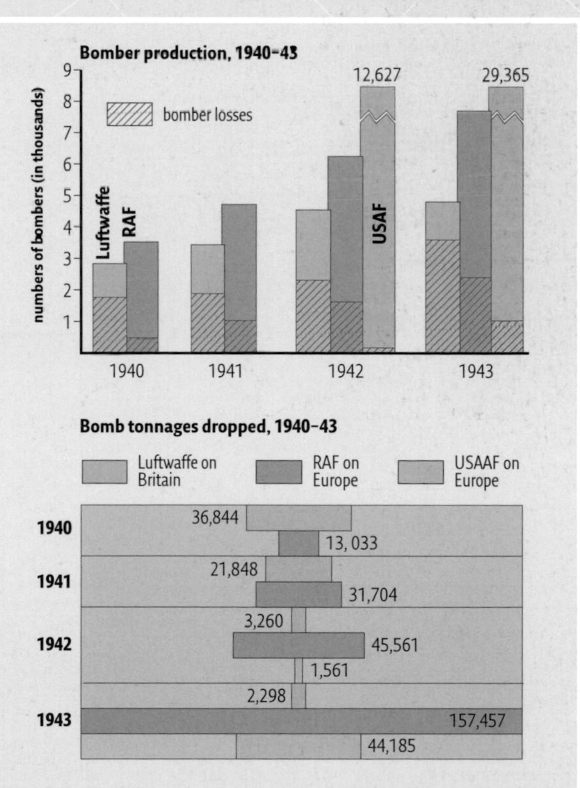

el alamein

august to november 1942

1942 (13 August) Montgomery made Commander-in-Chief Eighth Army

30 August Battle of Alam Halfa (to 2 Sept.)

30 September Eighth Army probing attacks at El Alamein

23 October Battle of El Alamein begins (until 4 No., when Rommel orders a retreat)

1 November Operation Supercharge – the Allied breakout from battlefield

12 November Eighth Army reaches Tobruk

13 December Rommel withdraws from El Agheila

1943 (28 January) Eighth Army captures Tripoli

Despite Auchinleck's success in holding Rommel at the Gazala-Bir Hakeim Line in July, a battle sometimes called First Alamein, Churchill decided to replace him following the Cairo conference, 4–10 August 1942. On 15 August General Harold Alexander was appointed in his place as Commander-in-Chief, Middle East; two days earlier Montgomery had been had been given command of Eighth Army.

Churchill's directive to Alexander was to destroy, as soon as possible, the Axis army in North Africa commanded by Rommel (who had been promoted to Field Marshal on 22 June). Montgomery's first order to Eighth Army was that it would retreat no further: it would hold any German offensive on its present line, Alam Halfa.

Rommel, who had been preparing to attack with his four German and six Italian divisions, opened the offensive on 31 August. By evening of 2 September he had made little progress and his armour was short of fuel. Next day he ordered a retreat. Montgomery did not pursue, fearing losses to his armour from German anti-tank defences, but staged heavy air attacks on the retreating Germans. By 7 September fighting had ended.

Montgomery now continued the reorganisation of Eighth Army he had begun on assuming command. During September and October reinforcements and new equipment reached Egypt, including 300 American Sherman tanks. By 23 October, the date chosen for the opening of his offensive on Rommel, Montgomery commanded 230,000 men and 1,030 tanks; Rommel commanded 100,000 men and 500 tanks (of which 218 were German). The British now had an air superiority of about 5:3. Montgomery resisted pressure from his superiors to open the offensive until he had sufficient troops and firepower to ensure success.

Rommel had fortified his position after Alam Halfa and intermingled his German troops with their Italian allies. Montgomery's plan for the battle, which would be called (El) Alamein, was to attack along the coast with the infantry of XXX Corps and to mount a simultaneous diversionary offensive with XIII Corps in the south. When XXX Corps had opened a corridor, the armour of X Corps was to attack through it, and drive Rommel's Panzer Armee Afrika back along the coast.

The attack opened on the night of 23 October with a hurricane of artillery bombardment, behind which four infantry divisions moved to the assault. Heavy fighting broke out, as the Germans committed 15th Panzer Division to hold the break-in. In the south the Germans resisted strongly and on 25 October Montgomery decided to transfer forces from that sector to the developing dogfight on the coast. Rommel, who had been absent sick in Italy, returned the same day.

The battle that ensued concentrated upon the key features of the coastal corridor, along which most lines of communication ran, and the commanding Kidney Hill position midway between the coast and the Qattara Depression. Despite Rommel's resourceful use of his Panzer divisions, Kidney Hill was gained, and from there Montgomery launched his decisive stroke. Following a heavy artillery barrage, a bitter tank battle ensued, reducing the German armour by the evening of 2 November to 35 serviceable tanks. Rommel decided to withdraw. Hitler countermanded the order but Allied troops broke the German line and armoured units poured through. The next day Rommel was forced to order a full retreat and the remnants of his army set off westwards along the coast road toward Tobruk.

Montgomery paused to regroup before launching a pursuit. When it began on 5 November he at first hoped to trap Rommel by encirclement on the coast. Frustrated by German elusiveness and bad weather, he accepted by 7 November that it would be a long chase, but resolved to give Rommel no rest. Over the next three months, with two long pauses at El Agheila and Wadi Zemzem, he sustained his harassment of Rommel, hampered by innumerable booby traps and by an increasing number of prisoners. Rommel's retreat did not end until he reached the temporary safety of the Mareth Line in Tunisia. The Eighth Army suffered 13,500 casualties in the Battle of Alamein. Rommel, though he preserved the manpower of his German divisions, lost almost all his tanks; his Italian formations effectively ceased to exist. But now he had some time to prepare for a vigorous defence of Tunisia.

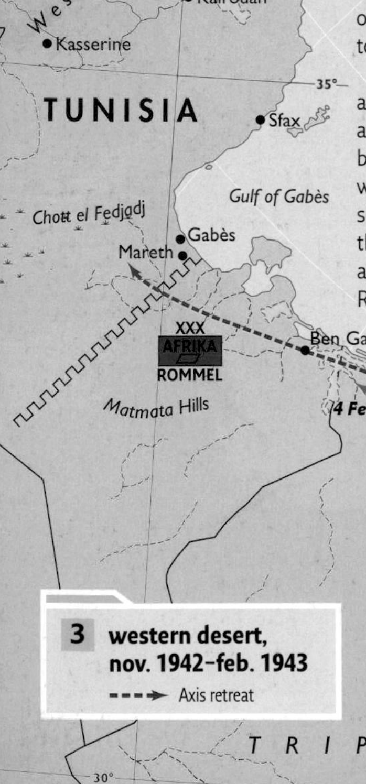

3 western desert, nov. 1942–feb. 1943

Axis retreat

www.bbc.co.uk/history/war/wwtwo/launch_ani_el_alamein.shtml
El Alamein; step-by-step battle animation
http://en.wikipedia.org/wiki/Bernard_Montgomery
Bernard Law Montgomery, Commander Eighth Army in North Africa

1-3 The conflict in the Western Desert reached a climax with a series of actions. Rommel began with an attack on Montgomery's Alam Halfa position lasting until 7 Sept. Montgomery prepared a major counter-offensive, which began with an attack at 22:00 hours on 23 Oct (*map 1*). XIII Corps' diversionary attack held 21st Panzer but 15th Panzer struck at the corridor opened near the coast. There was bitter positional fighting on 24–25 Oct. Montgomery, in order to accelerate progress, put his main effort into fighting for the coast, and by 1st Armoured Division, for Kidney Hill during 26–29 Oct. Rommel continually counter-attacked with 21st Panzer Division and (29 Oct.) brought 90th forward to support 164th on the coast. Montgomery therefore withdrew 1st Armoured and 2nd New Zealand into reserve as a preliminary to breaking out in the Kidney Hill area. The Alamein breakthrough (*map 2*) began on 2 Nov. at 01:00 hours north of and at Kidney Hill. The attack was led by 2nd New Zealand Division, supported by 1st Armoured, which during the day fought a violent tank battle with 15th Panzer. Rommel's tank losses were so heavy that he decided to withdraw that night but was forced by Hitler to continue the struggle. Counter-orders sowed confusion from which Montgomery profited. On 3 Nov. he sent 51st and 4th Indian Divisions in a night attack against Kidney Hill, and when they broke through, launched 7th and 10th Armoured Divisions into open country. Rommel now withdrew along the coast with Montgomery's forces in pursuit of their quarry (*map 3*). The 7th Armoured Division led the pursuit for most of the 1,600 miles, and although the Germans had not been decisively defeated as planned, the Western Desert was now cleared.

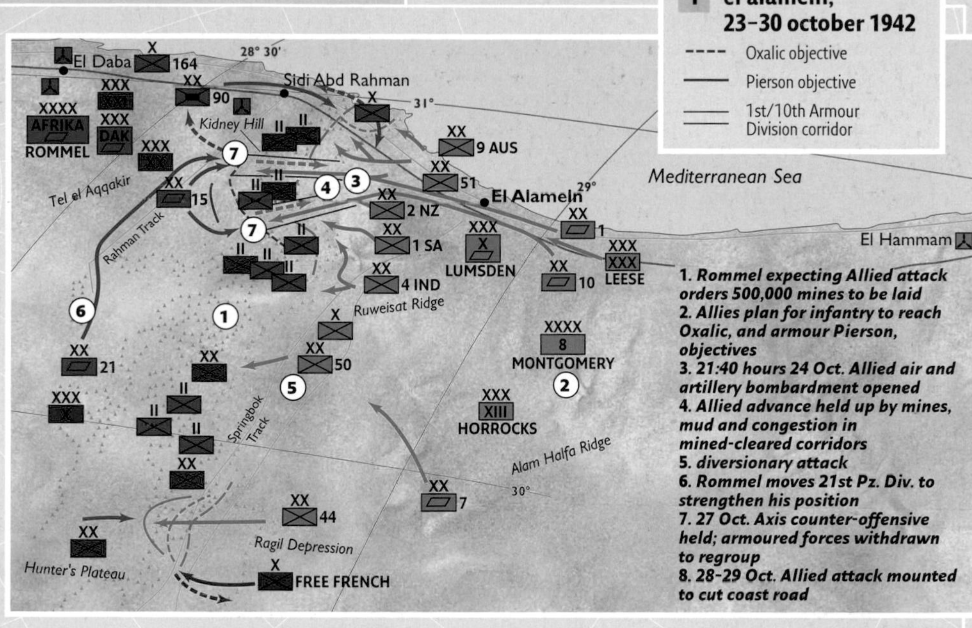

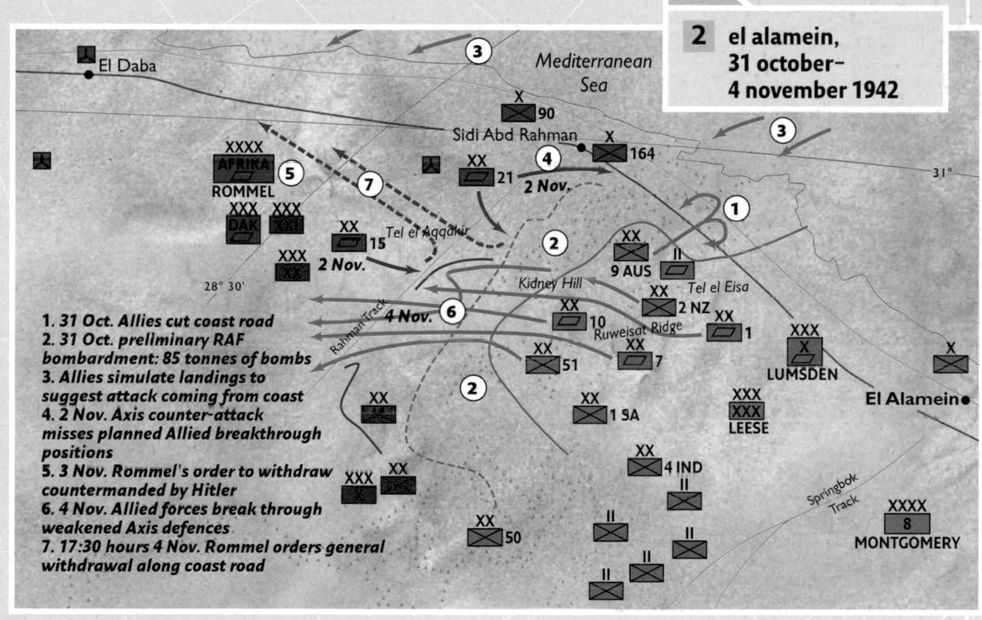

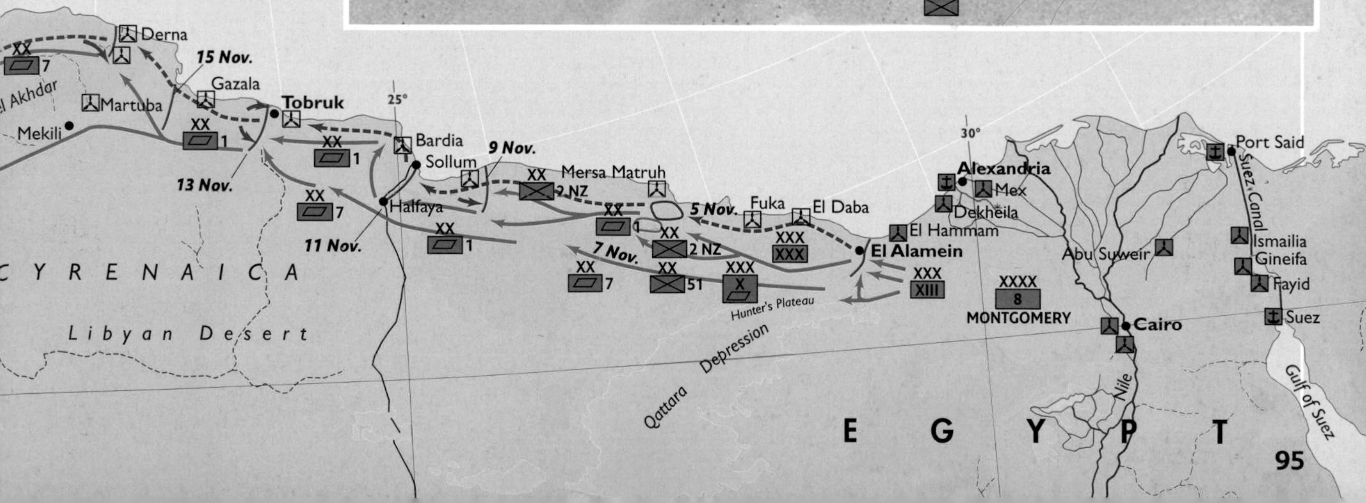

north africa

november 1942 to may 1943

1943 (8 February) Eighth Army enters Tunisia

14–25 February Kasserine campaign; heavy German counter-attack on 14 May, breaking through on 20 May; Allied recovery on 24 May

2 March German withdrawal in Tunisia begins

6 March Rommel leaves Afrika Korps

9 March Arnim takes command of Afrika Korps

20–28 March Eighth Army attacks and breaks through Mareth line

29 March Allies take Gabès

21 April Eighth Army takes Enfidaville

4–12 May last Allied offensive in North Africa

7 May Tunis falls to Allies

12 May Arnim surrenders all Axis troops

13 May Marshal Messe surrenders Italian First Army

The Anglo-American conferences of 1942 failed to concert a strategy for an early invasion of German-occupied Western Europe, which the British persuaded their Allies was too strong to be attacked with the forces available that year. At a London meeting, 20–22 July, a plan was drafted to use American forces, together with the British First Army, in an invasion of French North Africa. A headquarters for Operation Torch, as the offensive was code-named, was set up under Eisenhower in London on 14 August and the date of the landings fixed for 8 November.

French North Africa – Morocco, Algeria and Tunisia (the Maghreb) – was not occupied by German forces, but remained under the control of the Vichy Government. Since the conclusion of the Battle of Alamein however, Rommel's Panzer Armee Afrika had been in retreat to Tunisia from Egypt and Admiral Darlan, Vichy's commander in North Africa, was under orders to resist an Allied invasion. Of the three Allied Task Forces, Western, commanded by Patton, which had sailed directly from the United States, met the fiercest resistance in Morocco. Eastern, landing at Algiers, found the port in the hands of friendly forces and was opposed only when Vichy officers reasserted control late in the morning of 8 November.

The Germans had wrongly estimated that the Allied convoys were bound for Malta or Egypt and had therefore not heavily attacked them. On 10 November, however, on receipt of news that Darlan had been taken into protective custody and had negotiated a ceasefire with the Allies, Hitler ordered his troops into the unoccupied (Vichy) zone of France and extracted consent from Laval, Pétain's Prime Minister, to airlift and convoy troops to Tunisia. Italy meanwhile occupied Corsica. Confusion reigned among the French North Africa garrison, with some units welcoming the Allies, others seeking direction from Darlan and some obeying Pétain's original order to resist. The French Fleet at Toulon, which Darlan summoned to North Africa on 11 November (by which time he had made his ceasefire effective) was scuttled at its moorings.

The focus of action now transferred to Tunisia, where the Germans were building up a garrison and where the Allies were sending troops by air and sea from Algiers. The German forces were subjected to heavy aerial and artillery bombardment but the Allied overland advance on Tunis was halted by German counter-attack at Madjez-el Bab, outside the city, on 11 December. Elements of three German divisions had arrived from Italy, which were shortly to form the Fifth Panzer Army. To oppose them the Allies had two of their own and were supported by French units, led by Giraud, who assumed overall command after the assassination of Darlan by a dissident Frenchman on 24 December.

During January the fighting in eastern Tunisia was sporadic, although the Allied bombardment continued, and increasing pressure was exerted on Axis supply routes from Italy. But on 14 February, while Rommel was strengthening the defences of the Mareth Line (to which he had retreated from Egypt earlier that month), Fifth Panzer Army attacked the American II Corps between Faïd Pass and Gafsa and drove it back 50 miles. This offensive was not halted until 22 February. Eisenhower, who then had three divisions in line, counter-attacked on 26 February and by 3 March had regained his original positions.

Alexander had now arrived to act as Eisenhower's deputy in command of operations. He reorganised the Allied front to place the American II Corps opposite Bizerta, the British First Army opposite Tunis and the French XIX Corps to its south, with Montgomery's Eighth Army, which had broken the Mareth Line between 26 February and 31 March, in the south. On 4 May he unleashed a general offensive against the Axis forces and by concentric advances forced their total surrender on 13 May. Bizerta and Tunis, both held by German forces, surrendered on 7 May. The Italian First Army, remnants of Mussolini's garrison of Libya, was surrounded by Montgomery's Eighth Army and surrendered on 13 May. Some 125,000 Germans and 115,000 Italians became prisoners, including the German commander, Arnim (Rommel had been invalided on 9 March). The Axis presence in North Africa was at an end.

1 **Operation Torch, conceived to complete the destruction of Axis forces in North Africa, was a combined Allied operation of considerable complexity. The Allied Western Task Force, commanded by Patton, sailed directly from the US and landed on 8 Nov. at the Moroccan Atlantic coast ports of Safi, Casablanca and Port Lyautey. Light resistance by local French forces interfered neither with the landings nor the advance to Marrakech. Fighting ended on 11 Nov. Centre Task Force, commanded by Fredendall, entered the Mediterranean from British waters on 5–6 Nov., accompanied by Eastern Task Force. Fredendall's command landed around Oran on 8 Nov. A local force that entered Oran harbour was overcome and forced to surrender but the local French forces were beaten by 10 Nov. Eastern Task Force, commanded by Ryder, landed at Algiers on 8 Nov. Resistance was light and an armistice was negotiated on 10 Nov. Eastern Task Force at once set off across country to seize Tunis, 400 miles away. The British 1st and 3rd Parachute Brigades and American 509th Parachute Regiment were dropped ahead, near Bône and Tebessa, to seize airheads (12–16 Nov.) Dissatisfied by Vichy's actions, however, Hitler decided (10 Nov.) to invade the unoccupied zone of France, while launching the spearhead of the 10th and Hermann Göring Panzer and 334th Infantry Divisions into Tunis. Rommel was, meanwhile, working his way towards Tunisia from Egypt, surrounded by Montgomery's Eighth Army. Skirmishes between Allied and Axis forces began on 17 Nov. By 23 Nov. the two sides were in contact and the battle for Tunisia, which would last until 13 May, began.**

1 **the maghreb, 7 nov. 1942–1 apr. 1943**

Allied front lines:

- — — 30 Nov. 1942
- ········ 1 Jan. 1943
- –·–·– 14 Feb. 1943
- - - - - 22 Apr. 1943
- —— 31 Mar. 1943

http://www.worldwar2database.com/html/torch.htm
Operation Torch: the Allied landings in North Africa
www.diggerhistory.info/pages-enemy/vichy.htm
Vichy France and the Free French Forces

2 On 23 Feb. Rommel, now appointed as commander in Tunisia, began to withdraw, but then decided to attack Montgomery's Eighth Army, assembling outside the French fortified line of Mareth on 3 Mar. The attack failed and on 6 Mar. Rommel was invalided to Germany. While Patton mounted a diversionary attack at Gafsa, Montgomery went on to the offensive (20 Mar.). His main thrust was held by 15th Panzer Division, but a flanking movement by the New Zealanders (22 Mar.) turned the Mareth Line and forced its German-Italian defenders to retreat (31 Mar.). Montgomery renewed his offensive on 6 Apr. 4 and, assisted by Patton's attack at Maknassy, forced Messe's First Army to retreat (12 Apr.). The Allies then launched a series of concentric attacks on the Axis fortification around Tunis: Montgomery on 19 Apr., British First Army on 22 Apr. and Bradley's II Corps on 23 Apr. After regrouping, the attacks were resumed on 3 May and Bizerta fell to II Corps and Tunis to First Army on 7 May. On 13 May Messe's First Army surrendered to Montgomery.

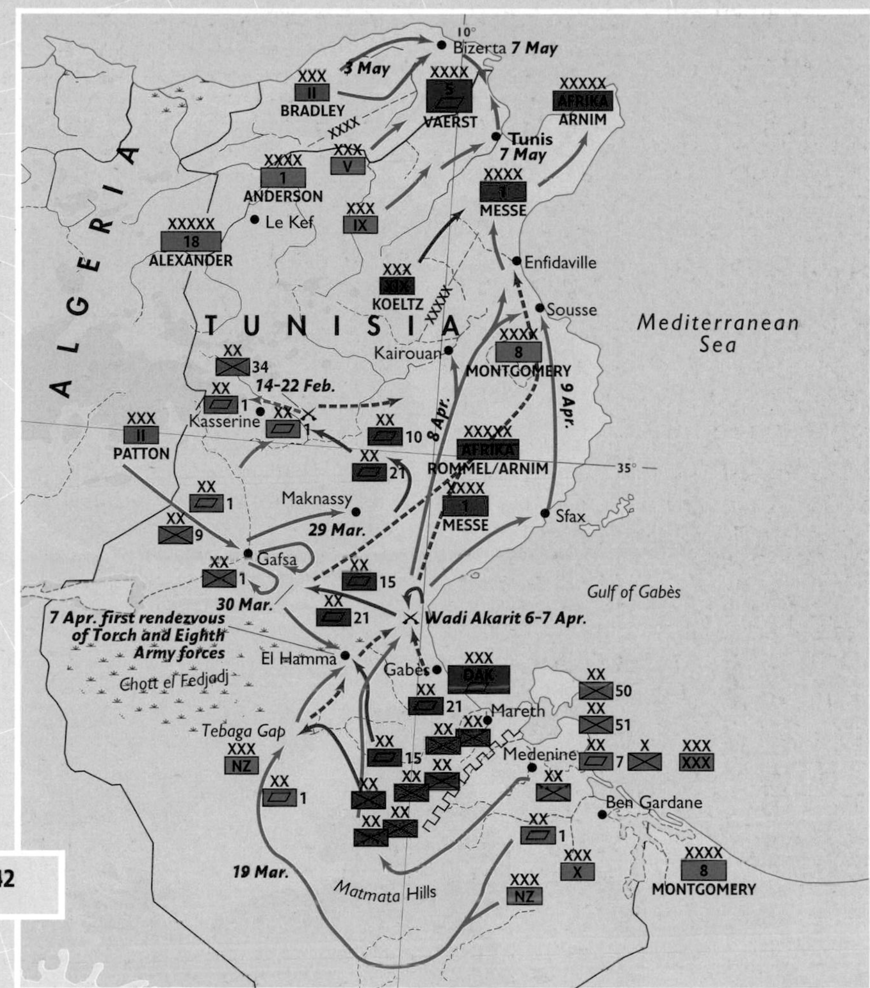

2 tunisia, 19 mar.–13 may 1942

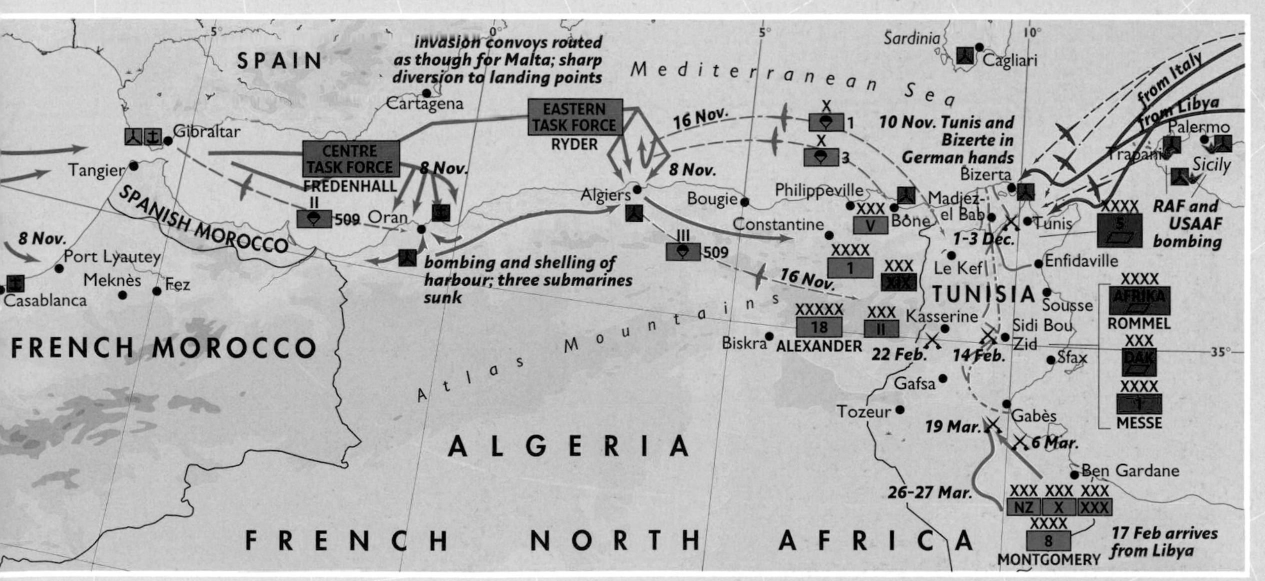

south west pacific

july to october 1942

- **12 July** Australians reach Kokoda
- **7 August** US Marines land on Guadalcanal
- **8 August** Battle of Savo Island; US Fleet defeated
- **21 August** Japanese driven back on Guadalcanal
- **23–24 August** sea battle east of Solomon Islands
- **26 August** Japanese land at Milne Bay
- **5 September** Australians force Japanese withdrawal from Milne Bay
- **11 September** Japanese halted in Owen Stanley Range
- **13 September** Japanese attack on Guadalcanal airfield heavily defeated
- **15 September** Japanese sink US aircraft carrier *Wasp*
- **11–12 October** Battle of Cape Esperance
- **14–17 October** Australians meet heavy resistance on the Kokoda Trail
- **26 October** Battle of Santa Cruz
- **2 November** Kokoda recaptured by Australians

In the spring of 1942 the Japanese planned operations throughout the South West and Central Pacific: following the Midway operation, the Japanese meant to proceed with the occupation of Port Moresby on New Guinea, New Caledonia, Fiji, Samoa and Johnston Island. The unexpected defeat at Midway cost the Imperial Navy the carrier force needed for the more distant of these operations, but did not lessen the Japanese determination to secure Port Moresby and to consolidate positions in the Solomons.

Assuming that no US counter-attack in the south-west Pacific could materialise before the second quarter of 1943, the Japanese sought to complete a network of bases in the area as soon as possible. For the Americans, victory at Midway provided the opportunity to dispute Japanese gains beyond Rabaul on New Britain. Determined not to allow the Japanese to recover from their defeat, the US High Command decided upon a step-by-step advance on Rabaul. In the south-west reaches of the Solomons, the Americans would seize Tulagi harbour and the airstrip that the Japanese were preparing on Guadalcanal; in eastern New Guinea, the Allies were to secure the Dobodura area by an overland advance to Gona and Buna. These two efforts were to begin in early and mid-August respectively.

Before the Allies had a chance to move in either theatre, however, Japanese forces were put ashore at Gona with the intention of advancing to Port Moresby along what was believed to be a motor track over the Owen Stanley Range. In reality, the Kokoda Trail was no more than a jungle track, the full length of which no white man had travelled in two decades. Neither the state of this trail nor the area's forbidding terrain and climate deterred the Japanese, who swept aside feeble Australian resistance around the beachhead, pressed rapidly inland and secured Kokoda on 27 July.

Thereafter the Japanese advance slowed as lack of numbers and supply problems took their toll; further, the second part of their effort – the seizure of Milne Bay at the south-east tip of New Guinea – miscarried on 25 August. Nevertheless, by 16 September the Japanese had fought their way from Kokoda to within 25 miles of Port Moresby, but exhaustion and the need to deal with the situation that had developed on Guadalcanal led the Japanese to halt operations on the Kokoda Trail and to settle for the consolidation of the Gona beachhead until the position in the Solomons was resolved. In the face of the threat posed by a massively reinforced garrison, however, the Japanese had to begin to withdraw along the Kokoda Trail on the 24th, and thereafter the Allies developed an outflanking attack and began to airlift forces to the Wanigela-Pongani area – directly threatening the Japanese beachhead around Buna and Gona.

In the Solomons, the Americans secured Tulagi harbour in the face of desperate resistance and had occupied Lunga airstrip – renamed Henderson Field – on 7–8 August. The Japanese response was immediate: a cruiser force hurried south from Rabaul, and inflicted a crushing defeat upon the Allied covering force off Savo Island on the night of 8/9 August. However, the Japanese failed to follow up this victory with an attack on the US transports in Tulgai harbour, and without the ground forces to dispute US control of Lunga, the Japanese were unable to prevent the Americans completing Henderson Field and bringing it into service on the 21st.

1 south-west pacific, 21 july–29 oct. 1942

www.history.navy.mil/photos/events/wwii-pac/guadlcnl/guadlcnl.htm
Guadalcanal overview with a selection of images
www.ibiblio.org/hyperwar/USN/USN-CN-SantaCruz/
The Battle of Santa Cruz, 25–27 October 1943

American possession of Henderson Field proved decisive in settling the Guadalcanal in the Allies' favour. With no large air bases in the northern and central Solomons, Japanese land-based aircraft could operate over Guadalcanal only at extreme range from Rabaul. Unless American air power could be neutralised, both landing troops on Guadalcanal and the naval bombardment of US positions there were fraught with hazards. Further, from the outset the Japanese had no clear idea of the size of the US forces on the island and the usual lack of coordination between the Imperial Army and the Japanese Navy fatally undermined Japanese plans. After the Savo Island action, battle was joined in a piecemeal manner, the Japanese gradually increasing their commitment but always at a pace behind the American build-up. In addition to control of Henderson Field, the support provided by the US carrier force operating to the south of Guadalcanal (despite the loss of the carrier *Wasp* on 15 September), provided the Americans with a power over and around the island that the Japanese could not overcome, even on the two occasions when they committed the fleet to the campaign. At the battle of the Eastern Solomons (23–25 August) two carrier forces fought a cautious and inconclusive action. At the Battle of Santa Cruz (25–27 October) the losses sustained by their air groups left the Japanese unable to exploit the tactical advantage that they gained by sinking the *Hornet* and damaging the *Enterprise*. Thereafter, with both Japanese and US carrier forces neutralised, the adversaries were compelled to commit their capital ships to the waters of Guadalcanal as the struggle entered a more urgent phase.

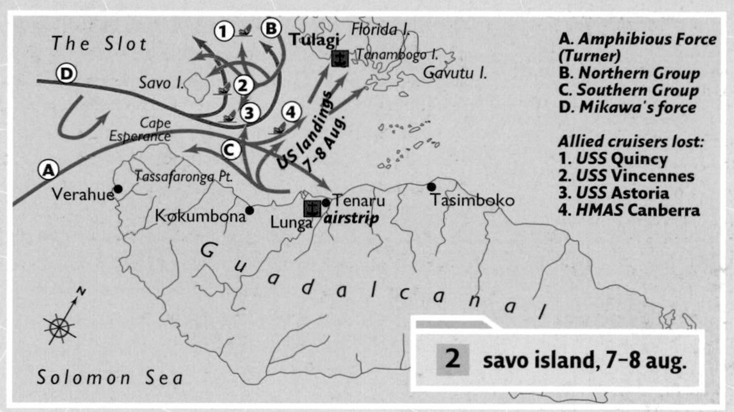

2 savo island, 7–8 aug.

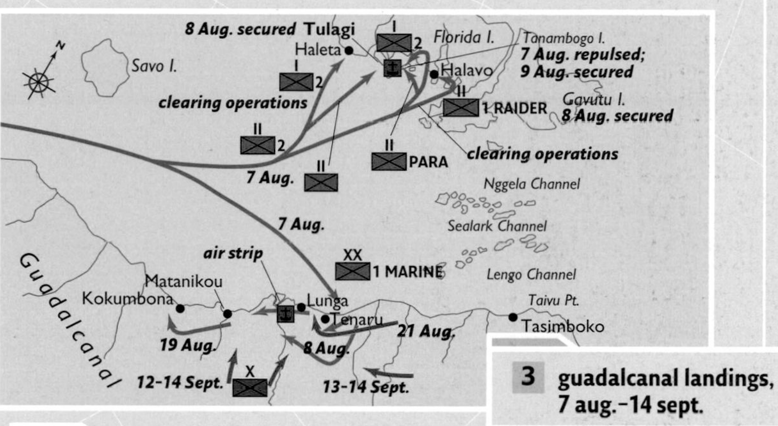

3 guadalcanal landings, 7 aug.–14 sept.

4 guadalcanal, 23–26 oct.

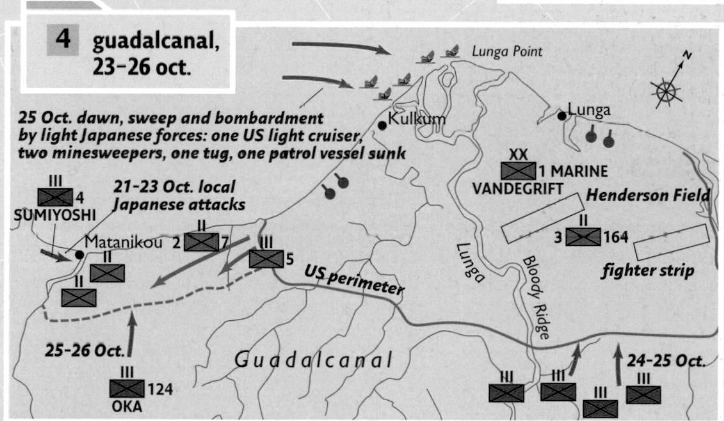

1 Before their victories at the Coral Sea and Midway, the Allies failed to strengthen effectively their forces in New Guinea; the Japanese, however, were keen to establish bases there, to extend their control. But the reinforcement of Port Moresby after July 1942 and the occupation of Milne Bay provided the Australians with the means to retain eastern New Guinea in the face of a Japanese attack following landings at Gona and Buna. The Japanese attempt to secure Milne Bay represented the high water mark of the Japanese effort in eastern New Guinea; thereafter the Allied advantage in numbers and ability to move forces by sea and air proved decisive in ensuring the Japanese defeat throughout the theatre. With Allied forces also advancing overland to the Solomon Sea, the Japanese position in eastern New Guinea was beyond recall, though November came with Japanese forces still occupying Kokoda.

Eastern Solomons 23–25 Aug. Japanese attempt to reinforce Guadalcanal: small carrier Ryujo *and destroyers* Jintou *and* Kinsyu Matsu *sunk, USS carier* Enterprise *damaged*

Santa Cruz 25–27 Oct. USS carrier Hornet *and destroyer* Porter *sunk; two Japanese carriers, two battleships, and three cruisers damaged; over 100 aircraft destroyed*

from New Caledonia, Efaté and Espiritu Santo, 7–8 Aug (Operation Watchtower)

Tulagi Malaita Tenaru Guadalcanal San Cristobal Santa Cruz Is Rennell 1 MARINE

2-4 The first Japanese landing on Guadalcanal, after the US invasion and resultant battle of Savo Island (*maps 2 and 3*), was on 18 Aug. when some 2,000 men were put ashore at Taivu Point. This force attempted to rush the Lunga position and was destroyed around Tenaru in the early hours of the 21st. The Japanese failure in the battle of the Eastern Solomons resulted in the force bringing troops to Guadalcanal being badly mauled by aircraft from Henderson Field on the 25 Aug., but over the next ten days some 4,700 troops were put ashore around Kokumbona and Tasimboko under cover of darkness. Problems of movement through dense jungle and of trying to coordinate various attacks ensured that the first major attempt to overrun Henderson Field collapsed in a series of costly defeats, most notably on Bloody Ridge (12–14 Sept.) (*map 4*). A further effort on 4 Oct., made in greater strength, also failed.

south west pacific

november 1942 to february 1943

- **1942 (30 November)** naval Battle of Tassafaronga
- **1943 (2 January)** Allies capture Buna, New Guinea
- **15 January** US offensive on Guadalcanal
- **22 January** end of fighting in New Guinea
- **1-19 February** Japanese 17th Army evacuated from Guadalcanal

October 1942 saw the Allies come within measurable distance of defeat in the struggle for control of the South West Pacific. The Japanese had almost reached Port Moresby, and even now their beachheads at Gona and Buna in eastern New Guinea were still strong although under increasing pressure. In the Solomons Japanese air attacks also led to the partial neutralisation of the newly completed American air base at Henderson Field on Guadalcanal Island. November, however, saw the Japanese defeated decisively both on Gaudalcanal and in eastern New Guinea, though both campaigns were to continue well into 1943.

Their inability to continue air attacks on Henderson Field thoughout October, and then either to secure the airfield or to defeat the US naval force off Santa Cruz, left the Japanese with no alternative, if they were to continue the battle, but to persist in their attempt to reinforce and resupply their formations on Guadalcanal, despite enemy air superiority. A series of convoys (nicknamed the 'Tokyo Express') down the Slot (a relatively narrow sea lane running through the Solomon Islands) produced a Japanese numerical superiority on Guadalcanal for the first time on 12 November, but in an attempt to ensure a potentially decisive reinforcement of their garrison, the Japanese decided upon a major convoy in mid-November, involving 11 fast transports and some 10,000 troops, after surface forces had pounded Henderson Field into passivity. This operation coincided, however, with American command changes in the South Pacific Area: as a result of these, the reinforcement of both Guadalcanal and the theatre in general were decided upon, when the US High Command identified winning the campaign in the Solomons as of sufficient priority to justify the transfer of naval forces from the Atlantic. However, this American resolve was tempered after the Battle of Santa Cruz by a refusal to risk a carrier north of or in the Solomons; thus the American reinforcement of the garrison on Guadalcanal on 12 November, in the face of heavy but ineffective air attack, was covered rather than supported by a task group, with the *Enterprise* and two battleships stationed well to the south of the island.

This situation resulted in a series of naval actions between 12 and 16 November, which effectively decided the outcome of the Guadalcanal campaign; at the same time Allied forces began to close around the Japanese beachheads at Gona in Eastern New Guinea. Two ferocious night actions off the north coast of Guadalcanal in Ironbottom Sound (12–13 and 14–15 November), the mauling of a Japanese bombardment force as it withdrew on 14 November and the annihilation of the transport convoy on 14–15 November as it tried to fight its way to Guadalcanal, resulted in the Japanese loss of two battleships, one heavy cruiser, four destroyers and ten transports; only 2,000 Japanese troops – and virtually no equipment and supplies – reached Guadalcanal on 16 November. Though the Japanese garrison was able to withstand the first major American offensive on the island in mid-November and a Japanese naval task group scored a notable tactical success off Tassafaronga (30 November) when it outfought a superior American formation, the Imperial Navy recognised that its mid-November losses were prohibitive. Concerned as it was with the preservation of its strength in readiness for 'the decisive battle', the Imperial Navy on 12 December proposed that the Guadalcanal campaign be abandoned. This was agreed by Imperial General Headquarters on 31 December.

1 **In New Guinea, the Japanese withdrawal along the Kokoda Trail quickly degenerated into a precipitate flight. By 30 Nov. the Japanese were confined to beachheads under a mile deep at Gona and Buna. The Gona beachhead was eliminated on 9 Dec., but the remaining Japanese positions, sited behind extensive swamps, were invulnerable to available artillery and could only be attacked by infantry. Disease and battle casualties reduced the Allied force considerably by the time Buna was secured (1 Jan.), and the area finally cleared (22 Jan.).**

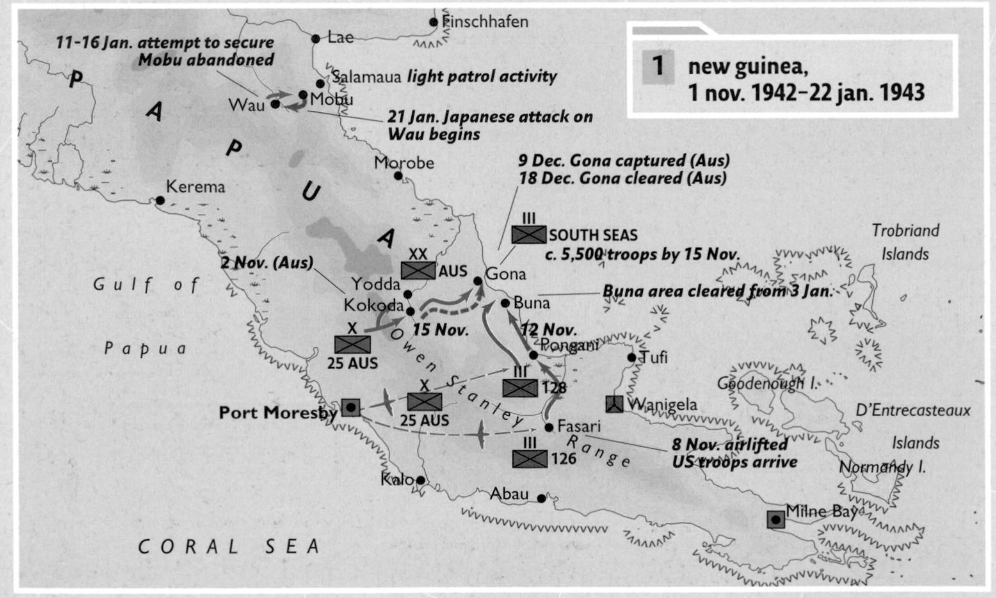

5-6 **In December, fresh US forces on Guadalcanal began a concerted push to clear the island: following steady American success the Japanese withdrew their garrison in early February, and converging US forces met around Tenaro (9 Feb.); the Guadalcanal campaign was over.**

www.combinedfleet.com/guadal.htm
The Guadalcanal naval battles
www.army.mil/cmh-pg/books/wwii/GuadC/GC-fm.htm
A further overview of the Guadalcanal camapign

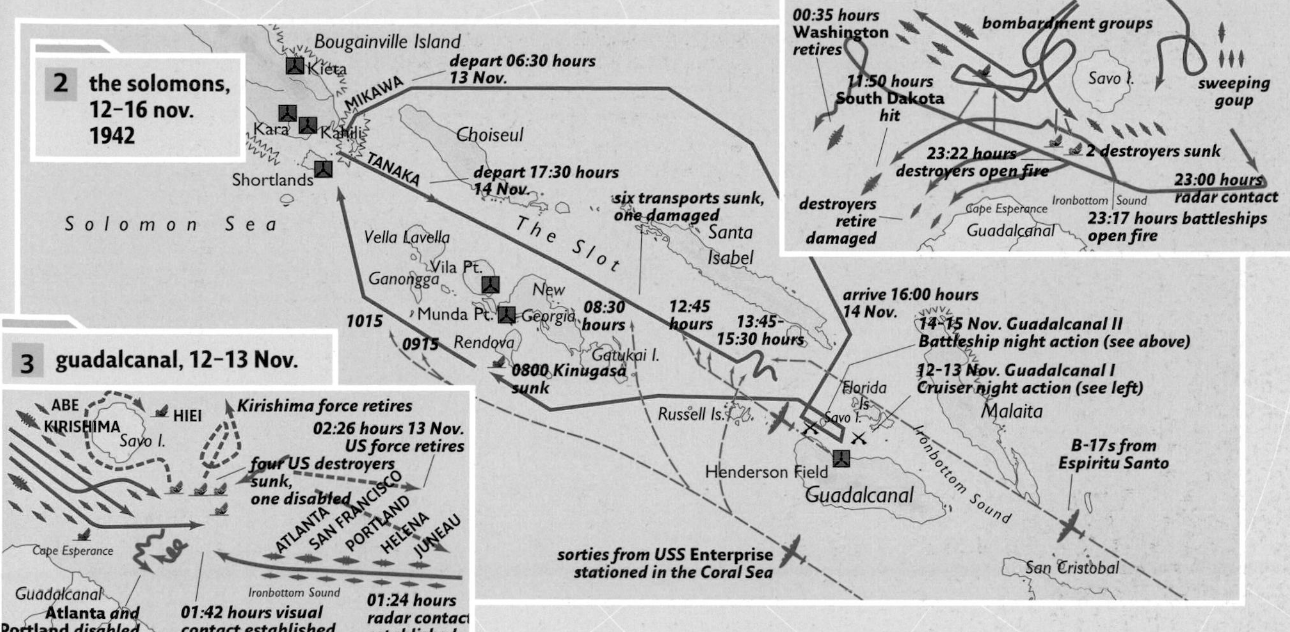

This decision came at a time when the Americans had replaced their forces on Guadalcanal with fresh troops, and the battles around Gona in New Guinea had clearly entered their final phase. Here the Allies had applied persistent pressure on the Japanese beachheads, the Australians pressing forward from the Kokoda Trail to Gona, while increasing numbers of American troops were airlifted from Port Moresby to the area south of Buna. Japanese resistance was bitter, but without any prospect of reinforcing or resupplying their forces around Gona, the Japanese abandoned their beachheads to their fate while concentrating their resources for the clearing of Australian forces further north, behind Lae and Salamaua.

The forces on Guadalcanal, however, could not be similarly written off, and under the cover of preparations to reinforce their garrison, the Japanese completed the evacuation of 10,652 troops from Guadalcanal on three nights between 2/3 and 7/8 February without the Americans being aware of what was afoot. This achievement, during which only one Japanese destroyer was lost, did not alter the fact that Guadalcanal had been lost at the cost of some 20,000 troops, 860 aircraft and 15 warships; with the concurrent collapse of resistance around Gona and the failure of a Japanese attempt to secure a forward position further north at Wau the truth became apparent. The failure of both the Guadalcanal and the eastern New Guinea campaigns revealed that the defensive perimeter that Japan had cast around her conquests could not be maintained. Further, while the Americans could not prevent the Japanese evacuation of Guadalcanal, they moved immediately to secure the nearby Russell Islands, thereby serving notice of their intention to continue the campaign – and to inflict further defeats on the Japanese – in the Solomons.

2–4 The Japanese attempt to win the Guadalcanal campaign reached a turning point by mid-November 1942. Two crucial naval actions were fought in Ironbottom Sound, both at night. The first was fought on 12–13 Nov. at ranges at which torpedoes would not arm: one Japanese battleship and one destroyer, and one US cruiser and four destroyers, were sunk or left sinking. Two nights later, after the Americans committed two battleships to the defence of the Henderson Field lodgement, a further Japanese battleship and single destroyer were sunk at the cost of two US destroyers; here the ranges were so close that large guns could not be lowered sufficiently to engage. Thereafter, the Japanese attempt to sail a convoy to Guadalcanal faltered when it was attacked by US aircraft from USS *Enterprise*, Henderson Field and Espiritu Santo; after turning back late on 14 Dec., four surviving transports were beached and later destroyed on Cape Esperance.

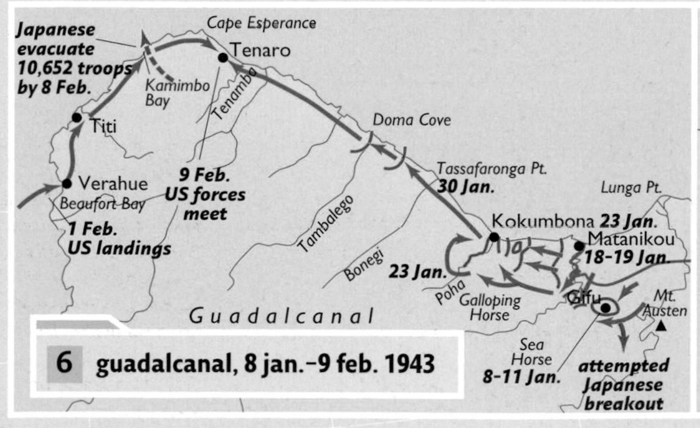

south west pacific

february 1943 to april 1944

- **1943 (2–5 March)** Battle of Bismarck Sea destruction of Japanese troop convoy to New Guinea
- **18 April** Admiral Yamamoto shot down and killed by US fighters
- **21 April** Admiral Koga commands Japanese combined fleet
- **30 June** amphibious Operation Cartwheel against Japanese on Rabaul; landings on New Guinea
- **12–13 July** sea battle of Kolombangara; Japanese defeated
- **2 October** Australians take Finschhafen
- **26 April** Australians take Alexishafen

1943 proved to be a year of consolidation in the Pacific as both the Americans and Japanese alike sought to strengthen their forces and positions in readiness for the battles that lay ahead. Notwithstanding their defeat in the campaign for Guadalcanal, the Japanese could draw comfort from the fact that securing the island had cost the United States six months, sustained effort and that after 14 months of war the Americans still remained thousands of miles from the Southern Resources Area.

In the event, however, the Japanese attempt to consolidate their holdings in the South West Pacific in the course of 1943 was flawed on three counts: first, their shipyards could not match the output of American yards that in this year alone put into service a warship tonnage equivalent to that of the total Imperial Navy at the outbreak of war; second, the air losses sustained over Guadalcanal could not be made good by Japanese naval air service and aircrew – the Americans could do both; third, the Guadalcanal campaign saw the strategic initiative pass to the Americans.

The underlying weakness of Japanese strategic policy was that without the means to defeat the Americans in the air and at sea, any Japanese island garrison could be either subjected to overwhelming attack, piecemeal reduction or simply bypassed by an enemy with the choice of when, where and in what strength to mount operations. The Americans developed a parallel strategy – a drive across the small islands of the Central Pacific and a concerted drive to advance in the Solomons and New Guinea (Operation Cartwheel).

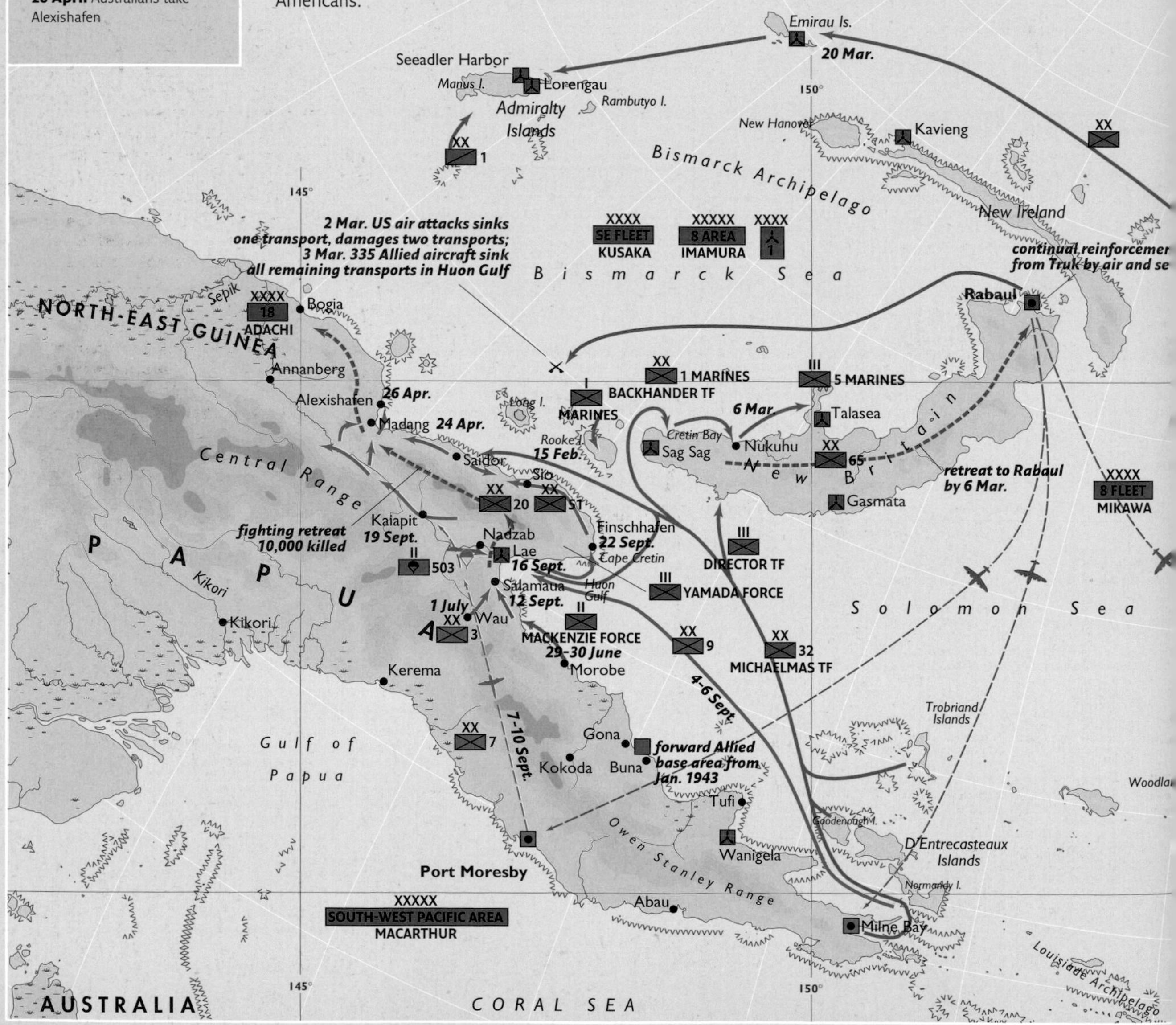

http://en.wikipedia.org/wiki/Operation_Cartwheel
Operation Cartwheel
www.diggerhistory.info/pages-battles/ww2/gona-buna-san.htm
The Australian campaigns at Buna, Gona and Sananda

The American occupation of the Russell Islands within two weeks of the end of the Guadalcanal campaign made clear their determination to carry the war into the central and northern Solomons; but even as the Americans adopted the island-hopping technique for the first time, with the landings on Vella Lavella and the bypassing of Japanese garrisons on New Georgia and Kolombangara, so American policy was in the process of change. Rather than aiming to recover Rabaul, the Americans decided to isolate and bypass what should have been the keystone of the Japanese defence in the area. Despite this decision, the neutralisation of Japanese garrisons in the northern Solomons would be a long and bloody struggle.

On the other side of the Solomon Sea, a complementary effort began after the annihilation of a Japanese reinforcement convoy in the Battle of the Bismarck Sea (2–4 March). After this the Japanese never attempted to reinforce their garrisons in eastern New Guinea. The slow but progressive reduction of Japanese positions around Huon Gulf continued throughout the year, though the main focus of US strategy attention remained the Solomons. It was primarily in the Solomons in April that the Japanese made their last offensive effort of the war (Operation I-Go), and it was in order to counter American moves into the northern Solomons that Rabaul was reinforced in October by carrier air groups and cruisers detached from the fleet at Truk. Both were to be savaged in raids on 5 and 11 November by US carrier formations. These were so successful that the Japanese fleet was thereafter left unable to meet the American moves into the Gilberts and around Rabaul. The isolation of the latter remained to be completed, but after November 1943 Rabaul's effectiveness was at an end – though it remained in Japanese hands until the general capitulation on 6 September 1945.

1 **The elimination of the Gona beachhead in January and the destruction of a reinforcement convoy bound for Lae in March, confirmed the Allied possession of the initiative in the South West Pacific theatre. Despite clearing operations in the Woodlark and Trobriand Is. it was not until September that Allied forces effected amphibious landings in Huon Gulf (4 Sept.) and one of the very few airborne operations of the Pacific war at Nadzab (6 Sept.) which brought the Allies control of Salamaua (12 Sept.) and Lae (16 Sept.), however, Japanese forces on the Gulf were able to avoid encirclement and fought for the Markham Valley. The Japanese were unable to prevent Allied landings on Cape Cretin, however, and at Finschhafen the Australians routed the numerically-superior Japanese – unique in the Pacific war. Thereafter, and with the start of the US offensive in the Central Pacific, the Allies moved against western New Britain to begin to isolate Rabaul, though 1943 ended with Allied forces in New Guinea still checked around Nadzab and Saidor.**

Operation Cartwheel was intended both to give the Japanese no respite after their defeat on Guadalcanal and to coordinate the southern flank of a broad US advance into the western Pacific. The Japanese made no attempt to dispute the US occupation of the Russell Islands as they set about strengthening their garrisons and positions in the New Georgia group, but over the next four months battle was joined in the air as both sides sought to secure superiority over the central Solomons. Though the Japanese committed carrier air groups to Rabaul in April in an attempt to halt or slow the US build-up in the southern Solomons, the Japanese decisively lost this struggle. Even Operation I-Go amounted to only four raids, none by more than 200 aircraft, against different targets. Having secured air superiority, the Americans moved against New Georgia and Rendova (30 June) but, despite subsidiary landings, the chaotic conduct of this enterprise prevented the capture of Munda Point airfield until 5 Aug. On the 15 Aug. US forces landed on Vella Lavella. The clearing of the island was left to the New Zealanders after mid-September. These various landings were punctuated by a series of naval clashes between light forces. The landings in the Treasury Islands (October) and Empress Augusta Bay on Bougainville (1 Nov.) brought the Allies within fighter range of Rabaul. Also, by landing on a difficult coast and opposite a swamp the Americans gained total strategic surprise; by the time Japanese forces on Bougainville came against the beachhead, the swamp had been drained, an airfield was operational and a secure perimeter established. Beaten in battles on these defences, Japanese forces remained on Bougainville until the end of the war, and were then hunted by tracking animals: but for practical purposes the island was in Allied hands. Meanwhile, US forces swept round New Ireland to the Admiralty Islands, thereby completing the isolation of Rabaul.

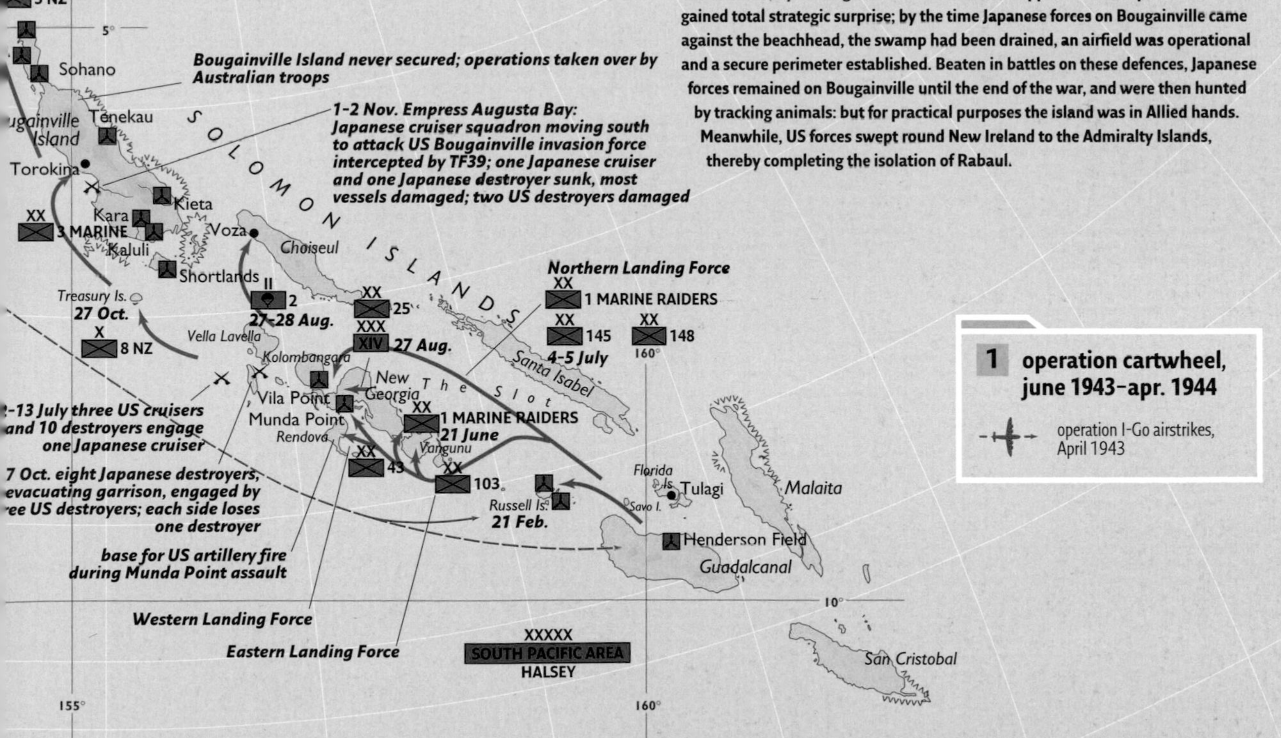

kursk

july to august 1943

- **5 July** Operation Zitadelle, the last German offensive at Kursk
- **12 July** Soviet counter-offensive begins on northern axis; largest tank battle in history
- **13 July** Hitler cancels Zitadelle
- **5 August** Red Army captures Orel and Bielgorod
- **18 August** Briansk recaptured

Soviet successes in early 1943 and German counter-attacks had left a great bulge or salient round Kursk between Orel and Kharkov. Hitler had once postponed Operation Zitadelle, as the plan to pinch out the Kursk salient was known, and had considered a proposal by OKW to build up a strong reserve instead, but on 18 June he decided to proceed: Zitadelle would demonstrate German strength, with 900,000 men 2,700 tanks and assault guns and 1,800 aircraft massed for the attack - although this was achieved by concentrating 70 per cent of German tanks and 65 per cent of the aircraft from the entire Eastern Front.

Kursk would also demonstrate the pros and cons of new German technology. Since the Battle of Moscow, where they encountered the powerful new T-34, the Germans had tried to develop a comparable tank. The answer was the Panther, which first appeared in May 1943. It had a 75mm gun and 70mm of frontal armour, but was beset by teething troubles. The Germans also used the heavy Tiger tank, with an 88mm gun and up to 100mm of armour, and the Ferdinand assault gun based on the Tiger chassis. The Red Army, meanwhile, had upgunned the T-34 from 76mm to 85mm.

Although often thought of as a tank battle, Kursk as a whole arguably demonstrated the triumph of artillery, infantry and engineers over armour. The Soviet plan was to soak up the German assault in a colossal web of defensive positions, and only then launch their armoured counter-attack. It was also an important air battle, in which the balance now shifted in the favour of the Soviets.

The Soviet *Lucy* spy ring gave Stalin the approximate time of the German attack - between 3 and 6 July. The Soviets were waiting. Battlefield intelligence on 4 July fixed H-Hour at 0:200 hours, European time, on 5 July. Soviet artillery fired the biggest 'counter-preparation' - smashing enemy forces as they prepared to attack - in the history of war. Six hundred guns and mortars in the Sixth and Seventh Guards Army areas (on the left of the planned breakthrough to the south) opened fire on the evening of 4 July, and each front (Rokossovsky's Centre and Vatutin's Voronezh) fired once more during the night.

2 prokhorovka, 12 july 1943

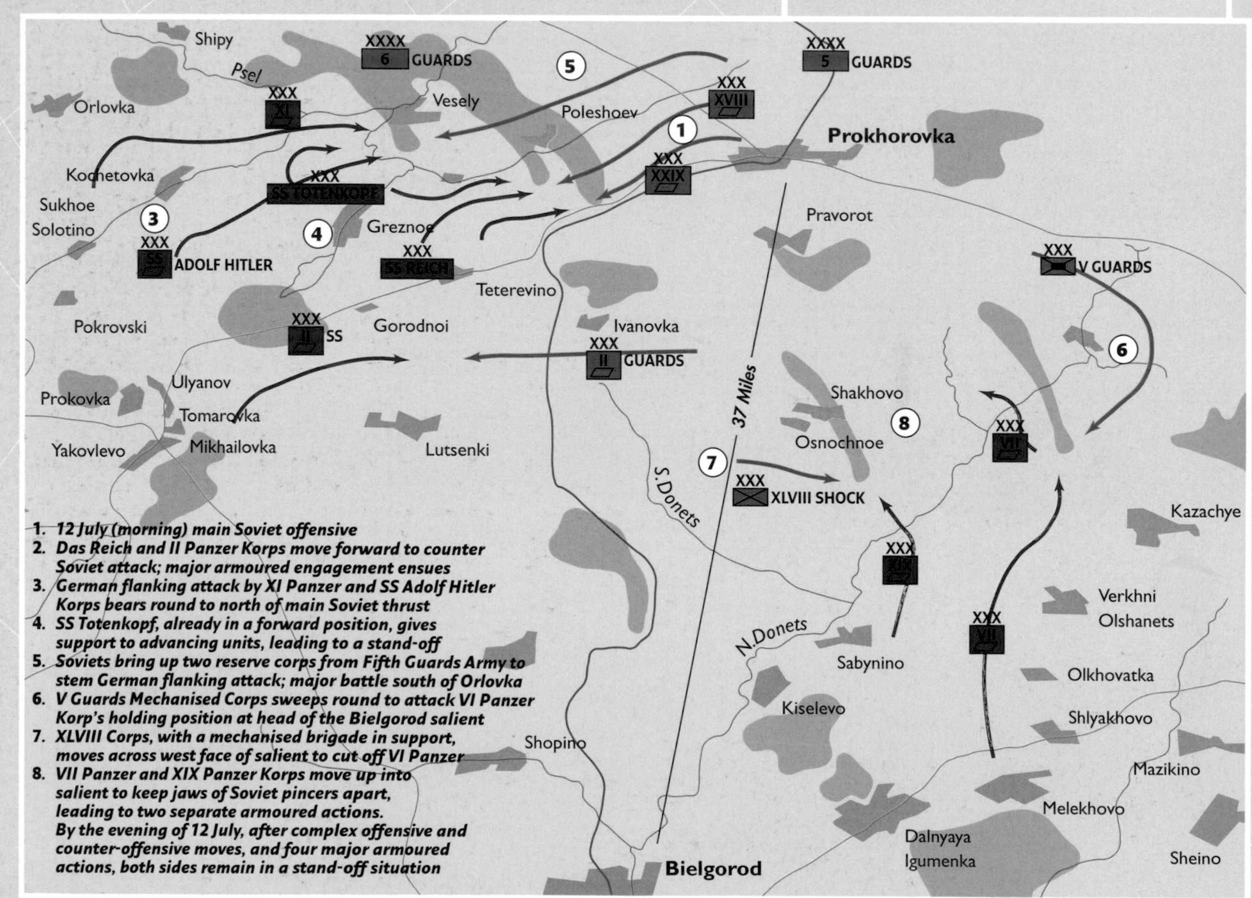

http://zhukov.mitsi.com/Kursk.htm
The Battle of Kursk
http://en.wikipedia.org/wiki/T-34_tank
The history of the Soviet T-34 tank

At 05:00 hours Hoth's Fourth Panzer Army, already shaken, attacked in the south in a wedge formation: motorised infantry at the base, Panthers and Mk IV tanks on the flanks, heavy Tigers and Ferdinands at the front. They drove into a merciless arc of fire, a 'ring of flame'. Many of the Panthers broke down. The heavy Ferdinands and Tigers ploughed on, only to be met by 'Pakfronts'– batteries of anti-tank guns all of which engaged one tank at a time in strict coordination. By 10 July the attack in the south had stalled, having covered barely 20 miles.

In the north, where Model's Ninth Army attacked at 05:30 hours, the Soviet Thirteenth Army put up fierce resistance, especially in the area of Ponyri (7–8 July) and by 10 July the Germans had only penetrated eight miles.

Only now that the assault was blunted were Soviet tank armies committed. In the south, Hoth's Fourth Panzer Army was used in a final bid to smash the Soviet defences by striking near Prokhorovka. They collided with Rotmistrov's Fifth Guards Tank Army, in the largest tank battle of the war so far. The hot, dry weather had ended on 7 July and Prokhorovka was fought in rain under a sky piled high with thunderclouds. Guderian recalled that he had never received 'such an overwhelming impression of Soviet strength and numbers as on that day'. Soon, T-34s were streaming 'like rats' over the battlefield. In this engagement alone the Germans lost 400 tanks and 10,000 men: Soviet casualties were greater, but they could afford them. At the end of this stage of the Battle of Kursk, the Soviet defensive phase, the Soviets claim to have killed 70,000 and destroyed nearly 3,000 tanks. The Germans claim to have destroyed or crippled 1,800 Soviet tanks on the south face alone. After Prokhorovka, Soviet tank strength was half what it had been eight days before.

The Soviet counter-attack had begun on 12 July, by which time the recent Allied invasion of Sicily had forced Hitler to abandon Operation Zitadelle. By 2 August the Red Army had recovered the ground lost in the German assault. On 3 August the full counter-offensive, the Bielgorod–Kharkov operation, which forms part of the Battle of Kursk, began. The counter-offensive was launched after massive artillery and air preparation. Bielgorod was liberated on 6 August and Kharkov on 23 August. The operation was launched in concert with partisan forces behind the German line. On the night of 2/3 August alone they fired over 600 demolitions. Whereas destruction of German communications before the counter-offensive might have made the Germans fight harder by impeding withdrawal, this hit them when they were most vulnerable – in flight. The Soviet use of partisans in close coordination with main forces in this way was more effective than the Western Allies' use of resistance movements.

Kursk marked the end of major German initiatives in the east. From now on, Germany and her allies would be on the defensive here, as everywhere else. At the end of the counter-offensive on 27 August, the Soviets were poised to move into Ukraine.

1-2 **The Red Army built defensive works in the Kursk salient and to the east to a total depth of 150–200 miles. On the Centre and Voronezh fronts there were 5–6 successive defence 'belts': two in the 'tactical' (division) zone that formed the first 10-12 miles, one in the army rear area and three in the front rear areas. Behind this was a defensive perimeter of the Steppe Military District (later Front) and finally a national defence zone on the east bank of the Don. Most of the Engineer effort (field fortifications, mines) was in the tactical zone. East belt comprised 2–3 positions, each about a mile deep. Each position in turn comprised 2–3 lines of trenches linked by communication trenches. Anti-tank defences were deployed to a depth of over 20 miles. The German plan envisaged Model's Ninth Army comprising XX and XXIII Corps, XLI, XLVI and XLVII Panzer Corps striking from the north. Hoth's Fourth Panzer Army, comprising LII Corps, XLVIII Panzer Corps and II SS Panzer Corps together with Armee-Abteilung Kempf, comprising III Panzer Corps, Corps Raus and XLII Corps, would assault from the south. But these assaults barely penetrated the Soviet 'tactical zone' (the first two defensive belts), before reaching the limit of their advance at Prokhorovka and Ponyri. At Prokhorovka, the Germans began their drive on 11 July. By dawn on 12 July they threatened to close on Prokhorovka and Rotmistrov's Fifth Guards Tank Army was ordered to prevent this. Rotmistrov had about 900 tanks; the Germans 600 tanks west of Prokhorovka and 300 to the south. There was thus rough parity, except that the Germans fielded about 100 Tigers. Over 1,000 tanks actually clashed. By nightfall on 12 July the Germans had lost over 300 tanks, but fighting continued far into the night and resumed the next day. This marked the beginning of the Soviet counter-attack, which, with the commencement of the Bielgorod–Kharkov operation on 3 Aug. became a full counter-offensive.**

ukraine

august to december 1943

- **5 August** Soviets capture Orel and Bielgorod
- **26 August** Soviet Four Front offensive in the Ukraine begins
- **22 September** Soviets take Poltava and cross the Dnieper
- **25 September** Soviets capture Smolensk
- **1 November** Soviets cut land routes to the Germans in the Crimea
- **3 November** operations against German-held Kiev begin

The battle of the River Dnieper is one of the historic great battles of the Soviet War. It was fought on an immense scale. Soviet forces comprised five fronts: Centre (Rokossovsky), Voronezh (Vatutin), Steppe (Koniev), South West (Malinovsky) and South (from 21 September, Tolbukhin). On 20 October these were renamed the Belarussian and First to Fourth Ukrainian Fronts respectively.

The Soviet grouping comprised 2,633,000 men, over 51,000 guns and mortars, 2,400 tanks and assault guns and 2,850 combat aircraft. German forces comprised Second Army from Army Group Centre (Kluge), Fourth Panzer, Eighth, First and Sixth Armies from Army Group South (Manstein): in all, 1,240,000 men, 12,600 guns and mortars, 2,100 tanks and assault guns and 2,100 combat aircraft. The Soviets, therefore, had about four times as much artillery as the enemy and twice as many men, but not much more armour or air power.

Soviet planning for the Dnieper battle began as the Battle of Kursk unfolded. The aim of the first phase was the liberation of 'Left Bank Ukraine' (east of the Dnieper), the industrial area of the Donbass, and Kiev. Several component operations, whose most distinctive feature was the need for assault river crossings, would take place along a front over 400 miles long. The second phase would see the Soviets establishing strategic bridgeheads on the west bank of the Dnieper and the recapture of Kiev. German forces withdrawing towards the Dnieper after the Soviet capture of Kharkov believed that the river line, though unfortified, would be enough of an obstacle to allow them to stabilise their eastern front for some time.

In the Ukraine, the right wing of the Steppe Front began its attack towards Krasnograd on 13 August, and on 16 August attacked from a bridgehead on the Northern Donets, as part of the Donbass offensive operation (13 August-22 September). The South West Front and Seventeenth Air Army, Southern Front and Eighth Air Army launched attacks against German Army Group South and Luftflotte 4: by 22 September they had reached the Dnieper south of Dnepropetrovsk. To the north, Centre Front forces attacked on 26 August. Sixtieth Army enjoyed the greatest success, creating a breakthrough south of Sevsk: by 31 August it was 60 miles wide and nearly 50 miles deep.

1 **The battle of the Dnieper took place on a huge front between the Sea of Azov in the south, and the vast Pripet Marshes in the north. Operations began (13 Aug.) in the southern sector with the Donbass operation, while the battle of Kursk was still underway. Operations to the north began at the end of August.**

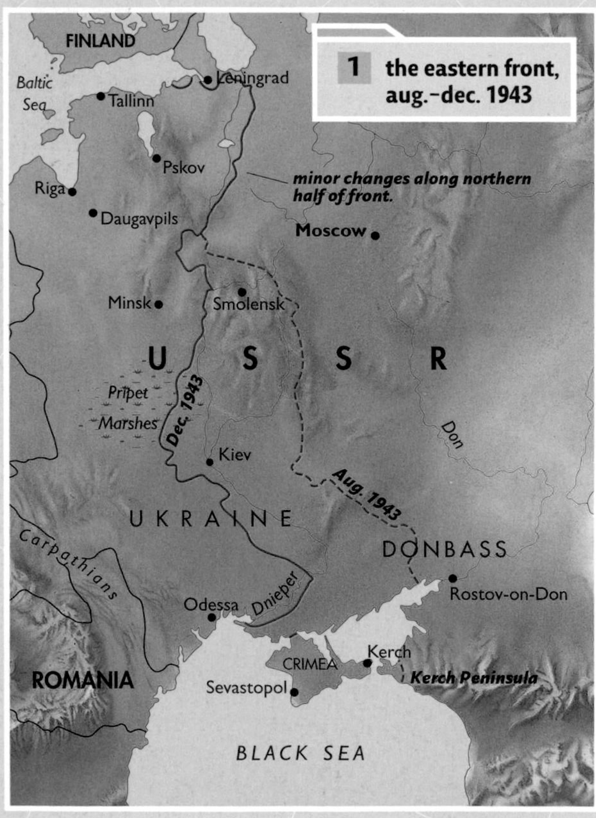

2 **Hitler opposed plans to shorten Kluge's Centre Army Group's front and withdraw it to the Dnieper line (14 Sept.), but agreed to von Manstein's Army Group South's withdrawal to the line of Melitopol and the R. Dnieper, and its reinforcement with four of Army Group Centre's divisions. The withdrawal was probably the most difficult operation performed by Army Group South during the 1943–44 campaign, according to von Manstein, 'in the face of unremitting pressure from a far superior opponent'. From a 440-mile-wide front, three armies had to converge on a maximum of five Dnieper crossing points. Once across, they had to fan out again on an equally wide front without letting the Soviets get a foothold. It was successfully completed by 30 Sept.**

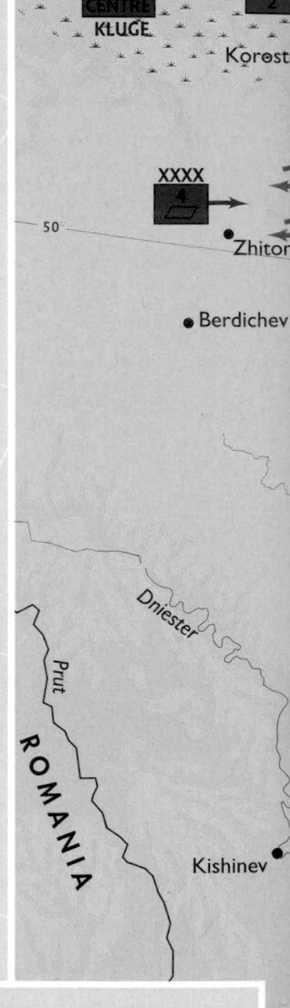

2 ukraine, aug.-dec. 1943

German counter-attack
front line, mid-Aug.
front line, mid-Sept.
front line, end Sept.
front line, end Dec.

www.infoukes.com/history/ww2/
The Ukraine during World War Two
www.joric.com/Conspiracy/Kluge.htm
Field Marshal Guenther von Kluge, Commander German Centre Army Group

At the beginning of September, Front commanders were ordered to seize bridgeheads by attacking straight from the line of march. By this time, Centre and Voronezh Fronts were driving for Kiev, Steppe Front for Poltava and Kremenchug, and South West Front for Dnepropetrovsk. During the second half of September Centre Front advanced westward towards the river north of Kiev, Voronezh Front south of it. Voronezh Front deployed a mobile group (a classic Soviet device to keep the enemy off balance); racing ahead of the slower main forces on a 45-mile front, this reached the Dnieper on the night of 21/22 September. On the next day, forward units established small bridgeheads at Rzhishchev and Veliki Bukrin. During the night of 24/25 September the Soviets tried an airborne assault to expand the bridgeheads, but with disastrous results. While the survivors fought behind German lines, main forces approached the river on a front of nearly 500 miles between 22 and 30 September.

The second phase of the great battle, from October to December, revolved around the 23 bridgeheads now established across the Dnieper. On 12 October Voronezh Front (renamed First Ukrainian) attacked towards Kiev, which was finally recaptured after fierce fighting on 6 November. Soviet forces pushed on nearly 100 miles establishing a strategic bridgehead west of the Dnieper.

By now the idea of liberating Soviet territory, rather than just destroying German forces, was becoming important. Further, the seizure of the strategic bridgehead across the Dnieper created the jumping-off point for the Belasoviet offensive. In the battle for the Dnieper, 38,000 settlements including 160 towns and cities were recaptured. By the end of December most of the difficult river obstacles were behind Soviet forward troops. The end of 1943 marked the conclusion, from the Soviet viewpoint, of the 'second period of the war' – seeing the fundamental shift in the balance of forces. The third period would see Germany finally and decisively defeated.

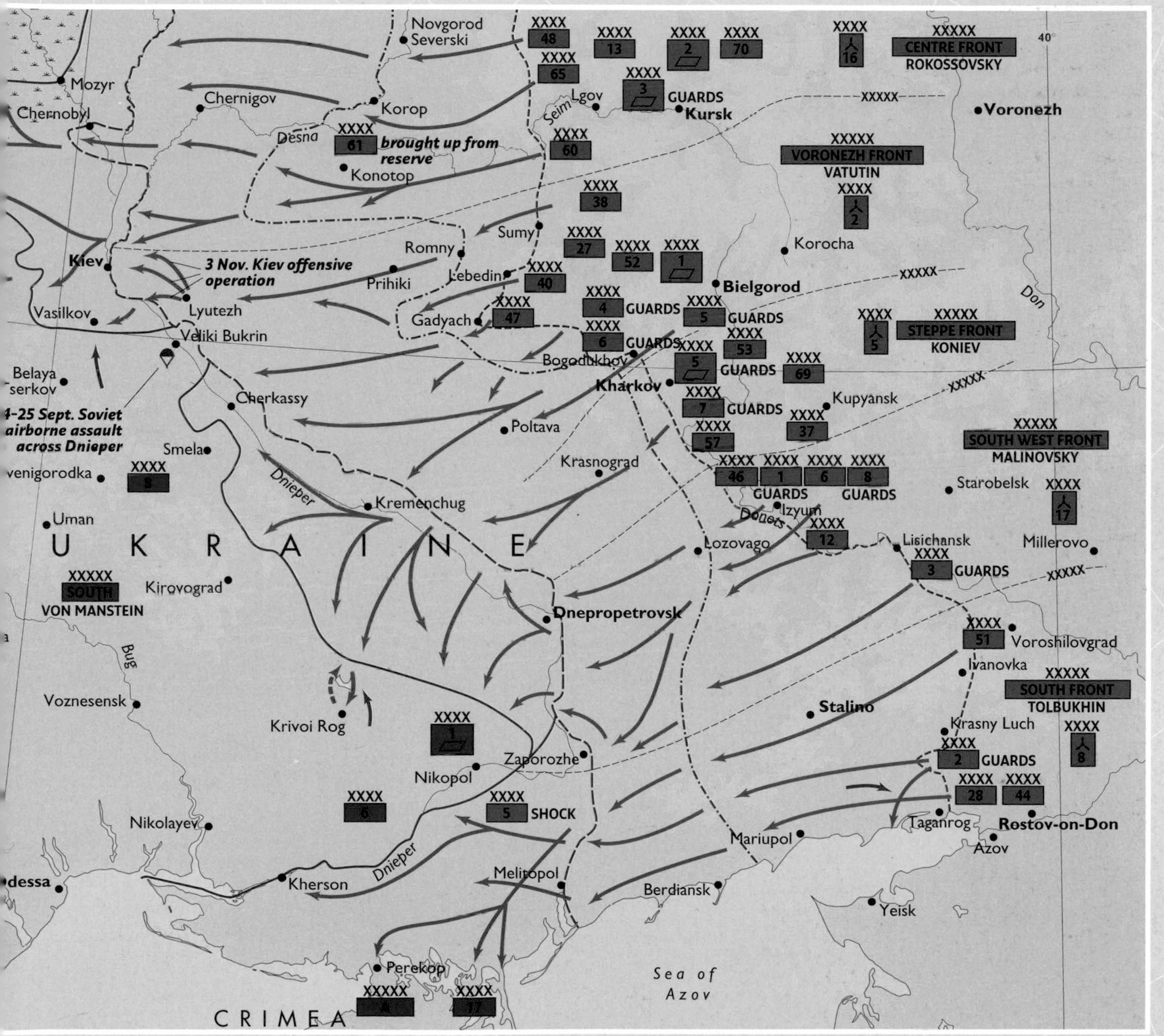

the **balkans**

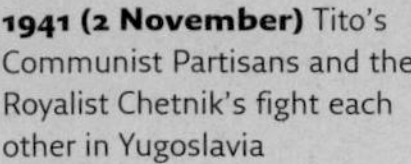

1941 to 1945

- **1941 (2 November)** Tito's Communist Partisans and the Royalist Chetnik's fight each other in Yugoslavia
- **1942 (24 June)** Tito's Partisans driven into retreat
- **1943 (15 May)** fifth Axis offensive against Yugoslav Partisans (until 9 June); Tito's forces almost destroyed
- **8 September** Yugoslav forces round up and disarm Italian forces
- **16 September** Partisans seize Split
- **1944 (4 January)** Yugoslav Partisans capture Banja Luka
- **6 September** Soviet forces reach Yugoslav border (enter 1 October)
- **14 October** Athens liberated
- **20 October** Belgrade liberated
- **1945 (3 January)** new Greek government under President Plastivas
- **5 March** Tito forms new Yugoslav government

Hitler's lightning conquest of Yugoslavia and Greece in April 1941, and his hastily improvised division of the spoils, created the conditions for anti-Axis resistance, civil wars, and Communist revolutions in the western Balkans. Wishing to exploit the area with the minimum commitment of troops, he relied on his allies for much of its garrisoning and governance. The punitive and exploitative 'New Order' offered nothing positive to the bulk of the region's inhabitants.

Even before the German invasion of the USSR impelled the Comintern to summon the underground Balkan Communist parties to launch a partisan struggle in defence of 'mother Russia', remnants of the Royal Yugoslav Army had taken to the woods. Known as Chetniks, this movement of Serb officers came gradually under the titular command of Col. Draga Mihailovitch. His aim was to organise a secret army that would be mobilised to restore the Serb-dominated monarchy and to punish the Serbs' enemies as and when the western Allies returned to the Balkans. He had not counted, however, either on competition from the Communists or on the spontaneous risings among the Serbs of the 'Independent State of Croatia' who were subjected (from May) to a campaign of genocide by their new Ustashi (from *ustasa*, rebel) rulers. In September 1941 the leader of the Communists, Josip Broz Tito, took to the field in western Serbia, where the units they had raised (now dubbed Partisans) were contesting with Mihailovitch for primacy in what had become a veritable insurgent republic.

Mihailovitch was appalled both by the Partisans' disregard for the costs of the unremitting warfare they proclaimed and by the revolutionary means they used to propagate it. Hitler's orders that the rebellion be crushed, and that 100 civilian hostages be executed for every German killed, underscored Mihailovitch's fears. In November he sought arms from the Germans with which to quash the Communists. They refused but neither the authorities they had installed in Serbia nor their Italian allies proved so punctilious. Meanwhile the Germans ejected the Partisans from Serbia and reduced Mihailovitch to a headquarters without an army.

The civil war that broke out in Serbia in November was soon replicated in much of the rest of the country. The year 1943 brought the Partisans the assurance of eventual victory. Their survival of two great Axis offensives (Weiss and Schwarz) in the first half of the year, their reception of missions and aid from the British after April, and the Italian surrender in September permitted them to claim recognition as the future rulers of a federated Yugoslavia. By 1944 Tito claimed to have 300,000 men and women at arms, and to be containing as many Axis troops as were the Allies in Italy. He worked to secure international recognition by making nominal concessions to the exiled King Peter, while pressing on with the destruction of the Royalist Chetniks in Serbia. He appealed successfully to Stalin to divert the Red Army to help in the latter enterprise. Belgrade fell on 20 October and the Soviets departed for Hungary. The Partisans were left to pursue the Germans and to make good their claims on Slovene and Croat unredeemed territory. The Yugoslavs entered Trieste hours before the Western Allies (1 May).

In Albania, the Communist Party established their National Liberation Movement in September 1942. The Communists' bid for control under Yugoslav influence led to the formation of a republican movement (Balli Kombëtar), which found anti-Communist collaboration with the Axis easy to rationalise. The Communists were able to destroy their rivals and supplant the Germans as they withdrew in Autumn 1944.

The Greek Communists were first in their country to gear up for resistance. They set up a National Liberation Front (EAM) in September and a National Popular Liberation Army (ELAS) in December 1941, although guerrilla bands did not form in the mountains until September 1942. By then non-Communist officers were also organising. The Communists concentrated on liquidating the officers' movements while levering their way into the councils of the exile government. Successful in both respects by summer 1944, they failed to capitalise on their effective control of the country (established as the Germans withdrew) and allowed the government and its British guarantors to return to Athens in October. Realising their error, they launched a confused struggle to recoup their position in December and failed to eject the desperately reinforcing British – unaware that Stalin had already consigned their country to a British sphere of influence.

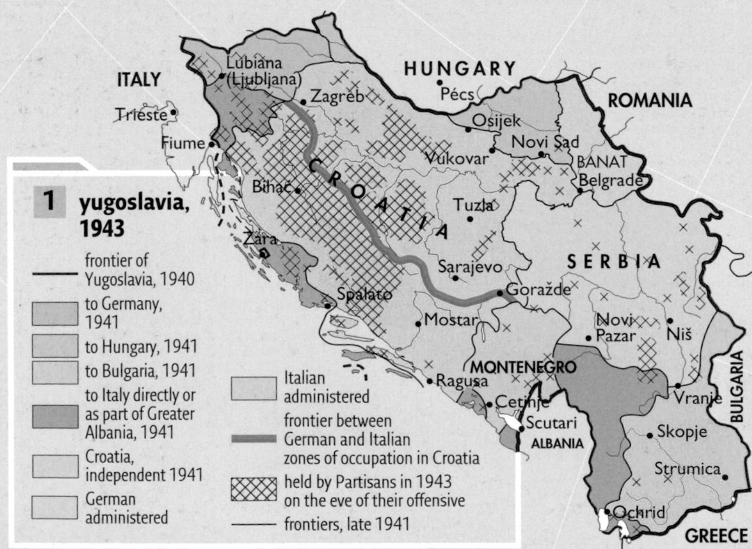

http://db.bbc.co.uk/history/war/wwtwo/partisan_fighters_01.shtml
The Partisan war in Yugoslavia
www.ushmm.org/wlc/article.php?lang=en&ModuleId=10005456
The Holocaust and Yugoslavia

2 yugoslavia and greece: the partisan war, 1943–45

- Partisan campaign, 1944–45
- Partisan areas in Greece
- successful Partisan operation in Greece
- Partisan base
- centres of Chetnik resistance
- Partisan Units

1-2 The new order in the Balkans (*map 1*) effectively redrew the political map of the region. After Germany and her Axis allies had annexed various portions of territory, an 'Independent State of Croatia' was formed, although this was effectively partitioned into German and Italian spheres of influence. Politically sensitive or strategically valuable areas were under Axis occupation, and German troops took over most of the former Italian areas, following that country's surrender to the Allies in September 1943. The leaders of both the Axis powers and the Balkan resistance movements were convinced that the Western Allies would invade the peninsula. The successful cultivation of this belief played a notable strategic role at the time of the landings on Sicily in July 1943: the Germans were deceived into reinforcing their garrisons in Greece and the resisters stepped up their efforts to eliminate their rivals in anticipation of liberation. Although Churchill advocated Balkan operations (sponsoring an ill-fated attempt in September to bring Turkey into the war by seizing the Dodecanese), the Americans opposed such diversionary schemes and the slow Allied advance in Italy precluded them. Hitler, however, continued to fear a Balkan invasion. He hastened to replace the defecting Italians in autumn 1943 and so continued to confer strategic importance upon the resistance. The most powerful and successful resistance grouping were Tito's Communist Partisans in Yugoslavia, based in the rugged Dinaric mountain zones (*map 2*). Their war against the Axis powers was hampered by internal struggles against the Royalist Chetniks, who were based in Serbia, Montenegro, Herzegovina and inland Dalmatia. The 1944 defections from the Axis of Romania (23–25 Aug.) and Bulgaria (5–8 Sept.) opened the way for the Red Army to advance into Hungary and to assist Tito in making good his civil war victory. Belgrade fell (20 Oct.) to a combined Soviet/Partisan assault, but German Army Group G was able to stabilise its front in northern Yugoslavia and Hungary and held on until the end of the war. But simultaneous German withdrawals from Albania and Greece permitted the Communist-led resistance to assume power in the former and to confront the British forces accompanying the returning exile government in the latter. Fighting broke out in Athens in December, but a precarious armistice was signed in February 1945.

PART 4 **ALLIED OFFENSIVES**

1943 (9 July) Allied airborne troops land by night on Sicily

10 July Operation Husky – main Allied landings on Sicily

19 July first Allied air raids on Rome

22 July Americans capture Palermo

25 July Mussolini resigns and is arrested; Fascist government dissolved

2 August Italians make peace moves through their embassy in Lisbon

17 August Allies take Messina

3 September armistice signed with Italy; Allies land in Calabria

8 September Italian surrender announced

9 September Allied landings at Salerno; British Airborne Division takes Taranto

13 October Italy declares war on Germany

The decision to invade Sicily, rather than transfer the bulk plans for the Allied invasion of the Allied armies out of the Mediterranean for an assault on North West Europe, once Tunisia had been cleared of Axis forces, was taken by Churchill and Roosevelt at the Casablanca Conference (14–24 January 1943). The Americans remained suspicious, however, that Husky, as the operation was codenamed, might become an open-ended commitment that would set back a North West Europe landing beyond early 1944 and therefore insisted that its aims be limited to securing the Mediterranean line of communications, diverting German divisions from the Soviet Union, detaching Italy from Germany and bringing Turkey into the war on the Allied side.

It was only at the Trident Conference (Washington, 12–25 May) that Churchill extracted Roosevelt's consent for Eisenhower, Allied Supreme Commander, to plan for Italy's elimination from the war by the exploitation of Operation Husky's results.

D-Day for Operation Husky was set for July and the force allocated consisted of the US Seventh (Patton) and British Eighth (Montgomery) Armies, comprising divisions drawn from Britain and the US as well as Tunisia and the Middle East. The Axis defence plan led to the reinforcement of Sardinia and Greece. The Allied assault, preceded by air attacks and airborne landings, was hampered by bad weather but was not seriously opposed. Landing respectively west and east of Cape Passero, the Americans and British each put four divisions ashore without serious difficulty. By 15 July the Allies had advanced to the Agrigento-Augusta Line and were landing reinforcements. While Montgomery advanced along the eastern coast towards Catania and Messina, Patton exploited westward to Palermo. On 20 July, however, Alexander ordered Patton to swing his troops east to outflank Axis forces, who were impeding Montgomery's advance beyond Mt Etna.

While the Germans were being reinforced, the Italians began to withdraw their troops from Sicily on 25 July: Mussolini had been removed from power by an internal parliamentary coup, and the Italians began seriously to question their allegiance to the Axis. Against weakening opposition, and aided by amphibious hooks, Patton reached the approaches to Messina on 15 August. Montgomery, who had pressed his divisions westward of Etna, arrived a day later. By then, however, the Germans were in full retreat across the Straits of Messina and when the city fell on 17 August, all 100,000 Axis troops had reached Italy.

In the light of Mussolini's overthrow, Eisenhower received permission to plan a landing on the Italian mainland. He decided to launch diversionary British attacks into the toe of Italy on 3 September and follow these with a major Anglo-American landing, commanded by Mark Clark, in the Gulf of Salerno on 9 September. Badoglio, who had succeeded Mussolini as head of the Italian government, meanwhile was negotiating an armistice with the Allies, which was signed on 3 September and made public on 8 September. Hitler, however, reinforced his troops in Italy. The Luftwaffe attacked and damaged the Italian fleet on its way to Malta (9–11 September) and German forces heavily opposed the US Fifth Army landings at Salerno. Counter-attacks were particularly heavy on 13 September and by 16 September, when Montgomery's Eighth Army (reinforced by 1st Airborne Division, which had landed at Taranto on 9 September) joined forces.

Naples was occupied on 1 October and by 12 October Fifth and Eighth Armies had established a line 120 miles long across the peninsula, from the River Volturno to Termoli on the Adriatic. Axis forces had, meanwhile, evacuated Sardinia (18 September) and Corsica (by 3 October). On 13 October, when Italy now entered the war on the Allied side, Fifth Army crossed the River Volturno and began an advance to the River Garigliano on 15 November. Between 20 November and 2 December Eighth Army fought its way across the Sangro. Difficult terrain and winter weather, bringing torrential rain, then allowed the Germans to hold the Allies, despite bitter hand-to-hand fighting (especially at Ortona on the Adriatic coast) on the Gustav (Winter) Line, which ran between Minturno on the Mediterranean to Pescara on the Adriatic, from 15 January 1944. Numbers on both sides were about level: 13 German opposing 18 Allied divisions under Alexander, who had assumed command of the Mediterranean theatre on Eisenhower's departure to prepare the Normandy invasion on 31 December; Montgomery, who had left on 30 December to act as his deputy, handed over command of Eighth Army to Leese.

Despite the reasonably rapid success of Allied operations in capturing Sicily and southern Italy, few German forces had been captured or destroyed, and the Allies now faced a protracted struggle north to the Alps.

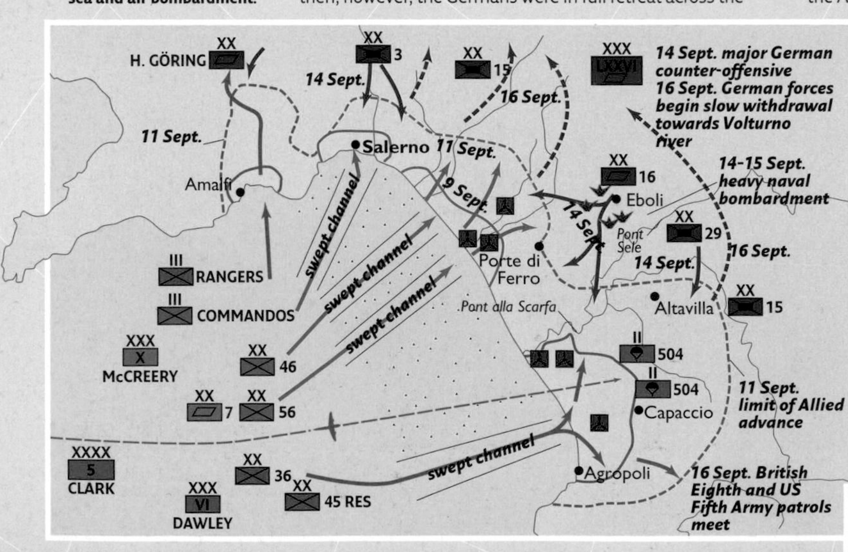

2 salerno, 9–16 sept. 1943

2 **The Salerno landing achieved surprise and the Germans reacted by shifting the weight of their local forces north to guard communications with Naples. When reinforcements arrived they staged heavy counter-attacks, but these were broken up by sea and air bombardment.**

www.combinedops.com/husky.htm
Operation Husky, the Allied invasion of Sicily
www.bbc.co.uk/dna/ww2/A1057411
Allied landings at Reggio, Salerno and Taranto

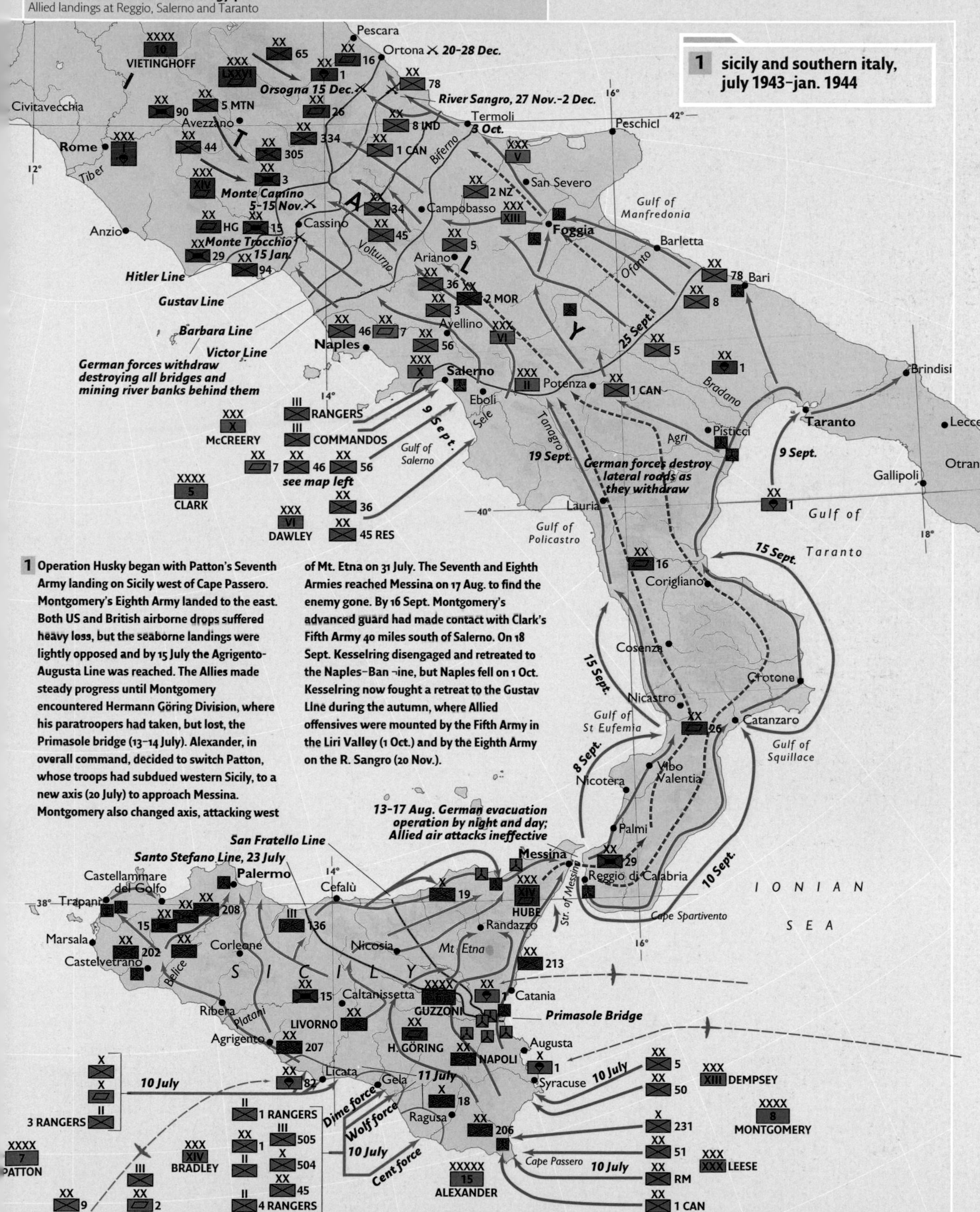

1 Operation Husky began with Patton's Seventh Army landing on Sicily west of Cape Passero. Montgomery's Eighth Army landed to the east. Both US and British airborne drops suffered heavy loss, but the seaborne landings were lightly opposed and by 15 July the Agrigento-Augusta Line was reached. The Allies made steady progress until Montgomery encountered Hermann Göring Division, where his paratroopers had taken, but lost, the Primasole bridge (13–14 July). Alexander, in overall command, decided to switch Patton, whose troops had subdued western Sicily, to a new axis (20 July) to approach Messina. Montgomery also changed axis, attacking west of Mt. Etna on 31 July. The Seventh and Eighth Armies reached Messina on 17 Aug. to find the enemy gone. By 16 Sept. Montgomery's advanced guard had made contact with Clark's Fifth Army 40 miles south of Salerno. On 18 Sept. Kesselring disengaged and retreated to the Naples–Ban ¬ine, but Naples fell on 1 Oct. Kesselring now fought a retreat to the Gustav Line during the autumn, where Allied offensives were mounted by the Fifth Army in the Liri Valley (1 Oct.) and by the Eighth Army on the R. Sangro (20 Nov.).

january to august 1944

- **15 January** Fifth Army takes Mt Trocchio; Germans withdraw across River Rapido
- **22 January** Allies land at Anzio
- **15 March** New Zealanders and Indians attack at Monte Cassino
- **22 March** attacks halted
- **18 May** Poles capture Cassino monastery
- **23 May** breakout from Anzio begins
- **5 June** Fifth Army enters Rome
- **4 August** Eighth Army reaches Florence

At the beginning of January 1944 the Allied armies in Italy had driven the German Tenth Army from the approaches to Kesselring's Winter Position in a series of hard-fought operations. Now, in accordance with a directive issued by Alexander on 8 November, Fifth Army undertook a succession of offensives, designed to open up a passage north to Rome through the Liri Valley.

Alexander's conception was that the city should eventually be taken by an offensive up the Liri, supported by an amphibious assault nearer the city, at Anzio. During December, Fifth Army had fought battles for Monte Cassino (1–10 December) and San Pietro (20–21 December), which barred the way into the Liri Valley. Between 5–15 January 1944, Fifth Army moved forward to the line of the Rapido River, which flows into the Liri near its confluence with the Garigliano, and on which the strongest point of the Winter Position, the Gustav Line, was established.

On 17 January the British X Corps, of Fifth Army, stormed and crossed the Garigliano. When the 36th (Texan) Division assaulted the Rapido, however, on 20 January, it was bloodily repulsed. The next day the Anzio landing (Operation Shingle) began. Four British and US divisions, with supporting Commandos and Rangers, got ashore without loss, having taken Kesselring by surprise. But Lucas, the VI Corps commander, then concentrated on building up force within the bridgehead rather than driving on Rome. An immediate drive might have been defeated; but Lucas's inaction allowed Kesselring to rush emergency units to Anzio. While forward reserves were transferred from other sectors of the Winter Position, by 15 February he had assembled sufficient force to mount a deliberate counter-offensive, which nearly bisected the bridgehead: it was checked only by heavy Allied air, artillery and naval bombardment.

The initial failure of the Anzio landing cast responsibility for rescuing the Italian campaign from stalemate back upon the troops of US Fifth Army, opposite the Gustav Line, despite a continuing depletion of Allied forces as troops and equipment were withdrawn to mount Operations Overlord and Anvil. The key to the Gustav Line was Monte Cassino, the fortress monastery that commanded the approaches to the Liri Valley. Clark, commanding Fifth Army, made four attempts to capture it, employing in the process two of the reinforcing contingents – the Free French Expeditionary Force and Polish II Corps – which had joined the Allied Army in Italy since the start of the battle for the Winter Position. Clark's US 34th Division attacked first on 24 January but was eventually defeated

1 monte cassino, 24 jan.–18 may 1944

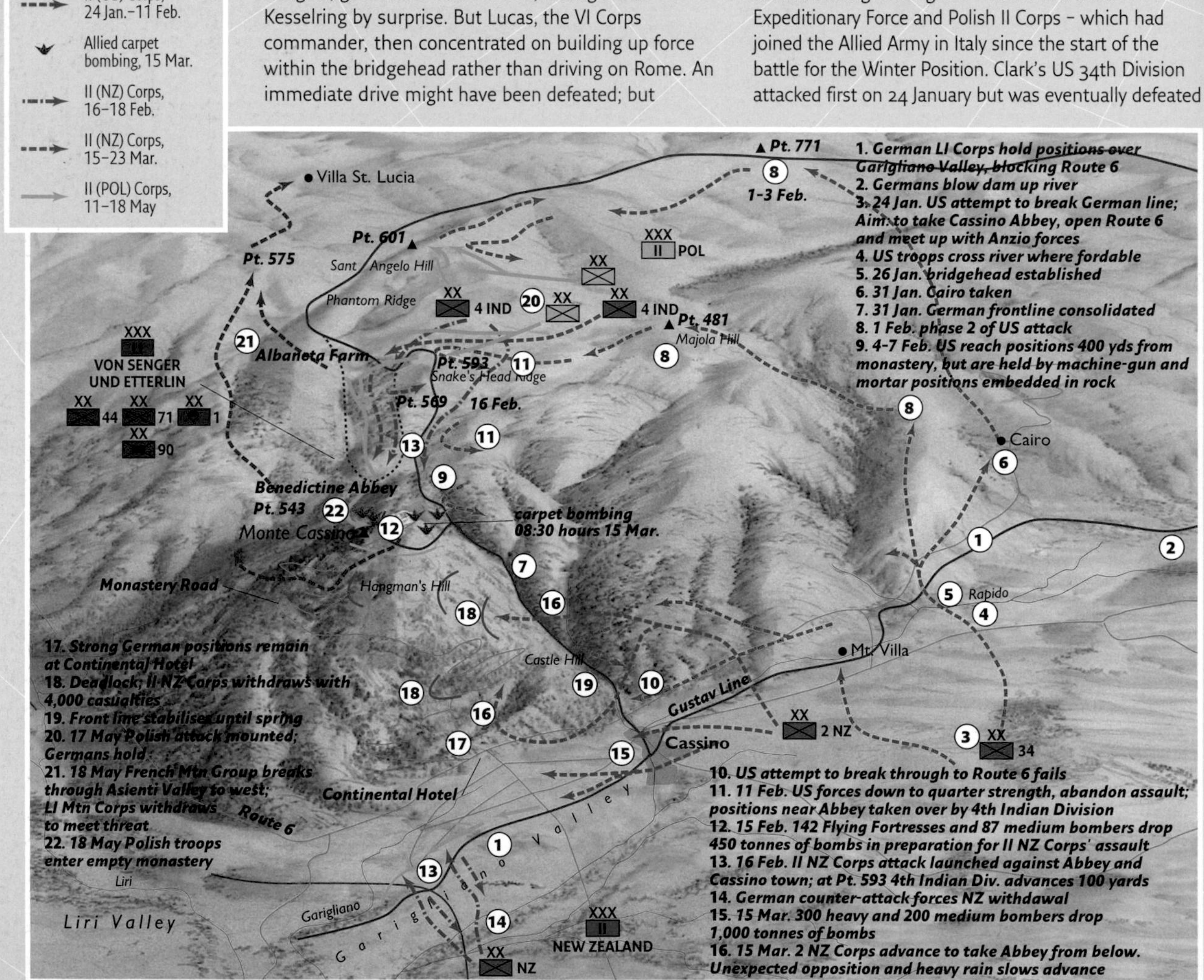

www.bbc.co.uk/history/war/wwtwo/battle_cassino_01.shtml
The Battle of Monte Cassino
www.militaryhistoryonline.com/wwii/articles/anzio.aspx
Operation Shingle: The Allied landings at Anzio

(12 February) by the German 1st Parachute Division, which defended the monastery heights. New Zealand Corps attacked in the second battle, 16–18 February, but despite the heavy bombardment of the monastery by B-17s on 16 February, was also defeated. New Zealand Corps tried once more, 15–23 March, again supported by bombers, but after winning more ground, was forced to desist.

Alexander's Chief of Staff, Harding, now devised a plan (Operation Diadem) to unlock the stalemate on the front south of Rome. VI Corps at Anzio had been reinforced. The final battle for Monte Casino began in May. The mountaineers of the Free French Expeditionary Corps bypassed the monastery to the west; after an initial and costly surprise Polish II Corps took the monastery on 18 May; the British XIII Corps breached the coastal line west of Cassino on 23 May. On the same day VI Corps began to break out from Anzio and II Corps advanced to join it on 25 May. Harding's plan – which was to trap the German Tenth Army between the Anzio-Cassino pincers – now seemed on the point of fruition. The next day, however, Clark, who was determined that the Americans be the first to enter Rome, shifted the axis of Fifth Army's advance to the north-west. German rearguards were then able to check VI Corps at Velletri and Valmontone until 2 June, allowing Tenth Army to join Fourteenth (formed the previous November and used to contain the Anzio bridgehead) in a retreat towards the Pisa-Rimini (Gothic) Line.

American troops entered Rome on 4 June, in the forefront of a general Allied advance. While Eighth Army cleared the Adriatic coast between Pescara and Ancona, Fifth Army moved along the Mediterranean. Livorno fell on 19 July, Florence on 11 August. Both Fifth and Eighth Armies were by then in contact with the Gothic Line but because of the withdrawal of the French Expeditionary and US VI Corps to mount the southern France landing, were forced to pause temporarily before launching an assault upon it.

3 central italy, may–aug. 1944

1-3 **The battles for Monte Cassino proved enormously costly for the Allies, but also provided acts of extraordinary bravery and endurance among all participants. The first battle was staged by the US 34th Division, which succeeded at heavy cost in capturing high ground to the north-east of the monastery. The monastery, unoccupied by the Germans, was nevertheless destroyed by Allied heavy bombing, to prepare the assault of New Zealand Corps (2nd New Zealand and 4th Indian Divisions) that day. Their attack, though it took more high ground, was terminated on 18 Feb. New Zealand Corps attacked again on 15 Mar., when Allied medium bombers saturated the German parachutist positions with carpet bombing, but on 23 Mar. was forced to call off the attack, having seized most of the southern approaches to the monastery and north of Cassino town. Finally in May, as part of the Operation Diadem, Polish II Corps opened the fourth battle. Repulsed at first, they eventually captured the ruins of the monastery on 18 May. Further north, at Anzio, VI Corps landed by surprise. Lucas, the Corps commander, did not press on to Rome, but consolidated his bridgehead, only six miles deep. Kesselring attacked and almost broke through to the coast but was halted by heavy Allied firepower. The battle then resolved itself with a bloody siege but by 23 May VI Corps had been built up to seven divisions and it easily broke out on that date to play its part in Operation Diadem. This was launched on 11 May as a means of breaking the Gustav line and encircling the German Tenth Army. While Polish II Corps attacked north of Cassino, British XIII, the Free French Expeditionary Corps and US II Corps all attacked between it and the coast. XIII and II Corps drove along the coast towards the Anzio bridgehead, out of which VI Corps broke on 23 May. Kesselring thus retreated back to his last line of defence, the Gothic Line.**

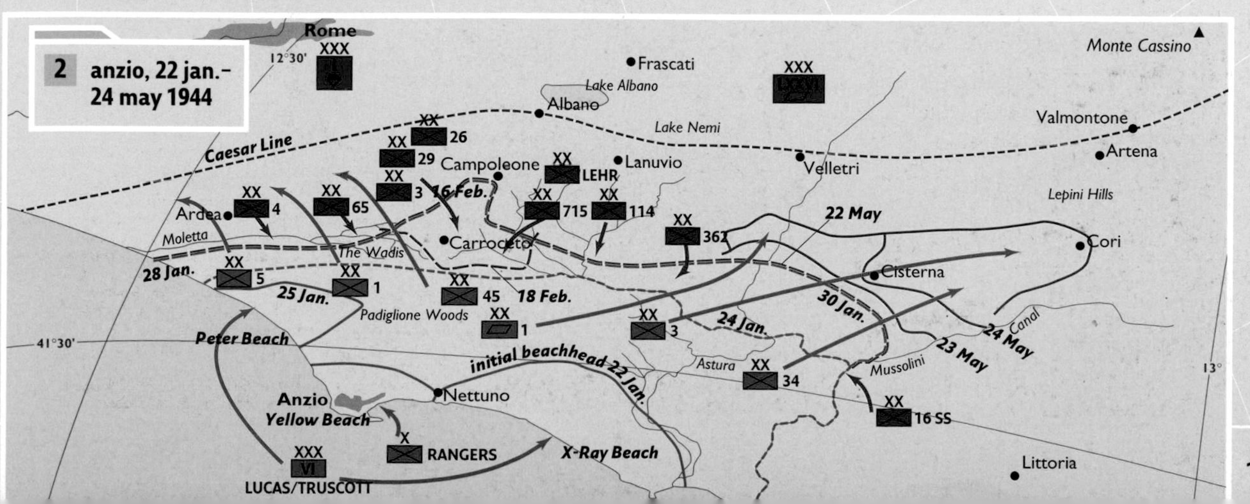

2 anzio, 22 jan.– 24 may 1944

politics and **strategy**

- **14–24 January** Casablanca Conference; Roosevelt demands unconditional surrender
- **26 March** Laval assumes reins of power in France; Pétain a figurehead
- **1 April** plans for the invasion of Europe begin
- **26 April** Soviet Union severs relations with Polish government in London over Katyn massacre
- **1 August** De Gaulle made President of French Committe of National Defence
- **28 November–1 December** Teheran Conference meeting of 'Big Three'
- **12 December** Rommel appointed Commander-in-Chief Fortress Europe

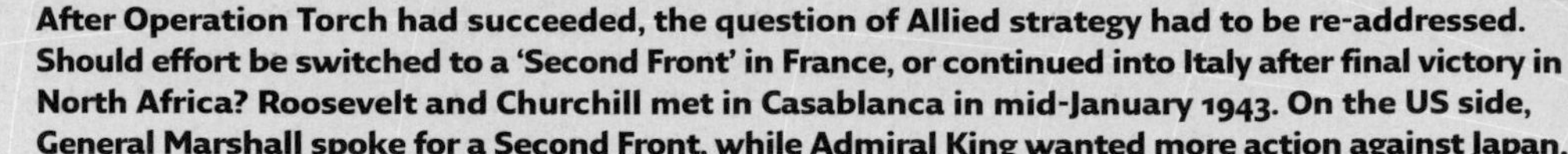

After Operation Torch had succeeded, the question of Allied strategy had to be re-addressed. Should effort be switched to a 'Second Front' in France, or continued into Italy after final victory in North Africa? Roosevelt and Churchill met in Casablanca in mid-January 1943. On the US side, General Marshall spoke for a Second Front, while Admiral King wanted more action against Japan.

The British doubted Allied capacity for a French landing before 1944, and they advocated action in the Mediterranean, against Italy and the Balkans; meanwhile, they claimed that their bombing of Germany was weakening Germany's effort on the Eastern Front. Eventually, Roosevelt sided with the British although two large-scale offensives were planned in the Pacific. Politically, Casablanca was important for the demand, made almost casually by Roosevelt, that the enemy powers would have to accept 'unconditional surrender'.

In May, Roosevelt and Churchill met again, in Washington, for a further conference (Trident). There were difficulties in reconciling the various claims made for a build-up of force in the British Isles for invasion of France, for an invasion of Italy, and for offensive action in the Pacific. At Trident a Second Front was agreed, for 1 May 1944, and a force of 29 divisions was to be set up for this. However, a landing in Sicily was also agreed, though not an invasion of Italy; in the Pacific, further aims were somewhat reduced, to the opening-up of the Burma Road into China, and the establishment of US air bases in the areas controlled by Chiang Kai-shek.

After the invasion of Sicily and the fall of Mussolini (25 July 1943) the American Joint Chiefs of Staff were won round to Churchill's view that the next effort should be launched in Italy. To work out details, and apportion supplies between the Channel, the Mediterranean and the Pacific, a further Anglo-American conference was held at Quebec in mid-August (Quadrant). Here, the Americans insisted on a cross-Channel invasion of France but also agreed that it would have to be very strongly backed and that there should be a further effort in Italy (still the chief ambition on the British side), but that part of that effort might be shifted to an invasion of southern France, coinciding with Operation Overlord. Meanwhile, there were further exchanges concerning the manufacture of the atomic bomb – now heavily concentrated in the US.

Major Axis conferences

1. Rome 24–28 Feb. Ribbentrop meets Mussolini to review African situation

2. Berchtesgaden 31 Mar.–18 Sept. Hitler receives allied Axis leaders to consolidate military and political support: King Boris of Bulgaria, Antonescu (Romania), Admiral Horthy (Hungary), Vidkung Quisling (Norway), Tiso (Slovakia), Pavelic (Croatia), Neditch (Serbia)

3. Salzburg 7–10 Apr. Hitler and Mussolini decide to attempt to hold positions in Africa

4. Berchtesgaden 29 Apr. Hitler reviews situation in French North Africa with Laval, now effectively in charge of occupied France

5. Verona 19 July Hitler and Mussolini discuss Africa and defensive measures for Italy

Major Allied conferences

6. Casablanca 14–24 Jan. Roosevelt and Churchill meet to decide future strategy; resolutions include cross-Channel invasion of France in 1944, subsidiary offensive in Italy, U-boat offensive and supplies to USSR given top priority, the Combined Bombing Offensive against Germany and unconditional surrender terms announced

7. Adana 30 Jan. Churchill meets President Inönü of Turkey, who refuses to join the war

8. Second Washington Conference (Trident) 11–27 May Roosevelt and Churchill reach compromise on all major issues: cross-Channel offensive date set (1 May 1944); immediate Pacific and Italian offensives approved

9. First Quebec Conference (Quadrant) 17 Aug. US and British military leaders to discuss details of cross-Channel offensive; also support of Italian offensive agreed; aid to China to continue; preliminary discussions for Burma offensive

10. Washington 2 Sept. Churchill and Roosevelt continue planning talks

11. Second Moscow Conference 18 Oct.–1 Nov. Allied foreign ministers devise provisional formulas for joint military/political decision-making in liberated countries

12. Atlantic City 9 Nov.–1 Dec. First United Nations Relief and Rehabilitation Administration (U.N.R.R.A.) meeting

13. First Cairo Conference (Sextant) 22–25 Nov. Roosevelt, Churchill and Chiang Kai-shek discuss Burma-China plans

14. Teheran (Eureka) 28 Nov. Stalin, Roosevelt and Churchill meet for first time; cross-Channel invasion approved, as are plans for invasion of southern France; Stalin promises to join war against Japan

15. Second Cairo Conference 4–6 Dec. Roosevelt and Churchill meet President Inönü of Turkey, who again refuses to join the war

www.yale.edu/lawweb/avalon/wwii/tehran.htm
The declaration of the Three Powers at the Teheran Conference
www.army.mil/cmh-pg/books/wwii/sp1943-44/chapter6.htm
The Trident Conference, Washington, May 1943

However, the Italian campaign went very slowly (despite Italy's change of side) whereas, on the Eastern Front, the Soviets were rapidly pushing the Germans before them. It was necessary to arrive at agreement on strategy – to reassure Stalin as to the Second Front, but also to cater for Soviet involvement in the war in the Far East. Before meeting Stalin, Roosevelt and Churchill met Chiang Kai-shek at Cairo (Sextant). It provided little except the Cairo Declaration of 1 December 1943, which laid down terms for Japan's surrender, and for the restoration of Manchuria to China and independence for Korea.

Roosevelt and Churchill then proceeded to Teheran, for a conference (Eureka, 28 November–1 December) with Stalin. The conference was preceded by a meeting of their three foreign ministers (Eden, Hull and Molotov) at Moscow (19–30 October), where various problems were discussed in an atmosphere of mounting Soviet victory. There, Soviet consent was gained to the formula for Italy's surrender and occupation – a tripartite political commission might advise a military commander who otherwise would take orders from the Combined Chiefs of Staff in the West. In addition, the foreign ministers agreed upon the restoration of Austria and the establishment of a European Advisory Commission in London to discuss the future of Germany.

At Teheran, Stalin promised that he would eventually intervene against Japan, and was satisfied as to prospects for a Second Front in Europe. However, he wanted assurance concerning Poland. The Soviet Union had annexed a large part of eastern Poland in 1939–40, mainly on the grounds that its population, being Ukrainian or White Russian, 'naturally' belonged to the USSR. The exiled Polish government expected support from London. At Teheran, Churchill and Roosevelt, recognising the fact of Stalin's power in the area, agreed, though not formally, that Poland should be compensated with industrially-rich German territory for her losses in the east. At the same time, the integrity of Persia, occupied by the Allies, was guaranteed, and post-war withdrawal promised. Returning to Cairo, Roosevelt and Churchill conferred, and by 7 December they recognised that, the Italian campaign having slowed down, Operation Overlord in northern France and Operation Anvil in southern France should now take priority.

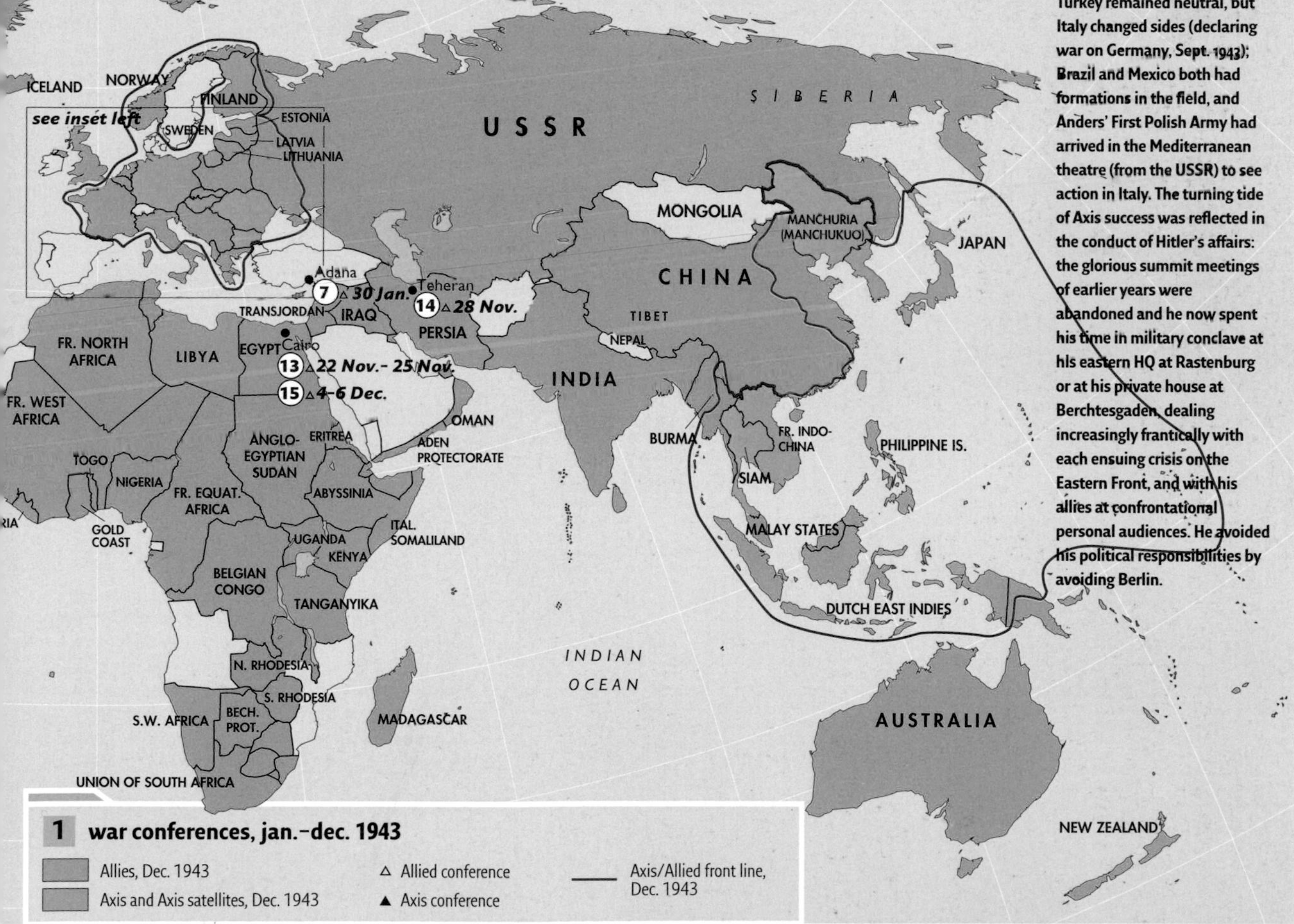

1 Nineteen Forty-Three was a year of important decisions for the Allies. The shape of grand strategy that would bring the war in Europe to an end was decided, and provisional plans were laid for the political restructuring of the post-war world. Although the Second Front in Europe was yet to open, the Western Allies had recovered North Africa and were invading Italy. The Red Army had liberated Stalingrad, and won critical battles at Kursk and Kharkov. By autumn it was beginning its victorious advance west, pushing the Germans and their allies back to the line of the Dnieper. In the South West Pacific, the Japanese were beating a retreat and preparing for an inevitable US drive into the western Pacific, although they were unaware of when or where it would occur. The Allied cause was still growing: Turkey remained neutral, but Italy changed sides (declaring war on Germany, Sept. 1943); Brazil and Mexico both had formations in the field, and Anders' First Polish Army had arrived in the Mediterranean theatre (from the USSR) to see action in Italy. The turning tide of Axis success was reflected in the conduct of Hitler's affairs: the glorious summit meetings of earlier years were abandoned and he now spent his time in military conclave at his eastern HQ at Rastenburg or at his private house at Berchtesgaden, dealing increasingly frantically with each ensuing crisis on the Eastern Front, and with his allies at confrontational personal audiences. He avoided his political responsibilities by avoiding Berlin.

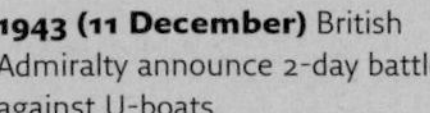

battle of the **atlantic IV**

october 1943 to may 1945

- **1943 (11 December)** British Admiralty announce 2-day battle against U-boats
- **26–27 December** Battle of North Cape, Royal Navy sinks *Scharnhorst*
- **1944 (7 February)** first use of snorkel equipment on U-boat
- **22 March** Admiral Dönitz orders U-boats to operate singly and give up convoy attacks
- **12 November** RAF sink *Tirpitz* in Tromsø Fjord
- **1945 (4 May)** Admiral Dönitz orders surrender of all U-boats

Never, even at its height, had British naval supremacy rested upon the outcome of a single battle; the command of the sea that Britain had exercised in successive wars was secured through consecutive victories but was never able to prevent substantial mercantile losses at the hands of enemies employing a *guerre de course*. After August 1943 the Allies had to repeat their summer victories over the U-boats in the Battle of the Atlantic, albeit on more modest scales, throughout the remaining twenty months of the European war.

During this period there were two quite distinct aspects to the Allied application of victorious sea power: a defensive success in continuing to thwart the German campaign against shipping, and an offensive success in carrying the war into North West Europe, and in completing the destruction of German seaborne commerce.

The last phase of the European war witnessed the effective neutralisation of the U-boat menace but not the defeat of the U-boat arm itself. In 1943 as a whole the German Navy commissioned 272 boats, in 1944 another 242, and with losses of 237 and 242 boats in these same years, the U-boat arm was able to maintain, indeed slightly increase its numerical strength until it reached its maximum wartime strength of 444 boats in commission in April 1945. In the whole of 1944, however, German submarines sank 432 merchantmen of 773,327 tonnes, fewer ships (but more tonnage) than the Allies lost to all causes in June 1942. However, in this final phase of the struggle at sea, the effectiveness of German submarines lay not in their sinking Allied commerce but in tying down disproportionately large Allied naval forces, while awaiting the entry into service of a new generation of submarine (Type XXIII with high-speed underwater performance) that would – it confidently was hoped – wrest the initiative from the Allies. The first operational mission of these new submarines began on 30 April 1945, the day that Hitler committed suicide, coming far too late to have any impact on the war at sea.

In this final phase of the war, the escort re-emerged as the main agency of U-boat destruction: the introduction of the snorkel breathing apparatus (which allowed submarines to recharge their batteries at periscope depth, thus avoiding surfacing, but reducing their mobility) provided German submarines with a degree of immunity from detection (and hence destruction) from the air, albeit at the cost of greatly degraded performance. The various technological developments of previous years provided the means whereby the Allies could now take the battle to the U-boats. When linked to increases in numerical strength, this meant that escort groups now became larger and capable of operating independently in waters known to be used by U-boats. The German introduction of the acoustic torpedo as the antidote to escort effectiveness proved counterproductive. Forced to operate at low speed in order to nullify these torpedoes, the escorts found themselves obliged, for the first time, to use forward-firing weaponry against submerged U-boats rather than employing high-speed depth-charge attacks. Such weaponry had been introduced in 1941 but had been little used; but, from 1944 it emerged as the most formidable means of attacking and destroying U-boats.

The Allied offensive campaign in the war at sea (apart from the movement, support and maintenance of field armies on the continental mainland), was primarily carried by shore-based air power. Eight of the nine major German warship losses in the last year of the war were to direct air attack, and such operations and mining brought about the collapse of the German minesweeping fleet and merchant marine in the last five months of

1 the north atlantic, sept. 1943–may 1944

- Allied merchant ships sunk by U-boats
- U-boats sunk
- major convoy routes

1 **After the defeat of August 1943, when they sank only two merchantmen in the North Atlantic, the U-boats made successive attempts to regain the initiative, but despite the introduction to service of acoustic torpedoes and snorkel breathing apparatus they were forced to withdraw from the Atlantic following severe losses in November 1943 and March 1944. Thereafter, the U-boats were concentrated for operations in British home waters and against Allied invasion forces, but against the latter they sank only 21 vessels before the evacuation of French ports. Subsequently, as the snorkel entered general service, success for both sides became increasingly rare, the U-boats being conferred with a high degree of immunity from detection and destruction, but at the cost of offensive effectiveness.**

www.usmm.org/libertyships.html
Liberty Ships (merchant ships), built by the US during World War II
www.royal-navy.mod.uk/static/pages/3531.html
The Battle of the Atlantic, 1939–45

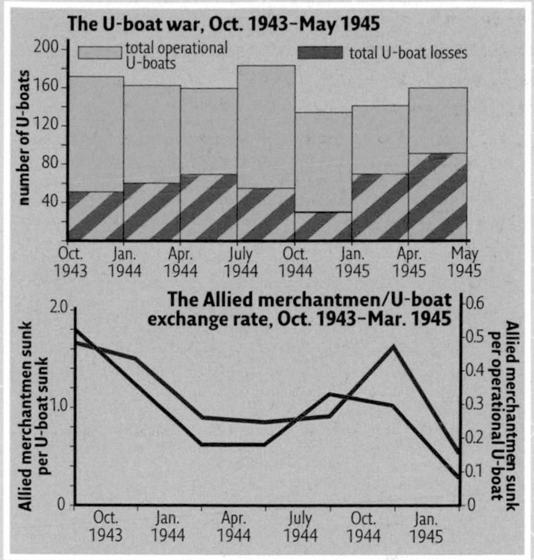

Allied merchant ship losses, Oct. 1943–May 1945 tonnages (nos. of ships)

date	U-boat	aircraft	mine	warship raider	merchant raider	E-boat	unknown and other causes	quarterly totals
Oct.–Dec. 1943	250,959 (47)	160,603 (28)	32,526 (9)	none	none	8,538 (4)	150 (1)	452,776 (89)
Jan.–Mar. 1944	328,145 (54)	45,853 (7)	14,352 (2)	7,840 (1)	none	2,280 (4)	755 (4)	405,450 (74)
Apr.–June 1944	144,448 (24)	31,636 (6)	24,654 (6)	none	2,280 (4)	10,735 (4)	213,753 (216)	213,753 (44)
July–Sept. 1944	205,448 (37)	none	16,745 (7)	none	none	14,395 (2)	5,277 (2)	241,865 (44)
Oct.–Dec. 1944	95,286 (17)	43,167 (6)	40,104 (13)	none	none	1,141 (1)	4,863 (2)	184,561 (39)
Jan.–Mar. 1945	187,298 (39)	14,353 (2)	70,508 (18)	none	none	10,222 (5)	7,036 (7)	289,417 (71)
Apr.–May 1945	82,979 (16)	29,998 (4)	8,733 (6)	none	none	none	none	121,710 (28)
June.–Aug. 1945	11,439 (1)	none	14,422 (4)	none	none	none	1,833 (3)	25,888 (7)

totals by theatre, Oct. 1943–Aug. 1945

Atlantic Ocean	Mediterranean	Indian Ocean	Pacific Ocean
497,895 (88)	371,012 (69)	417,938 (68)	120,023 (16)

the war. Conventional naval power, however, had driven German commerce from the oceans from the start of the war, but as a result of her own resources, requisitions and captures, Germany until 1944 possessed sufficient shipping to meet her modest seaborne requirements. In 1944, however, the withdrawal of Swedish shipping from the iron ore trade left Germany unable to cover the deficiency in this one area. The German Navy and Merchant Navy retained a degree of effectiveness until the end of the war, but by May 1945 the German Merchant Navy, which had totalled some 4,500,000 tonnes of shipping in 1939, retained only 1,500,000 tonnes, and it lost 1,052,000 tonnes of shipping – 42 percent of its 1944 strength – in the last 16 months of hostilities.

The Allied victory at sea was thus as comprehensive as the outcome of the struggles on land and in the air. In the course of the war as a whole, all forms of Axis action and natural causes accounted for 22,000,000 tonnes of Allied and neutral shipping, but Allied construction amounted to 42,000,000 tonnes of shipping. Further, the access to worldwide resources provided by their command of the sea gave the Allies the upper hand over Germany, which was increasingly obliged to wage war on the basis of her own resources. The German Navy had proved unable to maintain Germany's oceanic trade: also, ultimately, it failed to protect Germany's conquests and allies from invasion.

2 the north atlantic, june 1944–8 may 1945

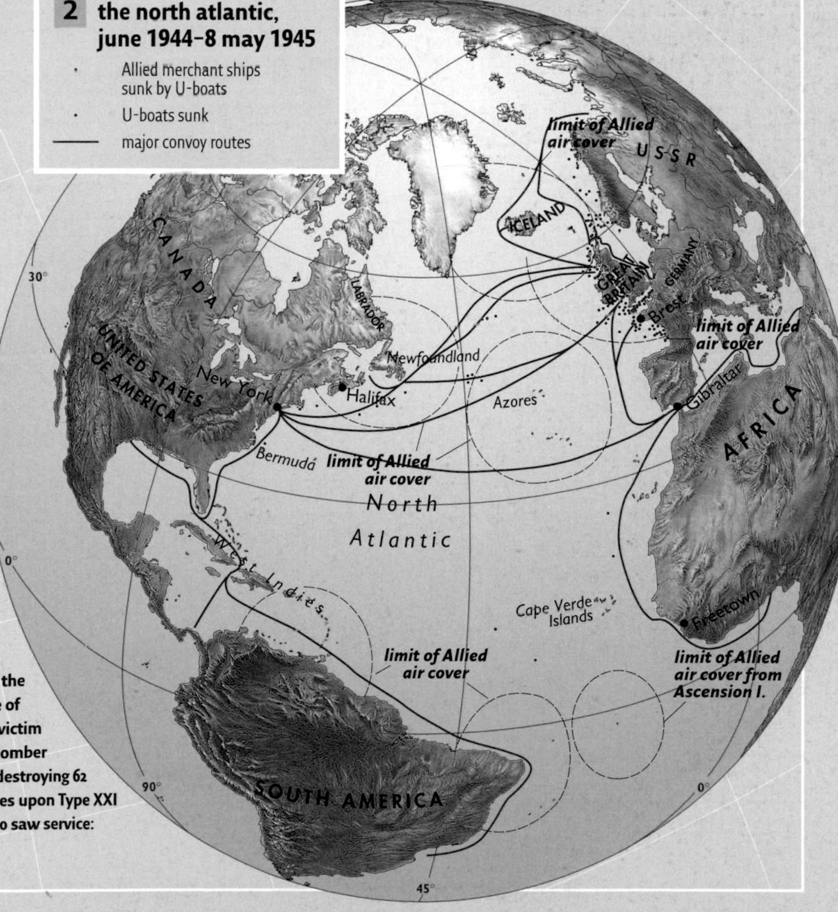

2 Apart from withdrawals before major invasions, Allied escort strength in the Atlantic increased throughout the war with the exception of the last months, when there was an increasing concentration of strength in British home waters in response to a changing pattern of German operations. Even with the snorkel, however, the U-boats were unable to reverse the general trend of the various exchange rates that were the best indicators of the course of the battle; the new coastal Type XXIII submarine claimed its first victim only in spring 1945. In the last months of the war Allied strategic bomber forces registered their only sustained success of the naval war in destroying 62 submarines and, critically, by imposing a series of delays and losses upon Type XXI and Type XXII construction. Of the 1162 U-boats that were built, 830 saw service: 784 were lost, and of these 696 were destroyed by Allied action.

1944 to 1945

- **1944 (20–27 February)** 'Big Week' bombing of German fighter factories
- **6 March** first major daylight raid on Berlin
- **13 June** first V-1 rockets land in Britain
- **15 June** first use of 22,000lb 'Tallboy' bomb by RAF
- **12 December** Americans capture V-weapon factory at Wittring
- **1945 (13–14 February)** destruction of Dresden in fire storm; 30,000 civilians killed
- **27 March** last V-2 rocket lands in Britain

The strategic bombing offensive, launched four years before by the RAF, finally came of age in 1944. Not until then did either Bomber Command or the United States 8th Air Force have enough bombers in the front line to inflict serious damage on the German economy.

Only in 1944 did the use of newly developed radio direction finding become general, and the accuracy of bombing improve; only in 1944 did the Allies develop the long-range escort fighter, the P-51 Mustang with drop fuel-tanks, which could fight the Luftwaffe over its own territory and win the air superiority necessary to permit further bombing. The vast numerical superiority enjoyed by the Allies was brought to bear with critical effect. By the summer of 1944 the Luftwaffe was no longer an effective fighting force, and the Allies could finally test the strategic value of the Combined Offensive.

Before that stage was reached the Allied supreme commanders insisted that the bombers, kept from the Reich by the strength of German air defences, should instead be used to help pave the way for the Allied invasion of mainland Europe. This help took two forms: first, Operation Pointblank aimed at the destruction of the German air force and its sources of supply; and second, a systematic destruction of tactical targets (bridges, railway lines and storage depots) to prevent the German armed forces from repelling the invasion of Normandy. The bomber commanders objected to the diversion of effort from what they saw as the major objective in the Reich.

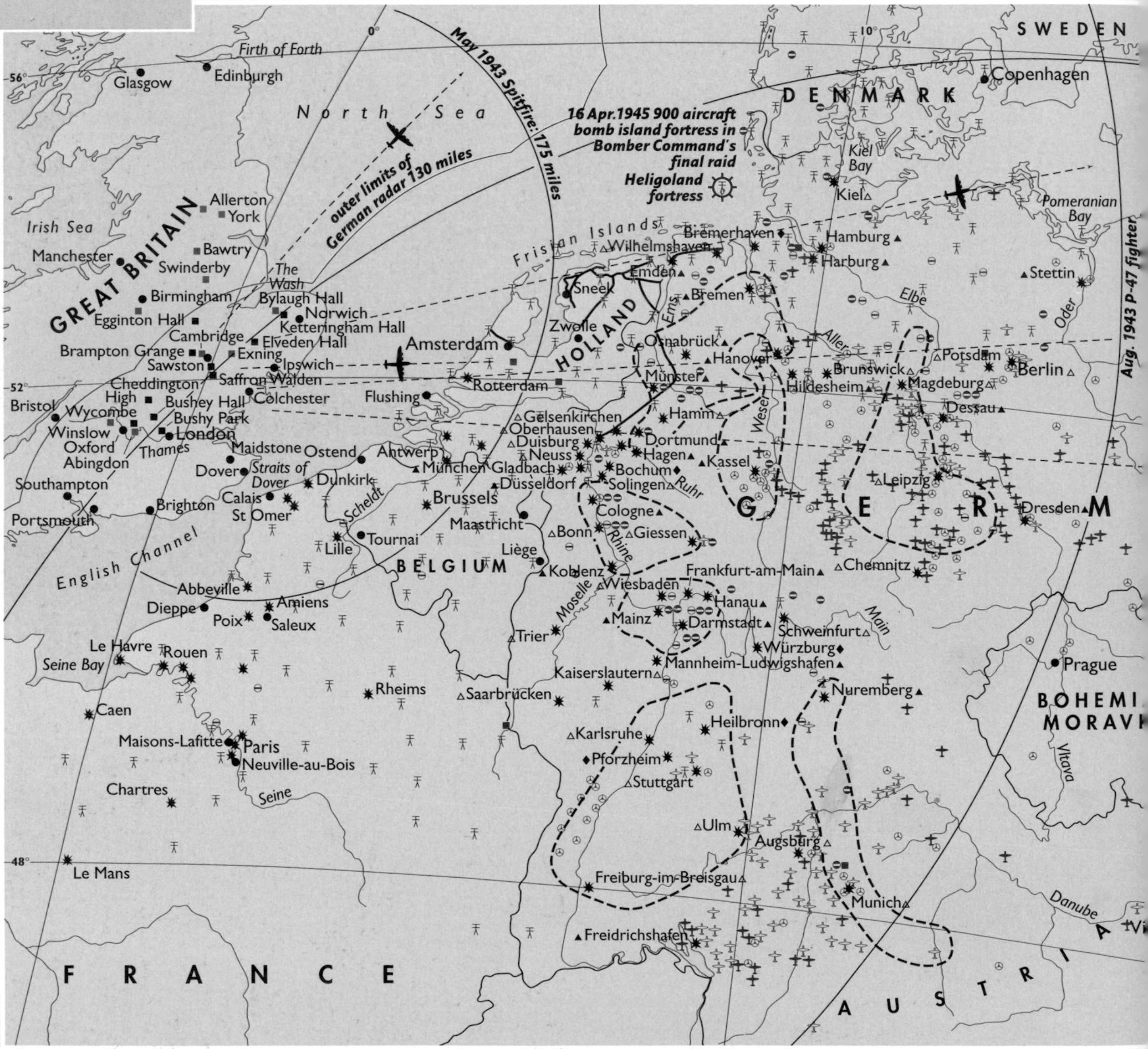

May 1943 Spitfire: 175 miles
outer limits of German radar 130 miles
16 Apr.1945 900 aircraft bomb island fortress in Bomber Command's final raid
Heligoland fortress
Aug. 1943 P-47 fighter
North Sea
Irish Sea
Firth of Forth
English Channel
Straits of Dover
Seine Bay
Frisian Islands
Kiel Bay
Pomeranian Bay
GREAT BRITAIN
HOLLAND
BELGIUM
DENMARK
SWEDEN
FRANCE
GERMANY
AUSTRIA
BOHEMIA MORAVIA
Glasgow
Edinburgh
Manchester
Allerton
York
Bawtry
Swinderby
Birmingham
Egginton Hall
Bylaugh Hall
Norwich
Ketteringham Hall
Cambridge
Elveden Hall
Exning
Brampton Grange
Sawston
Ipswich
Saffron Walden
Cheddington
High Wycombe
Bushey Hall
Bushy Park
Colchester
Bristol
Winslow
Oxford
Abingdon
London
Thames
Maidstone
Dover
Southampton
Portsmouth
Brighton
Amsterdam
Rotterdam
Flushing
Ostend
Antwerp
Dunkirk
Calais
St Omer
Scheldt
Brussels
Tournai
Lille
Maastricht
Liège
Abbeville
Dieppe
Amiens
Poix
Saleux
Le Havre
Rouen
Caen
Rheims
Maisons-Lafitte
Paris
Neuville-au-Bois
Seine
Chartres
Le Mans
Sneek
Zwolle
Emden
Wilhelmshaven
Bremerhaven
Bremen
Ems
Osnabrück
Münster
Hamm
Gelsenkirchen
Oberhausen
Duisburg
Neuss
München Gladbach
Düsseldorf
Dortmund
Hagen
Bochum
Solingen
Ruhr
Cologne
Bonn
Giessen
Rhine
Koblenz
Wiesbaden
Mainz
Moselle
Trier
Frankfurt-am-Main
Hanau
Darmstadt
Schweinfurt
Würzburg
Main
Mannheim-Ludwigshafen
Kaiserslautern
Saarbrücken
Karlsruhe
Heilbronn
Pforzheim
Stuttgart
Ulm
Augsburg
Freiburg-im-Breisgau
Munich
Friedrichshafen
Nuremberg
Kassel
Weser
Hanover
Aller
Brunswick
Hildesheim
Magdeburg
Potsdam
Berlin
Dessau
Leipzig
Chemnitz
Dresden
Hamburg
Harburg
Elbe
Kiel
Copenhagen
Stettin
Oder
Prague
Vltava
Danube

www.raf.mod.uk/bombercommand/
RAF Bomber Command
http://usaaf.com/8thaf/index.htm
US 8th Air Force in World War II

But in practice the attack on the German air force, most successfully carried out in 'Big Week' in February 1944, which destroyed a great deal of the German aircraft industry and of aircraft in the supply pipeline, benefited the strategic bombing offensive as well. The air battle preceding Operation Overlord finally destroyed the German air force, the 'intermediate target', and from June left Allied bombers free to roam over the German heartland.

Although the two Allied air forces still attacked separately by day and night, both now undertook to attack with greater precision, made possible by new navigational aids. In the second half of 1944, first the oil industry then transportation were systematically attacked. Both proved decisive in undermining the continuation of war production at a high level; although German output expanded into late 1944, the last, now irreplaceable, reserves of raw materials were being used up. Strategic attacks in late 1944 and early 1945 brought the German economy to the verge of disintegration. The Combined Offensive fatally weakened the Reich and permitted the armies from east and west to drive into Germany and end the war.

In all, the Combined Offensive dropped 906,000 tonnes of bombs on German and French targets. Most of this was on industrial targets: 224,000 on oil; 319,000 on transportation; 57,000 on the aircraft industry. In addition, the RAF dropped a further 674,000 tonnes on targets in Europe, mainly on German and Italian cities. By March 1945 the 8th Air Force had 7,100 aircraft on hand, Bomber Command 6,900. In total the two forces lost 21,900 aircraft, and 158,000 flying personnel. But the toll on Germany was great, with the destruction of huge areas of urban Germany, and an estimated 420,000 German dead, the great bulk women, children and old men. Indeed, the scale of destruction involved in the firestorm raids on Dresden invoked heated post-war debate concerning the ethics of area-bombing tactics.

Bombing did not bring the war to an end on its own as some of the bombing strategists had hoped. Yet the impact on Germany was very considerable. The bombing offensive required the diversion of enormous resources. By 1944, over two million Germans worked in anti-aircraft defence forces. A third of all artillery production and a fifth of all shells went to anti-aircraft defence, as did half of all electro-technical production and a third of the output of the optical industry. The aluminium used in the anti-aircraft defences would have built an estimated 10–15,000 more fighters. In addition, Allied precision bombing forced the dispersal of much arms production to less efficient and decentralised sites, and left the working population in constant fear of death and disruption. Morale did not collapse, but people reacted with apathy and passivity. Under these circumstances it was impossible for Germany to produce what was needed for the war effort. The German air force planned to produce 80,000 aircraft a year by 1945, but in 1944 could only produce 36,000, many of which were destroyed in transit or at the airfields, or could not be flown for lack of aviation fuel. Without the bombing Germany would have been much more heavily armed with battle front weapons and the Luftwaffe would have proved a much more effective opponent.

1–2 **In the last two years of the war the Combined Bombing Offensive was directed at Germany's industrial economy. The RAF bombed major cities and industrial centres, and the US 8th Air Force attacked precision industrial targets. Technical improvements permitted bombing over most of Germany, escorted by long-range fighter aircraft. In the summer of 1944 Hitler ordered attacks on London with the V-1 flying bomb and later the V-2 rocket. Some 2,420 V-1s and 517 V-2s reached London but this represented only a tiny tonnage of explosives. The effectiveness of the campaign was undermined by Allied bombing of the launch sites, and by fighter attack on the missiles. A large defensive zone – the Diver gun belt – was set up to intercept missiles.**

1 allied bombing, 1944–45

- city subjected to area bombing

percentage of city destroyed:

- 0–50%
- 50–75%
- 75–100%
- main transportation attack zones
- RAF group HQ
- USAAF HQ
- USAAF targets outside Germany

German aircraft industry targets:

- airframe factory established before 1944
- airframe factory established after 1944
- aero engine factory

German defence system:

- German radar station
- night fighter base
- fighter base
- Luftwaffe headquarters

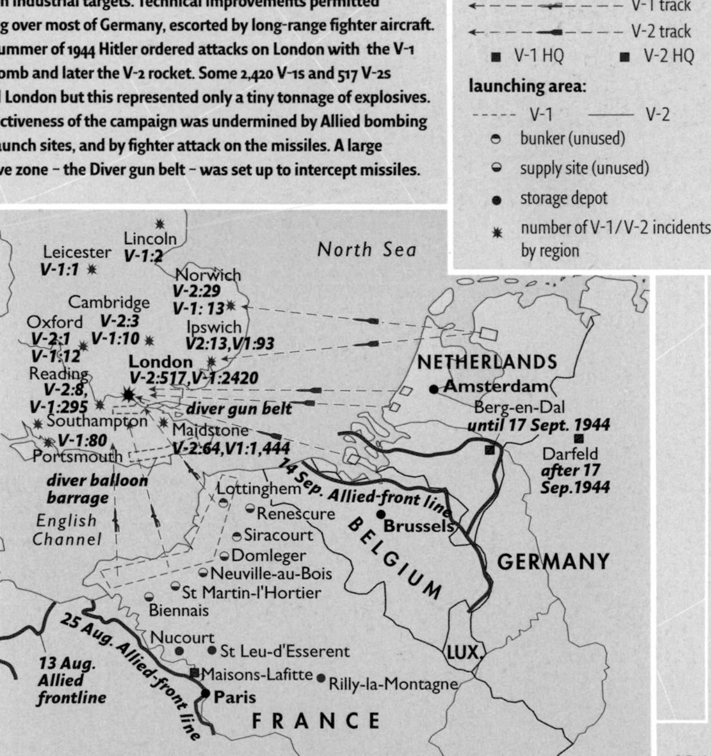

- **1943 (20 December)** US troops land on Makin and Tarawa Atolls (Gilbert Islands)
- **1944 (31 January)** US troops invade Kwajalein and Majura Atolls (Marshall Islands)
- **22 April** Americans land unopposed at Hollandia
- **26 April** Australians take Alexishafen
- **29–30 April** US TF58 attacks Truk Atoll
- **27 May** US troops land on Biak Island
- **14 June** first B29 Superfortress raid on Japan

Despite defeat on Guadalcanal and in eastern New Guinea, until October 1943 the Japanese High Command could console itself with the belief that its policy of waging a defensive war along an extended perimeter, with the aim of wearing down American resolve, was working: after nearly two years Japan's position in the Central and South West Pacific was barely compromised.

The recent reverses in the central Solomons were unpromising in their implications, but a recasting of strategic policy in September 1943 would solve the problem. Saipan–Truk–Timor was designated the main line of resistance in the Pacific, with garrisons to the east assigned a delaying role. The Japanese High Command did not now regard future operations with foreboding and despair. By November 1943, these Japanese assumptions concerning their strength and durability were shown to be an illusion.

Between September and November 1943 the Americans executed two parallel operations (Cartwheel) that had the effect of ripping open the Japanese defensive positions in the Central and South West Pacific, and which simultaneously revealed that Japanese calculations regarding the effectiveness of their fleet based on Truk were flawed. Rather than being able to check American advances in either the Central or the South West Pacific from Truk, the Imperial Fleet was shown to be unable to concentrate against either offensive. Carrier raids on the Japanese base at Rabaul in November 1943 effectively neutralised it; the base thereafter was bypassed, while in that same month a series of landings in the Gilbert Islands gave the Americans control of the island group and placed them in a position from which operations against the Marshall Is. could be successfully launched.

The prosecution of a two-front war in the Pacific by the Americans was largely the result of a major expansion of the US Pacific Fleet during 1943; for example, they could now afford to deploy 11 fleet and light fleet carriers in support of the Gilbert landings.

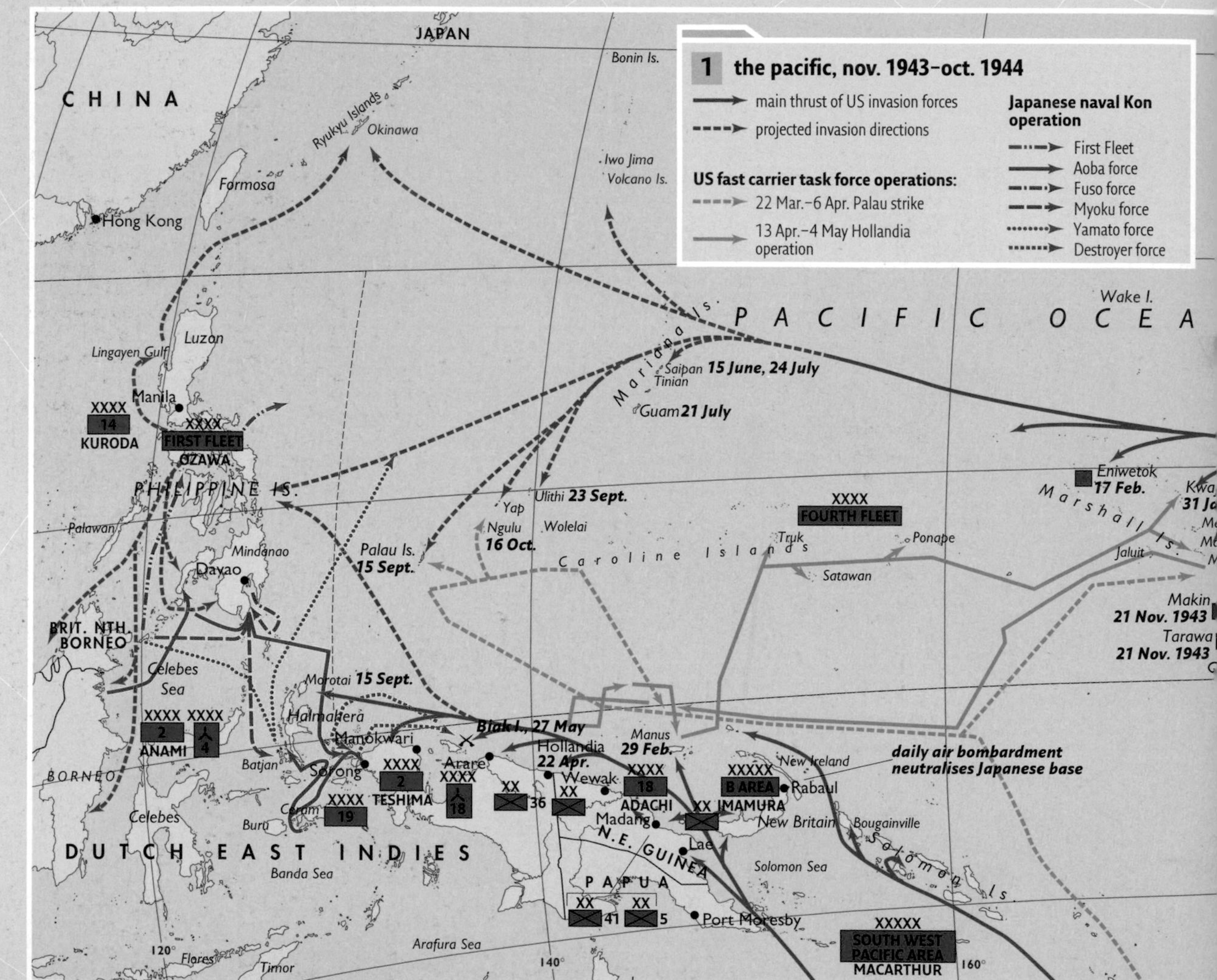

www.empereur.com/G._Douglas_MacArthur.html
General Douglas MacArthur, Commander-in-Chief, South West Pacific Area forces
http://ajrp.awm.gov.au/
Australia–Japan Research Project for the War in the South West Pacific

This greatly increased strength prompted the US Navy to insist upon an advance to Saipan in the Marianas, from which a bombing campaign against the Japanese Home Islands could be mounted. There was no agreement within the American High Command on the crucial questions of which of these offensives – Central or South West Pacific – was the major effort; further, no decision had yet been reached concerning which targets in the Western Pacific would be selected for the next major Allied offensive effort. The heavy losses sustained during the US invasion of Tarawa in the Gilberts temporarily strengthened the claims of MacArthur's South West Pacific command for primacy. However, a combination of policy decision and the momentum of events in the Central Pacific were instrumental in redressing the balance: the Marshalls and Eniwetok were cleared between 31 January and 23 April 1944, during which period an American carrier force rampaged through the Central Pacific, penetrating as far west as the Palaus, which forced the Japanese Combined Fleet to withdraw its main forces to Singapore.

With the Japanese base at Truk neutralised, the whole of the Central and South West Pacific was bared to American arms, despite the Japanese attempt to recast defensive plans around the Saipan–Truk–western New Guinea line. Long before such an intention could be translated into reality, however, the Japanese had been forced to withdraw their southern flank in the face of American coast-hopping advances along the northern shore of New Guinea. The Japanese now hoped that any future American move would be made against a target in defence of which the Japanese could concentrate their land- and carrier-based air power in such strength as to meet and defeat the enemy. The American landings on Biak on 27 May seemingly provided the Japanese with the opportunity to force battle upon the Americans, but even as the Imperial Navy tried to assemble forces for a counter-attack the main American effort was developed in the Marianas; US carrier forces first neutralised Japanese land-based air power in the island group and then effectively destroyed its carrier-borne air power in the Battle of the Philippine Sea.

Thereafter, the US Navy considered their target options in the Western Pacific. The Japanese defensive perimeter had been decisively ruptured, and their means of sustaining such an oceanic perimeter – the Combined Fleet – was falling back in disarray. A direct move might be made against Iwo Jima, which would place US bombers with fighter escorts in easy range of the Japanese Home Islands. A successful assault on Okinawa would drive a wedge between the Home Islands and the Southern Resources Area. However, MacArthur's claim that the Philippines be made the American priority received unexpected support in September 1944, when a US carrier raid encountered little resistance over the islands. As a result of this, the timetable that had scheduled amphibious landings on Leyte in the southern Philippines was urgently accelerated.

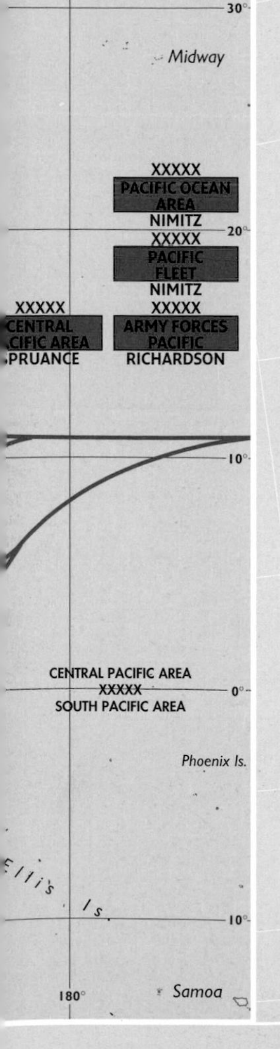

1 **Between 20–29 Nov. 1943 American forces successfully occupied six atolls in the Gilberts, thereby breaching the Japanese outer defensive perimeter in the Central Pacific. The results that flowed from this were enormously significant. From the Gilberts the Americans secured the undefended atoll of Majuro in the Marshalls, which thus became the first national territory lost by Japan in the course of the war. On the same day, American forces landed on the atoll of Kwajalein and secured Kwajalein Island by 4 Feb., and Eniwetok between 17–23 Feb. Thereafter the Americans completed the clearing of the Marshalls, but for the Japanese garrisons on Wotje, Maloelap, Jaluit and Mili. Throughout these operations the Imperial Navy was helpless to intervene, and instead collected its forces, in the Kon operation, for a decisive action in the Philippine Sea. The loss of the Gilberts, Maluro and Kwajalein rendered both Truk and Rabaul indefensible, and two massive carrier raids on Truk, on 17–18 Feb. and 29–30 Apr., completed the destruction of Japanese power in the Carolines.**

2 **The close investment of Rabaul was achieved by Allied landings on western New Britain and in the Admiralty Islands. between 15 Dec. 1943 and 20 Mar. 1944. Its distant blockade was completed as a result of landings at Hollandia and Aitape on 22 Apr., which bypassed the Japanese Eighteenth Army around Wewak. The loss of Hollandia forced the Japanese to substitute Biak and Manokwari as their twin centres of resistance in New Guinea but losses at sea led the Japanese to abandon these in favour of Sorong and Halmahera. US landings on Biak induced the Japanese to force 'the decisive battle' upon the Americans off the island, but it was not until June that battle forces were committed to action, and by the time that these reached Batjan US carrier forces had raided Guam, Tinian and Saipan. No decisive action was fought in the South West Pacific, but even without one the Allied front had advanced some 500 miles in two months.**

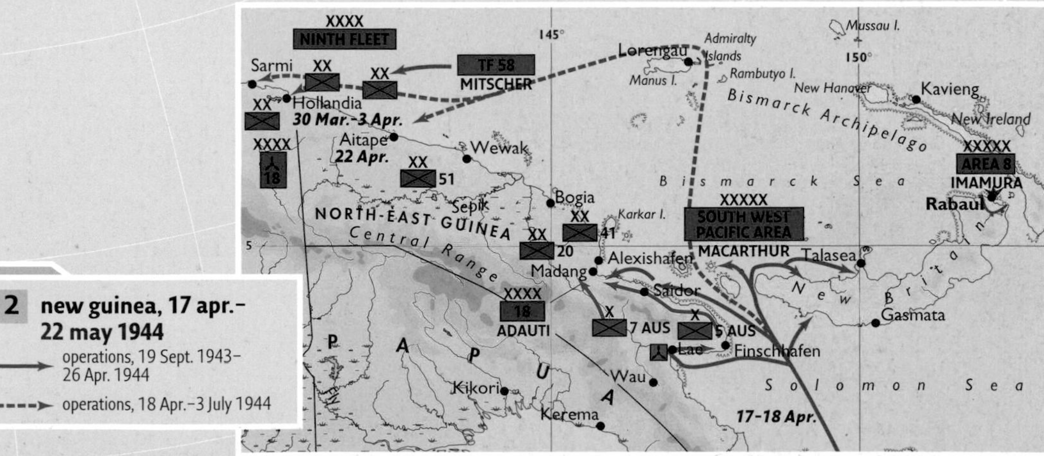

2 **new guinea, 17 apr.–22 may 1944**

operations, 19 Sept. 1943–26 Apr. 1944

operations, 18 Apr.–3 July 1944

june to august 1944

- **11 June** US TF58 begins bombardment of Marianas
- **15 June** US Marines land on Saipan
- **19–20 June** Battle of Philippine Sea: Japanese lose 300 aircraft and 14 ships sunk or damaged
- **27 June** heavy fighting on Saipan; Admirals Nagumo and Yano killed
- **7 July** Japanese wiped out on Saipan
- **21 July** US Marines land on Guam
- **21 July** US Marines land on Tinian (secured 1 August)
- **9 August** destruction of Japanese on Guam

After November 1943 the Japanese were presented with the problem of trying to counter a twin American offensive across the Pacific: without the means to meet even one of these thrusts, the Japanese Fleet was unable to prevent either the isolation of Rabaul or the collapse of the outer defensive perimeter in the Central Pacific. Nevertheless the Japanese could not decline battle as the Americans reached into the Western Pacific to positions from which they could menace the Southern Resources Area. By spring 1944 Japan was intent upon a policy of resistance in the Marianas, the Carolines and western New Guinea.

In a halting, irresolute manner the Japanese attempted to offer battle when the Americans landed on Biak in May, but the test of Japanese resolve occurred on 11 June when American carrier forces struck Guam, Saipan and Tinian as the prelude to landings in the Marianas. With Saipan as their first and main objective, the Americans sought to secure the Marianas as the base for further operations into the western Pacific and for bombing operations against the Home Islands. The result of this clash of aims was the first carrier battle in the Pacific for 20 months – and the greatest carrier battle of the war. The Battle of the Philippine Sea was an overwhelming victory for the United States, though the full extent of their victory was not readily apparent at the time.

By the time American forces came ashore on Saipan, on 15 June, the basis of an American victory had been established by the neutralisation of Japanese shore-based air power in the Marianas. The Japanese had planned to combine this with their carrier-borne air power in order that they each might compensate for the weakness of the other, thus allowing the Imperial Navy to give battle on the basis of numerical equality. With nine carriers and 450 aircraft under command, Ozawa's 1st Mobile Fleet was massively inferior in numbers and quality to America's TF58 (Mitscher), which had at its disposal 15 carriers and 902 aircraft. TF58 also had intelligence decrypts of Japanese intentions and plans, but divergent tasks to perform. In addition to the countering of shore-based air power, it had to provide cover for the US amphibious forces committed to the Marianas while dealing with the Japanese Fleet. Despite numerical and qualitative inferiority, the Japanese possessed two advantages over the Americans: the superior range of their aircraft and an advantageous position. The prevailing trade winds from the east allowed the Japanese to engage at long range an enemy that could not close because of the need to steam away from the wind in order to successfully launch and recover aircraft.

Faced with these tasks Vice Admiral Spruance chose to await an attack and to concentrate his fighter strength in defence of his groups. Despite all but running out of sea room, on 19 June these tactics worked. By the morning of 20 June only 100 serviceable aircraft remained to the Japanese carriers, and two of these had been sunk by submarine attacks (including Ozawa's flagship). Meanwhile, the US carriers continued to pound Japanese airfields in the Marianas.

2 philippine sea, 19–21 june

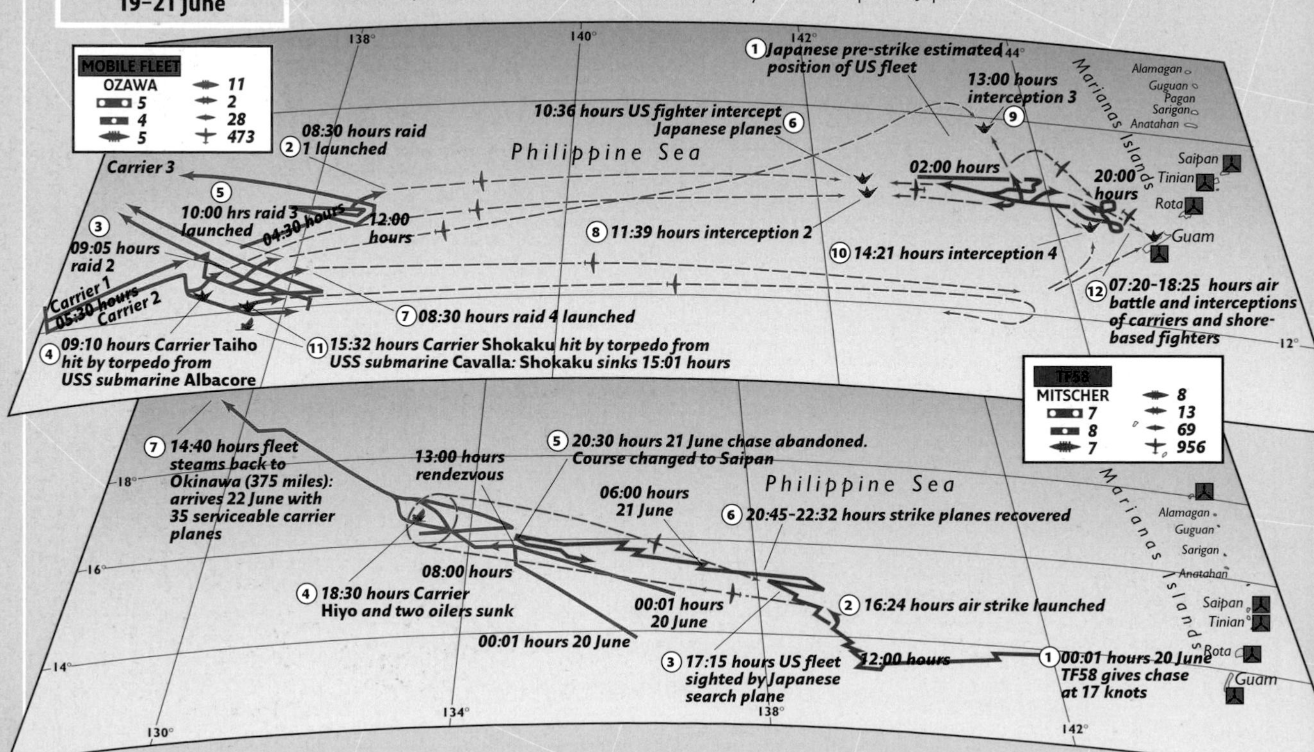

www.navyleague.org/sea_power/jun_04_46.php
The 'Great Marianas Turkey Shoot': the June 1944 air battle off the coast of Saipan
http://navysite.de/ships/lha2about.htm
The Battle for Saipan

Misled by claims of success by his own pilots and headquarters ashore, Ozawa intended to refuel his ships on 20 June and resume the battle on 21 June. He was out of touch with the battle after his flagship was sunk, and it was not until he reboarded a carrier at midday on 20 June that he became aware of the extent of his previous day's losses: Ozawa then ordered a retirement. But by then it was too late for the Japanese to escape. American carrier aircraft, operating at extreme range and in failing light, sank one fleet carrier and damaged four more carriers, one battleship, one cruiser and two oilers (both of which were scuttled). At the end of this attack the Japanese were left with 35 aircraft: the attack cost the Americans 99 of the 216 aircraft committed to the strike, 82 being lost in trying to return to their carriers.

Having failed to regain contact on 22 June, TF58 struck Pagan on 23 June and the Jimas on 24 June, its final toll of Japanese shore-based air power between 17–24 June being about 200 aircraft. The American victory off the Marianas – popularly known as the 'Great Marianas Turkey Shoot' – ensured the ultimate fall of any island in the group the Americans wished to take; it was also a victory from which the Japanese were not able to recover. Because of the speed with which the Americans were able to develop operations against the Philippines, in the wake of the Marianas battle, the Imperial Navy was never again able to challenge the Americans with a balanced fleet.

1-2 **The US decision to land on Saipan saw their fleet entering the Philippine Sea, thus crossing the Japanese perimeter defensive. Numerous air searches, however, failed to detect the Japanese fleet, which held off until the landings were under way. The mastery of ship-to-shore assaults under fire was essential to American success in the central and western Pacific. On the morning of 15 June a huge fleet of US transports steamed into their positions. While the landings went according to plan, the island was not secured for three weeks; 27,000 Japanese, almost the entire garrison, were killed. The US fleet remained off Saipan providing constant air and naval bombardment until 8 June, when it prepared to meet the advancing Japanese fleet. The Battle of the Philippine Sea revolved around a series of air strikes that saw approximately 280 Japanese planes shot down for the cost of approximately 20 US planes. The second half of the action, a chase by US forces on the retreating Japanese fleet, was subsequently abandoned to concentrate on providing support for the further landings on Guam and Tinian.**

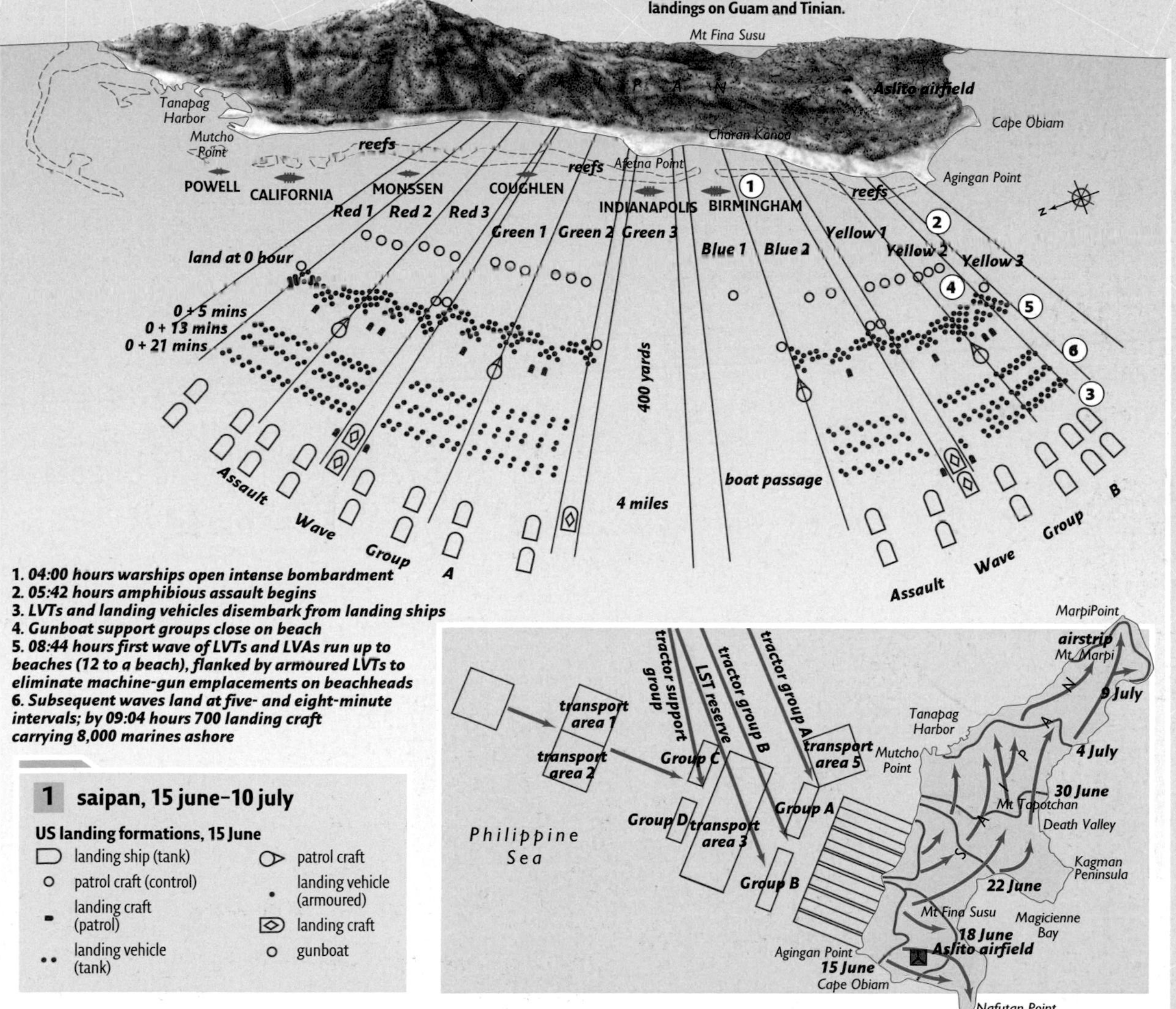

china

1941 to 1945

- **1941 (21 April)** Japanese occupy Foochow
- **8–13 August** Japanese air raids on Chungking
- **28 September** Japanese occupy Changsha
- **18 December** Japanese land on Hong Kong
- **1942 (10 March)** General Stilwell appointed Chief of Staff in China
- **11 May** Japanese offensives in Yunnan and Chekiang provinces
- **1943 (September)** Chiang Kai-shek becomes President of Chinese Republic
- **3 October** Japanese attack in central China
- **1944 (13 January)** Chinese occupy Hukawng Valley
- **18 April** Operation Ichi-Go: Japanese attack to control Peking-Hankow railway
- **18 June** Japanese take Changsha

The nature of the China theatre between 1939 and 1945 was dominated by the fact that in 1937 and 1938 the Japanese overran virtually the whole of China that was worth occupying, and apart from a series of coastal operations in the south in 1941, their basic stance in China thereafter was defensive. This left three main parties to struggle for power in China: the Kuomintang (KMT) regime of Chiang Kai-shek; the Communists of Mao Tse-tung and the Japanese.

Without the means to bring the Kuomintang regime to the peace table by further military victories, the Japanese were to be led into Indo-China and thence into the Pacific war in their attempt to ensure the isolation of Chungking, yet at the same time the Japanese authorities would not invest the puppet regime at Nanking (nor its Peking rival) with power sufficient to allow it to present itself as a credible alternative to the Kuomintang. For its part, the latter increasingly adopted a passive policy towards the Japanese forces of occupation to the extent that American liaison teams coming to China before the outbreak of the Pacific war were shocked to find that 'special undeclared peace' prevailed in much of the country and that a flourishing trade existed across no man's land: indeed, it was one standing American grievance that throughout the war the Japanese outbid the United States for Kuomintang-supplied tungsten.

Kuomintang acquiescence in Japanese occupation of much of China was primarily the result of Chiang's calculation that Japan's ultimate defeat was assured and that the Japanese would be forced to relinquish their holdings in China by the Allies. Moreover, Kuomintang strength had to be preserved in readiness for a resumption of the struggle with the Communists. Communist policy was no more than a mirror

www.militaryhistoryonline.com/wwii/articles/airlifttochina.aspx
The Allied airlift of supplies to China (the Hump air-supply route)
http://en.wikipedia.org/wiki/Operation_Ichigo
Operation Ichi-Go; the Japanese 1944 offensive in China

image of that of Chungking. The cooperation between the two factions established as a result of the Sian Incident was little more than nominal: the period between 1940 and 1945 was marked by many clashes between the Communists and Kuomintang. These soon badly compromised Communist offensive power and forced the Communists to attempt to reconsolidate their position in Yenan rather than actively pursue operations against either of their enemies.

The limited offensive capacity of all three parties in effect led to the observation of de facto truces between the Japanese and each of the Chinese factions, though these were punctuated by periodic rice raids and by a series of ferocious pacification operations, in which the Japanese adopted policies of systematic and widespread slaughter and destruction. But the main threat of these various accommodations was presented by the American determination to develop China as an active theatre of military and air operations as a complement to the US naval and amphibious efforts in the Pacific. A Chinese army of 90 divisions was raised for large-scale offensive operations and air bases developed in south-east China for a bombing campaign of the Japanese Home Islands.

Practical difficulties of supplying China from India on the scale needed to realise these intentions, and Chungking's procrastination in meeting American expectations, ultimately led to the trimming of American aims, with the result that the strategic air offensive came to represent the main American undertaking. In the event, however, this policy produced the very situation that the air effort was supposed to forestall: a general Japanese offensive – Operation Ichi-Go – throughout southern China, aimed at eliminating the air bases from which the US bombers were to attack Japan.

This Japanese effort, the last major Japanese offensive effort of the war, began in April 1944 with the clearing of that part of Honan that had remained in KMT hands since 1938: the collapse of KMT resistance in the province led to massacres of fleeing Nationalist troops by an enraged and deserted peasantry. Thereafter the main Japanese effort across the middle Yangtze began on 27 May and over the next six months various converging Japanese offensives slowly resulted in linking up existing holdings. By late November, the Japanese were able to claim the establishment of uninterrupted overland communications between Singapore and Manchuria: the elimination of US air bases throughout southern China was all but completed at the same time. However, the decision to capture the Marianas had freed the Americans of the need for air bases in China, and whatever gains the Japanese had made were illusory. By spring 1945, the Japanese had begun to withdraw from their recent conquests as a result of belated awareness of over-extension and the need to consolidate their positions in northern China and Manchuria: as they did so they were followed, usually at a respectful distance, by KMT and Communist forces seeking to steal a march on one another in anticipation of the resumption of the 'real' war.

1-2 **For most of the period between 1941 and 1945 China represented an untidy patchwork of various factions contending for control within it. Though nominally all of northern China was under Japanese control, in reality Japanese occupation extended primarily over the main centres of population, industrial and mining areas, and lines of communication: rural areas were mostly under KMT or Communist control or under no formal control whatsoever. In general terms, however, Communist influence prevailed in northern China, whereas KMT power extended over 'unoccupied' China, and it was in the latter areas that the Americans had to develop the airfields from which to stage operations against Japan. The main concentration of these airfields lay along the Changsha–Kweilin axis, and it was here that the Japanese made their main effort – the Operation Ichi-Go offensive – between May and December 1944. This offensive provided the essential background to the final denouement of US policy in China. It brought to a head the rivalry inherent in American plans for both air and military operations. The predominance of the air plan in 1944 owed much to Chiang Kai-shek's willingness to sanction an offensive requiring minimal KMT involvement. The ranking American officer in China, Stilwell, was opposed to both Chiang because of KMT passivity and to the air plan because of the lack of ground forces needed to ensure the security of the air bases. When the Japanese offensive began to fulfill Stilwell's prediction, Washington demanded of Chiang that Stilwell be given effective control of the whole KMT regime. But without the means to enforce this demand, Washington had to recall Stilwell when Chungking demanded his removal: thereafter the US administration found itself bound to the Chungking regime. The KMT were, however, eventually to lose the struggle for control of those areas formerly in Japanese hands, their forces in the south being steadily eroded by the northern-based Communists.**

2 china, 1945

- areas re-occupied by KMT in 1945
- areas under full Communist control, Aug. 1945
- areas under partial Communist control, Aug. 1945

ukraine and **crimea**

december 1943 to **may 1944**

- **1943 (3 December)** Red Army advances on wide front
- **14 December** Cherkassy captured; Soviets begin winter offensive
- **31 December** Red Army takes Zhitomir
- **1944 (6 January)** Red Army advances into Poland
- **24 March** River Dnieper reached by Red Army
- **10 April** Red Army captures Odessa
- **9 May** Red Army captures Sevastopol, ending German presence in Crimea

The end of 1943 marked the completion of a fundamental shift in the balance of forces on the Eastern Front. The next phase of the war witnessed the final expulsion of enemy troops from Soviet soil, and the beginning of Germany's slide towards total military defeat. The Teheran conference in November 1943 had firmly fixed the date of Operation Overlord – the opening of the second front in the west – in the late spring of 1944. This gave Stalin encouragement that a major effort drawing off German forces was not far away, and also kept rival Allied armies away from his southern flank, giving the Soviet Union a free hand.

By 23 December 1943 Soviet forces had reached a line west of Kiev and north of the Crimean peninsula. In Ukraine, the Red Army resumed offensive operations on Christmas Eve 1943. These operations, collectively known as those for the 'Right Bank Ukraine' (west of the Dnieper), lasted from 24 December 1943 to 17 April 1944 and extended over a front of 900 miles. The objectives were the destruction of German Army Groups A and South (von Manstein). Simultaneously with the right bank Ukraine operations, Soviet forces also attacked at Leningrad and Novgorod (14 January to 1 March 1944). In Ukraine, Stavka launched a strategic offensive operation with five Fronts (1st (Vatutin), 2nd (Koniev), 3rd (Malinovsky) and 4th Ukrainian (Tolbukhin) and 2nd Belarussian (Kurochkin)). Stavka representatives co-ordinating the actions of the several Fronts were Zhukov (1st and 2nd Ukrainian) and Vasilevski (3rd and 4th Ukrainian). The operations fell into two phases: winter (to the end of February) and spring (4 March to 17 April). Right bank Ukraine comprised no fewer than ten component operations.

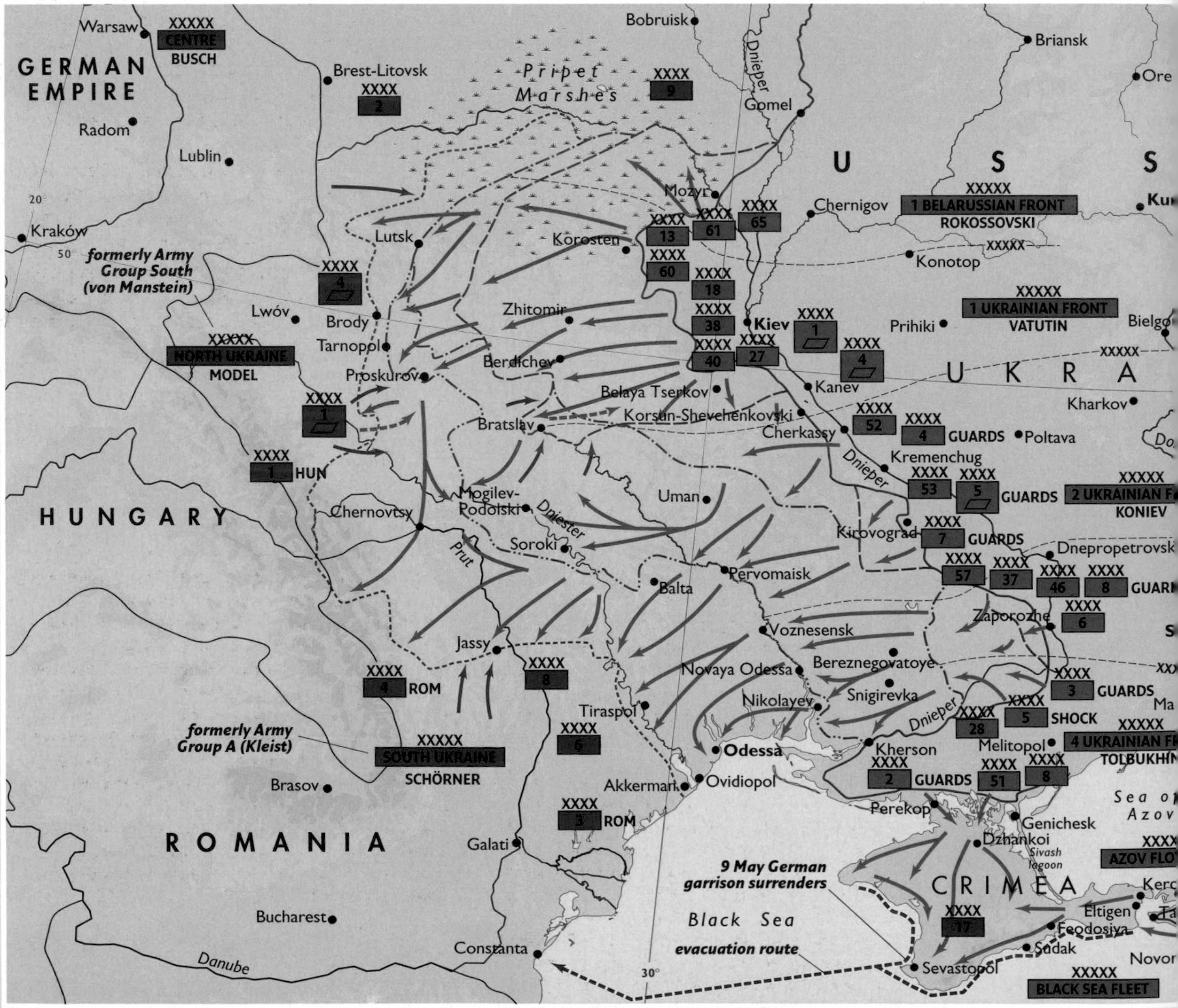

www.infoukes.com/history/ww2/
The Ukrainian experience in World War Two
www.worldwar2database.com/html/sovietoffensive.htm
The Soviet Offensive, July 1943–May 1945, with images and further web links

In the last days of 1943 1st Ukrainian pushed German armies away from Kiev, clearing Belaya Tserkov and Berdichev by 5 January. On that day 2nd Ukrainian, working in cooperation with 1st, attacked near Kirovograd. The weather helped the ground forces, light snow and frost hardening the ground, but low cloud hindered aircraft. Neither 1st nor 2nd Ukrainian Fronts could collapse the German salient jutting out as far as the Dnieper around Korsun-Shevchenkovski, where hilly country aided the defence by 12 German divisions from First Panzer and Eighth Army from von Manstein's Army Group South. This became the object of a special operation (24 January to 17 February), a classic encirclement battle by both fronts that ended with carnage and debris strewn across the snow. The encircled grouping had comprised about 73,000 officers and men. In addition, 15 German divisions attacking the outer front of the encirclement suffered severely.

The southern grouping of 1st Ukrainian broke through to Tarnopol and Proskurov, splitting the German First and Fourth Panzer Armies. The 2nd Ukrainian Front defeated the German Eighth Army, its forward detachments reaching the southern Bug and preventing First Panzer Army's withdrawal. Mobile Groups also cut off the withdrawal of the Bereznegovatoye–Snigirevka groupings. A huge hole had also been smashed between Army Groups South and A. Between 11 and 13 March, Stavka approved Zhukov's plan to carry on over the Dniester and as far as Chernovtsy, on the Prut near the Romanian border. The effect of this was finally to split German forces in Poland from those in the southern Soviet Union, the latter backing nervously onto the Danube.

The Germans had held onto the Crimea for longer than might have been expected. As a result of the Melitopol and Kerch-Eltigen (amphibious) operations of 1943 the Red Army was at last in a position to assault the peninsula, with its key naval base at Sevastopol and its ability to command the Black Sea and the Romanian and Bulgarian littoral. By early 1944 Soviet troops had broken through the 'Turkish Wall' and seized bridgeheads over the wide, salty Sivash lagoon. The 4th Ukrainian Front attacked from Sivash–Perekop, and the Independent Primorsk Army (Yeremenko) from the Kerch peninsula bridgehead in the east. The Soviet operation was launched on 8 April, reaching the approaches to Sevastopol on 5 May. The speed with which the Soviets recaptured the fortress-port was remarkable.

Throughout, German reactions were divided. Hitler constantly expected exhaustion to bring the Red Army to a halt; others expected the rasputitsa, to halt them in March. Von Manstein was less optimistic, in February expecting the Red Army to sever the Lwów–Odessa railway behind the northern flank of Army Group South. He did not, however, expect operations on the scale of the second (spring) phase, with four Fronts attacking from the Pripet Marshes to the Black Sea, which aimed to utterly destroy German forces in the south. Gehlen, in charge of German military intelligence, reeled off cold statistics and reported on 30 March that the Soviets could sustain continuous operations; they would undoubtedly move on to the eastern frontier of the Reich.

By 17 April the Red Army had been on the unbroken offensive for four months and destroyed the entire southern wing of the German armies, except for Seventeenth Army locked in the Crimea, and by mid-May the Crimea was also recovered. Four million Soviet troops, over 45,000 guns and mortars, over 4,000 tanks and assault guns and 4,000 aircraft had attacked on a 900-mile-wide front in one of the most gigantic operations of the war, penetrating 150–300 miles to the Carpathians.

1 ukraine and crimea, dec. 1943–may 1944

—— 24 Dec. 1943	—··— 21 Mar. 1944
— — 23 Jan. 1944	------ 12 May 1944
—·—· 4 Mar. 1944	——▶ German counter-attack

1 **On 23 Dec. 1943 Soviet forces had advanced to a line stretching from Leningrad in the north to Sivash lagoon in the south, the boundary of the Crimean peninsula. By May 1944 they had recovered the Crimea and Ukraine; but Axis forces still possessed Belarus. Operations to recover Ukraine west of the Dnieper ('Right bank Ukraine') began on 23 Dec. 1943. This comprised component operations that lasted until 17 Apr. In addition, the Crimean Operation (8 Apr.–May 1944) constituted an 11th operation. Soviet forces totalled 470,000 men, 6,000 guns and mortars, 560 tanks and assault guns and 1,250 aircraft. In addition, the Black Sea Fleet and the Azov Flotilla would support the offensive. German forces comprised 150,000 German and Romanian troops (11 divisions), and the bulk of the German Seventeenth Army withdrawn from Taman, under General Jänecke. Jänecke's forces could have considerable confidence in their three defensive belts opposite the Sivash bridgehead, two on the Perekop isthmus and four against the Kerch bridgehead. However, against Soviet superiority they crumpled quickly. The attack from north and east was launched on 8 Apr. By 12 Apr. Soviet forces were pursuing Axis troops withdrawing from the east of the peninsula, initially along the Feodosiya–Sudak–Sevastopol route. By 9 May Sevastopol's German garrison had surrendered, the remnants of Seventeenth Army withdrawing along the Kherson head. Massive Soviet air superiority made it possible to massacre troops attempting to withdraw from Sevastopol to Constanta and Varna. The Soviets also attacked convoys carrying troops out with aircraft and submarines, major attacks occurring midway between the Romanian coast and the Crimea on 23 Apr., 3 and 12 May, and off Sevastopol on 12 Apr. and 11 May. By noon on 12 May, 25,000 German troops had surrendered at Kherson. Soviet estimates of German losses – the destruction of Seventeenth Army – total 110,000 killed, wounded and prisoners.**

1944

- **3 January** Red Army takes Olevsk and cuts railway to Warsaw
- **27 June** Red Army crosses River Dnieper
- **1 July** Red Army crosses River Berezina
- **3 July** Minsk falls to Soviet forces
- **17 July** Red Army crosses River Bug into Poland
- **28 July** German forces encirled at Brest-Litovsk
- **31 July** Soviet armies 10 miles from Warsaw

Soviet planning for the Belarussian operation began in spring 1944. The Soviet High Command reached the conclusion that White Russia and its capital Minsk was the next priority for liberation, a conclusion anticipated by German Army Group Centre. The latter's large salient still appeared threateningly close to Moscow, and still posed a potential air threat to the northern flank of the three Ukrainian Fronts, preventing any offensive by the latter further west. The Belarussian salient also represented the shortest route for Soviet forces to the heart of Germany.

The operation was code-named Bagration, after one of the heroes of 1812, and the sense of grand opera was maintained in the timing of the assault, to begin on 22 June, three years to the day after the German invasion of Russia. In May the scope of the operation was extended, to a depth of 400 miles, in order to take it well clear of the Pripet Marshes and seize the 'land bridge' between the Dvina and Neman rivers. The operation would extend almost as far from north to south. It would also take place after the Allied landing in Normandy, exploiting the Anglo-American challenge to German land power and any confusion arising from German involvement in a two-front land war.

Soviet forces comprised 19 all-arms and two tank armies, in all 1.4 million men, 31,000 guns and mortars, 5,200 tanks and assault guns, supported by over 5,000 aircraft. The principal military objective, agreed at a Stavka conference on 22–23 May 1944, was destruction of the German Army Group Centre, with a simultaneous breakthrough on six sectors (each forward Soviet division in these sectors thus having a front of 1.5 kilometres), and with the three Belarussian Fronts converging on the main forces of Army Group Centre in the Minsk area. German forces had adopted a deeply echeloned defensive position, up to 17 miles deep and comprising in all 1.2 million men, 9,500 guns and mortars, 900 tanks and assault guns and 1,350 aircraft.

On 10 June, German intercepts picked up an order to partisans behind German lines ordering them to step up the 'rail war' and cripple troop movements from 20 June onwards. Railway lines west of Minsk were attacked on 19–20 June. On the night of 22–23 June, Soviet long-range aircraft attacked, first airfields and railway lines, then artillery positions and reserves and troops on the move. German reports noted new, more skilful infantry tactics and the employment of air forces 'on a scale not previously experienced'.

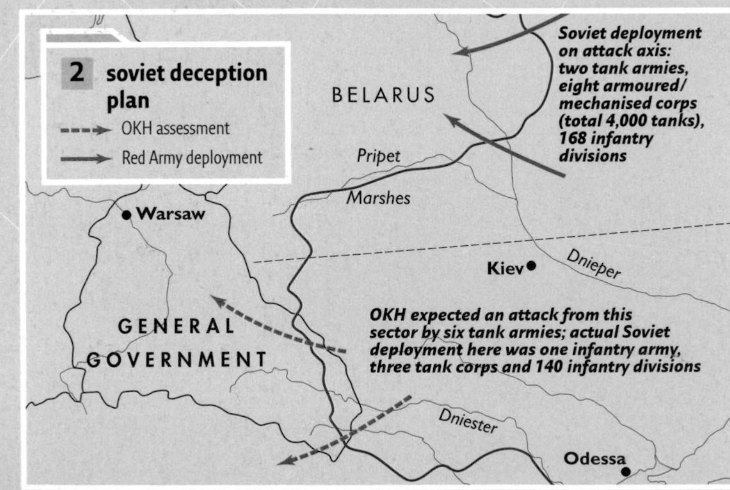

The first phase, from 23 June to 4 July, comprised the Bobruisk, Vitebsk-Orsha, Mogilev and Polotsk operations and completed the encirclement of the Minsk grouping. By the evening of 26 June 1st Belarussian Front forces were breaking into Army Group Centre positions in the Bobruisk area and 3rd Belarussian between Vitebsk and Orsha, two cities, which, together with Mogilev, Hitler had ordered should be held as 'firm positions' (*Feste Plätze*): to the last round and the last man. By the evening of 3 July, XXVII Panzer Corps, 110th Division and Task Force Müller were on the run and encircled east of Minsk, with the rest of Army Group Centre being pushed back west of Minsk. In the second phase (5 July to 29 August) the Fronts conducted five more offensive operations: Siauliai, Vilna, Kaunas, Białystok and Lublin-Brest- Litovsk. The grouping encircled east of Minsk was destroyed (5–11 July). By 8 July, Model, who had taken command of Army Group Centre from Busch on 28 June, requested a meeting with Hitler, seeking to extricate the Vilna garrison. Hitler, characteristically, ordered it to be held at all costs. He agreed, at Model's insistence, to some reinforcement of Army Group Centre from Army Group North, but refused to countenance the latter's withdrawal, Admiral Dönitz insisting that the Baltic ports be kept open. Vilna fell on 13 July, Pinsk on the 14 July and Grodno on the 16 July. On 15 July the Russians gained their first bridgehead over the Neman at Alytus.

Hitler's insistence on holding 'firm positions' and refusal to allow withdrawal had contributed to the entrapment of large German forces. Army Group Centre had been destroyed in a classic *Kesselschlacht* (cauldron battle), with 17 divisions totally annihilated and 50 losing half their strength. On 20 July, the day when the destruction of the Army Group was finally accomplished, German officers, dismayed at Hitler's conduct of the war, made an attempt on his life. It failed. Meanwhile the Soviet advance, inevitably, ran out of steam. They had reached a line just east of Kaunas. In the next month they pushed forward, just touching the frontier of East Prussia. In the south, they pushed on another 60 miles, to Warsaw. While the restoration of territory was symbolic and significant in terms of prestige, the Belarussian Strategic Offensive Operation underscored a classic rule of war: that the enemy's main forces must be the primary objective.

http://victory.archives.gov.by/e_arx_doc/e_osvob.html
Images of the liberation of Belarus
http://en.wikipedia.org/wiki/Operation_Bagration
Operation Bagration, the Soviet advance through Belarus

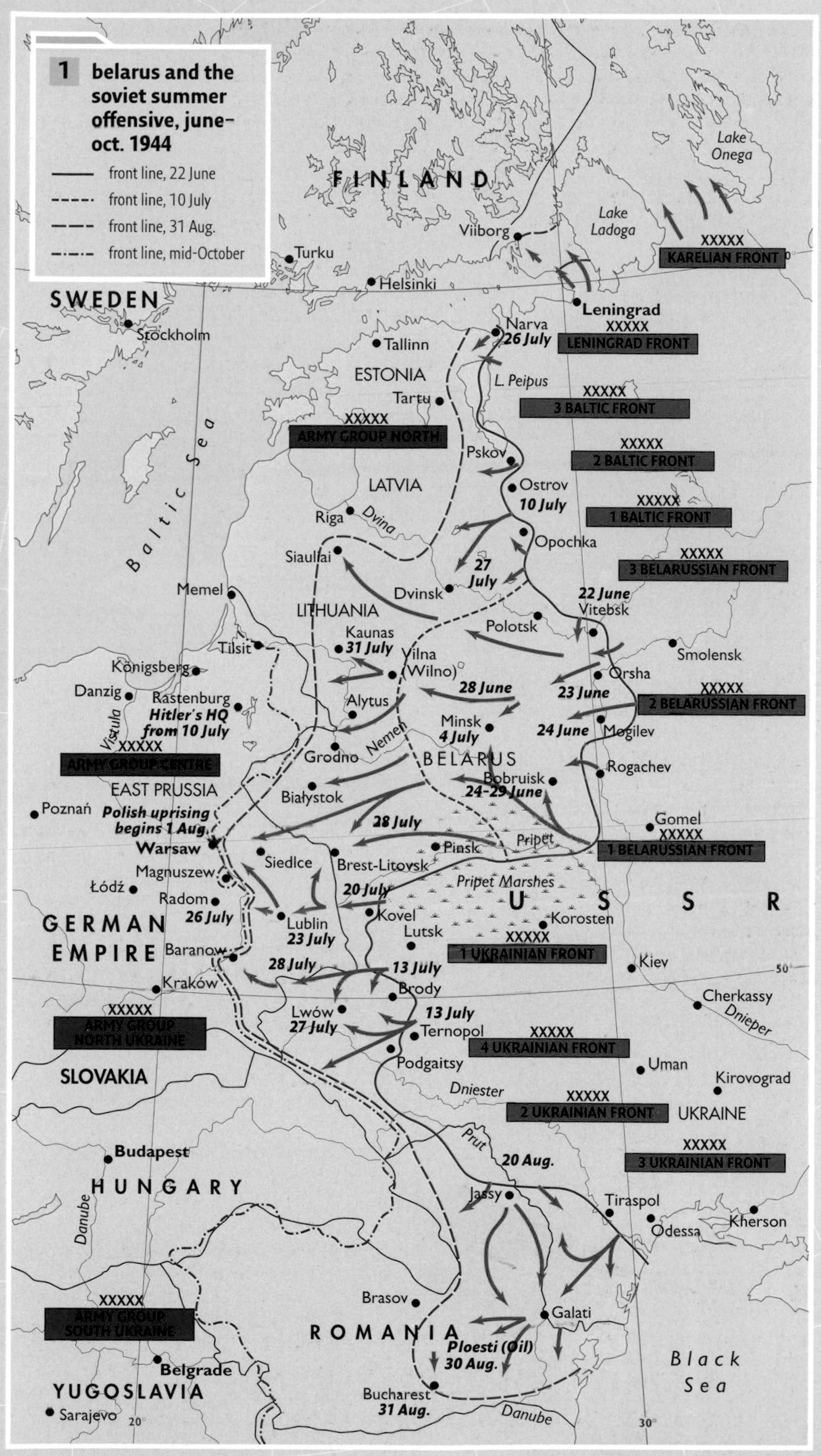

1-2 The Belarussian Strategic Offensive Operation (23 June to 29 Aug.) was one of the largest Soviet operations of the war. The Soviet plan involved a vast strategic deception (*map 1*). In the area of 3rd Ukrainian Front, to the south, the Russians feigned a major concentration of forces for the attack, while in Belarus the real concentration was carefully concealed (*map 2*). The German command was fooled to some extent. Of 30 Panzer and mechanised divisions on the Soviet German front, 24 were concentrated south of the Pripet Marshes. Within the context of German Army Group Centre's front, north of the Pripet Marshes, Soviet deception was also maintained. The order of battle of Soviet forces was clarified in good time, and the Germans noted that air forces in the south remained markedly stronger than those on the central and southern sectors. But the Germans underestimated the strength of the Soviet forces facing them. The Bobruisk operation (24–29 June), on the southern flank of the attack on Army Group Centre, formed an important part of the Belarussian operation. The Soviet aim was to drive for Bobruisk, encircling the main Bobruisk grouping. 'Reconnaissance by Battle' took place on 23 June and on the 24 June, Soviet forces attacked after a two-hour five-minute artillery preparation. Soviet forces penetrated to a depth of 3–5 miles and then I Guards Tank Corps was pushed in to exploit the breakthrough. On the second day, the KMG, which had been waiting between Sixty-Fifth and Twenty-Eighth Armies was inserted to drive deeper, by-passing the encircled force, driving north-west. Another important manoeuvre was a massive regrouping of artillery forces to strengthen the southern wing of the Soviet assault, between 5 and 13 July. Once the breakthrough was accomplished in the Bobruisk area, and the Germans fell back reaching a line west of Minsk on 4 July, 3,500 artillery pieces were moved through the wild Pripet Marshes area to new positions east of Kovel, increasing artillery strength on 1st Belarussian's left flank to 9,000 pieces and around 300 pieces per mile of front. As a result, 1st Belarussian was able to push into Poland later in July, just ahead of the other Front clearing Soviet territory.

the **baltic**

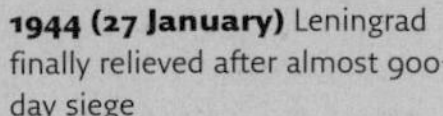

1944 to 1945

- **1944 (27 January)** Leningrad finally relieved after almost 900-day siege
- **1 March** Soviet forces attack across River Narva
- **31 July** Soviet Baltic Fleet lands troops on Hiiumaa and Saarema
- **17 August** Red Army reaches East Prussian border
- **2 September** provisional treaty ends fighting between Finland and Soviet Union
- **26 September** Soviet forces occupy Estonia
- **10 October** Riga falls to Red Army
- **23 October** Red Army enters East Prussia
- **1945 (19 January)** Red Army takes Tilsit
- **29 January** Germans evacuate two million troops and civilians from East Prussia
- **9 April** Soviet forces capture Köningsberg

It was not until the beginning of 1944, as a result of Soviet victories at Kursk and in Ukraine and Donbass that the Soviets were able to undertake a general offensive to the north-west to clear German troops right away from the city of Leningrad, under siege since September 1941, and restore something approaching wartime normality.

The Leningrad-Novgorod operation involved the Leningrad, Volkhov (to 15 February 1944) and 2nd Baltic Fronts, long-range aviation (the nearest Soviet equivalent to British and American strategic bombers) and 35,000 partisans. The offensive began on 14 January 1944. Novgorod was recaptured on 20 January, and by 1 March the Soviets had pushed forward to the borders of Latvia. Only now was the 900-day Siege of Leningrad truly over. By the end of winter Soviet forces had pushed almost as far as Lake Peipus.

Between July and November 1944, Soviet forces advanced through the Baltic States, incorporated into the Soviet Union only in 1940 with Hitler's tacit approval under the terms of the German-Soviet Pact. The 1st Baltic Front (Bagramyan) conducted the Klaipeda (Memel) operation from 8–10 October, securing the city on the Lithuanian coast, while 2nd Baltic (Yeremenko) captured Riga, the capital of Latvia. This left a pocket of German troops from Sixteenth and Eighteenth Armies of Army Group North, 33 divisions in all, on the Courland peninsula. It was renamed Army Group Courland on 26 January 1945. The Stavka of the Soviet High Command assessed, correctly, that while the Courland grouping was an annoying anomaly, it was a lesser priority than pressing on into Poland and East Prussia, and the Soviets contented themselves with blockading it by land and sea. The Soviet Navy in the Baltic had suffered severely from Stalin's purges and many of its sailors had been used for fighting on land. Its ships and submarines had been bottled up by German mining and blockade of the Gulf of Finland for most of the war, and the ships had been used principally as heavy firepower to enhance land artillery. Only with the capture of Narva in Estonia in July 1944, and Finnish withdrawal from hostilities on 19 September, which made bases on the northern shore, including Hangö, available to the Soviets, was the Soviet Navy able to break out into the Baltic. The Soviet Navy, however, did not have the ships, the men or the skills to take on first-rate German warships like the *Admiral Hipper*, and the Germans were able to evacuate large numbers of men and much material from Courland. Only 21 divisions and one brigade – 189,000 officers and men plus 42 generals – remained on Soviet territory to surrender on 9 May 1945.

Meanwhile, Soviet forces skirted the pocket and from 13 January to 25 April 1945, and concurrently with the Vistula–Oder operation, conducted the East Prussian operation using 2nd (Rokossovsky) and 3rd (Chernyakovski, then Vasilevski) Belarussian and part of 1st Baltic Fronts. On 10 February, 2nd Belarussian broke away west to conduct the East Pomeranian operation (until 4 April).

As the Russians broke into German territory, many felt they had scores to settle. Numerous sources speak of massacre and rape on a large scale. Soviet troops believed that raping German women and girls would go unpunished, and it appears that these events were widely condoned, if not officially encouraged. Stories of atrocities contributed to the panic-stricken flight of civilians and service personnel to the Baltic ports: Gdynia, Danzig, Königsberg, and at the end of an isolated spit, Pillau. The sea route was arguably the safest and certainly the most efficient way of moving large numbers of troops and sailors, refugees, wounded and stores. Admiral Dönitz, who was to succeed Hitler briefly as Führer, masterminded the evacuation of a reported 2,022,602 persons from pockets along the Baltic: Courland, East and West Prussia and Pomerania between 23 January and 8 May 1945. The Soviet Baltic Fleet was ordered to step up its activities against German lines of communication. As a result, three large ships, crammed with refugees, were sunk sailing from Danzig-Gdynia: the greatest loss of life in any recorded ship sinking (probably over 7,000 people) occurred on 30 January when the *Wilhelm Gustloff* was torpedoed by Soviet submarine S-13 off Stolpebank. Other ships were the hospital ship *Steuben* (9 February) and the *Goya* (16 March). Catastrophic though these losses were, they represented only 1 per cent of the number evacuated by sea: 99 per cent got out safely. Gdynia fell on 28 March and Danzig on 30 March. The last major port was Pillau, captured by the Soviets on 25 April. After this, the Germans continued a Dunkirk-style operation, picking up people from the beaches to take them to the west, where they would fall into British or American hands as the Soviets closed in. Admiral Dönitz, in a little known but masterly operation, had supervised the greatest seaborne evacuation in history.

1 Between the beginning of 1944 and May 1945 Soviet forces advanced along the Baltic coast from Leningrad to Wismar, a distance, of over 800 miles. The Courland grouping was bypassed in pursuit of more vital strategic objectives. The Germans had constructed a powerful defensive scheme, with no less than seven defensive perimeters, strengthened with concrete pill-boxes, dragon's teeth and other permanent fortifications, and six fortified regions. In the East Prussian operation, Soviet forces numbered nearly 1.7 million men, over 25,000 guns and mortars, nearly 3,900 tanks and assault guns and over 3,000 aircraft. The Germans had 8,200 guns, 700 tanks and 775 aircraft. The 3rd Belarussian Front attacked north of the Mazurian Lakes in order to cut off Army Group Centre from the rest of Germany (13 Jan.). The 2nd Belarussian Front attacked on the axis Marienburg–Elbing on 14 Jan. By the end of January, the Soviets had reached the Vistula Lagoon, severing most of East Prussia from the rest of Germany, and on 10 Feb. 2nd Belarussian was directed west, into East Pomerania, leaving 3rd Belarussian to liquidate German forces in East Prussia. This involved the reduction of the fortress city of Königsberg. The Germans succeeded in evacuating many civilians and military personnel from East Prussia and the Polish corridor by sea, which included Operation Hannibal, to evacuate valuable U-boat personnel. One of the ships, the *Wilhelm Gustloff* with over 8,000, people left Gdynia on 30 Jan. At 23:08 hours Soviet time the USSR submarine S-13 fired three torpedoes. One chalked 'for Stalin' failed to fire: one of those that struck was chalked 'for Leningrad'. Over 7,000 died in the worst ship sinking in history.

www.answers.com/topic/evacuation-of-east-prussia
The evacuation of East Prussia, 1945
www.feldgrau.com/wilhelmgustloff.html
The *Wilhelm Gustloff*, torpedoed during the German evacuation of East Prussia

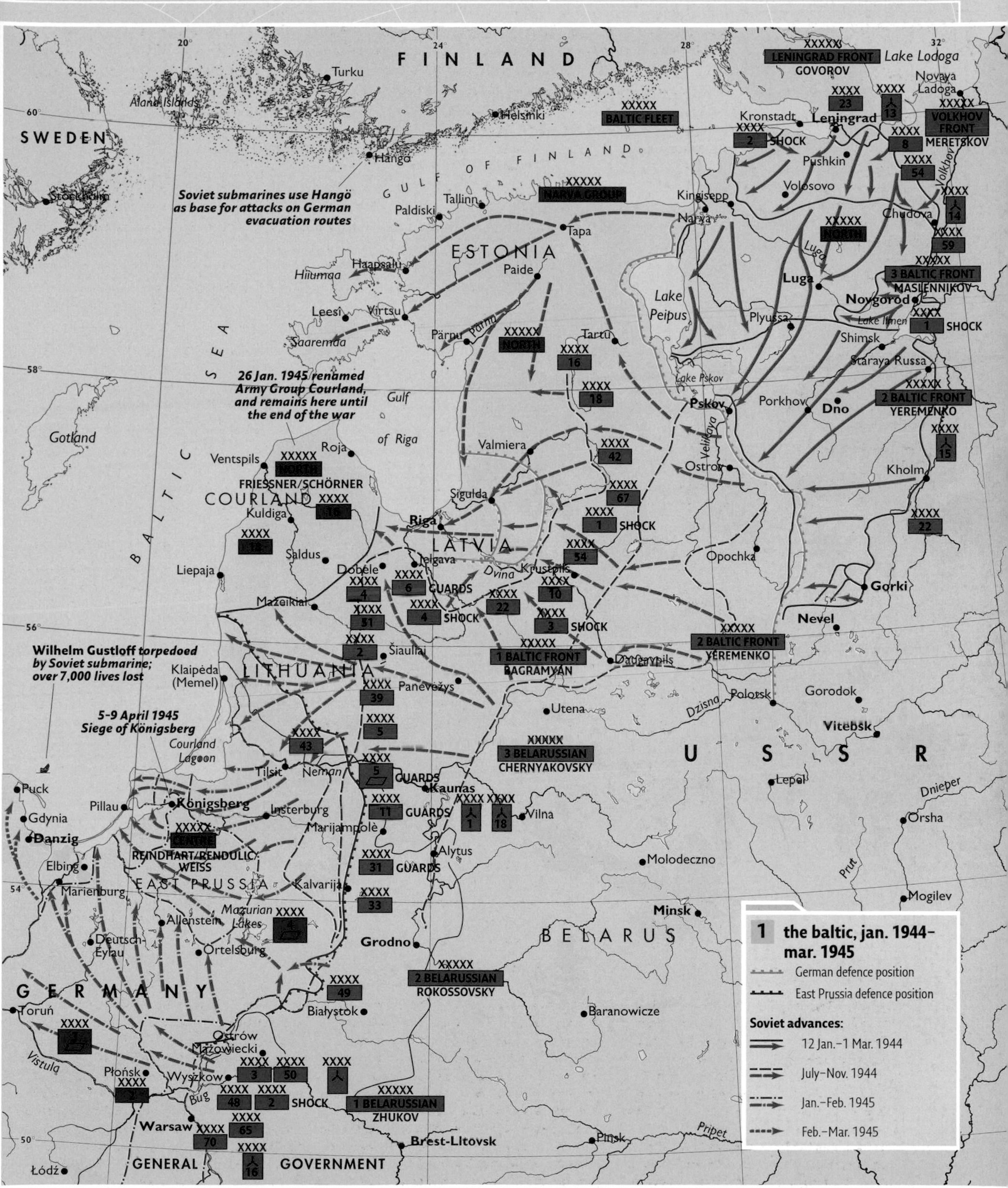

normandy

june to july 1944

- **4–6 June** Resistance disrupts communications in French hinterland
- **6 June** D-Day landings between Cherbourg and Le Havre on the Normandy coast
- **9 June** Allied aircraft begin operating from French airstrips
- **12 June** all Normandy landing zones linked up
- **26 June** Americans capture Cherbourg
- **9 July** British Second Army captures Caen
- **17 July** Rommel badly wounded
- **18 July** Operation Goodwood begun by British Second Army. US troops take St Lô
- **29 July** Germans counter-attack along River Odon

Plans for the invasion of occupied Europe via northern France had been discussed by the British and Americans since early 1942, but strategic weakness and then strategic disagreement forced a series of postponements in favour of a 'Mediterranean' strategy. At the Quebec Conference (August 1943), the British agreed to name commanders. In December, Eisenhower was appointed Supreme Allied Commander; he directed Montgomery to prepare detailed invasion plans and act as commander of the invasion ground forces.

Hitler, embroiled on the Eastern Front, delayed preparing plans for the defence of the West until November 1943. Then, in Führer Directive 51, he gave it new priority. In December, he appointed Rommel to take charge of defensive preparations as commander of Army Group B; Rundstedt remained Supreme Commander West over Army Groups B and C. In all, Rundstedt disposed some 50 infantry and ten armoured divisions. But German strategy was hampered by the need to defend all coasts, because of the Allies' success in disguising their intentions. Too many infantry divisions were, therefore, left in the south (Army Group C). Rommel and Rundstedt also disagreed about the deployment of armour, the former wanting it on the beaches, the latter in central reserve. Hitler imposed a compromise, and unwisely took some of the armoured units under his direct control.

The Allies had decided in March to invade Normandy. It lay within fighter cover from British airfields and was thought – correctly – to be judged by the Germans a less likely landing point than the Pas de Calais. But Montgomery altered the plan for Operation Overlord so as to land five rather than three seaborne divisions, as well as three airborne. He retained the scheme of using the airborne divisions to secure the flanks of the bridgehead, to build up a strong 'lodgement', to follow-up with seaborne divisions; to secure Caen early and fight a battle to destroy the German armour; and eventually to unleash US divisions from the western end of the bridgehead to break out into mainland France. But the timetable foreseen was a lengthy one. It was not expected that the Franco-German frontier would be reached until 1945.

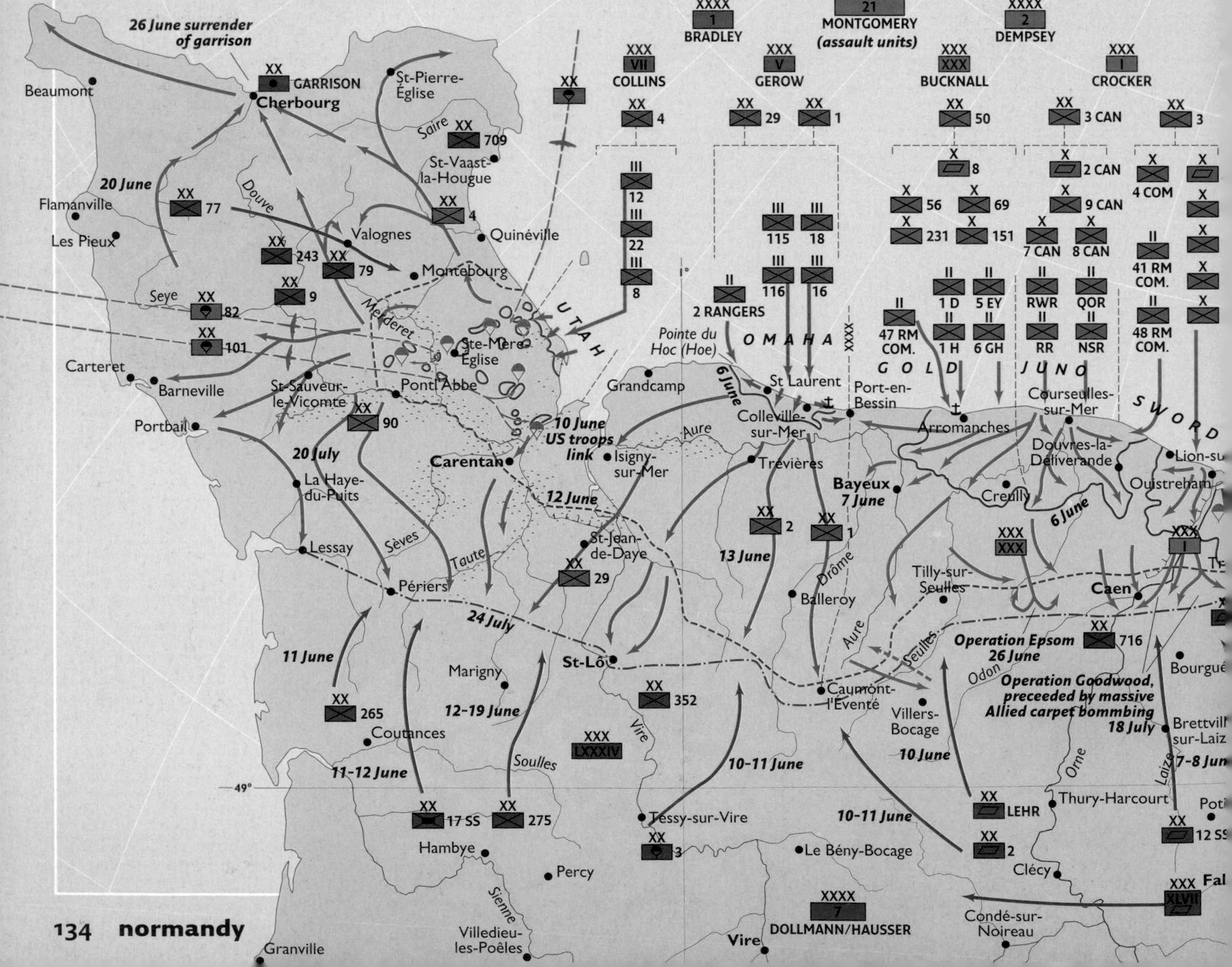

www.bbc.co.uk/history/war/wwtwo/index_special.shtml
Overview, images, maps and participant interviews
www.dday.co.uk/
In-depth look at all aspects of D-Day, 6 June 1944

1-3 The operational radius of a Spitfire was a crucial factor in the Operation Overlord plan, for it determined the area in which landings could be mounted (*map 1*). Despite a carefully disguised build-up of troops and equipment on the south coast, Allied convoys also had to be brought from Wales and East Anglia to rendezvous off the Isle of Wight in order to reach Normandy in one night. Air cover hid them and bombardment threw the Germans into disarray. Airborne troops landed in darkness, while the convoys reached the Normandy coast at dawn, 6 June (*map 2*). Rundstedt reacted to the landings by sending 21st Panzer Division against the British beaches that evening. He and Hitler then released their own armoured reserves (1st and 12th SS, Panzer Lehr). Allied power and ground resistance held them at bay. Meanwhile the Allies reinforced the lodgement area, pushed inland and built up strength for a breakout. Mulberry floating harbours (*map 3*), one British at Arromanches, one American at St Laurent, were assembled directly offshore. The American harbour was wrecked by a gale but the British harbour remained in use, discharging up to 11,000 tonnes of supplies daily. At Utah beach, where US parachutists had seized much inundated territory, German resistance was slight. At Omaha, on beaches dominated by high cliffs, defended by the best German coastal division in Normandy (352nd), the US infantry suffered heavily. Following the consolidation of the Allied beachheads into a defensible lodgement, Operation Epsom was intended to isolate Caen. In heavy fighting, German armoured reinforcements halted it. Operation Goodwood (18–20 July) was also checked. Its object had been to isolate Caen from the east and secure an opening towards Paris. However, both efforts soaked up German resistance, freeing the US forces for the forthcoming breakout.

The cross-Channel passage of some 6,500 naval and transport craft, forming 75 convoys, was to be protected or supported by 12,000 aircraft, against which the Germans could deploy only 170 fighters. Air power was vital to the success of the invasion. On the night of 5/6 June, the convoy began to cross the Channel, while widespread Allied air raids blinded or distracted the German warning and command systems. Heavy naval and air bombardments covered the disembarkation of the 3rd British, 3rd Canadian, 50th British and 1st and 4th US Divisions on Sword, Juno, Gold, Omaha and Utah beaches. Meanwhile 6th British and 82nd and 101st US Airborne Divisions had landed during the night east of Sword and west of Utah respectively.

The seaborne divisions were accompanied by amphibious armour and got ashore without serious loss or delay, except at Omaha, where the armour had been launched too far from shore and swamped. Losses there of 3,000 were the heaviest in the toll for D-Day. By nightfall, however, all beachheads were secured, a German armoured counter-attack checked and reinforcements were coming ashore. By 10 June, the separate beachheads had been consolidated into a single lodgement and the Americans were making ground inland and towards Cherbourg. The British, having beaten off German Panzer attacks, were preparing to take Caen.

Despite heavy bombardment of Caen and positions to the south, an attempt to outflank the city via Villers-Bocage failed on 10–12 June. A second attempt, made in greater strength by 15th Scottish Division (Operation Epsom, 24 June–1 July), was also checked. Meanwhile the Americans were occupying the Cotentin peninsula and forced the surrender of Cherhourg on 27 June. The Germans had begun to withdraw infantry divisions from First and Nineteenth Armies to reinforce Normandy, but Hitler, fearing a follow-up invasion of the Pas de Calais, refused to allow withdrawals from Fifteenth Army until 30 July. The third British attempt to capture Caen, 18–20 June, by a strong armoured thrust east of the city (Operation Goodwood) was again contained by local forces. Operation Goodwood had the effect, nonetheless, of holding and attracting German armour at the eastern end of the lodgement area. When the Americans, who had been creating a reserve to the west, unleashed it in the powerful Operation Cobra (25 July), it met little resistance. The breakout had begun.

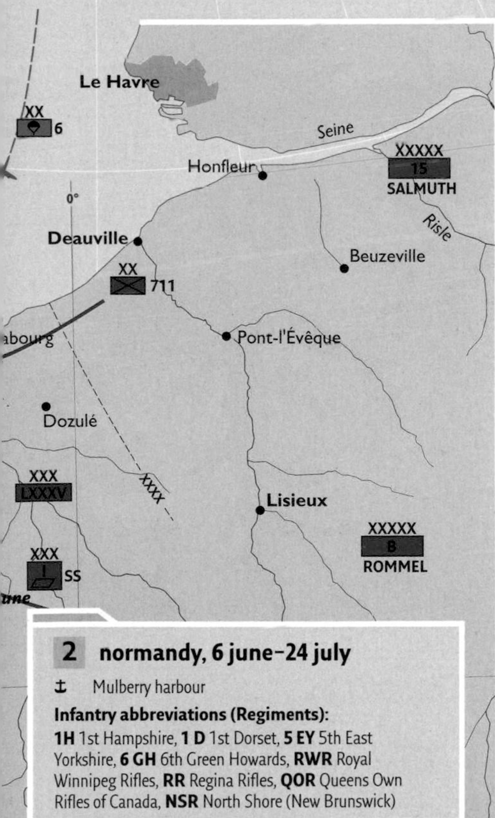

2 normandy, 6 june–24 july

⚓ Mulberry harbour

Infantry abbreviations (Regiments):
1H 1st Hampshire, **1 D** 1st Dorset, **5 EY** 5th East Yorkshire, **6 GH** 6th Green Howards, **RWR** Royal Winnipeg Rifles, **RR** Regina Rifles, **QOR** Queens Own Rifles of Canada, **NSR** North Shore (New Brunswick)

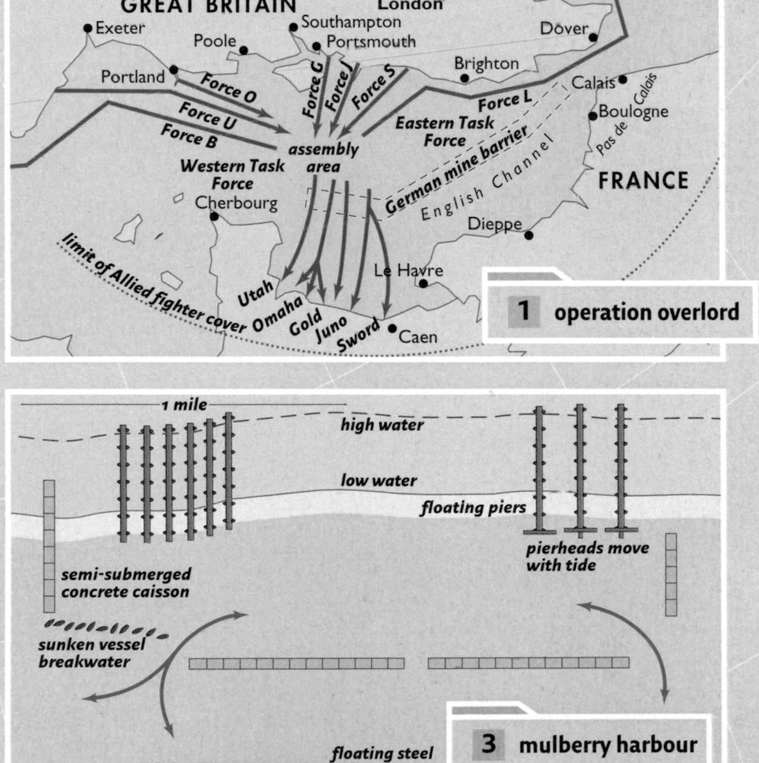

1 operation overlord

3 mulberry harbour

northern france

july to august 1944

- **2 July** Kluge replaces Rundstedt as Commander-in-Chief West
- **20 July** von Stauffenberg's plot to blow up Hitler fails; plotters tried and executed, 4–8 August
- **6 August** US Third Army takes Nantes and reaches Brest
- **12 August** PLUTO pipeline provides oil across English Channel
- **16 August** Canadians surround Falaise
- **20 August** Falaise gap closed; bridgehead established over River Seine
- **22 August** rising in Paris
- **23–25 August** liberation of Paris

In the six weeks following the D-Day landings the Allies had consolidated a substantial beachhead, and, at considerable cost, achieved their secondary objective. The Germans were not slow to respond and moved up all available units to contain the problem. The size and quality of these reinforcements were somewhat less than the Allies had anticipated, as commitments on other fronts were beginning to reveal the amount to which German manpower was overextended.

Operation Cobra, which opened on 25 July, originally intended to seize ground west of St Lô, from which an Allied breakout could be mounted; but the extent of its success was not foreseen. That was the outcome of two factors: the destructive effect of the preparatory aerial bombardment and the absence of German reserves behind the chosen attack sector. The dropping of 4,000 tonnes of bombs – some of which fell short, killing hundreds of Americans on the start line – wrecked the only German Panzer division (Lehr) behind the front. Most of the others were still near Caen, drawn in that direction by Operation Goodwood.

Finding resistance weaker than expected, the US VII Corps advanced rapidly towards Coutances. East of St Lô, XIX Corps also made ground and acted as flank guard when Kluge (who had replaced Rommel, wounded in an air strike, on 17 July) redeployed two Panzer divisions against Bradley's army on 27 July. In heavy fighting around Tessy-sur-Vire, XIX Corps allowed VII and the reinforcing VIII Corps to reach Avranches and open the way into Brittany – but also towards the rear of the German positions in Normandy.

On 1 August Bradley transferred command of First Army to Hodges and became commander of Twelfth Army Group, controlling also the newly-formed Third Army under Patton. The latter now assumed control of the advance from Coutances, exploiting the talent for hard-driving leadership he had displayed in Sicily. By 4 August his spearheads had reached Mayenne and on that day Montgomery, still exercising control of ground operations, ordered the first change to the Overlord plan. Instead of advancing to occupy Brittany and the Atlantic ports, the Americans were to send only minor units in that direction. First Army was to continue its swing eastwards, thus encircling German positions in Normandy in a wide loop. Patton was to strike directly across the German rear towards Le Mans. The British Second and the new Canadian First Army (activated 23 July) were to continue attacking southwards from Caen.

The Germans were now threatened with a close encirclement in Normandy and a wider encirclement on the line of the Seine. Hitler, however, glimpsed opportunity. On 2 August he ordered Kluge to transfer all available Panzer divisions westwards and strike from Mortain towards the sea, with the aim of cutting

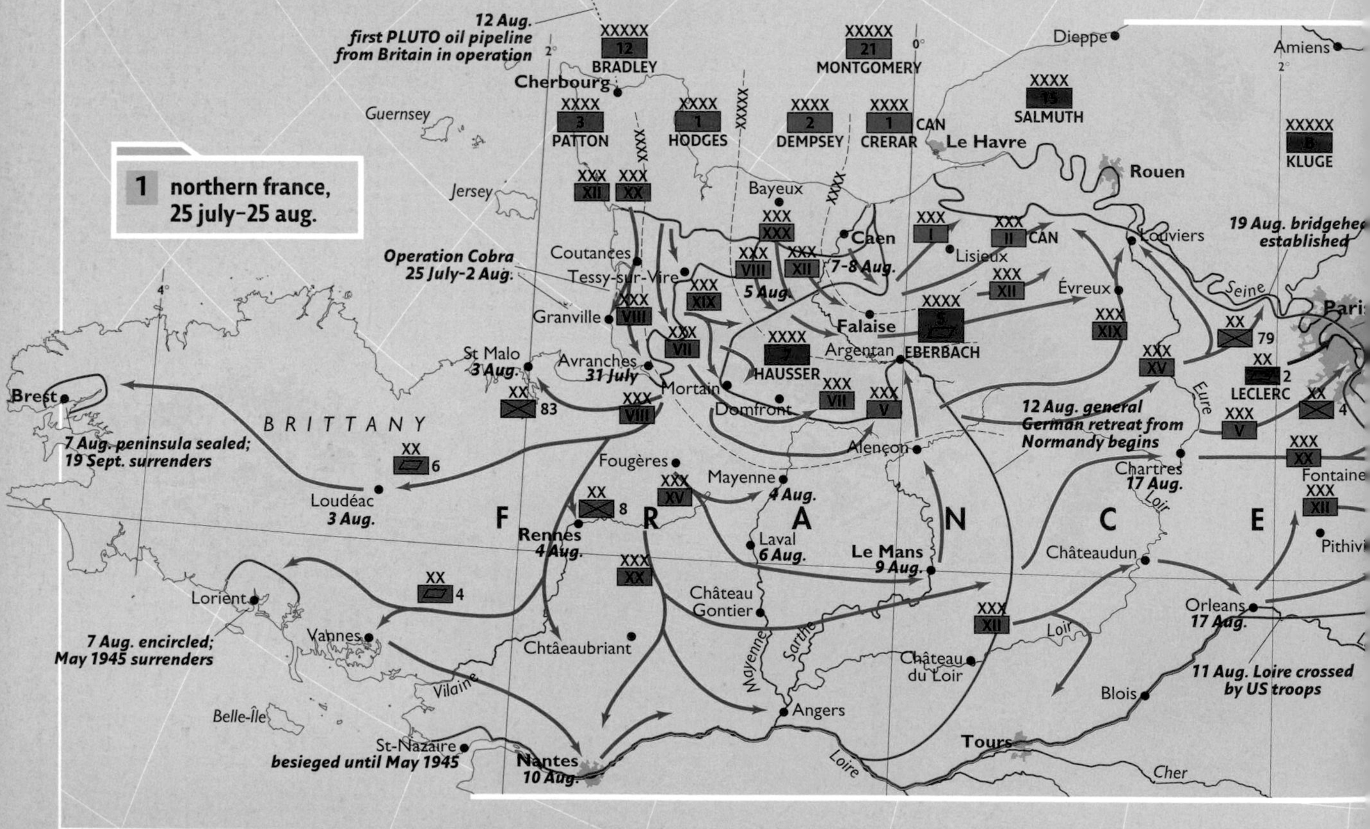

1 northern france, 25 july–25 aug.

12 Aug. first PLUTO oil pipeline from Britain in operation

Operation Cobra 25 July–2 Aug.

7 Aug. peninsula sealed; 19 Sept. surrenders

7 Aug. encircled; May 1945 surrenders

besieged until May 1945

12 Aug. general German retreat from Normandy begins

19 Aug. bridgehead established

11 Aug. Loire crossed by US troops

www.canadahistory.com/sections/conflict/conflict.htm
Operational maps of all the major campaigns of northern France, 1944
www.paris.org/Expos/Liberation/
Events, images and map of the liberation of Paris

off the American breakout at its root. This redeployment was detected by Ultra intercepts: when the Mortain counter-attack began on 6 August it was promptly halted by American forces, which had been hurried to the spot.

The defeat at Mortain, by attracting and then destroying the German Panzer divisions from Caen, opened the way for the British and Canadian armies to drive southwards towards Falaise. While they struggled to block the German retreat towards the Seine, the American First and Third Armies were sweeping westwards and then northwards to Argentan (reached 13 August). Bradley also sent units of XV Corps directly to the Seine, which was crossed at Nantes on 19 August.

The neck of the Falaise Pocket was finally closed on 20 August, trapping 50,000 Germans and all the heavy equipment of Seventh and Fifth Panzer Armies. The bulk of their personnel had, however, escaped and managed to cross the Seine by ferry and pontoon (all bridges downstream of Paris having been destroyed by Allied air attack) in the last week of August. Paris, in which an uprising orchestrated by various resistance factions had begun on 19 August, was liberated on 25 August by the French 2nd Armoured Division. General de Gaulle, who had arrived in France under his own auspices on 20 August, made a triumphal entry into the city the next day.

1-2 **The breakout from Normandy (*map 1*) proved a more effective campaign than the Allies had originally envisaged. Despite British difficulties in isolating Caen, and effecting a breakthrough there, the US build-up in the west soon forced an inevitable logic. The breakthrough would be effected by a push south, which would then sweep round to encircle German forces in what became known as the 'Falaise Pocket' (*map 2*). Operation Cobra had a false start when Allied aircraft, bombing short on 24 July, hit troops of US VII Corps. On 25 July the bombing was accurate, destroying the German defences, which led to rapid advances out of Normandy, towards the Atlantic ports (defended as fortresses by Hitler's order and to be besieged by the US Ninth Army, activated in September) and eastward towards the Seine. The Operation Overlord plan was amended on 4 Aug. to substitute an encirclement in Normandy for an occupation of western France. The line of the Loire was nevertheless reached (11 Aug.) and the Seine was crossed on 19 Aug. Brest fell on 19 Sept., but Lorient and St Nazaire held out until 1945, as did La Rochelle and Bordeaux further south. The US XV Corps reached Argentan on 13 Aug. and the Canadian First Army reached Falaise two days later. They were then separated by only 15 miles but, despite the heroic efforts of the Polish 1st Armoured Division to close the neck of the Falaise Pocket, the sheer press of German numbers held it open until 20 Aug. A popular uprising, in which the Resistance and the gendarmerie joined forces, broke out on 19 Aug., as soon as it became clear that the Allied armies were approaching. The response of the occupying Germans was half-hearted, and a plan to destroy the bridges and public services was not fulfilled. Nevertheless, nearly 1,000 members of the FFI were killed in the insurrection, although it was left to the advancing armed forces to claim the laurels of liberation. Eisenhower nominated the French 2nd Armoured Division to liberate the city. Leclerc, its commander, accepted the German surrender on the Ile de la Cité (19 Aug.).**

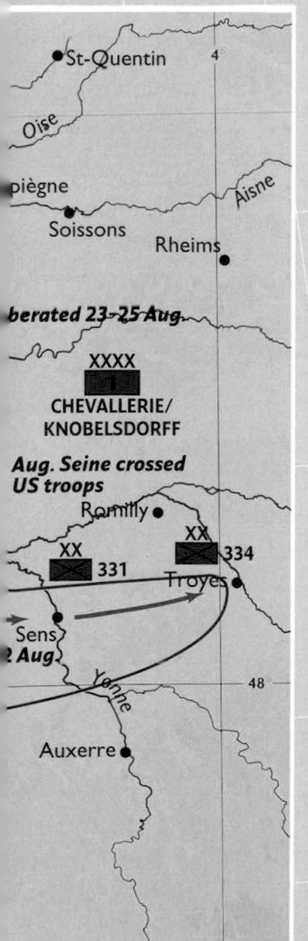

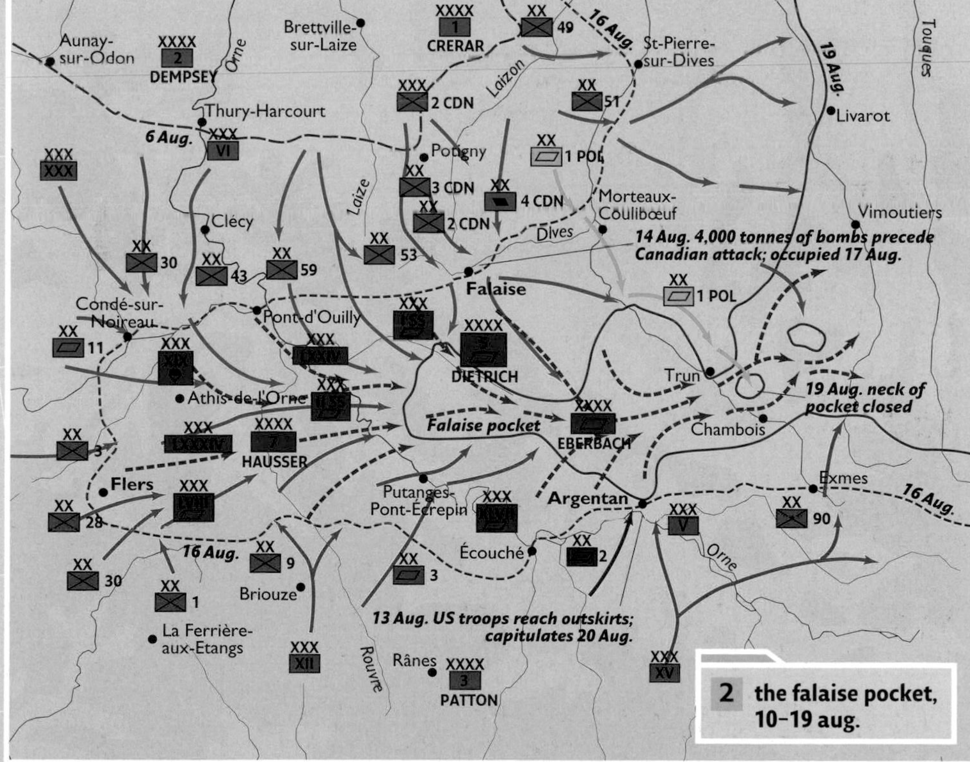

2 the falaise pocket, 10–19 aug.

southern france and northern italy

august 1944 to may 1945

- **1944 (15 August)** Operation Anvil/Dragoon begins; Allied Seventh Army invades southern France
- **31 August** Eighth Army attacks the Gothic Line
- **2 September** Fifth Army enters Pisa
- **8 September** Fifth Army breaks through Gothic Line
- **26 September** Eighth Army crosses the River Rubicon
- **10 November** Eighth Army captures Forlì
- **1945 (24 April)** Fifth and Eighth Armies cross the River Po
- **28 April** Mussolini captured and shot by partisans
- **2 May** German armies in Italy surrender

A landing in the south of France, timed to complement Operation Overlord, had been considered by the Combined Chiefs of Staff as early as August 1943 and was endorsed at the Teheran Conference in November. No date for Operation Anvil was fixed, however, because of the difficulty in providing shipping and troops to mount it. In January 1944 Eisenhower secured its postponement beyond the Operation Overlord date and as late as 11 June, five days after the Normandy landings, Churchill suggested that it should be cancelled in favour of an attack into the Balkans. Roosevelt, in view of an agreement made with Stalin, rejected this; Operation Anvil was finally fixed for 15 August.

The operation had also been opposed by the commanders in the Mediterranean, Wilson, Alexander and Clark, who felt it would rob them of the troops needed to prevent the Germans establishing strong positions on the Pisa–Rimini line. One French division was brought from North Africa; the rest – three US, three French – were indeed withdrawn from Clark's Fifth Army in Italy and, with US and Canadian paratroop Rangers, formed the US Seventh Army under General Patch. The formations sailed from Taranto, Salerno, Brindisi, Corsica and Oran to rendezvous off Provence on the night of 14/15 August.

There were eight German divisions in Nineteenth Army defending the sector but of these only one, 11th Panzer, was first class. Under a heavy air and naval bombardment, the landing was completed easily and while the French captured Toulon and Marseilles (28 August), the Americans set off to pursue the Germans, who had orders to retreat, up the Rhône Valley. Patch embarked on a breakneck chase because Ultra intelligence reassured him that he was in no danger of being attacked by Germans from northern Italy. Nineteenth Army, however, covered its withdrawal skillfully and although 57,000 of its soldiers were taken prisoner, its formations,

1 **During Operation Anvil, Delta, Camel and Alpha Forces landed between Toulon and Cannes (15 Aug.); only Camel Force met serious opposition. Four French divisions then captured Toulon and Marseilles, essential for their port facilities, while US divisions pursued the Germans up the Rhône Valley. Delaying action by the 11th Panzer Divison prevented the US 36th Division from blocking the German retreat. The US advance eventually reached Dijon (11 Sept.), close to where the Seventh Army and Patton's Third Army linked. The bulk of the German Nineteenth Army, however, escaped into Alsace.**

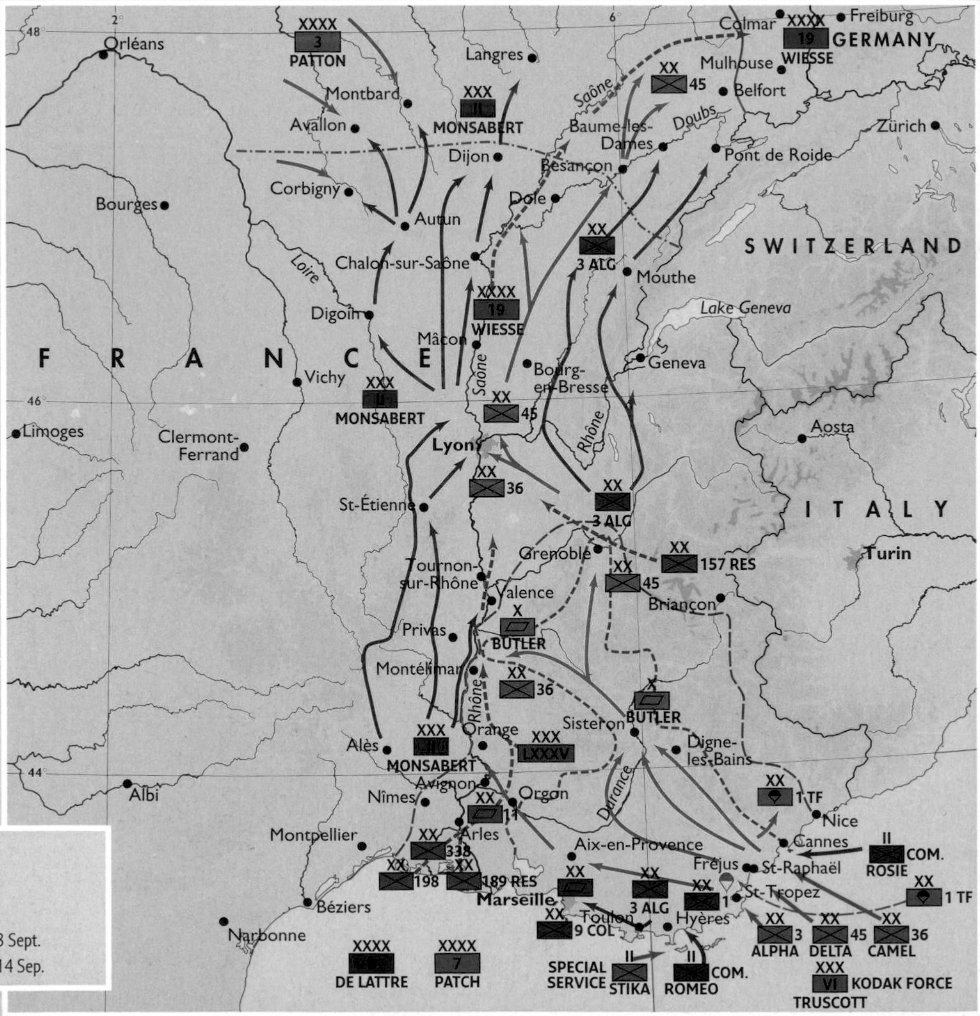

1 southern france, 22 aug.–14 sep.

front lines

- - - - - 22 Aug.
— — — 28 Aug.
– · – · – 3 Sept.
——— 14 Sep.

www.multimanpublishing.com/pp/anvil/anvil.html
Operation Anvil/Dragoon the Allied invasion of southern France
http://en.wikipedia.org/wiki/Benito_Mussolini
A biography of Benito Mussolini

including 11th Panzer Division, reached Alsace intact. Seventh Army made contact with Patton's Third near Dijon on 11 September .

Meanwhile, the Allied armies in Italy had been sustaining their pursuit of the Germans from the Winter Position towards the Gothic Line. Obliged to halt on 4 August by the transfer of troops for Operation Anvil, after an advance of 270 miles in 64 days, Alexander regrouped for a deliberate assault on what Kesselring had identified as the last strong position south of the Po Valley. The Eighth Army was repositioned on the Adriatic coast but the British XIII Corps left with the US Fifth Army, which was to launch a breakthrough towards Bologna as soon as Eighth Army had drawn the German reserves onto the east flank. After considerable engineering work had been done to repair the roads and bridges destroyed by the retreating Germans, Eighth Army attacked on 25 August. This initial assault carried Eighth Army through the Gothic Line and by 4 September it was fighting for Rimini. Kesselring transferred troops to hold the sector, weakening his centre, which was assaulted by Fifth Army on 1 September. Between 13 and 18 September the US II Corps made a rapid advance towards Bologna. Rimini fell to the British on 21 September and on 1 October Fifth Army opened its final assault on Bologna. Kesselring concentrated his reserves to hold the city, which allowed Eighth Army to advance beyond Rimini, but on 20 October Clark, though only nine miles from Bologna, was forced to halt.

Winter weather now halted operations. The number of German divisions in Italy (26) actually exceeded the Allied (20), though the Germans lacked armour and air power. While Eighth Army continued to inch forward between Rimini and Ravenna (despite a German counter-attack in the Serchio Valley on 26 December) the battle line hardly moved through the winter.

The final Allied offensive began in early April towards Spezia (5 April) on the Mediterranean, towards the Argenta Gap in Eighth Army sector (9 April) and in the centre, towards Bologna (14 April). By 20 April Bologna was outflanked and all Allied formations (except those at Spezia) had broken out into the plains of the Po. Exploitation was rapid. Eighth Army swung north-east to Venice, Fifth Army north-west to Milan; the US 92nd Division, which made the Spezia attack, moved along the coast to Genoa and Monaco. On 28 April Italian partisans captured and murdered Mussolini; the remnants of his Fascist army began to surrender the same day. On 29 April Vietinghoff, who had succeeded Kesselring, asked for an armistice. It became effective on 2 May.

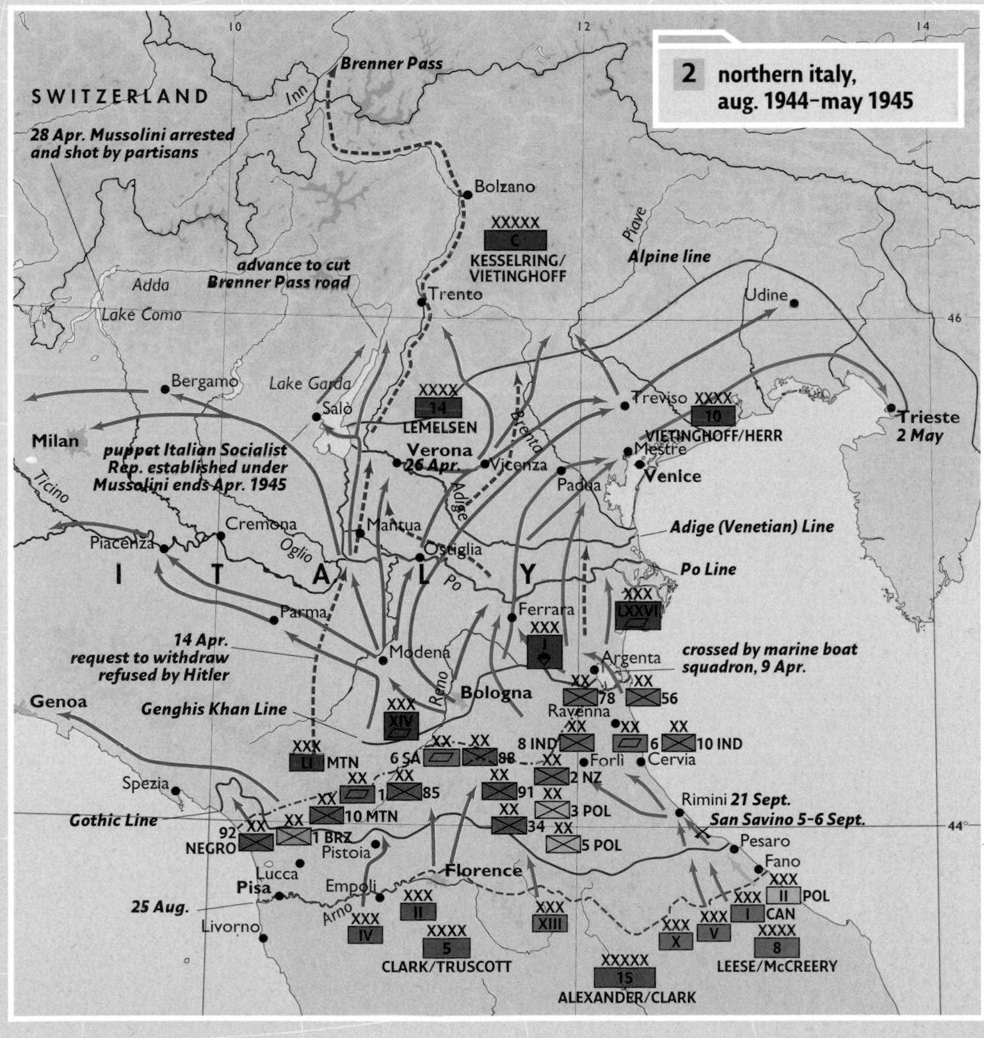

2 In Italy, an Allied bombing campaign destroyed every major bridge in the Po Valley by the end of July. The Allies then attacked Kesselring's Gothic Line south of Rimini (25 Aug.); US IV Corps penetrated the centre, bypassing the strongly defended Futa Pass (1 Sept.). Eighth Army crossed a succession of rivers up to Ravenna during December The US drive on Bologna was halted on 20 Oct. Following a harsh winter the Allied assault on the Gothic Line was renewed (9 and 14 Apr.), supported by air power. The US 10th Mountain Division breached the mountain positions above Bologna (14–17 Apr.), breaking out into the Po Valley (20 Apr.), by which time Eighth Army had passed through the Argenta Gap. German defensive withdrawals collapsed as the US forces exploited east and west of Verona, to cut the German retreat. The Eighth Army swept east through Venice, reaching Trieste by May, in advance of Tito's forces.

france, belgium and holland

1944

- **31 August** British First Army reaches Amiens and captures Somme bridgeheads; Montgomery made field marshal
- **1 September** Artois, Dieppe and Rouen captured by Allies
- **3–4 September** Allies liberate Antwerp and Brussels
- **7 September** US troops cross the River Moselle
- **12 September** Le Havre surrenders after bombing
- **17–26 September** Operation Market Garden results in destruction of Allied airborne forces

1 **The chase from the Seine to the borders of Germany began ten weeks after the Normandy landings. Patton debouched from his bridgeheads across the river on 26 Aug., Montgomery three days later. On 3 Sept. the British entered Brussels. Patton had crossed the Meuse near Verdun on 30 Aug. By 15 Sept. Luxembourg had been liberated by Hodges' First Army, Patton's Third was on the line of the Meuse and the British were at Antwerp and Maastricht in Holland.**

The extent of the German Army's defeat in the Falaise Pocket forced the surviving units of Army Group B to retreat at high speed across the Seine and then, since Hitler had earlier refused permission for a line to be prepared on the River Somme, to the next major water obstacle, the Meuse (Maas) and Scheldt in eastern France and central Belgium. The Allies pursued, hampered by a shortage of fuel and supplies.

Hitler had ordered the ports along the Channel coast to be held as fortresses; of these, Le Havre was besieged until 12 September, and Boulogne and Calais fell on 30 September, but Dunkirk held out until the end of the war. This obliged both Montgomery and Patton to draw on shipments landed across the Normandy beaches – necessarily both slowing the Allied advance and limiting the amount of supplies available to them. Each petitioned Eisenhower, as Supreme Allied Commander, to allot him a major share of the supplies available, thus provoking what came to be called the 'Broad versus Narrow' dispute over strategy. Montgomery insisted that he could break into Germany via Holland if given the lion's share; Patton similarly argued that he might rush the Siegfried Line through Lorraine. Eisenhower diplomatically distributed equal shares, with the result – probably inevitable in view of Hitler's mustering of reserves – that the Allied advance came to a halt on the approaches to the German frontier in early September.

In uncharacteristically headstrong mood, Montgomery then persuaded Eisenhower to allot him the Allied Airborne Army (82nd and 101st US, and 1st British Airborne Divisions) to mount an air-ground thrust across the Rhine in order to project the Allied advance into the German plain. Advance airborne units would secure certain bridges across the Rhine, paving the way for an armoured thrust by ground forces. The manoeuvre was code-named Operation Market Garden and was launched on 17 September. The assault was conceived in two parts: Market, the seizure of the Eindhoven and Nijmegen bridges by the Amercian divisions, worked perfectly but Garden, in which the British would gain control of the bridges at Arnhem, met with disaster. The airborne forces swiftly came under counter-attack by the 9th and 10th SS Panzer Divisions, who were at Arnhem recuperating from the battle in Normandy. Only the northern section of the main road bridge was taken, and the British were forced, after vicious house-to-house fighting, to relinquish it on 21 September. The British Armoured Division (Guards), meanwhile forcing its way through the airborne corridor on a 'one tank' front was held up by fierce resistance. Despite reinforcement by the Polish Parachute Brigade, 1st Airborne Division could not hold its positions after 25 September, abandoning them that night. Among the survivors, those that evaded capture attempted to make their way across the Rhine and back to Allied lines.

Montgomery's insistence on venturing the airborne crossing of the Rhine had left the Germans in his rear free to strengthen the defences of the Scheldt, with deplorable effect on the supply situation. Although Antwerp had been captured on 4 September, its port facilities, the largest in Europe, could not be used while the estuary remained in German hands. Operations to take it began on 2 October but were not completed until 8 November and were severely hampered by the flooding of certain areas by the Germans. The port was not opened until 20 days later. The '85 days' between the capture of Antwerp and its utilisation as a port was a period of logistic famine for the Allied armies on the German frontier. This was also the period in which Hitler developed his plan to isolate the advanced Allied armies in the west with a bold armoured thrust through the Ardennes to the North Sea coast.

The American generals Hodges, commanding First Army, and Patton, commanding Third, had meanwhile been fighting with the resources available to capture ground around Aachen and in Lorraine. Hodges, supported by Simpson's Ninth Army, painfully broke through the Siegfried Line (West Wall) into the Hürtgen Forest during November. They reached the River Roer in early December. Until the opening of the German Ardennes offensive in mid-December, they devoted their principal efforts to securing the Roer river dams. Patton, supported by the 6th Army Group of American and French troops, which had landed in Provence in August, made better progress in Lorraine. By mid-December, he had reached the line of the Rhine and the West Wall along most of his sector. The Allies now stood on the very threshold of the Reich.

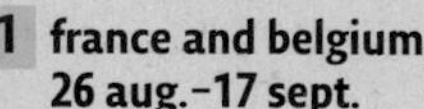

1 france and belgium, 26 aug.–17 sept.

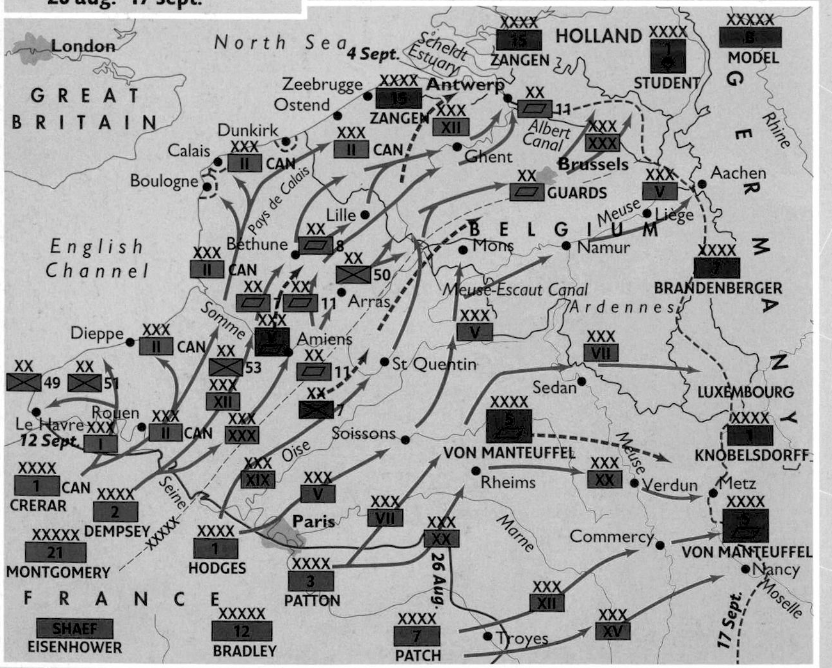

www.bbc.co.uk/history/war/wwtwo/battle_arnhem_01.shtml
Operation Market Garden
www.marketgarden.com/
Operation Market Garden: images, animated maps, history and veterans' role of honour

2 operation market garden, 17–26 sept. 1944

Allied parachute and glider landing zones

Arnhem front lines

17 Sept.

final perimeter 26 Sept.

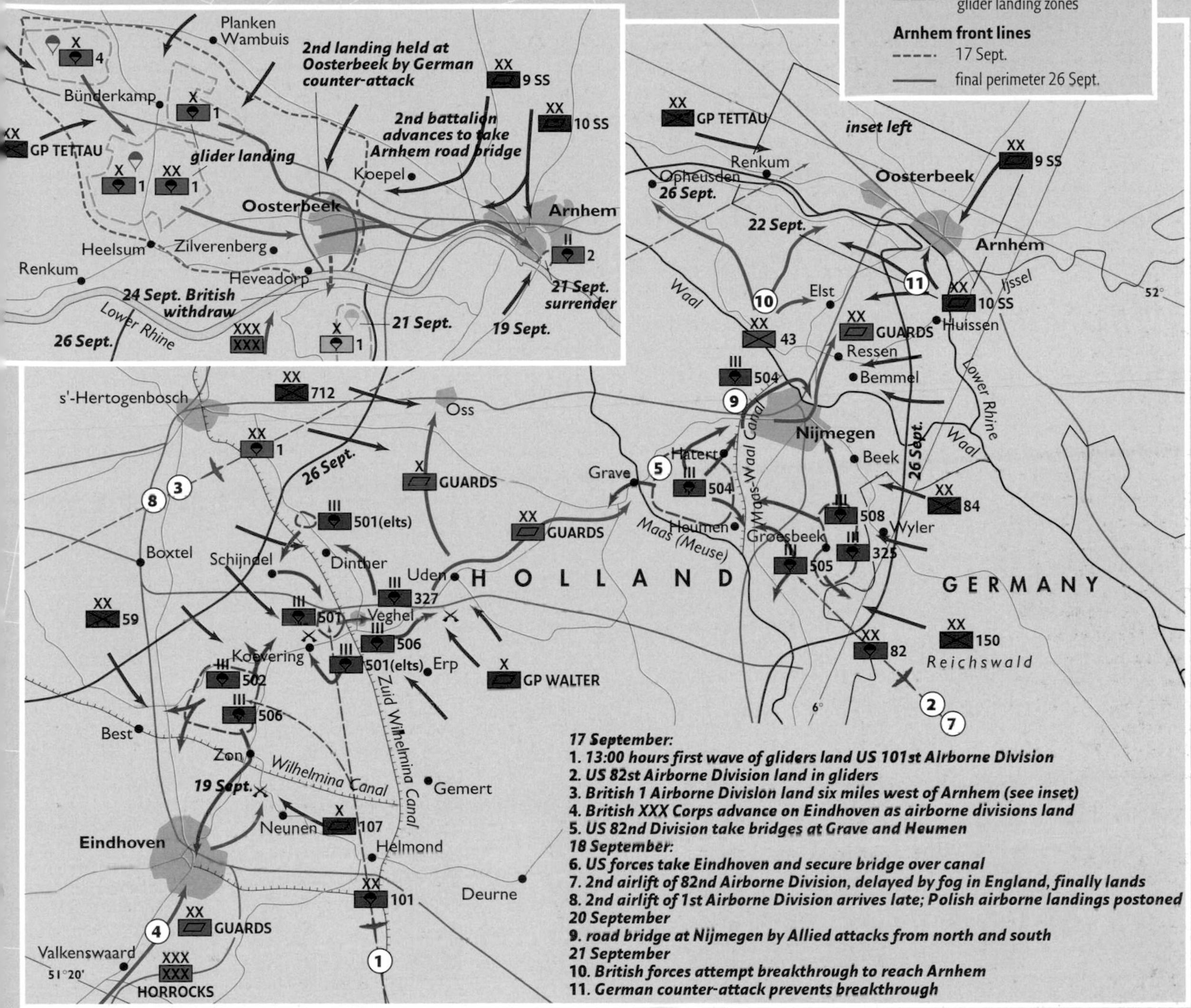

17 September:
1. *13:00 hours first wave of gliders land US 101st Airborne Division*
2. *US 82st Airborne Division land in gliders*
3. *British 1 Airborne Division land six miles west of Arnhem (see inset)*
4. *British XXX Corps advance on Eindhoven as airborne divisions land*
5. *US 82nd Division take bridges at Grave and Heumen*

18 September:
6. *US forces take Eindhoven and secure bridge over canal*
7. *2nd airlift of 82nd Airborne Division, delayed by fog in England, finally lands*
8. *2nd airlift of 1st Airborne Division arrives late; Polish airborne landings postoned*

20 September
9. *road bridge at Nijmegen by Allied attacks from north and south*

21 September
10. *British forces attempt breakthrough to reach Arnhem*
11. *German counter-attack prevents breakthrough*

2nd landing held at Oosterbeek by German counter-attack

2nd battalion advances to take Arnhem road bridge

glider landing

24 Sept. British withdraw

21 Sept. surrender

inset left

2 Mongomery's plan to use the Allied airborne arms to seize key Rhine bridges ahead of the ground advance was code-named Operation Market Garden. Market, the seizure by American divisions of the Eindhoven and Nijmegen bridges went according to plan. Garden was a partial, and eventually a total failure. Concerted German counter-attacks wrested within four days control of the one Arnhem bridge captured by the British. The advancing British ground forces were unable to reach Arnhem in time to save the beleaguered British force.

3 The British began a clearing of the Scheldt banks and islands in an operation from Antwerp on 2 Oct., the Canadians attacking on the south bank. Walcheren, the last German position, was secured in an amphibious operation, 1–8 Nov.

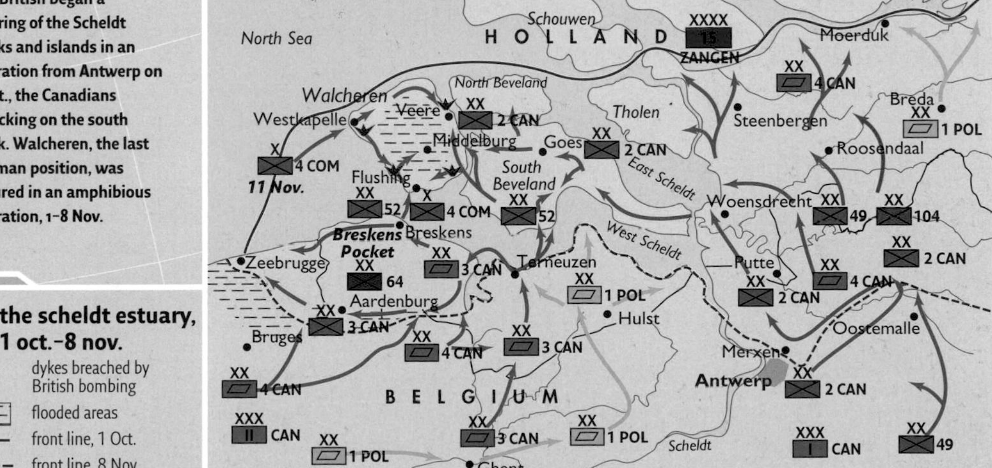

PART 5 **ALLIES VICTORIOUS**

the **ardennes** and the **battle** of the **bulge**

december 1944 to **february 1945**

- **Dec 16** German Panzer and infantry corps assault front line creating an almost 50-mile salient
- **Dec. 17** Malmédy massacre of US prisoners and civilians by members of the SS
- **Dec 19** Germans encircle Bastogne held by US 101st Airborne Division
- **Dec 21** Germans attempt to expand northern shoulder of salient; fierce fighting around St Vith; US 7th Armoured Division ousted
- **Dec 22** US and British mount counter-offensive
- **Dec 26** US 4th Armoured Division relieve Bastogne
- **Dec 28** US 12th Army Group counter-attacks; Hitler agrees to withdraw to West Wall
- **16 Jan. 1945** front line back to original position

Hitler conceived the idea of mounting a winter counter-offensive against the Allies even while his armies were reeling back in defeat from Normandy. He foresaw that, if the Allies could be held on the line of the West Wall and the Dutch rivers, and denied ports of supply along the Channel coast, their long lines of communication would hamper their offensive power and render them vulnerable to a counter-stroke.

He therefore ordered Le Havre, Boulogne, Calais and Dunkirk to be held as fortresses, and the mouth of the River Scheldt to be garrisoned, so that Antwerp, though lost to the Allies on 4 September, could not be used, and 25 new Volksgrenadier divisions to be created behind the West Wall for the coming operation.

Hitler's conception for Operation Autumn Mist, as it was eventually code-named, was of a drive by two Panzer armies from concealed positions in the Eifel Mountains, through the Ardennes forests and across the Meuse, to reach Antwerp 100 miles distant. The operation would not only recapture the port (which the Allies at last reopened on 28 November) but also separate the British and Canadian armies in the north from the Americans in the south. Profiting by the confusion this caused, and the time won, Hitler then planned to transfer his reserves eastwards to deal a similar blow against the Russians advancing on Berlin.

Rundstedt and Model, respectively Commander-in-Chief West and Army Group B commander, both thought the plan overambitious and during October argued for a 'small solution', designed merely to cast the Allies off balance by a drive to the Meuse. Hitler was adamant and laid down that as soon as a spell of bad weather promised protection from Allied air attack, the tanks were to roll. By early December they were ready. Eight re-equipped Panzer divisions and a Panzer grenadier division were to spearhead Sixth SS and Fifth Panzer Armies' attack on a sector of front held by four inexperienced and tired American divisions.

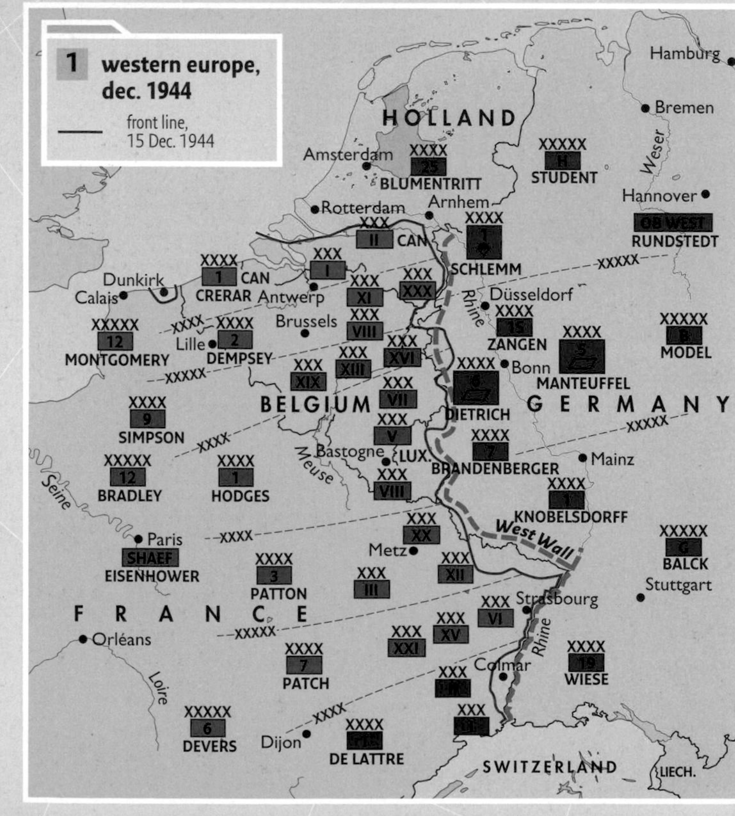

Allied intelligence had failed to detect signs of the impending attack, because strict radio silence gave Ultra no clues, and had discounted the likelihood of heavy fighting in the remote and difficult Ardennes. When the Germans appeared early in the morning of 16 December, therefore, they quickly overran the defenders, whose brave resistance nevertheless imposed delay. Eisenhower's quick reaction also forestalled German intentions. By sending the US 7th Armoured and 101st Airborne Divisions to hold the key junctions of St Vith and Bastogne on 17 December, he ensured that the timetable of advance was further set back. St Vith was abandoned on 23 December but Bastogne was held. It became the focus of the American counter-attack from the south, which Patton began on 22 December. On 20 December, Eisenhower had appointed Montgomery to coordinate the attack from the north, which was greatly assisted by an improvement in the weather, permitting the resumption of air operations, on 23 December. The Germans were also halted on that day by petrol starvation, having failed to capture the fuel dump on which they had counted for resupply. On 26 December the US 2nd Armoured Division halted 2nd Panzer at Celles, thus terminating the German effort to reach the Meuse. Rundstedt now proposed that the offensive be abandoned, but Hitler refused. During 27–30 December there was heavy fighting around Bastogne, which Patton had relieved on 26 December, while Hitler ordered the opening of a diversionary offensive in Alsace on 1 January (the day on which the Luftwaffe mounted its last large-scale operation, destroying 156 aircraft, at heavy cost to itself, on Allied airfields in Belgium).

Montgomery was, meanwhile, gathering his forces on the northern flank of the 'bulge' and unleashed a major counter-attack on 3 January. On 7 January the US VII Corps cut the Laroche-Vielsalm road, leaving German troops in the 'bulge' with only the Houffalize road as a line of supply. On 8 January Dietrich, commanding Sixth SS Panzer Army, requested and was granted permission to withdraw. The Wehrmacht had suffered 100,000 casualties and lost 600 tanks and 1,600 aircraft; the Allies had suffered 76,000 casualties. Hitler had set back the Allied drive into Germany by six weeks, but in the process lost his last armoured reserve. Operation Autumn Mist had proved a daring but costly failure.

www.mm.com/user/jpk/battle.htm
Battle of the Bulge experience and related facts
www.army.mil/botb/main.html
Overview of the Battle of the Bulge with images of US troops in action

2 the battle of the bulge, 16–25 dec. 1944

front lines

-·-·- 16 Dec.
----- 20 Dec.
—— 25 Dec.

-3 **In December 1944 the bulk of the Allied forces on the German border were concentrated for offensive operations against the Ruhr and in Lorraine (*map 1*). Hitler's plan was for the Sixth SS Panzer Army under Dietrich to drive for Antwerp, while von Manteuffel's Fifth Army supported it on the left flank. Special forces disguised as US forces were to sow confusion in the army rear and a parachute drop near Spa was to protect Dietrich's intial break-in (*map 2*). The Sixth Panzer's attack began with a drive to seize ground between St Vith and the Meuse, but was checked by the US 2nd and 99th Divisions. Dietrich's armour bogged down in the narrow roads of the Ardennes. Manteuffel secured quicker gains, but was weakly supported by the Seventh Army and so was drawn into a frustrating battle for Bastogne. On 26 Dec. Manteuffel's advance was checked at Celles. Thereafter the concentration of 33 Allied divisions strongly supported by air power gradually restored the situation (*map 3*). At its deepest the 'bulge' had penetrated 70 miles; by 16 Jan. almost all the ground taken by the Germans had been recaptured.**

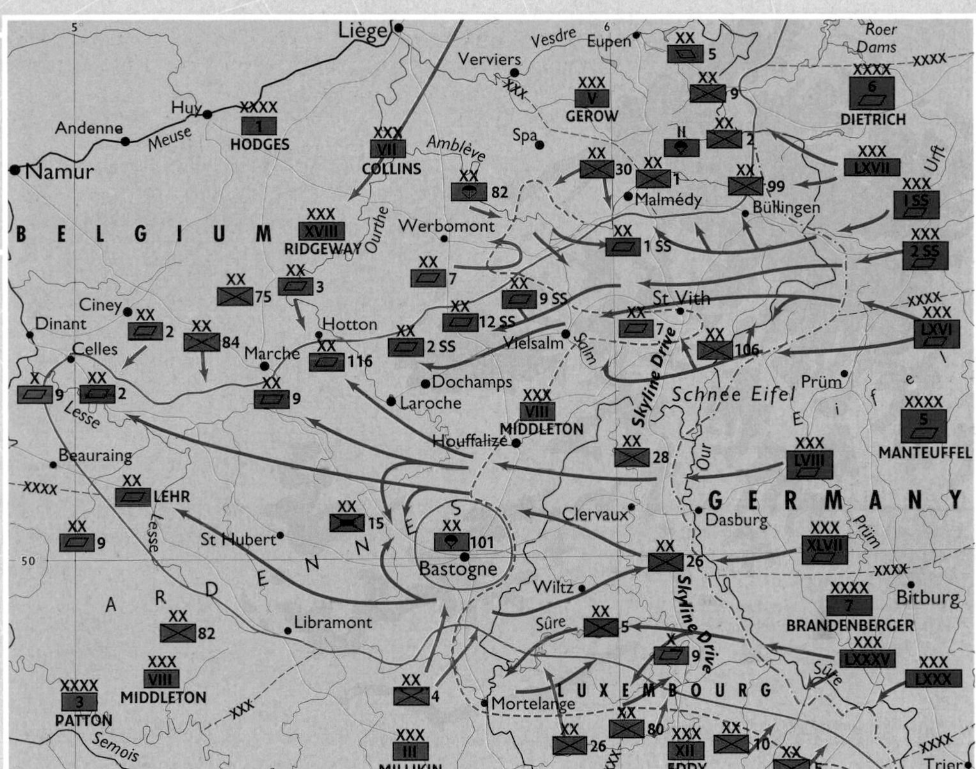

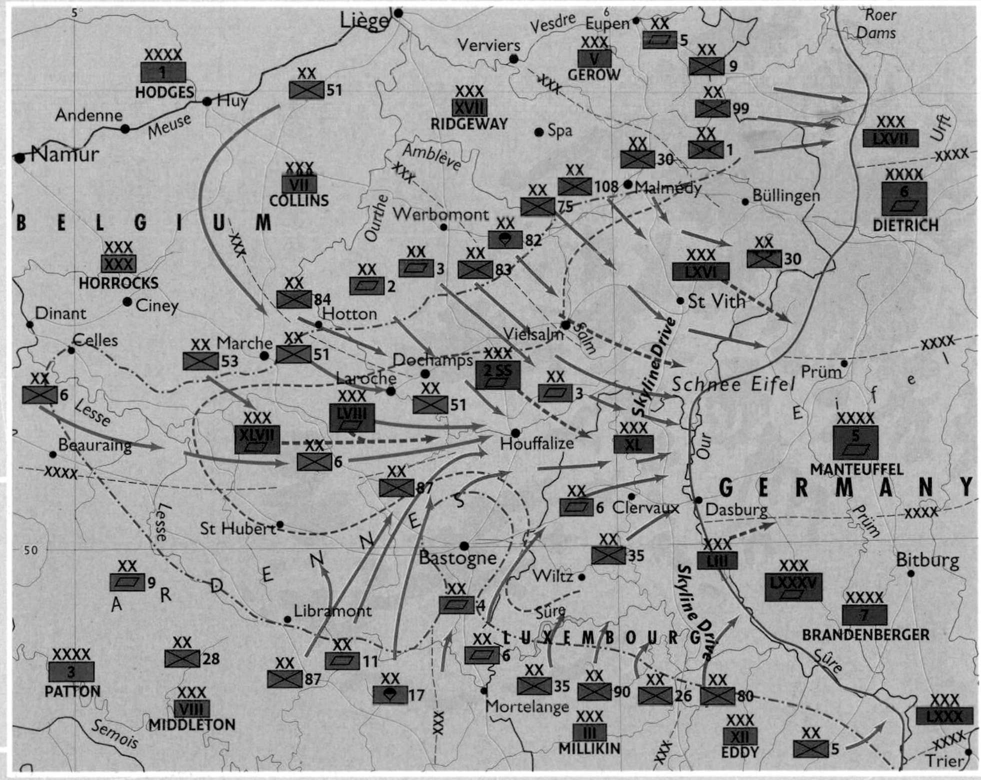

3 the battle of the bulge, 26 dec. 1944 – 7 feb. 1945

front lines

-·-·- 26 Dec.
----- 9 Jan.
—— 7 Feb.

burma

1942 to 1945

- **1942 (21 December)** British and Indian forces advance into Burma
- **1943 8 February** first Chindit raids of Wingate's 77th Indian Infantry Brigade
- **1 August** Burmese puppet government declares war on Britain and US
- **18 December** Stilwell appointed to command Chinese troops in India and northern Burma
- **1944 (6 January)** 'Merrill's Marauders' set up
- **8 March** Battle of Imphal begins, with the siege begining on 29 March
- **24 March** Wingate killed in air crash
- **18 July** Japanese retreat from Imphal-Kohima
- **1945 (4 March)** Allies take Meiktila
- **3 May** Indians capture Rangoon

The American strategic intention to develop China as an active theatre of military and air operations necessarily involved a campaign to recover Burma, because only by re-establishing overland communications with Chiang Kai-shek's regime at Chungking through Burma could China and KMT armies be made ready for offensive operations. The relevance of this intention, and the difficulties presented in attempting an overland reconquest of either Upper Burma or the whole of Burma from north-east India gave rise to a never-ending series of Anglo-American disputes between 1942 and 1944.

At the heart of these disputes was the difficulty of moving forces through the roadless mountains and jungles that divided India and Burma, against an enemy that could operate on good, secure lines of communication in the Sittang, Irrawaddy and Chindwin valleys to ensure superiority at the point of contact. Chinese forces in Yunnan were unable to play an effective containing role on the Salween river, without first being supplied and equipped by the road that was supposed to be opened by the Allies. The first Allied attempt to undertake even a limited offensive, in the Arakan in the 1942–43 dry season, resulted in the comprehensive defeat of the 14th Indian Division. However, a three-week foray behind Japanese lines by air-supplied columns – the first Chindit operation – proved more significant. In 1942 the Japanese Army had dismissed the suggestion of an overland offensive into north-east India as impractical, but this raid, though it achieved little apart from the temporary disruption of Japanese lines of communication, provoked the Burma Area Army into demanding (and Tokyo into accepting) the need for a pre-emptive offensive. This would secure Imphal and Kohima at the end of the 1943–44 dry season, the calculation being that the onset of the monsoon would preclude any effective Allied counter-attacks.

This Japanese effort began in February 1944 with a diversionary attack in the Arakan that drew into the battle six British divisions, plus transport aircraft from as far afield as the Mediterranean theatre. The offensive began after the American-controlled Northern Combat Area Command, with two Chinese armies, raised and maintained from US sources, began an advance in October 1943 with an advance in the Hukawng Valley that was to result in the taking of Myitkyina airfield in May 1944. There, Sino-Chinese forces were to link up with forces that remained in Upper Burma from the second Chindit operation that had begun in March, the combined Allied effort resulting in the capture of Myitkyina itself in August. By then, however, the Japanese offensive into north-east India had encountered disaster. Forewarned of Japanese intentions, British forces in front of Imphal were able to avoid encirclement in the first phase of the Japanese offensive and then establish themselves on the Imphal plain. Here their superiority of numbers and firepower, plus support and supply from the air, resulted in the siege being broken. The Japanese formations, lacking secure lateral lines of communication, could not secure superiority at any single point of the attack. Around Kohima the same first Japanese onrush was checked; the Japanese refusal to admit failure at either Imphal or Kohima, or to withdraw into Burma, resulted in the Fifteenth Army effectively being destroyed in a series of protracted battles, Imphal being relieved by overland advance from Kohima on 22 June. What amounted to the destruction of Japanese power during 1944 in north-east India exposed Burma itself to invasion and conquest from the north in 1945. While Chinese forces attended to the clearing of the north-east, the main Allied effort was undertaken by the British against Japanese forces concentrated in defence of Mandalay. Supported by a series of amphibious landings in the Arakan that secured airfields from which to support an

2 imphal and kohima, mar.–july 1944

airfields built in 1942

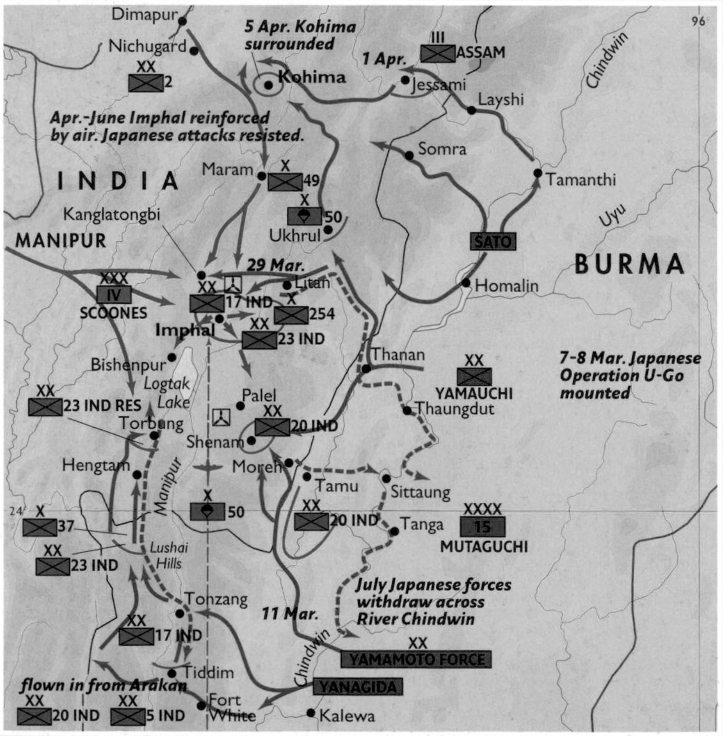

2 The Japanese decision to go over to the offensive at Imphal and Kohima was made in August 1943 and was to prove the decisive battle in Burma. The speed and timing of the Japanese advance (9 Mar.) caught the British off-guard. The Imphal Road was not cut until 29 Mar. The fiercest fighting was at Kohima. The siege at Imphal continued, but the British continued to fly in reinforcements. By 8 July the Japanese had decided to withdraw. The campaign had cost them 30,000 deaths. Allied casualties numbered 16,700.

www.army.mil/cmh-pg/books/wwii/marauders/marauders-fw.htm
Merrill's Marauder's, February–May 1944
www.bbc.co.uk/dna/ww2/A1122256
The Allied defence of Imphal and Kohima

1 **Between 1942 and 1943 the Japanese were happy to remain on the defensive. The US saw Burma in terms of opening up land communication with China by building a road from Ledo to the old Burma Road. The British considered it an impossible task. Chiang Kai-shek refused to commit any of his forces, unless sea and air dominance were established over the Bay of Bengal. In the absence of a major offensive, the British developed the idea of Long Range Penetration groups (LRPs), designed to operate behind enemy lines, and overcome communications difficulties by radio contact and supply by air. Known as Chindits, 3,000 men were dropped by air behind enemy lines in the first of these operations (Feb. 1943). Four months later 2,182 returned to India. Their main effect appears to have been to prompt the Japanese to take the offensive at Imphal and Kohima. Merrill's Marauders were the US equivalent to British LRPs. After Imphal and Kohima British forces, went onto the offensive. Ramree Island was secured (17 Dec. 1944). By 1 Feb. 1945 bridgeheads across the Irrawaddy were established. The crucial junction of Meiktila was taken by surprise, the Japanese believing the main effort was aimed at Mandalay. As airfields and communications lines were captured, the rate of advance was speeded up. Rangoon was secured on 3 May, by a land-based assault and amphibious landing.**

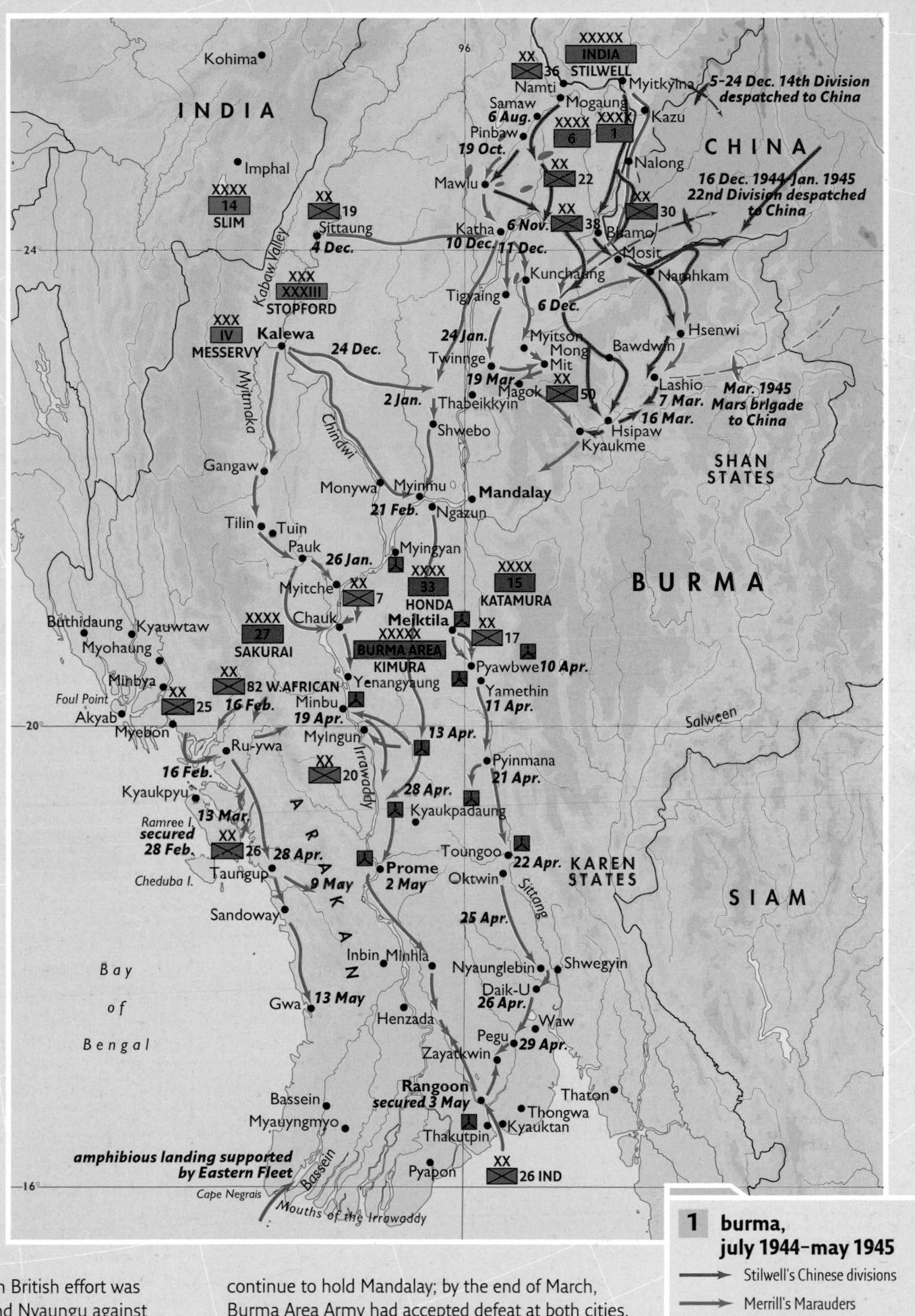

1 burma, july 1944–may 1945

assault on Rangoon, the main British effort was developed through Kalewa and Nyaungu against Meiktila, which was taken on 4 March. Forced to respond because of the threat to its lines of communication, the Burma Area Army committed itself to a major counter-attack that retook Meiktila airfield, but it could neither recover the town nor continue to hold Mandalay; by the end of March, Burma Area Army had accepted defeat at both cities. Thereafter the British were to continue their overland advances into Lower Burma, securing Rangoon by amphibious assault in May. The war ended with the Japanese attempting to reform their still numerous forces in Burma in defence of Tenasserim and Siam.

leyte gulf

22nd to 27th october 1944

- **12–18 October** US 3rd Fleet operations against Formosa
- **17 October** US Rangers land in Leyte Gulf
- **20 October** US Sixth Army invades Leyte
- **24–26 October** naval air battle over Leyte destroys remains of Japanese carrier fleet
- **27 October** Japanese Kamikaze attacks on US TF38 in Philippines

The Japanese defeat off the Marianas in June 1944 opened the whole of the western Pacific to an American advance. While American planners debated whether to take or bypass Luzon in favour of Formosa, the Japanese were facing starker choices. Without an effective carrier force to take the initiative they had to respond to landings that could be made anywhere between Okinawa and Mindanao.

American superiority and the threat to the links between the Home Islands and the Southern Resources Area demanded this. Once again the Japanese prepared to fight the 'decisive battle', committing all their effective sea and air power to what was to become the largest naval action ever fought: the Battle of Leyte Gulf.

American carrier raids over the Philippines in September, however, confounded early Japanese planning. Japanese air power was ravaged, and the US took advantage of Japanese weakness to accelerate their timetable to land on the Philippines. Further US strikes, using four naval task groups with 17 carriers and nearly 1,100 aircraft left the Japanese with only 200 aircraft on the Philippines. In addition a shortage of fuel oil on the Home Islands forced the Japanese to disperse their naval forces. The need to concentrate naval forces off Brunei in preparation for battle meant a longer reaction time to any US landing.

The final Japanese plan, drawn up in the days before the largest convoy in the Pacific war brought the American landings on the Philippines, took account of these operational difficulties. Japanese naval forces were split into three formations: Centre Force, Southern Force and Northern Force. Ozawa's Northern Force, which included four carriers with just 116 aircraft, was to act as a decoy to draw the bulk of the US Third Fleet, supporting the landings, away from the landing beaches, allowing Centre and Southern Forces to advance in a pincer movement north and south of Leyte, and there to destroy the landing forces.

On 23 October the naval battle was joined. Centre Force lost two cruisers to US submarines in the Palawan Passage. As Centre Force advanced into the Sibuyan Sea, US air strikes sunk a further cruiser. Southern Force, however, successfully advanced into the Mindanao Sea. A tightly organised US action with MTBs, destroyers and the last broadside in naval history blocked the passage of this force in the Surigao Strait. On 25 October, Ozawa's Northern Force was finally spotted by a US scout plane. Reading the presence of carriers as the greatest threat to the landings, US Third Fleet commander, Halsey, ordered the bulk of his forces to rendezvous off Catanduanes and to steam north, away from the landing beaches, in pursuit. The Japanese decoy had worked. Kurita's Centre Force was able to pass through the San Bernardino Strait unopposed, to sweep down on the US landing beaches, defended only by three Task Forces of escort carriers. A fierce action ensued, the Americans relying on their air power, the Japanese on fire-power, and towards the end of the action, Kamikazes. Unaccountably the Japanese commander decided to call off the action just as he had the upper hand. The Americans were given crucial time to regroup and the Japanese were forced to withdraw.

Overall, between 23–27 October, when the battle finally died, the Americans sank four carriers, three battleships, six heavy and four light cruisers and 11 destroyers from the 64 Japanese warships committed to the battle. Over 10,500 Japanese sailors and airmen were killed. The Americans lost the light cruiser *Princeton*, two escort carriers, two destroyers and a destroyer escort from a total force of 218 vessels. Leyte Gulf had confirmed the Americans' superiority at sea, and extinguished the ability of the Japanese to fight a major naval action.

2 surigao strait, 24–25 oct. 1944

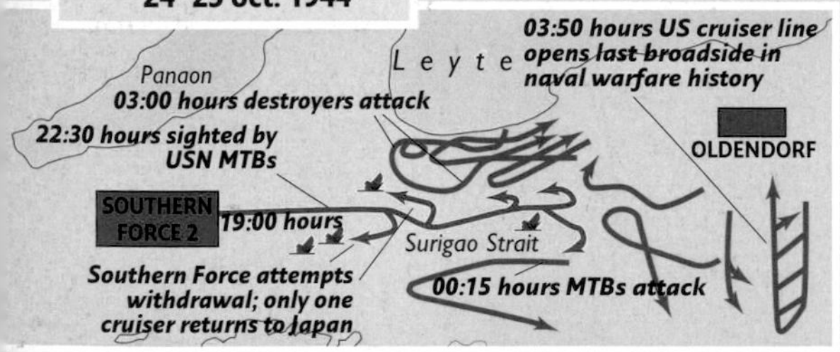

Panaon
Leyte
03:50 hours US cruiser line opens last broadside in naval warfare history
03:00 hours destroyers attack
22:30 hours sighted by USN MTBs
OLDENDORF
SOUTHERN FORCE 2
19:00 hours
Surigao Strait
Southern Force attempts withdrawal; only one cruiser returns to Japan
00:15 hours MTBs attack

3 samar, 25 oct. 1944

06:45 hours sights US escort carriers: general attack ordered
CENTRE FORCE KURITA
09:20 hours Centre Force withdraws
10:50 hours Kamikaze attack; USS St Lo sunk
Philippine Sea
07:30 hours US escort carriers launch air strikes
TU2 STUMP
TU3 C. SPRAGUE

1–2 The American campaign to recapture the Philippines was prefaced by US Task Force 38 carrier raids on Formosa and Luzon, and intense submarine activity. The landings began on 17 Oct. when a Ranger battalion secured the island of Dinagat. On 20 Oct. two US corps landed either side of Tanauan on Leyte and thereby opened a campaign that was to continue until May 1945 (*map 1*). Japanese Southern Army had decided that an American landing would be opposed wherever it took place, and within a matter of hours of these initial landings, Japanese naval forces were steaming to rendezvous off Brunei. It was not until 22 Oct., however, that the main forces were to sail for the Philippines. Kurita's Centre Force – with five battleships, ten heavy and two light cruisers and 15 destroyers – immediately encountered trouble as it negotiated the difficult Palawan Passage. Two US submarines sank two heavy cruisers and severely damaged a third on the morning of 23 Oct. Despite the setbacks Centre Force entered the Sibuyan Sea on 24 Oct. only to find that whatever air power remained to the Japanese had been committed to attacks on TF38 rather than to providing air cover for its passage. Sustained American carrier attacks sank the battleship *Musashi* and one destroyer and damaged five other warships of the Centre Force before, at 15:00 hours, Kurita reversed course to the west. The Japanese had one notable success on 24 Oct. when a lone *Judy* bomber sank the light cruiser *Princeton* east of Luzon. On the same day Southern Force 1 experienced only intermittent attacks as it crossed the Sulu Sea and entered the Mindanao Sea. As it did so, however, the various US support groups off Leyte were organised into successive MTB, destroyer, cruiser and battle lines within and across the Surigao Strait (*map 2*). The first clash took place about 22:00 hours but a running fight developed after 00:15 hours on 25 Oct. as the Japanese entered the Strait: by 03:19 hours all but the cruiser *Mogami* and one destroyer had been overwhelmed by torpedoes and gunfire. A second Japanese force – with one light and two heavy cruisers and seven destroyers – some 40

www.odyssey.dircon.co.uk/leytegulf.htm
The Battle for Leyte Gulf, outline images and maps
www.arlingtoncemetery.net/halsejr.htm
William Frederick Halsey, commander of the US 3rd Fleet

miles astern, suspected what awaited it and declined to enter the Strait. As it withdrew, however, one of its number collided with the *Mogami*: the latter, slowed, was to be caught after daybreak by US aircraft and pounded into a wreck. By dawn on 25 Oct. the Americans, despite the loss of the *Princeton*, had clearly had the better of the exchanges. At 16:40 hours on the previous day, however, a scout plane from TG38.3 located Ozawa's decoy carrier force (*map 1*). The US and Japanese carrier forces were now some 140 miles apart, and TF38 was immediately ordered to turn north in order to engage next morning. In so doing TF38 took with it its battleships and made no provision for the guarding of the San Bernardino Strait. It was through this strait that Centre Force passed soon after midnight on 25Oct. Coming around Samar, at 05:49 hours, the Japanese sighted the first of three escort carrier groups standing off the Leyte beachheads, and by 06:12 hours battle was joined with the other two US groups. Overall the three US groups had some 500 aircraft and these subjected Centre Force to successive waves of attacks until 11:36 hours, when the Japanese broke off the battle and retired northwards. To the north, battle was joined off Cape Engaño between the fast carrier formations of Halsey's Third Fleet and Ozawa's Northern (decoy) Force soon after 07:35 hours on the morning of 25 Oct. The Americans launched six attacks during the course of the day, which sank three carriers and a destroyer. During the initial strikes, however, TF38 received word of developments off Samar, and in response to desperate appeals for support, it ordered two TGs to make for Samar, and the battle force to turn to the south and close the San Bernardino Strait. Carrier planes from TG38.1 and TG38.2 joined US bombers in attacking the retreating Centre Force, which made it back to Brunei with the loss of one destroyer. The various naval and air actions known as the Battle of Leyte Gulf effectively extinguished the ability of the Japanese to fight a major naval action. In the face of American superiority they came to rely more on unorthodox methods, such as Kamikaze attacks, first used successfully in the action off Samar Island.

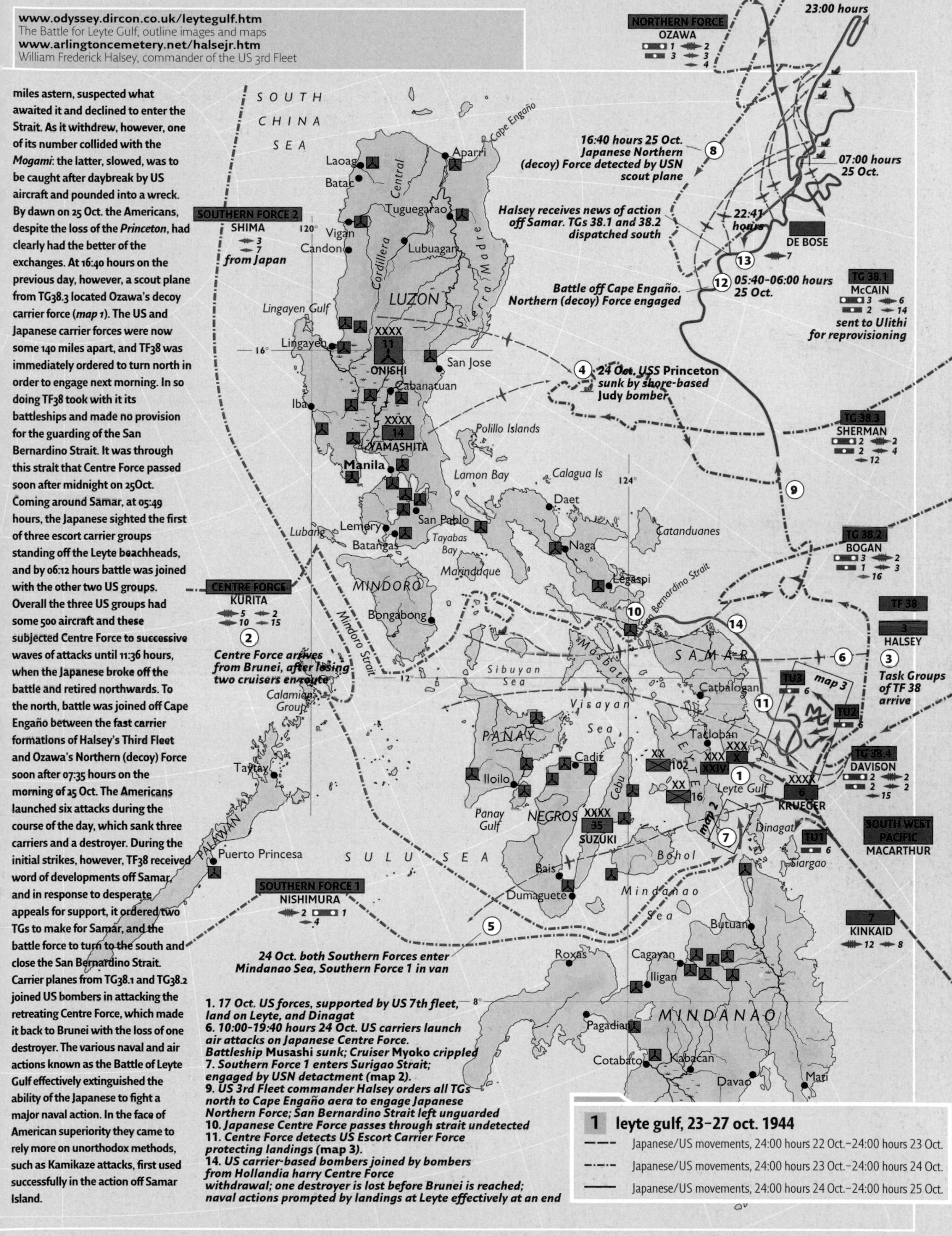

the philippines

1944 to 1945

- **1944 (11 October)** US 3rd Fleet aircraft attack Okinawa
- **11 November** US Navy bombards Iwo Jima
- **15 December** Mindoro airfield construction began by US forces; operational on 28 December
- **22 December** end of Japanese resistance on Leyte
- **30 December** ten US vessels lost to air attack off Mindoro
- **1945 (6 January)** Kamikaze attacks against invasion forces approaching Lingayen Gulf
- **1 February** US Sixth Army advances on Manila
- **17 February** US forces occupy Bataan peninsula
- **28 February** Corregidor secured by Americans
- **4 March** Manila falls to Americans
- **23 April** Americans control central Philippines
- **10 June** Australians land on Borneo

The outcome of the war in the Philippines was determined from the beginning of the campaign by the American advantages of surprise, concentration and position. The overwhelming American victory at Leyte Gulf in October served to compound these advantages in a campaign that thereafter conformed, in basic outline, to those campaigns that had been, and remained to be fought, in the Pacific; the American ability to isolate Japanese garrisons from outside support ensured their ultimate defeat. The Philippines campaign nevertheless proved protracted, and in different ways, costly to both sides.

Defeat at sea in no way lessened the Japanese determination to dispute the ownership of Leyte, and in seeking to reinforce its single division on the island, the Thirty-Fifth Army enjoyed some measure of protection against air attack because of the seasonal rains, the enforced withdrawal of TF38 after the Leyte Gulf battle and Kamikaze success. Between 24 October and 12 December some 45,000 troops drawn from five divisions were transferred to Leyte from other islands in the Philippines, but in the process the Japanese inevitably weakened their grip on the central and southern Philippines. Furthermore, they could not match the American build-up on Leyte. The Japanese sustained growing losses as the scale, intensity and effectiveness of American air operations increased. By December 1944 the Americans had some 200,000 combat troops on Leyte, but it was not until the middle of the month that Japanese resistance was broken in the north-west of the island following landings in Ormoc Bay and at Palompon. On 19 December, the Japanese abandoned the struggle for Leyte, though resistance on the island continued into May 1945.

What had brought the Americans to the Philippines, however, was the desire to liberate the islands from Japanese rule and the need to secure air and fleet facilities in the island. Control of Leyte provided the Americans with access to San Pedro Bay (first used by US fleet carriers in April) but continued Japanese control of air bases on other islands precluded its being rendered secure. Luzon alone offered the facilities sufficient to meet American requirements. Accordingly, on 15 December, American forces, having passed through the Mindanao Sea, landed on south-west Mindoro, and by the end of the year had two airfields around San Jose in service even though the island itself was not secured for another month. Then, with Task Force 38 pounding various targets between Luzon and Okinawa from 3 January, two corps of the US Sixth Army were put ashore in Lingayen Gulf on 9 January and moved rapidly inland – as had the Japanese before them in 1941 – across the central plain towards Manila. Clark Field and Calumpit were both secured on 31 January, the day that landings were made at Nasugbu. These achievements were made possible because the Japanese intention was not to offer serious resistance in front of the capital, but instead to concentrate forces in the mountains in an attempt to draw as many American formations as possible into a protracted struggle. The three Japanese commands on Luzon were thus ordered to withdraw into the mountains, the Zambales and the Sierra Madre, and behind Baguio; meanwhile, naval forces in Manila denied the Americans control of the capital until 3 March – despite Sixth Army having entered the city on 4 February and completed its encirclement by 12 February. With Corregidor secured on 28 February, however, the clearing of Manila – at the cost of an estimated 100,000 Filipino casualties – provided the Americans with effective control of everything of political and military value on Luzon.

1 the pacific, nov. 1944–aug. 1945

1 The elimination of effective Japanese naval and air power at Leyte Gulf left the Americans with the means to separate the Japanese from their southern resources area. The possibility of bypassing Luzon in favour of a campaign against Formosa was abandoned for political, as much as military, reasons. The campaign in Borneo was carried out by Australian forces and was essentially a mopping-up operation with the oilfields at Brunei, Tarakan and Balikpapan as its main objective. The oil, while it would prove useful to the US Pacific Fleet, had at this point no strategic value to the Japanese, who no longer had the means to transport it to the Home Islands. Little effort was made to clear the island of Japanese forces; instead the areas captured were secured. All these campaigns saw American and Australian chiefs of staff concentrating on political and prestige considerations, while the war to defeat Japan was carried onto Iwo Jima and Okinawa.

www.worldwar2database.com/html/philip44vid.htm
Newsreel footage of the war in the Philippines
www.ww2australia.gov.au/lastbattles/landings.html
The Australians' Borneo campaign of 1945

The Japanese had in effect abandoned Luzon on 13 January when the dispatch of further air reinforcements to the Philippines was halted. By that time the airfields remaining in Japanese hands had been rendered unviable and Japanese resources had to be preserved for the defence of the Home Islands. American naval losses, which in the month before this decision totaled 79 warships, merchantmen and amphibious vessels sunk or damaged by Kamikaze attack, now all but ceased. The Americans set about clearing the central and southern Philippines in order to free shipping routes through the islands. On 19 February, American forces landed on Samar and on 28 February at Puerto Princesa on Palawan. In the following seven weeks, a further 38 landings were conducted throughout the central and southern Philippines. In spite of the fact that they had some 110,000 troops spread across these islands, the Japanese could offer sustained resistance only on Negros and Mindanao; even on Luzon in mid-1945 the presence of 115,000 Japanese troops in the field failed to prevent a steady decline in the Imperial Army's ability to sustain its defensive campaign. This was tacitly recognised by the Americans in June when Sixth Army was withdrawn from operations. At the end of the war, four US divisions remained committed to operations in the Philippines, though responsibility for mopping up Japanese resistance was being passed to Filipino formations, with Australian troops designated the messy task of clearing and securing the now isolated Japanese garrisons in Borneo and the East Indies. With 16 US divisions having been committed to the Philippines, the securing and partial clearing of the islands cost the US Army nearly 146,000 casualties.

In a broader context, American control of key points in the Philippines by spring 1945 (Leyte, Manila) provided essential bases from which the approach to the Japanese Home Islands could be made. With the launching of Allied campaigns against Iwo Jima and Okinawa, the main focus of the war-winning effort shifted north.

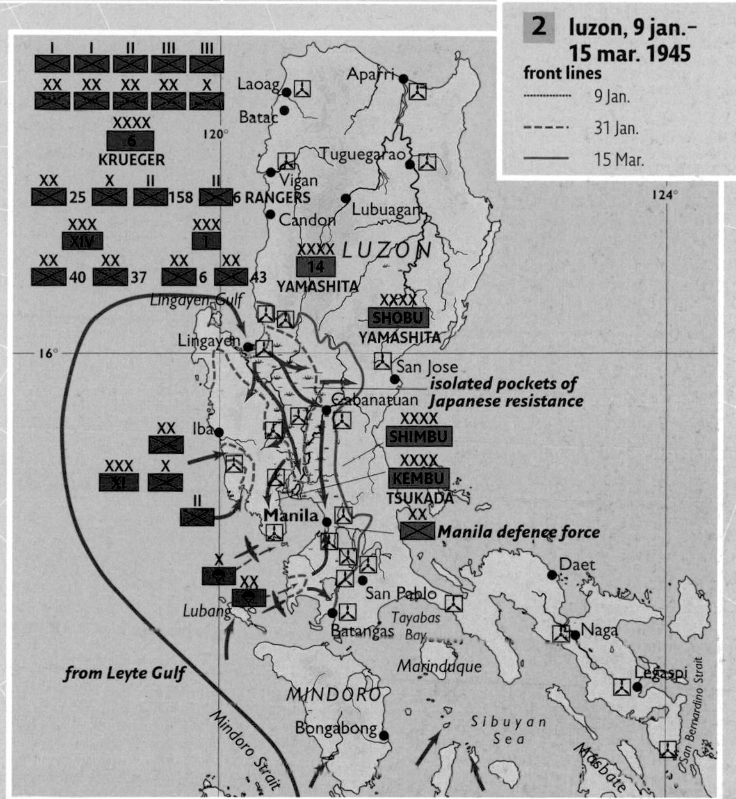

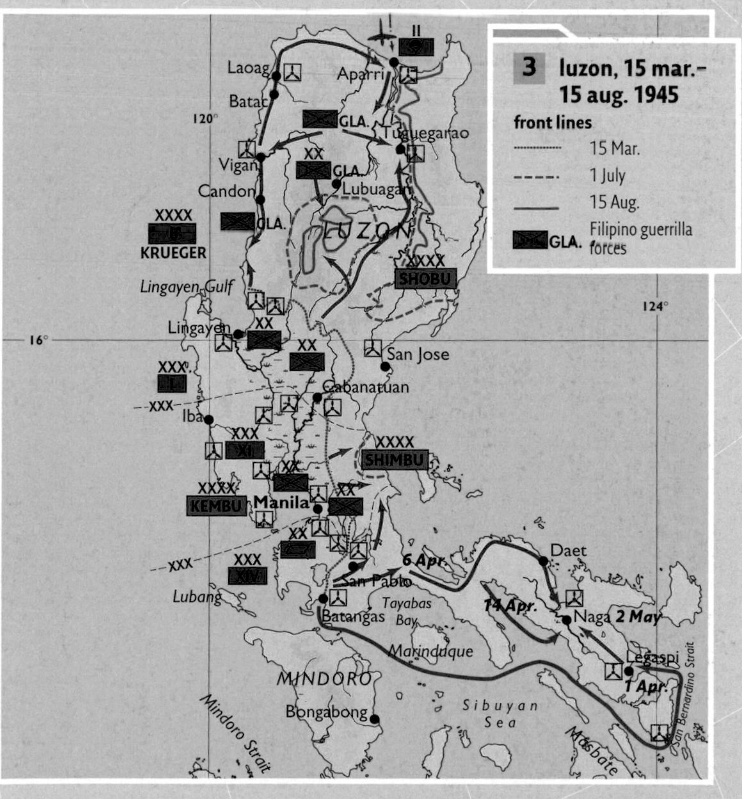

2-3 **The battle for Luzon was to become the most protracted campaign of the Pacific war. Huge logistical difficulties were overcome to land US forces successfully at Lingayen Gulf, and by 31 Jan. all the major airfields were in US hands. The Japanese adopted a policy of a static defence, and the use of isolated jungle troops. While most of the island was cleared at huge cost, the latter half of the campaign was left to Filipino guerrilla forces, marking an acceptance that Japanese troops would continue to occupy pockets of the island until the end of the war.**

iwo jima and okinawa

february to june 1945

- **16 February** Iwo Jima bombarded from air and sea
- **16–17 February** fast carrier raid on Japan
- **19–26 February** US Marines land on Iwo Jima
- **21 February** US carrier *Saratoga* badly damaged by Kamikaze attack
- **23 February** US Marines take Mount Suribachi on Iwo Jima
- **1 April** US Tenth Army invades Okinawa
- **11 April** Kamikaze attacks on US TF38 at Okinawa
- **18 May** US Marines take Sugarloaf Hill on Okinawa
- **4 June** US Marines land on north Oroku Peninsula
- **22 June** end of resistance on Okinawa

American planning for the advance across the Western Pacific had paid little attention to the islands of Okinawa and Iwo Jima until mid-1944, being mainly concerned with whether the Philippines were to be invaded or bypassed. When the US Navy's plans for invasion of Formosa were finally set aside, however, Okinawa assumed a significance previously denied it: air power based on the Philippines would still be too distant to support an invasion of the Japanese Home Islands, but Okinawa could provide an important base for both tactical and strategic air operations over Japan. Iwo Jima, however, was different in that even before June 1944 its importance, in terms of the planned bombing offensive from the Marianas, was recognised. The capture of both islands was thus authorised by the US Joint Chiefs of Staff in October 1944.

The strategic significance of Okinawa and Iwo Jima was obvious to the Japanese long before the Americans fought their way into the southern Marianas and the central Philippines, but the defence of the islands presented the Japanese with considerable problems. Iwo Jima, the largest of the Volcano Islands, was too small to be defended in depth, and Okinawa was only one of several Japanese defensive problems in the south-west approaches to Kyushu. The Japanese recognised that neither island could be denied the Americans, and thus the aim of any defence would be not to meet any invasion on the beaches, but to mount protracted campaigns that might sap the American will to proceed with an invasion of the Japanese Home Islands; such a strategy would also force the Americans to commit heavy naval forces to the beachheads, where they could be subjected to concentrated, and hopefully withering, air attack.

The scale of both operations was enormous, involving extensive preliminary carrier bombardments of the Home Islands, huge naval escort forces, and the transport of invasion troops across large distances – combined operations of greater complexity even than Overlord in Normandy. Delays in the campaign on Luzon forced the American High Command to postpone the invasion of Iwo Jima until 19 February and of Okinawa until I April. This left the US Fast Carrier Force with time for only one raid on Honshu before the assault on Iwo Jima but allowed more time for the preliminary bombardment of the island. Iwo Jima was bombarded both from the sea and by B-24 and B-25 raids from the Marianas for 72 days before the landing, the longest bombardment afforded any island in the Pacific war; heavy US warships joined the effort on 16 February. The assault itself was accompanied by a creeping barrage provided by warships (the first of the Pacific war); but the effectiveness of air and naval bombardment was largely offset by a combination of the soft lava of Iwo Jima – which covered the island in dust – and the Japanese preparation of a dense network of tunnels and defensive positions. The soft lava and the steep shelving of the beaches produced chaos amongst assault shipping on 19 February; after swift initial success, US forces confronted bitter resistance that continued for some five weeks before the island was declared secure on 26 March. The campaign cost the Japanese 23,300 dead

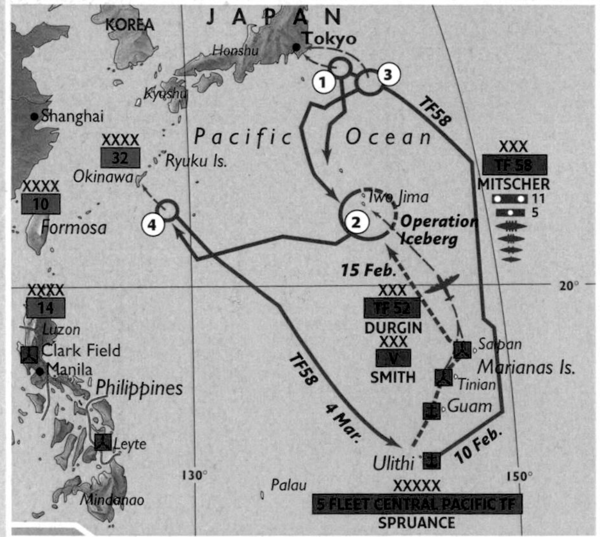

1 the western pacific, 10 feb.–4 mar. 1945

fast carrier operations; invasion force and escort operations

1. TF58 operational area for air strikes on Honshu, 16 Feb.
2. TF58 operational area for air strikes and tactical support on Iwo Jima, 1 Feb.
3. TF58 operational area for air strikes on Honshu, 25 Feb.
4. TF58 operational area for air strikes on Okinawa, 1 Mar.

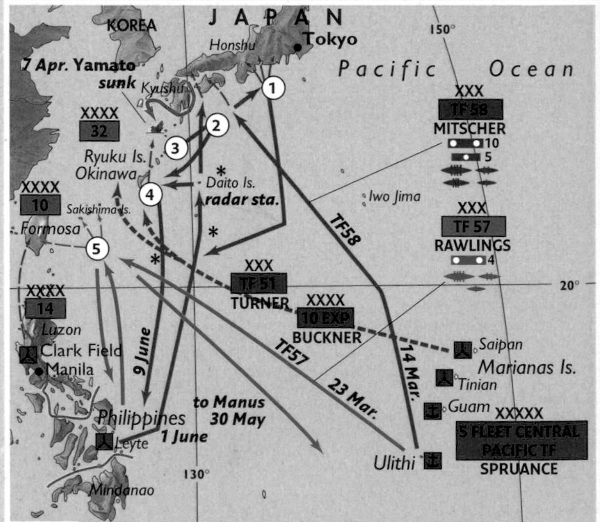

3 the western pacific, 14 mar.–13 june 1945

fast carrier operations; invasion force and escort operations; British carrier operations; * fuelling area

1. TF58 operational area for air strikes on Honshu, 18–19 Mar.
2. TF58 operational area for air strikes on Kyushu, 18–19 Mar.
3. TF58 area for 28 operational dates against Okinawa, Ryukyus and Japan, 26 Mar.–24 May
4. TF58 operational area for air strikes and tactical support on Okinawa, 28 dates between 23 Mar.–28 May
5. TF57 operational area for air strikes on Sakishma Is. and Formosa, 26 Mar.–20 Apr., 4–25 May

www.iwojima.com/
Images of the Battle of Iwo Jima
www.militaryhistoryonline.com/wwii/okinawa/default.aspx
The battle of Okinawa

and 1,000 prisoners; the Americans suffered 24,391 casualties, plus a fleet carrier badly damaged and an escort carrier sunk on 21 February. But the island was rapidly transformed into a base for the bombing campaign over Japan. By the end of the war, 2,251 Superfortresses had made emergency landings on Iwo Jima – the first on 4 March – and fighters operated from the island from 11 March.

Three days later, on 14 March, TF58 cleared Ulithi to begin operations in support of the landings on Okinawa; she remained at sea for 92 days, reflecting not simply the sheer length of the Okinawa campaign, but the intensity of operations over and off the island. Here support was also provided by a British carrier force. Again resilient Japanese defence led to a protracted and costly month-long campaign, which involved both clearing the outlying islands and dislodging the main Japanese force on the island, committed to a last-ditch defence.

Some 110,000 Japanese died defending Okinawa. The American losses totalled 20,195 dead and 55,162 wounded. For the first time in the war, however, Japanese surrendered in significant numbers – 7,400. The Allies lost 38 naval vessels sunk and 368 damaged, but in the course of the struggle for Okinawa, and at the cost of 763 aircraft, Allied naval power destroyed the last remaining Japanese naval force (the *Yamato* left Japan at the head of a relief task force, but was sunk by US bombers) and 691 Japanese aircraft, including some 190 suicide aircraft.

2 iwo jima, 19 feb.– 26 mar. 1945

1-5 **Astride the route of bombers operating against the Tokyo area from bases in the Marianas (*map 1*), Iwo Jima was assaulted on 19 Feb (*map 2*). The Americans successfully landed six regiments on the first day of the assault. By 23 Feb. the Americans had secured the heavily fortified outcrop of Mt Suribachi, which overlooked the invasion beaches, fought their way onto Airfield No. 2 and almost reached the Japanese main line of defence. Thereafter V Amphibious Corps, with three divisions committed, overran remaining Japanese positions by 16 Mar., but while the island was declared secure on 26 Mar., some 2,409 Japanese soldiers were killed or captured as resistance flickered on into June. Off Okinawa TF58 found itself committed to a protracted campaign in support of Tenth Army (*map 3*) because the latter, after considerable initial success, found itself opposed by a Japanese force that displayed a keen appreciation of terrain, a highly-developed sense of self-preservation, and great skill in the conduct of a defence that employed a great diversity and weight of artillery. On 26 Mar. the 77th Infantry Division secured the Keramas and the Keises (*map 4*), gaining positions from which southern Okinawa could be brought under fire. On 1 Apr. four divisions came ashore around Katena, and within 36 hours had thrust across the narrow waist of Okinawa to reach its eastern coast. The 6th Marine Division then set about securing northern Okinawa, encountering only scattered resistance except on the Motobu peninsula. By securing the latter, the Marines could bring fire down on Ie Shima, secured by the 77th Infantry Division between 16–21 Apr. With units of the 27th Infantry Division securing some of the eastern islands between 8–22 Apr., the main US strength advanced into southern Okinawa (*map 5*). Japanese resistance did not collapse until 17 June, though the 24th Infantry Division continued to offer organised resistance for a further four days. The Japanese Home Islands were now within striking distance.**

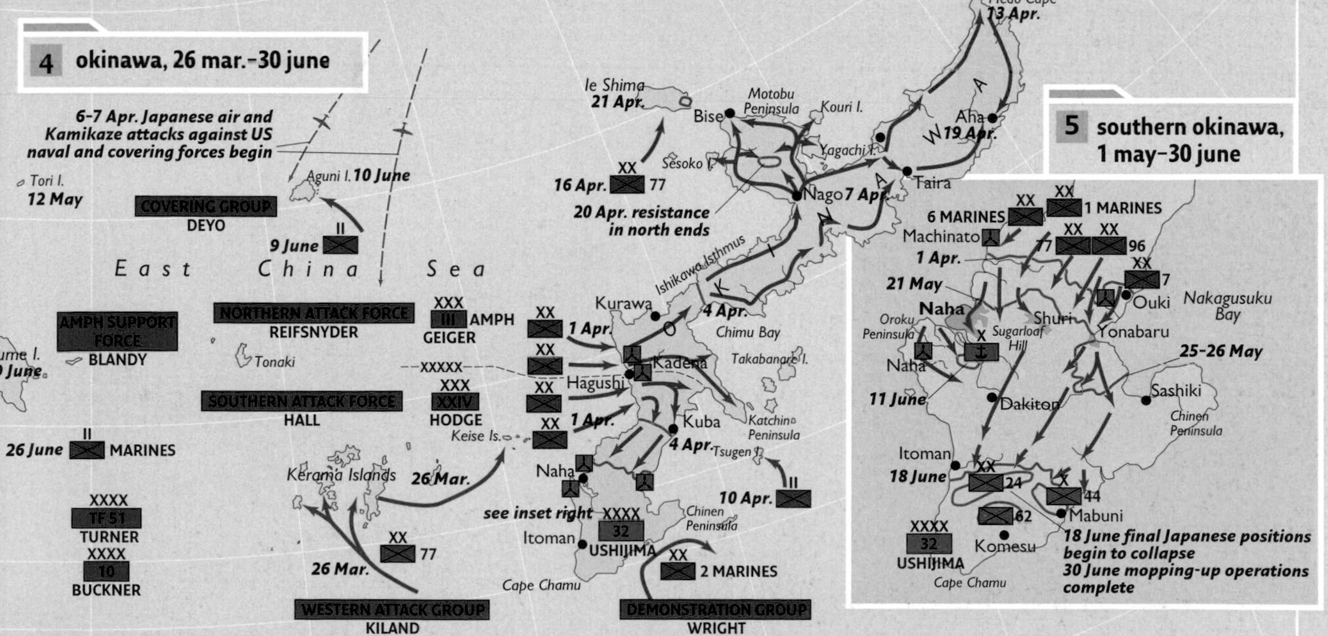

resistance in eastern europe

1941 to 1945

- **1941 (4 July)** Tito announces resistance in Yugoslavia
- **November** Chetniks and Tito's Partisans fight each other
- **1942 (27 May)** attempted assassination of Heydrich in Prague (dies of wounds four days later)
- **10 June** reprisal massacre at Lidice for Heydrich's death
- **22 July** first deportations from Warsaw Ghetto to extermination camps
- **1944 (1 February)** Polish resistance assassinate Major Kutschera, Chief of Gestapo in Poland
- **1 August** Polish Underground Army begins revolt in Warsaw

Whereas Hitler's 'New Order' in western Europe conceded a degree of fraternity and even independence to the conquered states, in the east, German rule was absolute and unbending. Nazi racial theories and ideology gave their administrators every justification to pursue ruthless policies of exploitation and repression in Poland, the Baltic states and the occupied areas of the Soviet Union.

This attitude naturally led to only limited success in promoting collaboration with the civilian population, although Nationalist elements (Belarussians, Ukrainians) within former Soviet territory were encouraged, and with German manpower shortages becoming an increasingly serious problem, Red Army prisoners were accepted into the Wehrmacht together with anti-communist volunteers. The harshness of German policies towards the civilian population in the east contributed, in part, to the growth of resistance. For, when Slavs recognised their ultimate fate as so-called 'useless eaters', many felt that they had little to lose by resisting. In contrast to the occasionally indulgent German reaction to minor acts of resistance in western countries, in the occupied east there was little opportunity to register opposition with strikes and demonstrations. Anti-Fascist demonstrations and industrial action were, however, more widespread in the now occupied Axis satellite countries of Central and South Eastern Europe. Schools and universities were suppressed and systematic attempts were made to eradicate Poland's intelligentsia and professional classes. Nevertheless, a flourishing illegal press was maintained in Warsaw and other cities. Furthermore, the Polish underground was able to provide the Allies with important intelligence and offered assistance to escaped prisoners of war.

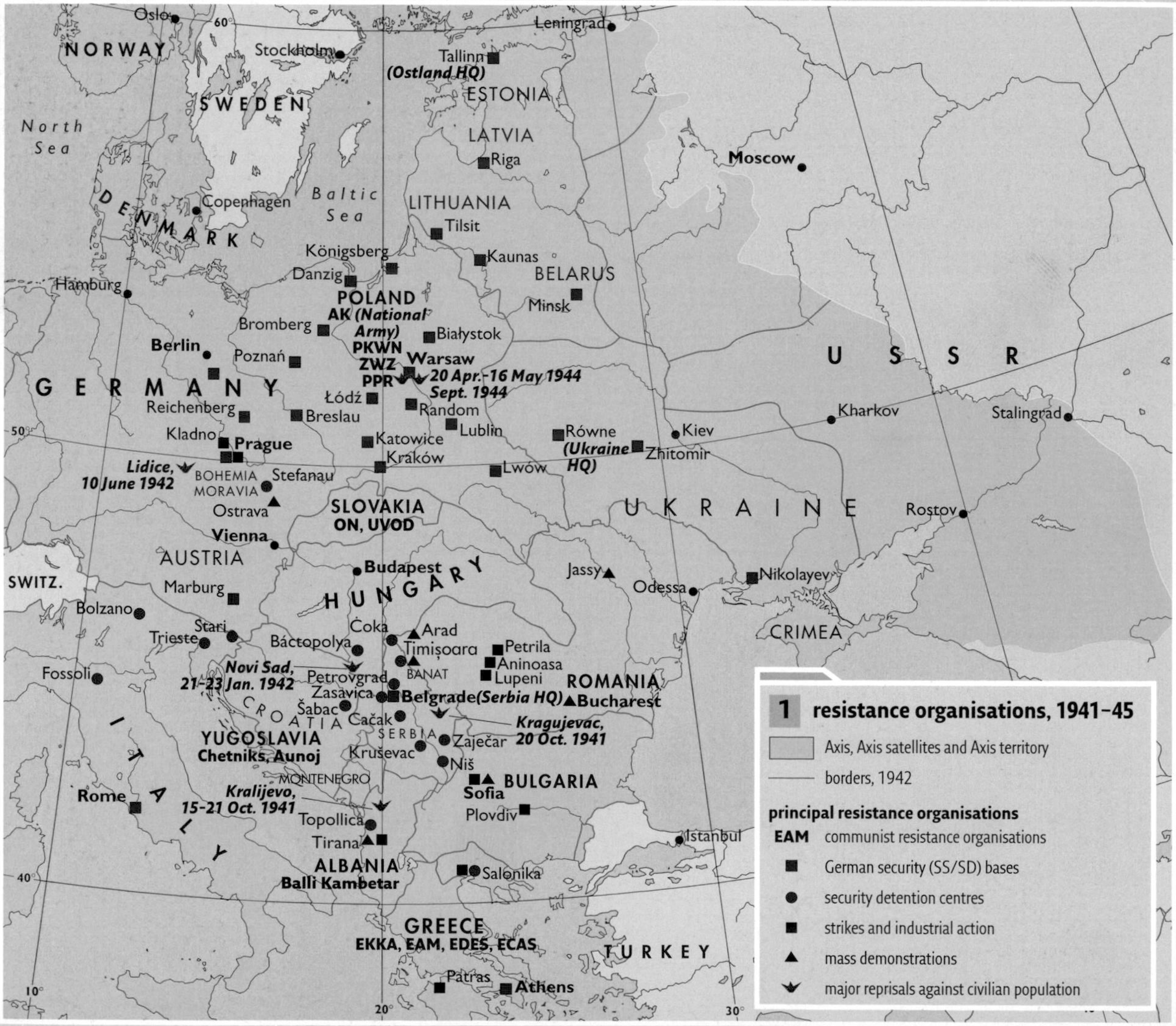

1 resistance organisations, 1941–45

- Axis, Axis satellites and Axis territory
- borders, 1942

principal resistance organisations

- EAM communist resistance organisations
- ■ German security (SS/SD) bases
- ● security detention centres
- ■ strikes and industrial action
- ▲ mass demonstrations
- major reprisals against civilian population

www.warsawuprising.com/
Images, movies, and information on the Warsaw Uprising, 1944
www.polishresistance-ak.org/
The Polish resistance during World War II

But resistance in the east was characterised largely by partisan warfare. The vastness of the area behind the German front lines and a terrain of marshes, forests and mountains lent themselves to guerrilla tactics. The partisan movement had stemmed largely from the presence in German occupied territory of whole Red Army units that had been cut off by the rapidity of the German advance in 1941. Although they hardly constituted a serious military threat, they nevertheless offered a base upon which to build effective partisan operations. In much the same way as Britain sought to ease pressure on its conventional forces by promoting resistance on the Continent, the Soviet Union was quick to exhort its civilian population to adopt guerrilla tactics against the invader. As early as July 1941 the Central Committee of the Communist Party called upon Soviet citizens to take up arms, and in May 1942 the Soviet High Command took steps to coordinate guerrilla activity by establishing a Central Staff of the Partisan Movement. Liaison officers, wireless equipment, weapons and supplies were provided in ever increasing numbers and partisan operations were fully integrated into Red Army strategy. In addition to widespread attacks on German communications, partisans made specific efforts in support of Soviet offensives, notably in 1943 to assist operations at Kursk. Similarly, guerrilla forces were able to ease the progress of conventional forces by securing bridges and key installations in the path of their advance. Such a role was markedly more effective than partisan attempts to engage German forces in open combat or to liberate or defend territory. For, in spite of diminishing numbers and resources, German units tended to be better and more heavily equipped than the partisans. Popular uprisings were consequently usually short-lived and armed resistance was crushed by determined German counter-insurgency operations in Warsaw and Slovakia in 1944.

The efficacy of partisan operations has been questioned, not least because of exaggerated post-war claims made to promote their activities. Similarly, it should be acknowledged that the large areas held under partisan control were often conceded to them by the Germans rather than conquered by guerrilla forces. Nevertheless, these facts should not discount the very real contribution made by partisan forces in eroding German dominance in Eastern Europe. Furthermore, Communist partisan groups were a reminder of Soviet intent to recapture the territory it had lost and to extend communist influence into the other occupied countries of Eastern Europe.

2 **In 1944 the Polish Home Army (*Armia Krajowa*) embarked upon an uprising in Warsaw. The rebels initially gained control of two-thirds of the city. However, its leaders, under General Bor-Komorowski, underestimated the ferocity of the German response. SS units launched a ferocious campaign, which, as supplies of food and ammunition became exhausted, forced the survivors literally underground into the sewers, where they were gradually reduced. The Poles had also relied upon both supplies airlifted from the Allies in the west (which were flown in with great difficulty) and the imminent liberation of the city by combined units of the Polish émigré and Red Armies. The latter did not materialise.**

1 **It was impossible for Germany completely to police all of its conquests in eastern Europe. The Germans relied upon the use of constant reprisals against the civilian population and major offensives against guerrilla groups. These failed to curtail resistance activity and tied down large numbers of troops – estimates in Soviet territory alone show approximately half a million Germans dealing with approximately 250,000 partisans. Even allowing for exaggeration, partisan activity was substantial, with vast tracts of German-occupied territory being virtually no-go areas, allowing the Soviets to coordinate partisan sabotage activities with conventional operations. In response, the Wehrmacht and the security forces carried out extensive anti-partisan sweeps, the largest of which, Operation Cottbus, took place in Belarus in June 1943 and involved nearly 17,000 men who failed to trap their quarry.**

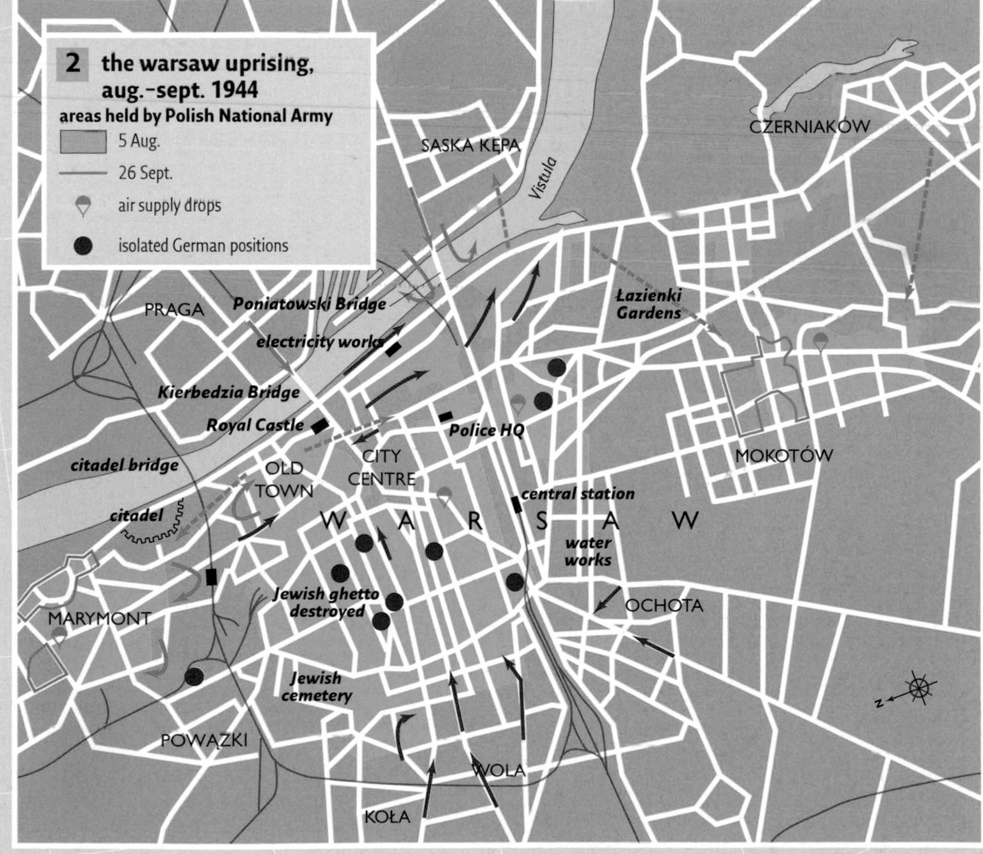

poland

january to march 1945

- **17 January** Soviets capture Warsaw
- **18 January** Polish provisional government set up
- **26 January** Auschwitz liberated
- **27 January** Soviets cross River Vistula
- **29 January** Poznań surrounded
- **11 February** Soviets advance towards Breslau and Dresden
- **15 February** Soviets attack Danzig and surround Breslau
- **23 February** Poznań captured
- **22 March** Soviets besiege Danzig and Gdynia
- **30 March** Danzig captured

The German counter-offensive in the Ardennes in December 1944 diverted Hitler from the gathering storm in the east. In spite of the attempts of Guderian and Gehlen (in charge of intelligence for the Eastern Front) to alert him, Hitler refused to believe that the Soviets were capable of launching another massive offensive. He remained mesmerised by the possibilities in the west and by illusions that Soviet tank armies lacked tanks.

In fact, operations by powerful Soviet tank armies were one of the distinctive features of the campaign. Gehlen predicted the Soviet offensive with amazing accuracy, expecting it towards the middle of January. On 9 January Gehlen announced that the Russians would aim to destroy the German will and ability to carry on the war completely, and three days later the attack began. It was probably brought forward to 12 January in response to Western Allied requests for help in the wake of the Ardennes, but possibly also to pre-empt German attempts to strengthen their defences.

The outline of the Soviet plan had been sketched in November 1944, taking the shortest distance to Berlin: straight through Warsaw. The operation was charged to 1st Belarussian Front (Zhukov) and 1st Ukrainian Front (Koniev), in cooperation with the left wing of 2nd Belarussian (Rokossovsky) and the right of 4th Ukrainian (Petrov). Zhukov aimed for Poznań, Koniev for Breslau. Their two fronts alone comprised 2.2 million men, 33,500 guns and mortars, 7,000 tanks and assault guns and 5,000 aircraft in 22 armies. Their mission was the destruction of Army Group A (Harpe) (from 26 January renamed Centre) and the conquest of Poland. Harpe's Army Group comprised 400,000 men, 1,136 tanks and assault guns and 270 aircraft in three armies: 30 divisions stretched from the Vistula north of Warsaw to the Carpathians. In addition, Reinhardt's Centre Group in East Prussia (580,000 men, 700 tanks and assault guns and 515 aircraft) posed a threat to the flank.

The operation fell into two phases: in the first (to 17 January), Soviet forces attacked from three bridgeheads – 1st Belarussian from Magnuszew and Puławy, 1st Ukrainian from Sandomierz. Bad weather hampered air support and placed even greater stress on artillery. 1st Ukrainian attacked on 12 January, the Sandomierz–Silesian operation, after a 107-minute artillery bombardment. 1st Belarussian attacked two days later, the Warsaw–Poznań Operation, after a 25-minute preparation in which double 'fire lanes' were ploughed into German positions, between which the Soviets advanced. The Soviets broke through on a 300-mile wide front to a depth of 60–100 miles. The first phase ended on 17 January with the fall of Warsaw. Whereas the Soviets had stood back as the Warsaw rising, led by the London-backed *Armija Krajowa* (National Army), had been wiped out, now the Soviet-controlled First Polish Army, in cooperation with 1st Belarussian Front fought its way into the city. In spite of Hitler's orders to hold, the German command in Warsaw was determined not to become another Stalingrad and hastily withdrew to avoid encirclement.

During the second phase, to 3 February, the Russians encircled and seized the Silesian industrial region, which Stalin ordered Koniev to capture intact in a typically oblique but unambiguous fashion – he pointed it out on the map and said one word: 'gold'. After advancing over 300 miles in two weeks, between 26 January and 3 February 1st Belarussian Front established bridgeheads over the Oder, the last major obstacle, 40 miles from Berlin.

1 The Germans fortified the territory between the Vistula and the Oder with some seven defensive zones, altogether 300 miles deep. Wide use was made of the natural features of the rivers and 'fortress cities'. The Soviet 1st Ukrainian Front attacked from the Sandomierz bridgehead on 12 Jan: 1st Belarussuan two days later. On the 1st Ukranian sector, all four tank armies broke through into the operational depth and pursuit phase. Some 200 German tanks, half of them heavy Tigers, were destroyed on the first day. The Russians prevented the Germans occupying prepared defence lines, keeping them constantly off-balance. By 31 Jan. I Mechanical Corps had crossed the Oder, seizing a bridgehead round Küstrin, which would play a key part in the subsequent offensive against Berlin. Armoured spearheads (tank armies deployed 25–55 miles ahead of the main forces), accelerated and maintained the Soviet rate of advance. The Third Guards and Fourth Tank Armies were particularly successful. A spectacular circuit by the former isolated a German Silesian grouping, capturing the region relatively intact. The advance by Fourth Tank captured Kielce and Łódź (19 Jan.), outmaneuvering the Grossdeutschland Panzer Corps. Substantial cavalry forces also ranged fast and far into the German rear. The Russians experienced some problems supplying their faster-moving forces. They used a prodigious amount of fuel and began to run out as they reached 400 miles from their supply depots.

www.polandsholocaust.org/1945.html
Chronology of events during the Polish campaign
http://en.wikipedia.org/wiki/Konstantin_Rokossovsky
Konstantin Rokossovsky, commander of the 2nd Belarussian Front

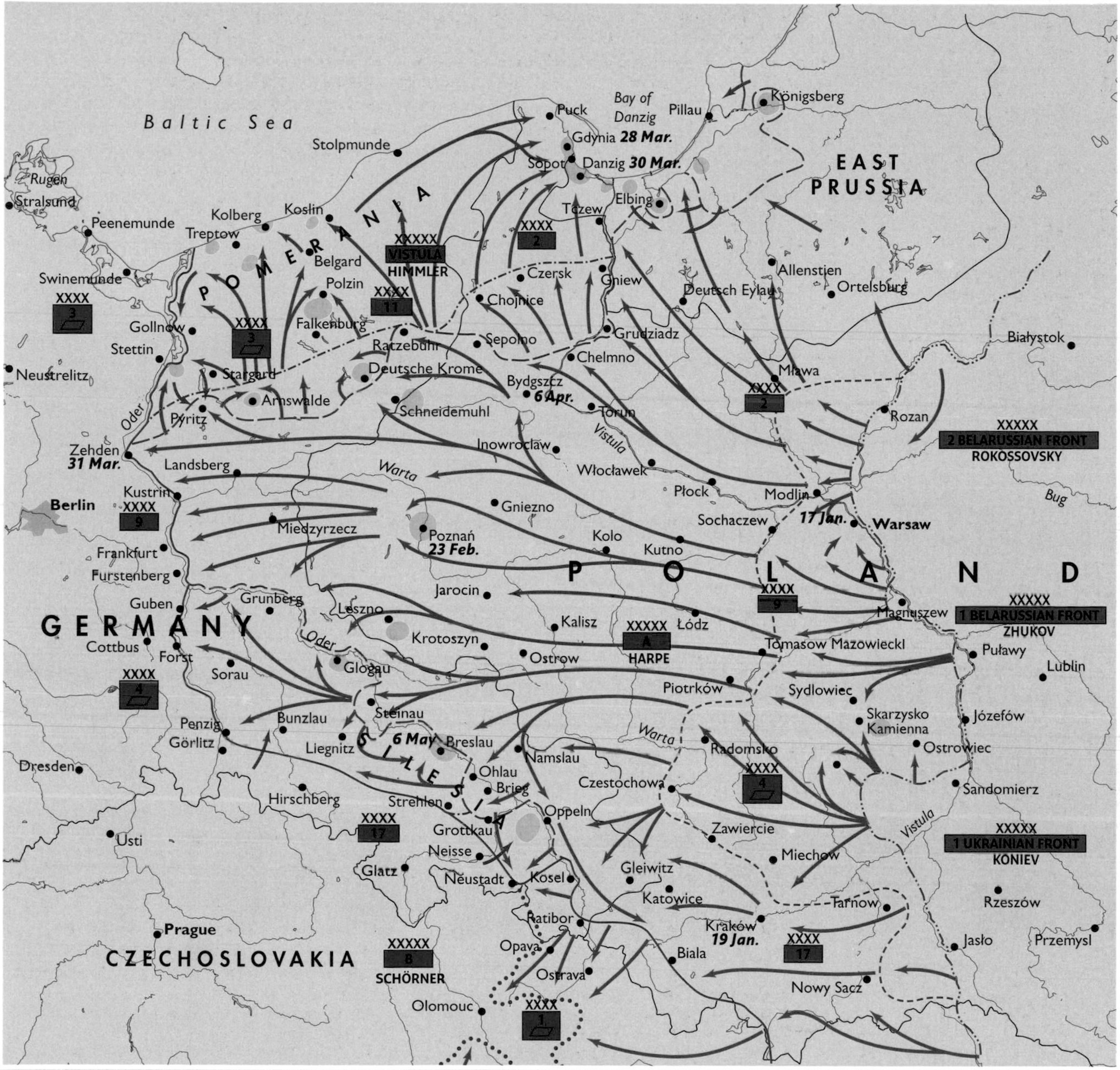

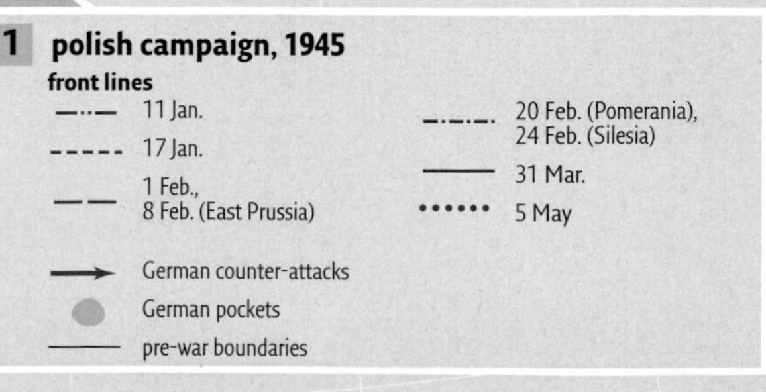

august to september 1944

- **6 August** Red Army takes Drohobycz oil centre
- **14 August** Red Army begins offensive from Vistula bridgehead
- **20 August** Red Army lands troops in mouth of Danube, attacking Romania
- **31 August** Bucharest taken by Red Army
- **20 August** Red Army enters Bulgaria unopposed

1 Lwów was a crucial link between German forces defending the approach to the Reich with those in Romania. The favourable terrain, including the barriers formed by the numerous tributaries of the Dniester, was used to establish three defensive belts 25–30 miles wide. The main German force held the axis covering Lwów, with infantry holding the first two defensive lines and the armour held some 10 miles back. Lwów was one of the axes of the Lwów–Sandomierz operation (13 July–29 Aug.), the other lay towards Rawa Ruska. The first phase lasted until 27 July; the second, until 29 Aug., and took Soviet forces to the Carpathians.

As Army Group Centre disintegrated under the hammer blows of Operation Bagration in mid-July 1944, the Soviet command extended its offensive to the area south of the Pripet Marshes, where Army Group North Ukraine (Harpe) held the German front down to the formidable natural barrier of the Carpathian range. Here, in West Ukraine and South East Poland, the Germans had expected the blow, which in fact fell in Belarus. Now, they had to move six divisions to Army Group Centre, leaving 34 infantry and five Panzer, to cover Lwów, the industrial region of Drohobycz-Borisław, the approaches to southern Poland, Czechoslovakia and Silesia, and their valuable industrial resources.

Stalin had proposed one thrust in the direction of Lwów but Marshal Koniev wanted two, the other towards Rawa Ruska, which Stalin allowed, on Koniev's 'own head'. This was the import of the Stavka directive issued on 24 June, for what would become Operation Lwów-Sandomierz (13 July–August). Koniev's 1st Ukrainian Front, already the strongest in the Red Army, was massively reinforced. The plan was to encircle and destroy German forces in the area of Brody and Lwów, then to split Army Group North Ukraine in two, driving one half west, the other half into the Carpathians, and advancing as far as the Vistula.

As the first phase of the operation began, on 13 July, German Fourth and First Panzer armies withdrew troops from the forward positions, a technique they had learned to mitigate the effect of the massive Soviet preparatory bombardment. Detecting this, the Russians in turn forgot about the bombardment and attacked immediately. For the first two days there was heavy fighting north-west of Brody, but by the evening of 15 July KMG Baronov (Cavalry-Mechanised Group) was committed to cut off the escape route for German forces in the area. The attack on the Lwów axis, for which the Germans were ready, fared poorly as mist and rain hampered the artillery bombardment. Soviet troops only made a shallow penetration when they attacked in the afternoon of 14 July, and the Germans immediately committed their tactical reserves. As the German counter-attacks were worn down, Rybalko's 3rd Guards Tank Army was committed on 16 July. The Russians succeeded in encircling up to eight divisions south-west of Brody, passing the two KMGs either side of the encircled force. The three tank armies were committed outside these, two to the south and one to the north. The Russians moved on to take Rawa Ruska, Przemysl, Lwów and Stanislawów and reach the River San.

The fall of Lwów on 27 July marked the end of the first phase of the operation, in which the Soviet objectives had been achieved exactly as planned. The axis now shifted from Lwów–Przemysl to Sandomierz (to the north), where the crucial Vistula crossings were nearer. As early as 30 July units of 3rd Guards Tank Army and KMG Sokolov were over the Vistula, but the bridgeheads were too small and precarious to be enlarged. A ferocious battle developed, Soviet units crossing the river parallel with withdrawing German ones. Like Army Group North Ukraine, 1st Ukrainian Front also found itself split. At the end of July, Koniev recommended that the armies on the left (Carpathian) axis come under separate command, and within a few days (8 August) a new Front command, Petrov's 4th Ukrainian, took control of First Guards and Eighteenth Armies, in operations in the Carpathian foothills.

Meanwhile, on 2 August, Stavka had issued the order for the attack on Romania. With Army Group North Ukraine split and shattered, it was now the turn of Army Group South Ukraine (Friessner) to be eliminated. Friessner had a nominal strength of 600,000 German and Romanian troops, the latter now about to stab the Germans in the back. Much of Army Group South Ukraine's armour had been moved north to cope with other massive Soviet attacks. Against this background Stavka framed the plan for the Jassy–Kishinev strategic operation to destroy Army Group South Ukraine and split the German–Romanian alliance by capturing Moldavia.

2nd Ukrainian launched its main blow north-west of Jassy on 20 August. 3rd Ukrainian attacked from the Kitsman bridgehead. The critical day of the campaign was 23 August. Some 18 German divisions were encircled south west of the city, and Third Romanian Army was similarly surrounded. Soviet armour reached the Prut at Leovo and Sixth Tank Army was racing on towards the Focsani gap, threatening the entire German Army Group. On the same day, Germany's position in South East Europe collapsed with the Bucharest coup. King Michael of Romania ordered Romanian troops to stop firing at the Russians, had Marshal Antonescu (who had seen Hitler

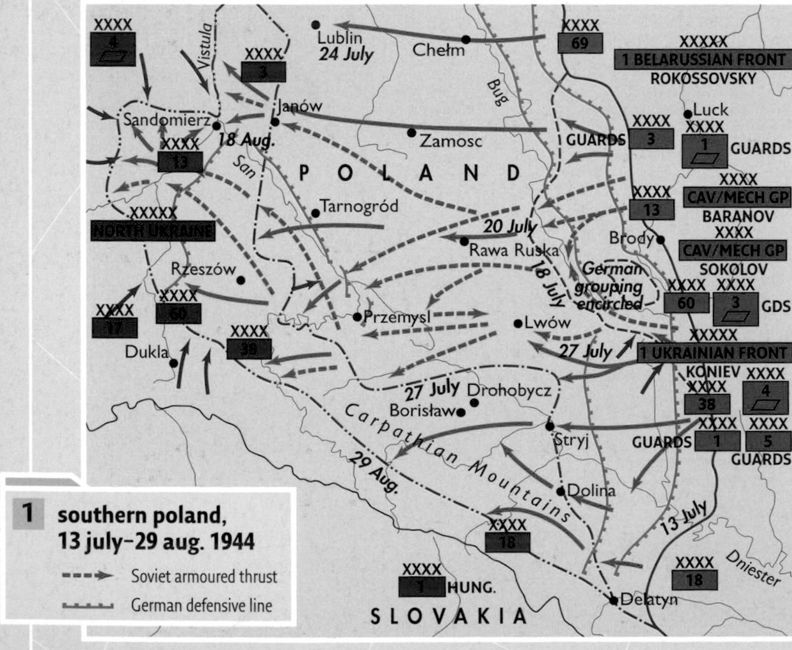

1 southern poland, 13 july–29 aug. 1944

Soviet armoured thrust

German defensive line

www.bulgaria.com/history/bulgaria/war2.html
Bulgaria during World War Two
www.iabsi.com/gen/public/Military_dukla_pass.htm
The battle for Dukla Pass, the Soviet advance from southern Poland into occupied Slovakia

as recently as 5 August) arrested, and surrendered unconditionally to the Allies. The Romanian change of sides took the Germans completely by surprise, the German ambassador in Bucharest committing suicide. The suggestion that the Russians halt their advance and that the Romanians deal with the remaining German forces was declined by Stavka, and Soviet forces entered Bucharest on 31 August.

After Romania seceded from the Axis, events in Bulgaria reached a crisis. On 26 August, with the Russians closing in, the Bulgarian government declared neutrality. This was not good enough for the Russians and on 5 September they declared war on Bulgaria. On 8 September Tolbukhin's 3rd Ukrainian Front crossed the Bulgarian frontier. There was no exchange of fire. On the following day the 'Fatherland Front' (Agrarians and Communists) seized power in Bulgaria and Soviet troops were ordered to halt military operations. It had been a bloodless victory.

On 29 August, the Slovak revolt had begun south of the Carpathians. 1st (Koniev) and 4th (Petrov) Ukrainian Fronts launched the East Carpathian operation on 8 September, in order to break Axis forces and seize control of the Carpathian passes, opening communications with the Slovak partisans. By 28 October, German forces had been driven out of eastern Czechoslovakia and north of the Tisza. With Romania and Bulgaria now also in Soviet hands, the massive Eastern Front was being rolled up from the right flank, which, as far as the defence of the Reich was concerned, now lay in Hungary and western Czechoslavakia.

2 The Jassy-Kishinev operation (20–29 Aug.), brought Soviet troops as far south into Romania as Bucharest, where there was a popular rising on 23 Aug., and Romania defected from the Axis. The Romanians tried to persuade the Russians to halt their advance, but Malinovsky, commanding 2nd Ukrainian Front, was ordered to continue his advance into Bucharest itself from 31 Aug. On 29 Aug., 2nd Ukrainian only faced the remnants of seven Axis divisions: the rest of the opposition had disintegrated. The Russians moved on towards Bulgaria, crossing the frontier on 8 Sept. Within 12 hours, after meeting no resistance, they were 40 miles inside. On 28 Sept., the Soviet LXXV Corps (Tolbukhin's 3rd Ukrainian Front) reached the Yugoslav frontier and the gunboats of Gorshkov's Danube flotilla approached Negotin, the first Soviet objective in Yugoslavia, which fell on 30 Sept.

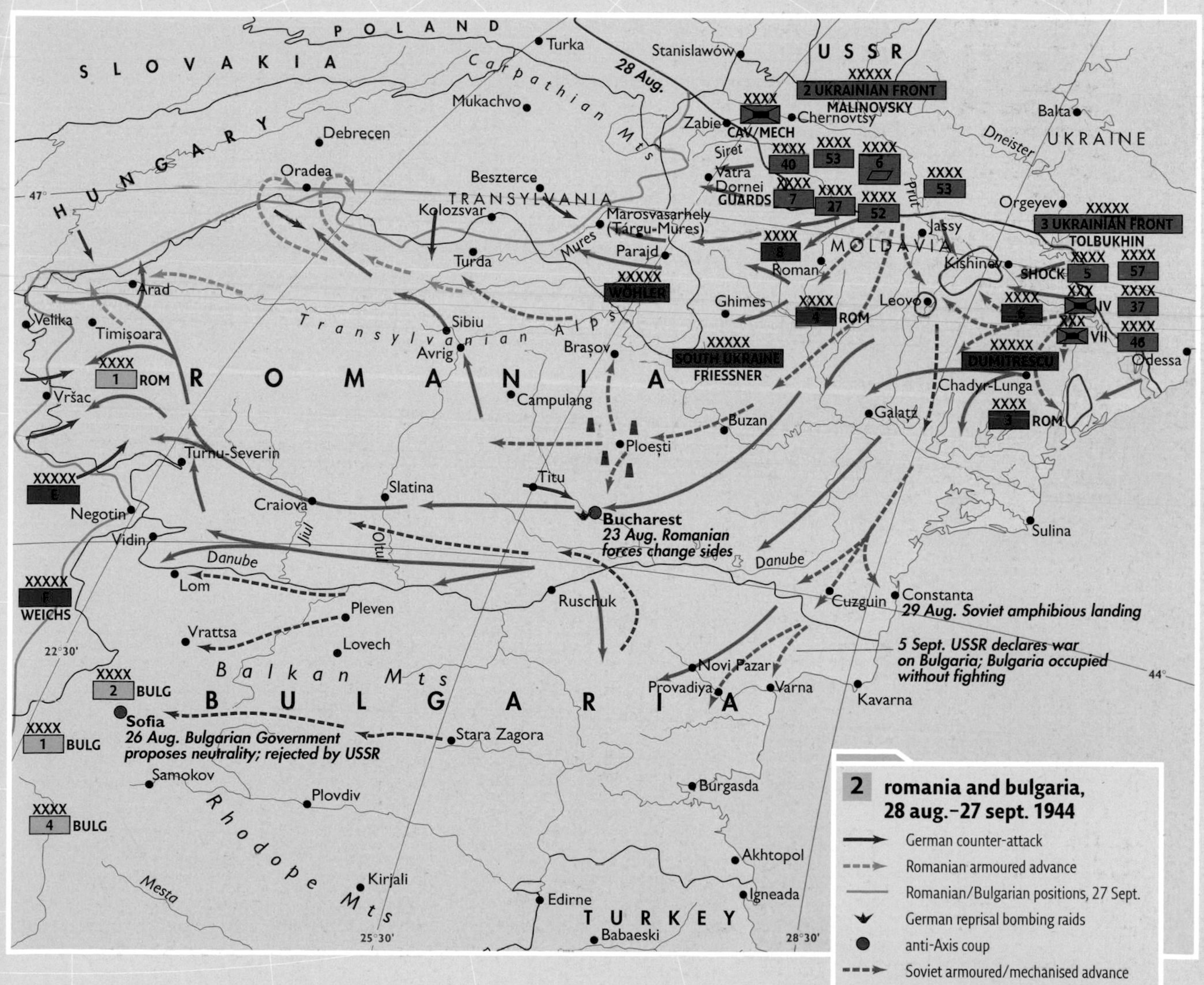

hungary

september 1944 to march 1945

- **1944 (10 October)** tank battle at Debrecen; Soviets lose three corps
- **18 December** Soviet forces cross River Sajó
- **27 December** Siege of Budapest begins
- **1945 (2 January)** Germans counter-attack at Budapest
- **20 January** Hungarian armistice
- **11 February** Soviet forces overrun Budapest
- **17–24 February** Germans wipe out Soviet Hron bridgehead
- **4 April** last Germans leave Hungary

By 24 September 1944, the Russians had overrun Romania and part of eastern Hungary as far as Târgu Mures. Hungary had been occupied by the Germans in March; now Malinovsky's 2nd Ukrainian Front mounted Operation Debrecen (6–28 October) to destroy Friessner's Army Group South and three divisions of Army group F in Hungary and northern Transylvania, in order to enable 4th Ukrainian Front (Petrov) to cross the Carpathians.

Soviet 2nd Ukrainian Front included two Romanian armies, First and Fourth, and two Cavalry-Mechanised Groups (KMG), KMG Pliev and KMG Gorshkov. The offensive began on 6 October and within three days KMG Pliev had penetrated 60 miles into the enemy rear, and by 20 October had reached the River Tisza along with units of KMG Gorshkov, cutting off the withdrawal of First and Second Hungarian and Eighth German Armies. By 28 October the Russians and their allies were 50 miles from Budapest.

Stalin wanted Budapest captured immediately. Malinovsky asked for five days, but was told to attack tomorrow, and immediately launched the Budapest operation (29 October–13 February), in cooperation with formations of Tolbukhjn's 3rd Ukrainian Front. Friessner's Army Group South and formations of Army Groups F, and to the north, A (renamed Centre on 26 January 1945) had fallen back to the north-west. By 10 December the Russians and Romanians had cut off the Axis retreat northwards from Budapest, which was completely surrounded by 26 December. Despite three strong German counter-attacks, Budapest finally fell on 13 February. By refusing Malinovsky's request for five days, Stalin may have lost three and a half months. The twin cities of Buda and Pest were terribly ravaged, and it became a sensitive subject with Stalin. Soviet efforts in Hungary had, however, drawn off substantial German forces (Army Group A) from the north, thus weakening the protection for Germany's heartland, to be reached through Poland. With the fall of Budapest a German–Hungarian force of 188,000 men was knocked out of the war. Meanwhile, a provisional government reached agreement with the Soviet Union on the conclusion of hostilities.

By 5 March Soviet and East European forces had reached a line level with the south-western end of Lake Balaton. Hitler ordered a counter-attack, code-named 'Frülingserwachen' ('Spring awakening') north and south of the lake. To the north Sixth SS Panzer Army was to strike north to Budapest, re-establishing a defence line along the major obstacle of the Danube. To the south, Second Panzer Army would do likewise, striking east. The advance hogged down in the muddy spring conditions, and ploughed into hastily improvised Soviet defences 15-30 miles deep, the Russians turning their anti-aircraft guns on German tanks and infantry. Battle with Tolbukhin's 3rd Ukrainian Front raged for ten days, with 800,000 men, 12,500 guns and mortars, 1,300 tanks and assault guns and 1,800 aircraft engaged on both sides. By 15 March 'Spring awakening' had ground to a halt and the Russians resumed their advance against Army Group South. By 4 April they had cleared the end of Lake Balaton and were within five miles of Vienna.

www.osa.ceu.hu/galeria/sites/siege/framee.html
The Siege of Budapest
http://en.wikipedia.org/wiki/Operation_Fr%C3%BChlingserwachen
Operation Frülingserwachen, the last German offensive of World War Two

1 The Soviet conquest of Hungary fell into two main phases: Operation Debrecen (to 28 Oct.) and Operation Budapest (29 Oct.– 13 Feb.). In the first phase a particularly prominent role was played by Cavalry-Mechanised Groups. Fighting in Budapest was particularly savage. On 24 Dec., 2nd and 3rd Ukrainian Fronts linked up, encircling the city, trapping 188,000 men with four divisions, IV SS Panzer Corps was shifted to Hungary from Army Group Centre, and participated in the attempt to relieve Budapest mounted on 1 Jan. By 17 Jan. almost all of Pest was in Soviet hands. The German garrison surrendered the following day. Fighting for Buda raged until 13 Feb., the Russians having to take one fortified building at a time. After the fall of Budapest, the Germans mounted a major counter-attack north and south of Lake Balaton. Sixth Army (Balck), transferred from the west, would attack between Lakes Balaton and Velence, breaking 3rd Ukranian in two. The Germans cut into Soviet Fifty-Seventh Army as far as Kaposvár but were fought to a standstill in a deep defensive battle. Tolbukhin asked permission from Stavka to commit Ninth Guards Army, but was told to hold it back for the counter-stroke (7 Mar.). After the Germans came to a halt on 15 Mar., Sixth Guards Tank Army was ordered to concentrate in the area of Ninth Army, west of Budapest. Fourth and Ninth Guards Armies attacked, and Sixth Guards Tank Army was committed to the breach. By 25 Mar., 2nd Ukranian had torn a 60-mile gap in the German defences, and the Russians pushed on through the Hron Valley and towards Bratislava.

As units of 1st Ukrainian Front reached the eastern boundaries of Czechoslovakia, Slovaks began an uprising, which was crushed in early October 1944 by German forces, with the Waffen SS playing a particularly prominent role.

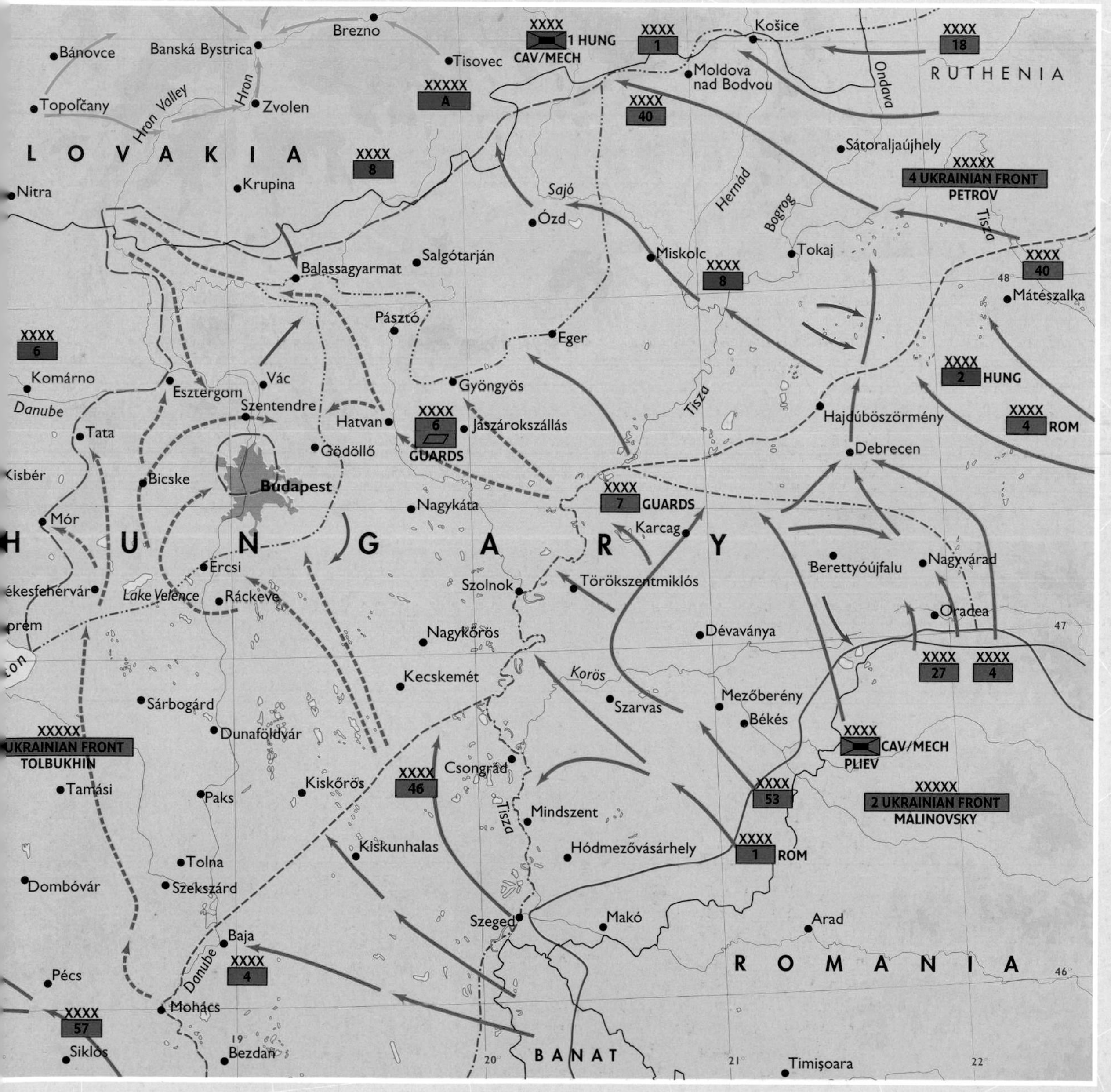

arctic warfare

1941 to 1945

- **1941 (26 June)** Finland declares war on Soviet Union
- **29 July** Soviets evacuate Karelian isthmus
- **1942 (4–9 July)** convoy PQ17 attacked and scattered with two-thirds losses; Arctic convoys postponed
- **1944 (9 June)** Soviet offensive begins on Finnish front; halted by Finns on 30 June
- **4 September** Finland changes side and fights against the Germans

As the geographical extent of the war zones in both Europe and the Pacific expanded, so the Arctic region proved increasingly important to the combatants. There were a number of reasons for this: the Arctic seas were an essential communication route, particularly between British, North American and North Soviet ports, for the transfer of war material to the Soviet Union; Arctic territories provided approach routes or land bridges to more populated and strategically significant regions below the Arctic Circle; they also yielded valuable mineral products, and weather stations established in the Arctic gave early warning of meteorological conditions affecting sea and air operations in lower latitudes.

German attempts to establish weather stations west of Norway were largely foiled. German forces briefly garrisoned Spitzbergen following a Commando raid (August 1941), and later returned in 1943 to destroy the wiring installations on the island.

The Germans used Norwegian coastal waters to ship minerals from the Arctic at the outbreak of the war. Admiral Räder's fears that the British would interrupt the traffic by mining, and his desire to seize bases for naval operations into the Atlantic, prompted him from October 1939 to urge Hitler to invade Norway. It was only, however, when evidence emerged that Britain and France might intervene in the Russo-Finnish war that Hitler decided to act.

The north Norwegian fjords then became important bases for the German Navy, which began to operate against British convoys to Murmansk and Archangel after June 1941; the arrival of the battleship *Tirpitz* at Trondheim in January 1942 greatly increased this threat. But the most important Arctic operations after the opening of Operation Barbarossa in June 1941 were fought on land. By August 1940 the Finns accepted assistance from Germany, seen as a means of securing their relations with the USSR. On 28 June 1941, the Finnish III Corps and the German Armeeoberkommando Norwegen attacked towards the Kola Peninsula, but this drive was stopped on 1 July. To the south, they made some headway in the Karelian peninsula but stopped before reaching Leningrad. The Germans also attacked towards Kandalaksha on the White Sea, an offensive which the Finns successfully took over (19 August–19 September). When the Germans, who had brought reinforcements from the Balkans, reopened the offensive to cut the Murmansk railway (which remained the principal link to the Soviet heartland for supplies arriving by Arctic convoy), the Finns at first cooperated successfully (3 November onwards) but then declined to cross their 1939 border. From 1942 until September 1944 the German Lapland Army, commanded by Hitler's favourite general, Dietl, made little progress and was occupied chiefly in protecting the Petsamo nickel mines. When Finland changed sides in September 1944, only weeks into a major Soviet offensive, Dietl made a slow and skilful withdrawal into northern Norway, retaining a foothold in Finland at Kilpisjärvi, which prevented its troops in the far north from being cut off, until April 1945.

2 finland, 1941–45

- frontiers, 1939
- limit of German/Finnish advance
- Soviet gains, 1944–45
- Finnish operations against German forces, 1944–45
- German retreat, 1944–45

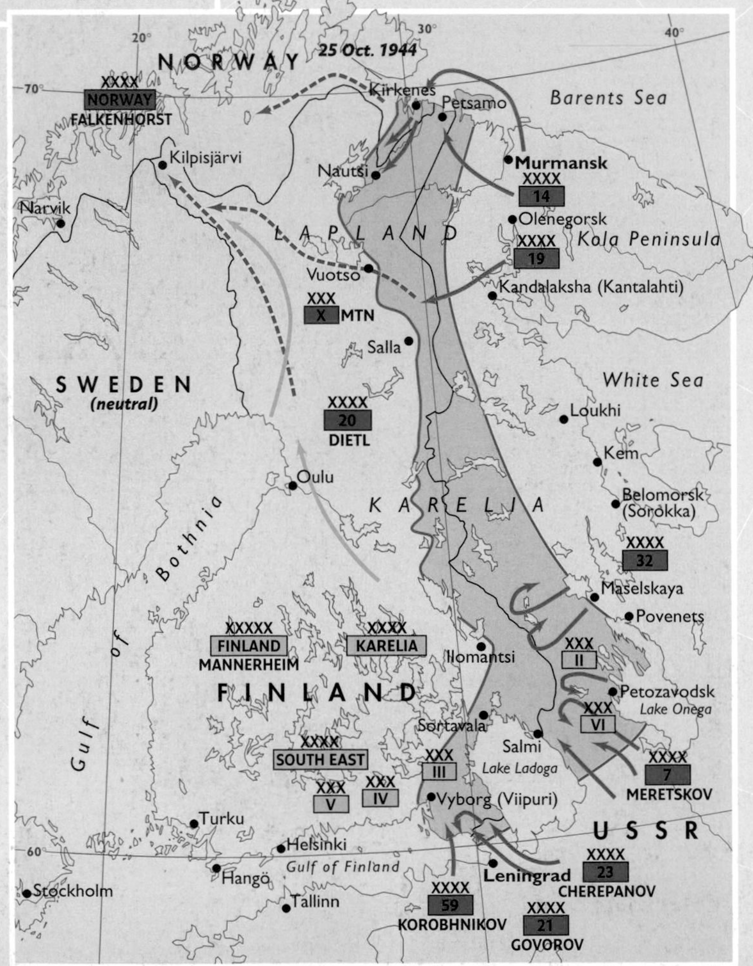

2 **As an adjunct to Operation Barbarossa (page 40) Finnish and German forces opened an offensive towards the Kola peninsula (28 June 1941), which was stopped by fierce Soviet resistance. In Nov., a new attempt was made to cut the Murmansk railway but the Finns refused to cross their 1939 frontier. In Sept. 1944, after the Finns changed sides, they and the Russians gradually forced the Germans back into northern Norway by Apr. 1945.**

www.geocities.com/Pentagon/9764/warfin1.html
The causes, events, and repercussions of the Russo-Finnish war
www.naval-history.net/WW2CampaignsRussianConvoys.html
Russian convoys, 1941–45

On the far side of the Arctic ice cap, the Japanese occupied Kiska and Attu in the Aleutian Islands during the Midway campaign, to open the threat of an offensive towards American Alaska, and were not expelled until two years later. The force deployed there did not, however, constitute a serious strategic threat to the North American continent, although a Japanese presence on US territory continued to constitute a major propaganda coup. The Japanese presence on American soil eventually provoked a heavy-handed response in the form of bombardments and naval demonstrations, which culminated in full force amphibious landings in 1943, by which time most of the Japanese garrisons had been evacuated. The important American convoys to Russia via the North Pacific and Bering Sea to Nikolayevsk were sustained.

The combatants', awareness of the potential that the Arctic region possessed, as a peripheral but strategically valuable theatre of war, was indicative of a major change in strategic thinking, which began to emerge after 1941: no longer was warfare limited to a two-dimensional battlefield, located in or near the geographical centre of the dispute. It had now become an exercise in power projection around a global arena.

1 The most important Arctic ports for convoys bringing Lend-Lease war materials to Russia were Murmansk and Archangel in the White Sea and Vladivostok in the Sea of Japan. Iceland, occupied by the British in May 1940 and taken over by the Americans in July 1941, was a vital intermediate base for air escorts to the North Atlantic and Arctic convoys. Iceland was also a major weather-reporting station, as were Greenland, Jan Maven Island and Spitzbergen. The Germans sent meteorological parties to the last territories, all of which were intercepted or captured by Free Norwegian, Royal Navy or US Coastguard patrols. The route to Vladivostok was threatened by the Japanese invasion of Kiska and Attu in the Aleutian islands on 6–7 June 1941. Following a Japanese-American cruiser action off the Komandorski Islands (26 Mar. 1943), Attu (11–30 May), and Kiska (15 Aug.) were recaptured. Out of 39 Allied convoys to North Soviet ports via the Norwegian Sea in 1941–42, 69 ships, of 533 escorted, were lost to U-boat, air or surface attack.

1945

- **1–17 January** Germans withdraw in the Ardennes
- **1 February** US Seventh Army reaches the Siegfried Line, breaking through on 9 February
- **1 March** US First Army captures München-Gladbach
- **5 March** Cologne captured; US Ninth and First Armies reach the Rhine
- **7 March** US 1st Army crosses Rhine by Remagen Bridge
- **23 March** US Third Army crosses Rhine
- **28 March** Eisenhower shifts emphasis of Allied advance away from Berlin
- **1 April** US First and Ninth Armies complete encirclement of Army Group B in the Ruhr
- **4 May** German forces in Holland Denmark and north-west Germany surrender
- **7 May** General Jodl signs unconditional surrender

The failure of the Ardennes offensive destroyed the counter-offensive potential of the German Army in the west and greatly reduced its defensive capabilities. In February it consisted of only three army groups, H (Student), defending Holland and the northern Rhineland, B (Model), defending the Ruhr, and G (Blaskowitz), in south Germany; all were under strength and lacked heavy equipment, particularly tanks.

Eisenhower, by contrast, deployed 85 full-strength divisions, of which 23 were armoured and five airborne, and enjoyed overwhelming airpower. His plan for the crossing of the Rhine and the advance into Germany fell into three phases. In the first, Montgomery's 21st Army Group was to clear the approaches to the lower Rhine, supported by Bradley's Ninth Army. In the second, Bradley's First and Third Armies were to drive the Germans out of the Eifel and secure the middle reaches of the Rhine. In the third, Seventh and Third Armies were to clear the banks of the Moselle, while Montgomery launched a deliberate assault across the lower Rhine, together with Ninth Army. In the exploitation phase, Ninth and First Armies, once they had crossed the Rhine, were to encircle Army Group B in the Ruhr, while the others advanced to the Elbe–Czech/Austrian border, where they would make contact with the Red Army advancing from the east.

Eisenhower's plan unrolled as anticipated, with two exceptions: the Canadians, under Montgomery's command, met heavier opposition than expected on the lower Rhine, while US First Army surprised the German

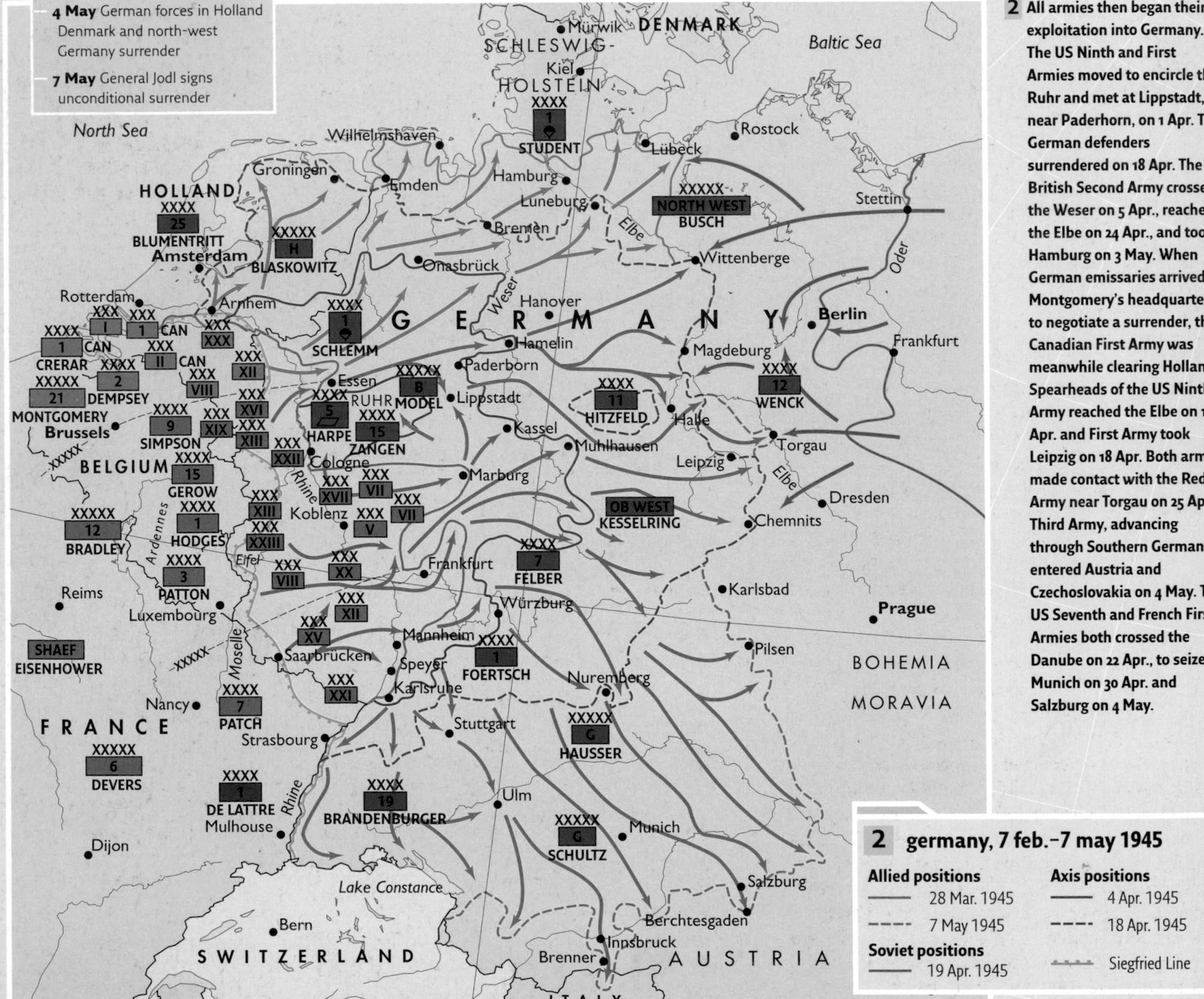

2 All armies then began their exploitation into Germany. The US Ninth and First Armies moved to encircle the Ruhr and met at Lippstadt, near Paderhorn, on 1 Apr. The German defenders surrendered on 18 Apr. The British Second Army crossed the Weser on 5 Apr., reached the Elbe on 24 Apr., and took Hamburg on 3 May. When German emissaries arrived at Montgomery's headquarters to negotiate a surrender, the Canadian First Army was meanwhile clearing Holland. Spearheads of the US Ninth Army reached the Elbe on 11 Apr. and First Army took Leipzig on 18 Apr. Both armies made contact with the Red Army near Torgau on 25 Apr. Third Army, advancing through Southern Germany, entered Austria and Czechoslovakia on 4 May. The US Seventh and French First Armies both crossed the Danube on 22 Apr., to seize Munich on 30 Apr. and Salzburg on 4 May.

www.worldwar2database.com/html/rhine.htm
The Allied crossing of the River Rhine
www.chanwww.bruecke-remagen.de/index_en.htm
The bridge at Remagen

defenders of the Rhine bridge at Remagen, between Bonn and Koblenz, on 7 March and thus secured an unopposed landing on the far bank. First Army used this bridge to establish a lodgement from which it began its drive into Germany on 25 March. By then the British and Canadians, together with US Ninth Army, had crossed the lower Rhine (23 March) and the US Seventh and French First Armies were to do so shortly afterwards.

The German Army in the west had been reduced to a strength of 26 divisions in the fighting west of the Rhine and could offer only patchy resistance to the Allied assault and advance. Most forces, as before, were concentrated against the Soviets; estimates of the latter in mid-April are as high as 214 divisions, including 34 Panzer and 15 motorised. Hitler had replaced Rundstedt with Kesselring on 10 March, but the successful defender of Italy altogether lacked the resources to organise a coherent defence of the Reich. The Ruhr was encircled by US First and Ninth Armies on 1 April and the remnants of Army Group B within the pocket surrendered on 18 April; Model, its commander, committed suicide. The other Allied armies were meanwhile advancing, at up to 50 miles a day, towards the agreed border of their occupation zones on the Elbe, where their patrols met the Russians on 25 April.

Berlin was by then under siege and Hitler was directing the movement of phantom armies from his bunker. He refused his last chance to escape on 22 April, allowing his OKW staff to join OKH and Admiral Dönitz in a flight to the north. They eventually set up headquarters at Mürwik In Schleswig-Holstein, which, after Hitler's suicide on 30 April, became the last seat of the government of the Third Reich.

By this time Soviet troops were in the suburbs of Berlin and by 27 April only a strip 10 miles long and three and a half wide remained. Ringed by Soviet guns and troops, the Führer reacted angrily on 28 April when he learned of Himmler's treachery in approaching Britain and the United States about a separate peace. That evening, Artillery General Weidling, commander of Berlin, reported on the state of the collapsing city to Hitler, whom he later described to a Soviet interrogator as a 'sick, broken man'. The final battle conference was held on 29 April in the *Führerbunker*, Hitler sounding tired but forbidding the surrender of Berlin. At 01:00 hours on 30 April, Keitel reported that all the German forces attempting to relieve Berlin had stalled, been encircled and forced onto the defensive. Hitler then, apparently, decided to kill himself. At 15:30, about an hour after the Soviet victory banner was hoisted from the second floor of the Reichstag, Hitler and his bride Eva Braun retired to his study and committed suicide, Hitler with a pistol, Eva Braun with cyanide. That evening Weidling was summoned to the *Führerbunker* and told by Bormann, Himmler and Krebs that Hitler was dead and his body burned. At 23:30 a German delegation informed Soviet officers that they had important news: at 03:50 on 1 May General Chuikov, commanding Eighth Guards Army, was told of Hitler's suicide.

1 **After the containment of the Ardennes offensive, the Canadian First Army moved to the attack. Operation Veritable (8 Feb.), designed to win ground west of the Rhine, encountered heavy resistance by First Parachute and Twenty-Fifth Armies. The US Ninth Army, delayed by German inundation in the Roer Valley, could not join in (Operation Grenade) until 23 Feb., when it advanced northward to meet the Canadians (and the British who had moved forward in between). The US First Army, meanwhile, kept pace with Ninth (Operation Lumberjack) and captured Cologne on the Rhine (5 Mar.). In the southern Rhineland the most dramatic event of the campaign was the capture of the Remagen bridge (7 Mar.), which fell to a surprise attack of First Army, after its German defenders had failed to set off demolition charges. Meanwhile, Third Army captured Trier, (1 Mar.) and cleared the region south of the Moselle by 11 Mar. Between then and 25 Mar., Third and Seventh Armies together occupied the Palatinate and the Saar and on 22 Mar. Third seized a bridgehead across the Rhine at Oppenheim. Operation Plunder, 21st Army Group's Rhine crossing, opened on 23 Mar. between Xanten and Rees. Ninth Army crossed at Wesel the next day, when the US 17th and British 6th Airborne Divisions were dropped across the Rhine to seize an airhead. By nightfall both were in contact with British Second and US Ninth Armies, which had established a bridgehead six miles deep. The US Third Army expanded its bridgehead on 25 Mar., entered Frankfurt the next day and linked bridgeheads with First Army (29 Mar.). The US Seventh Army crossed at Worms (26 Mar.) and the French First Army at Speyer (31 Mar.).**

1945

- **16 April** Soviet final offensive on Berlin begins
- **23 April** Soviet forces enter Berlin
- **26 April** US First Army and Soviet patrols meet at Torgau
- **30 April** Hitler commits suicide
- **2 May** Soviet forces hold Berlin; German casualties in battle for city: 150,000 dead, 300,000 captured
- **8 May** German surrender ratified in Berlin

On 1 April 1945 the Soviet Main Planning Conference (GKO, plus Zhukov commanding 1st Belarussian Front, Koniev commanding 1st Ukrainian, Antonov of the General Staff and Shtemenko of the Main Operations Directorate) met in Stalin's office. Stalin asked who was going to take Berlin: them or the Allies. Believing that the Western Allies were about to mount an operation to capture Berlin, there was no time to lose. Berlin lay in the path of Zhukov's 1st Belarussian, with 1st Ukrainian to the south, but as an extra incentive Stalin scrubbed out the fixed operational Front boundary lines from 40 miles east of the Nazi capital. From there on in, Zhukov and Koniev would race. Rokossovsky, whose 2nd Belarussian was still heavily engaged in East Prussia, was ordered to stand by to swing from east to west, across devastated country, and attack north of Berlin.

The two fronts vying for first place in Berlin approached the task in distinctive ways. Zhukov already had a bridgehead across the Oder, around Küstrin, into which he poured over 8,000 guns across 25 bridges. Zhukov would use over 140 searchlights to blind and confuse the defenders, but a short artillery barrage: only 30 minutes. Koniev, in contrast, opted for *Nacht und Nebel*: an attack under the cover of darkness and smokesceens, with a 145-minute barrage. Concealment was a real problem, especially for Zhukov's tightly-packed bridgehead. Spring came late that year and the leafless trees and sodden ground made camouflage and digging difficult. Soviet troops, many still wearing their winter fur hats, dug in their guns and brought seven million rounds of artillery ammunition to Zhukov's front line dumps.

The bombardment and assault were targeted with ruthless precision. Zhukov used a huge, elaborate scale model of Berlin for briefing and both Fronts used air photographs of the German defences to a depth of 60 miles, with Soviet aircraft overflying some sectors eight times. Artillery fire-plans used the combined results of ground and air observation, and the engineers built their own model to study problems of street fighting.

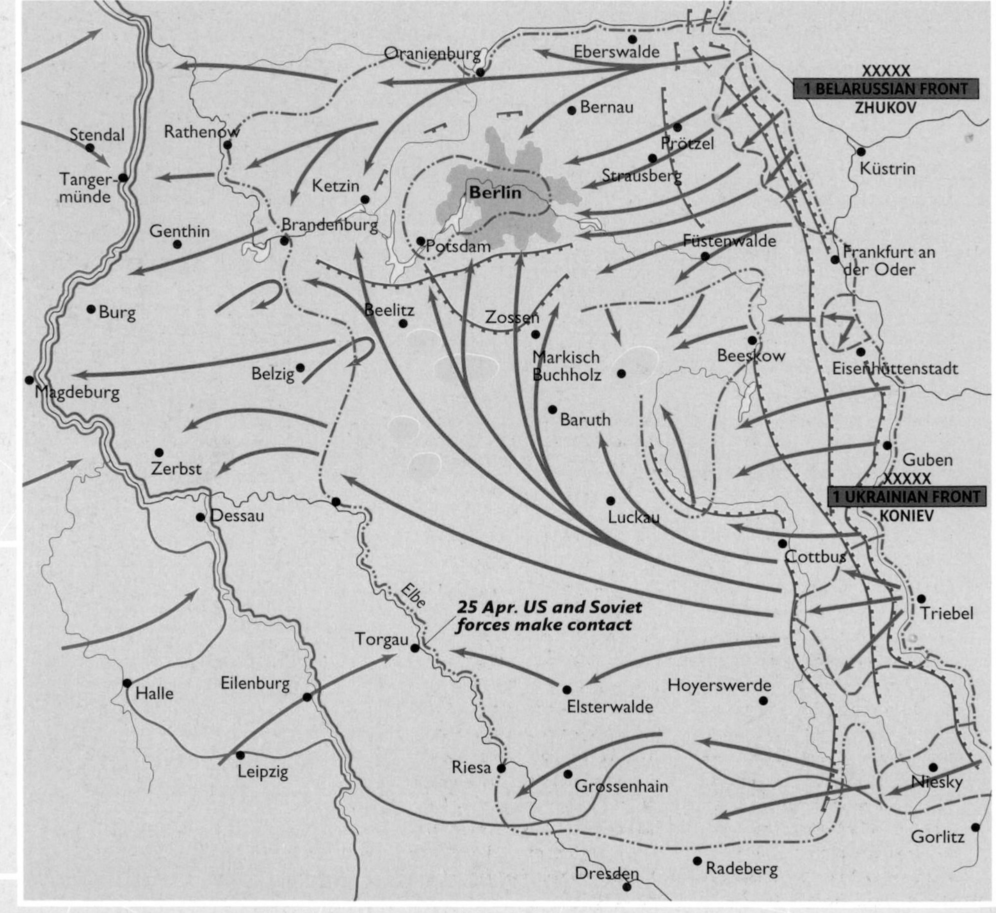

1 the advance on berlin, 15 apr.–6 may 1945

Soviet positions
- 15 Apr.
- 18 Apr.
- 25 Apr.

Allied positions, 6 May
German defence lines
German pockets

www.bbc.co.uk/history/war/wwtwo/berlin_01.shtml
The battle for Berlin
www.eyewitnesstohistory.com/berlin.htm
Eyewitness accounts to the fall of Berlin

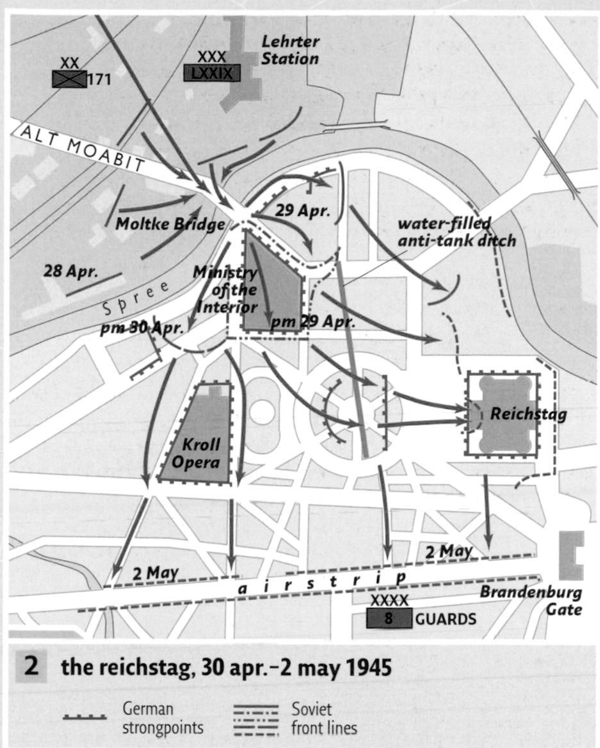

2 the reichstag, 30 apr.–2 may 1945

1-2 **At the start of the Berlin operation (16 Apr.–18 May), the army groups defending Berlin could, on paper, muster one million men. The German command had constructed five defence lines in the Oder-Neisse Defence Zone, some 12-25 miles deep, in three 'belts'. Behind this lay the Berlin defence zone. The urban setting and the numerous rivers and canals made Berlin a very tough nut to crack. On 26 Apr. half a million Soviet troops supported by 12,700 guns and mortars and 21,000 multiple rocket launchers attacked the city centre. In the centre of the city, the high Flak towers with anti-aircraft guns on their roofs, which could fire down on Soviet tanks, presented a major hazard. Inside, and in cellars throughout the city, civilians sheltered, some driven insane by the intensity of shellfire. On 28 Apr., the bridge on the Potsdamerstrasse was seized. In the face of ferocious SS opposition, the storming of the Tiergarten (Zoo) began. That evening forces of 1st Belarussian Front seized the Moltke Bridge over the Spree and the Ministry of Internal Affairs (Himmler's House). The Germans tried to blow the Moltke Bridge but failed. The Reichstag was a formidable defensive position and could not be taken until Soviet forces were across the Spree in strength. Soviet artillery (including heavy 6- and 8-inch guns firing over open sights) fired a barrage at the Interior Ministry at 07:00 hours on 29 Apr., and Soviet infantry broke into the Zoo, from where they could fire up at the Flak towers (from the Hippopotamus House, one of whose residents survived). At midday on 30 Apr. regiments of 150th and 171st Rifle Divisions took up final assault positions, and at 13:00 hours under a swathe of covering fire from heavy guns, Katyusha rocket launchers and even captured Panzerfausts, the Soviets careered across the open ground before the Reichstag and up the central staircase. Soviet troops raised the victory banner on the roof at 22:50, but the building was not entirely cleared until 2 May, the day the Berlin garrison ceased resistance.**

Reconnaissance in force began on 14 April, but Zhukov failed to identify the main line of resistance further back. Zhukov's Front attacked at 05:00 hours on 16 April, Koniev's at 06:15 hours. Koniev's attack across the Neisse went well, but Zhukov's troops stalled in the face of stiff resistance and the difficult obstacle of the Seelöw Heights. Stalin was furious at the delay, and that in his attempt to overcome it, Zhukov had launched both his tank armies (First and Second Guards Tank) early, against Stavka's instructions. Although behind schedule, by 19 April Zhukov had cracked all three defence belts in the Oder-Neisse zone and seized the Seelöw Heights and Müncheberg, west of Küstrin. On that night, Rokossovsky's 2nd Belarussian also began its attack. Koniev and Zhukov raced on, Koniev ordering his two tank armies (Third and Fourth Guards) to break into Berlin on the night of 20 April. By now, Soviet artillery was pounding the city itself, already largely reduced to rubble by Anglo-American air bombardment. However, as the Soviets knew, rubble makes a formidable fortress, even for boys and old men armed with Panzerfausts. On 23 April Stalin decreed that Zhukov had won the race: the Front boundary line would run just 150 metres west of the Reichstag, the outstanding prize, placing it in 1st Belarussian's sector. Berlin was completely encircled by 25 April, and the next day nearly half a million Soviet troops broke into the city centre. Late on 28 April, 79th Rifle Corps began to prepare its attack on the Reichstag. By 30 April, the 150th Division stood on the threshold of the symbolic seat of Nazi power, to the Red Army, 'target No. 105'. At 14:25 hours two sergeants, Yegorov and Kantariya, flew the Red Victory Banner from the second floor, and at 22:50 it was finally raised above the roof, although many German troops were still inside. For once, precious ammunition was fired off in a brief salute. That night, the Soviets learned of Hitler's suicide. Negotiations continued until the middle of the next day, when Chuikov, commanding Eighth Guards Army, exasperated at the unproductive talks, ordered artillery fire to be resumed. The Soviets also learned of Göbbels' death and improvised cremation on 1 May. Early in the morning of 2 May, Weidling, commanding the Berlin garrison, drafted an order for Berlin to surrender, which the Soviets approved. Germans hiding in the basement of the Reichstag began to surrender. At 15:00 hours Soviet guns ceased fire in Berlin. The Third Reich lay in ruins.

vienna and **prague**

1945

- **11 March** Czech government in exile leaves London for Slovakia
- **7–13 April** Soviet forces attack and occupy Vienna
- **4 May** civilian uprising begins in Prague, aided by defecting units of the anti-Communist Vlasov Army
- **9 May** Soviet forces occupy Prague, during which 5,000 civilians are killed
- **13 May** last pockets of German resistance in Bohemia crushed by Soviet forces

As a result of the operations around Lake Balaton, Soviet forces had gained the southern shore of the lake by 15 March 1945. To the north, the forward edge of the advance ran west of Budapest and along a fold of the Carpathians behind the River Hron. The Vienna operation would complete the destruction of German forces in Hungary, capture the Austrian capital Vienna, and carry Soviet forces over the Lesser Carpathians, the western limit of the Carpathian range and a natural phase line.

Stavka's aim was to launch two splintering blows, one towards Pápa, one towards Gyor. 3rd Ukrainian Front attacked on 16 March after a heavy artillery and air preparation. On 19 March weakened tank armies were committed. The Germans made good use of the numerous defiles, narrow mountain passes and rivers to hold off the Soviet armour. The grouping from 2nd Ukrainian attacked on 17 March and successfully broke through German defences south of the Danube. On 2 April Soviet forces reached the Neusiedler Lake and the frontier between Austria and Hungary. Hungary was completely cleared of German occupation by 4 April.

From 5 to 8 April, the Soviet Forty-Sixth Army was embarked on vessels of the Danube Flotilla and landed on the north bank of the Danube to encircle Vienna from the north. Fourth Guards Army attacked from the south-east. Between 5 and 9 April fierce street fighting raged in the suburbs of the city. On 6 April the Soviets appealed to the remaining citizens of Vienna not to allow the Germans to demolish what remained of the city, and on 9 April the Soviet Government announced that they would fulfil the Moscow Declaration on the independence of Austria. Savage fighting for the city continued, however, until 13 April, when Soviet forces took firm control of it; 130,000 German troops were taken prisoner. The advance halted at Stockerau, as attention turned to the last battle being fought for Berlin.

Immediately after the fall of Berlin, at the beginning of May, attention moved south again, to the last major concentration of Nazi forces in Europe: Schörner's Army Group Centre, now effectively encircled east of Prague by Soviet, and, more distantly, American forces. The Germans still hoped for a separate peace with the Western Allies: that was never on the cards, although Churchill and Eisenhower were agreed on the need to establish the demarcation line between the Russians and the Western Allies as far east as possible. This possibility encouraged the Russians to eliminate the last German groupings swiftly. Eisenhower proposed to the Russians that the Americans might now advance on Prague, but was sharply told that Western Allied forces should keep west of the demarcation line and out of Prague.

At the beginning of May Nationalist risings broke out all over Czechoslovakia and on 5 May there was a rising in Prague itself, following news of the US advance into Bohemia. The situation was further complicated by the presence of Vlasov's KONR divisions, Soviets in German employ. Vlasov himself urged his men to stand by the

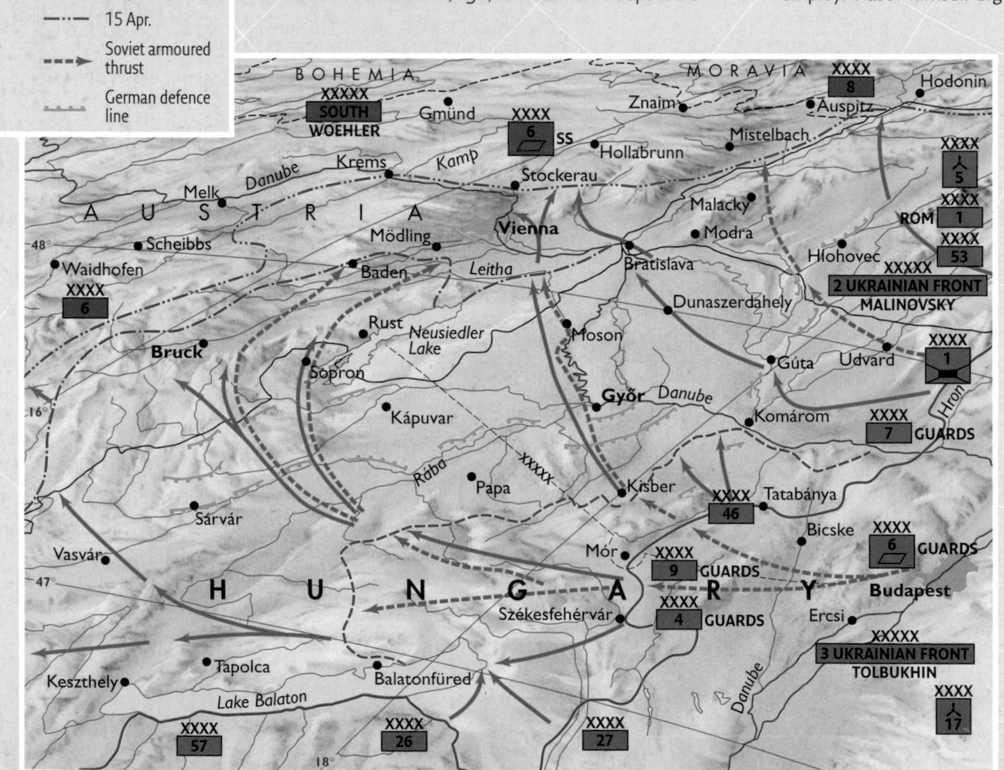

1 In the Vienna Operation (16 Mar.– 15 Apr., 1945), the Soviet 3rd Ukrainian Front comprised 18 Rifle Divisions, 3,900 guns and mortars, 800 aircraft but only 197 tanks and assault guns. The 2nd Ukrainian comprised 12 rifle divisions, 2,686 guns and mortars and just 165 tanks and assault guns. The low density of armour was in part due to the terrain. Despite the German defensive positions at Gyor, by 4th Apr. Soviet forces were five miles to the south of Vienna, defended by one mechanised and eight Panzer divisions and 15 independent battalions. Soviet progress into the city itself was slow, and Vienna did not fall until 13 Apr. Soviet advances in this region stalled for the rest of the month.

www.worldwar-2.net/timelines/war-in-europe/eastern-europe/eastern-europe-index-1945.htm
Timeline of events of the eastern European war
www.feldgrau.com/rvol.html
Russian volunteers in the German Army

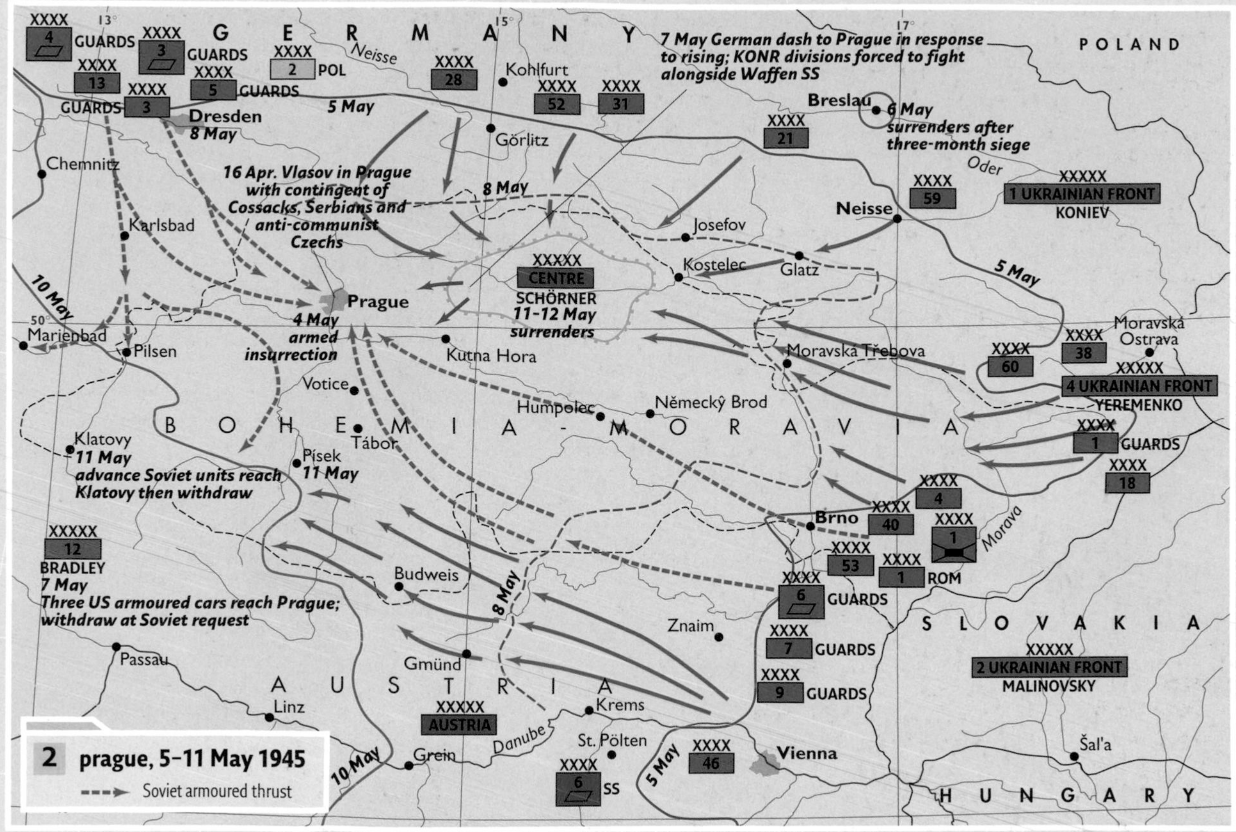

2 prague, 5–11 May 1945
Soviet armoured thrust

Germans; the Prague insurgents called on them as 'Russian and Soviet citizens' to desert the Germans and help them, while most of the Vlasov troops wanted nothing more than to surrender to the Americans and not be taken by the Red Army. Initially, Bunyachenko's 1st KONR Division helped the insurgents, but as German forces from Army Group Centre moved in to crush the rising, they were trapped and forced to fight alongside the Waffen SS.

The Germans had surrendered unconditionally at Rheims on 7 May, but there was no guarantee that German forces would obey their own High Command and Schörner's troops were still fighting. Marshal Koniev transmitted details of the capitulation to all German units in Western Czechoslovakia at 20:00 hours on 8 May, giving them three hours to respond. When they did not, the Russians fired a huge artillery barrage and resumed operations. Lelyushenko's Fourth Guards Tank Army raced into Prague in the early hours of 9 May to report: 'Remaining fascist resistance destroyed. Many prisoners. . . . there are no American forces'. Prague had fallen, but Soviet forces raced on to accomplish the tight encirclement of Army Group Centre. On 11 May, three days after the Western Allies celebrated victory in Europe, and two days after the Russians did so, the last major German force surrendered.

2 **After the fall of Berlin, German Army Groups Centre and Austria (a total of 900,000 men, 9,700 guns and mortars, 1,900 tanks and assault guns and 1,000 aircraft) remained the last centres of German resistance in Europe. Allied advances from the west and the uprisings in Czechoslovakia from 1 May added to the urgency, and the Russians mounted the Prague operation (6–11 May 1945). Three Soviet Fronts closed for the kill, 1st, 2nd and 4th Ukrainian; 1st Guards Cavalry-Mechanised Group, and various independent corps, including Second Polish, First and Fourth Romanian Armies and 1st Czech Army Corps. These forces totalled two million men, 30,500 guns and mortars, 2,000 tanks and assault guns and over 3,000 aircraft. The Prague uprising, in which some 30,000 insurgents fought behind 1,600 barricades, occurred on 5 May; on 6 May, the Soviet operation was launched, eliminating the German grouping at Breslau. On 8 May, Dresden was captured and on 9 May, after German forces in Czechoslovakia ignored the surrender signed at Rheims on 7 May, Soviet armoured formations raced into Prague. The possibility of US forces from the west reaching Prague ahead of the Russians had arisen in late April, but the Americans agreed to respect the agreed demarcation line in Czechoslovakia, since the Russians had deliberately halted their advance in Germany at the lower Elbe. The Russians fulfilled their undertaking to restore an independent Austria, although the last two Soviet divisions were not withdrawn from Austria until 1955. US forces vacated Czechoslovakia almost immediately. Excepting the Soviet gain of Ruthenia, in this area, unlike Germany and Poland to the north, the 1938 national boundaries were restored.**

politics and strategy

1944 to 1945

- **1944 (16 February)** Eisenhower assumes command as Supreme Commander Allied Expeditionary Forces
- **24 April** US War Department considers invasion of Japanese Home Islands necessary
- **1945 (12 April)** President Roosevelt dies; Truman becomes President
- **8 May** VE Day
- **16 July** first atom bomb test at Alamogordo in Mexican Desert
- **20 November** Nuremberg trials begin
- **27 November** UN Charter ratified by 29 nations
- **27 December** Britain, US and USSR hold meeting in Moscow to discuss Korea

The main lines of Allied agreement had been established by the end of 1943: there would be a great concentration of force for the invasion of Western Europe, whereas Stalin would be free to occupy such areas as his army conquered. Churchill continued to hope for an Allied thrust beyond Italy into Northern Yugoslavia, Hungary and Austria, at the expense of Operation Anvil in southern France. However, Operation Anvil went ahead slowing the Allied front in Italy after the capture of Rome in June 1944.

Following the success of Operation Overlord, Churchill and Roosevelt met again at Quebec (Octagon, 11–16 September 1944) where Eisenhower's plan for a thrust into north-central Germany was approved, and Roosevelt supported plans to parachute British troops into Greece, with a suggestion for landing an Anglo-US force in northern Yugoslavia and to relieve Chiang Kai-shek (under pressure, even in Chungking), by an attack on Rangoon and clearing of the Burma Road. Further, a division of post-war Germany into British, American and Soviet zones was adopted, and the Morgenthau Plan for turning the German economy into a pastoral one was accepted.

Churchill then flew to Moscow to confer with Stalin (9–20 October) and the US ambassador, W. Averell Harriman. Churchill proposed a division of Eastern Europe into zones of influence – the Soviets being preponderant in Bulgaria and Romania, the British in Greece, with rough equality in Yugoslavia and Hungary. There was a lengthy wrangle about Poland's future. Stalin remained adamant concerning those territories annexed in 1939–40 – the more so as his troops now occupied the entire area in question – and Churchill believed that the Polish exile government's

Major Axis conferences

1 Rastenburg 24 Jan. 1944 Hitler receives Quisling

2 Rastenburg 18 Mar. 1944 Hitler summons Horthy: arrests him

3 Helsinki 27 June 1944 Germans agree to send armed assistance to Finns

Major Allied conferences

4 Marrakech 12 Jan. 1944 Churchill and de Gaulle meet to discuss role of Free French in Allied operations

5 1–16 May 1944 Conference of Commonwealth Prime Ministers on strategy and foreign policy

6 Second Quebec Conference (Octagon) 10–16 Sept. 1944 Churchill and Roosevelt agree plans for continuing offensives in North West Europe and Italy; plans for attacks in Burma; British forces to join US campaigns in Western Pacific

7 Third Moscow Conference 9–20 Oct. 1944 Churchill, Eden and Stalin discuss future of Eastern Europe; Stalin insists on territorial rights in Poland, and claims Bulgaria and Romania as anti-Soviet sphere; Greece to come under British influence; Hungary and Yugoslavia shared; Stalin promises to join war against Japan

8 Malta 31 Jan.–2 Feb. 1945 Churchill and Roosevelt meet to plan Western Allied strategy at Yalta

9 21 Feb.–18 Mar. 1945 Inter-American Conference attended by all the American republics except Argentina; reaffirmation of collaboration in struggle against Axis

10 Yalta Conference (Argonaut) 4–11 Feb. 1945 Churchill, Roosevelt and Stalin agree plans for final defeat of enemy and building of lasting peace; Stalin gains promise of territorial gains in East Asia (S. Sakhalin, Kurile Is.) in return for joining war against Japan; post-war borders of Europe agreed including Polish losses (to USSR) and gains (from Germany); Stalin guarantees elections in Eastern Europe (but refuses Western supervision); occupation zones in Germany agreed; preliminary discussion of United Nations Organisation.

11 Potsdam Conference (Terminal) 17 July–2 Aug. 1945 Truman, Stalin and Churchill agree political and economic principles for future government of Germany and relations with German satellite states; also agreement on redrawing Germany's eastern boundaries; Stalin conveys Japanese peace moves but these are rejected; the Potsdam Declaration repeats demands for unconditional surrender; Truman makes Stalin aware of a new secret weapon (the atomic bomb)

War Crimes

London

31 May–4 June 1945 Conference of 16 National War Crimes Offices held; basis for United Nations War Crimes Commission (UNWCC) Europe (Nuremberg) War Crimes trials: 22 tried, 19 convicted, 12 sentenced to death; subsequently 177 tried, 142 convicted, 26 sentenced to death

Asia War crimes trials: 5,700 tried, 4,405 convicted, 984 executed

□ 18–26 Sept. 1944 United Nations Relief and Rehabilitation Agency (UNRRA) meets to discuss plans for sustaining post-war Europe

□ 1–22 July 1944 International Monetary Conference; agreement signed on funding for post-war development. Basis for International Bank for Reconstruction and Development (IBRD) and International Monetary Fund (IMF)

□ 21 Aug.–29 Sept. 1944 Meeting of representatives of Britain, US and USSR to discuss post-war security; draft charter for the United Nations organisation established

□ 25–26 Apr. 1945 United Nations Conference opens; Charter of United Nations signed by delegates on 26 June; permanent members of Security Council established (USSR, US, Britain, France and China) and power of veto agreed; International Court of Justice propo

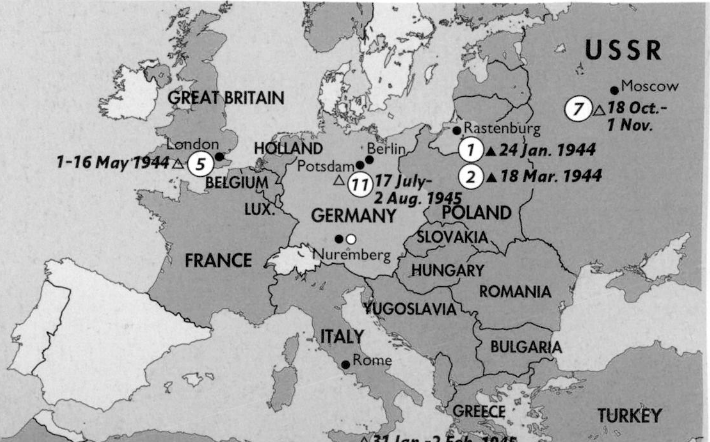

www.fordham.edu/halsall/mod/1945YALTA.html
Proceedings of the Yalta Conference
www.historyplace.com/worldwar2/timeline/nurem.htm
The Nuremberg war crimes trials

only hope of retaining independence from the Soviet Union after the war was to accept this, with territorial compensation at Germany's expense. The spheres of influence did, however, work tolerably well as far as immediate British interests were concerned: Stalin strongly discouraged the Greek Communists from seizing power in the winter of 1944–45, and the Italian Communists from disrupting the multi-party system in Italy. Western political influence in Yugoslavia appeared, also, to be secured through an agreement with the Communist leader, Tito.

The final meeting of Roosevelt, Stalin and Churchill was at Yalta between 4–11 February 1945. Here the Western Powers finally withdrew their recognition of the Polish exile government in London. The proposed compensation of Poland at Germany's expense was agreed in principle. In Germany, the Morgenthau Plan had already been dropped; instead, a conference in Moscow would determine how Germany should pay reparations for the damage that she had done. A fourth zone of occupation, for the French, was agreed, at British insistence; there would be trials of major war criminals; and as part of a general hand-over of each Allies' nationals, the Western Powers agreed that they would repatriate Soviet citizens found in German control. Stalin also promised that he would intervene against Japan. In return for this promise Stalin secured territorial gains in Sakhalin and the Kurile Islands.

Arrangements for the post-war world had been discussed during the war. In San Francisco, on 25 April 1945, the basis of the United Nations was agreed, the Charter of which, as drafted at Dumbarton Oaks, had been considered at Yalta. In 1943 the United States created a United Nations Relief and Rehabilitation Agency (UNRRA), which, after the war, helped resolve the stricken circumstances of most of Europe. But these arrangements did not prevent the development of rival power blocs and an arms race (the Cold War). However, a new Council of Foreign Ministers continued to hold meetings for some years to come. The final conference of the war (Terminal, 17 July–2 August 1945) was held at Potsdam. The late President Roosevelt was replaced by Harry S. Truman, who came with the new Secretary of State, James F. Byrnes; Stalin was present, as was Churchill until he was replaced by the new the Prime Minister, Clement Attlee. On 26 July, Japan was summoned to surrender by the Declaration of Potsdam, which through a still-neutral Moscow, she accepted, but with such qualification as amounted to a refusal in Allied eyes. The US now had atom bombs to use against Japan and Stalin was informed, in general terms, of this fact; he was also set to intervene in the Pacific War, although it was recognised that this would extend Soviet power over parts of China. Various other questions proved too difficult for Potsdam to resolve, and these were handed over to the new Council of Foreign Ministers. These questions included the drafting of peace treaties, but arriving at an agreement over the details of these would prove a long and arduous task.

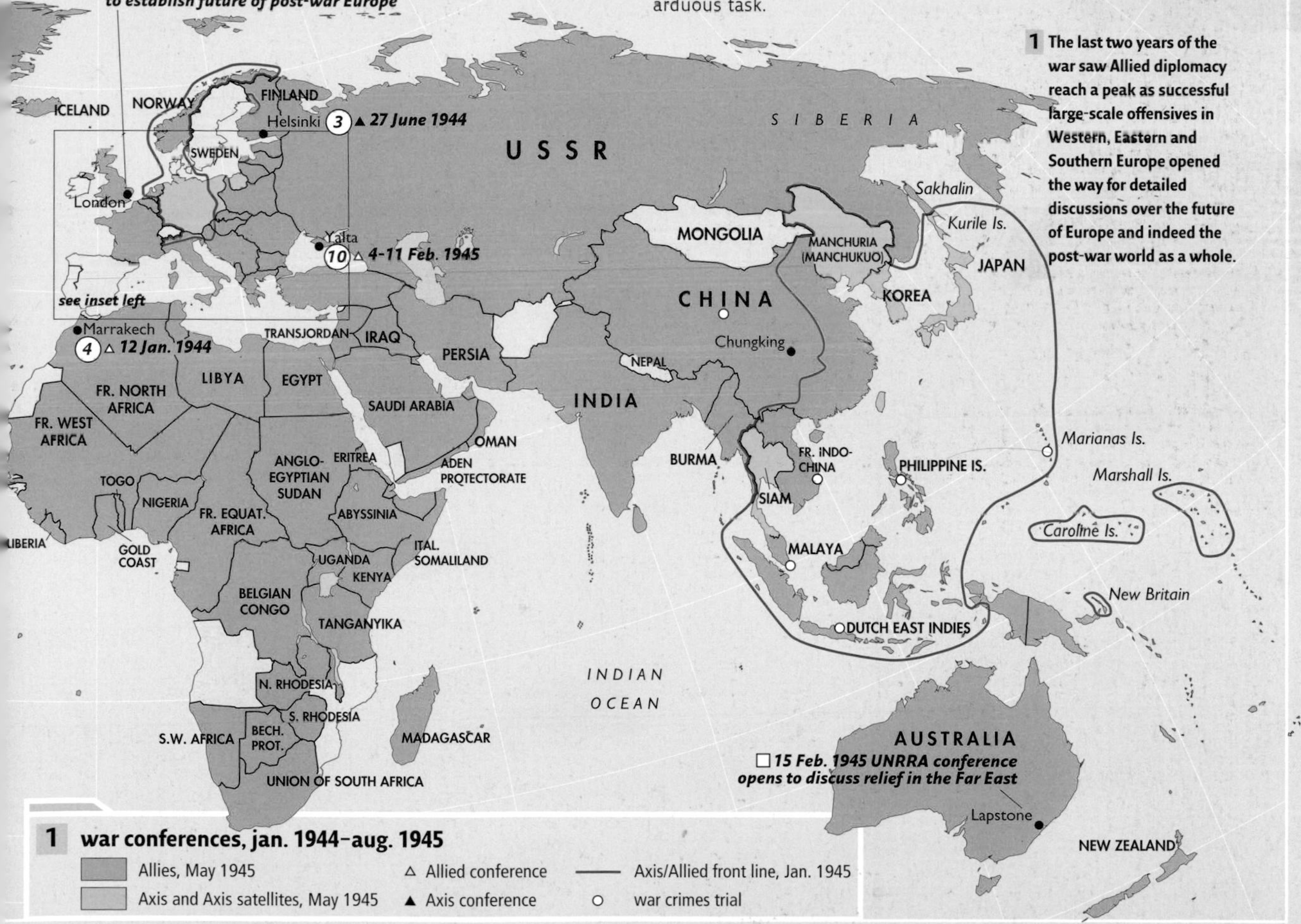

1 The last two years of the war saw Allied diplomacy reach a peak as successful large-scale offensives in Western, Eastern and Southern Europe opened the way for detailed discussions over the future of Europe and indeed the post-war world as a whole.

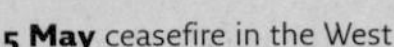

the **occupation** of **germany**

from 1945

- **5 May** ceasefire in the West
- **7 May** General Jodl signs unconditional surrender
- **8 May** VE Day
- **9 May** German surrender ratified in Berlin by all four major Allies
- **23 May** German High Command imprisoned; Himmler commits suicide
- **5 June** occupying powers partition Germany and Berlin
- **1 July** US, British and French troops move into Berlin

The Allied leaders, Roosevelt, Churchill and Stalin had agreed at Teheran in November 1943 to set up a European Advisory Commission, which, sitting in London, would draw up plans for the eventual occupation of Germany. These, which anticipated the advance of the Allied armies from the east and from Normandy, allotted Eastern Germany to the Soviets, North Germany to the British and South Germany to the Americans. Berlin was to be under tripartite control; a proposal of Roosevelt's for a corridor linking Berlin to the western zones was overlooked.

The Commission completed its plan in March 1944 and it was adopted at Yalta in February 1945; there, at Britain's suggestion, British and American areas were reduced to allot France occupation zones in the Palatinate, Baden and Württemberg, and also a sector of Berlin.

Knowledge that the boundary between the Soviet and Western zones of occupation was to follow the line of the River Elbe reached the Germans before their collapse; this prompted Admiral Dönitz, who assumed German leadership following Hitler's suicide, to prolong resistance against the Russians while seeking to persuade the British and Americans to hold open a line of retreat for the millions of Germans fleeing from the east. Dönitz sent Admiral von Friedeburg to negotiate a local surrender in North Germany with Montgomery on 3 May, but he was obliged to sign a capitulation that became effective on 4 May. Jodl was similarly treated at Eisenhower's headquarters at Rheims on 6 May. His delegates were forced to surrender unconditionally on 7 May. The terms became effective on 8 May and were ratified at Berlin on 9 May. The Western Allies did not, however, complete their withdrawals from east of the Elbe until 7 July, two days before they took possession, against marked Soviet reluctance, of their sectors of Berlin. The Allied Control Commission for Germany came into operation on 22 June, one month after Dönitz and his 'government' had been confined at Flensburg.

The first heads of administration in the four zones were military commanders: Clay (American), Montgomery (British), Zhukov (Russian) and Koenig (French). The Western commanders imposed policies of 'non-fraternisation' while 'denazification' began; the Soviets were more interested in stripping their zone of industrial plunder for war reparation. In all zones, however, the powers quickly permitted the revival of the pre-Nazi parties; local elections were permitted in the American zone in January 1946 and the revival of political life in the British and French zones resulted in the formation of a German Federal Republic, embracing all three, on 21 September 1949. Its creation, however, stemmed from the failure of the Western powers to agree terms for a general German peace settlement with the Russians, who quickly extinguished the non-Communist parties in their zone (through which they denied the Western powers land access to Berlin during the blockade of 1948–49) and sponsored its transformation into the German Democratic Republic, under a Communist-dominated government, on 7 October 1949. The United States, Britain and France terminated their state of war with the Federal Republic in 1951 and the Soviet Union followed suit in 1955.

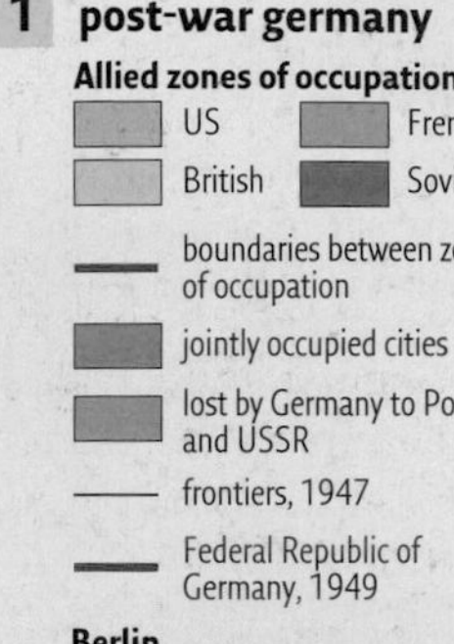

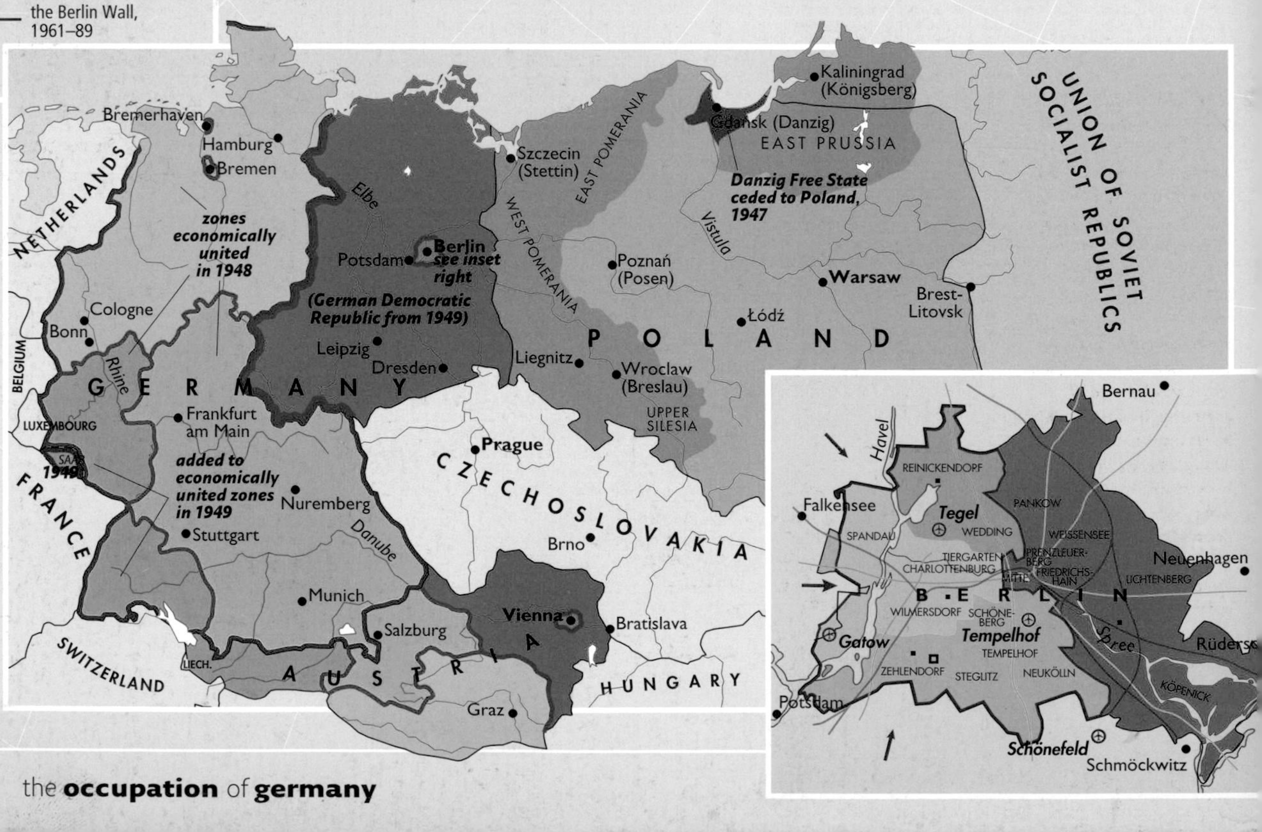

www.law.ou.edu/hist/germsurr.html
The German surrender documents
www.u-s-history.com/pages/h1886.html
West Germany since the end of the war

Zones of occupation in Austria were not agreed until Yalta, where Vienna was also placed under quadripartite status, with the centre as an international zone. On 29 April 1945, however, the *Anschluss* with Germany was renounced and the pre-1938 republic declared restored by a Soviet-sponsored government. The Western powers reluctantly recognised this government on 20 October but elections held in November returned a democratic majority. As Austria was deemed a 'liberated' state, its new government progressively assumed authority from the occupation powers and all foreign troops left Austria on the signing of the Austrian draft Treaty of Independence (1955).

The war left Europe in 1945 not only politically disorganised but also in a state of economic prostration, greatly exacerbated by large-scale population movements. Agriculture and industry in the war zone countries had been seriously impaired; the communications network (especially railways) crippled. Until 1949 the outlook was bleak, and political uncertainty, fostered by the growing antagonism between the US and USSR, hampered recovery. For Western Europe an injection of massive American aid (the Marshall Plan, 1948–52) helped lay the foundations for a new prosperity.

As a result of the 'Cold War' Europe divided into three blocs: Western, Communist and neutral. The first of these groups of countries was bound by a defensive alliance with the United States and Canada in the North Atlantic Treaty Organisation (1949), and by the emergence in stages of the European Economic Community. These developments were mirrored in Eastern Europe in the Warsaw Pact Organisation and Comecon. But it was not until the Helsinki Conference on Security and Cooperation in Europe in 1975 that frontiers in Europe were finally recognised by both factions, and accepted as inviolable.

1 Europe's new frontiers were negotiated at the Potsdam conference (July 1945). The Soviet-sponsored Polish government took over the administration of Eastern Germany up to the Oder-Neisse line. East Prussia was absorbed into Poland and the USSR. Poland was reconstituted, though much shrunken, Czechoslovakia reunited and Yugoslavia restored. Germany's western frontiers returned to the line of 1939. The western and eastern zones became separate republics in 1949.

2 The erasure of the Nazi map of Europe involved vast movements of population. Germans were expelled from Czechoslovakia and Poland, while 'ethnic' Germans fled from Yugoslavia, Hungary, Romania, the Baltic States and the USSR. Some ten million Germans reached the Western zones of occupation, but as many as three million may have died en route. Several million Russians who had made their way westward during the war were sent back, many to certain death. About one million 'displaced persons' of many nationalities were resettled in Western countries from the Western occupation zones and many Jewish survivors of the Holocaust made their way to Palestine (Israel after May 1948).

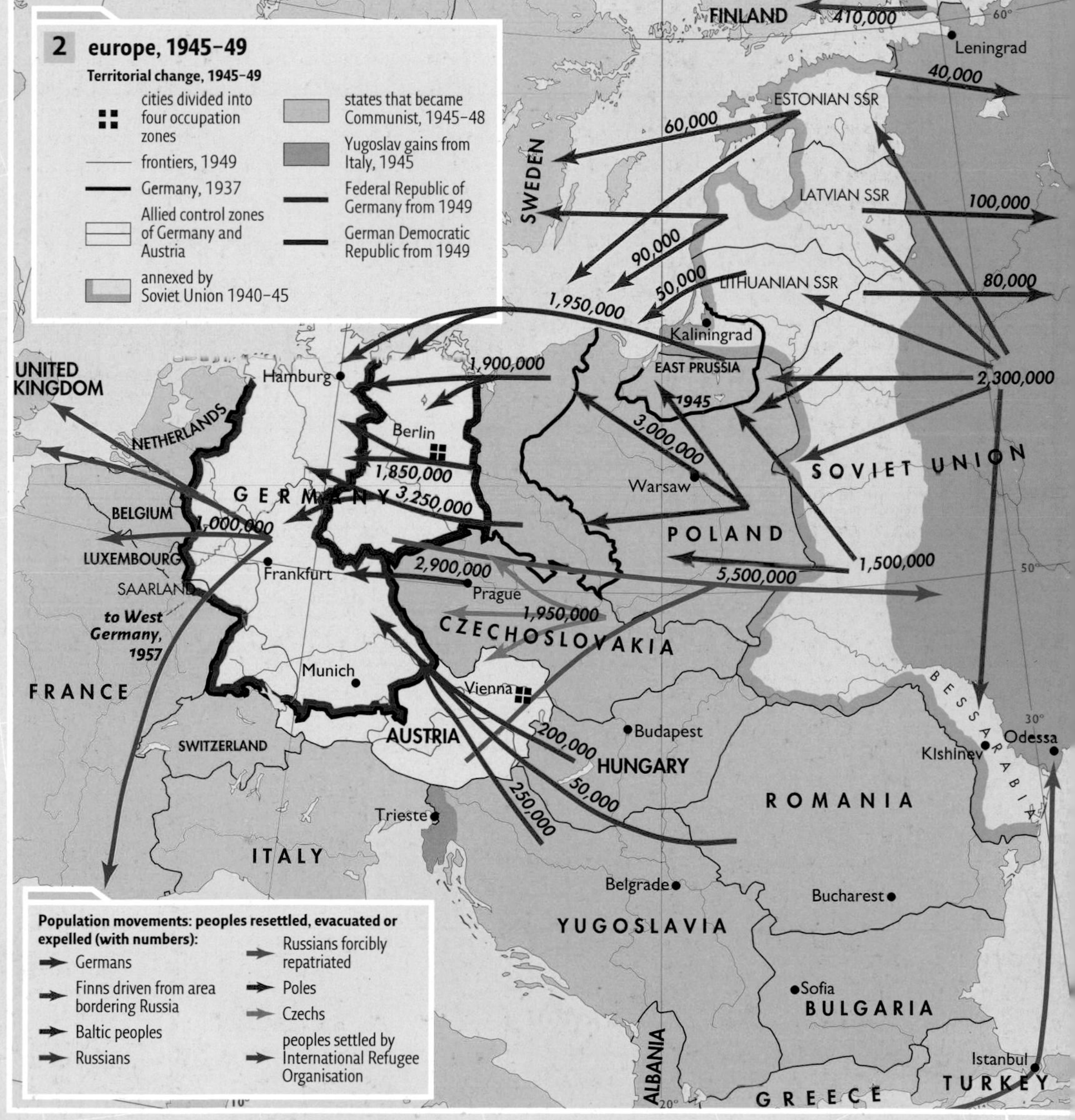

the **bombardment** of **japan**

1945

- **10 July** 1,000 bomber raid on Japanese mainland
- **17 July** 1,500 plane raid on Tokyo meets no air opposition; British Pacific Fleet and US 3rd Fleet raid Japan
- **3 August** complete blockade of Japan in effect
- **6 August** atomic bomb dropped on Hiroshima
- **9 August** atomic bomb dropped on Nagasaki

A mountainous empire, with few natural resources and many densely-populated cities, Japan was all but wholly dependent upon seaborne trade for the maintenance of both its civilian population and war effort. Japan was hopelessly vulnerable to campaigns against that trade and its major population centres.

Until June 1944 American planning for the Pacific War was based on the premise that an invasion of Japan might not prove necessary to enforce her surrender: thereafter planning proceeded on the basis that such an invasion was unavoidable. This switch of emphasis, nevertheless, coincided with the start of the strategic air offensive against Japan.

The first raid on Yawata (15 June 1944) by B-29 Superfortresses based in China, came as part of a bombing effort that had begun in March 1943 and which, over the next 14 months, extended across Indo-China, Southern China and Formosa. By June 1944, however, the Americans had decided to switch the base of their bombing effort from China to the Marianas, which were attacked that month. American raids on Japan from China thus ended in November 1944, the same month that XXI Bomber Command carried out its first raids on Japan from Saipan. For four months, however, this offensive failed to achieve any significant result; only a small number of Superfortresses were available at this time, and a lack of fighter cover over Japan forced the B-29s to bomb from high altitude, thereby decreasing accuracy.

In February 1945 the decision was taken to commit XXI Bomber Command to area bombing at night from low altitude. The effect was devastating against cities that were densely inhabited and largely built with timber and paper. In six months, in 1945, Japan sustained damage from air attack equivalent to that sustained by Germany in the last three years of the European War.

Operations by XXI Bomber Command against Japanese cities were underpinned by two other efforts: first, an escalating series of bombardments around the Home Islands by carrier forces and bombers, now based on Okinawa; and second, by its own mining operations, supported in the mining of Korean waters by naval aircraft, also operating from Okinawa. Operation Starvation was designed to reduce, to an impractical minimum, the flow of Japanese merchant shipping, and in the months between April and July 1945, it was largely successful. In 1945, the five great Pacific ports handled less than one-eighth of their 1941 trade. With the collapse of coastal trade, the Japanese were forced to transfer most of their Honshu trade to railways, which were, in turn, reduced by bombing to 25 per cent of their carrying capacity. Further, three-quarters of the Japanese fishing fleet was destroyed.

The scale of American mining overwhelmed the Japanese minesweeping force, though such ports as Yawata and Wakamatsu remained open to the last weeks of the war. After April 1945, however, what little shipping remained was largely directed to the import of coal and food, and with carrier and surface forces joining the bombardment, the war neared its end with Japan, not simply unable to defend herself, but realising that she could not feed herself into the next spring.

The bombardment of Japan was yet to reach its climax. The fanatical resistance with which the Japanese had met the Allies at every stage of the Pacific War led a special commission to recommend to President Truman, in July 1945, that the newly-developed nuclear weapon be used against the Home Islands. With the explosion of atomic bombs over Hiroshima and Nagasaki (6 and 9 August), the world entered the nuclear age. On 8 August the USSR declared war on Japan.

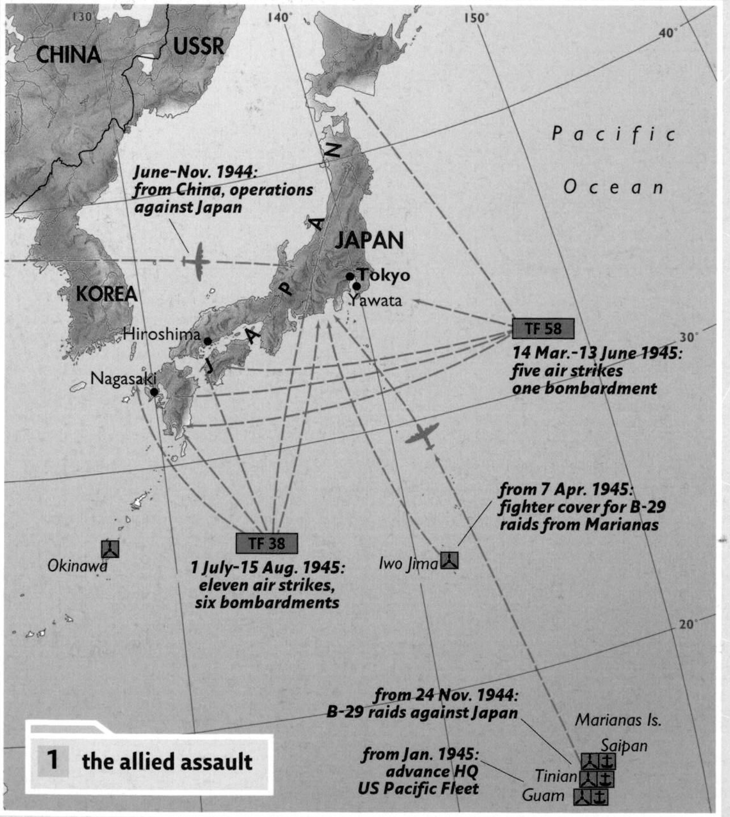

1 the allied assault

1 **Apart from the Doolittle Raid of April 1942 and operations against the Kurile Islands, the war did not come directly to Japan until 15 June 1944, when B-29 Superfortresses based in China bombed Yawata on Kyushu. From bases in China, however, Superfortresses could not reach the whole of the Japanese Home Islands, but the capture of the southern Marianas in mid-1944 provided bases from which to attack Japan's main islands and to mine her waters. By the end of the war these raids were complemented by operations based on Okinawa .**

www.worldwar2database.com/html/japanbom.htm
The strategic bombing of Japan, October 1944–August 1945
www.bbc.co.uk/history/war/wwtwo/nuclear_01.shtml
The use of the atomic bomb against Japan

2 japan, 1 mar.–15 aug. 1945

- major Japanese merchantman routes
- Japanese merchant ship losses
- the 'Big Six' fire-raid targets
- secondary fire-raid target
- major US mine-laying target
- coastal bombardment
- atomic bomb target

2 **Strategic bombing operations between June 1944 and February 1945 were conducted at high altitude against precision targets, with minimal results and at great cost in terms of engine life. In March 1945, General Curtis Le May adopted low-level area bombardment techniques: the first great raid, on Tokyo on 10 Mar., destroyed about 40 per cent of the city and killed more people than either of the atomic bomb attacks at Hiroshima or Nagasaki. With the five great cities of Japan singled out for similar treatment and American bombers ultimately raiding over 50 other cities, over 30 per cent of all buildings in Japan were destroyed, 13 million people made homeless and a further 8 million evacuated. The economy, too, heavily dependent upon small-scale enterprises and imported raw materials, was in ruins. An enormous mine-laying operation was directed against Japan's ports. Over 12,000 mines were laid, 2,100 in the crucial Shimonoseki Strait through which the bulk of surviving Japanese shipping had to pass in order to reach the major ports of the Inland Sea. In March, 796,200 tonnes of shipping passed through the Straits without loss; by July this shrank to 165,300 tonnes, 126 merchantmen being sunk in this four-month period. From April until the end of the war, mines destroyed 223 ships of 512,656 tonnes, all other causes – mostly aircraft – sinking a further 255 ships of 518,263 tonnes. The mining and air campaign between them caused Nagoya to be closed in April, Tokyo and Yokohama in May; virtually every one of Japan's 22 ports was closed at various times in spring and summer 1945 as a result of Allied operations.**

manchuria

1945

- **6 August** atomic bomb dropped on Hiroshima
- **8 August** Soviet Union declares war on Japan and invades Manchuria
- **18 August** Manchuria overrun by Soviet forces
- **21 August** Japanese Kwantung Army in Manchuria surrenders, although fighting continues until 1 September

Following their non-aggression treaty of April 1941, both Japan and the Soviet Union enjoyed the benefits of the other's neutrality in the conduct of their respective wars. In April 1945, however, when the Russians indicated an unwillingness to consider a renewal of the 1941 treaty after April 1946 when it expired, the Japanese concluded correctly that the Soviet Union would enter the war against her at the earliest opportunity, once Germany was defeated.

It was indeed the Soviet Union's intention, first indicated to the Americans and British at the Teheran conference in November 1943, to enter the war against Japan despite her non-aggression treaty; the breach of the treaty was rationalised in 1945 as necessary both under the terms of Soviet responsibilities to the United Nations and due to the request of her allies at the Potsdam conference. But though they correctly divined Soviet intentions, the Japanese anticipated that the Soviets could not begin operations in Manchuria until September, when the ground would have dried after the seasonal summer rains. In fact the Soviets planned to open operations in mid-August, the better to secure a measure of surprise and a potentially critical advantage of timing.

This Japanese miscalculation virtually assured the defeat of their armies. Though numbering about one million men, the Japanese order of battle contained various non-Japanese units and garrison, as opposed to field, formations; many of the latter were little more than training cadre replacements for divisions transferred to the Home Islands and the Western Pacific in 1944 and 1945. Moreover, in terms of firepower, mobility, communications and air support, the Japanese were no match for the three Soviet Fronts gathered around Manchuria, coordinated for a theatre of war the size of Western Europe, under a new strategic level of command: the Far East Command. The Japanese also underestimated their adversary in one crucial respect: they anticipated that any Soviet offensive would be halted for want of resupply after 250 miles and therefore planned to marshal their forces for a defensive battle on the central Manchuria plain. The Soviets were to confound this intention by ensuring that depths of advance far beyond 250 miles could be achieved.

With the natural and obvious routes into Manchuria covered by defensive positions the Soviets planned to make their main effort from the west, through the Gobi Desert and Greater Khingan Range with the Trans-Baikal Front. A secondary effort was to be made in the east by the 1st Far Eastern Front, especially strengthened with artillery, engineers and infantry in order to overcome the defences of the border area. The Far Eastern Front was assigned to hold the Amur River. In order to secure strategic surprise the start line for the Trans-Baikal Front was 300 miles from the nearest railhead, and the Front planned to use the second-grade Thirty-Sixth Army in a frontal assault on Hailar in order to hold Japanese attention at a time when the breakthrough was attempted on the flank.

The Soviet declaration of war, three months after victory in Europe as promised at Yalta, and the start of the Manchurian campaign occurred within hours of one another, on either side of midnight, 8/9 August. The timing was perfect, allowing the Soviet Union to enter the war against Japan before the Japanese could leave it after the US atomic bomb attacks. Within a week, as Soviet columns bit deep into Manchuria, Japan announced her decision to surrender, and on 17 August, following a direct order from Tokyo, the Kwantung Army signed the instrument of capitulation at Khabarovsk. Fighting in Manchuria and in the Kuriles nevertheless continued until 1 September.

Politically, the Manchurian campaign was of profound significance. Though not unexpected, the Soviet declaration of war came as a shock to the Japanese High Command. It ended Japanese hopes of securing a negotiated peace through Soviet auspices, and pointed to the hopelessness of Japan's position following the end of the war in Europe; the Allied resources thus released for redeployment in the Far East could not have been resisted. Moreover, though at the time defeat in Manchuria was incomplete, the Japanese High Command between 10–14 August rationalised the Emperor's decision to surrender in two ways: it was essential for Japan to capitulate while the United States remained her main enemy and it was imperative to avoid a final campaign on the Home Islands that could lead to social upheaval, revolution and Bolshevism. The fear of delaying a surrender until such a time as the Soviet Union would have a major voice in discussions regarding her future was also a strong factor. The Soviet Union was not a party to the 1951 peace treaty, and remains without a final settlement of the war with Japan, mainly because of her refusal to return (and Japan's refusal to cede) all or part of the Kurile Islands. Soviet commentators regard the destruction of Japan's last and largest concentration of ground forces as a cardinal factor in Japan's surrender. Western analysts maintain a particular interest in the campaign as a prototype for future Soviet strategic operations.

www-cgsc.army.mil/carl/resources/csi/glantz3/glantz3.asp#m10
Operation August Storm; the Soviet offensive in Manchuria
www.american.edu/projects/mandala/TED/ice/kurile.htm
The Kurile Islands dispute

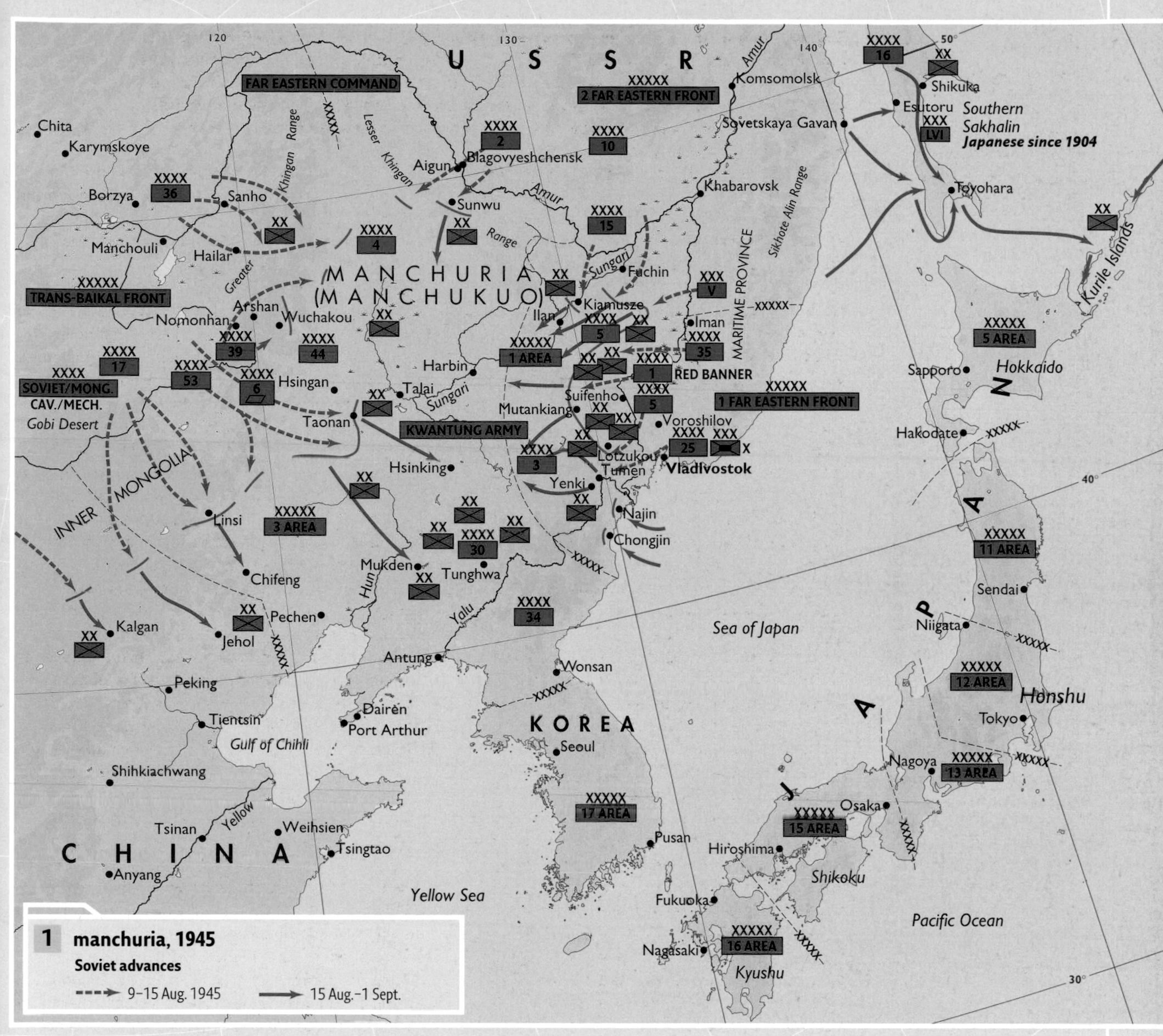

1 manchuria, 1945

Soviet advances

9–15 Aug. 1945

15 Aug.–1 Sept.

1 To oppose the one million men, 5,360 guns, 1,115 tanks and 1,800 aircraft mustered by the Japanese for the defence of Korea and Manchuria, the Soviets concentrated some 1.5 million men, 28,000 guns, 5,500 tanks and 4,370 aircraft across three Fronts controlled by a theatre command. By moving material direct from factories, the Soviets were able to transfer combat-experienced formations from Europe in time for a summer campaign, the Far Eastern Front being allocated the bulk of the second-grade formations already in the Far East. With formations that had fought in the close country and fixed defences of East Prussia drafted to the 1st Far Eastern Front in readiness for operations on the Soviet–Manchuria eastern border, in the west, the Trans-Baikal Front was assigned some 40 per cent of overall Soviet strength and the greater part of the assembled armour. The Soviet offensive was conceived as an envelopment by the Trans-Baikal and 1st Far Eastern Fronts, and the most obvious feature of the Manchuria campaign was the former's astonishing advance through the mountains to the central plain – a distance of 560 miles in 11 days. This advance was unopposed as the Japanese believed that the Soviets could not advance quickly and in strength through the mountains because of the problem of resupply. No less significant was the movement of light armour and cavalry of the mechanised group through the waterless Gobi Desert to positions from which Peking could be threatened. The main fighting in Manchuria came to an end on 17 Aug., but while isolated Japanese formations continued to fight until the end of the month, after 19 Aug. the Soviets used small airborne detachments to secure airfields, communications centres and local surrenders ahead of the main advances. The occupation of central Manchuria, of Port Arthur (22 Aug.) and of Korea north of the 38th parallel was unopposed for the most part. The Manchurian campaign remained the largest single Japanese military defeat of the Second World War. The campaign enlarged Soviet territory, as she was accorded the whole of Sakhalin and the Kurile Islands. Manchuria, however, was to be returned to Chinese control in 1946, while Korea was uneasily partitioned (along the 38th parallel) between a Soviet military government in the north and a US military government in the south.

japan and **east asia**

1945

- **14 August** Japanese agree to unconditional surrender terms
- **15 August** VJ Day
- **27 August** US and Allied naval units enter Japanese ports
- **28 August** Mao Tse-tung and Chiang Kai-shek meet in Chungking; Japanese sign surrender documents in Rangoon
- **2 September** Japanese sign instrument of surrender on board USS *Missouri* in Tokyo Bay
- **5 September** British land in Singapore
- **7 September** Japanese surrender in Shanghai
- **9 September** Japanese surrender in China
- **13 September** Japanese surrender in Burma
- **16 September** Japanese surrender in Hong Kong

The Second World War was formally brought to an end on 2 September 1945 when Japanese representatives signed the instrument of their country's surrender on the starboard veranda of the battleship USS *Missouri* in Tokyo Bay. However, a host of related conflicts continued, at least in East and South East Asia, until 1975, by which time the indigenous peoples of these areas had resolved most of their domestic affairs in a manner that suggested that they, not the great powers, now held the power of decision in such matters.

But these developments lay far beyond the reality that Japan faced in 1945. Such was her plight after the defeats at the hands of American forces in 1944 that court officials in early 1945 seriously, if discreetly, considered the possibility of the Emperor's abdication as the means of opening the way to peace, and in the spring and summer the American High Command was aware of Japan's hesitant and futile attempts to extricate herself from the war through Soviet mediation. The American decision to use atomic weapons against Japan (8 and 12 August 1945) was the result of a desire to bring about the quickest – and for the Allies, the most economical – end to the war, and to preclude effective Soviet intervention in the struggle. The Soviet invasion of Manchuria on 9 August nevertheless proved a crucial factor in the Japanese decision to accept the terms of the Potsdam declaration of 27 July 1945 – unconditional surrender. While the Japanese High Command rationalised Emperor Hirohito's personal decision to surrender in terms of the need to end the war while the United States retained the power of decision amongst Japan's enemies, fear of social revolution was no less important. Nevertheless, despite an unprecedented broadcast by the Emperor on 15 August announcing the decision to accept Allied terms, sections of the armed forces opposed national surrender. Their resistance was quickly stifled. Under the supervision of General MacArthur, Japanese society was reconstituted. Hirohito retained his position as Emperor, but revoked his divine status. He was not accredited with responsibility for war crimes.

Six years were to elapse, however, before the end of the war was finalised with the Treaty of San Francisco (8 September 1951) between Japan and most of her former enemies, and by that time East and South East Asia were in the process of a transformation. By exposing the fragility of the colonial empires Japan gave new impetus to the anti-imperial revolt of Asia, which would be a dominant feature of the post-war world. The Japanese had established governments in Burma (1942) and the East Indies and Indo-China (1945). After the Japanese defeat, these governments, enlarged or superseded by anti-Japanese Nationalist elements, won much popular backing. The war had also unleashed the forces of communism.

China after 1946 resumed full civil war between the communists and Kuomintang that had been barely suspended since 1940; the civil war was settled in 1949 with the expulsion of the Kuomintang Nationalists from the mainland to Formosa (Taiwan). With this victory the influence of both Chinese and Soviet Communism began to infiltrate other areas of the former Japanese empire.

The various imperialist powers found their return to former colonies opposed by indigenous forces. A precedent was set in the post-war affairs of South Asia. India, once the target of Japanese subversion and propaganda, was rapidly conceded independence in 1947 by the newly elected British Labour government. Two separate territories formed the Muslim state of Pakistan. Ceylon and Burma became independent in 1948. Nationalists in Java proclaimed an Indonesian republic upon the Japanese surrender in 1945. They advanced into Sumatra, Dutch Borneo, Celebes and the Moluccas, until by 1956 they controlled the whole of the former Dutch East Indies except West New Guinea. The British in Malaya fought a long war against Communist insurgents and resisted Indonesian attempts to annex Sarawak and Brunei. Independence from the United States in 1946 did not spare the Philippines a Communist-inspired insurgency campaign on Luzon. Indeed the most costly wars of the post-1945 era were to be fought within the former Japanese empire. In Korea (1950–53) US military attempts to ease the way to independence brought secession, civil war, and eventual partition. In Indo-China (from 1948) a similar move by the French authorities produced the same result. The crisis in both countries resulted in foreign intervention and ideological confrontation between Communist northern states, and Western-backed southern governments. In Korea compromise was reached, but in Vietnam Western influence was utterly eradicated by 1975.

National independence on the part of the states of East and South East Asia was accompanied in the first decades neither by peace nor stability, and areas that are among the most populous on the planet remain to this day beset by demographic pressure, racial tensions and political authoritarianism.

1 the allied invasion plans, aug. 1945

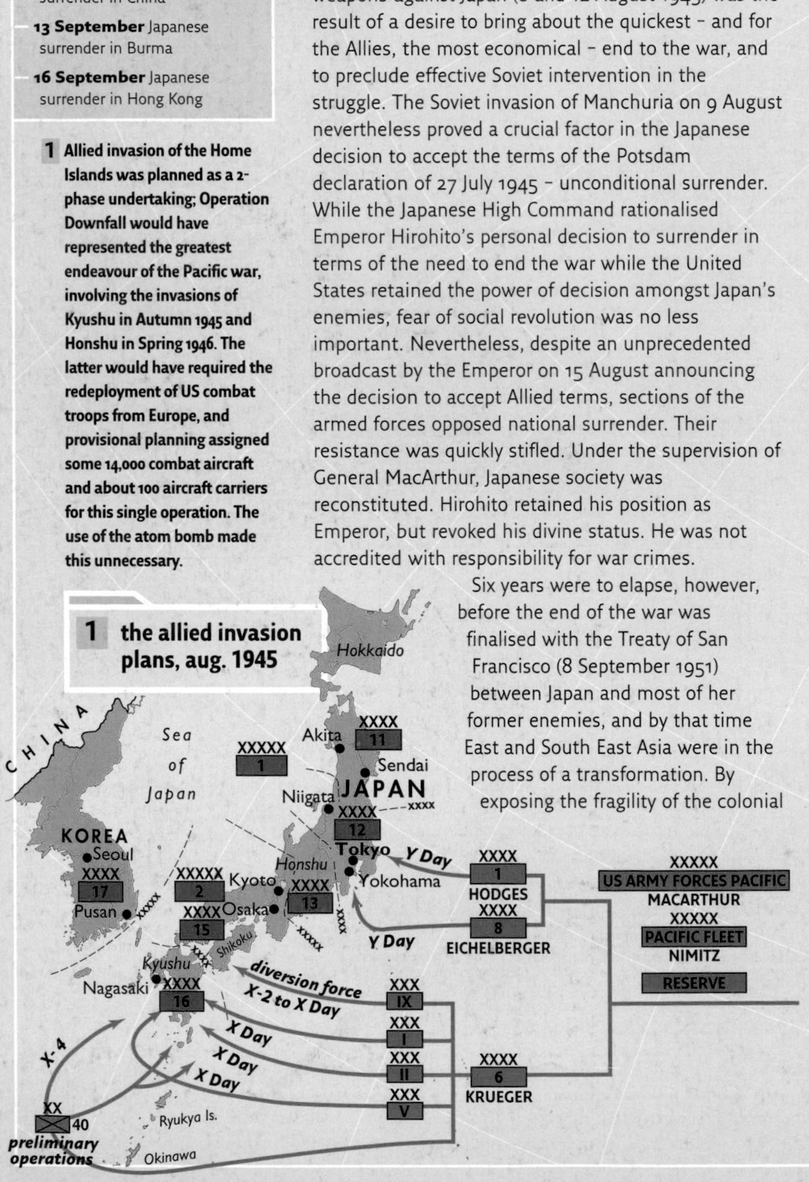

1 Allied invasion of the Home Islands was planned as a 2-phase undertaking; Operation Downfall would have represented the greatest endeavour of the Pacific war, involving the invasions of Kyushu in Autumn 1945 and Honshu in Spring 1946. The latter would have required the redeployment of US combat troops from Europe, and provisional planning assigned some 14,000 combat aircraft and about 100 aircraft carriers for this single operation. The use of the atom bomb made this unnecessary.

www.law.ou.edu/hist/japsurr.html
The Japanese surrender documents of World War Two
www.ww2pacific.com/downfall.html
Operation Downfall, the planned Allied invasion of Japan

2 The aftermath of the Greater East Asia war witnessed major political changes in most of the region:
Japan The Home Islands were placed under US military government, with General MacArthur at its head, until independence (1952). The armed forces were completely disbanded. Various Japanese pre-war territories were reallocated. Japan's Pacific territories were variously removed to US or UN control. Maintaining close relations with the US, successive governments concentrated on industrial development and new technology until in the 1970s Japan emerged as the world's third industrial nation.
Burma British control restored until independence granted in 1948. Communist guerrilla activity from 1948 leading to a series of military coups (1958–62), and subsequent military government.
China Civil war between Communists and Nationalist (Kuomintang) forces resumed (1945–49); Communists under Mao Tse-tung emerged victorious to form the People's Republic.
Indo-China French control restored until 1954, Laos and Cambodia granted independence, North Vietnam declared a Communist state (1954), South Vietnam an independent republic. Communist insurgency became open civil war in Vietnam in 1950s, with outside military involvement (France, UN, US), which spread to Laos and Cambodia. North Vietnam invaded South (1975).
Indonesia Declared independence 1945, negotiated end to Dutch control by 1949, effective control of most Dutch East Indies territory by 1956. Separatist and Communist rebellions from 1950s.
Korea Under US and Soviet military rule until 1948 when a Communist Peoples' Democracy declared in the North, and elected constitutional government established in the South. War between North and South 1950–53, involving UN troops (under MacArthur) and Chinese forces ended in stalemate.
Malaysia British colonial control restored (1945). Communist insurgency from 1948. Joined with Sabah and Sarawak to form Malaysia Federation (1963).
Philippines Short-lived US military government followed by independence (1946). Continuing Communist and Muslim insurgency. Pervasive US influence grew during the Vietnam War.
Thailand (Siam) Continuing constitutional monarchy (since 1932), with military governments and intermittent coups. Territories gained during war years stripped.

the **world war economies**

1939 to 1945

- **1940 (4 January)** Göring takes control of German war production
- **11 February** German–Soviet economic pact
- **29 May** German–Romanian arms and oil pact
- **1941 (10 January)** Lend-Lease Bill introduced to Congress
- **1942 (4 February)** Lord Beaverbrook becomes British Minister of Production
- **2 August** US begins supplies to USSR
- **1943 (11 January)** Roosevelt asks Congress for $100 billon war budget
- **1945 (August)** Lend-Lease terminated
- **1947** Marshall Plan for economic aid to Europe

From the beginning, the Second World War was about the mobilisation and supply of economic resources. All the major powers involved in the conflict expected it to be a total war in which industry and agriculture would play as vital a part as the armed forces. The First World War had taught them that industrialised warfare could only be fought with industrial weapons – economic rationalisation, the mass mobilisation of the economy, and mass production in all essential fields.

In the early stages of the war Germany was the largest economy, with access by 1941 to the resources of most of Europe. Britain was critically dependent on keeping open her worldwide supply lines, which were threatened everywhere by submarine. The Soviet Union cooperated with Germany; the United States helped the British Empire. The economic balance lay in the Axis, favour. With Hitler's decision to attack Russia and then America's entry into the war in 1941 the balance swung massively in favour of the Allies. It would be wrong to assume that from then on Axis defeat was inevitable, but there is a real sense in which the sheer quantity of resources available for the Allied cause, and Allied domination of the seas, made the Axis task almost impossible. Japan, Germany and Italy became siege economies, forced to build their war efforts on the resources of their captured empires, subjected to naval blockade, and, from 1943, to an increasingly heavy bombing offensive. The result was damaging pressure on production, the rapid decline of civilian living standards, and the savage exploitation of the captured areas.

The Axis problem can be expressed in a number of ways. In terms of population, the Allied powers could still call on 360 million against 195 million for the Axis. But this gap was partly made good by access to the labour resources of captured Europe, or China and Korea, and by exceptionally high levels of female employment, much of it on farms, in both Germany and Japan. The real gap lay in manufacturing potential. In 1938 Britain, the US and the USSR accounted for 60 per cent of the world's manufacturing capacity, the Axis for only 17 per cent. Even with the Axis occupation of western USSR in 1941 the gap was unbridgeable. The Allies had twice the steel output and three times the coal output of their adversaries. In 1938 Britain and France alone produced more motor vehicles and more shipping tonnage than the three Axis states together.

Though the Axis captured large additional resources, these only replaced overseas imports (the American embargo on steel and oil for Japan was not fully compensated for in Manchuria or the Dutch East Indies), or were exploited at well below optimum level. In the Soviet Union installations were so thoroughly destroyed by retreating Soviet forces that Germany acquired barely a fraction of the potential of the resources captured. In Fortress Europe hostility to Nazism, partisan activity and an increasingly disabled transport network reduced the gains from

1 **The Allies had the advantage of being able to operate on a global scale after American entry into the war. The US sent goods to every theatre and established a worldwide network of air bases and supply depots. The Allied powers had adequate access to oil supplies and their global tanker fleet expanded from 12 million to 21 million tonnes despite heavy losses to submarines. But even the Allies had problems with the loss of resources. The US had to build up a synthetic rubber industry to replace losses from Malaya using technical know-how from Germany. The US economy grew by 50 per cent during the war. The British, German and Japanese economies expanded more modestly.**

1 US supply lines, 1941–45

- USAAF supply lines
- US army supply lines
- maximum extent of Axis expansion, 1942

www.loc.gov/exhibits/marshall/
The Marshall Plan of 1947
www.qmfound.com/
The Quartermaster Corps, the US Army's logistical supply branch

exploitation. The steel industry of Lorraine, for example, worked at no more than 50 per cent capacity; Germany's oil imports during the war averaged less than half the level of 1939 even with virtual control of Romanian supplies. By contrast, the Allies had access to the resources of the whole western hemisphere, Africa, the Middle East, Australasia and South Asia. Only the submarine could undermine this economic advantage, and by 1943 that threat had been met. Moreover, the Allied states mobilised their economies more effectively than their enemies, leaving much of the task in the hands of industrialists and civilian experts rather than the military. The result was a degree of disparity in the output of finished weapons even greater than the gap in resources. In 1942 the Axis produced 26,000 aircraft, the Allies 101,000; the same year Allied tank production reached 58,000, Axis tank output a mere 11,000; the United States produced in 1943 ten times as many combat naval vessels as Japan and Germany together. Axis forces faced a relentless attrition cycle from 1942 onwards, which not even the revival of German production in 1944 could reverse.

The economic costs of the conflict were enormous. European industrial production was, by 1946, down to one-third of the pre-war level, food production to a half. France lost 46 per cent of her national wealth; Italy lost over one-third. The Soviet Union had 1,700 towns and 70,000 villages completely destroyed. Bombing damaged or destroyed the central areas of almost all German, Italian and Japanese cities. All states were faced with enormous increases in public debt. The main beneficiaries of the war were those states not directly affected by the conflict, where the huge inexhaustible demand for food, raw materials and weapons from the warring powers rapidly reversed the damage done by the Depression of the 1930s, paving the way for the development of a more open and prosperous global economy under US leadership.

2 the new economic order in europe, 1939–45

Axis and Axis-occupied areas 1942
coalfields and industrial regions
other industrial regions
crude oil plants
synthetic oil plants
2,438 cost of German war effort borne by occupied or allied states (in RM million)
tonnage of merchant shipping seized by Axis Powers (in thousand tonnes)

mineral resources:
bauxite
chrome
copper
iron ore
lead
magnesite
manganese
oil
potash
zinc

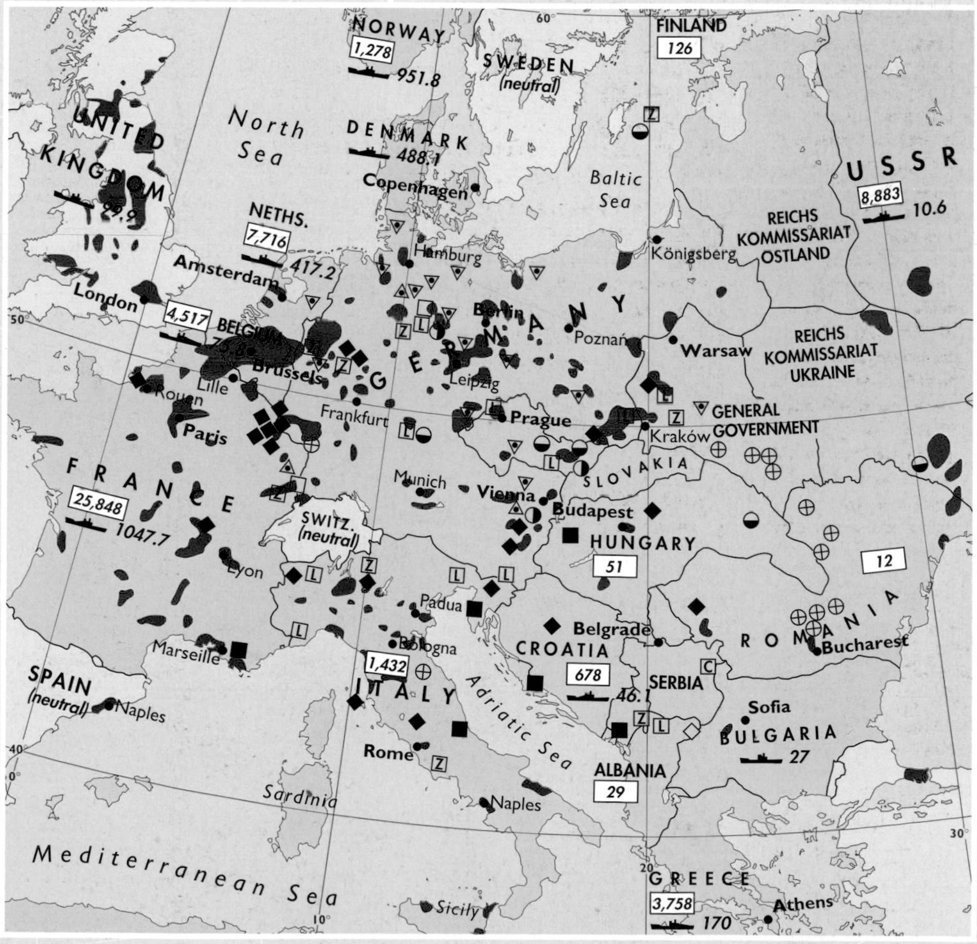

2 **During Germany's domination of Europe, plans were laid for a new economic order with Germany as the rich industrialised heartland surrounded by an outer circle of poorer agrarianised atates. In the captured areas living-standards were deliberately suppressed and resources taken for the war effort, though the home countries had to cut back on civilian consumption too. German daily intake of calories per day was higher than the occupied areas, but was well below levels in the United States or in neutral states. The occupied states of Europe were forced to pay more than 90 billion marks in war contributions, and to provide foodstuffs and labour for the Reich. By 1944 Germany owed the neutrals and her allies in Europe over 20 billion marks for goods bought during the war.**

the casualties

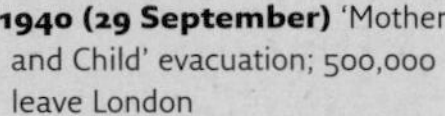

1939 to 1945

- **1940 (29 September)** 'Mother and Child' evacuation; 500,000 leave London
- **1941 (10 May)** climax of the London Blitz
- **October–November** Hitler orders extermination of European Jews
- **1943 (24–25 July)** Operation Gomorrah, the RAF's bombing of Hamburg, which killed 40,000 people
- **1945 (13–14 February)** destruction of Dresden in fire storm; 30,000 civilians killed

The cost of the Second World War in human life was the highest of any ever fought. It provoked a number of battles - Stalingrad, Normandy and Berlin - as destructive as the worst episodes of the First World War. It also caused very large loss of life away from the battlefield: by direct bombing attacks on the civilian population; by the deprivation imposed by siege (as at Leningrad, where over 500,000 civilians died between November 1941 and January 1944); by the disruption of agriculture and food supply; by massacre and reprisal in the course of guerrilla campaigns, particularly in Yugoslavia, which lost over one million of its population between 1941 and 1945; by flight and forcible expulsion, which accounted for the death of two million Germans in 1945 alone; and by organised extermination, particularly of the European Jews in Poland, who suffered up to six million deaths between 1941 and 1945.

The campaigns fought by the Axis powers against the Western Allies were governed by observance of the Geneva convention, which ensured humane treatment of prisoners, wounded and non-combatants. Axis prisoners in Allied hands enjoyed particularly good treatment, since many were sent to locations in North America and Africa where food was plentiful. Western prisoners in Axis hands fared less well, but most were correctly treated until, at the very end of the war, many were sent on forced marches away from the advance of the liberating armies. Western prisoners in Japanese hands suffered varied ill-treatment, including semi-starvation, subjection to scientific experiment, forced labour and incarceration in camps close to bombing targets. Soviet prisoners in German hands died in millions, at first because their numbers overwhelmed arrangements made for their containment, later because many were deliberately worked to death, or left to starve. The Soviets did not introduce regulations for dealing with prisoners of war until 1943. They took about three million Germans. Given shortages among Soviet troops, their treatment was at best perfunctory. Prior to the Japanese surrender in August 1945, the Allies took very few Japanese prisoners of war; they were determined to fight to the last man and most preferred suicide to the dishonour of captivity. However, in August–September 1945 the Soviets took over 600,000 Japanese prisoners, one-tenth of whom died in captivity.

1 The total number of war dead defies accurate calculation but is usually estimated at between 40 and 50 million worldwide. The Second World War, unlike the First, caused very high direct civilian casualties – by bombing, deprivation, maltreatment or deliberate extermination – which greatly exceeded military battle deaths. Casualties, both military and civilian, were higher in Europe than in Asia and much higher in Eastern than Western Europe, an indication of the brutality of the East European campaigns. The Red Army suffered some 8.6 million military deaths; another three million Soviet soldiers died as German prisoners. The Wehrmacht suffered almost three million battle deaths and Japan 1.5 million. The highest totals of battle deaths among the Western Allies were some 250,000 in the British forces, 300,000 in the American and 200,000 in the French. Civilian deaths were highest in the Soviet Union (an estimated 16 million), China (many millions, but unverified) and Germany, where some 600,000 were killed by bombing and nearly two million died in the flight from the east in 1945. Among individual countries, Poland suffered worst, losing six million, or some 18 per cent of its pre-war population; almost half of these were Jews, of whom almost six million throughout Europe were killed by deliberate Nazi policy during the war.

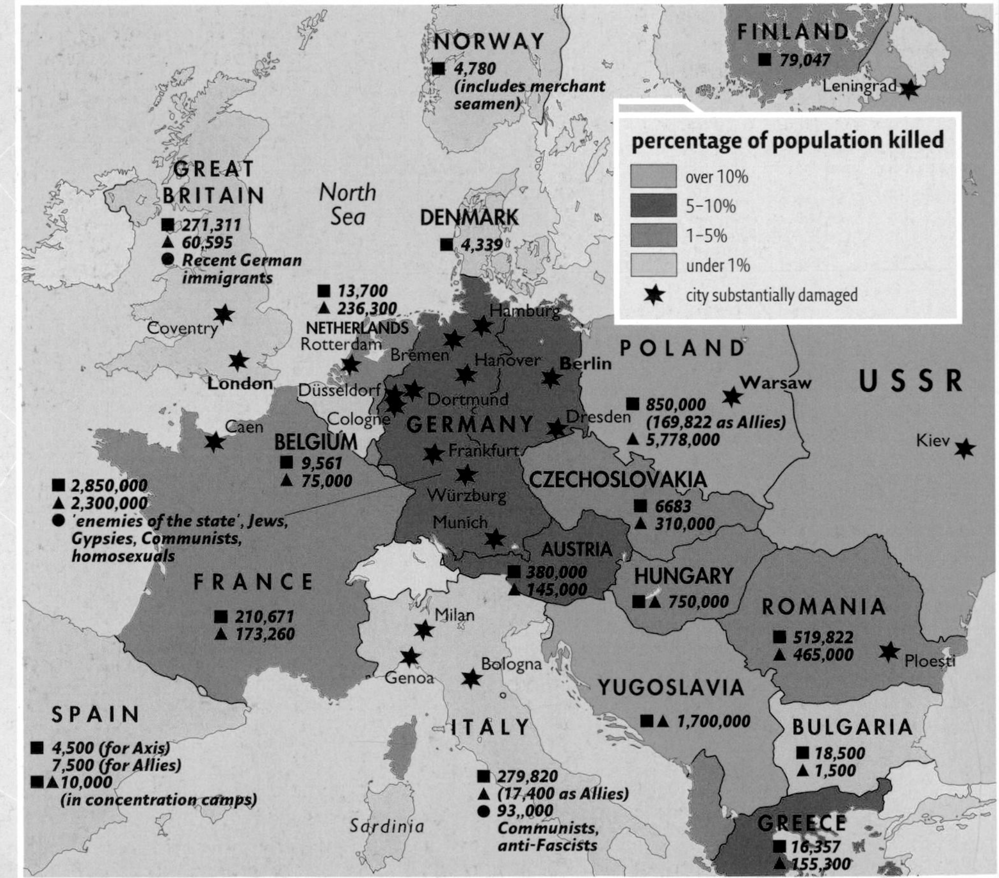

www.cwgc.org/cwgcinternet/search.aspx
The Commonwealth War Graves Commission
www.bbc.co.uk/dna/ww2/A1057349
Britain during the Blitz

The monitoring of the treatment of prisoners was in the hands of the International Red Cross, based in Switzerland. Its representatives were allowed access to prisoner-of-war camps in Germany, and those operated by the Western Allies; they also gained limited access to concentration camps before the war. However, both the Japanese and Soviet governments persistently refused to admit teams of inspectors.

After 1941, all the belligerents abandoned any reservations about attacking large centres of population. The devastation wrought upon the cities of Europe alone are an index to this – only Rome and Paris were nominally declared open cities, on the basis of their cultural importance. Warsaw, however, was utterly destroyed (November–December 1944) by the retreating Germans. The large-scale bombing of cities caused the deaths of some 420,000 in Germany, 500,000 in Japan and 60,000 civilians in Britain. There was also serious loss of life by bombing in Poland, France, Italy, Belgium and Holland. In the combatant states where the administrative machinery remained intact, however, there was no repetition of the death toll by deprivation and epidemic that afflicted the Central Powers during the First World War. Efficient rationing and medical care ensured that the health of civilian populations in Germany and the Western European states remained good; there were few war-related civilian deaths in the United States. In the USSR, Eastern and Southern Europe and China the toll of war-related civilian deaths was extremely high; some estimates put those killed by the Japanese in China at ten million.

Guerrilla warfare, internal disorder and forced movements of population, which afflicted the societies of Eastern and Southern Europe from 1939 to 1945 and wide areas of China from 1937 onwards, caused great loss of life. In Greece, where resistance to Axis occupation was strong, some 120,000 of the country's 140,000 war dead were victims of reprisal, factional fighting, massacre or deportation. A high proportion of the Soviet Union's 16 million civilian dead were victims of direct oppression or war-related deprivation. The largest single cause of death in the Second World War, however, was the battle between the Wehrmacht and the Soviet Army, which killed at least 11 million soldiers and wounded 25 million, of whom the vast majority were Soviet.

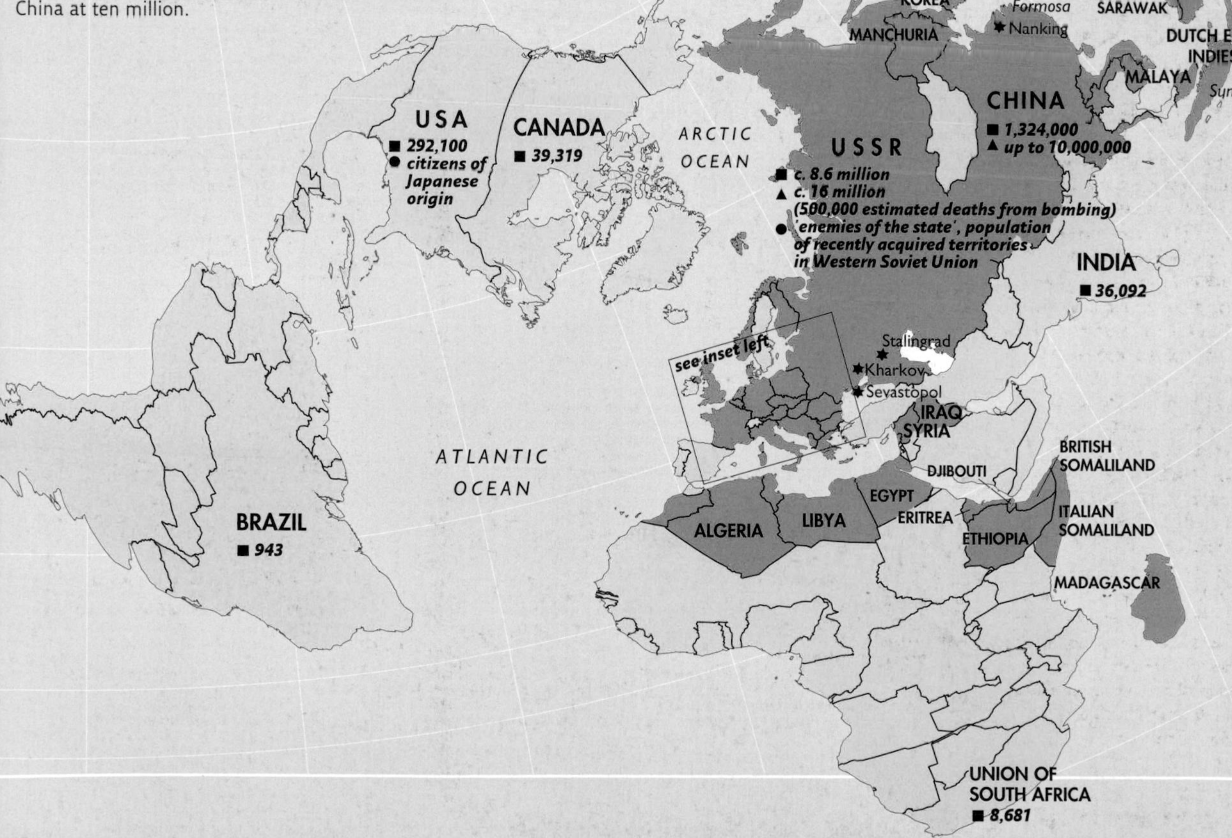

global war

1939 to 1945

- **1939 (3 September)** Britain, France, Australia and New Zealand declare war on Germany
- **1941 (7 December)** Japanese bomb Pearl Harbor and declare war on US
- **1945 (8 May)** VE Day
- **15 August** VJ Day

1 **By 1945 almost every sovereign state in the world was actively or technically a combatant in the Second World War. The involvement of the great imperial powers ensured that of their colonies in Africa and Asia. At the moment of Germany's collapse (May 1945) only nine sovereign states remained neutral. Every state in Latin America (including even previously pro-Axis Argentina) had joined the Allied cause.**

The Second World War, unlike the First, eventually engulfed the globe. In 1939, in Asia, the Japanese were pursuing a continuing war designed to bring them effective control of China. In Europe, it began as a local war mounted by Hitler to annihilate the Polish State. Though the armies mobilised in 1939 were large, numbering one million in Poland and three million each in France and Germany - Britain's regular army was only 200,000 strong - the numbers of men put into the field in the opening stage were smaller than in 1914.

The scale of the war grew apace thereafter. Britain continued its mobilisation programme after the defeat of France in June 1940 and, though Hitler temporarily reduced the size of the Wehrmacht at that time, he raised it again later that year when he had decided to attack the Soviet Union. By the time he unleashed the invasion, in June 1941, his forces were twice the size they had been in 1939, while his offensive brought into the war a Soviet force which was bigger still. It maintained a front-line strength alone of 11.5 million. Japan's decision to join Germany as an Axis combatant (enlarging the sphere of her ongoing war in China) further swelled fighting numbers, which would reach their fullest extent when the United States had completed the mobilisation of almost 12 million active servicemen.

As the war spread and developed, the nature of the arena in which it was fought began to change. Although trans- and inter-continental conflicts had occurred before, the battlefield now assumed a spherical, global form, with varying implications for all the combatants.

As an imperial power, with garrisons stationed around the world before 1939, Britain was committed to fight on almost every front of the Second World War. British troops, and those of her colonies and associated dominions, consequently fought in South East Asia, the Pacific islands, North and East Africa, Southern and North Western Europe and the Middle

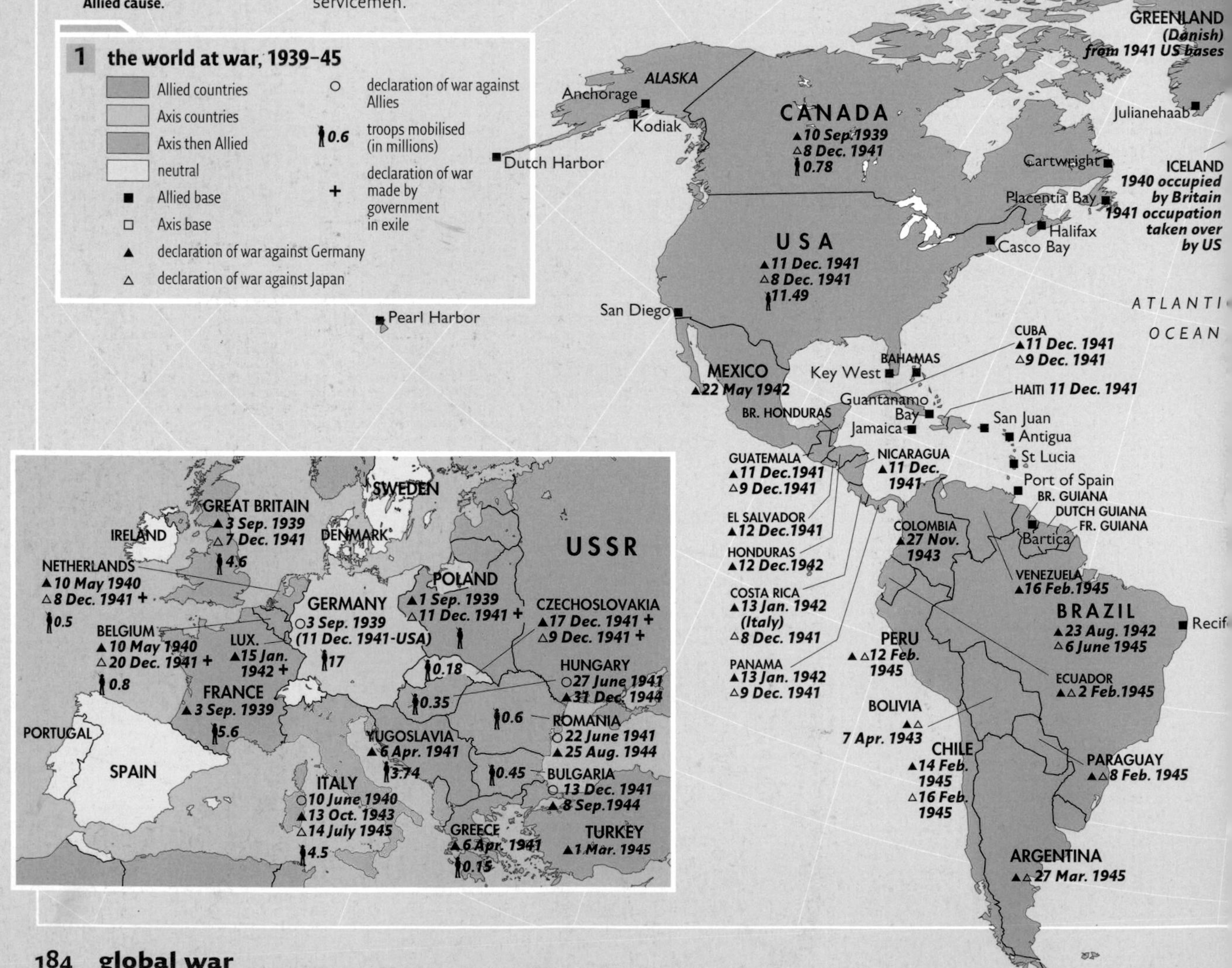

www.bbc.co.uk/history/war/wwtwo/
All aspects of World War Two
www.iwm.org.uk/
The Imperial War Museum

East, as well as in the Atlantic, Pacific, Indian and Arctic Oceans and all the skies of the northern hemisphere.

By contrast, the Soviet war was limited to its own territory and contiguous areas, of which the most distant from the centre was Manchuria, where it fought a victorious campaign against the Japanese in August 1945. Japanese forces ranged widely across the Western Pacific and adjacent territories, penetrating by 1944 deep into China. Germany, largely a land-locked power, succeeded in projecting its military force across the Mediterranean and, with its U-boats and surface commerce raiders, in conducting a maritime campaign which reached as far as the Caribbean in the west and the Indian Ocean in the east. But it was the United States that eventually achieved the widest global outreach. In 1944 it was conducting major land, sea and air campaigns in western and Southern Europe, in China, in South East Asia, and in the Central and Southern Pacific. The Second World War, at its apogee, was truly an American war.

The extension of the 'killing zone' beyond the immediate battlefield was a further global characteristic of the war. Aside from the ideological nature of civilian persecutions by the Axis powers, notably in China and Eastern Europe, civilians throughout Europe, Western USSR and East Asia came under direct military attack, largely as a result of bombing strategies or when caught in the path of a mobile battle front.

The experience of war was neither clear-cut nor decisive for many peoples and nations, especially those chosen by the major powers as targets for ideological policies. This was true of none more so than the Poles. Their country was invaded by Germany on the first day of the war and its forces were still active in the field, in strength on three major fronts, at the moment of Germany's surrender. In the interim, the country had suffered invasion by the USSR, appalling social and ideological persecution by both occupying powers and virtual political extinction. Some Poles volunteered or were coerced into both the Wehrmacht and the Red Army; many served as slave labourers for the Reich. Nevertheless, Poles in exile fought with the greatest valour and effectiveness at the side of the French, the British and the Soviets, while in Poland itself, the underground Home Army mounted the largest of all rebellions against German occupation forces (Warsaw 1944) to be staged by any resistance movement during the war.

INDEX